Multicultural Education in Middle and Secondary Classrooms:

Meeting the Challenge of Diversity and Change

Joan A. Rasool
Westfield State College

A. Cheryl Curtis
University of Hartford

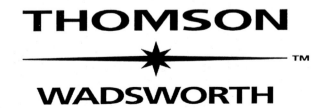

COPYRIGHT © 2004 by Wadsworth Group. Wadsworth is an imprint of the Wadsworth Group, a division of Thomson Learning Inc. Thomson Learning™ is a trademark used herein under license.

Printed in the United States of America

Wadsworth/Thomson Learning
10 Davis Drive
Belmont, CA 94002-3098
USA

For information about our products, contact us:
Thomson Learning Academic Resource Center
1-800-423-0563
http://www.wadsworth.com

International Headquarters
Thomson Learning
International Division
290 Harbor Drive, 2nd Floor
Stamford, CT 06902-7477
USA

UK/Europe/Middle East/South Africa
Thomson Learning
Berkshire House
168-173 High Holborn
London WCIV 7AA

Asia
Thomson Learning
60 Albert Street, #15-01
Albert Complex
Singapore 189969

Canada
Nelson Thomson Learning
1120 Birchmount Road
Toronto, Ontario MIK 5G4
Canada
United Kingdom

ALL RIGHTS RESERVED. No part of this work covered by the copyright hereon may be reproduced or used in any form or by any means—graphic, electronic, or mechanical, including photocopying, recording, taping, Web distribution, or information storage and retrieval systems—without the written permission of the publisher.

ISBN 0-534-65175-5

The Adaptable Courseware Program consists of products and additions to existing Wadsworth Group products that are produced from camera-ready copy. Peer review, class testing, and accuracy are primarily the responsibility of the author(s).

For permission to use material from this text or product, submit a request online at
http://www.thomsonrights.com
Any additional questions about permissions can be submitted by email to thomsonrights@thomson.com

Contents

Foreword by Beverly Daniel Tatum	vii
Preface	ix
Charge to the Reader	xii
Introduction by Cheryl A. Stanley	xiii

1 CREATING A CONTEXT FOR MULTICULTURAL EDUCATION **1**
  Brief History of Multicultural Education 2
  Definitions of Multicultural Education 5
  Readings 13
   Questioning the Status Quo: The Politics of Empowerment 13
   Multiculturalism as Compulsory Chapel 15
   Motivating Future Educators Through Empowerment: A Special Case 17
   Multicultural Education: For Freedom's Sake 24
  Discussion Questions and Activities 30
  References 31

2 THE ROLE OF RACE, CLASS, AND GENDER IN THE CLASSROOM 32
  Race and Racism 33
  Gender 37
  Class 39
  Connecting Race, Gender, and Class with Position and Privilege 40
  Readings 41
   Report: U.S. Gap between Rich, Poor Is Widening 42
   If Poverty Is the Question... 43
   White Privilege in Schools 46
   The Multicultural Me 48
   Anytown High School: A Profile of Pluralism 52
  Discussion Questions and Activities 56
  References 57

3 THE IMPACT OF CULTURAL LEARNING STYLES AND RACIAL IDENTITY ON LEARNING — 59

- Cultural Learning Styles — 60
- Summary and Implications for Learning Styles and Culture — 65
- Racial and Ethnic Identity — 66
- Racial Identity Theory — 66
- Educational Implications of Racial Identity Theory — 71
- Summary and Implications for Racial Identity Theory — 73
- Conclusion — 73
- Readings — 75
  - *Do You Know Why They All Talk at Once?: Thoughts on Cultural Differences Between Hispanics and Anglos* — *76*
  - *Learning, Chinese-Style* — *81*
  - *Praising My Individuality* — *84*
  - *Cultural Identity Groups Overview and Framework* — *87*
- Discussion Questions and Activities — 90
- References — 91

4 EFFECTIVE DECISION-MAKING, DELIVERY OF INSTRUCTION, AND CLASSROOM MANAGEMENT — 93

- Culturally Responsive Teaching — 94
- Motivation — 105
- Classroom Management and Diversity — 106
- Conclusion — 107
- Readings — 107
  - *Some Quick Cooperative Starters: Cooperation in the Classroom* — *108*
  - *Seven Strategies to Support a Culturally Responsive Pedagogy* — *110*
  - *Dangerous Minds: Decoding a Classroom* — *118*
  - *Supporting the Invisible Minority* — *123*
- Discussion Questions and Activities — 128
- References — 129

5 EFFECTIVE DECISION-MAKING IN PLURALIZING THE CONTENT — 130

- The Multicultural School Teachers' Blues — 132
- Guidelines for Pluralizing Curriculum Content — 134
- Curriculum Framework — 136
- Issues in Pluralizing Specific Content Areas — 141
- Steps to Becoming a Culturally Relevant Teacher — 147
- Readings — 148
  - *Incorporating Cultural Pluralism into Instruction* — *149*

Gender Balance: Lessons from Girls in Science and Mathematics   154
Afrocentricity for All   160
Western Mathematics: The Secret Weapon of Cultural Imperialism   162
Discussion Questions and Activities   175
References   176

6   SUPPORTING STUDENTS' READING, WRITING, AND LANGUAGE   177

Cultural Influences on the Construction of Meaning   178
Literacy Development within a Sociopolitical Context   182
Educational Implications for Cognitive and Cultural Perspectives on Literacy   186
Strategies to Enhance Literacy   187
Readings   191
    Instructional Strategies for Second-Language Learners in the Content Areas   192
    Black English: Its History and Its Role in the Education of Our Children   202
    Technological Literacy: More Questions Than Answers   209
Discussion Questions and Activities   211
References   212

7   CULTURALLY RESPONSIVE ASSESSMENT   214

What Is the Historical Context of Testing in the United States?   215
What Are the Current Trends in Classroom Assessment?   218
What Are the Trends in National Assessment?   221
What Responsibilities Do Culturally Responsive Teachers Have When Assessing Students?   224
Readings   227
    Alternative Assessment: Issues in Language, Culture, and Equity   228
    Successful Detracking in Middle and Senior High Schools   242
    Detracking Helps At-Risk Students   246
Discussion Questions and Activities   248
References   248

8   SCHOOL/FAMILY/COMMUNITY PARTNERSHIPS: RE-VISIONING TEACHING PRACTICES BEYOND THE CLASSROOM   250

Who Values School/Family/Community Partnerships?   253
Ties That Strengthen   255
What Schools Can Do   256
What Teachers Can Do   258

	Issues of Equity: Is the Partnership Fair to All Participants?	260
	Readings	262
	School/Family/Community Partnerships	*262*
	Tellin' Stories Project	*285*
	Eight Lessons of Parent, Family, and Community Involvement in the Middle Grades	*296*
	High Schools Gear Up to Create Effective School and Family Partnerships	*301*
	Discussion Questions and Activities	307
	References	308
	Further Reading	309
9	**DIVERSITY, SPECIAL EDUCATION, AND MULTICULTURALISM**	**310**
	A Brief History of Special Education Federal Legislation in the United States	312
	Inequities in Special Education Today	316
	Culturally Responsive Practices for Disabled Students from Diverse Backgrounds	327
	Readings	330
	Multicultural Education	*331*
	Culturally Sensitive Instructional Practices for African-American Learners with Disabilities	*338*
	Language Differences	*348*
	Discussion Questions and Activities	353
	Additional Readings	354
	References	355
10	**CHALLENGES FOR CHANGE AND DIVERSITY**	**359**
	Reform Themes	361
	Challenges and Obstacles to Change	364
	Stepping Forward: Being a Change Agent	366
	Concluding Thoughts	369
	Readings	370
	Why Teachers Must Become Change Agents	*370*
	Multicultural Education as Social Movement	*378*
	System Dynamics and Learner-Centered Learning in Kindergarten Through 12th Grade Education	*396*
	Discussion Questions and Activities	409
	References	410
INDEX		**411**

FOREWORD

Beverly Daniel Tatum, Ph.D.

It is an honor to write this foreword for this important and timely book. Every classroom teacher in the United States, whether in a rural, urban, or suburban setting, faces the challenge of educational reform and increasing diversity. Some may erroneously assume that multicultural education is not a concern of theirs because they teach in racially and ethnically homogencous enclaves. Even when this is the situation, every teacher must take seriously the task of preparing students for life beyond the borders of those communities. Every teacher must take seriously the challenge of preparing our children for effective participation in a multicultural world.

The young people we are educating are entering a new frontier. Certainly in the context of the United States, we have a society whose demographic portrait is changing rapidly: a much more pluralistic environment—racially, ethnically, religiously—than ever before. It is a much more pluralistic environment than the one experienced by most of today's teachers in their own youth. Though we are naturally inclined to teach the way we were taught, relying on the lessons of the past will not necessarily take us where we want to go.

Not long ago, this reality was vividly symbolized for me in a dream. In the dream, I was driving a car along a road, and all of a sudden the car went off the road and was on top of a pile of rocks. I said in surprise, "What happened to the road?" A voice answered, "There is no road." When I awakened, I thought, "This is a perfect metaphor for what we as multicultural educators are trying to do." We are living in a time where there is no clear road to where we are trying to go. Yet many of us have a vision of where we would like to be, a vision of schools where all children have the opportunity and the encouragement to achieve at a high standard. It is a vision of multiethnic communities characterized by equitable and just group relations rather than the present deeply ingrained power hierarchies that systematically advantage some and systematically disadvantage others. It is a vision of education that should not only foster intellectual development by providing students the tools of critical thinking, speaking, writing, and quantitative reasoning but should also provide all students the skills and experiences necessary for effective participation in a diverse society.

Joan Rasool and Cheryl Curtis share that vision. In this text, they have combined years of teaching experience with a critical synthesis of current research on such important topics as bilingual and special education, diversity and motivation, culturally relevant and responsive teaching, racial and ethnic identity development, and systems theory to begin to chart the road we might follow to bring this vision into being. Yet this is not a prescriptive process. Professors Rasool and Curtis practice what they preach throughout the text, asking us to be critical readers, inviting us to engage interactively with the text, challenging us to construct our own knowledge through the many questions for reflection and exercises for classroom application found throughout the text. This kind of critical self-reflection is an essential part of becoming an effective multicultural educator. We would be wise to follow their lead.

As we enter the twenty-first century, the challenges facing educators are real and the stakes are high. There is much our students need from us. We need the courage to travel on this unfamiliar road. We, like our students, need knowledge of the diverse cultures, communities and histories that comprise our society. We, like our students, need experiential as well as formal understanding of these topics, and we need, as they do, the capacity for collaborative, deliberative problem-solving abilities for use in a world in which unitary agreement does not exist and multiple perspectives must be acknowledged. We all need schools where educational equity is a lived reality and where students are empowered by their education to be full participants in a democratic society. I am grateful to Joan Rasool and Cheryl Curtis for pointing us in the right direction.

# PREFACE

In memory of Baidah and Hala's grandmothers: Nofa Haj-Hadi Al-Jaboury and Ada Margaret McCallum.

J.A.R.

"Black love is Black wealth." — to Tim, Melanie and Elizabeth and to my parents, George and Nora Freeman

A.C.C.

We confess that our motivation for writing *Multicultural Education in Middle and Secondary Classrooms: Meeting the Challenge of Diversity and Change* was self-serving. As instructors of courses in multicultural education and middle and secondary methods, we struggled to find resources that addressed the specific needs and questions of our middle and secondary pre-service and in-service teachers. So many of the texts and examples focussed on the implementation of multicultural education in elementary schools. Our concern was that future middle and high school teachers were left with the impression that "it" could be handled in the primary grades and as long as their content was "multicultural," they were meeting the needs of all their students.

We also wanted a text that would emphasize the link between multicultural education and teacher as change agent. Becoming a multiculturalist does not mean exchanging one curriculum for another; rather, it is a process of acquiring new knowledge and developing an ability to reflect critically on one's own and others' ideas about society, culture, and schooling. Finally, becoming a change agent involves having the courage to move forward and implement practices and policies that create a more equitable education for all students. In our experience, middle and secondary teachers need encouragement and support to overcome resistance in their schools and achieve this goal.

Multicultural Education in Middle and Secondary Classrooms can be used as an undergraduate and graduate text in multicultural education courses, courses in social justice or diversity, and middle and secondary methods courses. It can be a primary text or adapted for use as a supplementary text. Each chapter begins with a motivational excerpt, scenario, or diagram. Information and research are presented in a conversational tone that encourages readers to be active respondents to what they read. Several articles are included in each chapter that expand on concepts introduced in the text or offer alternative perspectives. Finally, each chapter ends with discussion questions and activities that allow students to integrate and think critically about the information presented.

Multicultural Education in Middle and Secondary Classrooms is divided into two sections. Part One presents basic concepts in the field of multicultural education, and Part Two addresses the application of multicultural education in the classroom. Chapter One, "Creating a Context for Multicultural Education," provides a historical and theoretical overview of multicultural education. Instructors could assign Chapters Two and Three before Chapter One; however, students should develop their initial definitions of multicultural education before reading about its application in Part Two.

Chapters Four, Five, Six, and Seven in Part Two address what happens in the classroom—instructional strategies, curriculum development, literacy practices, and assessment. Each chapter presents background information on the topic and instructional practices multiculturalists can use. Chapter Eight examines how middle and secondary teachers can involve families and community members in the education of adolescents, both in school and in the community. Chapter Nine takes a comprehensive look at special education legislation, the inequities of special education, and the needs of special education for students of color.

The discussion of teacher as change agent, first presented in the Introduction, comes full circle in Chapter Ten. The role of a change agent is a paradoxical one: "We are called upon to be leaders and team leaders as well, to work within the school culture and change the school culture, to take risks but get good teaching evaluations, to be silent but speak up, to be committed, but take 'time to smell the roses.'" *Multicultural Education in Middle and Secondary Classrooms* is our best attempt to help pre-service and in-service teachers find *their* way to becoming the most effective multicultural teachers possible.

Acknowledgments

We are pleased to acknowledge the numerous individuals who contributed to the writing of this book. First, we would like to thank Beverly Daniel Tatum for writing the forward—her words encourage us to do our best—and Sonia Nieto for her willingness to read and comment on our book. Cheryl A. Stanley's "Introduction" helps frame our discussion of teachers as change agents; John Gabriel's chapter reminds us of the importance of family and community in the education of young adults; and James Martin-Rehrmann offers valuable information about special education and students of color. Thanks to Carlton Pickron and Laurie Simpson for their suggestions on improving student-teacher interactions and to Anne Pelak for her insights on the role of technology in society. Frank Giuliano graciously contributed the section on science and multicultural education.

We wish to thank our students who engaged in our intellectual examination of multicultural issues, especially Amy Baker, who allowed us to use her autobiographical essay, and Alison Benoist for the use of her paper on pluralism in high schools.

Several people provided technical and research support when we needed it and for that we thank Linda Plasse and Jane Fox, and we thank Angela Dos Santos for her hard work on securing permissions for the articles. Many of the ideas found in this text began in collaboration with other friends and colleagues: Travis Tatum, Beverly Tatum, Sandra Lawrence, and Phyllis Brown. As always our extended families and support networks have been critical to the completion of our work: Walter A. Korzec, Amy Szlachetka, Nanci Salvidio, Susan Donner, Lisa Pickron, Judy Solsken, Rose Nuri, Lamees Hanna, Bruce King, Gerry Schamess, Jane Horvath, Anthony Rauche, Ed Weinswig, Frederick Sweitzer, and the women warriors of the PALM Society. Special thanks to the Freeman, Guercio, Davis, Archer, Curtis, Abdul-Rasool, McCallum, McCallion, Zgrodnik, and Morrell families who quietly supported aand anxiously awaited publication of the text.

We would like to thank the following colleagues for reviewing and commenting on our manuscript: Jeannette Abi-Nader, Gonzaga University; Jeri Jo Alexander, Auburn University, Montgomery; A. W. Anderson, Florida Atlantic University; Larry Arnoldson, Brigham Young University; Rose Chepyator-Thomson, State University of New York, Brockport; Kate Friesner, The College of Santa Fe; Maureen Gillette, College of St. Rose; Robert Gryder, Arizona State University; Betty Heath-Camp, Virginia Polytechnic Institute and State University; Holly Johnson, Texas Tech University; Steve O. Michael, Kent State University; Carolyn O'Grady, Gustavus Adolphus College; Lorrie C. Reed, Chicago State University; Thomas P. Ruff, Washington State University; Carole B. Shmurak, Central Connecticut State University; Ann D. Smith, Kennesaw State University; and Linda P. Ware, University of Rochester.

Finally, we appreciate the continued support from our editor, Dianne Lindsay, her assistant, Tangelique Williams, and our copyeditor, Robin Gold.

Charge to Reader: Becoming a Multicultural Teacher

Prescriptions for preparing students, particularly our increasingly diverse student population, to meet the demands of the twenty-first century abound. These remedies grow out of people's beliefs about what skills will be needed in the future, what knowledge and values will have privilege in society, and how power and wealth will be distributed.

Multicultural education offers one perspective. If we are advocates of multicultural education, however, we must take seriously its goal to develop students' critical thinking skills. We need to do more than explain multicultural education and how it can be implemented in the classroom. We believe that multicultural education "does not simply operate on the principle of substituting one 'truth' or perspective for another. Rather, it reflects on multiple and contradictory perspectives to understand reality more fully. In addition, it uses the understanding gained from reflection to make changes" (Nieto, 1996, p. 320).

We must also find ways that allow you, the reader, to critique the ideas that we present. We must find ways to allow you to "read between the lines" of what we say. We attempt to do this by presenting a variety of readings on a topic and by asking questions to prod your thinking. Your responsibility is to ask questions while you read, consider your own experiences and beliefs, discuss your ideas with others, and come to your own "working" conclusions. We hope that through this process you will learn more about multicultural education, the beliefs and perspectives of the authors, and your own views on multicultural education.

INTRODUCTION

Cheryl A. Stanley, Ed.D.

TEACHING IN THE TWENTY-FIRST CENTURY— BECOMING A CHANGE AGENT

Today many teachers—both novice and experienced—are leaving their classrooms because they feel inadequately prepared to teach their students. Teachers feel ineffective, but not because they lack certification, classroom experience, knowledge of their subject matter, or even a commitment to the profession. These teachers are realizing that how they were trained, the techniques they observed in their field placements, and their own teaching styles are being challenged: Perhaps their approach to teaching *doesn't* apply to all learners. Perhaps what they thought was "a natural way" to teach isn't the only way. Consequently, teachers have been forced to reevaluate their ideas about teaching and learning. This evaluation process is healthy; in fact, it is a catalyst for growth.[1]

Teachers aren't the only people concerned about ineffective instruction and poor student performance. There are as many reasons offered to explain this phenomenon as there are stakeholders: the economy, a lack of family values, too much technology—television and computers. Many educators look at the growing demographic diversity in our classrooms and wonder about "the match" between teachers and students. Census reports clearly show the complexion of our classrooms is changing. Today's classroom teachers encounter increased diversity in students' ethnicity, linguistic and cultural background,

---

[1] In a recent survey (1999) conducted by the U.S. Department of Education, 4,049 full-time, new and veteran teachers reported that they did not feel prepared to meet "'the four fastest changing aspects of the nation's schools': The demands for raising standards for public-school students, teaching students from diverse cultural backgrounds, helping students with special needs, and using technology in the classroom." (Basinger, J. Jan. 29, 1999. "Most New Schoolteachers Feel Unprepared for Recent Demands of the Classroom, Survey Finds," The Chronicle of Higher Education. http://chronicle.com/daily/00/01/9901290ln.hm)

family structure, socioeconomic status, learning style, and degree of learning disability (Davidman & Davidman, 1994).

Unfortunately, teachers are having difficulty meeting the needs of these diverse student populations in their classrooms. Numerous reports remind us that more students of color, low-income children, students with other than English language backgrounds, and students with special needs have higher rates of dropping out, violence, and truancy, and their academic achievement level is low and continues to remain low in some academic areas (Grant & Gomez, 1996).

As educators, we must address the issue that we are doing an inadequate job of reaching these students. Several educational reformists have scrutinized teacher preparation programs, school organizational structure, parental involvement, curriculum, textbooks and assessment, to name a few. Some researchers believe that one of the problems is the mismatch between home and school cultures. What is considered to be "the norm" often goes against the values of females, poor children, and children of color. "The customary ways of 'doing schooling,' the social, emotional, and valuative contexts and procedural rules that surround the formal curriculum, transmit certain powerful, pervasive, and persistent messages to students about which attitudes, values, behaviors, and personas are likely to be rewarded" (Gay, 1996, p. 43). Other issues are teachers' unfamiliarity with students' cultures and the communities in which they live and teachers' inability to teach to different learning styles and to assess students accordingly.

We agree with our colleagues that these issues must be addressed, and we are hopeful that teachers teaching in our multicultural and multiethnic twenty-first century can face these challenges. What will be needed, however, is that teachers gain the capacity to recognize and expand their vision of themselves as change agents.

TEACHERS AS CHANGE AGENTS

Change agents are individuals who are instrumental in bringing about change in their environments. The term *agency* is a critical part of the definition of a change agent. Agency refers to "the capacity to change the existing state of affairs," and, according to Datnow, policy makers act as though teachers have "the capacity to dramatically improve schools; all they need is freedom at the local level to do so" (Datnow, 1998, p. 10).

As a preservice teacher, you might be more concerned with becoming a good teacher and finding your first job than you are with reforming educational practices; part of being a good teacher, however, is developing those qualities that will allow you to advocate for students and their education. Teachers in the twenty-first century are entering the field at a time of unprecedented interest in education and educational reform. Reform means change, and novice teachers must be trained to initiate and critique change as well as to deliver instruction.

Politicians, business leaders, researchers, administrators, parents, and teachers all have ideas about what those changes should be. One of your tasks as a future teacher is to decide what changes you might want to make relative to the ways you've been taught, the curriculum you've been given, or the school environment you've experienced. You might decide that you support the reforms being promoted by your school, or you might believe that other changes are necessary. If your views are part of the agent group—the group that "has the power to define and name reality and determine what is 'normal,' 'real,' or 'correct' (Hardiman & Jackson, 1997, p. 17)—then you can expect institutional support. If, however, your ideas are outside the agent group, then your task—to find agency and make change—is quite different. What then are the characteristics of change agents and what are some obstacles that stand in the way of individuals making change?

Characteristics of Change Agents

First, change agents are lifelong learners who continuously engage in a reflective process that reexamines their personal vision of why they came to teach. Change agents use reflection to help shape and reshape their goals for teaching and use continual professional growth to develop their expertise. They practice self-examination, reflecting on the origin and consequences of their decisions and actions. In other words, they look inside and question what *they* are doing before they seek outside causes for students' academic failure. In sum, change agents are constantly asking questions and seeking answers.

Second, change agents have a philosophy that informs who they are as an educator, what they feel is important for students to learn, and how they teach in the classroom. This is what they preach to their colleagues about; their enthusiasm for teaching is exhibited in the classroom. Over time, a change agent's philosophy evolves as the educational needs of students change. Change agents are willing to give up some of their own classroom autonomy to work with administrators, parents, and teachers. These teachers are not afraid to make changes within their own classrooms—that is where they begin. Change agents are proactive teachers who participate in decisions that affect themselves, their students, the school, and the community.

Third, change agents don't act alone. They seek kindred spirits who share their vision; this shared vision forms the basis of the change process. For example, a group of teachers might share a similar vision of "schooling for democracy." As a community of learners, they see themselves and the students as having the ability to reshape knowledge to include and benefit all and to create a school that promotes equality for all learners. Each student, teacher, parent, and administrator should feel welcome in the school, regardless of cultural, racial, ethnic, or religious background. Expectations for student performance in reading, writing, and subject matter are high for all students. Change agents believe that school should promote independent thinking and encourage critical and creative problem solving. In this case, their humanistic approach is to empower the teachers (that is, themselves) and the learners by respecting the intellectual abilities and "voices" in the classroom and in the school at large. Change agents have a mission not just to build a better school but to build a better world for their students. How successful these teachers will be in translating this vision into an educational reality will depend on a variety of factors.

Obstacles to Change

Standing in the way of teachers initiating change is teachers' reluctance to give up familiar teaching practices (McIntryre & O'Hair, 1996). Teachers often believe that they are incompetent to implement change or feel overwhelmed at the task in front of them. To become change agents, teachers must be convinced that change will benefit *all* children. They must believe that what students learn and experience is meaningful and appropriate "for students in early elementary, intermediate, middle, and high school grades; for students of color and European-American students; for students in single- and multiracial school settings; for students in social studies and language arts as well as math and science; for school environments experiencing racial tensions and those that are harmonious" (Gay, 1996, p. 45).

Datnow (1998) takes a different view of obstacles to successful educational reform. She believes that administrators and teachers promoting change are naïve about the micropolitics present in schools and their power to prevent change. "Success is not simply guaranteed when teachers 'buy into' new ideas. In fact, teachers act in a variety of ways in response to reforms: Some teachers push or sustain reform efforts; others resist or actively subvert these efforts" (p.11). Datnow argues "that the literature on the school change process oversimplifies the role of teacher agency in reform and portrays culture as monolithic and shared, downplaying the importance of the micropolitical struggles that may ensue as teachers with varying ideologies grapple with reform" (p. 10).

At the micropolitical level, teachers with similar ideological views or commonalities based on age, race, or gender form subcultures and collaborate to "push" their own agendas which might not have the students and other teachers' best interests at heart. Unfortunately when change is initiated, these groups can exercise their power to maintain the existing structure or to influence the change process. Weiler (1988) reminds us that American schools are institutions that replicate society. Schools perpetuate the reproduction of existing class, racial, and gender divisions. Those who are in control, who dominate, and benefit from this structure, attempt in both conscious and unconscious ways to shape the schools to maintain their own privilege (see Chapter Three for a discussion of privilege). Attempting to engage in reform, without acknowledging the micropolitics of a school, can defeat your efforts. In fact, we must acknowledge these factions before we can address them (Datnow, 1998).

First Steps for Change Agents

Within their classrooms and schools, teachers have many opportunities to act on their beliefs about good education. Change happens when teachers are engaged in the process on different levels. In the classroom, teachers can take an active role by continually investigating and improving their teaching, asking why and thinking through alternatives. Teachers can also become part of curriculum reform committees and examine new challenges and ideas from a broader perspective. Teachers should include learning experiences that maximize the learning for each student and group in the school. These teachers select content that provides interdisciplinary connections, a multicultural perspective, gender equity, and adaptations to address the different learning styles of students. Change agent teachers also examine assessment practices, including alternative and authentic assessment, that complement curriculum.

Outside the classroom, teachers need to consider the cultural climate—the micropolitics—of their schools. Datnow (1998, p. 3) suggests examining the school culture for existing beliefs and practices to gain an understanding of those individuals or groups of teachers who can influence what happens in the change process because of their power and control over the other teachers. She poses three broad questions: "How are school cultures and structures contested and negotiated in the process of reform? Who has the power to shape schools, and how do these individuals accomplish their goals? How are professional relationships among teachers influenced by social location or, more specifically, gender?"

Finally, teachers must be part of the political process and find meaningful ways to involve themselves and parents in adopting school policies and electing school board members and administrators. To influence policies and representation, teachers must know how the system works. They must be willing to take risks and work with others to develop a shared vision that is crucial for the change process.

What we attempt to do in *Multicultural Education in Middle and Secondary Classrooms* is empower middle and secondary school teachers to become visionaries and change agents in a multicultural world. In this text, we encourage you to begin the change process by looking at your values and beliefs and how they influence your view of people and the world. We then challenge you to engage in a curriculum reform that makes learning accessible to all learners. We suggest ways in which reform can begin by first discussing basic concepts for understanding diversity and then offering readers several developmentally appropriate, culturally authentic instructional techniques for middle and secondary school students. We hope that this text inspires you to become a change agent in your classroom and then within the broader context of the teaching profession.

We return to the issue of teacher as change agent and "next steps" in Chapter Ten, "Challenges for Change and Diversity." You might want to skim over Chapter Ten before you begin the first chapter. Becoming a multicultural teacher or change agent is a process, and it can be helpful to revisit the ideas and suggestions more than once.

REFERENCES

Datnow, A. 1998. *The Gender Politics of Educational Change.* London: Falmer.

Davidman, L. M. and Davidman, P. T. 1994. *Teaching with a Multicultural Perspective.* White Plains, NY: Longman.

Eby, J. W., and Kujawa, E. 1994. *Reflective Planning, Teaching, and Evaluation: K-12.* New York: Merrill.

Gay, G. 1996. A Multicultural School Curriculum. In Grant, C.A., and Gomez, M. L. *Making Schooling Multicultural Campus and Classroom.* Englewood Cliffs, NJ: Prentice-Hall.

Grant, C. A., and Gomez, M. L. 1996. Journeying Toward Multicultural and Social Reconstructionist Teaching and Teacher Education. In Grant, C. A., and Gomez, M. L. *Making Schooling Multicultural Campus and Classroom.* Englewood Cliffs, NJ: Prentice-Hall.

Hardiman, R., & Jackson, B.W. 1997. In Adams, M, Bell, L. A., Griffin, P. (eds.) *Teaching for Diversity and Social Justice.* London: Routledge.

McIntyre, D. J., and O'Hair, M. J. 1996. *The Reflective Roles of the Classroom Teacher.* Belmont, CA: Wadsworth.

Nieto, S. 1996. *Affirming Diversity.* New York: Longman.

Passe, J. 1995. *Elementary School Curriculum.* Madison, Wisconsin: Brown & Benchmark.

Weiler, K. 1988. *Women Teaching for Change: Gender, Class & Power.* New York: Bergin & Garvey.

Chapter One

CREATING A CONTEXT FOR MULTICULTURAL EDUCATION

Situation one. You have a job interview tomorrow at an elite suburban high school (translate, mostly White student body). You have heard that the school is committed to diversity and multicultural education. You know you'll be asked a "multicultural question," and you want to get it right. What's the question, and what do you say?

Situation two. Your job interview the day after tomorrow is at an inner city middle school (translate, mostly Latino, African American, and low-income student body). You know they are going to ask you a "multicultural question," and you want to get it right. What's the question, and what do you say?

Are the questions the same? Are your answers the same? What definition of multicultural education is implicit in your answers? Some students think that multicultural education is only for minority students; others see multicultural education as focusing on being fair and treating everyone equally. Some students prefer not to see color and treat everyone as an individual, and some want to rewrite history to make it include everyone's experiences.

By now educators and prospective teachers have all heard of multicultural education and have formed some ideas about what it is and how it is applied in a classroom. A common response to multicultural education among middle and secondary school teachers is that it isn't relevant to their disciplines, except if they teach English or History/Social Studies, and in those disciplines it is important to include the writings and contributions of women and ethnic minorities.

Many believe that multicultural education is best "done" in the elementary grades where accepting and appreciating differences are part of the curriculum. These people might have heard of or seen many of the recent children's books that portray families of different ethnic, class, and ability backgrounds, but can't see how this relates to algebra class. Or how a discussion of Christmas, Chanukah, or Kwanzaa fits into chemistry class. Another response from middle and secondary school teachers is that although they are eager to try multicultural education, they simply don't know what to do. They are also acutely aware of the ACT and SAT tests their college-bound students will be taking and don't want to penalize students with what might be viewed as primarily a self-esteem building, feel-good frill. Finally, there are legitimate constraints on what one teacher can do in a 50-minute class that already has a set curriculum.

In Chapter One, we provide answers to the following questions: Where did multicultural education come from? What exactly does it mean? What does it take to be a multicultural teacher?

BRIEF HISTORY OF MULTICULTURAL EDUCATION

Ideas come with a history—a network of related ideas, circumstances, and events that are present at one time and on which an earlier idea is expanded or transformed or from which a new, but related, idea evolves. And of course no idea is static; once it is put forth, the idea can be changed by the number of people who think about it and try to understand and build on it. Scholars often cite the Civil Rights movement in the 1960s as the birth of multicultural education, but many of the ideas and goals embedded in multicultural education were part of an earlier discussion about cultural pluralism in the 1900s. Cultural pluralism refers to a belief that different ethnic or cultural groups should retain their heritage and culture while becoming a part of mainstream culture. Cultural and linguistic differences are accepted by the dominant culture.

Then, just as now, the United States was wrestling with changing demographics. Massive immigration by peoples from eastern and southern Europe between 1880 and 1920 had earlier immigrants concerned with the effect different cultures, languages, and histories might have on their status. The nativists were a political group that sought to restrict immigration and targeted these new immigrants for violence, including lynching. Others supported the Americanization movement that sought the assimilation of newcomers into mainstream predominantly White Anglo-Saxon Protestant (WASP) culture. Assimilation describes a process in which the culture, values, and language of new immigrants are suppressed, and the culture, values, and language of the dominant group are imposed.

Schools became a convenient place to foster (force) this assimilation. Children were taught English, "American" customs and values, and the importance of the melting pot in creating a new American society. "As a result of the nativists and Americanization movements, millions of White ethnics were forcibly and traumatically acculturated [assimilated] into the American mainstream. The almost total obliteration of the cultural identities of these groups, which are only now being painfully revived, testifies to the brutal effectiveness of these movements" (Suzuki, 1979, p. 44).

Within this context, cultural pluralists spoke out for a balance between assimilation and maintaining one's culture. In fact, Horace Kallen, a philosopher, "contended that the preservation of the culture and communal life of the different ethnic groups in American society would enrich the common [shared] culture and help extend and strengthen democracy" (Suzuki, 1979, p. 44; see also Garcia, 1991). W. E. B. Du Bois spoke out against accommodation—against changing one's culture to fit in. He was interested in developing Black leadership through higher education and "an Afro-American culture that would blend the African background of former slaves with American culture" (Spring, 1994, p. 55).

A Black American, educated at Fisk and Harvard Universities as well as at the University of Berlin, Du Bois opposed Booker T. Washington's views. Washington advocated an industrial arts education for Blacks that would develop good moral character and work habits. He believed that this education would enable Blacks to improve their economic conditions and, over time, gain them social acceptance from White Americans. His view supported a segregated school system.

> To Washington's program of accommodation, Du Bois proposed a strategy of "ceaseless agitation and insistent demand for equality [involving] the use of force of every sort: moral suasion, propaganda and where possible even physical resistance." He favored immediate social and political integration and the higher education of a Talented Tenth of the black population. His main interest was in the education of "the group leader, the man who sets the ideals of the community . . . " He therefore opposed Washington's exclusive stress on education of the hand and heart because without a "knowledge of modern culture" black Americans would have "to accept white leadership . . . " (Bennett, Jr., 1988, p. 332–333)

Du Bois's recognition of education as a tool for empowerment is integral to some scholars' definitions of multicultural education that we present in the next section. "What was most important for Du Bois was to educate Blacks to be discontented with their social position in the South" (Spring, 1994, p. 55).

Three other historical phenomena helped lay the foundations for multicultural education: early African American scholarship (Banks, 1996); the Service Bureau for International Education, established in 1933; and the progressive-education movement based on John Dewey's philosophy (Fereshteh, 1995). Early African American scholarship spanned four generations and includes the writings of such scholars as George Washington Williams, Carter G. Woodson, W. E. B. Du Bois, Horace Mann Bond, and Charles H. Wesley. The Service Bureau for International Education focused on teaching tolerance of other ethnic groups as a means of facilitating their assimilation and developed curriculum to overcome racism and discrimination. Although interest in this movement was not sustained, its emphasis on reducing prejudice is an essential component of present-day definitions of multicultural education. Dewey's emphasis on restructuring schools, on developing students' critical-thinking skills, and of fostering democracy are goals of multicultural education

(Fereshteh, 1995). "Multicultural Education: For Freedom's Sake" (Banks, 1996), one of the readings at the end of this chapter, discusses the links between multicultural education, western ideals, and democracy.

For the most part, we have been looking at the education of ethnic groups from the perspective of mainstream society; we have presented information that focuses on how institutions, such as the government and schools, responded to the education of "other" people. However, it is equally important to recognize the initiatives taken by members of these other groups as they worked to preserve their culture and attain educational equity. For example, according to Reyhner and Eder (cited in Spring, 1994), "By 1852 the Cherokee Nation had a better common school system than the neighboring states of Arkansas and Missouri" (p. 14). Blacks in Massachusetts fought, first for separate schools, and later for integrated schools. In 1861, Mary Peake established one of the first schools for Blacks in Fortress Monroe, Virginia, and in 1904, Mary McLeod Bethune established the Daytona Normal and Industrial School for Training Negro Girls. As early as 1819, Emma Williard, founder of the Troy Female Seminary, argued eloquently for women's rights to a substantive education before the New York legislature (Zinn, 1980). In addition, German Americans fought for the acceptance of their language, and by the late 1880s, eight states allowed for bilingual instruction in public schools (Garcia, 1991), while Puerto Rican teachers, their students, and the Puerto Rican Teachers Association fought to teach in Spanish (Spring, 1994).

Within the context of the 1960s Civil Rights Movement, educators again began to look more closely at the inequities of the United States educational system. Different ethnic and women's groups became vocal advocates for curricula that included their voices, stories, and contributions. Slowly the paradigm of assimilation and the melting pot gave way to cultural pluralism and led to the re-emergence of multicultural education.

At first, multicultural education referred only to ethnic and racial groups, but then expanded in the late 1970s and 1980s to include issues of gender, class, language, ability, religion, and sexual orientation, although not uniformly. For example, not all multiculturalists agree that sexual orientation should be included under the broad category of multicultural education. The inclusion of gay and lesbian issues in New York City's proposed multicultural curriculum generated considerable controversy. Other multiculturalists are concerned that as the term *multicultural* becomes synonymous with all kinds of *diversity,* "less often discussed are the growing tensions that exist between and among various groups that gather under the umbrella of multiculturalism . . . presuming a 'unity of difference'—that is, that all difference is both analogous and equivalent" (Ladson-Billings & Tate, 1995, p. 61–62). Multiculturalists favoring a narrower definition of multicultural education fear that as educators attempt to apply a multicultural framework to fit everyone's needs, it will meet no one's needs. Moreover, there is the distinct possibility that as multiculturalism becomes more "mainstream," it will be changed to fit the needs of existing institutions. In so doing, the potential for multiculturalism to radically challenge inequities will be undermined.[1]

In the next section, we look at several definitions of multicultural education. The history and definitions of multicultural education are naturally related. As you read, be aware of the links between the two and how some definitions respond to earlier educational goals for immigrants and students of color.

DEFINITIONS OF MULTICULTURAL EDUCATION

The term *multicultural education* only recently has become part of mainstream discussions about teacher training, but as we described earlier, the ideas have been around for quite some time. We will summarize the definitions of multicultural education as presented by Davidman and Davidman (1994) and Sleeter and Grant (1994). We have chosen these scholars because their works include a comprehensive overview of multicultural education definitions. Davidman and Davidman describe a more overlapping set of definitions, incorporating Afrocentric and global education, whereas Sleeter and Grant's approaches describe an evolving definition. Significant in the latter's definitional framework is an emphasis on the educational implications of the five approaches and the political ramifications of one's definition.

Definitions of multicultural education often refer to terms such as *race, ethnicity,* and *culture*. We will define these terms briefly and discuss them in greater depth in Chapter Two. *Race* categorizes individuals into groups (such as White, Black, Asian) based on certain outward physical characteristics. A person's *ethnicity* depends on "a sense of group identification, a common set of values, political and economic interests, behavioral patterns, and other culture elements that differ from those of other groups within a society" (Banks, 1991, p. 13). Some individuals identify strongly with a particular ethnic group (for example, Hmong, Italian, Turkish), but others feel little ethnic identification and identify more closely with the mainstream Euro-centric culture. "The classification of individuals by race and ethnicity is a complex and controversial undertaking. The concepts of race and ethnicity lack precise and universally accepted definitions. Their economic and social significance depend on a variety of factors, including how individuals identify themselves racially or ethnically and how others identify and treat them" (Council of Economic Advisors, 1998, p. 3). *Culture* refers to the specific shared values, beliefs, and attitudes of a group. Individuals often participate in more than one culture and may see themselves as bicultural. For example, one of the authors of this text would be identified racially as Black and would self-identify ethnically as African American. As a

---

[1] For further elaboration see Gloria Ladson-Billings; and William F. Tate IV, 1995. Toward a Critical Race Theory of Education. *Teachers College Record,* 97(1): 47–68; and Michael Olneck, 1993. Terms of Inclusion: Has Multiculturalism Redefined Equality in American Education. *American Journal of Education,* 101: 234–260.

member of American society, she participates in cultural traditions that reflect her ethnicity as well as those of the mainstream culture.

Begin thinking about which definition of multicultural education makes the most sense to you. You will need to consider your own underlying beliefs and assumptions about equality in American society, how children learn, and the goals of education. At this stage, you are beginning a process of making sense, constructing meaning, of multicultural education; be ready to reconsider whatever choice(s) you make as you proceed through this text.

Davidman and Davidman (1994) outline four overlapping categories for definitions of multicultural education: cultural pluralism; educational equity; reduction of racism, sexism, and other "-isms"; and integration with other philosophical movements. Cultural pluralism stresses acknowledging and celebrating diverse populations and their contributions to American society, whereas educational equity definitions focus on the necessity of providing ethnic minorities with an education that responds to their learning needs. It is important to note that equitable treatment doesn't necessarily mean treating students exactly the same (that is, equally). The reduction of "-isms" is a third category for definitions. The emphasis here is on helping students develop positive attitudes toward one another, overcome ethnocentrism, and confront racism, sexism, and so on within education and society.

The final category, labeled "multicultural education plus," links multicultural education with other philosophical approaches, such as, "social reconstructionism, multiethnic education, global education, and Afrocentric education" (Davidman & Davidman, 1994, p. 19). The combination of multicultural education with these other approaches broadens the scope and deepens the potential impact of multicultural education. We will discuss social reconstructionism when we present Sleeter and Grant's framework.

Multi-ethnic education underscores the educational and political needs of one historically oppressed ethnic group, such as Asian Americans or African Americans and instruction is designed to highlight the experiences, beliefs and values, and contributions of this group. Though recognizing the importance of class and gender, this perspective does not want these issues to overshadow the reality of oppressed ethnic groups. An integration of multicultural education and global education extends our understanding of differences to other nations and stresses the interconnectedness that exists between countries. James Banks has done extensive research in the area of ethnic studies (Banks, 1991). His pioneering work has been a source of information for educators, and his scholarship serves as a foundation for the field of multicultural education.

Afrocentric education is an example of a mono-ethnic curriculum where African history, values, and beliefs are at the center of learning. Davidman and Davidman describe several settings where this approach has been implemented; some where Afrocentric schools were developed in response to the needs of young African Americans, boys in particular; and others, such as in Portland Oregon Public Schools, where Afrocentric education was integrated with multicultural education.

In *Making Choices for Multicultural Education,* Sleeter and Grant (1994) present a detailed explanation and analysis of five broad approaches to multicultural education. Each category demonstrates a progression from accepting and accommodating to the present status quo in American education to calling for radically restructuring the purpose and goals of schooling. Sleeter and Grant analyze each category relative to how it responds to the present institutional structure and how it incorporates democracy into the classroom.

Teaching the Exceptional and the Culturally Different is primarily an assimilationist's approach to dealing with "special" populations. Even though this approach offers several sound pedagogical strategies, such as bridging school knowledge with the experiences and backgrounds of students, its ultimate goal is to provide students with the skills needed to make it into mainstream culture. "Most proponents regard immigrants, the poor, the unemployed, people with disabilities, and alienated members of society as lacking primarily the right skills, values, and knowledge. According to this approach, modifications are made in schooling to facilitate these students' academic achievement and their transition to the mainstream culture that White, middle-class children are learning" (Sleeter & Grant, 1994, p. 42). Some proponents of this approach see the differences in their students as deficits; others see them just as differences. A key distinction is that one view sees students with differences as inadequate, as having little "cultural capital" to add to the class, whereas the other view sees students with differences as having something unique to add to the class. Many middle and secondary school teachers are comfortable with this "culturally different" approach and see it as based on reality. Their argument goes something like this: "The ideals of social change and restructuring education are all well and fine, but students need to succeed in today's marketplace. Let's teach them the skills they need to write a good essay and the knowledge they need for the ACT or SAT. My students need help NOW."

The second approach, called Human Relations, draws on theories related to social learning, self-concept, and reference group identification. "The goals of this approach are to promote positive feelings among students and reduce stereotyping, thus promoting unity and tolerance in a society composed of different people" (Sleeter & Grant, 1994, p. 85). Much of what they say sounds similar to Davidson and Davidson's cultural pluralism category. Human Relations is an affective approach with its emphasis on appreciating the self and others. What is missing is recognition of the effect social and political institutions have on individuals. Students might treat each other nicely and not engage in individual acts of meanness, however, they will have learned nothing about injustices of the past and present. If teachers focus only on valuing diversity, they "can glorify the way people have adapted to poverty and powerlessness" (p. 117) without acknowledging the injustices that created this adaptation. In many ways, Human Relations is seen as an assimilationist approach.

Middle and secondary school teachers most assuredly want their students to respect one another and try to address these issues as they "come up" in class. Any name-calling is addressed immediately, and if students aren't working well in cooperative groups, teachers can teach a lesson on group dynamics or mediation techniques. In general, however, middle and secondary teachers view the Human Relations approach as part of the elementary curriculum and not a central focus of their work.

Single-Group Studies, an outgrowth of programs developed in the 1960s, are similar to Davidson and Davidson's multi-ethnic education category; however, Sleeter and Grant make the distinction that Single-Group Studies is broader in that it has evolved to include non-ethnic groups such as people with disabilities, gay people, or working-class people. A key assumption underlying this approach is that education and knowledge is not neutral and that it serves the needs/agenda of one or more powerful groups. Advocates of Single-Group Studies want to "promote social structural equality for and immediate recognition of the identified group" (1994, p. 124).

At the middle and high school levels, this approach is embodied in in-depth, comprehensive units about one group or courses in Black history, Latin American writers, or women's studies. Single-Group Studies pay particular attention to the curriculum being taught, and students learn about the history, contributions, and past and present discrimination of the identified group. The audience for these courses are both group and nongroup members. Sleeter and Grant characterize this approach as a good starting place, especially for teachers who do not have a strong background in ethnic studies and gender and class issues. Two criticisms of Single-Group Studies are that Single-Group curriculum is separate from the regular school curriculum and that Single-Group Studies don't often work together—thus overlooking points of connection and similar goals. Advocates of the Human Relations approach are afraid that Single-Group Studies are divisive, and Teaching the Exceptional and Culturally Different advocates view Single-Group Studies as shortchanging students by not providing them with the information and skills they need to succeed in a system that might be unfair. What usually happens in middle and secondary schools is that those teachers who support Single-Group Studies incorporate this approach into their courses or develop a single-group course to be offered to a few students. With the exception of some of the Afrocentric schools mentioned earlier, whole schools do not adopt this approach. In this way, the few advocates are allowed "to do their thing," a few students are exposed to new information, and most everything else stays the same.

The Multicultural Approach to multicultural education (Sleeter and Grant acknowledge the strangeness of this language) encompasses many of the beliefs and goals of the previous approaches, but it explicitly seeks to integrate these goals more fully across the curriculum and school setting. While advocates talk about appropriate instructional techniques and curriculum, they extend their discussion to appropriate evaluation techniques, school staffing, home and community-school relationships, and extra curricular activities. Multiculturalists are strong advocates of cultural pluralism, and increasingly they have incorporated gender and class in their analysis of pluralism. They argue "that because gender and class are also very important determinants of what happens, how it happens, and why it happens in society, these status attributes must also be considered in conceptualizing pluralism" (1994, p. 170). Another important concept for Multiculturalists is equal opportunity defined by equal outcomes for marginalized groups, rather than just equal access.

Sleeter and Grant present some of the problems associated with implementing the Multicultural Approach. First, to use this approach, teachers need to reeducate themselves about both content and pedagogy (that is, instructional strategies). Time for teachers is often at a premium; when the administration is not supportive, making change is difficult. Second, teachers often "treat multiple forms of diversity, especially race and gender, as parallel but separate" (p. 201). Teachers talk about race as if it were unrelated to class, gender, or disability. Finally, "the Multicultural Education approach directs too much attention to cultural issues and not enough to social structural inequalities and the skills [that is, analytical skills] that students will need to challenge these" (p. 202). Scholars such as Suzuki have cautioned against dwelling on culture and ethnicity and excluding the impact of "powerlessness, racism, and poverty" on people of color. Suzuki (1984) and Ogbu (1992) discuss how the culture of a group can change in response to oppression (that is, the use of power to institutionalize a group's privilege and prejudices). We discuss this concept further in Chapter Two. When the impact of oppression is not understood, multiculturalists can end up celebrating differences without recognizing social injustices that might have engendered these characteristics. Social injustice is the denial of an individual's full participation in society, economically, politically, or educationally. For example, teachers might misrepresent the reserve of Japanese Americans as a cultural trait and overlook the impact internment of Japanese Americans during World War II had on this group's behavior. Finally, critics of the Multicultural Approach feel that its proponents ought to be looking more closely at social class.

It is difficult to find middle and secondary schools or classrooms where the Multicultural Approach is being used. Teachers might be unconvinced of its need; they might subscribe to another less encompassing approach; they might have been told by school administration not to use the Multicultural Approach; or they might be unsure of or overwhelmed with how to implement such a program.

Education that is Multicultural and Social Reconstructionist integrates an understanding of social, cultural, political, and economic issues with the need for social action. The function of schooling is to "help students analyze their own lives in order to develop their practical consciousness about real injustices in society and to develop constructive responses" (Sleeter & Grant, 1994, p. 225). The goal of the Multicultural and Reconstructionist approach is to empower different groups by helping them "understand how their ascribed characteristics (e.g., race, class, gender, and their culture) impact on that oppression, which should lead them as a result to develop the power and skills to articulate both their own goals and a vision of social justice for all groups and to work constructively toward these ends" (p. 210). Education that is Multicultural and Reconstructionist views social behavior as more the result of group participation than of individual action. This approach maintains that groups keep power by controlling resources and ideas and develop economic, political, and social institutions that institutionalize their power. (See Reading 1, "Questioning the Status Quo: The Politics of Empowerment" at the end of this chapter.) Oppressed people do resist domination in a variety of ways, some leading to organized social change and others leading to individual acts of self-preservation. For example, Ogbu (1992) cites the behavior of many young African American males who resist doing well academically to reject what they believe are White cultural values. Their identity develops in opposition to a set of values African American males believe are part of the oppressive culture; this *oppositional identity* functions as a demonstration of resistance.

Proponents of Education that is Multicultural and Reconstructionist define learning as an active process in which students construct knowledge from personal experiences and by using their brains. (Students who are familiar with constructivism as a pedagogical approach will be familiar with this assumption.) These advocates cite Vygotsky who "believes that language is a social and cultural phenomenon that is central to the development of thinking and that cognitive development is greatly influenced by one's cultural and social environment" (p. 218). Multiculturalist/Reconstructionists draw on Dewey's desire to create mini sites in schools for developing democratic citizens. Students should be able to think critically and make decisions on social issues, a goal that W. E. B. Du Bois also envisioned. Culture should be studied not only to be appreciated but also to be understood in the context of other cultures and their social, political, and economic status. Collective activity and social action are essential goals of education that is Multicultural and Social Reconstructionist.

A very few teachers at the middle and secondary level are attempting to implement a Multiculturalist/Reconstructionist approach. Some view it as liberal hogwash, the result of too much political correctness. (George Will offers this view in Reading 2, "Multiculturalism as Compulsory Chapel" at the end of this chapter.) Others view the goals of this approach as too ambitious, difficult to achieve in isolation, or potentially frustrating for students. Once students are aware of these injustices, they are thwarted in not being able to resolve them constructively. A specific example of the Multiculturalist and Social Reconstructionist approach at the middle and secondary levels is found in ecology units where teachers feel comfortable in promoting student activism. They invite students "to think globally, act locally."

How a teacher implements multicultural education is a reflection of his or her implicit definition of the term. The "multicultural" instructional and assessment strategies employed, the curriculum topics included, and the relationships established with students express the teacher's underlying assumptions about society, students, and schooling. Sometimes future teachers are eager to embrace techniques, not caring about the theory behind them. Doing so leaves them poorly equipped to defend their choices and less reflective about the objectives they hope to achieve. (See the box, "A Definitional Analysis of Multicultural Education.")

A Definitional Analysis of Multicultural Education

Here, we present Bob Suzuki's (1979) definition of multicultural education, followed by a description of the teacher goals and student outcomes inherent in his definition. In parentheses, we have included our suggestions for making the definition more inclusive. As you read the following definition, ask yourself these questions:

- How does this definition compare with the others presented in the text?
- Do I share Suzuki's assumptions about American society, children, and education?
- Will this definition help me achieve the educational goals I have for my students?

Multicultural education is a multidisciplinary educational program that provides multiple learning environments matching the academic, social, and linguistic needs of students. These needs may vary widely due to differences in the race, sex, ethnicity, or sociolinguistic backgrounds of the students. In addition to enhancing the development of their basic academic skills, the program should help students develop a better understanding of their own backgrounds and of other groups that compose our society. Through this process, the program should help students learn to respect and appreciate cultural diversity, overcome ethnocentric and prejudicial attitudes, and understand the sociohistorical, economic, and psychological factors that have produced the contemporary condition of ethnic polarization, inequality, and alienation. It should also foster their ability to analyze critically and make intelligent decisions about real-life problems and issues through a process of democratic, dialogical inquiry. Finally, it should help them conceptualize a vision of a better society and acquire the necessary knowledge, understanding, and skills to enable them to move the society toward greater equality and freedom, the eradication of degrading poverty and dehumanizing dependency, and the development of meaningful identity for all people.

To understand the implications of this definition of multicultural education, let's look at its goals for teachers and outcomes for students.

Teacher Goals

1. Teachers should implement multicultural education in a variety of disciplines. (This would mean that multicultural education would be interdisciplinary and should be implemented in more than just a few select classes, such as English and history classes. To this we would also add "interdisciplinary.")

2. Teachers should offer students instruction that matches their needs based on factors such as race, sex, ethnicity, and sociolinguistic background. (We would add class and sexual orientation to the list of factors. Instruction would consider teaching and assessment techniques, student assignments, and learning styles. Many teacher-training programs today

continued on next page

A Definitional Analysis of Multicultural Education • *Continued*

only emphasize individualizing instruction based on students' abilities.)

3. Teachers should offer students basic academic skills as well as information about different groups in our society. (This would mean holding students to high academic expectations and providing them with academic and technological skills in reading, writing, computation, and critical thinking. It would also mean expanding curricula to include the contributions and experiences of people of color and women.)

4. Teachers should help students become aware of how sociohistorical, economic, and psychological factors have produced current conditions of inequality and ethnic polarization. (This moves multicultural education past the level of "celebrating" other cultures to a broadened understanding of how societies function and an awareness of social injustices.)

Student Outcomes

5. Students will develop respect and appreciation for cultural diversity.

6. Students will develop critical thinking and real-life problem solving skills. This definition of critical thinking means more than just decontextualized thinking skills. McLaren (1994, p. 169) states, "neoconservatives and liberals have neutralized the term critical by repeated and imprecise usage, removing its political and cultural dimension and laundering its analytic potency to mean 'thinking skills.' In their terms, teaching is reduced to helping students acquire higher levels of cognitive skills. Little attention is paid to the purpose to which these skills are to be put."

7. Students will develop a vision for a better society that is more humane, democratic, and egalitarian.

Now read the following definition by Sonia Nieto (1996, p. 307) and compare her definition with Suzuki's. Note common assumptions between the definitions and differences in word choice. Both offer comprehensive responses to the question "What is multicultural education?" Suzuki's definition was first published in 1979; Nieto's first appeared in 1992.

Multicultural education is a process of comprehensive school reform and basic education for all students. It challenges and rejects racism and other forms of discrimination in schools and society and accepts and affirms the pluralism (ethnic, racial, linguistic, religious, economic, and gender, among others) that students, their communities, and teachers represent. Multicultural education permeates the curriculum and instructional strategies used in schools, as well as the interactions among teachers, students, and parents, and the very way that schools conceptualize the nature of teaching and learning. Because it uses critical pedagogy as its underlying philosophy and focuses on knowledge, reflection, and action (praxis) as the basis for social change, multicultural education promotes the democratic principles of social justice.

READINGS

The four readings for Chapter One examine the relationship between politics and education. Shor's excerpt, "Questioning the Status Quo: The Politics of Empowerment," describes how education is never neutral—not even in math and science classes. Far from encouraging critical questioning, George Will maintains, in "Multiculturalism as Compulsory Chapel," that multiculturalism attempts "to inhibit debate" and "politicize and purge higher education curriculums." We counter Will's perspective indirectly in the third reading, "Motivating Future Educators Through Empowerment: A Special Case." We give examples of how we help our students develop critical questioning skills compatible with Sleeter and Grant's Multicultural and Social Reconstructionist approach to multicultural education. Finally, in "Multicultural Education: For Freedom's Sake," James Banks argues, "we can neither do away with the Western canon nor exclude the contributions of people of color." Banks sees multicultural education as essential to maintaining a free and democratic nation.

READING 1 *Questioning the Status Quo: The Politics of Empowerment*

Ira Shor

Education can be described in many ways. One way, suggested above, is to say that education is a contested terrain where people are socialized and the future of society is at stake. On the one hand, education is a socializing activity organized, funded, and regulated by authorities who set a curriculum managed (or changed) in the classroom by teachers. On the other hand, education is a social experience for tens of millions of students who come to class with their own dreams and agendas, sometimes cooperating with and sometimes resisting the intentions of the school and the teacher.

The teacher is the person who mediates the relationship between outside authorities, formal knowledge, and individual students in the classroom. Through day-to-day lessons, teaching links the students' development to the values, powers, and debates in society. The syllabus deployed by the teacher gives students a prolonged encounter with structured knowledge and social authority. However, it is the students who decide to what extent they will take

---

From Ira Shor, *Empowering Education*, pp. 13–15. Reprinted by permission of the University of Chicago Press.

part in the syllabus and allow it to form them. Many students do not like the knowledge, process, or roles set out for them in class. In reaction, they drop out or withdraw into passivity or silence in the classroom. Some become self-educated; some sabotage the curriculum by misbehaving.

To socialize students, education tries to teach them the shape of knowledge and current society, the meaning of past events, the possibilities for the future, and their place in the world they live in. In forming the students' conception of self and the world, teachers can present knowledge in several ways, as a celebration of the existing society, as a falsely neutral avoidance of problems rooted in the system, or as a critical inquiry into power and knowledge as they relate to student experience.

In making these choices, many teachers are unhappy with the limits of the traditional curriculum and do what they can to teach creatively and critically. Whether they deviate from or follow the official syllabus, teachers make numerous decisions—themes, texts, tests, seating arrangements, rules for speaking, grading systems, learning process, and so on. Through these practical choices, the politics of the classroom are defined, as critical or uncritical, democratic or authoritarian.

In class, as Apple suggested and as Giroux and Banks have also argued, the choice of subject matter cannot be neutral. Whose history and literature is taught and whose ignored? Which groups are included and which left out of the reading list or text? From whose point of view are the past and present examined? Which themes are emphasized and which not? Is the curriculum balanced and multicultural, giving equal attention to men, women, minorities and nonelite groups, or is it traditionally male-oriented and Eurocentric? Do students read about Columbus from the point of view of the Arawak people he conquered or only from the point of view of the Europeans he led into conquest? Do science classes investigate the biochemistry of the students' lives, like the nutritional value of the school lunch or the potential toxins in the local air, water, and land, or do they only talk abstractly about photosynthesis?

Politics reside not only in subject matter but in the discourse of the classroom, in the way teachers and students speak to each other. The rules for talking are a key mechanism for empowering or disempowering students. How much open discussion is there in class? How much one-way "teacher-talk"? Is there mutual dialogue between teacher and students or one-way transfers of information from teacher to students?

What do teachers say about the subject matter? Do students feel free to disagree with the teacher? Do students respond to each other's remarks? Do they act like involved participants or like alienated observers in the exchange of comments in the classroom? Are students asked to think critically about the material and to see knowledge as a field of contending interpretations, or are they fed knowledge as an official consensus? Do students work cooperatively, or is the class a competitive exchange favoring the most assertive people?

In addition, the way classrooms, schools, colleges, and programs are governed is political. Is there a negotiated curriculum in class, or is a unilateral authority exercised by the teacher? Is there student, teacher, and parent co-governance of the institution or an administrative monopoly on power?

School funding is another political dimension of education, because more money has always been invested in the education of upper-class children and elite collegians than has been spent on students from lower-income homes and in community colleges. Moreover, testing policies are political choices, whether to use student-centered, multi-cultural, and portfolio assessments, or to use teacher-centered tests or standardized exams in which women and minorities have traditionally scored lower than men and whites.

In sum, the subject matter, the learning process, the classroom discourse, the cafeteria menu, the governance structure, and the environment of school teach students what kind of people to be and what kind of society to build as they learn math, history, biology, literature, nursing, or accounting. Education is more than facts and skills. It is a socializing experience that helps make the people who make society. Historically, it has underserved the mass of students passing through its gates. Can school become empowering? What educational values can develop people as citizens who think critically and act democratically?

READING 2

Multiculturalism as Compulsory Chapel

George Will

The high school test asked students to identify the "Hellenic epic which established egotistical individualism as heroic." The correct answer was "The Iliad," the message of the question being this: Individualism is egotistical and egoism, rather than anything more noble, defines Western civilization. When a University of Pennsylvania student wrote of "my deep regard for the individual," an administrator underlined the word "individual" and wrote back: "This is a RED FLAG phrase today, which is considered by many to be RACIST. Arguments that champion the individual over the group ultimately privileges (sic) the 'individuals' belonging to the largest dominant group."

Asked what her fifth and sixth grade pupils learn about George Washington, a teacher says: "That he was the first president, that he was a slave owner, that he was rich—not much." She does teach about another white male: Eli Whitney. She says her pupils "know that he stole his invention from a woman who didn't patent it." How does the teacher know this? "Another teacher told me."

Reprinted by permission of Scribner, a Division of Simon & Schuster, from *A Woven Figure* by George F. Will. © 1997 by George F. Will.

During the 1992 quincentennial a public education group produced a study guide, "Rethinking Columbus," with chapter titles such as "Once Upon a Genocide" and "George Washington: Speculator in Native Lands." A Cornell residence hall director removed pictures of herself and her husband when she was accused, because of the pictures, of heterosexism. At a Cornell training session for resident advisers, an X-rated homosexual movie was shown and pictures were taken of the advisers' reactions, to detect homophobic squeamishness.

Some Brookline, Massachusetts, parents were denounced by public school officials as "censors" because they wanted to put back into the curriculum an advanced placement course on European history. The course had been found "incompatible with multiculturalism," presumably because it did not "validate" the self-esteem and contribute to the cultural "legitimization" of non-Europeans. Here is a multiple-choice exam question from Brookline: "A characteristic of the 13 English colonies was (a) complete religious freedom, (b) free high school education, (c) class distinctions, or (d) universal voting." "C" is the correct answer to this sly question that Richard Bernstein rightly says is "designed to demonstrate that something negative was the sole feature all the colonies had in common."

Critics of Bernstein's invaluable new book, *Dictatorship of Virtue: Multiculturalism and the Battle for America's Future,* from which these stories are culled, dismiss his meticulous reporting as "anecdotal," which is today's preferred description of inconvenient evidence. But a multitude of anecdotes makes a pattern, and the book frames with an explanatory theory the ugly picture of the depredations done in the name of "diversity." Bernstein, a reporter for *The New York Times,* is a liberal who is angry about the multiculturalists' attempts to smother intellectual diversity beneath "a thick glue of piousness."

What explains "the middle-class bureaucrats and education entrepreneurs, the guilty white liberals and aging flower children of the 1960s who most aggressively press the multiculturalist agenda"? Says Bernstein, "Thirty years ago, something shifted in the national mind." The broad contours of America's demography have not changed radically since the mid-1960s, and the foreign-born percentage of the population is much smaller than in 1920. What, then, accounts for today's multiculturalist frenzy?

Bernstein flinches from baldly stating the simple fact that many cultural institutions (including the Smithsonian, busy with vilifications of American history) have fallen into the hands of people who despise America. However, when he dissects the so-called "massive increase in hate crimes" in Minnesota—yes, Minnesota—he concludes, "There is a sizable industry of exaggeration that combines with a fear of appearing complacent about racism to create a misleading impression of American life." In fact, multiculturalism is a campaign to lower America's moral status by defining the American experience in terms of myriad repressions and their victims. By rewriting history, and by using name-calling ("Racist!" "Sexist!" "Homophobe!") to inhibit debate, multiculturalists cultivate grievances, self-pity and claims to entitlements arising from victimization. Hence the education trend that Bernstein calls "the curriculum as expiation of guilt."

Multiculturalism attacks individualism by defining people as mere manifestations of groups (racial, ethnic, sexual) rather than as self-defining participants in a free society. And one way to make racial, ethnic or sexual identity primary is to destroy alternative sources of individuality and social cohesion, such as a shared history, a common culture and unifying values. Hence the multiculturalists' attempts to politicize and purge higher education curriculums. Once universities are reduced to therapeutic institutions, existing to heal victimized groups and reform the victimizing society, our trickle-down culture produces similar distortions in primary and secondary education.

The multiculturalists' mantra is "diversity," but as Bernstein demonstrates, their assumption is that all authentic groups will share the sour leftism of the multiculturalists. Authoritarian politics and banal careerism have blended as "diversity" has become a growth industry, guaranteeing academic employment for the otherwise unemployable. Multiculturalists demand more jobs, honors, attention and subsidies, all in the name of the ultimate entitlement—a "right" to adore yourself and to make others express adoration of you.

The multiculturalists are invariably humorless and often ignorant, but these are not disabilities in today's academic settings. However, multiculturalists do have a fatal flaw as a political force: They manage to be simultaneously boring and ludicrous. Multiculturalism is, as Bernstein says, a kind of compulsory chapel. Yet in spite of all its bullying and occasional cruelties, it may by now be doing more good than harm because it is producing a libertarian backlash, of which Bernstein's not-at-all boring book is a splendid example.

READING 3

Motivating Future Educators Through Empowerment: A Special Case

A. Cheryl Curtis and Joan A. Rasool

Students enter our courses excited about becoming teachers, eager to "make a difference" in some child or adolescent's life and to open their pupils' eyes to the wonders of their disciplines. Most are ready to learn new instructional techniques, study the latest research on learning styles, and discuss how to implement multicultural education into their classrooms. Nevertheless, in motivating our prospective teachers to see themselves as future educational change agents, we regularly face polite and passive silence. Their interests are unwaveringly focused on students and their classrooms; few undergraduates enter teaching hoping to improve the profession as a whole. They define for themselves a narrow sphere of influence. Motivating them at least to consider, if not embrace, broader educational goals is practically impossible.

In addition, time is at a premium in many teacher-training programs. Educational reform has led to expanded subject-knowledge requirements and contracted pedagogical requirements for entry-level certificates. While providing students with a broad understanding of the field and specific pedagogical training, education courses are not very successful at inspiring students to view themselves as potential change agents. Under even the best of circumstances, instructors can hope to initiate a rudimentary process of reflection and critique—primarily around delivery of instruction—among prospective teachers. In sum, given their purposes and time constraints, teacher-training programs have scant opportunity to motivate preservice teachers and imbue them with the skills and perspectives to see themselves as educational change agents. Much of this work is left to a few elite teacher-training programs or graduate programs at research institutions.

Several educational reform measures—e.g., site-based management or career ladders—may allow for greater teacher participation. However, unless preservice teachers learn critical-analysis techniques, they will then be unable to engage in an expanded dialogue on the purposes and function of education.

How then can we hope to motivate our students to become socially and professionally empowered? Ironically, this empowerment is precisely what we want them to cultivate in their own pupils. For example, we tell our students that it is their responsibility to promote critical thinking among their pupils, in order to develop in them an understanding of social problems and to prepare them to take thoughtful action. However, given the licensing demands for teacher certification today, many departments do not have the flexibility to create a new course devoted to "teachers as change agents." We must look for opportunities in our present programs to motivate students.

Perhaps we can find the solution within courses that allow preservice teachers the opportunity to experience outcomes of instructional techniques that empower school children. Doing so makes for sound pedagogical practice. After all, we cannot expect teachers to teach skills effectively when they have had no experience. Empowerment for future teachers is a prerequisite to the authentic empowerment of public school children. Authentic empowerment is a radical concept that does not prescribe what any student might think to challenge or seek to change.

Many of our teacher-training programs already instruct preservice teachers on how to develop curricula that emphasize constructivist and cooperative activities and integrate higher-order thinking skills. We try to model these strategies in our methods courses. For example, we facilitate students' "discovery" of the lesson plan, set the stage for them to design their own methods course, or structure the design and execution of projects that include criteria for evaluation. We regularly group students for discussions and presentations. We ask them to evaluate themselves and other group members. We assign interdisciplinary units that teams of future content-area and special education teachers will complete. Finally, many teacher-training programs require reflective journals that encourage preservice teachers to make sense of their experiences. While these practices focus on the development and delivery of instruction and have the potential to empower future teachers to see themselves as confident knowers and capable learners, they do not ensure the development of teachers as change agents.

Teacher-training programs that incorporate critical and feminist perspectives and practices can create greater space for teachers' voices, help them expand their professional commitments, and motivate them to become catalysts of change. Inherent in critical and feminist pedagogies are beliefs in social reconstruction and the teacher as change agent. These pedagogies, incorporated into present educational courses, can provide a vital link between pupil and prospective-teacher empowerment and a necessary link between the prospective teacher and future change agent. We will briefly summarize some of the major tenets of critical and feminist pedagogies and then discuss three ways that we have brought these perspectives into our teacher-training programs.

Critical and Feminist Pedagogies

While we may define critical pedagogy in several ways, we draw specifically from the works of Paulo Friere and Ira Shor. Both focus on changing educational practices that perpetuate inequalities. They view learning as it is connected to social change. For example, they believe in learning that inspires students to create an economically and politically just society. Thus, we must view all curricula within a sociopolitical reality. Friere (1970) focused on the liberation of people from oppressive situations; thus, changing society and changing roles in society are important pieces of his message. Requiring future teachers to look at their relationships to society, examine the power of dominant and subordinate groups, and consider methods to change inequities are part of the teaching and learning process.

Feminist pedagogy emphasizes personal relationships, aesthetics, and affect in the construction of knowledge. Feminists nurture subjectivity rather than objectivity and emphasize working collaboratively and cooperatively. While feminist pedagogy may have some sociopolitical agenda, the focus is more on recognizing the role that subjective connectedness, voice, caring, and affect have in women's construction of meaning. It recognizes the significance of diverse perspectives and multiple voices. Feminists ask, "How is knowledge constructed? Whose stories get to be told?"

What is salient in the commonalities shared by critical and feminist pedagogy is the emphasis on democratic exchange in the classroom and liberation. Both dovetail nicely with constructivist and reflective pedagogies and offer an alternative to more traditional pedagogies that focus on a one-way transmission of knowledge. Rather than produce teachers who stand in front of classrooms as titular heads and dole out Truth, these pedagogies reflect the need to motivate students to become more empowered by the learning experience. In so doing, these theories are both constructivist and student-centered. Such classroom instruction requires that pupils become actively engaged—both cognitively and affectively—in their pursuit of making meaning. Such a classroom asks teachers to learn to silence their own voices and make room for student voices (Shor 1992).

Applying These Pedagogies in Teacher Education Classes

We can group the ways in which we integrate critical and feminist pedagogies in various ways. We can help students "read" the writer and the reader; provide students with questions to apply to curricula they develop and instruction they design; and heighten students' awareness of power dynamics in their professional relationships.

Using texts from our courses, we ask students to analyze the author's writing. We want students to "read" the writers of college textbooks, because many of them view textbooks as receptacles of objective truth. For example, we ask students to compare how two writers present the same topic in two textbooks. They are to note differences in treatment and tone, determine what information the author included or excluded, and reflect on how the author has constructed knowledge:

Excerpt #1 (Ornstein and Levine, 1993, 122):

> Although many of the concepts developed in *Emile* could be applied to the education of both boys and girls, Rousseau was writing about the education of the upper-class French male. Many of his comments are clearly sexist in that Sophy, who eventually becomes Emile's wife, is educated to become a pleasing companion for her husband. Despite the book's orientation to the education of the male, later educators, including many who were progressive or child centered, found much in Rousseau's writing that contributed to the liberation of both boys and girls.

Excerpt #2 (Smith and Smith, 1994, 226–228):

> Of the many educational thinkers during the Enlightenment, Jean Jacques Rousseau (1712–1778) stands out as offering a philosophy that influenced educators and schooling for centuries. In his novel *Emile,* published in 1762, he laid out the foundations. . . . Now, with the help of his tutor, Emile was to begin searching for a wife—whom he would find in the country. Her name was Sophie, and *her* ideal education would consist of learning how to please and care for men (because, in Rousseau's view, women were inferior intellectually and morally).
>
> Two women whose lives refuted Rousseau's views of femininity were Christine de Pisan (1364–1470?) and Mary Wollstonecraft (1759–1797). . . . Well-educated by her father, [Christine] began writing poetry—most notably, in response to a century-old French poem, *Roman de la Rose,* which characterized women as selfish, disloyal, untrustworthy, vicious, and easy victims of flattery. Her effective argument even suggested that women might be superior to men, and it supported both equal education and equal rights for women.
>
> This debate about women's political and educational rights continued for more than three centuries before it was joined by Mary Wollstonecraft, an

English feminist and pedagogical theorist. She thought that women's political rights should be equal to men's and that they should be educated through a curriculum that was as scholarly as men's.

Our students are quick to note that both writers admit that Rousseau was a sexist and then, with further questioning, to consider how the Pisan and Wollstonecraft information functions in our overall understanding. Here were women who argued capably in their own defense! Students then want to know the gender of the writers, which often leads to a discussion of how positionality—one's frame of reference for presenting information and interpreting and analyzing the facts—is never neutral or value free.

Positionality also requires students to "read" themselves. They begin to question their own interpretations, asking: What experiences influence my beliefs about who can learn and what should be taught? How does my background expand or contract my willingness to question or challenge my chosen profession?

We read to uncover writers' assumptions that can influence our understanding of the information. For example, students read the following passage (Ornstein and Levine, 1993, 29) and consider what the writers have not addressed or have left unspoken about the capabilities of preservice teachers of color and the fairness of standardized testing:

> Widespread testing of teachers has led to a growing concern about the performance of minority candidates for teaching, many of whom do not perform well on paper-and-pencil tests. In Alabama, for example, only about one-third of African-American students completing teacher-education programs passed the state teacher candidacy exams during the 1980s, compared to approximately three-fourths of nonminority candidates. Low passing rates for African-American and/or Hispanic candidates also have been reported in Arizona, California, Georgia, Mississippi, New Mexico, Oklahoma, Texas, and other states. Some observers believe that testing of prospective teachers has eliminated as many as 40,000 African-American and Hispanic candidates during the past decade.

How might a "minority" writer have reported this information? How can a writer influence our perceptions without realizing it? We expand our discussions to include racial privilege—the unearned assets and advantages that European Americans have because of their skin color. We study writers' use of language to show how they use positionality and privilege. Students compare Spring's (1994, 31) statement that, "after a long struggle for an independence that was quickly snatched away by an invading U.S. military, Puerto Rican citizens did not welcome subjugation by the U.S. government" with Ornstein and Levine's (1993) approach—"The history of Puerto Rican Americans, another large Hispanic group, dates to the Spanish-American War of 1898, when the United States acquired the island of Puerto Rico." As we ask students to relate the practice of reading the writer and reader to their roles as "dispensers" of knowledge, we hope that they become aware of their power and responsibility in instructing.

Developing Curricula and Designing Instruction

Methods courses offer students lots of practical advice for developing lesson plans and units. Students learn a variety of instructional techniques—both teacher-directed and student-centered—and how to assess and evaluate learning. Most instructors stress the importance of meeting individual needs of students based on language, culture, learning style, and special needs.

Developing curricula and designing instruction involves making numerous decisions. Tyler (1950) suggested asking four key questions: What shall we teach? How shall we teach it? How can we organize it? and How can we evaluate it? We have added to this list two other questions: Who does this lesson privilege? And Do my instructional practices create greater equity among my pupils?

In developing lesson plans, students must identify the lesson's assumed skills and knowledge and identify whom the plan "privileges." Any instructional approach will put some students at "an advantage," while others will be at "a disadvantage." Some lessons give good readers an advantage; others give good listeners and note-takers an edge. Others allow group workers or native speakers the chance to shine. Once future teachers are aware of this, they can vary their approaches and/or make adaptations for those who are not benefiting.

We also want students to place their classroom practices and lessons within a larger educational context. As background for our second question regarding practices that promote greater equity, we refer students to Rose (1989). His experiences with tracking and his work in remedial and developmental education highlighted how school-wide and classroom practices can lead to greater educational inequities. Students must step back from their curricula and instructional practices to consider whether their instruction reproduces existing inequalities among student populations or helps students gain more control over their lives: Is the purpose of education different for rural, inner-city, or suburban children? For public- and private-school children? Does the lesson plan reflect these larger educational inequities? We then link these questions to their teacher-training experiences: Does the instruction you receive reproduce existing inequalities among student populations, or is education helping you gain more control over your lives? If you were attending an elite private school, would you be receiving a different education? If yes, in what ways?

Finally, we weave a discussion of power throughout our courses. Students examine power differences among several groups: between students and teachers, among teachers, between teachers and administrators, the superintendent, the local school board, and the State Department of Education. When new teachers enter the profession with a practical understanding of some of these forces, they are more likely to get involved rather than frustrated. We tell our students that they cannot hope to escape into their classrooms and avoid the influence of outside forces telling them what to teach and what methods to use. As professionals, they will have to decide what role they want to play within the larger educational arena. Explicit discussions of power in our teacher-training programs offer students a more realistic view of the field and encourage them to see themselves as future contributors to the profession.

Power and Motivation

Nothing motivates quite like a sense of power over one's personal and professional life. It is true for both teacher and pupil, and for instructor and preservice teacher. Emancipatory practices in teacher training motivate prospective teachers to assume greater leadership roles within their profession and provide them with the necessary skills. As prospective teachers find their own voices, recognize the value of their own experiences, and learn to critique the education they are receiving and developing, they will transfer these tools to their pupils and their profession. Preservice teachers who have empowered themselves in their educational programs will feel motivated to continue that process in their careers.

The National Commission on Teaching & America's Future (NCTAF) (1996, 7), in its latest report on the status of education, addressed the need to "reinvent teacher preparation and professional development." The NCTAF (1996, 8) added, "All Americans have a critical interest in building an education system that helps people learn and work at high levels of competence, understand and respect other perspectives, take risks and persevere against the odds, and continue to learn throughout life." Future teachers, trained and encouraged to experience themselves as effective contributors to the field, will feel motivated to achieve these goals.

References

Cioffi, G. 1992. Perspective and experience: Developing critical reading abilities. *Journal of Reading* 36(1):48–52.

Freire, P. (trans. M. B. Ramos) 1970. *Pedagogy of the oppressed.* New York: Continuum.

Gore, J. M. 1993. *The struggle for pedagogies: Critical and feminist discourses as regimes of truth.* New York: Routledge.

Henderson, J. G. 1992. Curriculum discourse and the question of empowerment. *Theory into Practice* 31(3):204–209.

National Commission on Teaching & America's Future. 1996. What matters most: Teaching for America's future, Summary Report. New York: NCTAF. ERIC ED 395 931.

Ornstein, A. C., and D. U. Levine. 1993. *Foundations of Education,* 5th ed. Boston: Houghton Mifflin.

Rivera, J., and M. Poplin. 1995. Multicultural, critical, feminine, and constructive pedagogies seen through the lives of youth: A call for the revisioning of these and beyond: Toward a pedagogy for the next century. In *Multicultural education, critical pedagogy, and the politics of difference,* ed. C. E. Sleeter and P. L. McLaren, 221–244. Albany: State University of New York Press.

Rose, M. 1989. *Lives on the boundary: The struggles and achievements of America's underprepared.* New York: Free Press.

Shor, I. 1992. *Empowering education: Critical teaching for social change.* Chicago: University of Chicago Press.

Smith, J. K., and L. G. Smith. 1994. *Education today: The foundations of a profession.* New York: St. Martin's.

Spring, J. H. 1994. *Deculturalization and the struggle for equality: A brief history of the education of dominated cultures in the United States.* New York: McGraw-Hill.

Tyler, R. 1950. *Basic principles of curriculum and instruction: Syllabus for Education 360.* Chicago: University of Chicago Press.

READING 4

Multicultural Education: For Freedom's Sake

James A. Banks

In *The Dialectic of Freedom,* Maxine Greene (1988) asks, "What does it mean to be a citizen of the free world?" It means, she concludes, having the capacity to choose, the power to act to attain one's purposes, and the ability to help transform a world lived in common with others. An important factor that limits human freedom in a pluralistic society is the cultural encapsulation into which all individuals are socialized. People learn the values, beliefs, and stereotypes of their community cultures. Although these community cultures enable individuals to survive, they also restrict their freedom and ability to make critical choices and to take actions to help reform society.

Education within a pluralistic society should affirm and help students understand their home and community cultures. However, it should also help free them from their cultural boundaries. To create and maintain a civic community that works for the common good, education in a democratic society should help students acquire the knowledge, attitudes, and skills they will need to participate in civic action to make society more equitable and just.

Multicultural education is an education for freedom (Parekh, 1986) that is essential in today's ethnically polarized and troubled world. It has evoked a divisive national debate in part because of the divergent views that citizens hold about what constitutes an American identity and about the roots and nature of American civilization. The debate in turn has sparked a power struggle over who should participate in formulating the canon used to shape the curriculum in the nation's schools, colleges, and universities.

The Debate Over the Canon

A chorus of strident voices has launched an orchestrated and widely publicized attack on the movement to infuse content about ethnic groups and women into the school and university curriculum. Much of the current debate over multicultural education has taken place in mass media publications such as *Time* (Gray, 1991), *The Wall Street Journal* (Sirkin, 1990), and *The New Republic* (Howe, 1991), rather than in scholarly journals and forums. The Western traditionalists (writers who defend the canon now within the schools and universities) and the multiculturalists rarely engage in reflective dialogue. Rather, scholars on each side of the debate marshal data to support their briefs and ignore facts, interpretations, and perspectives that are inconsistent with their positions and visions of the present and future.

Reprinted from *Educational Leadership,* Dec 1991/Jan 1992, Vol. 49, No. 4, pp. 32–36, by permission of the Association for Supervision and Curriculum Development. © 1985 by ASCD. All rights reserved.

In his recent book, *Illiberal Education,* D'Souza (1991) defends the existing curriculum and structures in higher education while presenting an alarming picture of where multiculturalism is taking the nation. When multiculturalists respond to such criticism, they often fail to describe the important ways in which the multicultural vision is consistent with the democratic ideals of the West and with the heritage of Western civilization. The multicultural literature pays too little attention to the fact that the multicultural education movement emerged out of Western democratic ideals. One of its major aims is to close the gap between the Western democratic ideals of equality and justice and societal practices that contradict those ideals, such as discrimination based on race, gender, and social class.

Because so much of the debate over the canon has taken place in the popular media, which encourages simplistic, sound-byte explanations, the issues related to the curriculum canon have been overdrawn and oversimplified by advocates on both sides. The result is that the debate often generates more heat than light. Various interest groups have been polarized rather than encouraged to exchange ideas that might help us find creative solutions to the problems related to race, ethnicity, gender, and schooling.

As the ethnic texture of the nation deepens, problems related to diversity will intensify rather than diminish. Consequently, we need leaders and educators of good will, from all political and ideological persuasions, to participate in genuine discussions, dialogue and debates that will help us formulate visionary and workable solutions and enable us to deal creatively with the challenges posed by the increasing diversity in the United States and the world. We must learn how to transform the problems related to racial and ethnic diversity into opportunities and strengths.

Sharing Power

Western traditionalists and multiculuralists must realize that they are entering into debate from different power positions. Western traditionalists hold the balance of power, financial resources, and the top positions in the mass media, in schools, colleges and universities, government, and in the publishing industry. Genuine discussion between the traditionalists and the multiculturalists can take place only when power is placed on the table, negotiated, and shared.

Despite all of the rhetoric about the extent to which Chaucer, Shakespeare, Milton, and other Western writers are threatened by the onslaught of women and writers of color into the curriculum, the reality is that the curriculum in the nation's schools and universities is largely Western in its concepts, paradigms, and content. Concepts such as the Middle Ages and the Renaissance are still used to organize most units in history, literature, and the arts. When content about African and Asian cultures is incorporated into the curriculum, it is usually viewed within the context of European concepts and paradigms. For example, Asian, African, and American histories are often studied under the topic, "The Age of Discovery," which means the time when Europeans first arrived in these continents.

Facing Realities

If they are to achieve a productive dialogue rather than a polarizing debate, both Western traditionalists and the multiculturalists must face some facts. The growing number of people of color in our society and schools constitutes a demographic imperative educators must hear and respond to. The 1990 Census indicated that one of every four Americans is a person of color. By the turn of the century, one of every three will be of color (The Commission, 1988). Nearly half of the nation's students will be of color by 2020 (Pallas et al., 1989). Although the school and university curriculums remain Western-oriented, this growing number of people of color will increasingly demand to share power in curriculum decision making and in shaping a curriculum canon that reflects their experiences, histories, struggles, and victories.

People of color, women, and other marginalized groups are demanding that their voices, visions, and perspectives be included in the curriculum. They ask that the debt Western civilization owes to Africa, Asia, and indigenous America be acknowledged (Allen, 1986; Bernal, 1987). The advocates of the Afrocentric curriculum, in sometimes passionate language that reflects a dream long deferred, are merely asking that the cultures of Africa and African-American people be legitimized in the curriculum and that the African contributions to European civilization be acknowledged. People of color and women are also demanding that the facts about their victimization be told, for truth's sake, but also because they need to better understand their conditions so that they and others can work to reform society.

However, these groups must acknowledge that they do not want to eliminate Aristotle and Shakespeare, or Western civilization, from the school curriculum. To reject the West would be to reject important aspects of their own cultural heritages, experiences, and identities. The most important scholarly and literary works written by African-Americans, such as works by W. E. B. DuBois, Carter G. Woodson, and Zora Neale Hurston, are expressions of Western cultural experiences. African-American culture resulted from a blending of African cultural characteristics with those of African peoples in the United States.

Reinterpreting Western Civilization

Rather than excluding Western civilization from the curriculum, multiculturalists want a more truthful, complex, and diverse version of the West taught in the schools. They want the curriculum to describe the ways in which African, Asian, and indigenous American cultures have influenced and interacted with Western civilization. They also want schools to discuss not only the diversity and democratic ideals of Western civilization, but also its failures, tensions, dilemmas, and the struggles by various groups in Western societies to realize their dreams against great odds.

We need to deconstruct the myth that the West is homogeneous, that it owes few debts to other world civilizations, and that only privileged and upper-status Europeans and European-American males have been its key actors. Weatherford (1988) describes the debt the West owes to the first Americans. Bernal (1987), Drake (1987), Sertima (1984), and Clarke (1990) marshal considerable amounts of historical and cultural data that describe the ways in which African and Afroasiatic cultures influenced the development of Western civilization. Bernal, for example, presents linguistic and archaeological evidence to substantiate his claim that important parts of Greek civilization (technologies, language, deities, and architecture) originated in ancient Africa.

We should teach students that knowledge is a social construction, that it reflects the perspectives, experiences, and the values of the people and cultures that construct it, and that it is dynamic, changing, and debated among knowledge creators and users (Banks, 1991). Rather than keep such knowledge debates as the extent to which African civilizations contributed to Western civilization out of the classroom, teachers should make them an integral part of teaching. The classroom should become a forum in which multicultural debates concerning the construction of knowledge take place. The voices of the Western traditionalists, the multiculturalists, textbook authors, and radical writers should be heard and legitimized in the classroom.

Toward the Democratic Ideal

The fact that multiculturalists want to reformulate and transform the Western canon, not to purge the curriculum of the West, is absent from most of the writings of the Western traditonalists. It doesn't support their argument that Shakespeare, Milton, and Aristotle are endangered. By the same token, the multiculturalists have written little about the intersections of multicultural content and a Western-centric canon perhaps because they have focused on ways in which the established Western canon should be reconstructed and transformed.

Multicultural education itself is a product of the West. It grew out of a struggle guided by Western ideals for human dignity, equality, and freedom (Parker, 1991). Multicultural education is a child of the civil rights movement led by African Americans that was designed to eliminate discrimination in housing, public accommodation, and other areas. The leaders of the civil rights movement, such as Fannie Lou Hamer, Rosa Parks, and Daisy Bates, internalized the American democratic ideal stated in such important United States documents as the Declaration of Independence, the Constitution and the Bill of Rights. The civil rights leaders of the 1960s and 1970s used the Western ideals of freedom and democracy to justify and legitimize their push for structural inclusion and the end of institutionalized discrimination and racism.

The civil rights movement of the 1960s echoed throughout the United State and the world. Other groups, such as Native Americans and Hispanics, women, and people with disabilities, initiated their own freedom movements. These cultural revitalization movements made demands on a number of institutions. The nation's schools and universities became primary targets for reform, in part because they were important symbols of the structural exclusion that victimized groups experienced, and in part because they were easily accessible.

It would be a serious mistake to interpret these cultural revitalization movements and the educational reforms they gave birth to as a repudiation of the West and Western civilization. The major goals of these movements are full inclusion of the victimized groups into Western institutions and a reform of these institutions so that their practices are more consistent with their democratic ideals. Multicultural education not only arose out of Western traditions and ideals, its major goal is to create a nation-state that actualizes the democratic ideals for all that the Founding Fathers intended for an elite few. Rather than being divisive as some critics contend, multicultural education is designed to reduce race, class, and gender divisions in the United States and the world.

Given the tremendous social class and racial cleavages in United States society, it is inaccurate to claim that the study of ethnic diversity will threaten national cohesion. The real threats to national unity—which in an economic, sociological, and psychological sense we have not fully attained but are working toward—are the deepening racial and social-class schisms within United States society. As Wilson (1987) points out in *The Truly Disadvantaged,* the gap between the rich and the poor has grown tremendously in recent years. The social-class schism has occurred not only across racial and ethnic groups, but within these groups. Hence, the rush to the suburbs has not just been a white flight, but has been a flight by the middle class of many hues. As a consequence, low-income African Americans and Hispanics have been left in inner-city communities without the middle-class members of their groups to provide needed leadership and role models. They are more excluded than ever from mainstream American society.

Educating for Freedom

Each of us becomes culturally encapsulated during our socialization in childhood. We accept the assumptions of our own community culture and internalize its values, views of the universe, misconceptions, and stereotypes. Although this is as true for the child socialized within a mainstream culture as it is for the minority child, minority children are usually forced to examine, confront, and question their cultural assumptions when they enter school.

Students who are born and socialized within the mainstream culture of a society rarely have an opportunity to identify, question, and challenge their cultural assumptions, beliefs, values, and perspectives because the school culture usually reinforces those that they learn at home and in their communities. Consequently, mainstream Americans have few opportunities to become free of cultural assumptions and perspectives that are monocultural, that devalue African and Asian cultures, and that stereotype people of color and people who are poor, or who are victimized in other ways. These mainstream Americans often have an inability to function effectively within other American cultures, and lack the ability and motivation to experience and benefit from cross-cultural participation and relationships.

To fully participate in our democratic society, these students and all students need the skills a multicultural education can give them to understand others and to thrive in a rapidly changing, diverse world. Thus, the debate between the Western traditonalists and the multiculturalists fits well within the tradition of a pluralistic democratic society. Its final result will most likely be not exactly what either side wants, but a synthesized and compromised perspective that will provide a new vision for the nation as we enter the 21st century.

References

Allen, P. G. (1986). *The Sacred Hoop: Recovering the Feminine in American Indian Traditions.* Beacon Press.

Banks, J. A. (1991). *Teaching Strategies for Ethnic Studies,* 5th ed. Boston: Allyn and Bacon.

Bernal, M. (1987). *The Afroasiatic Roots of Classical Civilization,* Vol. 1: *The Fabrication of Ancient Greece 1785–1985.* London: Free Association Books.

Clarke, J. H. (1990). "African People on My Mind." In *Infusion of African and African American Content in the School Curriculum: Proceedings of the First National Conference,* edited by A. G. Hilliard III, L. Payton-Stewart, and L. O. Williams. Morristown, N.J.: Aaron Press.

The Commission on Minority Participation in Education and American Life. (May 1988). *One-Third of a Nation.* Washington, D.C.: The American Council on Education.

D'Souza, D. (1991). *Illiberal Education: The Politics of Race and Sex on Campus.* New York: The Free Press.

Drake, St. C. (1987). *Black Folk Here and There.* Vol. 1. Los Angeles: Center for Afro-American Studies, University of California.

Gray, P. (July 8, 1991). "Whose America?" *Time* 138: 13–17.

Greene, M. (1988). *The Dialectic of Freedom.* New York: Teachers College Press.

Howe, I. (February 18, 1991). "The Value of the Canon." *The New Republic:* 40–44.

Pallas, A. M., G. Natriello, E. L. McDill. (June–July 1989). "The Changing Nature of the Disadvantaged Population: Current Dimensions and Future Trends." *Educational Researcher* 18, 2: 2.

Parekh, B. (1986). "The Concept of MultiCultural Education." In *Multicultural Education: The Interminable Debate,* edited by S. Modgil, G. K. Verma, K. Mallick, and C. Modgil. Philadelphia: The Falmer Press, pp. 19–31.

Parker, W. P. (1991). "Multicultural Education in Democratic Societies." Paper presented at the annual meeting of the American Educational Research Association, Chicago.

Sirkin, G. (January 18, 1990). "The Multiculturalists Strike Again." *The Wall Street Journal,* p. A14.

Sertima, I. V., ed. (1984). (Ed) *Black Women in Antiquity.* New Brunswick, N.J.: Transaction Books.

Weatherford, J. (1988). *Indian Givers: How the Indians of the Americas Transformed the World.* New York: Fawcett Columbine.

Wilson, W. J. (1987). *The Truly Disadvantaged: The Inner City, the Underclass, and Public Policy.* Chicago: University of Chicago Press.

DISCUSSION QUESTIONS AND ACTIVITIES

1. We have spent a great deal of time presenting multiple definitions of multicultural education. Which definition or approach appeals to you the most? On what do you base this choice? How does your choice of definition affect how you might implement multicultural education in your field?

2. Look up the definition of multicultural education in another textbook (for example, foundations of education textbook), and analyze its meaning.

3. How can we ensure that our use of categories or generalized statements about groups of people and cultures will expand, not limit, our discussion and understanding of others?

4. The words we use and the way we structure our sentences can convey subtle differences in meanings and give an indication of our views and values. The following sentence is taken from Chapter One:

    Schools became a convenient place to foster (force) this assimilation.

    If we support the policies that were used to Americanize immigrants, then foster might seem like the appropriate term. If we oppose these practices, then force might seem like the more accurate term. How can the following sentence be rephrased to convey a different sense of who is responsible for the problem? "Our high school has become an integrated, multicultural school and it is being challenged to solve the problems created by its diverse student population." As a reader, you need to be aware of the nonobjective, non-neutral meanings conveyed by word choice.

    a. Using a textbook from your content area discipline, look for examples of word choice that convey political meanings. Be sure to look at introductory sections, such as the forward, preface, or instructions to the teacher.

    b. Look for additional examples in the text and readings in Chapter One.

5. In what ways does multicultural education support democracy?

6. What is Will's opinion of multicultural education? Make a list of all the reasons he presents in support of his position. How would you respond to his statements? (Keep your answers and refer to them after reading the textbook.)

REFERENCES

Banks, J. A. 1991. *Teaching strategies for ethnic studies,* 5th ed. Boston: Allyn & Bacon.

Banks, J. A. 1996. The African American roots of Multicultural Education. In J. A. Banks (ed.), *Multicultural education, transformative knowledge, and action: Historical and contemporary perspectives.* New York: Teachers College, Columbia University.

Bennett, Jr., L. 1988. *Before the Mayflower,* 6th ed. New York: Penguin.

Council of Economic Advisers. 1998. *Changing America: Indicators of social and economic well-being by race and Hispanic origin.* http://www.whitehouse.gov/WH/EOP/CEA/html/publications.html.

Davidman, L. M., and Davidman, P. T. 1994. *Teaching with a multicultural perspective.* New York: Longman.

Fereshteh, M. H. 1995. Multicultural Education in the United States: A Historical Review. *Multicultural Review, 4:* 38–45.

Garcia, R. L. 1991. *Teaching in a pluralistic society: Concepts, models, strategies,* 2nd ed. New York: HarperCollins.

Ladson-Billings, G., and Tate, IV, W. F. 1995. Toward a Critical Race Theory of Education. *Teachers College Record, 97*(1): 47–68.

McLaren, P. 1994. *Life in schools: An introduction to critical pedagogy in the foundations of education.* New York: Longman.

Nieto, S. 1996. *Affirming diversity: The sociopolitical context of multicultural education,* 2nd ed. White Plains, NY: Longman.

Ogbu, J. U. 1992. Understanding Cultural Diversity and Learning. *Educational Researcher, 21*(8): 4–14.

Olneck, M. 1993. Terms of inclusion: Has multiculturalism redefined equality in American education. *American Journal of Education, 101:* 234–260.

Shor, I. 1992. *Empowering education.* Chicago: University of Chicago Press.

Sleeter, C. E., and Grant, C. A. 1994. *Making choices for multicultural education: Five approaches to race, class, and gender,* 2nd ed. New York: Macmillan.

Spring, J. 1994. *Deculturalization and the struggle for equality.* New York: McGraw-Hill.

Suzuki, B. H. 1979. Multicultural education: What's it all about? *Integrated Education, 17*(97–98): 43–50.

Suzuki, B. H. 1984. Curriculum transformation for multicultural education. *Education and Urban Society, 16*(3): 294–322.

Zinn, H. 1980. *A people's history of the United States.* New York: HarperCollins.

Chapter Two

 **THE ROLE OF RACE, CLASS, AND GENDER IN THE CLASSROOM**

> Race and racism in the United States is at once an utter illusion and a material reality, a fiction and "scientific" fact. It is both a political wedge and unifying force. It is structured by legislation yet destabilized by judicial fiat, shaped by public opinion but also configured by academic consensus. The history and contemporary reality of race and racism in the U.S. forces individuals to negotiate daily between the ideological pillars of democracy—justice, freedom, and equality—and the constant evidences of racial inequality.
>
> *Lee D. Baker, Ph.D., Department of Cultural Anthropology,*
> *Duke University— Internet communiqué*

Ms. Stanley: I like to think of my students as individuals. I want to make sure each student is treated fairly and receives the same quality education. To do that I concentrate on developing interesting, content-rich lesson plans and use the latest innovative teaching techniques. I care about all my students and want them to be successful. I focus on work turned in and avoid thinking about a student's color, socioeconomic background, or gender.

Mr. Hill: I agree with Ms. Stanley, but I think I am more empathetic to the needs of my poor students, students of color, and girls in my classes. I know that not enough girls and students of color are going into the science fields, and it takes money in the home to buy a computer or pay for those trips to Sea World. I incorporate effort into the grades I give students. Let's face it, if students already have two strikes against them, why give them a third? I also make a special attempt to encourage these students to stay involved with their academics and develop a "can-do" attitude.

Does Ms. Stanley or Mr. Hill speak for you? According to your criteria, are these teachers multiculturalists? In this chapter, we explore the concepts of race, class, and gender and their relevance to middle and secondary school teachers. From a multicultural and reconstructionist perspective, these variables can have an important effect on how teachers teach and how students perform. What do we need to know to ensure that students don't get "a third strike" against them and do get a "quality education"?

A word of caution: Although issues around race, class, and gender permeate the media, current talk shows, and some academic circles, most of us have had little experience discussing these issues in public—and many feel that's the way it should remain. Our teaching experience, however, supports a more open discussion for several reasons. First, people become more aware of what they and others think and feel. Greater consciousness can help people uncover subtle attitudes that they were unaware of and lead to more effective student-teacher relationships. We are concerned with how teachers connect with their students, particularly students from different cultural or racial backgrounds. You might ask yourself what are some of the assumptions that Ms. Stanley and Mr. Hill make about their students or what perceptions underlie their interactions with students? Second, it is rare to find two people who hold the same view regarding the impact of race, class, and gender in the classroom. By exchanging views, prospective teachers practice a skill we hope they want to impart to their students—the ability to listen carefully and respond thoughtfully to another's opinion. Third, teachers tell us that by becoming more familiar and more comfortable with these issues, they feel less defensive and more proactive in their own and their students' lives.

Middle and secondary students are extremely sensitive to the unspoken attitudes and nonverbal messages we convey in class. We might deliver the best-planned lessons that incorporate the "most multicultural content" and use the "most diverse" teaching strategies but still not reach our students. The increased personal clarity that comes with dealing directly with issues of race, class, and gender can free teachers to develop more effective relationships with students, allow teachers to maintain high expectations for everyone, and create an atmosphere where they can "get on" with teaching their subject matter.

RACE AND RACISM

Race and Multicultural Education

Much of the early discussion of multicultural education has focused on race, a phenomenon consistent with what has been described as a "national obsession" with race relations in the United States. As noted in Chapter One, the focus on race in multicultural education is due largely to the historical evolution of multicultural education in American society. We suggested that the roots of multicultural education first sprouted in the cultural pluralism movement of the 1900s with the migration of immigrants from Europe. This short-lived movement attempted to fight off the assimilation promoted by American educational systems.

Cultural distinctiveness was not valued, and many Europeans acquiesced to the pressures of assimilation. For pragmatic reasons, European immigrants learned to accommodate. Being Caucasian made assimilation more probable. African Americans, Native Americans, and Asian immigrants were not extended the same invitation to blend in. Race was the most overt factor in keeping people of color separated.

Race: A Biological or Social Construct?

Debate rages over race as a biological and social construct. Traditionally, biologists have defined race based on physical characteristics—characteristics at one time believed to be obvious and distinctive. Skin color, hair type/texture and head shape, and others were among the defining features used as classification markers. This practice, however, is not without practical complications. For example, given added dimensions such as mixed heritage, racial distinctions are not easily ascertained. Moreover, some scientists have always questioned the accuracy of racial designations as a biological classification. The American Association for the Advancement of Science recently described deficits of using race as a classification tool. For example, new medical techniques now allow scientists to examine genetic characteristics that reveal commonalities across groups and diversity within them. Scientific proof of these commonalities speaks to the idea of a shared humanity and represents a shift away from some of the race-based research that has fueled racist beliefs in this country.

On the other hand, reaction to the possibility of adding a new multiracial category to the Census Bureau's questionnaire has raised a stir among those who feel this is yet another political act of dividing groups who share a common historical relationship with the dominant society. Perhaps social reality is a more powerful factor than biology in determining our understanding of race.

Some sociologists suggest that "the most appropriate definition of a racial ... group is that its members believe or *outsiders believe* [emphasis ours] that they share a common national origin, cultural traits, or distinctive physical feature" (Ferrante, 1995). Designated membership is the result of shared "social definitions." The People's Institute for Survival and Beyond defines race as "a specious classification of people, created by Whites, which ascribes or assigns for the purpose of establishing and maintaining power and privilege the notion of human worth and social status. White is the model of humanity to which everything else is measured."

As a social construct, racial categories have been widely manipulated politically and economically to oppress certain groups. *Racism* is the term applied to the practice of using institutional power to enforce racial preferences and prejudices. The ability to oppress others is directly linked to accessing institutional power. "In the United States at present, only Whites can be racists, since Whites dominate and control the institutions that create and enforce American cultural norms and values ... Blacks and Third World people do not have access to the power to enforce any prejudices they may have, so they cannot, by definition, be racists." (Education & Racism, National Education Association, 1973 cited by RURacist, nd). Even though prejudice and discrimination can be practiced by any individuals, including persons of color, racism is unique in its connection to those who have the power to affect all major institutions, such as government, schools, churches, courts, businesses, hospitals, and the media.

Personal Definitions of Racism, Positionality, and Privilege

Many students and teachers respond viscerally to the definition of racism presented earlier. They speak anecdotally of individual acts of intolerance and hatred perpetrated by all races and argue that these acts are just as odious as racist acts committed by Whites. Others claim that "things aren't so bad; oppression is more a thing of the past," or cite Rodney King's plea "Why can't we all just get along" or state that all people—even White heterosexual men—are oppressed in some way. The shortcoming in these statements is that they overlook issues of institutionalized and socialized position and privilege.

Positionality and privilege are frequently addressed in multicultural literature. Though these terms are not used interchangeably, we feel that they are grounded in similar interpretations of societal experiences. Understanding positionality and privilege is useful in our discussions of gender and class.

Positionality refers to those parts of our identity that develop out of our "positions" or roles we have in society including such factors as race, age, gender, socioeconomic class, and occupation. How we come to know and experience the world is partly a result of our personalities—Nenne will forever see the half-filled glass as half empty; Kevin will always see it as half full—and partly the result of the societal lens through which we look. Positionality is a lens through which we interpret our experiences. Nenne's interpretation of events will be filtered through her experiences as an African woman of great wealth; Kevin's views will be influenced by his working-class, White, male background. Positionality is our subjective accounting of the world. Positionality is not immutable and certainly can change as we have new experiences and are exposed to others whose positionality is different from ours, but we should be aware that certain kinds of knowledge and particular powers are often tied to positionality. Curtis offers insight into her positionality as an African American educator in the chapter reading, "The Multicultural Me."

Until recently scholars have conducted research and written textbooks without being aware of or making explicit their frames of references. These writers have been in powerful positions to influence whose story is told, whose view of the world is published, and whose knowledge is considered most important. Their findings, especially in the sciences, are viewed as "objective" and "value-free." Most educational research has been dominated by a White, male, middle-class, Eurocentric positionality with its results assumed to be universal. In the process, voices of people of color, women, the poor, and nonwestern ideologies have been excluded.

Some positions in society are more privileged than others are. People in these positions get more of society's "goods" and receive advantages of which they are often unaware. For example, McIntosh acknowledges the subtle effect that White privilege exhibits in our society.

> As a White person, I realized I had been taught about racism as something that puts others at a disadvantage, but had been taught not to see one of its corollary aspects, White privilege, which puts me at an advantage. . . .
>
> I think Whites are carefully taught not to recognize White privilege ... I have come to see White privilege as an invisible package of unearned assets that I can count on cashing in each day, but about which I was "meant" to remain oblivious. (1995, p. 76)

McIntosh further describes this unacknowledged privilege as the basis for unconscious oppression and racism. Getting Whites to recognize their privilege is a frustrating task particularly when there are layers of denial preventing an awareness of this deeply internalized phenomenon. (See the chapter reading, "White Privilege in Schools.") People want to believe that they have earned what they get, and many people work *very* hard to get what they have. The myth of a meritocracy, a social system where one's effort determines success, is a dearly held mainstream cultural belief. Students talk about parents and grandparents who worked three jobs to provide a better life for their families. It is hard to argue with visible and individual efforts, but the trick to understanding privilege is in understanding its invisibility. Some parents and grandparents have been "allowed" to work three jobs while some groups of people have been prevented from working one job. Regrettably, the overall system in place in the United States today still over-empowers one group. (The first set of chapter readings, "Report: U.S. Gap between Rich, Poor is Widening" and "If Poverty Is the Question . . ." further explore this reality.)

Implications of Race in the Classroom

When Cornel West titled his philosophical treatise *Race Matters,* he no doubt considered the double entendre implicit in the two words. The title signifies the contents of the book and reminds us that in this country, race is a significant social reality. Whether we like it or not, race matters, and it plays an important part in how we are socialized. Classrooms are not immune from the effects of racialized socialization and in many cases perpetuate it.

"Many faculty tend(ed) to look away from the problems of race and thereby deprive(d) themselves and their White students of the opportunity of becoming aware of their attitudes towards race and they deprive(d) their black students of the essential opportunity of being treated unequivocally as equals" (Katz, 1983, p. 30). Katz describes this as a defense mechanism used particularly by White faculty to avoid facing "their own almost unwilling prejudice" (p. 31), a prejudice borne out of their own limited experiences with people of color as either acquaintances or friends. This "psychological walling" cuts teachers off from even recognizing that there are racial concerns to be addressed.

Much of the research chronicles the negative effect of minority student-teacher interaction. Students of color are not expected to achieve as highly as are White students—except perhaps Asian students, but then only in math and science. When little is expected, little is received. Lowered expectations are frequently subtle and take many forms, including avoiding calling on students, seating students further away, demanding less, or allowing less wait time (Good, 1987; Simpson & Erickson, 1983). These patterns of proximity, latency, and other types of "aversion" are more examples of the "need to look away from and not hear the facts of discrimination ... not just a looking away from the Black student but also from one's own felt guilt. The unconscious wish is that it would be nice, at least in the classroom, if everyone were White. That is the wish of the faculty member who says that she or he treats all students alike regardless of skin color" (Katz, 1983, p. 34). Does this sound similar to Ms. Stanley's comments at the beginning of the chapter? We have seen in several anecdotal situations that teachers' affective responses to students of color send subtle dual messages—while verbally praising a student's good performance, the teacher's tone and facial expression convey surprise (not necessarily appreciative) or disbelief. Would Mr. Hill convey this kind of message? In the last chapter reading, "Anytown High School: A Profile of Pluralism," Alison Benoist investigates the ways in which her high school responds to its students of color.

Research on race and teachers' attitudes underscores the rich potential teachers have to affect student performance positively. Models, such as TESA (Teacher Expectation: Student Achievement), have been developed to address these issues. Developed in the late 1970s/early 1980s (Kerman & Martin, 1980) and currently taught in workshops sponsored by Phi Delta Kappa throughout the country, TESA focuses on teachers' perceptions of students and what behavior teachers exhibit as they communicate those perceptions. Believing that all students are capable of academic success and in the empowerment of and respect for all students regardless of race, gender, or class, TESA advocates that teachers be consciously aware of the effect their attitudes have on students. With this knowledge, teachers can then begin the task of raising expectations and developing strategies to address the needs of all students.

GENDER

In everyday conversation, the term *gender* often refers to biological and sociological concepts; however, *sex* is the term biologists use when distinguishing male from female. Sex relies primarily on physical characteristics, especially those related to reproductive abilities, to establish the distinguishing benchmarks. Gender, on the other hand, is a social construct. Ferrante (1995) defines genders as "social distinctions based on culturally conceived and learned ideas about appropriate behavior, appearance, and mental or emotional characteristics for males and females" (p. 394). We are particularly interested in information about male-female occupational stratification in education and how gender effects teaching and learning the classroom.

Gender in the Educational Work Force

The teaching profession is overwhelmingly female. Although the stereotypical view of teaching as a women's profession is changing, 70 percent of public school teachers are female. (Those percentages increase in the elementary and pre-K levels to 86 percent and 99 percent, respectively.) Despite the greater visibility of men at the high school level, women still represent a majority. Interestingly, however, females hold more classroom teaching positions, and males hold most of the higher paying administrative posts in public schools. Only among private schools do women hold a majority (52 percent) of administrative positions (U.S. Bureau of the Census, 1992).

What might these statistics mean relative to power and privilege between men and women working in education? Between White female teachers and women teachers of color? Between White teachers and teachers of color?

Gender in the Classroom

Research on gender bias and the inequities faced by females in the classroom documents a starkly negative picture from elementary school through college, including graduate school. Myra and David Sadker's (1994) extensive research on gender bias in the classroom spans thirty years and harkens back to Myra's years as a graduate student where she observed subtle and overt evidence of sexism among her college professors. The Sadkers' quarter-century-plus of research reveals repeatedly that girls are more likely to be "the invisible members" in the classroom. Despite changes in society and the advancement of women in all facets of American life, sexism remains "stubbornly persistent" in classrooms in this country. Even teachers who present themselves as caring and informed individuals and who would not describe themselves as biased in their approaches or interactions with students find, under closer scrutiny, that they are some of the "many well-intentioned professionals who inadvertently teach boys better than girls" (p. 3).

Using an observation system to record teacher-student interactions and trained coders to analyze the data, the Sadkers compiled consistently disturbing data on gender bias embedded in even the briefest of interactions. Their observations include the following general patterns:

- Teachers attend more to males and their comments (especially White males) than to females for all four types of teacher comments that they identified: praise, acceptance, remediation, and criticism. Boys are more likely to receive the "most precise and valuable feedback" (p. 55).
- Curriculum materials contribute to the "invisibility of females" in schools. Sexism is perpetuated by the lack of women's contributions included in course content or in textbooks and other instructional materials.
- Males are given more opportunities to answer and longer periods of wait time to formulate answers.
- An inequitable distribution of teacher contact coupled with inequitable distribution of course content sends negative messages to females and contributes to the self-esteem slide evidenced in significant numbers of females.

The 1992 AAUW Report, *How Schools Shortchange Girls,* notes that there are preliminary indications that teaching in certain subject areas (for example, science) may encourage "gender-biased teacher behavior."

CLASS

In the United States, discussions about class are centered around economic well-being. Though considerable research has been done on class systems based on talent, values, and ability, when it comes to class identification in American society, the critical factor is wealth. Wealth is a more comprehensive term than is yearly occupational income and includes multiple sources of income and property holdings and investments (Macionis, 1999). Class is a mirror of socioeconomic status.

The widening gap between rich and poor and the "incredible shrinking" middle class have generated greater interest in socioeconomic status as a significant factor in educational achievement. Recent research points to low socioeconomic status as a more consistent indicator of school failure than race is.

Jonathan Kozol has been a poignant voice in chronicling the devastating effect poverty has on children's total development. In 1967 in *Death at an Early Age,* he recounted stories of children living in poverty neglected and underserved by the Boston public school system. His 1991 *Savage Inequalities* reflects that the educational situation for poor children has not improved despite the two and a half decade time difference.

Most of us are surprised and saddened by the poverty statistics of the United States. We have internalized an image of this country as an advanced industrialized nation. That image, unfortunately, does not fit with the reality of poverty rates "three times as great as in most economically advanced nations" (McNergney & Herbert, 1995). According to Paul Wellstone (1997), one of every five children in the United States is poor, although we are one of the world's wealthiest nations. (See the chapter reading "If Poverty Is the Question....") In addition, the U.S. Census Bureau reports that in 1995 Black and Hispanic children are twice as likely to be poor as White children are.

Misperceptions about Poverty

Mainstream society frequently responds to the poor by blaming them for their problems. The poor are characterized as lazy and lacking family values. Linking morality with class is a convenient way to feel superior to *those* people because of *those* behaviors.

We have also internalized the myth that poverty is an urban, welfare subsisting, minority phenomena when evidence indicates that the rates for rural poverty are actually higher than for the inner city, including those who can be classified as the "working poor." Although people of color represent a disproportionate percentage of poor people, there are more Whites in poverty than any other ethnic group. According to the 1992 U.S. Bureau of the Census, the majority of poor children are White; most have a parent who works; and most live outside large cities, in rural and suburban America (cited by Leidenfrost, 1993).

Poverty and Education

Herbert Gans (in Frankel, 1995) maintains that "Education is still held out as the best escape route from poverty, but only if the class structure is not reproduced, so that poor children get the best schools, teachers, and equivalents for preschool preparations that more affluent parents can give their children" (p. 46). The grim reality is that, more often than not, the class structure *is* reproduced. Though, as a country we espouse equal educational opportunity with equal chances for success, our actions do not live up to these egalitarian and meritocratic ideals. Our ideals—that all human beings should have equal rights and advantages and that merit, or earned advantage, is the path to success—fall short in reality. Wealthy parents have the capacity to ensure a different educational experience for their children from those whose parents are poor and uneducated.

> Children in different social classes are likely to attend different types of schools, receive different types of instruction, to study different curricula, and leave school at different rates and times. As a result, when children end their schooling, they are more different from each other than they were when they entered, and these differences may be seen as *legitimating the unequal positions people face in their adult lives.* (emphasis ours). (Persell, 1993, p. 71)

Poverty in the Classroom

Social class has consequences for how students are perceived and treated in an educational environment. Research on teacher expectations related to social class reveals a similar pattern as for race and gender. Teachers expect less of children from lower socioeconomic classes than they do of middle-class children even when IQ and achievement are similar (p. 80). The Rockefeller Foundation reports that low-income students are at higher risk for dropping out of school and falling behind. As educators we must examine what part we play in communicating to students their value and potential in the classroom.

Bennett (1990) says, "Teachers must ask themselves the following question: Are we talking about groups of individuals whose backgrounds, attitudes, and general capabilities have failed to equip them adequately for a life of opportunities or are we talking about minority cultures of a country where the attitudes of the majority have inhibited the participation of the minorities in these opportunities? Do these children fail because their intellectual development is deficient from what is expected at school? Or do they fail because they can't fit in?" (p. 201). Teachers who accept the first explanation place the responsibility for change on the students; teachers who believe the second explanation is more accurate think the school needs to change. (Research supports the second explanation.)

CONNECTING RACE, GENDER, AND CLASS WITH POSITION AND PRIVILEGE

Obviously, race, gender, and class are inextricably intertwined. We write about them individually, but that is only an organizational structure used to simplify the writing task. The synergistic effect of race, gender, and class on the educational experiences of students is complex. Students who are poor, female, or of color all share a dubious relationship with a dominant power capable of negatively or positively affecting their success in political and legal, social and cultural, economic, and educational arenas. The outsider groups also have a number of possible responses—some more personally productive than others.

Paula Rothenberg (1992) suggests that race, class, and gender are central to understanding social, political, and economic institutions. She further challenges teachers to consider the interconnectedness of these issues and to "reflect on the way these elements function together, to determine how we see ourselves and each other and to circumscribe the opportunities and privileges to which each of us has access" (p. 1). In the classroom, we must consider how our privilege and positionality effect what we teach and how we choose to teach it. What positive advantages do we enjoy by virtue of our race, sex, or class? How can those advantages be shared more equitably? What does this mean for redistributing unearned power? First, we must examine what it is we value and the origins of those values. This can be an arduous process, but if as Pogo suggests "I have seen the enemy and he is us," there is ample rationale for starting here. Second, we must be able to instruct and empower our students to examine their lives in the same way.

As society becomes more diverse, the need for schools to respond to this call of reflectivity becomes increasingly more urgent. Educators face the task of preparing students to live in a rapidly changing society, and also of examining how their own past socialization helps or deters educators from providing the most productive and conducive atmosphere for learning.

READINGS

The first three readings in Chapter Two elaborate on the concepts of privilege, positionality, and meritocracy. "Report: U.S. Gap between Rich, Poor Is Widening" and a brief excerpt from "If Poverty Is the Question..." provide us with current statistics about how wealth and income are distributed among different income levels. In "White Privilege in Schools," Ruth Anne Olson highlights several examples of her "family's" experiences of White privilege in schools. The third reading, "The Multicultural Me," is written by A. Cheryl Curtis. She admits that writing this piece was "cathartic and somewhat self indulgent—self-disclosure to the max." Her essay gives us a good example of the complexity of positionality.

The final reading, "Anytown High School: A Profile of Pluralism," is written by a high school French teacher who examines how her high school is responding to a more diverse student population. Within this context, she gives us her impressions of how teachers and students interact. Although many of her examples are critical of what is happening, she sees the potential for positive change in the future.

READING 1a

Report: U.S. Gap between Rich, Poor Is Widening

The gap between haves and have nots is greater in the United States than in other Western countries and appears to be widening, the *The New York Times* reported today, citing new studies.

Federal Reserve figures from 1989 show that the richest 1 percent of American households owned nearly 40 percent of the nation's wealth. Their net worth started at $2.3 million.

The same year in Britain, where the richest 1 percent possessed 59 percent of the wealth in the decade just after World War I, the figure was 18 percent.

The top 20 percent of American households, families worth $180,000 or more, had 80 percent of the wealth, a bigger share than in any other industrial nation, the *Times* said.

In Finland, where distribution of income is particularly even, the lowest-earning 20 percent of the population gets 10.8 percent of the income. In the United States, the figure is only 5.7 percent.

The *Times* said inequality has risen in the United States since the 1970s and explanations include the spread of automation that eliminates unskilled income, low tax rates for the rich, a relatively low minimum wage, the decline of trade unions and rising stock and bond markets.

"We are the most unequal industrialized country in terms of income and wealth, and we're growing more unequal faster than the other industrialized countries," said New York University economics Professor Edward N. Wolff.

In two forthcoming papers, Wolff compared wealth patterns in Western countries. They are among research the *Times* cited.

The *Times* also said that Census figures show the gap widened past the period of Wolff's research into 1993, the first year of the Clinton administration. While the two-fifths most wealthy American households enjoyed higher incomes as the economy expanded, everyone else in this country saw their incomes fall when adjustments are made for inflation.

© 1995 by Associated Press.

READING 1b

If Poverty Is the Question...

Paul Wellstone

What does it mean to be poor in America? We can offer no single description of American poverty. But for many, perhaps most, it means homes with peeling paint, inadequate heating, uncertain plumbing. It means that only the very lucky among the children receive a decent education. It often means a home where some go to bed hungry and malnutrition is a frequent visitor. It means that the most elementary components of the good life in America—a vacation with kids, an evening out, a comfortable home—are but distant and unreachable dreams, more likely to be seen on the television screen than in the neighborhood. And for almost all the poor it means that life is a constant struggle to obtain the merest necessities of existence, those things most of us take for granted. We can do better.

More than 35 million Americans—one out of every seven of our fellow citizens—are officially poor. More than one in five American children are poor. And the poor are getting poorer. In 1994, nearly half of poor children under the age of 6 lived in families with incomes below half the poverty line. That figure has doubled over the past twenty years. The number of people who work full time and are still poor has risen dramatically as well. In 1975, 6 percent of young children who lived in families with one full-time worker were poor. By 1994, that figure had gone up to 15 percent.

Poor people are increasingly hemmed into poor neighborhoods, with everything that entails: poor schools, crime, violence, lack of accessible jobs and all the rest. The number of people living in concentrations of poverty (in neighborhoods of more than 40 percent poverty) went up by 75 percent from 1970 to 1980 and then doubled between 1980 and 1990. More than 10 million Americans (that constitutes about 4 million poor families) now live in very-high-poverty neighborhoods.

Minorities are poorer than the rest of Americans: 29.3 percent of African-Americans and 30.3 percent of Hispanics were classified as poor in 1995. Female-headed households are even poorer—44.6 percent of the children who lived in such families were poor in 1994, and almost half of all children who are poor live in female-headed households.

It's an old saw that the rich get richer and the poor get poorer. For nearly two decades that cliché has been a painfully demonstrable fact. Nearly all of America's economic growth has benefited the wealthiest among us, and the tiny slice of the pie allotted to the poor has actually gotten smaller. From

© 1997 by *The Nation.*

1977 to 1992 the richest 1 percent of Americans gained 91 percent in after-tax income, while the poorest fifth lost 17 percent of their income. The top 1 percent's total income equals that of the entire bottom 40 percent of the population. . . .

Poverty has many faces. There are the elderly, now less poor than the rest of America because of the success of Social Security and Medicare and Supplemental Security Income, as well as our private pension system. But women and minorities among the elderly are disproportionately poor. Our challenge for the elderly is to find the right way to protect Social Security and preserve Medicare. There are the disabled, protected by the historic Americans With Disabilities Act but experiencing a back-lash in recent benefit cuts. But even for those who can work, there is still very high unemployment. There are dislocated workers forced out of jobs by downsizing and plant relocation. There are women and children made poor by divorce or abandonment. There are rural poor who live far from available work, and farmers who work as hard as anyone but still can't make ends meet.

I will visit all of these and help to tell their stories. Their problems are real and pressing, and we are not doing enough about them. But here are four groups—four overlapping groups—that tend to set off the bumper-sticker talk and the political hot buttons and the simple-minded solutions. (H.L. Mencken once said, "For every problem there is a solution that is neat and simple—and wrong.") These groups are the working poor, welfare recipients, the inner-city and rural poor, and poor children and youths.

If there is any group of "deserving poor" in the United States—although that is a term I greatly dislike—it is the working poor. We have raised the earned-income tax credit substantially. We have now raised the minimum wage a little. But both are still too low, and we look the other way when it is pointed out that the lousy jobs that too many Americans have don't provide health coverage. We do a little shuffle when the real cost of child care is mentioned—a small calculation on the back of an envelope would reveal that the parents with the lousy jobs can't afford the child care, especially if they are single parents with one lousy job.

And now we are about to flood the labor market with a new supply of low-wage workers, pushed out there by the bumper-sticker command of our new welfare law to find a job, any job. The vast majority of them are women, who still earn less than men, and minority women at that, who earn less than white women, so these new workers are especially likely to end up in low-wage jobs. And elementary labor economics says they are—if anything—going to depress wages further for everyone at the low-wage end of the labor market.

Simply put, there are not enough jobs available that are geographically accessible and sufficiently undemanding of technical skills for all the long-term welfare recipients who have now been told to enter the job market or else. In real life, people of color will encounter discrimination when they try to find a job. But for a huge proportion of those who do find work, there will be a different, serious issue—how do I make ends meet? To add to the problem, in the same welfare bill there are large food-stamp cuts that by 2002 will reduce benefits by 20 percent for everyone, including the millions of working poor who get a little help from food stamps in their constant struggle to keep things together.

The answer is not ending welfare as we know it. The answer is dealing honestly with the real causes of poverty. We have to do this by genuinely making work pay, including providing access to health care and child care to go along with it. But we have to do it in two other fundamental ways as well: by committing ourselves to a genuine, positive, realistic developmental and educational strategy for children and young people so that they reach adulthood with the tools and attitudes they need to be responsible, self-sufficient adult citizens; and by reclaiming our neighborhoods of endemic poverty and helping parents and other decent people there to create a safe and healthy environment in which to raise children and bring them along the road to responsible adulthood.

We need to pay particular attention to young men. The welfare law primarily focuses on women, although not exactly in a positive way. It focuses on men in its tough new provisions on child support. But we need to be promoting responsible fatherhood, and that means marriage and involvement with the children and two earners in the family. One reason marriages do not form is lack of opportunity. Communities need to work on strategies to help young women and young men both to make it successfully into the job market. We have had a strategy for young men, but it is the wrong strategy: It is called prison, and it is eating its way through higher education budgets and school budgets across America. We will stop feeding the correctional appetite only if we stop supplying new customers.

But if too many parents find it terribly hard to meet all their responsibilities, and too many young people are falling by the wayside, communities cannot do the job of helping all by themselves. We need government, and we need the federal government now.

There are some steps we can take as a nation—right now—that would make an enormous difference in the lives of children. It is a scandal that 10 million children in America do not have basic health care to help them reach their full potential. It is a scandal that despite irrefutable and irreducible evidence that the Women, Infants and Children program is successful at giving women and children a healthy and nutritious diet, we have yet to fund it fully. We know WIC works, but currently it reaches only 74 percent of the eligible population. We can and must do better. It is a scandal that while we know that Head Start is effective in helping children from diverse backgrounds and circumstances to prepare for school, we have yet to fund it fully. Currently only 30 percent of children eligible for Head Start are enrolled!

There are hundreds and thousands of marvelous initiatives occurring in so many ways all over this nation that are making a major difference in the lives of poor people. We do not lack ideas. We do not lack knowledge. We do not lack committed people. But we lack a national commitment. We lack a genuine national debate about the underlying questions—the way our economy is structured and the very real issues of race and gender that are so deeply infused in so much of what goes on.

Without such a debate, without enlisting the energies of our fellow citizens, these problems will never be resolved. I have spent enough time in Washington and read enough history to know they will not be solved from the top. It was a combination of the civil rights movement and the activist movements of the sixties that generated our last truly national attack on the problems of poverty. That effort expired in the conflagration of Vietnam. But the successes of civil rights activists and the women's movement were a clear demonstration of the truism that in a democracy significant social change comes from the bottom up from an aroused opinion that forces our ruling institutions to do the right thing.

I think we can do bettah. That is what Robert Kennedy always said. I think we can do better too. Won't you join me in the effort?

READING 2

White Privilege in Schools

Ruth Anne Olson

It is important to distinguish between prejudice and privilege. Whereas racial prejudice is negative action *directed against* an individual, privilege is passive advantage that *accrues to* an individual or group. Good teachers recognize and actively address prejudice. But as Petty McIntosh (1988) points out, most White people are blind to the privileges accorded to White children and parents in schools.

I tried to identify my own family's experience of White privilege in schools and without much effort, it became clear that we have, indeed, benefited from privileges to which we have given little thought. Using McIntosh's format I could elaborate on her work and add observations from my own experience.

- Whatever topics my children choose to study, they are confident that they will find materials that link people of their race to the accomplishments in those areas.

- My children know that they will always see faces like their own liberally represented in the textbooks, posters, films, and other materials in the hallways, classrooms, and media centers of their schools.

- When my children talk about celebrations, holidays, or family observances in show-and-tell or in other informal exchanges at school, they know that their teachers will have experienced similar events and will be able to reinforce their stories.

Olson, R. A., 1992. *Eliminating White privilege in schools: An awesome challenge for White parents and educators.* Reprinted by permission of the author.

- My children are confident that the musical instruments, rhythms, harmonies, visual design forms and dramatic traditions of their culture will be generously recognized in the formal and informal uses of music, theater, and visual arts in their schools.

- The color of my children's skin causes most adults in school offices, classroom, and hallways to have neutral or positive assumptions about them.

- My children know that the vast majority of adults in their schools will be of their same racial background, even in classrooms where many or most of their fellow students are of races different from theirs.

- My children are confident that they will never be embarrassed by being called on to tell the class about their race, culture, or special ways of celebrating events.

- When I visit their schools, my children know that school staff members will reserve judgement about my economic class, my level of education, and my reason for being in the school until I make them known.

- My children take for granted that the color of any crayons, bandages, or other supplies in their classroom labeled "flesh" will be similar to their own.

- I take for granted that the tests used to judge my children's achievement and to determine placement in special classes have been developed with groups that included significant numbers of students who share our racial history and culture.

- My children are confident that they will never be embarrassed by hearing others suggest that the problems of the school (low levels of achievement, the need for special support services, etc.) are caused by the high numbers of children of their race.

- I am confident that policy decisions that affect my children's school experience will be made by state and local bodies dominated by people who understand our racial history and culture.

This list can go on. My family never asked for these privileges; principals and teachers didn't purposely create them for us; and, frankly neither they nor we have been consciously aware these privileges exist.

But stating that no one is to blame does not erase the fact that privilege has allowed my family to take for granted things that others must spend time, energy, and resources trying to earn. And while I have been blind to the existence of our privileges, people who don't share them cannot help but see them and feel resentment, puzzlement, disappointment, and rage at the fact that their children are excluded from the privileged class.

References

McIntosh, P. 1988. White privilege and male privilege: A personal account of coming to see correspondences through work in women's studies. Wellesley, MA: Working Paper Series, Wellesley College.

Discussion Questions

1. Can you think of other privileges that could be added to this list?
2. What are the implications for children of color if Whites have these privileges?
3. How can the system be changed so that these "privileges" become rights for everyone?
4. What actions can you take to help the system change?

READING 3

The Multicultural Me

A. Cheryl Curtis

Today I urge you to accept several challenges around exploring your positionality and what you can do to become a more culturally skilled practitioner and educator.

I challenge you to learn more about people from other cultures and balance that against your own cultural background and assumptions. It is important to discuss ways in which we may be different from each other, but equally as important to examine closely how we respond to those differences and why we respond in the ways we do and whether or not we need to learn new responses.

For several semesters, I have struggled with how I can encourage my students to move toward those goals and become more culturally skilled. Today as we continue to talk about diversity and differences, I wonder what perceptions and experiences you bring to trying to understand differences.

I must admit that I enter today's discussion with some fear and frustration, but I do so out of a sense of personal and professional investment. Ninety percent of the teachers in this country are White, and I assume that the statistics are similar for human service workers. You will be educating my children and grandchildren. I want to know that I have contributed to your being more aware as an educator.

A tee shirt that was popular a couple of years ago said, "It's a Black thing. You wouldn't understand it." And I have been in many conversations with Black people who echo that sentiment. This suggested that communication really isn't possible because the divide is just too great to be crossed. Recent events in our culture suggest that the divide has not been lessened and bridging the gap may be an impossibility. A few semesters ago Maya Angelou was on campus doing a poetry reading; she mentioned the tee shirt slogan and suggested that rather than take that attitude, she hoped some people would say instead "It's a Black thing. Let me help you understand it."

I see this as a more positive tact and have made conscious efforts in that direction. It is hard to say whether I've been successful at this. I'm not always around to see the fruits of the seeds that I try to plant. The failures are more immediately noticeable, and thus my frustration is compounded. I stifle a heavy sigh when my future middle and secondary teachers tell me "I don't need to know anything about multicultural education because I'm not going to teach in a multicultural setting"—as if to suggest that only minority populations have something to learn from such a curriculum. I listen to students say "But I'm not a racist. I didn't—and my parents didn't—own slaves"—as though they haven't in some way enjoyed the benefits of a racist culture. I listen to students who are content to live with historical amnesia: "That was the past. That was then. Things are different now."

I hope that parts of what I have to say to you bother you—but in a good way. This was not easy to write; it may not be easy to listen to. Some discomfort seems to be a natural by-product of a discussion of race. I welcome the discomfort because in that chaffing is the potential for self-examination. But please listen well—note where you are confused or indifferent. Indifference is more insidious. It will require more self-awareness. Note where you are uncomfortable for therein lies the work that is cut out for you on the road to becoming more culturally skilled. Note where you are empathetic—therein lies hope for the beginning of real understanding.

You might recall a song that was popular a couple of years ago. The song was by the group En Vogue, and it was entitled "Free Your Mind." In the song, the "funky divas" entreat us, "Before you can read me, you have to learn how to see me." Today I want to help you learn how to read and see me.

I am not complimented by well-intentioned people who say to me "But, Cheryl, when I look at you, I don't see color." On one hand, I understand the sentiment of pluralism and acceptance that is intended in the comment; on the other hand, I am incensed by the casual denial of an essential part of who I am. I interpret the statement as insensitive and potentially racist. That attitude of denial usually comes from someone who has lived all of his or her life with "white skin privilege." It usually comes from someone who has not experienced the world the way I have. If this were truly "a people are people are people world," it would be okay, but it is not. I can be encouraged by the hopes of "should be," but I live in the day-to-day reality of what is.

As an ethnic minority I present myself to you for examination—to consider the different microcultural pieces that make up who I am, pieces that are important knowledge for you to consider if you are to become culturally skilled:

I am a Black, Southern-born, 40-something, African American, heterosexual, recovering homophobic, bi-dialectical female. I am a registered Democrat, lapsed Catholic, raised by a Baptist mother and a Methodist father. My mother was a domestic (that is, maid), and my father was a laborer in a fertilizer factory. I am the youngest of seven children and have three brothers and three sisters, several of whom spent periods of time living out of our household being raised by my mother's sisters in the north. My mother had an eighth-grade education, which was as about as advanced as most Black people from the south in her era ever achieved. My father had a second-grade education. He left school to go to work to bring extra income into his family household. My father does not read or write, and my mother handled many household responsibilities.

I learned from my parents that I had to be respectful and deferential to Whites even when it was not reciprocated. Knowing one's place was important for economic and physical survival. As a child, I learned respect for elders, and I dared not question that upbringing. I was to call all elders by their proper titles of Mr., Miss, or Mrs. I learned that this was not an expectation of the little White children in the households where my mother worked who were ironically allowed to call her by her first name.

I learned that the eyes of the Black community as an extended family were upon me. My success was shared success. My failure was collective failure.

The Catholic school I attended began as a missionary school, and at Christmas time the parish children received gifts from some philanthropic source. One of the last gifts I remember receiving was a White doll with long brown hair. When the school was no longer a missionary school and began to charge tuition, my parents somehow found the money to keep us there—four girls and one boy—as they believed, first, that education was a precious gift that would bring us better conditions in life than they had experienced. I can still hear my mother saying to me that an education was something that "they"—referring to the White man—could not take away from me once I had it. Second, my parents believed that the education offered by the White Immaculate Heart of Mary nuns and the Passionist priests was more valuable than that offered by the segregated Black school in our town.

In the segregated South, I became aware of racism while I was fairly young. I was not allowed to sit at the lunch counter at the local Woolworth's. I could not go through the main entrance of the local movie theater, having instead to go through a back ally and up a flight of stairs to the balcony. Although I was pleased I did not have to pay the same admission price as Whites, I had to walk past the stench of unkempt toilets reserved for the coloreds. On occasion when I had to walk to my Aunt's house after school through White neighborhoods past the "Whites only" school I was called *nigger* and spat at. In our daily newspaper when perpetrators of crimes were Black, their race was clearly identified in the news stories. When the perpetrators were not Black, no mention was ever made of race. That's how we knew they were White.

As a high school student, I received messages from society that limited my career options to being a teacher or a nurse. My three older sisters are all involved in the medical profession either as nurses or technicians and moved to New York where job opportunities were supposed to be better. I chose teaching. I was the first person in my immediate family to graduate from a four-year college. My youngest brother fought in the Vietnam War. As a young coed, I pondered the irony of the possibility of his dying for a country that had laws that legally barred him from being buried in a Whites-only cemetery.

I eat collard greens and chitlins—if I know who has cooked them—and sweet potato pie. I am conscious about eating fried chicken and watermelon in certain circles because of the racial stereotype associated with them. I learned to say "greasy" instead of "greazy." I worked on getting rid of my country Southern accent. On White women, it is considered a throwback to the antebellum South and conjures up images of gentility and femininity; on Black women, it is associated with mental slowness and ignorance.

I have received ethnocentric messages from the macroculture that I am different, I am other, I am inferior, lazy, promiscuous, exotic, animalistic. I embraced the Black is Beautiful movement of the 1960s and 1970s with open arms. I have received messages from the macroculture that I must assimilate. I must become like them. At the same time, the macroculture shows me that it would never be truly possible for me to assimilate. The images of beauty from the television, the music videos, the print ads tell me that I will never have waxen, flaxen, bouncing and behaving hair, preferably blond. I will never naturally have blue eyes, thin lips, thin nose, thin hips. What pluralistic messages I receive are all viewed with a fair dose of mistrust of a society whose history is hard to overcome and for me cannot be "gotten over," ignored, or forgotten. It is a mistrust I know will be a legacy for my two daughters. In October, my eight-year-old daughter came in from school to ask me if nigger was another name for Black people. When I asked her why she was asking, she told me that her friend, a White boy who lives two doors down and someone whom she has played with since she was three, had called her a "nigger." We have come a long way but not nearly far enough.

The educational experts tell me that the macroculture in this society is based on a worldview that is individualistic, competitive, and achievement oriented. I must constantly reconcile the differences with my worldview that is community and consensus oriented, conformist, and distrustful of the macroculture. The *Black Women's Health Book* reports that 50 percent of Black women in this country live in states of emotional distress. I count myself among that number and find a small degree of comfort in knowing I'm not alone.

In 1903, W. E. B. Du Bois in the *Souls of Black Folks* wrote that Blacks in this society exist with a "double consciousness—a sense of always looking at one's self through the eyes of others, of measuring one's self by the tape of a world that looks on in an amused contempt and pity." I contend that the contempt and the pity are an internalized part of the worldview of the macroculture. I used to end this essay asking students if they can, indeed, read and see me. I have recently read some research by a feminist who contends that this seeing can not be done without crucial examination of one's own culture. She writes, "You do not see me because you do not see yourself and you do not see yourself because you declare yourself outside of culture." Maria Lugones calls this "dis-engagement" and labels it a radical form of passivity that privileges the dominant culture as the only culture to "see with."

So today I ask, can you see me? Can you see yourself?

READING 4

Anytown High School: A Profile of Pluralism

Alison R. Benoist

Since I began teaching there in 1971, Anytown High has changed from the typical all-White suburban bedroom community high school to one where pluralism is more evident each year. Racial tensions are beginning to be felt. Prejudice and stereotyping are increasing. According to this year's school census, out of a total enrollment of 1352 students, 72 are Hispanic, 27 are Russian, 22 are Asian, 17 are Black, 9 are Polish, and 1 is Israeli. Of these, 49 are unable to perform ordinary class work in English. For 102 of our students, English is not their first language. One-hundred six students are from low-income families. Anytown High has become an integrated, multicultural school, and it is being forced to solve the challenges created by its diverse student population. How has AHS chosen to deal with these problems? Does its response fit the "business-as-usual," the "assimilationist," the "pluralistic coexistence," or the "integrated pluralism" models suggested by H.A. Sagar and J.W. Schofield? Could a multicultural education approach be of help in solving the problems caused by desegregation?

I have had two personal experiences which may help to answer these questions. A few years ago, I wrote a new curriculum for the French IV course at AHS. It is called the History of France. At the time, I was completely unaware of the concept of gender-equity. I did not know that "girls are less apt than boys to see themselves reflected in the materials they study" and that this could significantly affect their success in school. I chose a text from those available, and taught the students what was in it. In retrospect, I probably should have called the course the History of French Men, for that is what we studied. My male students were enthusiastic and dominated the classroom discussions. My female students, though bright, were less enthusiastic and tended to listen rather than participate. I decided that I had to make the course more appealing to the girls. Also, as a woman, I was curious about the contributions of French women to history. I did some extensive research and supplemented the text with what I had learned. At the end of the second year, several of the girls told me that it was the best history course they had ever had. When I asked why, they all replied that it was the only history course at the high school which made women seem important. Anytown High has made many opportunities available to its girls: There is a teen-parenting program, girls are playing more sports than I ever could have imagined when I went to high school, and they are very much a presence in all other extracurricular activities. However, my interviews with students and faculty showed that the curriculum is not gender-equitable, nor is there much race- or culture-equity either.

Reprinted by permission of the author.

In the same history class discussed above, we have occasion to discuss homosexuality in the French court. I have always treated this subject matter-of-factly and have insisted that my students refrain from making disparaging remarks during the discussions. Recently, one of my students sought me out after school to thank me for the way I deal with homosexuality. He stated that the subject is treated in quite another way in most of his other classes, and that, as a gay male, he is often made to feel uncomfortable because teachers denigrate gays openly and do not discourage their students from doing so as well. I feel strongly that it is our responsibility to create a comfortable environment—a "climate of acceptance"—in which all of our students can learn. If students who are in any way "different" are made to feel uncomfortable, then we are creating a climate where failure is more likely and the dropout rate will continue to climb.

While my research has shown that other minorities are not openly ridiculed or denigrated in classes, some of them are made to feel ill-at-ease by more subtle means. One of my Black students told me that during a discussion of slavery in history class, the teacher asked her if she would rather sit in the corridor until the discussion was finished. The teacher felt that a Black student might be "uncomfortable" with the subject of slavery. This same student also told me that whenever students in her classes have to refer to Blacks in the course of discussions, they usually say something like: "I'm sorry. I hope that term doesn't offend you." Many teachers do likewise. It is obvious that, though well-meaning, these people are assuming that "to recognize race is to be racist." All of the students I interviewed who did not speak English as a first language reported that many students and teachers became very impatient with them if they did not speak English, or even if they speak English with an accent. They felt strongly that no one wanted to bother with them unless they spoke unaccented standard American English. A student from Israel told me that the students treated him differently after they heard him speak in his heavily accented English. He said he felt "like a Puerto Rican" and also stated that students told jokes about Jews and Israel in his presence. Most of the students with language problems, especially the Hispanics, felt that the teachers have low expectations of them, and that they are put in the low level classes as a matter of course. The bilingual teacher reported resistance from the administration to giving his students "academically demanding work instead of the watered-down and mechanical curriculum that is so often the norm for many ethnic- and language-minority students." He tries to mainstream them as quickly as possible but is often prevented from doing so by the administration—the reasoning behind this eludes him. The Russian teacher made it abundantly clear that, in most cases, the expectations of the teachers are not positive, that "the belief by teachers that all students can succeed and the communication of this belief to students" generally does not prevail. The Asian students, on the other hand, told me that they were encouraged to take regular classes as soon as possible, and were put into the upper levels, especially in math. Moreover, some of them felt that they had been pushed out of the bilingual program too soon. This shows that even positive stereotyping can be detrimental to students.

I have found that Anytown High School has some of the characteristics of each of the first three desegregation models mentioned in the introduction. Although now we have both a bilingual and an ESL program, and a very successful teen-parenting program, the curriculum is basically the same one that was taught in 1971. The academic and behavioral standards are essentially the same as well. In general, the students are expected to adjust to the school, not vice versa. In this regard, AHS fits a "business-as-usual" model. By and large, the color-blind attitude of the "assimilationist" model is also present; AHS does seek to make its minority students more like white students, in many cases, however, with the complicity of minority parents. The Asian students told me that their parents want them to learn English quickly, to "blend in" and "be American"—at school. At home, the cultural traditions are maintained. One of the Black students, whose parents are from Georgia, told me her family moved to this town specifically so that she could go to a predominately White high school with a very small Black minority. Her mother has also very consciously taught her the "codes of power"; she even prohibits the use of the Black vernacular in their home. As in the "pluralistic coexistence" model for dealing with school diversity, there are separate turfs, especially for the Puerto Rican students and the Russian students, but for different reasons. The Puerto Rican students separate themselves with greater frequency when they feel alienated by the language barrier, and possibly also because of their greater need for peer support, coming as they do from a high-context culture. The Russians separate themselves because they belong to an extremely separatist religion; they came here to be able to practice their religion freely, and for no other purpose. At the present time, little attempt is made, with the singular exception of an extremely successful International Day, to encourage students to mix—another characteristic of "pluralistic coexistence."

How can Anytown High move toward the ideal of "integrated pluralism"? I have concluded that we view "student diversity as a problem rather than as a resource." This must be changed. The teachers must be taught, perhaps through in-service programs, "to help students learn the culture of the school while maintaining identification and pride in the home culture." We need to organize more activities like International Day; an International Christmas/New Year's Bazaar, or an International Music Day might be possibilities. The Student Council is planning workshops in the fall for area schools; one of their activities will be anti-bias sensitivity training. The Governor's Commission on Gay and Lesbian Youth has asked us to create a team to be involved in making teachers aware of the problems of homosexual teenagers; we will begin attending workshops in the fall. These are steps in the right direction. "The process does not need to be helped along by indoctrinating people but only by educating them." "Cross-culturalism must seep into the curriculum as well." This is an area in need of much modification, but I sense a willingness on the part of some members of the faculty to move forward; they just need some direction. "Surely we can use a text written by a feminist, a gay, a Jew, a Black and many others to teach the suffering of those at the receiving end of prejudice; it does not have to be *To Kill a Mockingbird*." Two members of the English department have already asked to "pick my brain" about what I have learned in my Multicultural Education class, and several of my colleagues have expressed interest in taking the course. The culinary arts class would be a great place to explore cultural diversity as would the art and music classes. "Most music curricula in educational institutions still stress European musical traditions brought to the U.S. more than 100 years ago and ignore the beauty of the vibrant new arrivals and the transformations of many older surviving traditions." If teachers can be convinced to have positive expectations for all their students, if the learning environment encourages positive intergroup contact, and if a multicultural curriculum can be developed, Anytown High will be more successful in helping its students to fit into the pluralistic society in which we live. To paraphrase Jay Walljasper in his article, *Multiculturalism and me:* I think a school that recognizes and respects the richness of its many cultures will be a better place to learn.

References

1. *Individual Public School Report:* Westfield High School, October 1, 1992.
2. Bennett, Christine I. *Comprehensive Multicultural Education.* Boston: Allyn & Bacon, 1990.
3. The American Association of University Women. "Changing Schools That Shortchange Girls." *The Education Digest,* Oct. 1992: 41–45.
4. Fox, Judith R. and Roth, Stephanie. *Building a Climate of Acceptance in a School of Diversity.* Scarsdale High School. 1992.
5. Zeichner, Kenneth M. *Educating Teachers for Cultural Diversity.* University of Wisconsin-Madison, 1993.
6. Delpit, Lisa R. "The Silenced Dialogue: Power and Pedagogy in Educating Other People's Children." *Harvard Educational Review,* Aug. 1988.
7. Gambino, Richard. "From the One, Many: The Multiculturalist Threat." *Current,* Nov. 1992: 35–36.
8. Etzioni, Amitai. "Social Science as a Multicultural Canon." *Society,* Nov./Dec. 1991: 10–18.
9. Seeger, Anthony. "Let Music Teach Cultural Diversity." *The Education Digest,* Oct. 1992: 69–77.
10. Walljasper, Jay. "Multiculturalism and me." *Utne Reader,* Nov./Dec. 1991: 154–155.
11. Seeger, Anthony. "Let Music Teach Cultural Diversity" *The Education Digest,* Oct. 1992: 69.
12. *Comprehensive Multicultural Education* (24).

DISCUSSION QUESTIONS AND ACTIVITIES

1. a. The article, "Report: U. S. Gap between Rich, Poor Is Widening," states that the top 20 percent of American households has 80 percent of the wealth. Using a calculator, figure out how much classroom space and how many chairs, tables, and so forth constitute 80 percent of class wealth. Allow 20 percent of the students to occupy this space.

   b. Wellstone, in "If Poverty Is the Question...," states, "The top 1 percent's total income equals that of the entire bottom 40 percent of the population." For example, suppose that members of the top 1 percent each earned $250,000 per year. What would the average member of the bottom 40 percent of the population earn? How do these statistics relate to the myth of an American meritocracy?

2. Consider the common expression "It's not what you know, but who you know." How many people have gotten jobs because they knew someone, had a friend tell them about a job, or heard about a job through a network of acquaintances or organizations? Is being hired more often a function of knowing someone, being qualified, or being qualified and knowing someone? How does this relate to the myth of an American meritocracy?

3. What aspects of positionality are captured in the following picture?

Reprinted by permission of the Norman Rockwell Family Trust. Copyright ©1964 the Norman Rockwell Family Trust.

Describe your positionality by writing a brief autobiography or by creating a series of pictures or graphics. Share your work with other students.

4. Read the following excerpt. How might Ruth Anne Olson respond to what is being said? What would you say to the author?

> The term "privilege" connotes an advantage conferred upon a few to the exclusion of others. While there are certainly some revolting privileges present in our economic system, the possession of white skin does not automatically confer privilege upon an American citizen. I would argue that it is important to distinguish between a privilege based upon race and disadvantage based upon race. No one in their right mind would dispute that Black Americans have suffered profound impediments to their economic and political vitality. This doesn't mean that being a member of the White race is, in and of itself, a privilege. There are many undereducated and economically deprived White males in the country whose lives would belie . . . a privileged status. . . . uniformly placing guilt upon an ill-defined group that doesn't necessarily share in the spoils of the truly privileged few is no solution.
>
> *Jeff Roberts, The Valley Advocate, March 11, 1999, p. 4.*

5. Check the local and regional newspapers for two weeks and collect articles dealing with race, class, and gender. Describe the context and areas where these issues are reported. How might these articles be relevant to middle and secondary high school teachers?

6. Review the opening chapter statements by Ms. Stanley and Mr. Hill. What information regarding issues of race, class, and gender might be useful to them? How might this knowledge affect their relationships with students? How might it affect their teaching?

REFERENCES

Banks, J. A. 1991. *Teaching strategies for ethnic studies,* 5th ed. Boston: Allyn & Bacon.

Bennett, C. I. 1995. *Comprehensive multicultural education,* 3rd ed. Boston: Allyn & Bacon.

Cones, J. H. , J. F. Noonan, and Janha, D. (eds.). 1983. *Teaching minority students: New directions for teaching and learning #16.* San Francisco: Jossey-Bass.

Ferrante, J. 1994. *Sociology: A global perspective,* 2nd ed. Belmont, CA: Wadsworth.

Frankel, M. 1995. What the poor deserve. *New York Times Magazine,* 6(October 22):46.

Gabriel, S. L., and Smithson, I. (eds.) 1990. *Gender in the classroom: Power and pedagogy.* Urbana: University of Illinois Press.

Gay, G. 1975. Teacher's achievement expectations of and classroom interactions with ethnically different students. *Contemporary Education,* 66: 166–171.

Good, T. 1987. Two decades of research on teacher expectations: Findings and future directions. *Journal of Teacher Education,* 38(July-August): 32–47.

Hale-Benson, J. 1988 (revised ed). *Black children: Their roots, culture, learning styles.* Baltimore: John Hopkins University Press.

How schools shortchange girls: The AAUW report. A study of major findings on girls and education. 1992. Commissioned by the AAUW Educational Foundation, researched by the Wellesley College Center for Research on Women. Washington, D.C.: AAUW Educational Foundation, National Education Association.

Katz, J. 1983. White faculty struggling with the effects of racism. *Teaching minority students—New directions for learning, #16.* San Francisco: Jossey-Bass, pp. 29–38.

Kerman, S., and Martin, M. 1980. *Teacher expectations and student achievement: Teacher handbook.* Bloomington, IN: Phi Delta Kappa.

Kozol, J. 1967. *Death at an early age: The destruction of the hearts and minds of Negro children in the Boston public schools.* Boston: Houghton Mifflin.

Kozol, J. 1991. *Savage inequalities.* New York: HarperPerennial.

Leidenfrost, N. 1993. Fifty facts about poverty. Hungerweb. http://garnet. berkeley. edu:333/faststats/poverty stats. html

Macionis, J. 1999. *Sociology.* Upper Saddle River, NJ: Prentice Hall.

McIntosh, P. 1995. White privilege and male privilege: A personal account of coming to see correspondence through work in women's studies. In M. L. Anderson and P. H. Collins, *Race, class, and gender: An anthology,* 2nd ed. Belmont, CA: Wadsworth.

McNergney, R. F., and Herbert, J. M. 1995. *Foundations of education.* Needham Heights, MA: Allyn & Bacon.

Persell, C. H. 1993. Social class and educational equality. In J. A. Banks & C. A. M. Banks (eds.), *Multicultural education issues and perspectives.* Boston: Allyn & Bacon.

Rakow, L. F. 1991. Gender and race in the classroom: Teaching way out of line. *Feminist teacher, 6*(1): 10–13.

Rosenthal, R., and Jacobson, L. 1968. *Pygmalion in the classroom: Teacher expectations and pupils' intellectual development.* New York: Holt, Rinehart, and Winston.

Rothenburg, P. 1992. *Race, class and gender in the U.S.: An integrated study.* New York: St. Martin's.

Rowser, J. F. 1994. Teacher expectations: The forgotten variable in the retention of African American Students. *College Student Journal. 28*(l): 82–87.

"RURacist." http://leevalley. co. uk/yush/rewind/yush01081/ruracist.htm. No date.

Sadker, M. and D. 1994. *Failing at fairness: How America's schools cheat girls.* New York: C. Scribner's.

Simpson, A., and Erickson, M. 1983. Teacher verbal and non-verbal communication patterns as a function of teacher race, student gender and student race. *American Educational Research Journal, 20*: 83–98.

Sleeter. C. E., and Grant, C. A. 1994. *Making choices for multicultural education.* New York: Merrill.

Tetreault, M. K. T. 1993. Classrooms for diversity: Rethinking curriculum and pedagogy. In J. A. Banks and C. A. M. Banks (eds.), *Multicultural education: Issues and perspectives,* 2nd ed. Boston: Allyn & Bacon, pp. 129–148.

U. S. Bureau of the Census (http://www. census. gov)

Wellstone, P. 1995. If poverty is the question .... *Nation, 264*(14): 15–18.

Chapter Three

THE IMPACT OF CULTURAL LEARNING STYLES AND RACIAL IDENTITY ON LEARNING

Scene One: Baby Nicholas is a loved and cherished addition to the Cook household. Sitting in his highchair, his food on the tray in front of him, he begins to negotiate the task of getting food from plate to mouth. Family members are on hand to encourage his first attempts with smiles and kisses. Almost instinctively, his mother begins a language lesson letting her voice emphasize key words. "Look Nicholas, this is a SPOON." "See the BEAR on your plate." "This is your CUP." Lunch over, Nicholas's face and hands are wiped clean with a wash cloth, and he is turned over to Grandma who decides to take him for a ride in his stroller. The world is a big place, and it is time to explore!

Scene Two: Across town Baby Lamees is a loved and cherished addition to the Nuri household. She and her two cousins sit semi-circle on the living room carpet while Grandma feeds them. Grandma pops the food into each one's mouth while family members carry on any number of conversations around the three little ones. There is music in the background and *Headline News* is about to come on. Grandma knows that if she tells them a story, she will get them to eat more. And so she begins "Once upon a time, when your Great Grandfather was a young boy, he met a ghost on his way to town...." Lunch over, Grandma takes her hand, dips it in water and proceeds to wash each child's hands and face. Each one gets a big squeeze and a kiss. Finally, Lamees and her cousins are returned to the larger group. The world is a wonderfully connected place in which to live!

Moms and dads around the world love their children and do their very best to help them become well-educated, adjusted, and productive members of society. Although the parents' goals are the same, they might do very different things. What differences do you see in how Nicholas and Lamees are being raised? What effect might these differences have on how these children come to *know* the world or how they come *to be* in the world? What implications does this have for middle and secondary students' learning?

In this chapter, we consider the potential impact of cultural learning styles and racial identity on learning. Each section provides a context for understanding the concepts and their educational relevancy. Our example looks at differences in child-rearing practices—differences which are "being teased out through studies that link cultural [learning] differences to child-rearing practices and community/family norms" (Carter & Goodwin, 1994, p. 291). Racial/ethnic identity theory looks at differences among same racial/ethnic group members and between different racial/ethnic groups. Both areas offer prospective teachers valuable information about themselves and their students that can be useful in developing and delivering instruction.

CULTURAL LEARNING STYLES

Research on the relationship between cultural influences and learning style is controversial: Scholars haven't agreed on a precise definition for learning style; some dispute the instruments used to measure learning style and therefore what actually can be measured; and to date, researchers have not been able to pinpoint those cultural factors that determine learning style. Moreover, the dangers of overgeneralizing and misusing findings are high. As Bennett (1995) suggests, "The notion that certain learning styles are related to certain ethnic groups is both dangerous and promising" (p. 164). Educators are wary of fostering old or creating new stereotypes in their search to clarify the effects of culture on learning. Despite some misgivings, we believe that strong evidence suggests that culture does affect student learning (Banks, 1988; Bennett, 1995; Ogbu, 1992; Ramirez & Casteneda, 1974; Shade, 1989; Witkin, & Goodenough, 1981).

Researchers offer various definitions of *learning style*. It has been described as the "characteristics that students bring to situations that influence how they learn" (Shaw, 1996, p. 57); "the ways in which individuals receive and process information" (Nieto, 1996, p. 139); and "a consistent pattern of behavior and performance by which an individual approaches educational experiences" (National Task Force on Learning Style and Brain Behavior cited by Parkay & Stanford, 1998, p. 288). Research findings that we report encompass all these definitions. As we present the various findings, you will notice that many characteristics refer to how individuals from a culture process information (cognitive processing), types of behavior, patterns of communication, and social cognition.

Two broad categories of learning characteristics often discussed with learning styles are *field-independent* and *field-dependent/sensitive*. Field-independent learners are described as relying more on internal clues (such as personal feelings, values, experiences), whereas field-sensitive learners rely more on information picked up in social contexts (for example, peers, teachers). Field-independent learners prefer to work alone, but in competition with others, to deal with abstract material, and they respond more readily to monetary or material rewards. On the other hand, field-sensitive learners prefer to work cooperatively, deal with social issues or contextualized problems, and respond more readily to verbal praise. "Researchers tell us that field-independent students do better work in low-structure–inductive-learning situations whereas field-dependent students do better in high-structure–inductive-learning classes" (Clark & Starr, 1996, p. 263).

According to Grossman (1995), research from 1970s indicates that "some ethnic groups tend to be primarily field-sensitive (for example, African Americans and Hispanic Americans) whereas other groups are predominantly field-independent (for example, European Americans). Within most ethnic groups, females tend to be more field-sensitive than males are" (p. 287). Witkin's research on the cognitive styles of field independence and field dependence/sensitivity has been expanded to include the effect of child-rearing practices on those orientations and the subsequent connection to learning styles (Witkin & Goodenough, 1981). Cohen (1969) found evidence supporting two conceptual styles, relational and analytical, linked to how families (including extended families) share functions and power. Relational learners came from families that shared functions, such as parenting, with other members of the group and where authority lines were somewhat fluid. Analytical learners were raised in families where members had more defined roles (that is, big sister did not also function as mom) and authority was hierarchical.

Our goal is to highlight the wide-ranging evidence that scholars and educators are currently considering. Much of the research on culture and learning styles conducted over the past twenty-five years has focused on African Americans, Native Americans, Hispanic/Latino Americans, Asian Americans, and women. The inclusion of women among this group does not negate women as part of other racially/ethnically identified groups but speaks to significant research done on women's orientations to learning. There is a smaller but emerging body of research on cultural issues and gender as it relates to learning styles (Grossman & Grossman, 1994; Harpole, 1987; Wilkinson & Marrett, 1985).

Before presenting an overview of findings that describe cultural learning styles for various racial/ethnic groups, we need to distinguish between generalizations and stereotypes and *caution our readers to avoid turning generalizations into racial/ethnic stereotypes.* Generalizations are statements supported by data, whereas stereotypes are general statements based on incomplete or missing data. For example, statements such as "Most Italians are Catholic" or "Less than half of non-Hispanic householders own their own homes" (Changing America, 1998) can be supported by data. Stereotypes are often based on misperceptions and usually involve a negative judgment. Stereotypes emerge from personal experiences and observations; they are the result of misinterpreting data or from taking information out of a historical context. The distinction between the two terms can be seen in the following example: One Friday morning, while driving to your 8:30 Managerial Accounting class, you notice a woman driver make an illegal left turn up a one-way street and proceed to have an accident. Based on your idiosyncratic observation and previous jokes you have heard about women drivers, you conclude that women *really* are bad drivers. You arrive at class only to find your Business professor lecturing on actuarial studies on driving accidents. She compares statistics on accidents by women and men, and you learn that women have fewer accidents than men do and consequently have better accident records. "Women are bad drivers" is a stereotype; "Women have fewer accidents than men" is a generalization.[1]

African American Learners

A good deal of attention has focused on the cultural learning styles of African Americans (Hale-Benson, 1986; Hilliard, 1989, 1992; Shade, 1982, 1992). Some scholars speculate that African American learning styles draw from a worldview that has its roots in African philosophy handed down through generations, despite contact with an American culture that is more Western and European centered (Bell, 1994). Hilliard (1992) suggests that culture accounts for differences in how African American children think and behave and can often result in the mislabeling, misplacement, and mistreatment of African American children in educational assessments. Schools mistake this cultural mismatch as "student deficiency" and do little to respond to or validate different orientations to learning. The following characteristics are often cited as typical of African American learners:

- Learners are more global. They tend to focus on the whole picture, rather than on the parts.
- Learners often approximate space, numbers, and time rather than being tied to precise accuracy.
- Learners are more field dependent/sensitive (a perceptual style involving the ability to see embedded figures).[2]
- Learners prefer inferential reasoning.
- Learners are more relational than analytic when learning concepts.
- Learners rely on nonverbal as well as verbal communication patterns.
- Learners distrust mainstream people and institutions.
- Learners prefer visual and aural cues.

---

[1] Example based on conversation with Travis Tatum on March 28, 1999.

[2] Witkin has written of a correlation between field/dependence and independence and cultural learning styles. Research indicates that differences in how individuals approach perceptual tasks can be related to how one learns. African American, Latino, and Native American learners all tend to exhibit more field dependent learning styles characterized by a preference for working in groups, "an awareness of social cues with an orientation to the environment along with sensitivity to others' views and feelings," and a global approach to learning (Timm, 1996, p. 184).

Hispanic/Latino Learners

It is extremely important to remember earlier caveats about stereotyping and overgeneralizing when discussing Hispanic/Latino students because they represent a variety of cultures and cultural beliefs. Language is the most common unifying variable for Hispanic/Latino students, but we need to be especially cautious and not assume that all group members share characteristics (Dunn & Dunn, 1978; Ramirez & Casteneda, 1974). Following is a list of general characteristics associated with Hispanic/Latino learners:

- Learners are more field dependent/sensitive.
- Learners are group oriented and inductive thinkers.
- Learners are peer oriented and are more likely to perform well in small groups.
- Learners have a more external locus of control (that is, outside control over what happens to them rather than personal or internal locus of control).[3]
- Learners prefer more personal and informal relationships with authority figures.

Native American Learners

Native Americans may be the ethnic group most failed by the American educational system. Many Native Americans continue to live in isolated and culturally homogeneous settings; this is an advantage or disadvantage depending on your perspective. Much of their experience has been with mainstream educational systems that are "alien to and in conflict with their cultural heritage" (Sadker & Sadker, 1997, p. 452). General learning style characteristics are listed here:

- Learners prefer sharing and cooperative learning versus competitive learning environments. They do not seek personal, individualized recognition for achievement; group achievement is valued over individual achievement; performance must benefit the peer group. Learners prefer community participation to individual participation.
- Learners have a different concept of time from the mainstream perspective.
- Learners frequently exhibit behaviors that seem to indicate a lack of interest in learning and a lack of motivation. Mainstream educators' expectations of eye contact and extensive verbal participation as signs of interest can wrongly interpret Native Americans' behavior as non-interest.

---

[3] Locus of control refers to an individual's perceived source of control. For example, people with an internal locus of control see themselves as in charge of what happens to them; they are "confident about control over their environments, as they are about their intellectual problem-solving abilities" (Shaw, 1986, p. 59). People with an external locus of control do not see themselves as the sole master of their fate. They are aware of external factors that can, and do, often influence outcomes in their lives. Therefore, they do not necessarily equate individual effort with a determined outcome.

- Learners are more reflective than impulsive. They prefer to watch and then perform, rather than approach learning in a trial and error fashion. They are more visually and imagery oriented than verbally oriented.
- Learners more often have an internal locus of control and are self-directed.
- Learners view teachers as facilitators of learning.

Asian American Learners

As with Hispanics/Latinos, a wide range of cultural diversity exists among the many nationalities that constitute Asian populations in this country. A persistent stereotype for Asian American students is the myth of the "model minority." Because many Asian Americans have achieved academically in mainstream schools, they are labeled with this ostensibly "positive" stereotype. There might be fewer "culture clashes" between Asian Americans and mainstream classrooms because their cultural patterns might be more congruent with the values found in most schools. This could account for the scarcity of research on the learning styles of Asian Americans—the perception of them as hard working and academically successful doesn't appeal to the problem-solving mode of many researchers. Suzuki, however, cautions that the stereotype of Asian Americans as "quiet, hardworking, and docile . . . tends to reinforce conformity and stifle creativity" (Suzuki, 1983). A summary of the research on Asian American learning styles follows:

- Learners prefer formal relationships with teachers and other authority figures.
- Learners are autonomous and conforming.
- Learners are obedient to authority.
- Learners are usually conservative and reserved.
- Learners are more introverted.

Female Learners

Research on gender differences in learning style gained greater credence with the publication of works such as *Towards a New Psychology of Women* (Miller), *In a Different Voice* (Gilligan) and *Women's Ways of Knowing* (Belenky, Clincy, Goldberger, & Tarule, 1986). A growing body of evidence chronicles the impact socialization has on women's schooling behaviors, behaviors that are intricately interwoven with their academic performance. Gabriel and Smithson (1990) concede that although it seems likely "that women and men speak, write, read, think, and therefore, learn differently ...it is difficult both to identify the specific differences in the ways male and female students learn and to develop strategies to accommodate the different gender-based learning strategies that have been identified" (p. 8). These researchers also cite the need for more definitive and dependable research in this area.

An added variable is women's obvious inclusion in other cultural groups. There are variations in women's learning across different racial and ethnic cultural groups, but some patterns are common and appear to be specific to women as a culture.

- Learners prefer more community and cooperative learning oriented environments, rather than competitive ones.
- Learners are more relational than analytic in their conceptual learning. (Gilligan's ethic of caring, connection and responsibility.) Learners focus more on people and their activities rather than on decontextualized events and things.
- Learners feel unempowered/disempowered by schooling experiences; they often feel silenced.
- Learners view themselves less confidently than males do, especially in mathematics and science.

Another way to make sense of this information is to look at learning characteristics that tend to clump together, especially at the ends of the continuum. For example, learners who have relational conceptual styles are often field dependent and have an external locus of control. They learn information best when it is contextualized—when information is related to "the big picture" and, preferably, includes a social and affective component. On the other hand, learners who have analytical conceptual styles are often field independent with an internal locus of control. They are quite comfortable learning "the parts" and do not seek an emotional or affective connection to what they are learning. In general, students of color and females tend towards the relational end of the continuum, and White, middle-class students, particularly males, lean more toward analytical learning styles.

Because mainstream society often glamorizes independent, take-charge, "show me no emotion" kinds of people, future middle and secondary teachers must be careful not to value one kind of learning style over another or to assume that one student is more intelligent than another. In all likelihood, a teacher's own school experiences have reinforced a preference for independent, analytical learners. In schools, the ability to confront issues and argue against another's opinion is rewarded with high marks. The kinds of instruction, assignments, and assessment that favor (privilege) one group over another continues today; however, in the "real" world, students will be dependent on and need to work with others. Context is important. With this in mind, middle and secondary teachers can recognize the significance of affirming the different skills of all their students as well as helping them build additional skills.

SUMMARY AND IMPLICATIONS FOR LEARNING STYLES AND CULTURE

Though research on learning styles is debated, the discussion alerts us to the potential incompatibility in learning styles between teacher and students and sensitizes us to students' frustrations, especially for students whose learning styles differ from mainstream approaches. Any information that aids in our recognition of differences that can affect learning and directs us toward responsive and responsible strategies will better serve all students. In *Affirming Diversity* (1996),

Sonia Nieto proposes that "rather than being viewed as a burden, a problem, or even a challenge, cultural diversity will be approached as a key factor that must be taken into account if we are serious about providing all students with educational equity" (p. 137). Knowledge of the types or the nature of the differences in learning can help us create educational environments that tap strengths and develop skills necessary for students' academic success.

Sound pedagogical practice calls for diverse teaching practices, "instructional pluralism" (Shaw, 1996), that build on and expand students' abilities. It is important for teachers to understand that though everyone might have a predominant learning style, most of us use a variety of styles. In addition, we are certainly capable of expanding the styles we use. Good instruction should allow students and teachers to develop confidence in using a variety of styles. Instructional and curricula pluralism are discussed in Chapters Four and Five.

RACIAL AND ETHNIC IDENTITY

In Chapter Two, we talked about how race remains a powerful sociopolitical reality despite its inherently flawed biological basis. Banks (1991) prefers to distinguish between *ethnic groups* and *ethnic minority groups*. Members of an *ethnic group* "share a sense of group identification, a common set of values, political and economic interests, behavioral patterns, and other cultural elements that differ from those of other groups within a society" (p. 13), whereas members of an *ethnic minority group* have "unique physical and/or cultural characteristics that enable people who belong to mainstream groups to identify its members easily and thus to treat them in a discriminatory way" (p. 14). So, for example, Polish Americans are an ethnic group, but Latino Americans belong to an ethnic minority group. Carter and Goodwin (1994) use the term *visible racial/ethnic groups* to refer to members of both racial and ethnic groups who are potential targets of discrimination because of visibility of skin color, language, or physical features. The term *people of color* has become a common term used to describe members of visible racial/ethnic groups.

Racial identity is defined as "a person's psychological orientation toward his or her racial group rather than to racial group membership per se" (Carter & Goodwin, 1994, p. 292). Everyone belongs to a racial group; however, one's identification with that group can vary substantially.

RACIAL IDENTITY THEORY

Racial identity theories describe the beliefs and assumptions characteristic of the different ways individuals identify as members of racial/ethnic groups and the process by which they might move from one stage to another. Theories assume that a positive racial identity contributes to a person's psychological health.

The racial identity theories most often cited deal with Black and White racial identity development, specifically the researched models of William Cross (1991) and Janet Helms (1990), respectively. Theoretical and research evidence (Brown, 1996; Highlen, et al., 1988; Phinney, 1990; Tatum, 1992, 1997; Zavala, 1995) also suggests that the stages are applicable to other visible racial/ethnic groups. In addition, Poston (1990) has put forward a biracial identity development model outlining the process by which biracial individuals positively integrate multiple cultures to arrive at a healthy sense of self.

The application of racial identity theory to educational settings is proving to be a valuable tool in helping prepare pre-service teachers to work with diverse student groups. First we will present a brief overview of stages of racial identity for people of color and Whites and then look at the educational implications of racial identity theory for middle and secondary school teachers.

Stages of Racial/Ethnic Identity Development—People of Color

Individuals in the *Pre-encounter* stage identify themselves with the dominant culture. For example, James believes that "White is right" and that by playing by the White man's rules, he will be successful. He might admire and emulate the norms and beliefs of the Anglo-European American culture and at the same time distance himself from his own racial/ethnic group. Accepting the positive stereotypes about Whites and the negative stereotypes about his own people, James believes that lack of effort is what holds back other group members.[4] Race as a mitigating factor in one's experience is minimized.

Over time as James experiences the overt or subtle racial barriers in his life, he begins to question his former belief in inclusion. The racial blinders come off. In the *Encounter* stage, he becomes increasingly aware of how individuals and, more significantly, how societal institutions work to deny him full participation. The sense of having been duped can lead to feelings of anger, confusion, and betrayal. James must now come to terms with what it means to belong to a group targeted for discrimination. Individuals often enter this stage in early adolescence when they start dating cross-culturally, are followed by store clerks, or stopped by the police.

His worldview and sense of self being challenged, James begins identifying strongly with his racial/ethnic group. During the *Immersion-Emersion* stage, James begins to forge a new identity based on a greater understanding of his ethnic background. Time and energy are devoted to exploring his history, culture, and language. Initially he directs a lot of anger toward the dominant culture, and contacts across racial/ethnic lines may be difficult. Same peer-group support can be significant for individuals in this stage (see P. Brown's overview of her cultural identity group project conducted with fifth and sixth graders in the readings at the end of this chapter). As James's understanding of and immersion into his culture deepens, he moves from Immersion to *Emersion*. In

---

[4] Research suggests that "a preference for the dominant group is not always a characteristic of this stage. For example, children raised in households and communities with explicitly positive Afrocentric attitudes might absorb a pro-Black perspective, which then serves as the starting point for their own exploration of racial development" (Tatum, 1992, p. 10, citing Parham [1989] and Phinney [1989]).

the Emersion phase, James has a growing internalized racial/ethnic identity based on a nonstereotypic view of his racial/ethnic group. Being a person of color is no longer defined by the external perceptions of different groups. Freed from external dictates about what it means to be a person of color, James can decide to listen to both Bach and Puff Daddy, to play basketball and take up skiing. Grounded in a stronger sense of self, his anger toward Whites lessens and his sense of self is affirmed.

In the next stage,[5] *Internalization,* James has achieved a positive racial/ethnic identity and is now ready to reexamine his relationships with the dominant culture. He is willing to form meaningful relationships with individual Whites "who acknowledge and are respectful of his or her self-definition" (Tatum, 1992, p. 12). He can analyze White culture for its strengths and weaknesses and is ready to combat other forms of oppression.

Stages of Racial/Ethnic Identity Development—Whites

Contact, the first stage of White racial identity development, can be described as a stage of "racial bliss." In this stage, Whites consider themselves color-blind; they try not to see skin color and don't see themselves as racist. They are unaware of institutional racism or the privilege that comes with whiteness. They take the values and beliefs of the dominant culture as standards and have little understanding of ethnic and cultural differences. Naiveté, curiosity, and fear are common characteristics of individuals in this stage. For example, Jennifer might believe that people of color don't live in her neighborhood because they don't want to.

Whites might stay at the Contact stage for their entire lives, particularly if they have little or no contact with people of color. In our example, Jennifer enrolls in a new elective course, *Ethnic Studies.* Through lectures, readings and class discussions, her awareness of racial issues expands. In this stage of *Disintegration,* Jennifer can feel anxious, confused, and guilty. She must now reconcile her previous beliefs with this new data. She might try to educate her friends and family and change their attitudes. If she is not successful, then she risks being rejected by her own group. Her friends might accuse her of having "gone over" or having become "too sensitive, too politically correct."

The pressure to remain in one's group can push a person into *Reintegration.* Jennifer tells herself that the inequality that exists is not her fault; that Whites have earned their privileges and people of color should do more for themselves. Any leftover feelings of guilt or anxiety are turned into anger and fear towards people of color. A "blame the victim" mentality sets in. Jennifer might start skipping class, stop participating in class, and avoid any contact with students of color.

---

[5] Cross's theory includes a fifth stage, *Internalization-Commitment.* It differs only slightly from Internalization, but is characterized by a sense of action—wanting to proactively get involved in dealing with issues of social justice.

If, however, Jennifer continues on her path of racial discovery and is supported in her efforts to sort out what it means to be White, she moves into the *Pseudo-Independent* stage. Helms believes this is the first stage toward constructing a positive White identity. However, Jennifer's first steps to redefining her White identity still use a White cultural lens to explain racial and cultural differences. She counts on people of color to teach her about racism and affirm that she is not a racist. She wants "to help" oppressed people and doesn't yet see how racism hurts her. Jennifer might decide to disassociate herself from her White friends and identify with a particular oppressed group. Doing so can leave Jennifer feeling isolated: Whites reject her because she has broken with White norms, and people of color are suspicious of her motives.

As Jennifer continues to come to terms with her Whiteness, she enters the *Immersion or Emersion* stage. What does it mean to be White in this society? Who are the White role models for an anti-racist identity? Jennifer might begin to take an activist role on issues of equity and is eager to know about other Whites who have taken pro-active roles. Stereotypes for Whites and people of color are replaced with accurate information, and Jennifer develops feelings that support a positive anti-racist White identity.

As Jennifer internalizes a positive racial sense of self and lets go of personal, institutional, and cultural racism, she enters the final stage of *Autonomy*. Similar to the Internalization and Internalization/Commitment stages for people of color, the Autonomy stage is a proactive stage where individuals engage in ongoing efforts to work toward social justice and eliminate oppression. Jennifer realizes that this process is lifelong; she will continue to learn new information, perhaps revisit previous stages, and continue a process of self-reflection.[6]

Stages of Biracial Identity Development

Although no one has precise figures for the number of biracial individuals in the United States—estimates in 1990 ranged from one to ten million (Poston, 1990)—everyone agrees that the numbers are rising quickly.[7] Research on this population is in its infancy. Recent theories of biracial identity development (Poston, 1990) and research (Kerwin, Ponterotto, Jackson, & Harris, 1993) have begun to look at the unique experiences of biracial individuals, rather than assume that "the identity development of people who are of 'mixed race' is problematic and . . . their adjustment and identity development as 'marginal'" (Poston, 1990, p. 153). We will look briefly at Poston's five-stage model for

---

[6] See *Education of a WASP* (Lois Stalvey) and *Autobiography of Malcolm X* (Malcolm X) for illustrative examples of racial identity development.

[7] "In 1992 the U.S. Census indicated that the biracial birth rate was higher than the monoracial birth rate. Since 1970 the National Center for Health Statistics reports that the number of monoracial babies has grown at a rate of 15 percent, while the number of multiracial babies has increased by more than 260 percent. In 1989, although the percentage of multiracial births was small (3.4 percent when race was recorded for both parents), this figure translates into more than 100,000 births per subsequent year. Since 1989, almost 1 million first-generation biracial individuals have been born in the United States" (Root, 1996).

developing a positive racial identity among biracial individuals, a model he admits is tentative and may more appropriately be described as changes in reference group orientation attitudes (p. 153).

Personal Identity is the first stage and reflects an identity stage based primarily on factors such as "self-esteem and feelings of self-worth that they develop and learn in the family" (Poston, 1990, p. 153). Like most persons in this stage, Liang is quite young. His parents have told him he is both Asian and European American and that he should be proud of both heritages, but this information doesn't hold much saliency for him. Liang enters stage two, *Choice of Group Categorization,* when circumstances (such as classmates, relatives, census forms) force him to choose between an identity with one group or the other. Ostensibly, he has two choices: "One is to choose a multicultural existence, emphasizing the racial heritage of both parents; the other is to choose one parent's culture or racial heritage as dominant over the other" (p. 153). Poston believes that most individuals in this stage do not yet have the cognitive development to select a multiethnic identity, and therefore Liang will probably make a choice between either his mother or father's background. This choice will depend on such indicators as *social support* factors related to parents' influence and acceptance and participation in the community; *status factors* involving status of parents' ethnic background, the ethnic make-up of the neighborhood, and Liang's peers; and personal factors addressing physical appearance, "cultural knowledge, age, political involvement, and individual personality differences" (p. 153). For example, Liang lives in a predominantly Asian community and is learning to speak Chinese from his grandparents. His Asian features make him racially identifiable as Asian and thus, he might choose to identify himself as Asian American.

Confusion and guilt are hallmarks of stage three, *Enmeshment or Denial.* The guilt, self-hatred, and exclusion adolescent Liang feels at having to choose one identity leaves him conflicted. He might hide the fact that he celebrates Christmas or be ashamed for not wanting his Asian friends to see his White mother. "Eventually the child must resolve the anger and guilt and learn to appreciate both parental cultures, or stay at this level" (Poston, 1990, p. 154). Gibbs (1987) believes that supportive social networks, including schools, will help Liang through this stage, although biracial students might move more slowly than adolescents of either race might.

Stage four, *Appreciation,* marks the beginning of the development of a biracial identity. "They may begin to learn about their racial/ethnic heritage and cultures, but they still tend to identify with one group" (Poston, 1990, p. 154). Previously learned or new information broadens Liang's reference group orientation. In college, Liang has the opportunity to meet other biracial students who share similar experiences.[8] *Integration* is the final stage and it signifies "whole-

---

[8] See *Skin Deep,* a video that includes several biracial college students discussing their feelings about being made to choose between one race or the other.

Table 3-1 Summary of Racial Identity Stages Leading to a Positive Racial Identity

People of Color	Whites	Biracial
Pre-encounter: identification with dominant culture; denial of racism	*Contact:* unaware of institutional racism; color blind; naïve and curious about other racial/ethnic groups	*Personal Identity:* identity is based on self-esteem and self-worth learned in the family
Encounter: awareness of institutional racism and racial privilege; anger and betrayal	*Disintegration:* awareness of institutional racism and societal inequities; confusion and guilt	*Choice of Group Categorization:* societal pressure to identify with one ethnic/racial group
Immersion-Emersion: identification with own racial/ethnic group and immersion into one's own culture; less anger and stronger sense of self within one's culture	*Reintegration:* pressure to maintain status quo; blame the victim mentality; anger and fear	*Enmeshment-Denial:* conflict over having to choose one ethnic/racial idenitty; confusion and guilt
Internalization: positive racial/ethnic identity; more open to relationships with dominant culture	*Pseudo-Independent:* redefinition of White identity; affirmation of worth sought from members of oppressed groups; condescention and isolation	*Appreciation:* knowledge about both cultural heritages is learned; reference group orientation is broadened; development of a secure integrated multi-ethnic identity
Internalization-Commitment: desire to be proactive in dealing with issues of social justice	*Immersion; Emersion:* desire to understand Whiteness and find anti-racist White role models; development of a positive anti-racist White identity	
	Autonomy: ability to let go of personal, institutional, and cultural racism; proactive engagement in social justice	

ness and integration." Hall's research (cited in Poston) indicates that "67 percent of her participants (all adults) reported a multicultural existence. At this level, individuals develop a secure, integrated identity" (p. 154). See Table 3-1 for a summary of racial identity stages leading to positive racial identity.

EDUCATIONAL IMPLICATIONS OF RACIAL IDENTITY THEORY

Racial identity theory provides educators with an additional tool to interpret their own and others' behaviors and interactions. It can be a useful reference point for trying to understand inter–racial/ethnic communications and school achievement for some students. Our goal in presenting racial identity theory is not to train teachers to diagnose and label students but, rather, to introduce new variables to a discussion of student behavior and success. Racial identity theory is also a vehicle for teacher reflection. We caution readers to remember that racial identity theory isn't necessarily a lock-step stage theory where an individual must go through stage one to get to stage two (see Tatum footnote regarding starting point of racial identity development). Moreover, it is possible to revisit stages, although one's perspective might be from a different vantage point (Parham, 1989). "The image that students often find helpful in understanding this concept of recycling through the stages is that of a spiral staircase. As a person ascends a spiral staircase, she may stop and look down at a spot below. When she reaches the next level, she may look down and see the same spot, but the vantage point has changed" (Tatum, 1992, p. 12). For example, as a White person, Rasool has spent several years investigating and reflecting on racial issues. Even though she hopes to be "well along" in her racial development, she is acutely aware of "my feelings of disbelief and shame when I heard about the recent discrimination at a major corporation, or my pride and relief in knowing that White abolitionists supported the case of enslaved Africans who revolted against their captivity in the Amistad Revolt." On the other hand, Curtis, an African American woman teaching at a predominantly White institution, is still angered "when students and colleagues make generalizations about 'you people'" or when teachers tell her that "maybe your child just doesn't test well."

A teacher's stage of racial identity development can influence the lives of her students in very meaningful ways. In our example, we will assume that the teachers are White—an overwhelming reality—and that they have both White and students of color in their classes. Research indicates that many students of color at the middle and secondary levels are having encounter experiences, particularly as they enter puberty and begin dating; moreover, many students of color are seeking to find out what it means to be members of a targeted group. Our experience teaching White students at the college level indicates that many of these students are still in the Contact stage of racial development.[9] Imagine a classroom then in which teacher and students begin a discussion of democracy, the Civil War, or current media representation of "minorities." What kinds of statements could be made? What kinds of feelings could come up?

What kinds of assignments do teachers integrate into their curriculum when they are aware of racial identity theory? What information do they want to provide to Whites, biracial students and students of color? How might teachers monitor discussions among their students? How might they respond to White students, who upon hearing Latino students speak Spanish among themselves, declare themselves skinheads? How might teachers respond to students of color who only want to learn about their own cultural backgrounds? Who ostracize biracial students by calling them "half-breeds"? Or who defend their right to sit in racial/ethnic groups in the cafeteria?

---

[9] We assume that many biracial students in middle and high schools might be in Choice of Group Categorization or Enmeshment/Denial stages.

Racial identity theory provides a strong rationale for multicultural education. White students in the Contact stage need accurate information about themselves and others. They need to become aware of the powerful system of racial advantage that operates in our society as well as the unearned privileges they experience. All students need information about people of color who have resisted oppression and Whites who have stood against racism throughout American history. Biracial students also need to learn about the contributions of other biracial figures. An inclusive curriculum helps all students find role models and helps them construct an accurate picture of historical and present reality. Allowing students the opportunity to meet in racial affinity groups can foster the development of a positive racial identity. (See the chapter reading "Cultural Identity Groups Overview and Framework.")

Summary and Implications for Racial Identity Theory

An understanding of racial identity theory is a useful tool for educators. Teachers have the capacity to help their students develop a more positive racial identity by recognizing the curricular and social needs of students in the process. However, teachers must participate in self-examination and reflection to bring clarity to their own racial development. It is our hope that this textbook helps in the process. Teachers in training must be aware of the relationship between their own growth and development and that of their students. If we want future teachers to be prepared to teach all students, we need "to emphasize the transformation of the individual teacher as a necessary prerequisite to the transformation of practice" (Carter & Goodwin, 1994, p. 325; see also Lawrence, 1997).

Conclusion

Understanding cultural learning styles and racial identity theory are important underpinnings to becoming a culturally relevant teacher—our focus in Chapters Four and Five. We caution our readers not to become overwhelmed by the ways in which our students can differ but, rather, to allow an expanded awareness of these topics to inform their instructional practices, curriculum, and reflections on student learning. Most middle and secondary methods textbooks encourage future teachers to develop "an extensive repertoire" of teaching strategies even when they say little about cultural learning styles or racial identity. Information in this chapter helps teachers understand the strong rationale for using some of those techniques as well as the need to create an environment in which students are invited to learn.

When Real Dialogue and Feelings Are Part of Classroom Discussion

Teachers hope that as instruction begins to better meet students' needs, their students will become actively engaged in their own learning. Everyone will eagerly participate in class discussions; ideally, a variety of opinions and perspectives will be shared in a climate of respect and appreciation. But what if the discussions lead to controversial topics related to race, gender, socioeconomic class, or sexual orientation, and chaos threatens? Racial/ethnic identity theory tells us that we are not all in the same place in our development. Won't some students, no matter how well intentioned, offend others? Won't some students be unwilling to listen?

Real dialogue among students and teacher is a goal of every multiculturalist, but the consequences of true dialogue cannot be predicted. Contextualized learning connects students to the learning, and honest thoughts are tied to affective responses. In addition, adolescence is a time for strong feelings and opinions. Beginning teachers are concerned that they will not be able to handle a volatile situation or to prevent a discussion from collapsing into a conversational "free for all" where nothing substantive is said. However, as Frederick (1995) states, "A genuine 'intercultural' education only begins to happen when students of different cultures, classes, ethnicities, ages, sex, and learning styles interact with each other in classrooms and living units" (p. 83). Our goal is not to prevent feelings from arising but to develop some effective strategies for using these occasions to move individuals along in their thinking, when possible, or to provide a safety valve, when necessary. What follows are some suggestions that might help teachers as they support genuine dialogue in their classrooms:

1. Lay the groundwork for discussion at the start of the school year. Students and teachers need to develop rules for class behavior and discussions collaboratively. What guidelines need to be in place for students and teachers to feel safe to express their ideas? How should students let each other know when they disagree or have been offended by what has been said? It is better to establish class rules before any class discussions and display them as a reminder for everyone to see.

2. Let students know that you are not looking for "right answers," but an exploration of thought. The goal is not to achieve "political correctness." Model good listening skills and employ a nonjudgmental attitude about what is said. Repeating or rephrasing what a student says can help clarify statements that might have offended others. Avoid lecturing students on their feelings; people don't change because you tell them they are wrong.

3. Discuss conflict in general with students, and help students see the benefits of respectful confrontation and disagreement.

4. Introduce the concept of *triggers*:

    "Targeted group members usually have a long history of developing sensitivity to certain negative cues. They have been subjected to them, suffered from them, discussed, and thought about them throughout the course of their lives. Therefore, most are very sensitive to such

Continued

> ### *When Real Dialogue and Feelings...* • *Continued*
>
> signals. Typically, members of non-targeted groups have been so effectively and monoculturally socialized that they consider their language "natural." They are usually unaware of whom they are cueing and are shocked when someone takes offense. We call these cues and signals *triggers*." (Weinstein & Obear, 1992, cited in Wlodkowski & Ginsberg, 1995, pp. 43–44).
>
> 5. Ask students to address each other by name and avoid "some people say" statements. Ask students to speak from their own experiences. Arrange student desks so that students can see each another.
>
> 6. Provide students with material that challenges their thinking. Let the author's words be the focus of the discussion. As the teacher-facilitator, your job is to introduce key ideas from the readings and perspectives not yet voiced.
>
> 7. Thank students for their contributions, especially those that take courage to express.
>
> 8. If necessary, have the class take a "time-out." Have students write about both the content and the process up to that point and share it with one or two classmates. Then ask for a large group discussion.
>
> 9. Remind students that true dialogue is difficult. Celebrate your efforts. Stress that the confidentiality of individual statements should be maintained. Students are welcome to discuss topics that come up in class outside of class but should take care not to attribute statements to particular class members.

READINGS

The readings in Chapter Three extend our understanding of cultural learning styles and racial identity. Suzanne Irujo's "Do You Know Why They All Talk at Once?" offers insights into performance patterns and nonverbal behavioral differences between Anglos and Hispanics. Understanding differences in behaviors and the perception of that behavior can "help minimize misunderstandings." Howard Gardner's article "Learning, Chinese-Style" is useful in two ways: First, we read to understand what Gardner is saying about cultural teaching practices in China as he explains how the Chinese philosophy of education influences the delivery of instruction, and, second, we read to understand the cultural perspective of the writer! Make note of the author's tone and point of view.

"Praising my Individuality" is Amy Baker's racial autobiography and provides us with insights into how she first became aware of her whiteness and how privilege operates in her daily life. Finally, in "Cultural Identity Groups Overview and Framework," Phyllis Brown describes a pilot project in which students participate in cultural identity groups. Her work supports students' racial identity development in explicit and concrete ways.

READING 1

Do You Know Why They All Talk at Once?: Thoughts on Cultural Differences Between Hispanics and Anglos

Suzanne Irujo

Nancy was a bilingual teacher whose students came mainly from Puerto Rico. Her Spanish was excellent, and she prided herself on being bicultural since she had lived in Spain for many years and had traveled to several other Spanish-speaking countries. In her travels, she had often participated in conversations where everybody seemed to be talking at the same time, so she was not bothered when the students in her class did the same thing. She did try to teach them that their behavior was considered rude by many North Americans, but she accepted it as a normal part of their cultural background. There was another aspect of their behavior, however, which really bothered her. When she was correcting papers, all her students would push their papers under her nose at the same time, expecting her to correct each of theirs before she had finished the one she was working on. Her irritation over this often came out in nasty remarks to the children about why they weren't able to see that she could only do one thing at a time. Later, she was always sorry that she had allowed the children to see her irritation, but she didn't know what to do about it.

Nancy's problem here is that her understanding of her students' behavior is based solely on her own experience with similar behaviors. While that kind of understanding is better than none at all, it does not allow Nancy to generalize to other behaviors which she has not experienced. She needs to understand the underlying patterns and value orientations which influence particular behaviors. In this case, talking at the same time and expecting people to be able to do many things at the same time are both manifestations of an underlying polychronic ("many-things-at-one-time") orientation. Whereas most Anglos are monochronic and can only pay attention to one thing at a time, many Hispanics, and especially Puerto Ricans, are polychronic. Nine-Curt (1976) reports that store clerks in Puerto Rico routinely wait on several customers at the same time, and if Anglos patiently wait their turn to get the clerk's undivided attention, they will never get waited on.

This article will discus some of the differences between Hispanics and Anglos in the areas of nonverbal behavior, perception, and cognition. It will also examine culturally determined value and belief systems which can help explain why these differences occur, so that readers will be able to apply this

From *Equity & Choice*, May 1989. Reprinted by permission of Sage Publications, Inc.

understanding to new situations. It is important to remember, however, that all of the examples which follow are based on broad generalizations which are useful in characterizing groups as a whole, but which do not necessarily apply to sub-groups or individuals. Hispanic culture can vary in many aspects from one country to another, and individual members of any culture do not necessarily exhibit all of the characteristics of the culture in general.

Nonverbal communication, perception, cognition, and values were chosen for discussion because they are part of subjective culture which operates at a level outside of our conscious awareness. Most teachers have learned about various aspects of their students' material culture: food, clothing, daily routines, customs, festivals, and so on. They often incorporate that culture into the classroom in order to provide familiar examples for their students and to affirm the value of the native culture. However, cultural misunderstandings are more often due to differences in the beliefs, attitudes, and values which shape subjective culture and which determine material culture and behavior.

Nonverbal Behavior

Nonverbal behavior is an area of subjective culture which has great potential for causing misunderstandings. In verbal communication with speakers of another language, we expect difficulty and are alert for possible misunderstandings. In nonverbal communication, however, we often unconsciously feel that everyone should act the same way we do. Based on this feeling, we assign our own meanings to the behavior of others, thus creating a situation of miscommunication. It is therefore important for teachers to be aware of the major areas of differences between Hispanics and Anglos in nonverbal behavior.

Differences in the use of space often cause problems. Hall (1966) has described the distances which North Americans choose for intimate, personal, social-consultative, and public interactions. These distances differ from those preferred by most Latin Americans (Nine-Curt, 1976). What is personal space for a Hispanic is intimate space for an Anglo, and in a conversation between the two, the Anglo often attempts to back away while the Hispanic tries to maintain the space. The result is that Anglos may see Hispanics as being too close, too pushy, or too sexy, while Hispanics may see Anglos as being aloof, cold, or uninterested.

Hispanics not only interact at a closer distance than Anglos do, they also touch each other more. Touching is a natural part of all interactions, except those between two people of the opposite sex who are not related. Greetings between women always include a hug and a kiss; between men it is a hug and back-slapping. Children are constantly hugged, patted, and squeezed. Most Hispanic children expect to be touched in these ways by their teachers, and respond well to it.

Differences in smiling and eye contact are also evident. For many Hispanics, and especially Puerto Ricans, a smile can mean "hello," "please," "thank you," "you're welcome," "may I help you?" and much more (Nine-Curt, 1976). For them, the Anglo's constant use of words to perform these functions appears overly formal. For the Anglo teacher working with Hispanic children, it is important to realize that their smiles mean "please" and "thank you," and they are not being abrupt or rude when they fail to supply the words. It is also important to know that Hispanic children are taught to lower their eyes when they are being reprimanded. Many Anglos interpret lowered eyes as a sign of evasiveness or guilt, and demand that children look them in the eye when they are being spoken to. For the Hispanic child, prolonged eye contact in this situation is a sign of defiance and lack of respect.

Cognition and Perception

To many people it might appear that cognition and perception would be universal faculties, operating in much the same way in all cultures. However, research has shown that cognitive learning styles are influenced by culture (Brown, 1980). Two broad styles have been identified, field independence and field sensitivity, which are related to Anglo and Hispanic cultural patterns respectively. Field independence is the ability to perceive a particular relevant item or factor in a field of distracting items; this field may be perceptual, or it may be an abstract set of thoughts, ideas or feelings from which subsets are perceived. Field sensitivity is the ability to perceive the whole field more clearly as a unified whole, while the parts embedded in the field are not as easily perceived. These cognitive styles are tied to culture through child-rearing patterns. Authoritarian, agrarian societies which are highly socialized and have strict child-rearing practices tend to have more field sensitive children, while democratic, industrial, competitive societies with freer child-rearing norms produce more field independent children. In school, field independent children are more competitive, independent, and self-confident; they have self-defined goals, are less affected by criticism, and learn analytically. Field sensitive children are more socialized and cooperative, and derive their self-identity from people around them; they seek externally defined goals, are more affected by criticism, and learn globally. Clashes between teaching and learning styles can occur when Anglo teachers, who are probably field independent, work with Hispanic children, who tend to be more field sensitive.

Another way in which perception is influenced by culture becomes apparent when people from different cultural backgrounds are shown the same picture and "see" different things. People perceive that which makes sense to them based on their own experience. The squiggle in Figure 1 might represent a tornado for some people; others could see a corkscrew. The two joined circles suggest eyeglasses to some, and barbells to others, yet everyone is "seeing" the same lines. When shown the drawing in Figure 2 and asked where they think these people are, most Americans answer that they are inside a house. People from certain African cultures, however, would insist that they are outside under a tree, based on their experience with houses which have neither square corners nor windows. Besides that, dogs are never found inside a house. If asked to explain the incongruous square in the middle of the picture, they might respond that it is obviously a can of water balanced on the young woman's head.

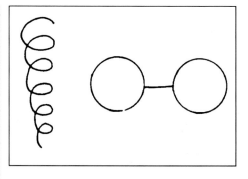

Figure 1

Figure 2

It is important to realize that Hispanic students may be employing a different cognitive style when they fail to perceive the equivalent fractions shown in diagrams in math books, or that their experience may be influencing their perception when they misinterpret a story because a picture has a different meaning for them than it has for an Anglo student.

Values

An examination of the differences in underlying value and belief systems of two cultures is necessary in order to be able to generalize from knowledge of specific cultural differences to understanding of why these differences occur. This will enable us to correctly interpret new behaviors which we have not previously encountered. This may be difficult for many people, however, because we are often not aware of our own value systems. We must also be careful not to assume that a value or belief which is generally held by a particular cultural group is necessarily held by all individual members of that group.

The major areas of contrast between Hispanic and Anglo value systems have been summarized by Zanger (1984). They include: (1) independence vs. interdependence; Anglos value independence as the basis of their own identity and their relations with others, while Hispanics build relationships of interdependence, especially within the family. (2) Equality vs. social hierarchy; Anglos believe in equality in personal relationships and are uncomfortable with shows of deference and situations that emphasize inequalities between people, while Hispanics accept the established social hierarchy which is the basis of most interaction. (3) Technological orientation vs. fatalism; Anglos believe that man is capable of controlling his own destiny, whereas Hispanics accept man's limited ability to influence fate. (4) Individualism vs. solidarity; Anglos expect to do things for themselves through self-reliance and competence, whereas Hispanics identify with a group and emphasize cooperation and loyalty. (5) Future vs. present; for Anglos, change is seen as positive and sacrifice for the future is common because of a strong future orientation, while for Hispanics, an orientation toward present time means that it is important to enjoy life to the fullest. (6) Tasks vs. people; the task-orientation of most Anglos is reflected in their striving for efficiency and practicality, while the Hispanic people-orientation is shown by their attention to relationships. (7) Protestant influence vs. Catholic influence; the Protestant heritage in North America is the source of many Anglo values such as the work ethic, practicality, and puritanical attitudes, while many Hispanic values, such as fatalism, piety, and respect for authority reflect the Catholic heritage of Latin America.

These underlying value systems create implicit cultural assumptions about why things happen. For example, an Hispanic might see an early death as being God's will, in contrast to an Anglo who could see it as a need for more control over environmental factors which caused the death. Value systems are also the basis for many culturally determined behaviors. Many Hispanics have a very different attitude toward money than most Anglos. Even if they have very little money, they are extremely generous, and what little money they have is used for social purposes. This is a reflection of the value of people orientation. In the area of clothing, Hispanics are usually well-dressed, clean and neat regardless of the limits of their budgets, and it is disrespectful to visit someone without being properly dressed. These behaviors reflect the value of social hierarchy. The well-known lack of importance of time in Hispanic cultures is due to their orientation to present time. The prevalence of laughter, play, and parties in Hispanic societies reflects people orientation, solidarity, interdependence, and present time orientation. Playing, enjoyment, and relationships with other people are what life is all about.

Conclusion

It is obvious that knowledge of cultural differences can help to minimize misunderstandings. It is equally obvious that nobody can know about all possible differences between two cultures. It is therefore important that teachers who work with students from a different culture be aware of potential misunderstandings, and be willing to accept behavior which they might not understand because it stems from a value system which they know is different. The key word here is acceptance. Culturally different students must not be made to feel that their behavior is wrong, strange, or unacceptable. The road to biculturalism includes both maintenance of one's own cultural identity and adaptation to dominant cultural patterns. It is the teacher's responsibility to help students do this by accepting their native cultural patterns, and at the same time guiding them through the discovery and adoption of new ways of thinking, perceiving, and valuing.

References

Brown, H. Douglas, *Principles of Language Teaching and Learning,* Englewood Cliffs, NJ: Prentice-Hall, 1980.

Hall, Edward T. *The Hidden Dimension.* New York: Doubleday and Co., 1966.

Nine-Curt, Carmen Judith. *Non-Verbal Communication in Puerto Rico.* Cambridge, MA: National Assessment and Dissemination Center for Bilingual/Bicultural Education, 1976.

Zanger, Virginia Vogel. *Exploración intercultural-Una guía para el estudiante.* Rowley, MA: Newbury House Publishers, Inc., 1984.

READING 2

Learning, Chinese-Style

Howard Gardner

For a month in the spring of 1987, my wife Ellen and I lived in the bustling eastern Chinese city of Nanjing with our 1 1/2-year-old son Benjamin while studying arts education in Chinese kindergartens and elementary schools. But one of the most telling lessons Ellen and I got in the difference between Chinese and American ideas of education came not in the classroom but in the lobby of the Jinling Hotel where we stayed in Nanjing.

The key to our room was attached to a large plastic block with the room number embossed on it. When leaving the hotel, a guest was encouraged to turn in the key, either by handing it to an attendant or by dropping it through a slot into a receptacle. Because the key slot was narrow and rectangular, the key had to be aligned carefully to fit snugly into the slot.

Benjamin loved to carry the key around, shaking it vigorously. He also liked to try to place it into the slot. Because of his tender age, lack of manual dexterity and incomplete understanding of the need to orient the key just so, he would usually fail. Benjamin was not bothered in the least. He probably got as much pleasure out of the sounds the key made as he did those few times when the key actually found its way into the slot.

©1989 Sussex Publishers, Inc. Reprinted by permission of *Psychology Today.*

Now both Ellen and I were perfectly happy to allow Benjamin to bang the key near the key slot. His exploratory behavior seemed harmless enough. But I soon observed an intriguing phenomenon. Any Chinese attendant nearby would come over to watch Benjamin and, noting his lack of initial success, attempt to intervene. He or she would hold onto Benjamin's hand and, gently but firmly, guide it directly toward the slot, reorient it as necessary, and help him to insert it. The "teacher" would then smile somewhat expectantly at Ellen or me, as if awaiting a thank you—and on occasion would frown slightly, as if to admonish the negligent parent.

I soon realized that this incident was directly relevant to our assigned tasks in China to investigate the ways of early childhood education (especially in the arts), and to illuminate Chinese attitudes toward creativity. And so before long I began to incorporate this key-slot anecdote into my talks to Chinese educators.

Two Different Ways to Learn

With a few exceptions my Chinese colleagues displayed the same attitude as the attendants at the Jinling Hotel. Since adults know how to place the key in the key slot, which is the ultimate purpose of approaching the slot, and since the toddler is neither old enough nor clever enough to realize the desired action on his own, what possible gain is achieved by having the child flail about? He may well get frustrated and angry—certainly not a desirable outcome. Why not show him what to do? He will be happy, he will learn how to accomplish the task sooner, and then he can proceed to more complex activities, like opening the door or asking for the key—both of which accomplishments can (and should) in due course be modeled for him as well.

We listened to such explanations sympathetically and explained that, first of all, we did not much care whether Benjamin succeeded in inserting the key into the slot. He was having a good time and was exploring, two activities that *did* matter to us. But the critical point was that, in the process, we were trying to teach Benjamin that one can solve a problem effectively by oneself. Such self-reliance is a principal value of child rearing in middle-class America. So long as the child is shown exactly how to do something—whether it be placing a key in a key slot, drawing a rooster or making amends for a misdeed—he is less likely to figure out himself how to accomplish such a task. And, more generally, he is less likely to view life—as Americans do—as a series of situations in which one has to learn to think for oneself, to solve problems on one's own and even to discover new problems for which creative solutions are wanted.

Teaching By Holding His Hand

In retrospect, it became clear to me that this incident was indeed key—and key in more than one sense. It pointed to important differences in the educational and artistic practices in our two counties.

When our well-intentioned Chinese observers came to Benjamin's rescue, they did not simply push his hand down clumsily, hesitantly or abruptly, as I might have done. Instead, they guided him with extreme facility and gentleness in precisely the desired direction. I came to realize that these Chinese were not just molding and shaping Benjamin's performance in any old manner: In the best Chinese tradition, they were *ba zhe shou jiao*—"teaching by holding his hand"—so much so that he would happily come back for more.

The idea that learning should take place by continual careful shaping and molding applies equally to the arts. Watching children at work in a classroom setting, we were stunned at their facility. Children as young as 5 or 6 were painting flowers, fish and animals with the dexterity and panache of an adult; calligraphers 9 and 10 years old were producing works that could have been displayed in a museum. In a visit to the homes of two of the young artists, we learned from their parents that they worked on perfecting their craft for several hours a day.

Interested as I was in the facility of the young artists, I wondered whether they could draw any object or only something they had been taught to portray. After all, in the practice of calligraphy, the ordinary method involves painstaking tracing of the same characters over and over. Suddenly I had a minor inspiration. I decided to ask three 10-year-olds to draw my face. The assignment at first nonplussed my three guinea pigs, but soon they undertook it with gusto, and each produced a credible job. To be sure, one picture had me looking like one of the Beatles, the second like a Chinese schoolboy, the third as Charlie's aunt is usually portrayed, but each of them bore at least a family resemblance to its subject. I had found out what I wanted: Chinese children are not simply tied to schemata; they can depart to some extent from a formula when so requested.

Creativity: Evolutionary or Revolutionary?

If I had to indicate the typical Chinese view of creativity, it would run as follows: In every realm, there are accepted means for achieving competence—prescribed and approved performance. There is really no good reason for attempting to bypass a long-established route, although a modest degree of latitude can be tolerated as the traditional form is acquired. Though the point of acquisition may never be totally reached (Zen Buddhist masters ask their charges to create the same sound or form or movement thousands of times), competent performers are sanctioned to introduce increasing departures from the approved forms. By this distinctly evolutionary path, the products of the master eventually come to be reasonably deviant from the canon. This is "approved creativity." Even so, the relationship to the canon continues to be evident, and critical discussion of an adult master may center on fruitful as opposed to idiosyncratic deviations.

While these views of the creative realm are not the modern Western ones, they seem entirely viable to me. We might contrast the Western, more "revolutionary" view, with a more "evolutionary" view espoused by the Chinese. There is a virtual reversal of priorities: the young Westerner making her boldest departures first and then gradually reintegrating herself into the tradition; and the young Chinese being almost inseparable from the tradition, but, over time, possibly evolving to a point as deviant as the one initially staked out by the innovative Westerner.

One way of summarizing the American position is to state that we value originality and independence more than the Chinese do. The contrast between our two cultures can also be conceptualized in terms of the fears we both harbor. Chinese teachers are fearful that if skills are not acquired early, they may never be acquired; there is, on the other hand, no comparable hurry to inculcate creativity. American educators fear that unless creativity has been acquired early, it may never emerge; on the other hand, skills can be picked up later.

However, I do not want to overstate my case. There is certainly creativity in China: creativity by groups, by selected individuals in the past and by numerous Chinese living in diverse societies around the world today. Indeed, as a society, China compares favorably with nearly every other in terms of the scientific, technological and aesthetic innovations that have emerged over the centuries.

There is also the risk of overdramatizing creative breakthroughs in the West. When any innovation is examined closely, its reliance on previous achievements is all too apparent (the "standing on the shoulder of giants" phenomenon). Perhaps as Claude Levi-Strauss has argued, it is misleading to speak of creativity as though it ever occurs from scratch; every symbolic breakthrough simply represents a certain combination of choices from within a particular symbolic code.

But assuming that the antithesis I have developed is valid, and that the fostering of skills and creativity are both worthwhile goals, the important question becomes this: Can we glean, from the Chinese and American extremes, a superior way to approach education, perhaps striking an optimal balance between the poles of creativity and basic skills?

READING 3

Praising My Individuality

Amy Baker

Looking back at your life can be an amazing experience. But, it can also be rather daunting when you think about all of the events that have made you the person that you are today. Family may play a major role in your development,

---

Reprinted by permission of the author.

because your family is a part of who you are and what you believe. The environment that surrounds you growing up has the ability to mold the way you think and act. All of these aspects of your cultural upbringing form cause-and-effect relationships that provide explanation for who you are. This is not to say that you do not have input into your own life, but these instances that have touched your life in some way have shaped you.

I am intimidated by the thought of analyzing my life to see how my cultural influences have shaped the kind of person that I am. It is always interesting to look at aspects of your life that you have packed away in a remote part of your mind. But, you also stand a chance of finding something you never realized existed in your experience thus far. This is where my ambivalence lies. However, I am now intrigued to proceed with an autobiography that highlights the possible cultural influences on my development as a person.

There are many roles to which I associate myself. I am a White, female, twenty-one-year-old of mixed-nationality. More than that, I am a sister, a daughter, a student, a teacher, and a friend. These roles have their advantages and disadvantages, but they are all a part of me. Through in-depth analysis, I have noticed that it is my whiteness and my femaleness that have dominated my life, although I was not keenly aware. I do not think about the fact that I am White or that I am female in my daily routines, probably because I have not found it to be an issue of concern. But, I am now more aware of it than ever. There have been several instances where my gender or my race has had influence on my decisions and reactions to different situations. Now that I have become aware of them, it seems almost ridiculous that I never realized how much my gender and my race affect who I am. This is part of that fear that I talked of earlier, because I have realized that I have been naïve to many common truths in my life.

I would like to talk about my experience as a White individual, as it has been rather startling over the years. It suddenly occurs to me that almost every place I go I can be sure to find people of my race surrounding me. I can choose to be in the company of other White individuals, or I can find a quiet place to myself where I will not be disturbed. My race has always been predominant at every school I have attended. Of course, there are generally samplings of other cultures, but a White majority for most of my life has surrounded me. Undoubtedly I have never complained, but I am now starting to wonder if that has played too large a role in my development.

The first significant realization I had about my skin color occurred when I came to Hartford three and a half years ago. My fieldwork for my educational studies brought me to several different schools in the Hartford area. This was the first time in my life that I felt like a minority. As I walked through the halls of an elementary, middle, and high school in Hartford, I was startled to realize the only other White people in the schools were teachers. This was such a new experience for me, coming from a predominantly White suburb in Massachusetts. My fieldwork experiences had a profound affect on the way I look at my whiteness.

I would like to share some of the feelings I had upon entering an all-black school. I consider these reactions unconscious, or at least I hope they are, because otherwise I feel guilty for even thinking them. A distinct image that pops into my head is finding myself peering over the tops of a sea of black faces, searching for a kindred spirit. Unfortunately, at the time, that kindred spirit would have been any other person from my own race. It now seems embarrassing to me looking back at it. But, at the time, that is exactly how I felt. I could not feel comfortable with myself until I formed a relationship with the students. However, I was rather close-minded upon my first step into the building. That is why I say it is an unconscious thought, because I was not aware of it at the time. Now it seems clear-as-day.

It is unsettling to think that I had not even tried to see the individuals for who they were, because I was too busy seeing who they weren't—White. I am ashamed of the thoughts that went through my head. I felt uncomfortable, different, afraid, and lonely. Fear is a powerful word. I was not afraid because I thought I was in danger or anything of the kind. I was afraid that I would say or do something that would give away my identity. I am referring to my identity as a White individual. It is ridiculous because the students could obviously tell I was White by my skin color and hair texture. But, I thought if I tried to blend in I would not give away any part of who I was. It now seems comical that these ideas ran through my head.

These experiences in my fieldwork placement influence the way I look at the cultural assumptions that I make. There is also another defining moment I recall as I look at the cultural influences in my life. I went abroad for a semester last spring to study in England. I never realized how much my culture defined me, especially my ties to the American culture. I felt so alone in England because I was singled out as an American. Although I have pale skin and may seem like I would fit in with English people, I felt extremely separate. My clothing, my language, everything about me set me apart from everyone else. I felt similar to the way I did in the Hartford schools because I was different. Again, I was afraid to give myself away. I tried not to speak, so as not to give away my American accent. I tried to dress similarly to the English students so I would blend in more appropriately. But, at the same time, I felt ashamed of myself for being embarrassed by my American heritage. I did not want to deny who I was, but that seemed the only way to accommodate the fact that I was foreign. It seemed like the easy thing to do. But, sometimes the easiest route may not be the best in the end.

Denying where you come from may be quite easy, but it is impossible to deny the fact that I am female. Although, there were many times as a child I tried endlessly to fit in with the males I hung around with. I grew up in a close-knit extended family and was constantly surrounded by cousins, aunts, and uncles. The girls in my family were several years older than me, so I tended to join in the boys' activities. The easiest way for me to fit in was to become a "tom-boy." I played the sports that they played, and tried to act as tough as I could so they would let me stay. All this was going on while the girls were upstairs playing dress-up and office. I found that I was too young to fit in with the girls and too female to fit in with the boys. Being stuck in the middle did nothing for my self-esteem. Eventually, I realized that I would start to lose the person I really was if I kept acting all the time. The male and female traits that I had acquired would allow me to fit in anywhere I chose to include myself. This goes back to that freedom I have to choose my own company and my own comfortable environment.

I no longer feel afraid to give myself away in unfamiliar crowds, because my experiences have made me who I am. I am a White, twenty-one-year-old female who is proud to be a sister, a daughter, and a friend. The cultural influences in my life, such as race and gender, have created a unique individual. Although I may not examine my cultural background all that often, I do acknowledge that it is a part of me. I know that being a female sets me apart from my male counterparts. And being White emphasizes my difference from individuals of other races. Looking at these differences does not hinder my ability to form relationships with people of other cultural backgrounds. In fact, I have learned a lot more about myself that will enable me to form closer relationships with more meaningful connections, based on these inherent, unique qualities.

READING 4: *Cultural Identity Groups Overview and Framework*

Phyllis C. Brown

The Cultural Identity Group Project model was piloted at Fort River Elementary School in collaboration with the University of Massachusetts in 1993. In 1994 and 1995 the project involved 70 young people, in grades 5 and 6, (Asian American, African American, Biracial American, Cambodian American, European American, Latino/American), and sixteen facilitators.

The goal of the cultural identity groups is to provide young people with an opportunity to explore issues of race/ethnicity, racism, and racial identity. The issues of race are ongoing and prevalent in school and in society and have a profound impact on children. Young people, although directly affected, are rarely given an opportunity to speak their mind, explore and discuss such matters openly with others. Tatum (1992) states "when offered the opportunity to discuss the psychological legacy of racism for both Whites and people of color, all students gain a new framework for understanding their interactions both

---

Reprinted by permission of the author.

within their own racial group and across racial boundaries" (p. 332). Thus, providing young people with an opportunity to voice their opinions and experiences will empower them to address feelings of isolation and incidents of bias that occur regularly in school and in the community, enlighten facilitators as well as school officials to the impact of such incidents on behavior and academic achievement, improve interethnic relations and prepare youth with the skills to address such issues in a constructive manner. Further, the skills developed will be useful in addressing similar concerns in junior high and high school where such issues manifest in ways that affect friendships, dating, and academics.

Empowerment here refers to an affirmed sense of self-efficacy, greater racial pride and a feeling of unity with others who share the same concerns, sociopolitical and psychological experiences. Empowerment also relates to greater appreciation for people of other racial, ethnic, and linguistic backgrounds. For example, one skill that is developed through this process is how to be an ally for people or a person being discriminated against.

The issues of equity and oppression are dealt with from the vantage point of the young people's understanding and experience with it. While the subject matter is complex, the group should also be fun and full of activities that are appropriate for the age group(s) involved. Facilitators must role model racial pride and positive interethnic relations. The activities should also be complementary and sensitive to the pre-existing knowledge, psychosocial, and racial identity developmental level of the young people.

The cultural identity group process is intended to be student-centered. A general outline, structure, and curriculum of the cultural identity groups are in place; however, students will be asked for their input on how and what the group should become. Because it is inappropriate to assume what knowledge the youth may or may not possess about their racial and cultural identity, or that all members will know each other, the groups will begin with simple "icebreaker" type exercises to foster community building within the group. The icebreaker is a pre-test to gauge the young people's sense of belonging.

This project is a two-stage model consisting of two phases that are conjoined by a large group community building activity and that concludes with an awards ceremony and multicultural festival. In brief:

- **Phase I:** focuses on the same race experience in which children are discussing the aforementioned issues in "Affinity" groups and addressing the leading question of adolescence, "Who Am I?". In this phase children are developing a greater appreciation for their own cultural, racial/ethnic heritage both as individuals and as members of a group.

- **Phase II:** focuses on multiracial groups in which children discuss the aforementioned issues in "Blended" groups. In this phase children are developing skills that will help them interrupt acts of discrimination and build stronger interethnic relations.

Cultural Identity Group Structure:

The group size should be small, 10–12 students maximum. Groups should be scheduled to meet at least once a week for 45–60 minutes. The sessions consist of a variety of activities that range from "Getting to Know You" to discussions that focus on constructive ways to confront issues of discrimination, build interethnic relations as well as celebrate and make visible racial and ethnic groups that are underrepresented. Music, literature, poetry, geography, current events (media literacy), theater, school experiences and food are used as tools for discussing issues of culture, racial and ethnic identity as well as racism. Parents are also invited to become involved through participation in group meetings and by working with students on home assignments given by the facilitators.

Cultural Identity Group Objectives:

1. Provide youth with an opportunity to discuss issues of cultural heritage, race/ethnicity, and racism in a safe setting;
2. Build on the students' pre-existing knowledge regarding issues and experiences with race and racism;
3. Facilitate the enhancement and building of self-esteem;
4. Help students to appreciate differences and consider the long-term implications of this awareness;
5. Provide students with an opportunity to express their feelings and/or concerns to school officials;
6. Create options for confronting racism (conflict resolution, peer mediation) which can minimize the harmful effects to youngsters.

Desired outcomes for Cultural Identity Groups are as follows:

1. Enhanced self-esteem and self-efficacy;
2. Appreciation of diversity and unity;
3. Empowerment and awareness of how racism affects individuals and groups and what individuals and groups can do to fight the effects of racism;
4. Developed mediation skills for dealing with interethnic conflicts;
5. Opportunity for students from different racial and ethnic backgrounds to meet and discuss issues of race and racism and develop appropriate social action plans to address such concerns;
6. Development of a joint inter-ethnic student project to synthesize the learning of the group and;
7. Documentation of this project for dissemination and replication of model.

Discussion Questions and Activities

1. Review the characteristics for field-independent and field-dependent learners. Would you describe yourself as a field-independent or field dependent/sensitive learner? Explain your answer. What cultural factors do you think have influenced how you learn? How compatible is your style with the way schools teach? How do you cope when a teacher's instructional style doesn't match yours? Given your answers to these questions, how would you describe your learning style? As a teacher, how can you accommodate students with different learning styles?

2. It is easy to become overwhelmed by the ways in which students differ in their learning styles. We make general statements about the learning styles of members from a particular group only to caution readers not to overgeneralize. There seems no end to the amount of information middle and high school teachers must store in their heads as they develop curriculum and deliver instruction for 150 diverse learners! What strategies can teachers employ to help them deal with the reality of being overwhelmed at times?

3. What are some of the major differences between the Chinese philosophy of teaching as described by Gardner and the American approach to teaching? How might a Chinese author describe those differences?

4. Write your own racial identity biography. Make note of changes that might have occurred over time. When did you first realize that you were [racial background]? Describe the events. How did you feel? What does being [racial background] mean to you? Have you ever thought before about what it means to be [racial background]? Who has been an influential role model in your life in helping you understand your racial identity? In what ways can teachers support the racial identity development of their students?

5. Read Martin Espada's poem "The New Bathroom Policy at English High School" (Nueva norma para el bano en la English High School). Using racial identity theory, how might you explain the actions of the principal and the use of Spanish by the students?

6. Is it useful to teach middle or secondary school students about racial identity stages or cultural learning styles? Explain your answers.

7. Your principal is considering establishing cultural identity groups in your middle school. She asks you to read the Brown "Cultural Identity Groups Overview and Framework," and offer your opinion. What would you say? Explain your answer.

REFERENCES

Banks, J. A. 1988. *Multiethnic education: Theory and practice,* 2nd ed. Boston: Allyn & Bacon.

Banks, J. A. 1991. *Teaching strategies for ethnic studies,* 5th ed. Boston: Allyn & Bacon.

Belenky, M. F., Clincy, B. M., Goldberger, N. R., and Tarule, J. M. 1986. *Women's ways of knowing: The development of self, voice and mind.* New York: Basic.

Bell, Y. R. 1994. A culturally sensitive analysis of Black learning styles. *Journal of Black Psychology, 20*(1): 47–61.

Bennett, C. 1995. *Comprehensive multicultural education: Theory and practice,* 3rd ed. Boston: Allyn & Bacon.

Brown, P. 1996. *Cultural identity groups overview and framework,* unpublished abstract.

Carter, R. T., and Goodwin, A. L. 1994. Racial identity and education. In L. Darling-Hammond (ed.), *Review of research in education,* vol. 20. Washington, D.C.: American Educational Research Association.

Changing America. 1998. http:/www. whitehouse. gov/WH/EOP/CEA/html/publications. html

Clark, L. H., and Starr, I. S. 1996. *Secondary and middle school teaching methods,* 7th ed. Englewood Cliffs, NJ: Prentice-Hall.

Cohen, R. A. 1969. Conceptual styles, culture conflict, and nonverbal tests of intelligence. *American Anthropologist, 71*: 828–856.

Cross, W. E., Jr. 1991. *Shades of Black: Diversity in African-American identity.* Philadelphia: Temple University Press.

Dunn, R. S., and Dunn, K. J. 1978. *Teaching students through their individual learning styles: A practical approach.* Reston, VA: Reston.

Frederick, P. 1995, Summer. Walking on eggs: Mastering the dreaded diversity discussion. *College Teaching, 43*(3): 83–92.

Gabriel, S., and Smithson, I. 1990. *Gender in the classroom: Power and pedagogy.* Urbana: University of Illinois Press.

Gibbs, J. T. April 1987. Identity and marginality: Issues in the treatment of biracial adolescents. *Journal of Orthopsychiatry, 57*: 265–278.

Gilligan, C. 1982. *In a different voice.* Cambridge, MA: Harvard University Press.

Grossman, H. 1995. *Teaching in a diverse society.* Boston: Allyn & Bacon.

Grossman, H., and Grossman, S. 1994. *Gender issues in education.* Boston: Allyn & Bacon.

Hale, J. E. 1994. *Unbank the fire: Visions for the education of African American children.* Baltimore: Johns Hopkins University Press.

Hale-Benson, J. 1986. *Black children: Their roots, culture and learning styles.* Baltimore: Johns Hopkins University Press.

Harpole, S. H. 1987. *The relationship of gender and learning styles to achievement and laboratory skills in secondary school chemistry students.* Paper presented at the Mid-South Educational Research Associations, Mobile, Alabama. ERIC ED 288 728.

Helms, J. E. (ed.). 1990. *Black and White racial identity: Theory, research, and practice.* Westport, CT: Greenwood.

Highlen, P. S., Reynolds, A. L., Adams, E. M., Hanley, T. C., Myers, L. J., Cox, C., and Speight, S. 1988, August 13. *Self-identity development model of oppressed people: Inclusive model for all?* Paper presented at the American Psychological Association, Atlanta, GA.

Hilliard, A. 1989. Teaching and cultural styles in a pluralistic society. *National Education Association, 7*(6): 65–69.

Hilliard, A. 1992. Behavioral style, culture and teaching and learning. *Journal of Negro Education, 61*(3): 370–377.

Kerwin, C., Ponterotto, J. G., Jackson, B. L. and Harris, A. 1993. Racial identity in biracial children: A qualitative investigation. *Journal of Counseling Psychology, 40*(2): 221–231.

Lawrence, S. 1997. Beyond race awareness: White racial identity and multicultural teaching. *Journal of Teacher Education,* 48(2): 108–117.

Miller, J. 1986. *Towards a new psychology of women.* Boston: Beacon.

Nieto, S. 1996. *Affirming diversity: The sociopolitical context of multicultural education.* New York: Longman.

Ogbu, J. U. 1992. Understanding cultural diversity and learning. *Educational Researcher, 21*(8): 5–14.

Parham, T. A. 1989. Cycles of Psychological Nigrescence. *Counseling Psychologist, 17*(2): 187–226.

Parkay, F. W. and Stanford, B. H. 1998. *Becoming a teacher,* 4th ed. Boston: Allyn & Bacon.

Phinney, J. 1989. Stages of ethnic identity in minority group adolescents. *Journal of Early Adolescence, 9*: 34–39.

Phinney, J. 1990. Ethnic identity in adolescents and adults: Review of research. *Psychological Bulletin, 108*(3): 499–514.

Poston, C. W. S. 1990. The biracial identity development model: A needed addition. *Journal of Counseling and Development, 69*(2): 152–155.

Ramirez, M., and Casteneda, A. 1974. *Cultural democracy, bicognitive development and education.* New York: Academic.

Root, M. P. P. 1996. The multiracial experience: Racial borders as a significant frontier in race relations. In M. P. P. Root (ed.), *The multiracial experience: Racial borders as the new frontier,* pp. xiii–xxviii. Thousand Oaks, CA: Sage.

Sadker, M. P., and Sadker, D. M. 1997. *Teachers, schools, and society,* 4th ed. New York: McGraw Hill.

Shade, B. J. 1982. Afro-American cognitive style: A variable in school success. *Review of Educational Research, 52*: 219–244.

Shade, B. J. 1989. *Culture, style, and the educative process.* Springfield, IL: Charles C. Thomas.

Shade, B. J. 1992. *Afro-American patterns of cognition.* Madison: University of Wisconsin, Madison Research and Development Center for Education Research.

Shaw, C. C. 1996. Instructional pluralism: A means to realizing the dream of multicultural, social reconstructionist education. In Grant, C. A. and Gomez, M. L., *Making schooling multicultural.* Englewood Cliffs, NJ: Merrill.

Suzuki, B. H. 1983. The education of Asian and Pacific Americans: In introductory overview. In D. T. Nakanishi and M. Hirano-Nakanishi (eds.), *Education of Asian and Pacific Americans: Historical perspectives and prescriptions for the future.* Phoenix, AZ: Oryx.

Suzuki, B. H. 1984. Curriculum transformation for multicultural education. *Education and Urban Society, 16*: 294–322.

Tatum, B. D. 1992. Talking about race, learning about racism: An application of racial identity development theory in the classroom. *Harvard Educational Review.* 62(1): 1–24.

Tatum, B. D. 1997. *Why are all the Black kids sitting together in the cafeteria?* New York: Harper Collins.

Timm, J. T. 1996. *Four perspectives in multicultural education.* Belmont, CA: Wadsworth.

Wilkinson, L. C., and Marrett, C. B. (eds.). 1985. *Gender influences in classroom interaction.* Orlando: FL: Academic.

Witkin, H. A., and Goodenough, D. R. 1981. *Cognitive styles, essence and origins: Field dependence and field independence.* New York: International Universities Press.

Wlodkowski, R. J., and Ginsberg, M. B. 1995. *Diversity and motivation.* San Francisco: Jossey-Bass.

Zavala, M. 1995. *Who are you if you don't speak Spanish?: The Puerto Rican dilemma.* Paper presented at the 1996 Annual Meeting of the American Educational Research Association, New York.

Chapter Four

EFFECTIVE DECISION-MAKING, DELIVERY OF INSTRUCTION, AND CLASSROOM MANAGEMENT

Your cooperating teacher is ready to let you take over her third period Biology class. You've assigned Chapter 7, "The Biosphere," for homework and now are wondering what you will do in tomorrow's class. You must make several decisions: How much material can I cover tomorrow? Should I lecture? Should I put students in groups? What kinds of activities would they do? Your decisions will be based on the material you want to teach, the students you will be teaching, and the objectives and goals you have for their learning. Chapter Five deals with decisions about *what* you might teach; in this chapter we want to consider *how* you would teach.

Your beliefs about education (objectives and goals) and learning (how students learn) will largely determine the *how* of your teaching. Figure 4-1 shows several continua reflecting the various positions teachers can take in relationship to the delivery of instruction. For example, in general teachers might be more interested in *what* students learn, rather than *how* they learn it, or more concerned with covering a lot of material, rather than covering less material but in more depth. Teachers might have strong feelings about *who* should dispense knowledge, or how important or relevant it is to connect the material to students' lives. Take a minute to see where you would place yourself.

You never make your choices in a vacuum, and good teachers are always reflecting and evaluating the impact of their instructional plans. On any day, given specific information and a particular goal, teachers can feel perfectly justified in being at one end of a continuum or the other. For example, there are

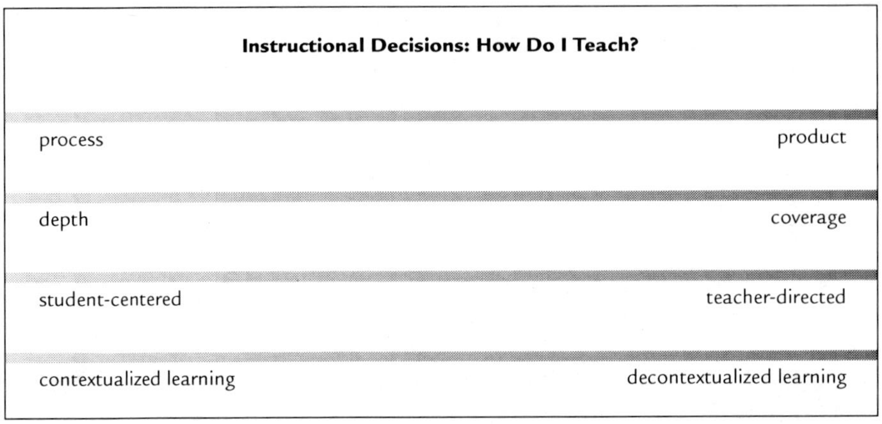

Instructional Decisions: How Do I Teach?	
process	product
depth	coverage
student-centered	teacher-directed
contextualized learning	decontextualized learning

Figure 4-1. Instructional Design Continuum

thirty minutes left in class and to complete the homework assignment students will need to understand "x, y, and z." Quickly you start lecturing, reminding students to take notes. You write down essential information on the board, provide students with a semantic map for structuring your ideas, and offer several examples to amplify your points. You end your lecture just as the bell rings and students scramble out the door.

Considering the information we learned about culture and learning style preferences (Chapter Three), however, where might multiculturalists place themselves along the continua? What kinds of instructional decisions would they make? How would they develop a culturally responsive approach to teaching? First, we will define culturally responsive teaching and then describe teaching strategies that support this approach.[1] We will look at motivational methods that respond to cultural differences and teacher expectations. Finally, we will consider classroom management.

CULTURALLY RESPONSIVE TEACHING

Definitions

Wlodkowski and Ginsberg (1995) describe culturally responsive teaching as "An approach to teaching that meets the challenge of cultural pluralism . . . [It] has to *respect diversity; engage the motivation of all learners; create a safe, inclusive, and respectful learning environment; derive teaching practices from principles that cross disciplines and cultures; and promote justice and equity in society.*

---

[1] Culturally responsive teaching encompasses both what is taught and how it is taught. Chapter Five deals with developing a culturally responsive curriculum.

These are the *essentials* of culturally responsive teaching. They foster effective learning for all students with attention to the collective good of society, so that systems of oppression, whether they are conceptual or institutional, do not continue to proliferate. This teaching is guided by a vision of justice, a pedagogy that seeks to transform as well as inform" (p. 19).

Gloria Ladson-Billings (1994, pp. 17–18) refers to culturally relevant teaching "as a pedagogy that empowers students intellectually, socially, emotionally, and politically by using cultural referents to impart knowledge, skills, and attitudes. These cultural referents are not merely vehicles for bridging or explaining the dominant culture; they are aspects of the curriculum in their own right."

We quickly see that these definitions of culturally responsive (relevant) teaching are compatible with definitions of multicultural education (see Chapter One). Such phrases as a pedagogy that "empowers students intellectually, socially, emotionally, and politically" and a "pedagogy that seeks to transform as well as inform" place culturally responsive teaching within Grant and Sleeter's fifth approach—multicultural education that is both multicultural and social reconstructionist.

Teaching Strategies

Culturally responsive teaching strategies are about teachers' ways of doing, being, and believing. These strategies refer specifically to the physical environment teachers create in their classrooms, how teachers connect with their students and encourage students to relate to one another, the teaching strategies teachers employ, and the expectations teachers have for students' learning and performance.

A **classroom's physical appearance** is the first piece of evidence students have about class climate. How the seats are arranged, what is posted on the walls, what materials and resources are on display, and what is written on the board all help set the tone in a classroom. A quick survey of how middle and secondary methods textbooks treat class climate and environment helps uncover the subtle differences between "good" and "culturally responsive" approaches. Standard textbooks (Armstrong & Savage, 1994) instruct novice teachers to pay attention to such factors as floor space, traffic patterns, location of the teacher's desk, materials storage, and classroom ambiance when planning for instruction. "Reflective teachers come to school several days before their contracts call for them to be there. They hang posters, decorate bulletin boards, and consider carefully ways to arrange the students' desks, tables, bookcases, and other furniture to fit their curriculum plans and the needs of their students" (Eby & Kujawa, 1994, p. 29). Ornstein (1992) encourages teachers to create a positive class climate by building a sense of community in their classrooms. Students should have "classroom partners" with whom they can share ideas, complete work together, and make joint decisions and choices. Finally, Armstrong and Savage (1994) emphasize the positive classroom ambiance that results "when the teacher pays attention to establishing an orderly overall classroom appearance and makes good decisions regarding nature of lighting, decoration of wall space, and control of temperature" (p. 230).

Shade, Kelly, and Oberg (1997), in *Creating Culturally Responsive Classrooms,* also offer teachers some of the same advice on the positioning of the teacher's desk and flexible seating arrangements; however, many of their comments are framed by a desire to "ensure that . . . students have a positive sense of belonging and are affirmed. . . . Students need to see themselves and their cultures reflected through pictures, displays, artifacts, room arrangements, and inclusion of different languages" (p. 110). Shade, Kelly, and Oberg recommend playing music of different cultures in the background as students write in their journals, prepare for tests, or reflect on what they are learning. Color and designs from different cultures should be present on the walls, including artwork, fabric, and artifacts, and students should participate in planning room arrangements. In a culturally responsive classroom, teachers make an *explicit* attempt to create a culturally inclusive student-centered learning environment.[2] One group of middle and high school students who often feel excluded and invisible in the classroom are gay, lesbian, and bisexual youth. Anderson, in the chapter reading, "Supporting the Invisible Minority," describes how educators in Stratford, Connecticut, have tried to address this concern.

Equally important to students is how teachers interact with them. **Teacher interactions**—how teachers connect with their students—directly influences learning and classroom management. A teacher's stage of racial identity is significant. Teachers who have little knowledge about how their own cultural, racial, class, and gender lenses affect interpersonal relationships, will have greater difficulty connecting with students whose backgrounds are dissimilar from theirs. For example, White teachers in the Contact stage who deny that racism exists will not be credible to students of color. Teachers who say, "Hey, I teach students" are denying the real-life experiences of their students of color (see Chapter Two) and perpetuating a sense of privilege among White students. Teachers of color in the Pre-encounter stage participate in their own form of collusion and provide a disservice to both White and students of color. Being perfect isn't a necessity, but being thoughtful about these issues is.

Awareness of one's background must be coupled with an understanding of different communicative styles. Communication is a marvelously complex process in which individuals intend to convey a message, but cultures develop a variety of acceptable modes of verbal and nonverbal communication that can confuse and misinform outsiders. Take for example the following exchanges:

---

[2] We are reminded of the banner "Feminism Spoken Here" posted on the class bulletin board. Other banners we have seen are "Spanish Speakers Welcome Here" and "This is a safe space for all students" printed below a pink triangle signifying acceptance of gay, lesbian, and bisexual students.

Example #1:

Mother-in-law:	Aunt! Aunt!
Daughter-in-law:	Yes.
Mother-in-law:	What did you want?
Daughter-in-law:	Yes, I am coming. (Turning to her female visitor) Get up, it is time to go meet my brother-in-law.

The daughter-in-law appears to understand what is expected of her, but certainly an outsider might not. First, the mother-in-law calls her daughter-in-law using the name that the daughter-in-law uses for her. Second, the mother-in-law asks a question in response to which the daughter-in-law responds that she is coming and tells her visitor that it is now time to meet the brother-in-law. How was the daughter-in-law able to understand? And if the mother-in-law wanted the daughter-in-law to bring over her friend for an introduction, why didn't she just say so? And why doesn't the mother-in-law call the daughter-in-law by her name? Making sense of what was said is difficult without a context for events occurring at the time of the exchange and an understanding of the culture. First, the title *aunt* reflects a close familiar relationship between the mother and daughter-in-law. Second, introductions between single men and women are constrained by proper social practices that do not encourage someone saying directly, "Come over and meet this man." In this case, the mother waits until her son is present and then calls to get her daughter-in-law's attention. The daughter-in-law sees her brother-in-law and, understanding the cultural mores, turns to her friend and tells her it is time to meet her brother-in-law. This exchange is a good example of contextualized and indirect speech that also takes into account recognized differences in status and roles.

Example #2:

Several British consultants sit around a large circular table. The consultants are vying for the same contract with a prestigious Middle Eastern architectural firm. The conversation among the consultants remains calm and subdued; however, a close analysis of what is being said reveals the acrimonious nature of the exchange. What sounds like a quiet discussion is actually one insult being hurled after another! One of the consultants leans back in his chair, crosses his leg, and thereby allows the sole of his shoe to face the Middle Easterner sitting next to him. The Middle Eastern quickly gets up and moves. At this moment a secretary enters and says "I'm sorry, but my key to the file cabinet has been lost."

The exchange between the consultants demonstrates a communicative pattern that does not allow for much emotional expression of thought and feelings. Communication also includes body language, and without knowing it, one of the consultants has insulted his host with his foot posture. Finally, the secretary's statement about the key being lost does not attribute any responsibility to her. The key was under her care and now it is gone. Some cultures use different language forms that do not require that they admit to mistakes.[3]

When multiculturalists say that it is important for people to learn about different cultures, they are also talking about patterns of communication. The scope of this text does not allow for an extensive discussion of different cultural communicative styles; however, we will look at several categories and examples. Keep in mind that the descriptors used to explain different styles are also a function of the cultural groups' perspective. So for example, explicit requests for something can be described as "being forthright" by one group and as "being tactless, or rude" by another. Rodriguez (cited in Grossman, 1995) explains that Mexican American children expect others to anticipate their needs; they become sensitive to the needs and feelings of others and rarely ask for help themselves. (They also expect a close, familial relationship with their teachers that includes respect for elders.) Native Americans also do not make direct requests (Shade, Kelly, & Oberg, 1997) in contrast to European American children who are socialized "to speak up." "How am I supposed to know what you want, if you don't tell me? I'm no mind reader." However, *demands* made by middle-class European American adults often are phrased indirectly (Delpit, 1988; Heath, 1983). For example, teachers might say to their students "Now we don't want to leave the room a mess for the next teacher, do we?" instead of the more direct statement, "I want everyone to put their desks back in rows and check the floor for litter."

Asian Americans often go "a linguistic mile" to disagree indirectly or not at all; European American males will disagree, logically and dispassionately, whereas African Americans are "up front" and ready to "tell it like it is." Research (Belenky, Clincy, Goldberger, & Tarule, 1986) on females indicates that girls prefer getting into the mindset of the speaker rather than arguing with one another.[4] Mexican Americans might prefer to use humor or jokes to release tension and avoid arguments that might be seen as disrespectful (Locke, 1992). European American teachers might interpret disagreements from African Americans as confrontations, Asian American behavior as evidence of compliance or passivity, girls' responses as lacking substance, and Mexican American comments as not taking the matter seriously.

In discussions, African Americans might enthusiastically join in, speak quite passionately, and then wonder why no one else cares or participates. Asian Americans are taught to think a lot and say little. Native Americans

---

[3] Grossman (1995) states, "Students who have difficulty accepting responsibility for their errors and mistakes or apologizing to others for cultural reasons may be misperceived as defiant or stubborn" (p. 176). Grossman goes on to say that although we might want all students to accept responsibility verbally, ". . . some students may be willing to accept the consequences of their behavior whereas they resist admitting their responsibility to others. In such cases, it may be more effective to permit them to avoid having to admit their errors and mistakes" (p. 177).

[4] Research findings report that girls often apologize in discussions before they make a point. This is probably because of internalized beliefs about the value of women's ideas.

value silence and observation, patience more than action; they avoid being "outwardly excitable in manner or speech" (Shade, Kelly, & Oberg, 1997, p. 28). When speaking, getting to the point is not necessarily the objective, and all group members are given time to speak.

Effective cross-cultural communicators do not take understanding for granted. Listeners and speakers question basic assumptions underlying communication. As Walsh's (1987) research indicates, even speakers using the same words, such as *family, neighborhood,* or *respect,* can have very different meanings for the words. Other areas for potential miscommunication involve degrees of formality, including how much self-disclosure is considered appropriate or what are acceptable discussion topics, proximity of speakers, relationship to time, and body language. "The communications styles of Hispanic Americans and some Asian and Pacific American groups tend to be much more formal than either the African American or European American communication styles" (Grossman, 1995, p.173). The Spanish language includes a formal and informal second person singular (you) form that establishes a linguistic hierarchical structure. In many Asian American families, respect and obedience to elders is expected.

Personal space is also negotiated within cultures. For example, European Americans usually require more distance between themselves and another speaker than do African, Mexican, or Arab Americans. Middle and secondary teachers who stay behind their desks and physically distant from their students, can be seen as uncaring and aloof.

Cultural differences around time are difficult to explain. Some cultures do not measure time as a commodity to be saved and carefully scheduled. Members of these cultures focus on what is presently happening, and beginning and ending times are flexible. Many European Americans who socialize across cultures are aware of a different sense of time used by Latinos and African Americans. If the host says come at 8 o'clock and the guests show up at 10, no one is offended. Teachers sometimes ask if cultural differences to time means they should excuse tardiness in certain students or allow them to turn in their work late. Although we don't agree with establishing multiple rules for turning in assignments, we do see this information as helping teachers understand student behaviors. In the dominant culture, when someone is late, it is considered insulting to the person waiting (that is, the teacher). Understanding a groups' relationship to time might prevent teachers from taking a student's lack of punctuality (or strict adherence to time schedules) personally or from judging them so harshly.

Next, we look at body language and how it affects communication. Students of color who have been targeted for racism will have a heightened awareness of teachers' facial expressions, gestures, and body movements. Latino and African American males, especially, are aware of being seen as threatening. We have already mentioned proximity in speaking. Eye contact is also important.

> Speakers in Native American cultures usually face each other and avoid fidgeting or changing postural positions. Giving one's undivided attention to the

> person with whom they are involved is an important social value as is showing politeness. When engaged in conversation, one does not interrupt the speaker and avoids the direct gaze or direct eye contact because it represents a sign of disrespect. (Shade, Kelly, & Oberg, 1997, p. 27)

Blacks and Latinos also lower their eyes to show respect, but European Americans show respect by looking at the person talking to them. Teachers who are not aware of these differences can easily misinterpret their students' body language or use body language that offends their students.

As always, we must avoid turning these general statements about communication styles into stereotypes. Some culturally responsive teachers call attention to different communication styles as a way of affirming everyone's style and as a way of making explicit some of the unstated rules and assumptions operating in the classroom. They might do this at the start of the semester, within the context of a content area lesson, or as part of a discussion on how the group will work with and talk to each other. Explicit discussions can also lay the foundation for the future, particularly if tension arises.

Finally, teacher expectations, explicitly or implicitly stated, form the backdrop to all teacher-student interactions. "If you have high expectations for your students, they will rise to meet them" is a pedagogical mantra. Principals, teachers, pre-service teachers, faculty involved in teacher training programs say it automatically and almost without thought. Beware the self-fulfilling prophecy! However, translating high expectations into action is a lot of work. Teachers must first believe that all their students can learn. Having higher expectations is a mind-set and attitude. (See the box, "Being Real: Pointers for Teacher/Student Interactions.") Unfortunately, several research studies (Everhart, 1983; Moody, 1990; Rist, 1971; Veldman & Worsham, 1982) have documented how teacher expectations for students of color and working-class students are lower than for middle-class European American students. "Study after study indicates that Anglo-European teachers make a difference between their perceived ideal student, who is usually an Anglo-European, and those who differ in skin color, language, or just behavior in general" (Shade, Kelly, & Oberg, 1997, p. 45). Second, teachers must translate their expectations into action by using instructional techniques, assignments, and assessment measures that stretch and challenge their students. On the surface, lower expectations might appear to make teaching easier; in our experience, however, the trade off is in increased classroom management problems. Having higher expectations for students means higher expectations for teachers. These require time and thought, but when teachers work together to pool resources, the workload is lessened.

Teachers, however, should not be held totally responsible for student achievement. Nieto (1996) cautions against seeing teachers as having "sole responsibility" for a student's achievement. It "places the blame on some of those who care most deeply about students and who struggle every day to help them learn. Thus, the use of *teachers' expectations* distances the school and society from their own responsibility and complicity in student failure" (p. 43). We will return to the issue of expectations in Chapter Eight.

Culturally responsive teaching also includes a number of relevant **instructional strategies** that are commonly presented in middle and secondary methods books and can be used effectively in multicultural classrooms. These strategies include mini lectures, questioning, discussions, cooperative learning, the three "s's"—stories, skits, and simulations—and revision. The judicious use of lectures can provide students with a framework or schemata (see Chapter Six) for learning. This allows teachers to relate subject matter to students' cultural backgrounds and support nonnative speakers' understanding. Important concepts and vocabulary can be presented through demonstrations, graphics, and visuals. Through lectures, teachers can move students' thinking from the concrete to the abstract. A well-organized lecture has a clear structure with several examples to clarify key points. Some middle and secondary teachers begin the school year using a sheltered lecture approach. Before class, the teacher writes on the board an outline of the lecture, with major points listed. As students develop their note-taking skills, the amount of information printed on the board decreases, although the teacher might make notes available to students with special needs. Good lecturers also make a habit of frequently checking for student questions and comprehension.

Questioning is an integral part of culturally responsive teaching and a vehicle for student empowerment. The Multicultural and Social Reconstructionist Approach to multicultural education emphasizes developing students' critical thinking skills not only to analyze content but also to recognize the politics behind information, to look for whose voices are included or excluded. (See Chapter One.) Teachers need to point out the differences between *real* or *honest* questions and school-type questions; the former are questions that students genuinely want answers for; the latter are questions someone else wants an answer for. Too often teachers and students collude in the classroom by going through the motions of asking and answering questions without actually becoming involved in the process: Teachers ask the questions, and the students provide the textbook answers.[5]

The other side of the questioning coin is responding. When students respond to genuine questions, they tend to speak in paragraphs. Through genuine dialogue, students explain, elaborate, and expound on their ideas in greater depth than when they respond to school-type questions. In the process of responding to genuine questions, students integrate information, add to their background knowledge, and make valuable connections. The process allows them to "know what they mean" and provides them with an audience that wants to hear them. The desire to communicate, rather than recite, can encourage the most hesitant speakers, including nonnative speakers, to offer their ideas. The emphasis is not just on products (the answers), but on the thinking process that leads to the answers.

---

[5] See Chapter Six for discussion of styles of questioning and cultural differences.

Being Real: Pointers for Teacher/Student Interaction

> Before we even attempt to teach children, we want them to know each of them is unique and very special. We want them to like themselves, to want to achieve and care about themselves.
>
> Marva Collins in *Working Woman*, October 1988

Following are the observations of two educators from the perspective of educator, counselor, and student. Through these excepts we offer educators-in-training the opportunity to see the outcomes of both effective and less effective teacher/student interactions.

To be effective teachers, you must be fully aware of who you are. What baggage (your ideas of race, gender, class, and so on) do you bring to the classroom? Before you can be "real" with your students, you must "deal" with yourselves.

To have effective interactions, teachers must care about, listen to, trust, be honest with, be respectful of their students. In evaluating their students' work, teachers must be sure to critique only the work and not the person who did the work.

A student relates this story:

"I can remember being asked a question by the teacher in a classroom of about 25 of my peers. I responded with what I thought was an appropriate answer and the teacher replied, 'What kind of answer is that? What would ever make you believe that?' At that point, I could feel my face turning red. I felt so embarrassed. I could have just crawled out of the room. Well, from that point on, I decided that I would never speak up in class again."

If a student answers a question inaccurately, a "sandwich approach" may be more effective. Indicate that the student's response was appreciated, offer the correct response, and follow up with an additional positive comment. A student should feel safe enough in your classroom to speak, right or wrong, and not feel intimidated.

An effective interaction must be consistent. With regard to consistency, one student relates,

"What a great teacher, I thought to myself. This is the kind of teacher who I know I can trust and be up front with. He is so open and friendly and funny in the class-

---

Experienced middle and secondary teachers know that there is an art to structuring effective discussions. To prevent class discussions from breaking down into a verbal free-for-all, and thereby convincing teachers that they are a waste of time, prior planning is required. What is the purpose of the discussion? The goal might be to have students share their interpretations of a reading, describe the way they solved a math problem, discuss how material relates to their experiences, or debate the author's opinion. Given the purpose, what is an appropriate format and who will participate? Large group or small group discussions are two options.[6] Students can respond to a set of questions or be

---

[6] For an interesting discussion format called KIVA based on the ancient Pueblo Native American tradition, see Shade, Kelly, and Oberg (1997).

> ### Being Real: Pointers for Teacher/Student Interaction • Continued
>
> room, yet, on more than one occasion, I asked him for assistance outside the classroom, and he was unapproachable. He made me feel as if I were imposing on him."
>
> In order to be consistent, a teacher must be real, in and out of the classroom. Who you are in the classroom needs to reflect who you are as a person. If you are not "real," it will come through in your teaching and interactions.
>
> Another student speaks of a "comfortable classroom":
>
> "From the first classroom experience, I knew that, while within those walls, I was safe. The teacher set the ground rules for active participation in the class. Some of the ground rules were: Use "I" statements, be open and honest, speak only from your experiences, listen and respect other students when they are speaking, agree that anything that goes on in the class, stays in the class, agree to disagree, respectfully. This class dealt with social issues (that is, race, class, and gender), and some of the proposed topics were potentially volatile. By supporting these ground rules, the teacher also supported a comfortable classroom climate."
>
> It is evident that this student felt empowered by this experience. Empowered because she was able to be herself, see herself, and free herself from the traditional role of passive listener to active classroom participant without fear of reprisal.
>
> We close with three additional recommendations on improving effective teacher/student interactions:
>
> - Think back to your own experiences. You may think that your teachers were the best, but you must strive to be even better than they were.
> - Genuinely believe that *all* students can learn and *all* students can achieve. (If you do not genuinely believe, than teaching is not the profession for you.)
> - Do unto your students as you would have them do unto your child.
>
> Carlton Pickron, Ed.D.
> Associate Dean of Academic Affairs
> Director of Academic Achievement Center
> Westfield State College, Westfield, MA
>
> Laurie Simpson, M.A., Psychology
> Assistant Academic Counselor
> Westfield State College, Westfield, MA

asked to generate their own questions. Fishbowl approaches place speakers in a circle surrounded by observers. Students in the outer circle are not allowed to speak during the discussion, but might be asked to respond later. Who leads the discussion? Teachers can act as the facilitator or assign the task to another student(s). It is important to have ground rules established so that everyone feels comfortable speaking. (See Chapter Three.) Here is an opportunity for teachers to talk about different communicative styles. Someone could be assigned the role of inviting students who haven't spoken to speak, or students could take journal-writing breaks during the discussion. If students are accountable for the material discussed, how will they be assessed? Teachers can ask students to jot down important points to an argument or to summarize main ideas presented. If the discussion has a clear focus and format, students find it easier to meet teachers' expectations for learning, and teachers are inclined to share more of the floor with their students. Teaching becomes more student-centered, and learning becomes more contextualized because students use both new information and their own experiences and knowledge to participate.

Cooperative learning is a cornerstone to culturally relevant and multicultural teaching. It is consistent with the learning styles of African Americans, Asian and Pacific Americans, Mexican Americans, Native Americans, and females. Cooperative learning is "in tune with the affective orientation and social, cooperative preferences of students from shared-function families [families whose members play a variety of roles]" (Shaw, 1996, p. 62) and those with a cooperative learning style. Shaw goes on to say that "[of] 68 studies reviewed by Slavin (1990), 49 showed positive effects in terms of academic achievement for the groups involved in cooperative learning. In five studies investigating cooperative learning's effectiveness, Black students and students with learning and physical disabilities outperformed both their control counterparts and White, high-achieving, and nondisabled treatment students" (p. 62).

However, cooperative learning does not guarantee positive learning results for everyone. According to Grossman (1995), European American males, both high and low achievers, "respond better to competitive and individualistic situations . . ." (p. 276). In addition, even though some studies of mixed-race cooperative groups indicate a positive impact on ethnic relations, other researchers (Piel & Cromwell, 1989, cited in Grossman, 1995) suggest that if White students are the only ones who assume dominant leadership roles in a group, then the experiences for Blacks might be "similar to the negative experiences of many females" (p. 278). According to research, females do better in single-sex cooperative groups where they are required to assume leadership roles. In mixed-sex groups, "although they tend to be the providers of assistance, they are rejected by males when they ask for assistance" (p. 227). Given this research, cooperative groups might be more successful when groups consist of at least two members from a group (for example, females, students of color).

Middle and secondary teachers have several cooperative learning techniques from which to choose. "Some Quick Cooperative Starters," one of the readings in this chapter, lists several activities and briefly describes their uses. Having teachers prepare students to work together is important to the success of cooperative learning. Adolescents are old enough to participate in a discussion about group dynamics and what makes cooperative learning effective. Students can self-identify as preferring cooperative, competitive, or individual assignments and discuss what strengths and weaknesses they bring to a group. "Students, especially those who are likely to dominate others and those who tend to allow others to assume dominant positions, must be prepared for cooperative learning in order for all of the members of the group to reap the benefits associated with this approach" (p. 278). Finally, teachers need to supervise group work, allow students to reflect on the group process, and provide students with feedback.

We group several instructional techniques under the heading "Stories, skits and simulations" because of their commonalities. These techniques draw on a student's ability to think visually and contextualize information. They require student imagination, the inclusion of multiple perspectives and affect, and the application of knowledge into a real world context. Creating "once upon a time" stories using information helps field dependent learners retain information. Skits and simulations are holistic learning experiences that meet the needs of kinesthetic learners. Moreover, these activities allow for a presentation style that resonates with the cultural backgrounds of many students of color.

Our final instructional technique is not usually defined as such; however, our combined teaching experience bears out the significance of revision as an instructional strategy. Revision places the responsibility for doing well in the hands of students, if the student chooses to do so. Instruction that plans for revision is freeing for both students and teacher. Teachers can hold students to higher academic standards, and students have an incentive to continue learning. Academic achievement does not depend on how fast one can learn. Often, students only begin to learn at the point of revision. Meeting in small groups or individually, teachers can assess a student's difficulty and provide appropriate instruction. This provides an opportunity for teachers to connect with students and establish a more personal relationship. A policy of revision creates a pool of willing students and a chance to save wear and tear on secondary school teachers trying to maximize their energy and time. (See "Seven Strategies to Support a Culturally Responsive Pedagogy" in the readings section for further suggestions.)

MOTIVATION

An inviting classroom atmosphere combined with effective teacher interactions can help motivate students to want to learn, but the interest and effort of middle and secondary students, especially, are critical to all external attempts to motivate adolescents. Several scholars (Ogbu, 1992; Solomon, 1992) have offered resistance theories to explain the lack of motivation of some students.

> Many non-European and poor students are alienated, distrustful, angry, and disillusioned about the schools they attend and the teachers that instruct them because of the prejudice and discrimination they encounter. They believe that even if they do well in school, they will not obtain the same benefits that European American upper-class males receive from succeeding in school, particularly in the vocational area, and some of them are pressured by their peers not to conform or to do well in school because to do so is to act White. (Grossman, 1995, p. 272)

Girls might also turn away from learning because they fear rejection by males or view ambition and individualism as conflicting with women's traditional preferences for collaboration and equality. Among non-European communities, there is the fear that educated girls will assimilate too much into the mainstream culture.

Given what we have learned about cultural differences, it should come as no surprise to learn that motivation is linked to culture. Wlodkowski and Ginsberg (1995) define motivation as "the natural human capacity to direct energy in the pursuit of a goal" (p. 22). Motivation cannot be separated from emotion, and what brings "forth the reactions of frustration or joy may differ across cultures, because cultures differ in their definitions of novelty, hazard, opportunity, gratification, and appropriate responses" (p. 22). Basing motivation on ambition or achievement might not reflect cultural norms or values. Some cultural groups don't define success by individual achievement; personal ambition is not a cultural goal.

In *Diversity and Motivation,* Wlodkowski and Ginsberg (1995) lay forth a "macrocultural pedagogical" framework for developing students' intrinsic motivation regardless of culture. Their Motivational Framework for Culturally Responsive Teaching is based on teachers addressing the following four questions:

What do we need to do to feel respected by and connected to one another? (Establishing inclusion)

How can we use relevance and choice to create a favorable disposition toward learning? (Developing attitude)

What are active ways to increase the complexity of what we are learning so that it matters to us and contributes to a pluralistic democracy? (Enhancing meaning)

How can we create an understanding that we are becoming effective in [the] learning we value? (Engendering competence) (p. 33)

Be sure to note the ways that LouAnne Johnson motivates her students in the chapter reading "Dangerous Minds: Decoding a Classroom."

CLASSROOM MANAGEMENT AND DIVERSITY

Body language is a wonderful way to express emotions, and adolescents are often skilled in conveying their feelings and attitudes by using a variety of postures, gestures, and behaviors. But do their teachers always understand the messages being sent? We discussed eye contact in a previous section on communicative patterns. For example, Hispanics and African Americans lower their eyes to show respect, and European Americans lower their eyes to convey guilt. According to Grossman (1995), European Americans express their innocence with strong denials whereas African Americans do not. Some cultures emphasize admitting mistakes; others don't require verbal statements. In the Middle East, friends "care about you so much," they lie to you, but westerners admonish their friends, "If you don't tell me the truth, who will!" European Americans might be angry and glare at their teachers, African Americans might roll their eyes, and Asian Americans might smile.

Appropriate ways of disagreeing or resolving conflicts can be culturally based. This information is important for teachers attempting to manage their classrooms and maintain discipline. Because we often unconsciously register another's body language, we can easily find ourselves disgruntled with a student and not really know why. Teachers might misread the emotional responses of certain students as aggressive and interpret the silences of others as passivity. Teachers often respond negatively to students who aren't behaving or responding in anticipated ways. Middle and secondary teachers, who have opportunities to see how parents discipline their children at the grocery stores, in the libraries, or at houses of worship, can have an advantage over other teachers when it comes to managing their classrooms.

CONCLUSION

Culturally responsive teaching is the foundation of multicultural education. It reminds us that behind the "best" multicultural textbooks, the "best" multicultural curriculum, and the "best" multicultural teaching strategies is the teacher. The extent to which you see, understand, affirm, and connect with your students, determines, to a large measure, student learning and achievement in your classroom. We return to an underlying assumption of this textbook: You, the teacher, are critical to successful multicultural teaching.

READINGS

The first two readings in this chapter offer practical techniques for implementing a culturally responsive pedagogy. "Some Quick Cooperative Starters" lists several cooperative learning strategies and gives a brief description of each. "Seven Strategies to Support a Culturally Responsive Pedagogy" describes strategies that are can be used at any grade level and in any discipline. Strategies 6 and 7 are the focus of upcoming chapters in our text. The author underscores the need to take "a proactive stance toward the problem of miseducating or undereducating whole generations of students from culturally varied backgrounds. In "Dangerous Minds: Decoding a Classroom," Christensen critiques the teaching of LouAnne in the recently popular movie, Dangerous Minds. Christensen employs critical thinking skills that challenge the story being told and points out the ways in which LouAnne could have helped her students "reflect on real social inequities that impact their life opportunities." The fourth reading addresses the needs of an invisible minority—gay and lesbian students. Statistics indicate that gay and lesbian youth are three times more likely than their schoolmates are to commit suicide, and school officials are increasingly aware of the obstacles gay and lesbian students face in school. "Supporting the Invisible Minority" looks at how Stratford, Connecticut, has attempted to meet the needs of these students.

READING 1

Some Quick Cooperative Starters: Cooperation in the Classroom

W. W. Johnson, R. Johnson, and E. J. Holubec, 1988

1. **Learning Partners.** Ask the students to turn to a neighbor and ask him/her something about the lesson; to explain a concept you've just taught; to explain the assignment; to explain how to do what you've just taught; to summarize the three most important points of the discussion; or whatever fits the lesson.

2. **Reading Groups.** Students read material together and answer the questions. One person is the Reader, another Recorder, and the third the Checker (who checks to make certain everyone understands, agrees with, and can explain the answers). They must come up with three possible answers to each question and circle their favorite one. When finished, they sign the paper to certify that they all understand, agree on, and can explain the answers.

3. **Jigsaw.** Each person reads and studies part of a selection with a partner, practices teaching the section with a new partner (student studying same section from another group), then teaches what he or she has learned to the other members of the group. Each then quizzes the group members until satisfied that everyone knows all parts thoroughly.

4. **Bookends.** Before a film, lecture, or a reading, have groups of three students summarize together what they already know about the subject and come up with questions they have about it. Afterwards, the groups answer questions, discuss new information, and formulate new questions.

5. **Drill Partners.** Have students drill each other on the facts they need to know until they are certain both partners know and can remember them all. This works for spelling, vocabulary, math, grammar, test review, etc. Give bonus points on the test if all members score above a certain percentage.

6. **Reading Buddies.** In lower grades, have students read their stories to each other, getting help with words and discussing content with their partners. In upper grades, have students tell about their books and read their favorite parts to each other.

7. **Worksheet Checkmates.** Have two students, each with different jobs, do one worksheet. The Reader reads, then suggests an answer; the Writer either agrees or comes up with another answer. When they both understand and agree on an answer, the Writer can write it.

Reprinted by permission of the authors.

8. **Homework Checkers.** Have students compare homework answers, discuss any they have not answered similarly, then correct their papers and add the reason they changed an answer. They make certain everyone's answers agree, then staple the papers together. You grade one paper from each group and give group members that grade.
9. **Test Reviewers.** Have students prepare each other for a test. They get bonus points if every group member scores above a preset level.
10. **Composition Pairs.** Student A explains what she/he plans to write to Student B, while Student B takes notes or makes an outline. Together they plan the opening or the thesis statement. Then Student B explains while Student A writes. They exchange outlines, and use them in writing their papers.
11. **Board Workers.** Students go together to the chalkboard. One can be the Answer Suggester, one the Checker to see if everyone agrees, and one the Writer.
12. **Problem Solvers.** Give groups a problem to solve. Each student must contribute part of the solution. Groups can decide who does what, but they must show where all members contributed. Or, they can decide together, but each must be able to explain how to solve the problem.
13. **Computer Groups.** Students work together on the computer. They must agree on the input before it is typed in. One person is the Keyboard operator, another the Monitor Reader, a third the Verifier (who collects opinions on the input from the other two and makes the final decision). Roles are rotated daily so everyone gets experience at all three jobs.
14. **Book Report Pairs.** Students interview each other on the books they read, then they report on their partner's book.
15. **Writing Response Groups.** Students read and respond to each other's papers three times:
    a. They mark what they like with a star and put a question mark anywhere there is something they don't understand or think is weak. Then they discuss the paper as a whole with the writer.
    b. They mark problems with grammar, usage, punctuation, spelling, or format and discuss it with the author.
    c. They proofread the final draft and point out any errors for the author to correct.

    Teachers can assign questions for students to answer about their groups members' papers to help them focus on certain problems or skills.
16. **Skill Teachers/Concept Clarifiers.** Students work with each other on skills (like identifying adjectives in sentences or showing proof in algebra) and/or concepts (like "ecology" or "economics") until each can do or explain it easily.
17. **Report Groups.** Students research a topic together. Each one is responsible for checking at least one different source and writing at least three

notecards of information. They write the report together; each person is responsible for seeing that his/her information is included. For oral reports, each must take a part and help others rehearse until they are at ease.

18. **Summary Pairs.** Have students alternate reading and orally summarizing paragraphs. One reads and summarizes while the other checks the paragraph for accuracy and adds anything left out. They alternate roles with each paragraph.

19. **Elaborating and Relating Pairs.** Have students elaborate on what they are reading and learning by relating it to what they already know about the subject. This can be done before and after reading a selection, listening to a lecture, or seeing a film.

20. **Playwrights.** Students write a play together, perhaps about a time period recently studied, practice, and perform it for the class.

READING 2

Seven Strategies to Support a Culturally Responsive Pedagogy

Francesina R. Jackson

American demographers report that even as public school populations are becoming increasingly more ethically, linguistically, and economically diverse, the teaching force in the U.S. is becoming more homogeneous (Evangelauf, 1988; Nea, 1987). Coupled with these data is the fact that many economically disadvantaged students, students of color, and students for whom English is a second language generally perform academically less well than their mainstream counterparts.

These data suggest a continued inability of the schools to adequately address the academic needs of a large proportion of U.S. student populations. One must have faith that teachers could develop multicultural competencies focused on teaching to diversity and thus improve the achievement of these students (Delpit, 1988; Heath, 1983; Villegas, 1992).

School administrators have begun to respond by providing inservice workshops on teaching diverse student populations. Too often, however, these workshops prove ineffective. Sleeter's (1990) analysis of multicultural workshops offered in various school systems shows that the workshops focused on awareness or sensitivity training and on enhancing intercultural understanding and recognition—laudable goals, yet teachers continue to say "OK, I now

---

Reprinted by permission of the author and publisher.

know how nonmainstream students differ from mainstream students, but how can I change my delivery of instruction to address these differences?"

Essentially, these workshops fall short in providing modification strategies. Too little attention is given to helping teachers recognize the strengths that culturally different students bring to the class and capitalize on these strengths, especially if they do not match the teacher's preconceived notion of the norm.

Baruth and Manning (1992) believe that effective teachers in a multicultural setting possess appropriate knowledge, attitudes, and skills, and that there are specific strategies that most American teachers already employ but may not recognize as ones they can use to enhance multicultural learning. I too assume that most classroom teachers already possess the prerequisite attitudinal competencies, such as having high expectations for all students and of attempting, to the extent possible, to avoid stereotypical thinking that may negatively skew their perceptions of students' abilities.

Not only must teachers focus on enhancing their own professional competencies but they must create a classroom climate that promotes positive intercultural interactions between students. Among the generic strategies to address this, teachers need to include conflict resolution, active listening, and procedures to discuss controversial topics.

This article asks teachers to view some of the common strategies that they currently employ in literacy instruction, and then review them from a culturally sensitive perspective. In this article I describe seven strategies. Although all seven are standard strategies in and of themselves, they are also integral components of a culturally responsive pedagogy.

Attendees at several recent multicultural workshops that I have given have identified these seven strategies as providing immediate payback for their efforts. It is important to note that the seven can be used across grades and disciplines. They are not presented here in hierarchical order; rather they are to be viewed as recursive and interrelated.

Strategy 1—Build Trust

An often overlooked component of an effective classroom is mutual trust between teachers and their students. Teachers who build trust have been able to engender in their students a level of confidence and belief that what they do in that classroom is worthwhile. Concentrating heavily on the cognitive aspects of teaching comes at the expense of developing the affective aspects. Teachers need to examine their relationships with their students to determine how effectively they are building the trust factor.

One strategy for building trust might include learning students' names and pronouncing them correctly. All first names have some unique meaning and are of interest for discussion, but students from nonmainstream cultures may have nonmainstream names of special significance. Since the late 1970s, an increasing number of African-American parents have given their children African first names. Teachers can capitalize on this practice by according recognition and interest to these given names and asking students to research the country where their names originated and their meaning.

Another way to build trust is to have students research and share information about their family's ethnic background. For example, I have asked students in groups of four to answer questions adapted from Covert's (1989) model:

1. What generation in the United States do you represent? Are you and your siblings the first of your family to be born in this country? Were you foreign born?
2. Where did you or your ancestors migrate from? Within the U.S.? From outside the U.S.? What made them wish to come here?
3. Does your immediate family or extended family practice ethnic or cultural customs that you or they value or identify with? For example: foods, celebrations, traditions, social behaviors, manners, beliefs. What customs do you prize the most? Do you or your relatives speak your ethnic group language?
4. What occupations are represented in your family background?

After sharing, students analyze information in terms of their similarities and differences. Participants have said this activity gives them an opportunity to share their background in a nonthreatening way. The discussions have also heightened mainstream participants' interest in and appreciation for their own ethnic backgrounds. Many European-Americans have commented that this activity sensitized them to their own ethnic roots.

Strategy 2—Become Culturally Literate

Historically, "minority" people have had to be bicultural, bidialectical, and bicognitive (I do believe that people in different cultures think rather differently) in order to achieve in mainstream U.S. society. By the same token, few demands were made on mainstream members, including teachers, to learn about diverse cultures. To avoid mistakes of the past, teachers will have to assume responsibility for becoming at least biculturally and if possible multiculturally aware. Teachers need to learn about their students' language, interactional styles, learning styles, and values.

Delpit (1988) recommends that teachers use ethnographic procedures to learn about their culturally diverse students. These procedures may include observing students in nonschool settings: visiting community churches, talking to community leaders, and making home visits, thus allowing teachers not only to learn about nonmainstream communities, but also to tap the community's rich resources to incorporate in their classes. These visits will provide opportunities for teachers to dispel the mistrust that nonmainstream community members hold toward representatives of the power structure. The teacher's mere presence conveys to the community a sense of genuine concern for and interest in the nonmainstream youngsters.

I have observed some nonmainstream youngsters perform in an exemplary way in community organizations, but receive little recognition for these efforts in the school. School administrators might recognize and reward service rendered outside the school.

Becoming bilingual is an obvious plus for a teacher, but even demonstrating serious interest and engaging in steps toward understanding their students' language, whether it is Black English, Spanish, or Vietnamese, is a sure-fire step in Strategy 2.

Strategy 3—Build a Repertoire of Instructional Strategies

While the research shows that students have their preferred learning styles (Dunn, Beaudry, & Klavis, 1989) and that these are culturally specific (Hillard, 1989), U.S. schools remain entrenched in a culture that is Eurocentric and middle class. According to Shade (1982), the traditional educational setting rewards students who exhibit the following characteristics: an attentional style that focuses on tasks and verbal instructions rather than on the people in the environment; an information processing approach that is logical, linear, sequential, and analytical; the ability to sit for long periods and attend to one idea, event, or task; the desire to be independent, self-starting, and competitive; the ability to deal with ideas and concepts without concrete replication of them; a perceptual style that helps in the differentiation of relevant from irrelevant information (field independence).

In contrast to the American school culture, students from culturally different backgrounds are often more field dependent (Ramirez & Castaneda, 1974), process information in nonlinear ways (Hillard, 1989), tend to be physically active (Shade, 1982), and may value group affiliation above individual competitiveness (Hillard, 1989).

Educational research demonstrates that instructional strategies such as cooperative learning provide a more appropriate cultural match between instructional styles and learning styles for some minority students and result in improved learning (Little Soldier, 1989; Slavin, 1987).

An interesting variation on presentation is described by Hollins (1982), who suggests that Marva Collins's instructional strategies might be especially culturally relevant for African-American students. Hollins states that Collins uses interactional patterns commonly found in the African-American church, such as choral and responsive readings. In this instance, the teacher will ask a question or give a prompt, and students will respond in unison, sometimes in a rhythmic fashion. Teachers will wish to evaluate this suggestion in the context of their particular classroom milieu.

It may be wise for all teachers to consider limiting the amount of assumptive teaching that takes place in the classroom. Some teachers assume that all students are able to perform academic tasks, but that some are simply unwilling to do so. In fact, some students really cannot do so, not because they lack the ability to perform these tasks, but rather because their culturally different environments have not laid the groundwork for such behavior.

It is further important for teachers to teach explicitly the underlying thought processes used to study a particular discipline. Scholars refer to this ability to control and monitor thought processes as metacognition. Specifically, metacognition is defined as "thinking about one's own thinking" (Brown, Campione, & Day, 1981). Students who are aware of their thought processes can modify how they approach tasks so as to choose the approach best suited to the discipline.

Much of metacognitive skill development takes place in the home and the community. Because of the close cultural match between school demands and mainstream, middle-class ideals, European Americans have a clearer perspective of the kind of thinking skills needed for academic achievement. On the other hand, a basic cultural mismatch occurs as students from diverse cultural backgrounds come to school valuing intuitive learning and prizing nonverbal behavior (Hillard, 1989; Shade, 1982) more highly than institutional norms that assume that students will think in a linear, analytical manner and value precise language. This condition suggests the need for American teachers to model explicitly the thinking processes needed to master a discipline area.

Strategy 4—Use Effective Questioning Techniques

Researchers highlight the fact that teachers directed too few higher order questions to all students, especially to those for whom they had low expectations (Allington, 1983; Durkin, 1978–1979). Higher order questions are important for several reasons:

First, they promote the development of analytical and evaluative thinking skills.

Second, higher order questions affirm the students' self-perceptions as learners. (Essentially, higher order questions suggest to students that they possess the knowledge, values, and characteristics that will allow them to be successful. Most importantly, open-ended questions that require students to synthesize, analyze, and evaluate information convey to students that their opinions are valued.)

Third, higher order questions allow students to see themselves as knowledge producers rather than knowledge consumers. In this instance students learn that appropriate responses are not always found in the text or with the teacher but within themselves.

Literal level questions, on the other hand, implicitly teach that the knowledge that is worth knowing and valuing lies outside themselves. More often than not, these sources of knowledge in a U.S. school come from a Eurocentric perspective.

Strategy 5—Provide Effective Feedback

The research shows that American White, middle-class males receive feedback that is more concrete, specific, and directed toward academic learning than that given to other population groups or to females (Baker, 1986; Irvine, 1986;

Jones, 1989; Oakes, 1985). Too often students of color receive feedback that relates to personality variables or the neatness of their work rather than to academic quality. Teachers need to make a conscious effort to analyze the quality of feedback they give all students, and apply a special degree of sensitivity to their feedback to nonmainstream students.

Three points are crucial to improving the quality of feedback teachers give students: First, accentuate some positive feature of the students' work. Second, be specific and focus comments on the academic components of the work. Third, communicate to students how to correct errors and how to improve the overall quality of the work.

Strategy 6—Analyze Instructional Materials

Banks (1981) advocates that teachers become familiar with criteria for assessing the quality of cultural sensitivity in instructional materials used. Some of these criteria might include the following:

1. Accurate portrayal of the perspectives, attitudes, and feelings of the groups being studied.
2. Inclusion of strong ethnic characters in fictional works.
3. Ethnic materials devoid of racist concepts, clichés, phrases, or words.
4. Historically accurate factual materials.

I further urge teachers to develop their own instructional materials with student appeal. For example, when teaching a group of African-American middle school students to locate the main idea in a paragraph, I developed the following text: "The rap group Public Enemy encourages youngsters to stay in school and get a good education. The group Heavy D and the Boyz sings about the dangers of drug use. Some rappers sing about events in Black history."

I observed students' paying closer attention to this paragraph than to previous paragraphs used for the same activity. Information in the paragraph focused on content with which they were familiar. The purpose was for them to learn the skill of locating the main idea, and they had such interest in the content, they understood easily and enjoyed the assignment.

Strategy 7—Establish Positive Home-School Relations

Educators are well aware of the importance of parental support in the educational process, even at the middle and high school levels. However, we generally fail to take a proactive stance toward establishing positive relationships or eliciting parental support early in the school year. Educators typically call parents when students experience difficulty. This is especially true for nonmainstream students who are disproportionately identified as showing behavioral problems.

An analysis of longitudinal data collected over a 7-year period showed that preservice teachers expressed a lack of confidence in their ability to communicate effectively with nonmainstream parents. Their response was one indicator of the teacher education program's ineffectiveness in preparing the university students to interact appropriately with culturally diverse populations (W.I. Burke, personal communication, October, 1991).

At the beginning of the year, teachers can send home a note to express their enthusiasm for having the student in the class. It is especially important to follow up these notes with a telephone call to discuss the student with the parent. Examples of questions might be to ask parents what they perceive to be the student's strengths, weaknesses, and interests. Teachers can incorporate this information as they plan future lessons. They can then address those areas of parental concern and of pride in the future. It is important for teachers to encourage parents and students to talk about the students' academic goals.

It is also critical that nonmainstream and mainstream students see adults representing diverse populations in the school. Given the dire statistics regarding the diminishing pool of American minority teachers (Graham, 1987), teachers must invite adults who represent diverse population groups to visit the class and assist with the educational program. Scholars suggest that young African-American males in particular need "touchable role models."

Activities at the middle school might include Grandparents' Day where students invite their grandparents or substitute to visit the school. At the secondary level, activities may be organized around content or disciplines. For example, teachers can organize panels to discuss open-ended topics such as the Great Depression, World War II, Malcolm X, John F. Kennedy, the Vietnam War, famine and U.N. intervention in Somalia.

One way to encourage parental participation at this level is to invite parents to respond to open-ended questions. For example when teaching ninth-grade American history I asked my students to interview their parents about the civil rights movement in the 1950s and 1960s. After reading the interviews, I invited parents representing diverse groups to describe their experiences to the class.

Act Now

U.S. educators no longer have the luxury of waiting to develop new and innovative techniques that address the pressing needs of minority students. We must act now to tackle these concerns. Using time-honored techniques and sensitive strategies from a culturally aware perspective provides one way to approach the problems. Although we have no panacea and must continually expand our knowledge base, the seven strategies discussed here offer a basis for taking a proactive stance toward the problem of miseducating or undereducating whole generations of students from culturally varied backgrounds. We need to reach out to each other, to recognize and accord value to each other's cultures. We need a basic ingredient—the ability to respond to each other in the teaching and learning enterprise.

References

Allington, R.L. (1983). The reading instruction provided readers of differing abilities. *Elementary School Journal, 83,* 548–559.

Baker, D.R. (1986). Sex differences in classroom interactions in secondary science. *Journal of Classroom Interaction, 22*(2), 212–218.

Banks, J.A. (1981). *Multiethnic education: Theory and practice* (2nd ed.). Boston, MA: Allyn & Bacon.

Baruth, L.G., & Manning, L.E. (1992). *Multicultural education of children and adolescents.* Needham Heights, MA: Allyn & Bacon.

Brown, A.L., Campione, J.C., & Day, J.C. (1981). Learning to learn: On training students to learn from texts. *Educational Researcher, 10*(2), 14–21.

Covert, R. (1989, June). *Cultural diversity training.* Paper presented at an individual conference addressing the issues in multicultural education. Chapel Hill, NC.

Delpit, L.D. (1988). The silenced dialogue: Power and pedagogy in educating other people's children. *Harvard Educational Review, 58*(3), 280–298.

Dunn, R., Beaudry, J.S., & Klavis, A. (1989). Survey of research on learning styles. *Educational Leadership, 46,* 50–58.

Durkin, D. (1978–1979). What classroom observations reveal about reading comprehension instruction. *Reading Research Quarterly, 14,* 481–533.

Evangelauf, J. (1988, January 3). Plan to encourage minority students to pursue teaching careers is proposed. *Chronicle of Higher Education,* p. 2.

Graham, P.A. (1987). Black teachers: A drastically scarce resource. *Phi Delta Kappan, 68*(8), 598–605.

Heath, S.B. (1983). *Ways with words.* Cambridge, MA: Cambridge University Press.

Hillard, A.G. (1989). Teaching and cultural styles in a pluralistic society. *National Education Association, 7*(6), 65–59.

Hollins, E. (1982). The Marva Collins story revisited: Implications for regular classroom instruction. *Journal of Teacher Education, 33*(1), 37–40.

Irvine, J.J. (1986). Teacher-student interactions: Effects of student race, sex, and grade. *Journal of Educational Psychology, 78*(1), 14–21.

Jones, M.G. (1989). Gender issues in teacher education. *Journal of Teacher Education, 40*(1), 33–38.

Little Soldier, L. (1989). Cooperative learning and the Native-American student. *Phi Delta Kappan, 71,* 161–163.

National Education Association. (1987). *Status of the American public school teacher* 1985-86. Washington, DC: Author.

Oakes, J. (1985). *Keeping track: How schools structure inequality.* New Haven, CT: Yale University Press.

Ramirez, M., III, and Castaneda, A. (1974). *Cultural democracy, bicognitive development and education.* New York: Academic Press.

Shade, B.J. (1982). Afro-American cognitive style: A variable in school success? *Review of Educational Research, 52,* 219–244.

Slavin, R.E. (1987). Synthesis of research on cooperative learning. *Educational Leadership, 48*(5), 72–82.

Sleeter, C.E. (1990). Staff development for desegregated schooling. *Phi Delta Kappan, 72,* 33–40.

Villegas, A.M. (1992, February). *The competence needed by beginning teachers in a multicultural society.* Paper presented at the annual meeting of the American Association of Colleges for Teacher Education, San Antonio, TX.

READING 3

Dangerous Minds: Decoding a Classroom

Linda Christensen

Too often, teachers close their doors and teach. This is not just a lonely approach to teaching; it reinforces bad pedagogy. For years, I invented lessons, practiced, praised, and criticized my teaching all alone. Of course, there were students present, and even when I didn't formally ask for feedback and critique, they gave it—sometimes ruthlessly. Sure, an administrator wandered in once every other year, but that's hardly an ongoing discussion about the practice of teaching.

So when teachers flock to see movies like *Dangerous Minds* or *Stand and Deliver*, I understand the pull. We want to peer in other teachers' rooms and see why they are being applauded. What accounts for these teachers' supposed brilliance in the classroom? What can we steal? What can we learn?

Dangerous Minds is a summer movie based on LouAnne Johnson's book, *My Posse Don't Do Homework*. The book jacket reads, "They were called the class from Hell—thirty-four inner-city sophomores she inherited from a teacher who'd been 'pushed over the edge.' She was told 'those kids have tasted blood. They're dangerous.'" The movie condenses the book's timeline into one year and sets the high school in Palo Alto, where Michelle Pfeiffer, playing LouAnne, teaches a class of mostly Black and Latino kids. Johnson is "an ex-marine with an attitude" who, of course, believes in her students and dazzles and succeeds, where others have failed.

Although I liked *Stand and Deliver* better, *Dangerous Minds* does portray a growing reality that *Stand and Deliver* doesn't—a White middle-class teacher in a community of color. For that reason, it's worth examining and critiquing the teaching represented in the film.

Respecting Community

As a White teacher in a school with a student population that is largely Latino and African American, LouAnne's first obligation is to study the community, roam the streets, shop in neighborhood store, attend services at local churches, read the community newspapers, eat in restaurants owned by her students' families, find the writers, historians, artists, and activists who live among her students. She should talk with teachers, parents, students, and building administrators who could tell her about the school, the students, the world she has entered. In the best of situations, the school would provide this as a service to in-coming teachers; in the real world, first-year teachers must do this on their own.

But LouAnne doesn't. Instead she imposes a White middle-class curriculum on her students. Certainly, she does this without malice, because she apparently

---

Reprinted by permission of the author.

doesn't know about the cultural heritages her students bring to class or that flourish in their neighborhoods. In fact, I think she believes they need her curriculum in order to "make it," and to a certain extent they do. But because of her racial and cultural blindness, her lack of acknowledgment implicitly tells students that their lives, their cultures are second class, unworthy of study.

After a fight between three students, Emilio, Raul, and Gusmaro, LouAnne's class is angry with her. They believe she "snitched" on the students and caused their suspensions. It wasn't true, but it made for a tense class session. During this exchange one young student tells LouAnne, "You don't come from where we live. You come into my neighborhood and see what's going on before you try to tell us how to live."

LouAnne quickly responds that unlike the students in her class who choose to finish school, there are people in their neighborhood who don't choose to get on the school bus. They choose to sell drugs. Now, LouAnne needs a reality check. Her student is right. What does she know about the neighborhood? Is she making assumptions about these students and their families? Does she assume that because the neighborhood is poor and diverse that everyone is selling drugs? More fundamentally, is she assuming poverty is a choice that her students' parents made?

During this discussion, she proclaims, "There are no victims in this classroom." What is that supposed to mean? Their families aren't the victims of a profit-first economy? Who is most likely to lose jobs these days? Who is least likely to be hired? Who is most likely to be picked up or harassed by the police? Are LouAnne's students in full control of their lives? While I understand the point LouAnne wants to make—that students can choose to make their lives different—LouAnne's White, middle-class appraisal suggests that students and their parents are solely responsible for the conditions in which they live. This "I'm in control, you're in control" stance infects her whole curriculum, and prevents LouAnne from encouraging her students to reflect on real social inequities that impact their life opportunities.

Now don't get me wrong, LouAnne loves her students. And in many ways, she is a good teacher. She values the young people in her room as individuals, and she cares deeply about what happens to them. When her student Emilio's life is threatened, LouAnne brings him home, fixes him dinner, and convinces him to speak with the principal instead of killing the young man who is out to get him. In another incident, she gives Raul $200 to pay for a coat he bought on credit off the street because she doesn't want him to miss school or get harmed by the thief who sold it to him. She also goes out of her way to fight for pregnant Callie's right to stay in school. It's obvious that she thinks a lot about her lesson plans and tries to capture students' attention. Because she cares so much about her students, they are willing to work for her. Unfortunately, her approach is Eurocentric and elitist, because she doesn't acknowledge the cultural heritage of her students.

LouAnne looks out at a sea of beautiful mostly brown faces and then brings Bob Dylan to class. And Dylan Thomas. Two white male poets. LouAnne is undoubtedly the victim of stunted education herself, but she needs to look outside of the traditional canon to find writers who honor and connect with her students. She asks Hal, her teaching buddy, who his favorite poet is, but she doesn't ask Mr. Grandey, the African-American principal, or the students themselves. Margaret Walker, Luis Rodriguez, Lawon Inada, Li-Young Lee, Sherman Alexie, June Jordan . . . The list of poets of color is endless. There are too many good, contemporary writers for LouAnne to ignore them. Because of the narrowness of LouAnne's education, she might have come to believe that students must read only within the canon in order to be prepared for college or to be considered educated. While it's true that some teachers err by eliminating the canon totally, it's still more common to find teachers like LouAnne who seem oblivious to great writers from other racial/cultural backgrounds. As my friend and fellow English teacher Bakari Chavanu wrote about the movie, "Isn't it ironic that a school of mostly Black and Latino students would not even have developed a curriculum that addresses their history and culture?"

I like Bob Dylan and Dylan Thomas, too. They have important things to say, but I think students would have actually discovered "poetry is its own reward," as LouAnne sarcastically says to her principal, if LouAnne would have broadened the list of poets. Whether by design or good luck, she struck a "generative theme"—as Ira Shor and Paulo Freire call the mother lode that occurs when a teacher hits a topic that generates not only an interest with students, but which also connects the students' lives with broader social issues. For LouAnne, the topics were death and choice. She might have included poems by *Boston Globe* writer and poet, Patricia Smith. Smith, who wrote the poem "Undertaker" after interviewing people in the African-American community about the annual statistics condemning young Black men to death or prison, speaks in plain English about death. Smith's poem would have grabbed students' attention without the candy bars and amusement ride bribes Ms. Johnson doles out as rewards for studying:

> When a bullet enters the brain, the head explodes.
> I can think of no softer warning for the mothers
> who sit doubled before my desk,
> knotting their smooth brown hands,
> and begging, fix my boy, fix my boy.
> *Here's his high school picture.*
> And the smiling, mildly mustachioed player
> in the crinkled snapshot
> looks nothing like the plastic bag of boy
> stored and dated in the cold room downstairs . . .

No translation needed.

Curriculum and Students

We watch LouAnne's students decode published writers, but we never observe them writing or listening to their classmates' writing. They are given vocabulary lists and taught grammar, but we never see them use their skills in real work—like writing poetry or even essays unraveling the meaning of difficult poetry. Her early exasperated comment that "these kids don't even know what a verb is" is a clue to this omission. Perhaps LouAnne thinks that people need to know grammatical terms before they can write. This is simply untrue.

Students learn to write by writing, receiving feedback, and rewriting—and even by reading. Knowing grammatical terms might make it easier for students to talk with their teacher if they make an error, but it doesn't make them better writers. My experience is that many students actually know the names of the most basic parts of speech, but withhold them as a kind of resistance. When LouAnne brings candy bars as "prizes" for learning, students quickly identify the correct part of speech. Granted students, especially students whose "home language" is not "Standard Edited Written English," need to look at their own patterns of errors and learn how to "fix" those, but this should happen *while* they are writing their own pieces, not by correcting manufactured lessons on grammatical terms.

LouAnne's students teem with poetry. We hear their raps before she walks in that first day. We hear them spontaneously spout poetry whenever she pauses for a moment, but she always hushes it up so she can push on with the lesson. Why not encourage them to write poetry about death? or life? or music? or education? Why not nurture and guide her students' poetic impulses? Why not take their lives and their words as subjects of study?

LouAnne missed the opportunity to link the topic of death and choice with the students' lives, but she also missed the link with the larger economic and political picture: Why were there so many deaths? What was happening in the community that created death as a by-product? What had happened to the community in recent years? Had family-wage jobs been replaced with unemployment as manufacturing plants migrated to Mexico or Thailand? Poet/activist Luis Rodriguez points out that 300,000 manufacturing jobs were lost in California during the 1980s and early '90s [*Nation,* Nov. 21, 1994]. Did this job flight contribute to increased poverty and violence in the East Palo Alto community of LouAnne's students?

A Community of Support

LouAnne has contempt for the African-American principal. She thinks his rule about knocking before entering a closed office door is petty because she doesn't understand his "hidden curriculum." She lies when he tries to point out the rules regarding field trips. She sucks candy, slouches, and rolls her eyes while he tries to engage her in a conversion about the classroom techniques and content. Mr. Grandey does come off as a rigid rule maker and rule keeper. (In fact, both African-American adults in the movie are portrayed as obstacles in students' education.) But she never tries to engage him in a discussion about why she sees the established curriculum as a waste of time. Again, she assumes she knows more than this African-American educator about what students at the school, many of whom are African-American, need. She needs a little humility; she needs to develop contacts with people who might help her understand the students, the community. She can't afford to cut people off before the dialogue even starts.

Her failure to develop ties with other teachers isolates her. She is always the one, the great White heroine coming in to save these kids from the ignorance of others. She might be more effective if she built relationships with other teachers and worked with them to change the rules of the school. For example, the administration pushes pregnant girls out of school because they think "pregnancy is contagious." Ms. Johnson fights for Callie's right to stay in school, but she battles the administration by herself. Certainly, other teachers might know and see how unfair the administration's stance is. If she gathered allies before cussing out the administration in a public office, she might change the rule rather than just get Callie back. She might also confer with them about changing the curriculum which she deems unsuitable.

Similarly, LouAnne needs to build alliances with her students' parents. She is stung when an African-American mother withdraws her two sons from school. I found the scene unconvincing. In 20 years, I've never encountered an African-American mother, or mother of any race who withdrew her children from school because they "don't need it." But let's take it at face value. The mother says that her sons don't need to learn poetry. The mother might be right. As far as we in the audience can tell, these kids discuss poetry every day. I love poetry. I teach poetry. But the mother has a point: how is this going to help her sons negotiate a highly inhospitable world? What real-life skills is LouAnne teaching them? LouAnne again assumes she knows more than the parents about their children's needs. Why didn't she ask the mother what her children need to learn? Why doesn't she tell the mother about her plans, how she sees poetry fitting into their lives?

Making the Implicit Explicit

According to reviews I've read of *Dangerous Minds,* and according to LouAnne herself as she's packing her crates to leave the school, LouAnne was teaching a college level curriculum. I don't think so, but let's pretend she was. Why did she wait until the very end of the year to tell students? And why did she tell just one student, Raul? Very early in their schooling, students learn their place. If LouAnne was attempting to teach students the discourse of the academy by asking them to read and decode difficult literary texts, she should have let the students in on the secret.

I teach in a school where many bright students have either been told or have learned that they are not "college material." Students have to unlearn that lesson. One way of unlearning it is to be explicit about the curriculum, to let students know that they are deciphering college material. There's no need to hide the fact. This helps them readjust their self concept, so they can see themselves as succeeding in college. But LouAnne also needs to unmask the process and name the skills they are learning—whether it's scrutinizing SAT vocabulary, decoding difficult poetry, or writing essays documented with historical or literary references.

The more information first generation college-bound students have, the more likely they are to attempt the leap. The language and atmosphere of the "academy" is likely to be a barrier, so instead of taking students to fancy restaurants and teaching them to treat grown male waiters with disrespect as she does in the film, LouAnne should take students to a college and allow them to see themselves as part of that world.

Becoming the Light

I loved the end of the movie when students used the language of the Dylan Thomas poem she taught them and declared they were raging against her leaving the school because she was their light. And I was also troubled. Teachers can be "lights" for their students; we can show the way, guide, find the beauty and dignity in students when students sometimes don't see it themselves. Certainly, we can do what we're paid to do—teach students to read, write, or conduct experiments. But we also need to teach them to find that light within themselves.

LouAnne needs to teach students to become their own lights. She must help them develop the skills to work in the world, but also the skills to critique the world so they can unlock, not only Dylan Thomas poems, but everything from political pronouncements to films about inspirational teachers. She needs to equip them to recognize and combat the racism, sexism, and homophobia that will follow them from their neighborhoods to their college classrooms and beyond. Instead of buying them candy and taking them to amusement parks, she must teach them how to listen and talk together so they can light the way and convince each other as Margaret Walker urges in her poem "For My People":

> Let a new earth rise. Let another world be born. Let a bloody peace be written in the sky. Let a second generation full of courage issue forth; let a people loving freedom come to growth. Let a beauty full of healing and strength of final clenching be the pulsing in our spirits and our blood. Let the martial songs be written, let the dirges disappear. Let a race of men [and women] now rise and take control.

READING 4

Supporting the Invisible Minority

John Anderson

In every school, there is a group of forgotten children—a hidden minority of boys and girls whose needs have been ignored, whose existence has been whispered about, whose pain is just beginning to surface. These are our gay, lesbian, and bisexual students.

Copyright © 1997 by John D. Anderson. Reprinted by permission.

A Harris poll, released in June 1992, said that 86 percent of high school students would be very upset if classmates called them gay or lesbian. A 1989 report from the federal government suggested that gay and lesbian youth were three times more likely than their peers to commit suicide (Remafedi 1994). Historically these teens have been given derogatory names by society and ignored by their schools, except as the butt of jokes. As teens come out, or go public with their sexual orientations, this oversight is becoming increasingly unacceptable. Studies show that the mean age of coming out for sexual-minority youth is declining, at least in urban areas. For 1993 the mean age for males was 13.1 years; for females 15.2 (Baily and Phariss 1996).

In the two places where a child should feel safe and supported, gay and lesbian youth are routinely reviled: family and school. Gay or lesbian children who are taunted usually have nowhere to turn.

Educators have a clear professional mandate to address the needs of sexual minorities. Organizations such as the National Education Association, the American Federation of Teachers, and the National Association of State Boards of Education have passed resolutions that protect the rights of sexual-minority students and staff. Even most businesses acknowledge the necessity of respect for diversity of all kinds (Carson 1993, Mickens 1994).

Educational leaders often deny there is a problem when it comes to sexual minorities in the schools. In a statewide survey of Connecticut teachers and administrators in 1991, respondents indicated that they recognized the plight of gay and lesbian students, admitted that next to nothing was being done for them, and expressed hope for a solution. The results showed a dichotomy between the perceptions of teachers as a group and those of administrators: Teachers called for action; administrators claimed there was no need or that programs were already in place to address these issues (Woog 1995). The good news is that even in such an environment, great strides can be made, as they have in Stratford.

The Coming Out of Leadership in Stratford

What makes Stratford Public Schools unique in the state and perhaps in the United States? The school system has an openly gay high school teacher, an openly gay elementary school principal, an openly gay middle school teacher, and a middle school assistant principal who openly accepts that one of her sons is gay. In our district, the actions of a few have had unimagined consequences, even in the face of administrative reluctance or objection (Anderson 1996).

I began teaching in Stratford in 1985. In 1991 three events converged to change my life as a teacher. First, in October, Connecticut extended civil rights protection to gay and lesbian citizens, one of nine states to do so to date. Second, during the summer of that year, I began writing a bimonthly column on gay and lesbian concerns for the *New Haven Register.* Third, as my official evaluation goal, I chose to examine the needs of gay and lesbian students and to evaluate how the school system was meeting those needs.

I found that little is being done in U.S. schools to ameliorate the educational opportunity for gay and lesbian students (Harbeck 1992; see also Rienzo et al. 1996). Nevertheless, in Stratford, we have raised sensitivity levels and provided increased support for gay and lesbian students and staff. We have found that most educators are caring people, but they are fearful and look in vain for direction from our educational leaders (Anderson and Edwards 1996).

In lieu of leadership and policies, many educators in Stratford and in other cities and states have taken steps on their own to help reduce discrimination in our schools against those who are gay, lesbian or bisexual. The amazing thing is the progress made with this scattered approach. It is discouraging, however, to note that few schools are replicating successful programs.

Fragmented State and National Leadership

Kevin Jennings (1994) and David Woog (1995) have chronicled the stories of U.S. educators who are gay, lesbian, or bisexual. Yet the stories illustrate that schools have no unified procedure or policy concerning sexual orientation of educators or students.

Another researcher, Harbeck (1992), describes a program called Project 10, which began at a dropout-prevention center founded in 1984 by Virginia Uribe at Fairfax High School in Los Angeles. Project members produced a video documentary on the plight of gay and lesbian students. It was entitled "Who's Afraid of Project 10?"

In another isolated example, the New York Public Schools in 1985 opened the Harvey Milk School, an alternative high school, to provide psychological, social, and academic support to gay, lesbian, and bisexual students. This school is part of the youth advocacy work of the Hetrick-Martin Institute, which also publishes posters and resource materials.

These are partial solutions to local manifestations of a national problem. Until recently, Project 10 and the Harvey Milk School were the extent of organized efforts to address the needs of sexual-minority students in concrete terms.

Two states have begun using data to make decisions about gay and lesbian students and education. In Massachusetts, the Governor's Commission on Gay and Lesbian Youth (1993) produced an excellent study of the issues affecting gay and lesbian students, from poor school performance to suicide. The study makes recommendations for schools, for families of gay and lesbian youth, and for state agencies and the Massachusetts legislature. An important result of this report is that the State Board of Education now requires all teacher certification programs in the state to include sensitivity training on gay and lesbian issues.

The Minnesota Department of Education (1994) published a source booklet that addresses how to include issues related to homosexuality in school policy, instruction, and student services. This text challenges schools to examine their environment and then to develop a more sensitive, inclusive place of learning.

A third state, Connecticut, began addressing homophobia in the schools in 1991, through the *Sex Equity Newsletter* of the State Department of Education.

This newsletter features resources, information, and guidelines similar to those of Massachusetts and Minnesota.

All three states are addressing five important issues (Anderson 1994). Stratford has made progress in all five.

Effective Approaches to Sex Equity

Professional development. In the past few years, Stratford has begun to provide workshops and forums that address sexuality issues. In the first, during the 1992–93 school year, about 30 teachers attended voluntarily; only one administrator participated. At a 1994 workshop on "The Invisible Minority," no administrators attended. One of the presenters was Garret Stack, an openly gay elementary school principal—and my life partner. Another presenter was Ann Edwards. Other forums have included limited presentations—mostly on sexual harassment and cultural minorities—at the annual "World of Differences" workshops.

Support staff and services. Stratford guidance personnel have increasingly been supportive of gay and lesbian issues. Several guidance counselors displayed posters that I provided. One poster declared "Homophobia Is a Social Disease." One counselor has a rainbow sticker, pink triangle, and other gay paraphernalia on her bulletin board. The school psychologists, school nurses, and social workers also provide support to students.

Sexuality in the health curriculum. Like most high school health textbooks (Baily and Phariss 1996), Stratford's text contains only one paragraph on homosexuality. The high school health teachers, however, are supportive and articulate. One teacher, Lea Dickson (1995), has written a resource directory for ASCD's Gay and Lesbian Network. After two years of lobbying the central school administration for permission, two teachers recently invited me to address their senior health classes on homosexuality. At one class session, a panel of "adults in relationships" included both heterosexual and gay couples. I proudly participated, representing Garrett Stack and myself. Student response to these classes has been overwhelmingly positive.

Library resources. The Stratford High School library held a diversity exhibit in 1993. It included noted gay and lesbian Americans—James Baldwin, Martina Navratilova, Col. Margarethe Cammermeyer, Audre Lorde, and Walt Whitman—as well as members of other minority groups. The exhibit occurred without incident. One librarian posted a list of 20 possible topics for research papers, including "civil rights for gays and lesbians." One high school recently held a "Stop the Violence Week." The library exhibited Elaine Landau's (1986) *Different Drummer: Homosexuality in America,* as well as works from two series for adolescents by Chelsea House Publishers: *Lives of Notable Gay Men and Lesbians* and *Issues in Gay and Lesbian Life* (see Gough and Greenblatt 1992).

Curriculum support. We have found that any teacher can transform the curriculum into an inclusive experience for students. For example, a social studies teacher included sex equity issues in a unit on civil rights; in an English class, a student wrote a research paper on gay parenting. In another English class, an

Advanced Placement student developed ways to include gay and lesbian material in the curriculum. I used the TV drama *Serving in Silence* about Col. Cammermeyer, as well as some of my *New Haven Register* columns, as extra-credit activities in my English classes (see Resources).

Conversations and Civility

Most of our efforts in Stratford have focused on *educating the educators*. The administration has been less comfortable with services and support for students (Anderson 1996; see also Riddle 1996, Rensenbrink 1996). Despite the lack of policy, we are slowly creating a supportive environment for our gay, lesbian, and bisexual students and staff.

A highlight of our equity movement was a 1995 conversation with the superintendent. The superintendent listened to parents, teachers, and students express concerns about equal educational access. He encouraged us to continue in our support for equal education for all and cautioned moderation in our choice of actions. We have found that careful planning, mutual respect, and civility go a long way toward achieving real progress.

References

Anderson, J.D. (1994). "School Climate for Gay and Lesbian Students and Staff Members." *Phi Delta Kappan* 76, 2: 151–154.

Anderson, J.D. (1996). "Out as a Professional Educator." In *Open Lives Safe Schools,* edited by D. Walling. Bloomington, Ind.: Phi Delta Kappa Educational Foundation.

Anderson, J.D., and A. Edwards. (1996). *Out for Life.* Las Colinas, Tex.: Idea House.

Baily, N., and T. Phariss. (1996). "Breaking Through the Wall of Silence: Gay, Lesbian, and Bisexual Issues for Middle Level Educators." *Middle School Journal* 27, 3: 38–46.

Carson, C. (1993). "Perspectives on Education in America: An Annotated Briefing." *Journal of Educational Research* 86, 5: 259–310.

Dickson, L. (1995). *Lesbian, Gay, and Bisexual Issues in Education, An ASCD Resource Directory 1994–1995.* Fairfield, Conn.: Garden Gates Communication.

Gough, C., and E. Greenblatt. (1992). "Services to Gay and Lesbian Patrons: Examining the Myths." *Library Journal* 117, 1: 59–63.

Harbeck, K., ed. (1992). *Coming Out of the Classroom Closet: Gay and Lesbian Students, Teachers, and Curricula.* Binghamton, N.Y.: The Haworth Press.

Jennings, K. (1994). *One Teacher in Ten.* Boston: Alyson Publications.

Landau, E. (1986). *Different Drummer: Homosexuality in America.* Englewood Cliffs, N.J.: J. Messner.

Massachusetts Governor's Commission on Gay and Lesbian Youth. (1993). *Making Schools Safe for Gay and Lesbian Youth: Breaking the Silence in Schools and in Families.* Boston: Author.

Mickens, E. (1994). *The 100 Best Companies for Gay Men and Lesbians.* New York: Pocket Books.

Minnesota Department of Education. (1994). *Alone No More: Developing a School Support System for Gay, Lesbian, and Bisexual Youth.* St. Paul, Minn.: Author.

Remafedi, G. (1994). *Death by Denial.* Boston: Alyson Publications.

Rensenbrink, C. (1996). "What Difference Does It Make? The Story of a Lesbian Teacher." *Harvard Education Review* 66, 2: 257–270.

Riddle, B. (1996). "Breaking the Silence: Addressing Gay and Lesbian Issues in Independent Schools." *Independent School* 55, 2: 38–47.

Rienzo, B., J. Button, and K. Wald. (1996). "The Politics of School-Based Programs Which Address Sexual Orientation." *Journal of School Health* 66, 1: 33–40.

Woog, D. (1995). *School's Out: The Impact of Gay and Lesbian Issues on America's Schools.* Boston: Alyson Publications.

Resources

American Federation of Teachers, Gay-Lesbian Caucus, 1816 Chestnut St., Philadelphia, PA 19103.

American Library Association, Gay and Lesbian Task Force, 50 E. Huron St., Chicago, IL 60611.

ASCD Network, Lesbian, Gay and Bisexual Issues in Education, P.O. Box 27527, Oakland, CA 94602.

Chelsea House Publishers, 300 Park Ave. S., New York, NY 10010.

Gay and Lesbian High School Curriculum and Staff Development Project, Arthur Lipkin, Harvard School of Education, 210 Longfellow Hall, Cambridge, MA 02138.

The Gay, Lesbian and Straight Teachers Network (GLSTN), 122 W. 26th St., Suite 1100, New York, NY 10001.

Hetrick-Martin Institute, Inc., 2 Astor Place, New York, NY 10003.

National Education Association, Gay-Lesbian Caucus, P.O. Box 314, Roosevelt, NJ 08555.

Parents and Friends of Lesbians and Gays (PFLAG), P.O. Box 27605, Washington, DC 20038.

Sexuality Information and Education Council of the United States (SIECUS), 130 W. 42nd St., Suite 2500, New York, NY 10036.

World Wide Web

The Gay, Lesbian and Straight Teachers Network (GLSTN): http://www.glstn.org

"Programs in Gender and Lesbian, Gay, and Bisexual Studies at Universities in the USA and Canada": http://www.duke.edu/web/jyounger/lgbprogs.html

University of Maryland "Sexual Orientation Specific Resources": http://www.inform.umd.edu:8080/EdRes/Topic/Diversity/Specific/Sexual_Orientation/

DISCUSSION QUESTIONS AND ACTIVITIES

1. *Consider the variety of ways in which people attempt to communicate with one another. Reflect on your communicative patterns. Have there been occasions when you might have been misunderstood because of cross-cultural miscommunication? Share your answers with others.*

2. *Turn to the "Instructional Decisions: How Do I Teach?" continuum at the start of the chapter. Review your first responses and see if you would now change your place on the continuum for any of the categories. Explain your choices.*

3. *Watch the movie* Dangerous Minds *and compare your opinion of the film with Linda Christensen's comments in "Dangerous Minds: Decoding a Classroom."*

4. *Ask several middle and secondary school teachers working in different schools what, if anything, their schools are doing to meet the needs of gay and lesbian students.*

5. *Develop questions and discussion formats for specific content area materials. In class, take turns facilitating discussions using these materials or work with small groups of middle or secondary students. Share your experiences with class members.*

REFERENCES

Armstrong, D. G., and Savage, T. V. 1994. *Secondary Education,* 3rd ed. New York: Macmillan.

Belenky, M. F., Clincy, B. M, Goldberger, N. R., and Tarule, J. M. 1986. *Women's Ways of Knowing: The Development of Self, Voice and Mind.* New York: Basic.

Delpit, L. D. 1988, August. The Silenced Dialogue: Power and Pedagogy in Educating Other People's Children, *Harvard Educational Review. 58*(3): 280–298.

Eby, J. W., and Kujawa, E. 1994. *Reflective Planning, Teaching, and Evaluation: K-12.* New York: Merrill.

Everhart, R. 1983. *Reading, Writing, and Resistance.* Boston: Routledge.

Grossman, H. 1995. *Teaching in a Diverse Society.* Boston: Allyn & Bacon.

Heath, S. B. 1983. *Ways with Words.* Cambridge: Cambridge University Press.

Ladson-Billings, G. 1994. *The Dreamkeepers.* San Francisco: Josscy-Bass.

Locke, D. C. 1992. *Increasing Multicultural Understanding.* Newbury Park, CA: Sage.

Moody, C. 1990. Teacher Effectiveness. In J. G. Bain and J. E. Herman (eds.), *Making Schools Work for Underachieving Minority Students.* New York: Greenwood, pp. 159–163.

Nieto, S. 1996. *Affirming Diversity: The Sociopolitical Context of Multicultural Education,* 2nd ed. White Plains, NY: Longman.

Ogbu, J. U. 1992, November. Understanding Cultural Diversity and Learning. *Educational Researcher, 21*(8): 5–14.

Ornstein, A. C. 1992. *Secondary and Middle School Teaching Methods.* New York: HarperCollins.

Rist, R. C. 1971. Student Social Class and Teacher Expectations: The Self-Fulfilling Prophecy in Ghetto Education. In *Challenging the Myths: The Schools, the Blacks, and the Poor,* Reprint Series no. 5, Cambridge, MA: Harvard Educational Review.

Shade, B. J., & Kelly, C., and Oberg, M. 1997. *Creating Culturally Responsive Classrooms.* Washington, D.C.: American Psychological Association.

Shaw, C. C. 1996. Instructional Pluralism: A Means to Realizing the Dream of Multicultural, Social Reconstructionist Education. In C. A. Grant and M. L. Gomez, (eds.), *Making Schooling Multicultural: Campus and Classroom.* Englewood Cliffs, NJ: Merrill.

Solomon, R. P. 1992. *Black Resistance in High School.* Albany: State University of New York Press.

Veldman, D. J., and Worsham, M. 1982. Types of Student Classroom Behavior. *Journal of Educational Research, 76*: 204–209.

Walsh, C. 1987. Language, Meaning, and Voice: Puerto Rican Students Struggle for a Speaking Consciousness. *Language Arts, 64*(2): 196–205.

Wlodkowski, R. J., and Ginsberg, M. B. 1995. *Diversity and Motivation.* San Francisco: Jossey-Bass.

Chapter Five

EFFECTIVE DECISION-MAKING IN PLURALIZING THE CONTENT

"School Teachers' Blues" (excerpts)

> Refrain
>
> School teacher blues (school teacher blues)
> I got them school teacher blues (school teacher blues)
> School teacher blues
> Nothing to lose but ma pay . . .
> And that ain't nothin'
> You know my fingers have turned purple
> My master is like I chewed it
> My mind is gettin' warped
> From inhalin' ditto fluid
>
> Refrain
>
> And the problem when in public
> Don't know what parents might say
> They don't pay me quite enough
> To make me act that way
>
> Refrain
>
> They say Johnny can't read
> But what does Johnny have to know
> Look at the competition
> It's the age of video
>
> Refrain

Written by Gaye T. Adegbalola. Recorded by Saffire-The Uppity Blues Women. Reprinted by permission.

> Ohh, noble education
> Rising tide of mediocrity
> I points my finger to the home
> And I views hypocrisy
>
> Refrain

The women's blues group, Saffire, sings the "School Teachers' Blues." They lament the energy required to teach pitted against those perennial questions about the worth of the effort. Middle and secondary content-area teachers faced with pluralizing their curricula sing their own version of the blues. They express any number of concerns as they move toward pluralizing their curricula, making it more inclusive and multicultural. Change—even the idea of change—is often met with resistance. This is true for individuals as well as institutions, including educational organizations. Conservative by nature, schools experience the tension of the push toward curricular reform and the pull to maintain the status quo.

Chapter Five addresses the question, "*What* do culturally responsive teachers teach?" Many curriculum decisions are out of their hands with school departments, school districts, and state mandates directing what is taught, but that is why teacher participation and input in curriculum development is so critical; teachers, individually and to a greater degree collectively, can and should find ways to influence the curriculum taught in their schools. Many curriculum decisions will be based on their assumptions about knowledge, student learning, and the needs of students.

Curriculum development is often the area where teachers who want to be change agents first see themselves assuming this role and experiencing institutional resistance: As a beginning middle or secondary teacher, you have been able to concentrate on developing relationships with your students and have been able to implement culturally relevant teaching practices. By mid-year you are ready to be a more active member on the departmental curriculum committee, and it is then that you realize that your ideas of a more inclusive curriculum are up against state mandates for curriculum content and pressures to improve students' scores on statewide tests. Now might be a good time to reread the Introduction at the beginning of this text and turn to the section on change agents in Chapter Ten.

Implementing a multicultural curriculum at the elementary level is usually received enthusiastically; the expectation is that teachers will talk about famous women, men and women of color, and respect and appreciation for all kinds of differences.[1] The most controversial aspect of multicultural education at the elementary level often revolves around whether to acknowledge families

---

[1] See Louise Derman-Sparks and A. B. C. Task Force 1989. *Anti-Bias Curriculum: Tools for Empowering Young Children.* Washington, D. C.: National Association for The Education of Young Children. This text is an excellent resource for early childhood educators and offers an in-depth approach to implementing multicultural education that moves beyond the level described in the text and toward social reconstructionist.

with same-sex partners. Concerns at the middle and secondary level focus on "whose stories" should be told and whose privileges should be unmasked. Will culturally relevant curriculum fractionalize us into ethnic/cultural/gender camps?[2] Empowering middle and secondary students is seen as potentially more threatening.

In this chapter, we look at the various "blues" teachers face when they think about implementing multicultural education and present some general guidelines for pluralizing curricula. Banks's curriculum framework provides a good overview to different multicultural curriculum approaches. We conclude the chapter with a discussion of multicultural curricula for specific subject areas, a general plan for getting started, and the benefits of a culturally relevant curriculum for middle and secondary students.

THE MULTICULTURAL SCHOOL TEACHERS' BLUES

The "Too Much Information—Not Enough Time" Blues

Learning "multicultural information" for a specific discipline takes considerable time and energy. This information is not readily available in textbooks, and teachers must engage in independent research to find and include appropriate materials in their courses. There is also the concern over which perspectives to include. One of the myths about a multicultural curriculum is that all perspectives must be included. Teachers rightly panic at the thought of trying to mount that enormous task within the confines of a yearlong or, worse yet, semesterlong course.

We can apply the argument of too much information to any discipline. A natural by-product of the information age is that we are continually bombarded with new information or new perspectives on existing information. As teachers, we are dealing with an overabundance of information no matter what curriculum goals we have, and teachers will need to work together formally and informally. Diaz (1992) suggests that teachers need to develop multicultural literacy and integrate this information into their teaching repertoire so that they can be "congruent with the heterogeneity present in this nation as well as in the world" (p. 194).

We take seriously teachers' concerns for finding more time. How *do* teachers find more time? Obviously, developing priorities and recognizing that you can't "do it all" are general guidelines. In addition, experience at teaching also helps teachers become more efficient—they are more familiar with instructional preparation, they learn how to streamline grading, and they develop relationships with students and better techniques for classroom management. We cannot stress enough that teachers need to work with others. They should start small and look for new ways to restructure practices while synthesizing

---

[2] This question reflects the concerns of the mainstream. It assumes that groups are unaware of their own histories and experiences and that the present Eurocentric curriculum is creating unity.

new information. Many districts have grants available to teachers to support their developing new curricula. Many states mandate professional development that requires teachers to take courses or attend conferences and workshops to retain certification. A small group of committed colleagues could take advantage of professional development opportunities to advance their goals. As a change agent, you might be interested in radical and immediate change, but systemic change—change that alters the traditional ways institutions or professions operate—needs both consensus around a vision and leadership.

The "What to and How to Cover" Blues

Critics claim that a multicultural curriculum is too political or too politically correct. Was Columbus a hero or a heel? Did Edison invent the light bulb or did he take credit for work done by a Black man? Teachers are concerned about the truth, but what is the truth and whose version will be studied? Particularistic visions (such as Afrocentricism or Eurocentrism) are adversarial to more culturally pluralistic ones (those of Sleeter and Grant and Banks). Do we risk reducing the curriculum to the latest revelations of revisionist history or the most recent group who grabs our attention in the headlines?

Multiculturalists recognize the political nature of education (see Chapter One). In fact, making explicit the links between knowledge and the power behind it are goals of multicultural education. According to Banks (1996a), "the positions of both the Western traditionalists and the multiculturalists reflect values, ideologies, political positions, and human interests. Each position also implies a kind of knowledge that should be taught in the school and university curriculum" (p. 5). Multiculturalism's emphasis on developing students' critical thinking skills means providing them with a broad range of information from which they can draw their own conclusions.

The "My Content is Not Multicultural" Blues

Some middle and secondary teachers view their disciplines as outside the scope of multicultural education. Even as math and science teachers embrace culturally relevant instructional and assessment approaches, they might believe that their subject matter is "culture neutral." Efforts to include famous women mathematicians or scientists of color are seen as incidental to the real content; force fitting multicultural information into the class is an inauthentic stretch.

Fortunately, several useful texts have been published in recent years that provide a sound rationale and framework for developing an inclusionary approach in the content areas. We will describe this further in the section dealing with specific subject areas.

The "My Students Are Not Diverse" Blues

Some teachers believe that because they teach in racially or ethnically homogeneous communities that multicultural education has less relevance for them. They question the significance of multicultural content for their students.

Moreover, sometimes the community is vocal, challenging teachers about the importance of such content.

Such concerns reflect a limited definition of multicultural education. Although some communities are less racially diverse than others are, cultural differences are still present. To recognize multicultural education as the purview of only urban centers or more racially heterogeneous communities overlooks the cultural impact of gender, social class, ability, and sexual orientation on an individual's identity. It also denies the reality of the global community young adolescents will live in!

The "This Won't Help My Students on the SATs" Blues

Parents, teachers and administrators are concerned that multicultural education, no matter how noble, good, or just, will take away from the "real" purpose of education. Won't the "basics," that is, mathematical problem solving and reasoning abilities and skills in writing/composing and verbal reasoning be ignored? Won't this subsequently affect students' performance on standardized tests like the SATs or the ACTs?

Recent changes in the structure of the content and format of many standardized tests including the SATs and ACTs underscore test makers' recognition of the link between culture and assessment. Such tests increasingly reflect the diversity of students in schools and the goals of multicultural education. The content of test items has become more inclusive, and more items require critical thinking and interpretations of multiple points of view. For many questions, students are asked to produce responses, rather than merely recognize answers. Instead of being penalized by the adoption of multicultural themes and strategies, students in these classes would be better prepared!

GUIDELINES FOR PLURALIZING CURRICULUM CONTENT

Teachers who have battled the blues and want to make a commitment to pluralizing their content need to think about knowledge in new ways. Multiculturalists view knowledge as a social construction. We have already looked at several examples of how language is never neutral (see Chapter One) and seen how multiculturalists are called to dig below the surface structure of language to understand its hidden meanings, power, and privilege. Knowledge, even information that has all the trappings of "hard evidence," is influenced by the kinds of questions a society asks and the methods people use to obtain answers. If we videotaped two people talking, the tape would not be a neutral recording of events. Why, for example, have we chosen to record *this* conversation and not someone else's? How do the speakers change their conversation because of the taping and how does their understanding of *why* they are being taped affect them? The cameraperson chooses the angles, the close-ups, and the lighting, which can influence what we see. Moreover, our eyes take in only a small fraction of the sensory data available. In the end, the lens is never neutral. "The knowledge construction process relates to the extent to which teachers help students to understand, investigate, and determine how the implicit cultural assumptions, frames of references, perspectives, and biases within a discipline influence the ways in which knowledge is constructed within it" (Banks, 1996a, p. 337). This applies to the sciences as well as to the humanities.

Teachers do not have to know everything their students are to learn, but they need to understand the concept of knowledge construction and present students with examples from different vantage points. Teachers sometimes need to research marginalized voices and perspectives to supplement traditional texts.[3] These curriculum changes involve not only including additional sources of information, but also the framing of assignments and teaching students new ways of interacting with the material. Students must also learn how to see themselves as constructors of knowledge.

Teachers are constantly faced with decisions about how much to cover and at what depth. A curriculum that responds to Sleeter and Grant's Multicultural and Multicultural and Social Reconstructionist approaches takes time and requires depth. However, the issue of too much information is not solely a problem for multiculturalists. The "too much information—not enough time" blues face everyone. All teachers (and school districts) will make decisions about what is included and what is excluded. For multiculturalists the "center of the curriculum no longer focuses on mainstream Americans, but on an event, issue, or concept that is viewed from many different perspectives and points of view. This is done while at the same time helping students to understand our common U.S. heritage and traditions" (Banks, 1996a, p. 339). As we will see, this statement is not just about history, but also relates to modes of scientific inquiry, for example.

Future middle and secondary teachers can use several criteria to guide the development of a culturally responsive curriculum, regardless of their disciplines. The curriculum should do the following:

1. *Acknowledge that multicultural education and a multicultural curriculum is crucial for all students.* This statement represents an assumption held by those developing the curriculum. The curriculum will reflect the underlying definition of multicultural education of the curriculum specialists and will evolve out of their thinking and experiences with the benefits to all students being an inclusive curriculum. A curriculum that views multiculturalism as critical for everyone will not save learning about people of color until their "week, month, day" of celebration, nor will it be an add-on to the traditional curriculum.

2. *Develop materials that help students understand and appreciate diversity.* Appreciation is a difficult outcome to predict. You might remember adults

---

[3] Thanks to the work of many scholars coming out of ethnic studies departments (including ethnic/cultural studies, women's studies, and so forth) the amount of information available is steadily increasing.

trying to help you develop an appreciation for okra or salsa. They might or might not have succeeded, but one thing is certain: You needed to have some contact or exposure to have a chance. If we look at diversity as including the voices, culture, contributions, and perspectives of many groups, then as a start, you need to expose your students to this information. The nature of how students are exposed to information also makes a difference. Are there certain contexts in which you might have been more inclined to develop a taste for okra or salsa?

3. *Include multiple, nonstereotypical perspectives and voices through the use of primary sources.* Students need to be taught the difference between primary and secondary sources—they can also be included in the search for locating these sources—as well as how individual positionality (see Chapter Three) affects how information is presented and understood. In Chapter One, we pointed out that differences in meaning can result from slight changes in word choice.

4. *Teach students how to recognize power and privilege inequities in society.* To develop curriculum that recognizes power and privilege, teachers must be sure that they maintain a level of awareness. Nieto's definition of multicultural education spoke of a process. Part of that process for multiculturalists is to keep those concepts in the forefront of their thinking. They continue to ask themselves "In what ways are power and privilege operating in my life?" Pedagogically, the best way to teach students this awareness is by modeling our own awareness and through the kinds of questions we continue to ask them—questions that allow students to draw conclusions around power and privilege.

5. *Adopt a critical thinking dimension that incorporates complexity and responds to multiple interpretations.* Discuss problem solving strategies and generate appropriate options for action. Determine the relevance of content to students in the class and connect to current local and global issues.

6. *Incorporate ways of involving parents/families and community leaders in the classroom.* Draw on the expertise and experiences of family members and community leaders. Provide students with opportunities to listen to adults and help them understand how individuals interpret their experiences and construct knowledge. Link what students are learning to what others in the community are doing. (See Chapter 8.)

CURRICULUM FRAMEWORK

Educators approach pluralizing their curriculum in a variety of ways. Their first resource is usually a textbook. "However, the content about ethnic groups in textbooks is usually presented from mainstream perspectives, contains information and heroes that are selected using mainstream criteria, and rarely incorporates information about ethnic groups throughout the text in a consistent and totally integrated way" (Sleeter and Grant as cited in Banks & Banks,

1997, p. 232). Teachers can't rely on publishers to create their curricula and must find additional ways to make their materials be more inclusive.[4]

Banks (1997) has categorized the strategies teachers use to address the lack of ethnic and multicultural content in elementary and secondary classrooms and has identified four levels into which curriculum materials and assignments can be classified. These levels correspond to different multicultural goals and objectives. Again, we see how critical a teacher's definition is in determining how multicultural education is implemented in her classroom. You might also want to check how each level matches our yardstick (that is, criteria) for culturally relevant curricula and how the levels reflect Sleeter and Grant's approaches to multicultural education. (Also see "Incorporating Cultural Pluralism into Instruction" in the readings for a list of assignments related to Banks's curriculum levels.)

Contributions (Level 1)

At this level, heroes, holidays, and some cultural elements such as food and music are inserted into the curriculum. For example, a teacher might do a unit on "Great Mexican American Writers" or "Women Who Have Made a Difference" or ask students to do research on sports played around the world. These units act as corollaries to the mainstream curriculum whose goals and structure remain unchanged. A social studies teacher might assign a project on famous Native Americans. "The criteria used to select ethnic heroes for study and to judge them for success are derived from the mainstream society and not from the ethnic community" (Banks, 1997, p. 233). Who is a hero, and what is deemed heroic, therefore, is filtered through a mainstream lens and might not fully reflect perspectives from the ethnic community. Lessons focus on an occasional "citing/sighting of the exotic." Themes are discussed or studied on a special day (Martin Luther King's birthday) or during a designated month (Women's History Month) with little or no reference to these individuals or groups elsewhere in the curriculum. In middle schools, "Celebrate Diversity" days are popular events, and middle school teachers often find Level 1 an easy starting point, but sometimes they stay at this level. Turn to page 149 and read the examples of the Contributions Approach listed. How many of these lessons have you experienced either as a student or a teacher?

Additive (Level 2)

This approach pluralizes the curriculum with the "addition of content, concepts, themes, and perspectives to the curriculum without changing its basic structure, purposes and characteristics" (Banks, 1997, p. 235). Through this approach, a book (for example, Toni Morrison's *Beloved*) or a unit (Women and the Vietnam War) or even a course (The Psychology of Women) might be added to the curriculum. Although pluralized content is added, it is usually

---

[4] Teachers should start by evaluating the materials they have on hand. The criteria, particularly items 2–6, listed in the previous section, can be a useful yardstick.

done within the context of an existing curriculum that again reflects mainstream perspectives. Again, there is no rethinking or restructuring of the curriculum and adding more material to an already overloaded course can overwhelm the most committed of educators! The Additive approach is popular among secondary school teachers.

Despite its shortcomings, however, Banks sees this level as a possible precursor to transformative curricula (level 3). Moreover, Banks suggests that implementing levels one and two is better than ignoring ethnic and multicultural input, altogether. Both provide some visibility that is lacking in mainstream curriculum. He sees the Additive level as a necessary first step to moving to more relevant and inclusive levels. Others are not as generous in their assessment of these levels. There is concern that the accomplishments of people of color will be presented in a way that limits the depth of their significance and contribution. For example, was George Washington Carver the only Black scientist taught about in your school and were his contributions reduced to discovering peanut butter? This approach becomes a facile way to perpetuate the "illusion of inclusion." The addition of a few select historical figures or authors relegated to limited classroom exposure can do little to change a Eurocentric focus or value system. See page 150 for a list of examples that reflect the Additive approach to multicultural education. How many of these types of activities have been part of your education? What is your opinion of this approach?

Transformation (Level 3)

Unlike the Contributions and Additive approaches the structure, goals, and perspectives of curriculum are changed at the Transformation level and students are able to "view concepts, issues, themes, and problems from several ethnic perspectives and points of view" (Banks, 1997, p. 237)—points of view that include multiple voices that are traditionally left out of the curriculum. As previously discussed, many novice and experienced teachers find this curriculum revision a daunting task. "Does this mean I need to include the viewpoints of every ethnic group in our country?" This, however, is not the goal; the goal is to empower students to view concepts and issues from multiple perspectives and especially from the perspectives of those groups most actively involved and influenced by the events. The goal is to encourage students to think critically about the complexities of society by examining various perspectives.

Although applications of the Transformation level are perhaps more obvious in areas such as social studies, music, and art, there are also ways to recognize the importance of diverse points of view, social customs, vocabularies, and experiences in science and mathematics.[5]

Consider, for example, an inquiry-based lesson in which students have been asked to determine the Earth's circumference as though they were

---

[5] The authors are indebted to Dr. Frank Giuliano for contributing, both conceptually and in writing, the science examples included in this section.

astronomers living 500 years ago. The *National Science Education Standards* (NRC, 1996) advocate that, in such a lesson, the teacher should help students discover how, "in Columbus' day," it was known that the distance between a town in Scandinavia and a town in Italy was about 3000 miles (calculated by measuring the North Star's angle from the horizon at both locations). It is easy for many teachers to engage students in such a Euro-centered lesson. A more inclusive approach, however, might engage students in a role-playing activity in which they are members of the great University of Alexandria. Eratosthenes, born around 274 B.C., was the first scientist to measure the Earth's circumference. This was done more than 2000 years ago, using the shadows cast by the Sun in two different cities in North Africa. This approach allows students not only to learn the content, but also to immerse themselves in the social context of how ancient scientists lived and worked.

More contemporary, and perhaps more compelling, examples of applying the Transformation level in science center around environmental issues. During the past few decades, our attitude toward the environment has moved closer to the Native American view and is moving slowly away from the view of the Europeans who took over the land. In addition, it is becoming increasingly obvious that environmental issues cannot be separated from social and cultural issues. The recent controversy surrounding the hunting and fishing rights of the Ojibwe tribe in Minnesota is one example of the connections among cultures, societal issues, and environmental concerns.

The relationships among environmental issues, cultural issues, and societal issues are exemplified by the contemporary issue of environmental racism. This refers to situations in which the costs and effects of some environmental degradation fall disproportionately on some groups of people. Those same groups are often those who have been marginalized or have faced discrimination because of their race or ethnicity. This issue raises questions regarding which neighborhoods are more likely to be on the receiving end of pollutants or which towns are more likely to be the site of chemical plants, paper mills, or other sources of unpleasant substances and odors. Arguments are made that those who are most likely to be on the receiving end of such pollution are members of groups in society likely to experience discrimination and racism. One could argue that lack of political, social, or economic influence by poorer neighborhoods and minorities effectively translates into those same neighborhoods and groups bearing more of the environmental costs.

One final example deals with integrating multicultural content into mathematics. In a recent gathering of faculty to discuss considering multicultural issues in course content, a colleague from the math department balked at the idea, falling back on the rationale that teaching mathematical concepts did not necessarily fit in with "multiple perspectives." When it was suggested that examples used to solve problems could be taken from relevant, real world examples, he conceded that yes, perhaps he could use examples from poverty statistics or employment data but that information was so depressing! What the professor's remarks seemed to miss is that even though the statistics are alarming and depressing, especially for women and members of racial minority groups, the opportunity to think critically about issues of inequality and to raise awareness could be a part of his curricular agenda.

As illustrated in these examples, pluralism and multiculturalism are not ideas that one puts in education; rather, they are inherently part of, and necessary to, understanding math, science, and the scientific process. Math and science, like culture, are not objects to be manipulated or described, but are negotiated, temporal, and emergent (Good, 1995). Exploring culturally embedded assumptions regarding the nature of math and science by using their histories and philosophies will help students better understand the dynamic, complex nature of science. Additional examples of the Transformation approach are listed on page 151.

Social Action (Level 4)

The Social Action approach takes the Transformation level a step further. Students are educated for "social criticism and social change" (Banks, 1997, p. 239) and are given instruction in decision making.[6] Students are encouraged to analyze and question authority rather than to accept it passively. To many, this is a radical redefinition of education—education designed to produce change and question reproduction of the status quo. This approach links education to democratic action that asks educators to change long-held ideas about the purpose of school. It puts into practice several of the criteria of culturally relevant curricula we have listed earlier.

Action, especially in the name of social justice, turns teachers into change agents, proactive in empowering students to address some of society's problems. Students become problem solvers, investigating social issues, promoting democratic ideals, while critically analyzing the consequences of their actions. For example, in an American government class dealing with censorship, students develop a survey of students' interests in reading materials. Among the books most listed by students as ones they'd like to read are three that have been banned by the Board of Education (such as *Mein Kampf* by Adolf Hitler; *Kaffir Boy* by Mark Mathabane; and *Huckleberry Finn* by Mark Twain). Students interview several factions of the school community including parents, administrations, students, and community leaders. Students research cases regarding censorship of literature, write letters to the school and local newspaper editors, and schedule open debates. The culminating activity might be a proposal to the School Board to lift the ban. Whether students are successful or not in getting the ban lifted, they have learned valuable information and have put into *practice* the civic skills extolled in our textbooks. Examples of the Social Action approach are listed on page 153. What social action is likely to result from completing these activities?

---

[6] Sleeter and Grant's Multicultural and Reconstructionist approach to multicultural education is relevant here as are Dewey's education for citizenship and Banks's multicultural education for democracy.

Issues in Pluralizing Specific Content Areas

Specific academic areas have their own unique struggles as they move towards curricula that are more inclusive. Some disciplines are concerned with who has the right to teach which content; others are engaged in discussions of historical accuracy, new political agendas, and what constitutes truth—scientific or otherwise. We look briefly at some of the issues being discussed among English, history, and math and science educators. Some of the issues are really debates over which curriculum approach to multiculturalism should be implemented.

A Culturally Relevant Literary Curriculum[7]

Many English teachers have diversified their readings to include authors of color, and textbook publishers have facilitated that process by marketing a number of texts that respond to the American "mosaic." Given that teachers have at their disposal a wider selection of primary sources than in the past, can we feel confident that their students are receiving a culturally relevant curriculum? The answer is, "It depends." Teachers using the Additive curriculum approach don't change the basic framework of their course, and students, though gaining some new information, will probably not engage in any transformative construction of knowledge.

From current statistics on the ethnic background of teachers, we know that most English teachers are White, and, therefore, are the ones introducing authors of color to their students.[8] In *Seasons of the Witch,* Gail Griffin (1995) writes honestly about her experience teaching African-American literature as a White teacher to primarily White students. The experience has been a "crucial site of self-discovery" (p. 162). She says,

> A reading is never any better than the reader. Instead of asking Black literature to do my work for me, I'm learning to assume that it will function as a touchstone, revealing much about its White readers that I need to know to make the interventions and translations that can liberate the novel's power, to clear away some of the web of distortions, omissions, and outright lies about African Americans in which many White students are stuck, and to dislodge the ignorance of themselves on which racism depends.

Griffin speaks of the privilege Whites often assume in their ability to teach African American literature when they have "precious little genuine understanding of the cultural context [. . . .] not to mention wholly unexamined assumptions (like mine) about their competence to understand and 'right' to teach anything they happen to enjoy reading. . . . I want to begin to think about, and to teach about, African American texts [authors of color] as lenses through which we whose vision is compromised by white privilege can come to see our own whiteness more clearly" (1995, pp. 137–138).

---

[7] We discuss culturally responsive reading and writing in Chapter Six.

[8] Although our text separates pedagogy (teaching strategies) from curriculum, the separation is artificial. We recognize how interconnected instructional approaches and curriculum are.

Cheung (1994) cautions teachers not to present works by authors of color as representing an entire group. They should also make students aware of the link between politics and book publications.[9] In addition, "it is important to show that race and gender do not merely affect the literary production of women and ethnic minorities but that they shape the work of canonized authors as well. (How anxiety about White ideology informs Melville's *Moby Dick* has been brilliantly illustrated by Toni Morrison" [Cheung, 1994, p. 147]). Finally, students must be made aware of how oppressed people create culture and celebrate their heritage; too often students see marginalized groups as only victims (Griffin, 1995, p. 144; Wood, 1994, p. 229).

As our comments suggest, a culturally responsive literary curriculum is more than the introduction of non-White writers. In Chapter Six, we define reading as a process of constructing meaning and emphasize the role cultural background plays in comprehending. A culturally responsive curriculum seeks to empower students and encourages readers to assume some ownership over the text. It also diffuses the position of the White teacher as the authority in discussions.[10] The challenge for English teachers is to help facilitate these processes for their students while not colluding in their appropriating the text in ways that "[annihilate] critical racial self-awareness" (Griffin, 1995, p. 155).[11]

A Culturally Relevant Social Studies/History Curriculum

Popular debates about multicultural education usually focus on the curriculum for social studies and history classes. Anxiety centers on answers to the following three questions: Whose story should be told? Whose knowledge is more valid? What are the consequences of implementing an inclusive curriculum? We will respond briefly to each question.

Multiculturalists believe that students should be exposed to a variety of perspectives. Boyle-Baise's (1995) uses feminist standpoint theory to frame her presentation of multiple perspectives. "According to standpoint theory, there is no one stance that fully explains the 'truth' of social reality, rather there are varying standpoints or social positions from which reality is perceived . . . The search for truth requires consideration of many standpoints, including minority and majority points of view" (p. 162).[12]

This concept is consistent with the Banks (1996a) typology of knowledge types: personal/cultural, popular, mainstream academic, transformative

---

[9] Cheung refers to bell hooks's comments on the greater marketability for books depicting Black male oppression of Black females than White oppression of Blacks.

[10] Dr. M. D. Purinton is credited for reminding us of this point.

[11] A major shortcoming in our presentation is a discussion placing students of color as the students reading the texts. G. Ladson-Billings (1994. *The Dreamkeepers: Successful Teachers of African American Children.* San Francisco: Jossey-Bass) is an excellent source despite its focus on elementary grades.

[12] *Lies My Teacher Told Me* by James W. Loewen (1995) is an excellent source of transformative academic knowledge for history teachers. It is published by The New Press.

academic, and school. Personal knowledge is based on an individual's experiences in the home and immediate community; popular knowledge is primarily the information we obtain through mass media; mainstream academic knowledge derives from traditional Westerncentric sources of history and the social sciences. Transformative knowledge is defined as "the facts, concepts, paradigms, themes, and explanations that challenge mainstream academic knowledge and expand and substantially revise established canons, paradigms, theories, explanations, and research methods" (p. 9). School knowledge is what teachers find in their textbooks and curriculum guides—the implicit "facts, concepts, generalizations, and interpretations."

Thus, the multiculturalist's answer to "Whose story should be told?" is, "As many peoples as possible."

The debate over whose knowledge is more valid has been heated. George Will (1990) extols the virtue of Western civilization. "'Eurocentricity' is right, in American curricula and consciousness, because it accords with the facts of our history, and we—and Europe—are fortunate for that. . . . Saying that may be indelicate, but it has merit of being true and the truth should be the core of any curriculum" (p. 10). Ladson-Billings's comments serve as a rejoinder:

> When scholars who take a different position—one that looks at a longer continuum of Western tradition and asserts that both Africa and Asia have contributed to the European scholarship and thus are joint heirs to the western tradition (Asante, 1987; Bernal, 1987)—they are castigated and accused of sloppy scholarship. And while most conservative scholars will acknowledge the influence of Egypt on the West, there is a subtle pattern of distortion that lifts Egypt out of Africa and reconstructs the racial composition of Egyptian society. (1995, p. 331)

Multiculturalists believe that "All types of knowledge are needed." Each kind of knowledge represented in Banks's typology offers student insights into how knowledge is constructed, how it reflects the views, experiences, hopes and goals of a particular group. "Teaching students various types of knowledge can help them to better understand the perspectives of different racial, ethnic, and cultural groups as well as to develop their own versions and interpretations of issues and events" (Banks, 1996, p. 8).

Whether a social studies/history teacher decides to develop curricula at Banks's Transformative or Social Action level will depend on her or his overall learning goals. Too often textbooks, if not teachers, are used to organizing information around historical periods highlighting famous heroes, laws, and battles. An inclusive curriculum is theme and issues based. Inquiry methods of teaching are used and students have opportunities to read primary sources and historical fiction. They collect oral history and record social history. Reflection and decision-making skills are incorporated into the learning. We can see how Banks (1996b) links social studies to his Social Action level. "The main goal of the social studies is to help students acquire the knowledge, skills, and values needed to make reflective personal and public decisions so they can take action, consistent with American values—such as equality, justice, and human dignity—that will improve and reform society" (p. 231).

Multicultural critics fear that this approach will undermine students' individuality. Are we teaching students to see themselves as belonging only to an ethnic, cultural, or gender group and as victims, as well? How will national unity be preserved? Although legitimate, these questions narrow the goals of multicultural education and overlook other essential characteristics of a multicultural curriculum. Historians are quick to tell us that it is unfair to judge past events by the standards of today; however, providing students with multiple perspectives will allow for a more balanced and complex story. Students will be taught to reflect on ways in which Western ideals have not yet been met and how their participation can move us toward those ideals. Social studies and history is not just about victims, but about the "surviving and thriving" of people who have had to struggle.

By the year 2020, an estimated 46 percent of our school-age population will be students of color. "Students from diverse ethnic, cultural, and linguistic groups must have an opportunity to see themselves and their heritages represented in the curriculum if they are to ultimately see themselves as Americans. At the same time, White students will find themselves in work and living environments that are increasingly diverse. They will need perspectives and skills that prepare them to successfully encounter diversity" (Ladson-Billings, 1995, p. 332).

From a multiculturalist's perspective, an inclusive curriculum is integral to our preserving national unity!

A Culturally Relevant Math and Science Curriculum

We group these two subject areas together because of the common attributes used to describe the disciplines—objective, definitive, value neutral, and scientific, and the belief by many that math and science aren't multicultural material. However, as with our earlier example of videotaping two people talking, even math and science lenses are never neutral. Issues around implementing a multicultural curriculum in math and science classes center on redefining educational goals in this area, expanding our understanding of these fields (that is, what constitutes scientific knowing, what makes math so powerful), and who will be our future mathematicians and scientists.

Both The National Council of Teachers of Mathematics (NCTM) and the American Association for the Advancement of Science (AAAS) have made strong statements in support of multicultural education:

> Students should have numerous and varied experiences related to the cultural, historical, and scientific evolution of mathematics so that they can appreciate the role of mathematics in the development of our contemporary society. (NCTM)
>
> It is important . . . for students to become aware that women and minorities have made significant contributions in spite of the barriers put in their way by society; that the roots of science, mathematics, and technology go back to the early Egyptian, Greek, Arabic, and Chinese cultures; and that scientists bring to their work the values and prejudices of the cultures in which they live. (AAAS)
>
> *(Both cited in* Multiculturalism in Mathematics, Science, and Technology, *1993, p. 4)*

Nevertheless, math and science teachers are often skeptical about what to do after hanging up posters representing the contributions of women and people of color and completing a time-line around the room pinpointing the origins of significant mathematical and scientific concepts or discoveries. (We can see the additive curriculum approach at work here.)

A transformative approach to math and science "centers the student in the knowledge-acquisition process" (Tate, 1996, p. 194). Instruction is situated in or contextualized by students' interests, cultural knowledge, and experiences. Tate (1996) relates the story of why so many students got the wrong answer to the problem: "It costs $1.50 each way to ride the bus between home and work. The weekly pass is $16.00. Which is the better deal, paying the daily fare or buying the weekly pass?" The test question assumed that the person working only had one job and worked 5 days a week, a reality that did not fit with students' lives whose parents often had two jobs and worked weekends. Many of us may remember fussing over certain questions only to be told by our teacher "Just answer the question. Don't read so much into it." A culturally responsive curriculum allows for "reading into" the problem. A social reconstructionist (Social Action) approach would include information on how mathematics is used in our capitalist society. (See "Western Mathematics: The Secret Weapon of Cultural Imperialism" in the readings.) In addition, teachers might develop interdisciplinary units around social issues that integrate math skills.

The adjectives we used earlier to describe math and science reflect a Eurocentric perspective. The scientific method is considered the only valid tool for understanding our world (Barba, 1995). Science and math come to us as static, rule-bound procedures with little recognition of the conflict found in the discipline, "conflicts over data interpretation, credit for discovering ideas, censorship . . ." (Eva as cited in Tate, 1996, p. 196).

Inventions and discoveries are presented as the works of single individuals. "Group discoveries of knowledge are rarely acknowledged within the androcentric tradition of science [crediting one person for a discovery]" (Barba, 1995, p. 58). Native Americans, Chinese, Africans, and women scientists have long histories of group discoveries. Knowledge passed down through an oral tradition is discredited by Western science, despite the fact that yesterday's folk remedies are often tomorrow's medicines. For example, consider recent studies which "proved" that chicken soup can help make you better! Moreover, Western society has regularly assigned European names to principles developed by Asians and Africans.[13]

---

[13] "(1) the Pythagorean Theorem was developed in Babylonia 1000 years before Pythagoras, (2) Pascal's Triangle was created by Chinese and Persian mathematicians hundreds of years before Pascal, (3) a part of Fibonacci's book was copied line-for-line, diagram-for diagram from a book that abu-Kamil wrote in Egypt 400 years earlier" (Multiculturalism in Mathematics, Science, and Technology, 1993, p. 5). This text is also a valuable resource for teachers.

Pluralizing Mainstream Curriculum

Hillis (1993) provides the following example of how mainstream curriculum could be changed to reflect the additive and transformative levels.

Mainstream (Eurocentric) Model: Traditional model; materials selected from a monocultural, Eurocentric perspective. Dominant ideology taught—other views neglected.

Example: Mrs. Haines is a high school English teacher beginning a unit of American Literature. Her curriculum consists of three readings: *The Catcher in the Rye* by J. D. Salinger, a novel that explores the life of an adolescent male in the 1940s; *The Snows of Kilimanjaro* by Ernest Hemingway, a short story about a man dying on the plains of Africa; and *The Great Gatsby* by F. Scott Fitzgerald, a novel about the "American Dream." Through these readings, Mrs. Haines is able to explore with her class the problem of human suffering.

Dominant voice: white male, American society.

Ethnic Additive Model: Added content to the existing curriculum. Mainstream perspective remains fundamental but is supplemented with ethnic material.

Example: Mr. Hernandez is an English teacher in the same building as Mrs. Haines. Like his colleague, Mr. Hernandez teaches Salinger, Hemingway, and Fitzgerald. However, he feels that he needs to expand the curriculum to include divergent perspectives. To accomplish this, he adds two additional novels: *The Color Purple* by Alice Walker, an exploration of the life experiences of an African-American woman, and *The Chosen* by Chaim Potok, a story portraying the relationship between a father and son in a Jewish community. Mr. Hernandez, like Mrs. Haines, facilitates class discussion on the problem of human suffering by examining each writer's ideas.

Basic nature of the curriculum; dominant voice supplemented with isolated alternative views.

Multicultural Model: Goal is a transformation of the curriculum. Does not disregard the mainstream perspective but views it as one perspective among many.

Example: Ms. Gibbs has constructed a unit on American literature. She has decided to present a multicultural curriculum that represents the contributions of all people. Instead of limiting the unit to Salinger, Hemingway, and Fitzgerald, she alters and expands the cultural perspectives presented. Her unit consists of Fitzgerald, Walker, and Potok. Ms. Gibbs's choice of material provides the soil for rich, insightful and critical dialogue. In this way, the students are not simply taught about one perspective of American literature. Rather, in Ms. Gibbs's class the students see that American Literature consists of writers who are men and women, of different ethnic and religious backgrounds. This multicultural view provides students with the opportunity to gain a broad understanding of the richness and heterogeneity that exist in our nation and culture, in both past and present.

Allows a more comprehensive picture; allows opportunity to examine such critical concepts as culture, conflict, and identity. Transforms a Eurocentric curriculum into one of balanced ethnic and cultural perspectives. [Authors' comment: We hope that in time Ms. Gibbs would expand her readings to be even more inclusive. The addition of short stories, poetry and Latino/a, Asian, Middle Eastern, and Native Americans would be welcome.]

From Hillis, M. 1993. Multicultural Education and Curriculum Transformation *The Educational Forum,* 58(1): 50-56.

Finally, math and science teachers are concerned about the numbers of girls and students of color going into these fields. Certain math courses, sometimes taken as early as middle school, are critical to the pipeline for future math- and science-related occupations. The underachievement of girls and students of color in these fields continues, as does their underrepresentation in the fields of engineering, banking, and accounting. Based on these facts alone, many schools have decided to evaluate their math and science curricula and instructional approaches. Equally important has been their willingness to consider changes in the times and sequencing of courses so that students who need prerequisites will have access to them, their experimentation with all-girl math and science classes, and their movement away from ability tracking. (See Chapter Seven for a discussion of tracking.)

STEPS TO BECOMING A CULTURALLY RELEVANT TEACHER

It has been our intention in the first five chapters to provide the reader with a foundation for culturally relevant teaching. How the various pieces of information fit can best be demonstrated by outlining steps teachers can take as they move towards this goal. It also provides a review of the material we have been covering and a preview of what we will cover.

1. Teachers who can find someone to work with will have the built-in support needed to begin this process. It is very hard to be a change agent by yourself. Find allies to work with you—other teachers, administrators, parents, and students.
2. Do your homework. By that we mean:
   a. Develop a personal working definition of multicultural education. (Chapter One)
   b. Reflect on your own cultural/ethnic background. What lens are you using to view the world? Be aware of your positionality, and power and privilege, if applicable. (Chapter Two)
   c. Understand the role culture plays in students' learning and how conflicts between home and school culture can influence academic achievement. Be aware of your and your students' racial identity and its instructional implications. (Chapter Three)
   d. Review instructional approaches and cultural patterns of communication. Create a welcoming and affirming classroom environment. (Chapter Four)
3. Develop a culturally relevant curriculum.
   a. Evaluate the curriculum materials you have on hand.
   b. Get to know your students' backgrounds—what they know and what interests them.

c. Start slowly by setting specific goals for pluralizing your content. (You may realize that you are starting at the Additive level, but you are starting.)
d. Find transformative information that will support your learning objectives.
e. Check out books or surf the Internet for multicultural lesson plans in your content area. Evaluate materials for compatibility with your definition of multicultural education.
f. Develop curriculum materials. Have a colleague review your materials.
g. Teach and assess instruction and learning.
4. Continue the process. Periodically review your definition of multicultural education.
5. Learn about culturally relevant literacy practices. (Chapter Six)
6. Develop alternative ways of assessment. (Chapter Seven)
7. Reach out to families and communities to support your students' learning. (Chapter Eight)
8. Become knowledgeable about special education and students of color. (Chapter Nine)
9. Keep yourself informed. Listen to critics; their voices are valuable. They challenge and clarify your ideas.
10. Remember that both you and your students are learners in this process. If empowerment is a goal you have for your students, then it's your goal too.

READINGS

The readings for Chapter Five are a mixture of the practical and philosophical. "Incorporating Cultural Pluralism into Instruction" is an excerpt from an article by Branch, Goodwin, and Gaultieri. They have developed a list of twenty-five activities and assignments that correspond to Banks' curriculum frameworks. Their suggestions are useful by themselves, but also as a guide for teachers who have developed their own materials and want to check "the level" of their lessons. Pollina's article, "Gender Balance: Lessons from Girls in Science and Mathematics," reminds us of the inseparable relationship between curriculum and instruction. The successes she reports are worth noting.

A chapter on multicultural curriculum would not be complete without reference to Afrocentricity.[14] Schiele's "Afrocentricity for All" is a thoughtfully written piece that challenges readers to move beyond a Eurocentric perspective. Bishop's "Western Mathematics: The Secret Weapon of Cultural Imperialism"

---

[14] See Asante, M. K. *The Afrocentric Idea* 1987. Philadelphia: Temple University Press, for a comprehensive treatment of this topic.

investigates the impact of western mathematics on indigenous cultures. Both articles represent transformative knowledge and readers are encouraged to see their applications in the classroom.

READING 1 *Incorporating Cultural Pluralism into Instruction*
Robert Branch, Yvonne Goodwin, and Jill Gualtieri

Level I: Contributions Approach
Examples:
1. Write a poem about a personal experience with nature. Read it aloud.
2. Construct a calendar containing the birthdays of noted American women (authors, scientists, politicians, mathematicians, artists, etc.).
3. Inform students about local cultural events and encourage students to bring such announcements to class.
4. Bring in newspapers from different countries in Africa, Asia, Europe, South America, or the Pacific.
5. Create a picture file of homes from different cultures.
6. Organize a food fair. Each child brings in a dish that is traditional in their family. Decorate the table with country flags and share recipes.
7. Discuss sporting events around the world, such as the running of the bulls.
8. Discuss family ethnic backgrounds during a "Who am I?" unit. Encourage students to bring in pictures of family members.
9. Display money from a variety of countries.
10. Construct "A day in the life of. . . ."
11. Decorate the room with pictures of heroes, artists, scientists, and other famous people from various ethnic groups.
12. Arrange a Festival of Nations; have students grouped to display their cultures.
13. Celebrate Black History Month with displays, videos, observation of holidays, and discussion of heroes.

Reprinted by permission of Kappa Delta Pi International. Ideas are based on the work of J. Banks. Banks, J. A. 1989. Integrating the curriculum with ethnic content: Approaches and guidelines. In *Multicultural education: Issues and perspectives,* ed. J. A. Banks and C. A. McGee Banks, 189–207. Boston: Allyn & Bacon.

14. Create a photograph collection of notable women.
15. Introduce art work, dance, and music from other countries to your students; ask them to note similarities in technique or effect.
16. Compare elements of various folk literatures.
17. Have a buffet luncheon for the student body; students sit next to someone they don't know.
18. Celebrate Winter Solstice (or other seasonal celebrations of different cultures).
19. Create a time line of notable contributions of American women in science and technology; combine with photograph collection in item 14 above.
20. Read literature in which an adolescent from another country is portrayed; ask students to discuss similarities and differences between the fiction and their own lives.
21. In March, celebrate Women's Herstory Month and include a study of women's contributions to society.
22. Discuss different climates around the world in geography or science, perhaps related to the study of homes from different cultures (item 5 above).
23. Discuss lives and contributions of ethnic heroes.
24. Create an annotated bibliography including authors of both genders from different ethnic backgrounds.
25. Discuss the origins of names of the children in the class, including both first names and family names; note any similarities among children's names and differences in spelling.

Level II: Additive Approach

Examples:

1. Discuss how a worldwide adoption of the metric system would affect your subject area.
2. Study the origins of mathematics as it relates to topics within your subject area.
3. Assign students to write and present perspectives on topics different from those described in the textbook.
4. Discuss how import and export policies impact topics in your subject area.
5. Include words originally from other cultures on spelling lists.
6. Tell a Native American story about how an animal developed a body part to introduce a lesson in adaptation.
7. Try class cooking projects that utilize recipes from different cultures.
8. Present a mini-unit on Native American language and poetry to introduce a more "traditional" poetry unit.
9. Discuss the lives of black soldiers within Confederate and Union troops.

10. Include Australian art in art curriculum.
11. Add a literature study of ethnic minorities within American society.
12. Ask students to write a story or make a book about their own or a different culture and publish a class collection; have students record their book or story for sharing.
13. Include the Holocaust in your studies of the twentieth century.
14. Add works by authors of different cultural backgrounds when teaching reading.
15. Try a cross-cultural approach to literary themes; for example, read *Little Red Riding Hood* and *Lon Po Po,* the Chinese version.
16. Develop a unit showing the influence of other cultures on the development of American spoken language.
17. Present a whole unit on Native Americans, including pre-Columbian cultures as well as contemporary issues facing Native Americans in the United States.
18. Discuss food, clothing, and shelter found in different areas of the world.
19. Highlight the contributions of the Black Muslim movement in a social change unit.
20. Have students research an event and role play key elements of the event.
21. Have children present food menus and heritage costumes in class.
22. Distribute a list of cultural differences between the industrialized world and the developing world and discuss the reasons behind the differences.
23. Talk about how it would feel to trade positions with other cultures; for example, what it would mean if Europeans had only one month to talk about their history in an Afrocentric curriculum.
24. Describe the problems that specific immigrant groups have encountered with nativism.
25. Based on monthly themes, invite guest speakers to teach about mores from other cultures, such as rites of passage in Egypt, Japan, New Zealand, Thailand, and Botswana.

Level III: Transformation Approach

Examples:

1. Investigate the effects of sustainable development on the local people in the rain forests of Brazil and on the Brazilian government.
2. Have students research individuals historically omitted from the curriculum.
3. Contrast the reasons and patterns of migration to the United States for Italians, Asians, Slavs, and Africans.
4. Incorporate creation myths from a wide range of cultural traditions in Greek mythology.

5. Prepare a book that includes information about the children in the class based on questions they have about children living today in faraway places.
6. Ask adolescent students their opinions about communication skills, community involvement, leadership skills, workplace composition, self-concept, and conflict resolution.
7. Present a conceptual perspective of mathematics of different cultures in both ancient and present times.
8. Add literature units that include multicultural themes.
9. Explore the relevance of math or math games and their uses in other countries.
10. Engage students in social studies mapping exercises that include native or ancestral lands of students represented in the classroom.
11. Entertain arguments that Alexander Graham Bell did not invent the telephone.
12. Describe how current politics are affecting individual cultures.
13. Examine the American experience through literature written across cultural and political perspectives, such as the African-American experience in the nineteenth century, as described in *The Adventures of Huckleberry Finn*.
14. Compare civil rights problems from the 1960s to problems of today within a play written and performed by students.
15. Investigate how technology has changed the way students live.
16. Investigate how different cultural groups perceive media events.
17. Calculate and discuss the distortion of various map projections of the world. Examine one with the land area of all countries in the appropriate scale, e.g., the Peters projection.
18. Show a film about women in different countries; arrange for persons from those countries to address students, exploring points of view of different cultures.
19. Role-play a family situation in several cultures e.g., going on a date.
20. Consider alternatives to Columbus's "discovery" of America and Pizarro's and Cortes's conquests of native peoples.
21. Watch a movie of a historical event from a non-American culture and compare it to a movie on the same event made in the United States.
22. Have students participate in activities that involve developing a relationship with people from other countries, such as pen pals or international computer networking.
23. Teach students to determine universal cultural concepts such as belief in the unknown, economics, and traditions.
24. Have students discuss differences in manufacturing practices among the United States, Japan, and the European Community.

25. Discuss "westward" expansion from multiple perspectives, including that of the Native American. Emphasize the complex political motivations of this era.

Level IV: Social Action Approach

Examples:

1. After reading literature of cultural conflict such as *Othello, Heart of Darkness,* and *Apocalypse Now,* ask students to recommend ways to reduce social tension.
2. Have students form an organization to promote pluralism within school activities.
3. Have students examine different forms of media as shapers of "the norm," with particular attention paid to how cultural and gender stereotypes are perpetuated.
4. Arrange for students to telecommunicate with a school outside the United States.
5. Discuss prejudice and how prejudicial perspectives limit human development; identify ways students can act responsibly in their own lives.
6. Have students conduct research on environmental issues and formulate solutions; publish these in the school newspaper or another public forum.
7. Ask French language students to react to the same event, literature, or music (for example, the song "Telegraph Road" by Dire Straits) as French citizens of similar age; send their written reactions to a recording company.
8. Have students write an editorial on a news event, including their cultural viewpoints.
9. Produce a school play that compares the civil rights era of the 1960s with current civil rights legislation.
10. Develop a conservation strategy for a recently established national park.
11. Have students conduct a newspaper survey on current issues in state politics and write letters to the local newspaper editor reflecting their conclusions and concerns.
12. Report the desirable and undesirable effects of technology on people of the United States and other countries.
13. Invite police officials to the class to discuss problems and how students can help.
14. Sponsor a debate about whether pornography should be protected by the Constitution under freedom of speech.
15. Arrange switch-role debating from different cultural viewpoints; students first interview people from each culture to get needed information.
16. Accept community service as a class project.

17. Publish a collection of poetry written by women.
18. Have students critically analyze current textbooks for cultural bias.
19. Encourage students to rewrite certain pages of their textbooks to reflect multicultural perspectives.
20. Use class meetings to discuss how today's social issues are related to the class subject.
21. Have each student choose a Francophone country (region) and present it as if he or she were a part of it.
22. Discuss how household duties can be shared equally between men and women.
23. Teach reading by encouraging students to write or develop their own books and newsletters about issues or topics relevant to their cultural heritage.
24. Assign extra credit for class projects in which students mentor peers from cultural backgrounds different from their own.
25. Coordinate a student performance written by the students about alternative and less popular perspectives to topics related to your subject area.

READING 2: Gender Balance: Lessons from Girls in Science and Mathematics

Ann Pollina

Are we emphasizing the right issues when we talk about gender in the mathematics, science, and technology classroom? We are and we aren't.

The need for equitable treatment of girls and women is beyond dispute: women are still greatly underrepresented in fields like physical sciences, engineering, and technology. As a matter of simple justice, there should be no field of academic inquiry closed to women.

The economic necessity argument is valid as well, particularly as women make up a greater share of our work force. And if we are to remain competitive in a world market, U.S. women must be well trained in mathematical, scientific, and technological fields.

From *Educational Leadership*, Sept. 1995, Vol. 53, No. 1, pp. 30–33. Reprinted by permission of the Association for Supervision and Curriculum Development. © 1995 by ASCD. All rights reserved.

But as important as these issues are, we cannot allow them to overshadow a third critical argument: The characteristic approaches that many girls and women bring to learning and scientific inquiry are vital to science and to science education.

Feminizing Scientific Inquiry

Too often in the past, we have focused on girls as if they were the problem. If not enough girls took math and science, we asked, "What is wrong with them, and how do we fix them?" How do we make them more aggressive, more analytical, more competitive, tougher, so that they will survive in these disciplines? For years, we gave girls what researchers at Smith College have called courses in remedial masculinity. Then we wonder why many girls lack self-esteem.

Instead of trying to change the way our female students approach mathematics, science, and technology, we need to study the ways they *do* learn. We need far more than a grudging willingness to change our pedagogy to simply accommodate girls' learning styles. We must be willing to learn from them. Even more important, we must come to believe that the messages they have for us are of real value.

The work of a number of women scientists demonstrates how profoundly a woman's perspective can enrich and enliven scientific study. The unusual insights of Barbara McClintock, for example, opened a new window through which to view the study of genetics. In 1983, McClintock won the Nobel Prize for her discovery that genes can rearrange themselves on a chromosome. The direction of her research was informed by a "feeling of the organism" (Keller 1983).

Jane Goodall and Dian Fossey, who revolutionized the understanding of primate behavior, did not hypothesize and then corroborate by observing a group of apes. Instead, they took a relational approach and focused on a single ape, tracing that primate's interactions. Their work has become a model for wildlife observation.

These women's formation of questions and approaches to problems represented a new way of looking at science: They introduced feelings and relationships into the discipline.

Ten Tips from Girls' Schools

How do we begin to learn lessons from girls in the classroom? The collective wisdom of teachers from girls' schools can provide all educators with insight into the learning styles of girls. Believing girls' schools to be an untapped resource in our country's efforts to find ways to inspire young women to study mathematics, science, and technology, the National Coalition of Girls' Schools has sponsored three symposiums in these fields. Two were held at Wellesley College, in June 1991 and 1995; and a third in conjunction with the Dudley Wright Center at Tufts University in March 1993. Each brought together educators from public, independent, single-sex, and coeducational schools to examine research and proven strategies for teaching girls in the classroom.

Here are some of the messages from these workshops that I use in my high school classroom at Westover, an all-girls school in Connecticut.

1. *Connect mathematics, science, and technology to the real world.* My students remind me how much richer mathematics is when we do not divorce it from its history, its philosophical underpinnings, and its functions. Connecting any subject to the lives of real people and the good of the world is a powerful hook for girls.

Some specific exercises:

Collect examples of decorative borders from different cultures. My geometry students study transformation and isometry using these.

Establish links with other disciplines. Both the calculus and the European history classes at my school spend some time looking at the powerful effect Newton's laws of motion had on the thinking of the Enlightenment, and we share presentations between classes.

Divide a class into groups and ask them what sort of mathematics a prehistoric hunter-gatherer clan might need to survive. You will have a wonderful discussion about the nature of mathematics.

2. *Choose metaphors carefully, and have students develop their own.* For years we have asked girls to *tackle* problems and master concepts using metaphors and real-world problems more closely tied to boys' life experiences. We have taught fractions using batting averages and presented parabolas as paths of missiles and rockets. Presenting images of mathematics and science that are comfortable and meaningful for girls is more than a sign of our current preoccupation with political correctness.

In my classes, I often ask students to create their own metaphors. A teacher may gain valuable insights into students' own perceptions of learning style by asking questions such as:

"If math were a food, for me it would be _____ because _____."

My favorite response to this question was from a 9th grader entering Algebra I:

If mathematics were a food, for me it would be a sandwich because sometimes I like what's on a sandwich and sometimes I don't. When there's too much stuff on a sandwich, I can't fit it in my mouth.

After reading this, I knew what that student needed in a math classroom. This exercise is the kind of "window on students' thinking" that the National Council of Teachers of Mathematics speaks of in its *Teaching Standards* (Leiva 1993–95). Dorothy Buerk, who teaches mathematics education at Ithaca College, has developed a wealth of these exercises (Buerk 1985).

3. *Foster an atmosphere of true collaboration.* Collaborative learning has become the classroom panacea of the '90s. Although a collaborative environment *is* attractive to many girls, pulling desks into a circle does not assure a collaborative, noncompetitive experience. Small groups work for girls if all members are taught to listen and are responsible for one another's learning. Some teachers insist that a true group project is one that no single group member can complete without the group's help.

4. *Encourage girls to act as experts.* When the teacher is the touchstone for all knowledge and answers, students rarely exhibit self-confidence. Only when the group is responsible for verifying its own logic and when students critique their own work and that of their peers do they begin to see themselves as scientists. The technique of the teacher refusing to act as an expert has been used successfully for over a decade in the SummerMath program at Mount Holyoke College. The program is designed for high school girls to address underrepresentation of women in mathematics-based fields.

5. *Give girls the opportunity to be in control of technology.* The issue of the expert is also a critical one in technology. Both boys and girls need to recognize the masculine cast of the computer industry. Taking any computer magazine and comparing the number of men and women pictured or mentioned in advertisements will stimulate a good class discussion.

At Westover, the computer room is staffed and serviced by students, usually from our Women in Science and Engineering (WISE) program. These girls are responsible for basic repairs, for teaching software, and for dealing with data emergencies. At times they teach the required computer literacy course. Girls need to see other girls in control of technology. In coed settings, an all-girls computer club may allow girls to develop more computer expertise.

6. *Portray technology as a way to solve problems as well as a plaything.* Girls use computers differently than do boys. Few girls will play with a computer just because it's there; most often girls use it as a tool, not a toy, and they need to see its relevance to their lives. One way to encourage girls to play on the computer is to emphasize the networking and communication capability. Single-use work stations can be isolating; pairing girls creates a comfortable atmosphere and stimulates discussion.

When asked to create a dream machine, girls want to create things that can help make our lives better. Cornelia Brunner and Margaret Honey of the Center for Children and Technology have crafted a variety of exercises to explore technological imagination (Brunner and Honey 1990).

7. *Capitalize on girls' verbal strengths.* Strong writers and good readers—both girls and boys—have valuable tools at their disposal. Yet, often, we are not creative enough in teaching them how to use those tools to their advantage in a mathematics or science classroom.

At the Coalition of Girls' Schools' symposiums cited earlier, teachers presented a wealth of situations in which they used writing. Students were encouraged to express the logic behind their solutions in essay or picture form. Proof might be essays and well-constructed arguments with a minimum of mathematical notation.

My calculus students keep journals in which they reflect on their experiences in the course, comment on their progress, and set goals for themselves. Two possible journal questions:

You died while doing your physics homework. Write your physics obituary.

You are a spider on the wall of your room observing you doing your mathematics homework. What do you see?

8. *Experiment with testing and evaluation.* Assessment methods must reflect the research suggesting that girls do not think in linear right/wrong categories. Multiple-choice testing that requires forced choices or contains out-of-context questions and topics unrelated to real-world experiments make no use of girls' ability to synthesize, make connections, and use their practical intelligence. The work of Maryellen Harmon and her colleagues at Boston College's Center for the Study of Testing, Evaluation, and Educational Policy suggests that, for this reason, such assessments inhibit science education reform (Madaus et al. 1992).

Alternate strategies that do work well for girls include *embedded assessments*—activities in which students, usually working in groups, perform experiments, discover patterns, and arrive at hypotheses. A teacher circulates and observes student performance to evaluate them. Another form of assessment is the *circus,* where stations with reflection questions or experiments are set up around a room. Students go from station to station and are evaluated on the quality of their investigation at each.

9. *Give frequent feedback, and keep expectations high.* Because girls still may not expect to do well in mathematics and science, they tend to need more encouragement than do boys. The role of the teacher in praising students and verbalizing expectations is critical. Teachers at the girls' schools forums found it vital to provide frequent feedback in the form of homework checks, quizzes, and comments, thereby reinforcing students' belief in their control of the material. Many said they use this strategy to develop the kind of self-reliance that all students need to survive in an inquiry-based classroom.

10. *Experiment with note-taking techniques.* Girls are dutiful learners. They can get so absorbed in taking down every note and diagram that they are too preoccupied to take part in discussions. Teachers at the symposiums suggested a variety of techniques to counter this tendency, ranging from the "no note taking allowed" classroom to handing out copies of lecture notes or having them available on the computer. My algebra and geometry students take notes on reading material before coming to class. Most teachers at the symposiums included some standard note-taking situations so that students could learn this important skill.

Single-Gender versus Coed Settings

The number of single-gender experiments in schools from New Hampshire to California bears witness to our interest in equity and our willingness to change. Those experiments are also steeped in controversy, and for good reason. If the purpose of such experiments is to divide girls from boys because girls can't compete in a "real" mathematics or science classroom, then our experiments, by conveying this message to girls, can do infinite harm. But if we begin these experiments believing that our female students have something to teach us, then what goes on in such a classroom can be more subtle and powerful than the absence of boys: it can be the empowerment of girls.

A recent, well-publicized experiment at the Illinois Mathematics and Science Academy in Aurora illustrates this point dramatically. In 1993, the academy, an experimental, residential school serving gifted and talented students, offered an all-girls' section on mechanics as part of a yearlong calculus-based physics course. David Workman, the physics teacher involved, did not simply import his usual classroom methods, but was willing to learn from the young women. He found some approaches successful—collaborative processes, hands-on experimentation, connection of abstract concepts with practical application—and he made these the cornerstone of his class. Then—and this is most vital—he tried to import these methods into his coed setting.

Workman made it clear to the girls that there was nothing wrong with the way they related to physics or to the physical world. His powerful message:

> I'm not just doing these things because you are incapable of learning physics the 'right way'; I am using the teaching methods that appeal to you because they are valid and important methods of scientific inquiry.

A report on the experimental section (Dagenais et al. 1994) showed it mirrored much of the atmosphere of all-girls' classrooms that other academy teachers describe: a spirit of co-learning, with both teacher and students feeling free to ask questions, admit mistakes, take risks, express confusion, and so on; a profound sense of responsibility for one's own learning and that of others; and a special rapport between and among the teacher and the students.

He Said, She Said

Workman's initial efforts to replicate this collaborative atmosphere in his coeducational classes was foiled: many boys tended to blurt out answers to questions posed to the class as a whole, with predictable results. The other students were suddenly diverted from collective problem solving and inquiry to an explain-the-answer-to-me mode. "In this environment," said Workman, "all except the boldest and fastest hesitate to be open, ask questions, and take risks."

To get around this problem, Workman has his students write down answers rather than speak them. Then, moving from table to table, he confirms whether an answer is right or whether the student or group of students needs to work through the problem again.

These difficulties notwithstanding, the single-gender experiment has already helped to level the playing field. Last year, for example, girls performed on a par with their male peers (in prior years their performance declined relative to boys' as the semester went on); more girls enrolled in and successfully completed the yearlong physics course than ever before; and girls in the single-gender section gained more self-confidence than did those in coeducational sections.

Workman and his colleagues plan to further analyze the results of the experiment. "We're going to take what we learned and think harder about how we can preserve the strengths of both male and female modes of learning in mixed classes in order to benefit everyone," he said.

In single-gender class experiments, the culture that surrounds a class is as vital as teaching itself. If we are willing to stop trying to change girls and ready to let a feminine approach to science inform our pedagogy, we may see some exciting results for boys and girls and for science and technology.

References

Brunner, C., and M. Honey. (1990). "Hampton Hills Gazette—An Instrument for Evaluating Technological Imagination." New York: Center for Children and Technology.

Buerk, D. (1985). "The Voices of Women Making Meaning in Mathematics." *Journal of Education* 167: 3.

Dagenais, R., E. Moyer, D. Musial, M. Sloan, L. Torp, and M. Workman. (December 1994). "The Calculus-Based Physics Exploratory Study Summary Report." Aurora: Illinois Mathematics and Science Academy.

Keller, E. F. (1983). *A Feeling for the Organism.* New York: W.H. Freeman and Co.

Leiva, M. A., series ed. (1993–1995). *Curriculum and Evaluation Standards for School Mathematics.* Reston, Va.: The National Council of Teachers of Mathematics.

Madaus, G. F., M. M. West, M. C. Harmon, R.G. Lomax, and K. A. Viator. (1992). *The Influence of Testing on Teaching Math and Science in Grades 4–12.* Boston: Center for the Study of Testing, Evaluation, and Educational Policy, Boston College.

READING 3

Afrocentricity for All

Jerome H. Schiele

In recent years, the concept of Afrocentricity has been used to convey several meanings. One consequence of this is that the higher education community has received a distorted conception of Afrocentricity, which has diminished Afrocentricity's true meaning. The objective of this discussion is to clear up some of the misunderstanding about Afrocentricity by offering it as an instrument for societal and human transformation for all.

Afrocentricity, or Afrocentrism, has probably received the greatest attention in primary and secondary education. There, Afrocentricity has been mostly associated with the exposure of African-American children to the historical accomplishments of people of African descent. Known as the curriculum of inclusion, the integration of Afrocentric content in primary and secondary schools is predicated on the assumption that the academic performance of

---

Reprinted by permission of Cox, Matthews & Associates, Inc.

African-American children will improve if they have knowledge of the past accomplishments of their ancestors. Another prevailing view in the popular literature is that Afrocentricity is a new Black nationalist movement that promotes racial separation and exposes white racism. This form of Black nationalism is said to have emerged because of the disenchantment of African Americans with the post civil rights era, that is, with the perceived failure of civil rights legislation and philosophy to ameliorate the economic, social, and psychological status of African-Americans.

Although Afrocentricity is significantly related to African history, and can be said to have emanated from Black nationalist thought, it has been more appropriately described as a philosophical model predicated on traditional African philosophical assumptions. Indeed, Afrocentricity is one of three traditional philosophical models of this world (the others are the Eurocentric and Asiancentric models). Like the other models, Afrocentricity has a distinct set of cosmological, ontological, epistemological and axiological attributes. In other words, Afrocentricity is one means through which people can understand phenomena and define reality—a way through which the world, and all its elements, can be viewed.

Cosmologically, Afrocentricity views the structure of phenomena from a perspective of interdependency. All elements of the universe, such as people, animals, inanimate objects, etc.—are viewed as one. There is no demarcation between that which is spiritual or material. All elements are as seen as functionally interconnected. Ontologically, Afrocentricity assumes that all elements of the universe have a spiritual base, that is, are created from a similar universal substance. This is precisely why the cosmological perspective of Afrocentricity assumes the interconnectedness of elements. Thus, phrases such as "oneness with nature," "human-nature unity" and "harmony with nature" have been used to describe the cosmological character of Afrocentricity.

Epistemologically, the Afrocentric perspective places just as much emphasis on an affective way of knowing as it does on a cognitive way of knowing. Knowing (i.e., understanding events and reality) through emotion or feeling is deemed valid and important from an Afrocentric viewpoint. Axiologically, Afrocentricity significantly underscores the value of interpersonal relationships. This "person to person" emphasis fosters a human-centered orientation to life rather than an object or material orientation. Therefore, from an Afrocentric perspective, the value placed on material objects does not override the value in maintaining and strengthening interpersonal relations.

Though Afrocentricity is predicated on traditional African philosophical assumptions, and has special meaning for people of African descent, it is erroneous to believe that people of African descent are the only beneficiaries of Afrocentricity. Its philosophical attributes can and should be adopted by any group or person. Indeed, one of the primary reasons underlying the promotion of Afrocentricity over Eurocentricity, which is the philosophical foundation of western societies, is that Afrocentricity is viewed as a more humanistic philosophical model. This is because of Afrocentricity's emphasis on spirituality, which is more likely to encourage higher standards of morality and compassion than the Eurocentric model's emphasis on domination and control, materialism and individualism. It cannot be overstated that the major criticism levied against Eurocentricity is not that it is a "white" or European system but that it is an unlikely philosophical model to facilitate human and societal transformation towards spiritual, moral and humanistic ends.

It is because of the latter reason that Afrocentricity is offered to all racial and ethnic groups, especially those interested in promoting spirituality and humanism. Indeed, Afrocentricity provides hope for a decadent society, like the United States, that is deteriorating socially and morally. As noted psychologist Na'im Akbar has observed, a society that has abundant technology but at the same time is socially and morally decadent cannot be considered an advanced civilization. The adoption of the Afrocentric philosophical model can assist the United States in offsetting its emphasis on material affluence. This would truly help engender advanced civilization.

With its emphasis on a spiritual and collective understanding of human beings, Afrocentricity also offers a way for people to understand and highlight the similarities among all racial and ethnic groups. A major premise of Afrocentricity is that all people, regardless of racial and ethnic differences, are spiritual beings, created from a similar, universal source.

Finally, Afrocentricity provides a mode through which all people can liberate themselves from the restricted conceptions of human beings found in the Eurocentric philosophical model. When human beings are conceived primarily as material and physical beings, as is found in the Eurocentric model, considerable understanding about the extensive capabilities of people is precluded. In this regard, Afrocentricity's greatest advantage is that it offers a means through which all people can better realize their unlimited and vast potential as human beings.

READING 4

Western Mathematics: The Secret Weapon of Cultural Imperialism

Alan J. Bishop

Of all the school subjects which were imposed on indigenous pupils in the colonial schools, arguably the one which could have been considered the least culturally loaded was mathematics. Even today, the belief prevails. Whereas educational arguments have taken place over which language(s) should be

Reprinted by permission of the Institute of Race Relations.

taught, what history or religion, and whether, for example, "French civilisation" is an appropriate school subject for pupils living thousands of kilometres from France, mathematics has somehow always been felt to be universal and, therefore, culture-free. It had in colonial times, and for most people it continues to have today, the status of a culturally neutral phenomenon in the otherwise turbulent waters of education and imperialism.

This article challenges that myth, and places what many now call "western mathematics" in its rightful position in the arguments—namely, as one of the most powerful weapons in the imposition of western culture.

Up to fifteen years or so ago, the conventional wisdom was that mathematics was culture-free knowledge. After all, the popular argument went, two twos are four, a negative number times a negative number gives a positive number, and all triangles have angles which add up to 180 degrees. These are true statements the world over. They have universal validity. Surely, therefore, it follows that mathematics must be free from the influence of any culture?

There is no doubt that mathematical truths like those are universal. They are valid everywhere, because of their intentionally abstract and general nature. So, it doesn't matter where you are, if you draw a flat triangle, measure all the angles with a protractor, and add the degrees together, the total will always be approximately 180 degrees. (The "approximate" nature is only due to the imperfections of drawing and measuring—if you were able to draw the ideal and perfect triangle, then the total would be exactly 180 degrees!) Because mathematical truths like these are abstractions from the real world, they are necessarily context-free and universal.

But where do "degrees" come from? Why is the total 180? Why not 200, or 100? Indeed, why are we interested in triangles and their properties at all? The answer to all these questions is, essentially, "because some people determined that it should be that way." Mathematical ideas, like any other ideas, are humanly constructed. They have a cultural history.

The anthropological literature demonstrates for all who wish to see it that the mathematics which most people learn in contemporary schools is not the only mathematics that exists. For example, we are now aware of the fact that many different counting systems exist in the world. In Papua New Guinea, Lean has documented nearly 600 (there are more than 750 languages there) containing various cycles of numbers, not all base ten.[1] As well as finger counting, there is documented use of body counting, where one points to a part of the body and uses the name of that part as the number. Numbers are also recorded in knotted strings, carved on wooden tablets or on rocks, and beads are used, as well as many different written systems of numerals.[2] The richness is both fascinating and provocative for anyone imagining initially that theirs is the only system of counting and recording numbers.

Nor only is it in number that we find interesting differences. The conception of space which underlies Euclidean geometry is also only one conception—it relies particularly on the "atomistic" and object-oriented ideas of points, lines, planes, and solids. Other conceptions exist, such as that of the Navajos where space is neither subdivided nor objectified, and where everything is in motion.³ Perhaps even more fundamentally, we are more aware of the forms of classification which are different from western hierarchical systems—Lancy, again in Papua New Guinea, identified what he referred to as "edge-classification," which is more linear than hierarchical.⁴ The language and logic of the Indo-European group have developed layers of abstract terms within the hierarchical classification matrix, but this has not happened in all language groups, resulting in different logics and in different ways of relating phenomena.

Facts like these challenge fundamental assumptions and long-held beliefs about mathematics. Recognising symbolisations of alternative arithmetics, geometries, and logics implies that we should, therefore, raise the question of whether alternative mathematical systems exist. Some would argue⁵ that facts like those above already demonstrate the existence of what they call "ethno-mathematics," a more localised and specific set of mathematical ideas which may not aim to be as general nor as systematised as "mainstream" mathematics. Clearly, it is now possible to put forward the thesis that all cultures have generated mathematical ideas, just as all cultures have generated language, religion, morals, customs and kinship systems. Mathematics is now starting to be understood as a pan-cultural phenomenon.⁶

We must, therefore, henceforth take much more care with our labels. We cannot now talk about "mathematics" without being more specific, unless we are referring to the generic form (like language, religion, etc.). The particular kind of mathematics which is now the internationalised subject most of us recognise is a product of a cultural history, and in the last three centuries of that history, it was developing as part of western European culture (if that is a well-defined term). That is why the title of this article refers to "western mathematics." In a sense, that term is also inappropriate, since many cultures have contributed to this knowledge and there are many practising mathematicians all over the world who would object to being thought of as western cultural researchers developing a part of western culture. Indeed, the history of western mathematics is itself being rewritten at present as more evidence comes to light, but more of that later. Nevertheless, in my view, it is thoroughly appropriate to identify "western mathematics," since it was western culture, and more specifically western European culture, which played such a powerful role in achieving the goals of imperialism.⁷

There seem to have been three major mediating agents in the process of cultural invasion in colonised countries by western mathematics: trade, administration, and education.⁸ Regarding trade and the commercial field generally, this is clearly the area where measures, units, numbers, currency, and some geometric notions were employed. More specifically, it would have been western ideas of length, area, volume, weight, time, and money which would have been imposed on the indigenous societies.

If there was any knowledge of indigenous measure systems at all, or even currency units, there is little reference made to them in the literature. Researchers have only fairly recently begun to document this area, and it is perfectly clear that many indigenous systems did (and do) exist.[9] Nevertheless, the units used in trade were (and still are) almost entirely western, and those local units which have survived are either becoming more and more westernised or are in the process of dying out. In some cases, there were simply no local units for measuring the kinds of quantities needed to be used by the western traders—as Jones' informant showed in Papua New Guinea in a recent investigation: "It could be said [that two gardens are equal in area] but it would always be debated" and "There is no way of comparing the volume of rock with the volume of water, there being no reason for it."[10]

The second way in which western mathematics would have impinged on other cultures is through the mechanisms of administration and government. In particular, the numbers and computations necessary for keeping track of large numbers of people and commodities would have necessitated western numerical procedures being used in most cases. According to the research evidence, the vast majority of counting systems in the world are and were finite and limited in nature, and with a variety of different numerical bases. There is certainly evidence of some systems being able to handle large numbers in sophisticated ways if the societal needs are there (e.g., by the Igbo people and the Incas),[11] but though these, and presumably others, did exist, there was little evidence that they were even known by the colonial administrators, let alone encouraged or used. The one exception would have been the use by the Chinese, and by other people, of the abacus in certain colonies, which clearly was felt to be a sufficiently sophisticated system for administrative purposes.[12]

The other aspect to be imposed through administration would have been the language of hierarchy, through structuring people and their functions. It may seem a relatively insignificant example to choose, but it is very difficult for anyone used to the western obsession with naming and classification to imagine that there exist other ways of conceptualising and using language. The research of Lancy and of Philp have made us aware of this. As Lancy, for example, says:

> In Britain, parents teach their children that the most important function of language is reference. They prepare their children for a society that places a premium on knowing the names and classes of things. The Kaluli of the Southern Highlands of PNG invest—if anything—more time in teaching language to their children than do the British, but their aim is very different. The Kaluli child learns that the most important language functions are expressive; specifically, that the competent language user is one who can use speech to manipulate and control the behavior of others.

Any enforced use of other language structures is thus likely to cause difficulties and confusion,[13] but, more than that, any western European colonial governmental and administrative activity which concerned system, structure and the role of personnel would inevitably, and perhaps unwittingly, have imposed a western European mode of linguistic and logical classification.

The third and major medium for cultural invasion was education, which played such a critical role in promoting western mathematical ideas and, thereby, western culture. In most colonial societies, the imposed education functioned at two levels, mirroring what existed in the European country concerned. The first level, that of elementary education, developed hardly at all in the early colonial period. In India for example, the "filtering down" principle, whereby it was assumed that it was only necessary to educate the elite few and the knowledge would somehow "filter down to the masses," was paramount. In some of the mission schools and in the latter years of colonialism when elementary schooling began to be taken more seriously, it was, of course, the European content which dominated. The need was felt to educate the indigenous people only in order to enable them to function adequately in the European-dominated trade, commercial and administrative structures which had been established. Mathematically, the only content of any significance was arithmetic with its related applications.[14]

Of much more interest to the theme of this essay is the secondary education given to the elite few in the colonised countries. In India and Africa, schools and colleges were established which, in their education, mirrored once again their comparable institutions in the "home" country.[15] The fact that the education differed in French-controlled institutions from their English counterparts merely reflected the differences existing in the current philosophies of French and English education.

At best, the mathematics curriculum of some of the schools was just laughably and pathetically inappropriate. Mmari quotes some typical problems from Tanzanian colonial textbooks (recommended for use in schools by British colonial education officers)[16]:

> If a cricketer scores altogether r runs in x innings, n times not out, his average is $r/(x-n)$ runs. Find his average if he scores 204 runs in 15 innings, 3 times not out.
>
> Reduce 207,042 farthings; 89,761 half-pence; 5,708 1/2 shillings to £.s.d.
>
> The escalator at the Holborn tube station is 156 feet long and makes the ascent in 65 seconds. Find the speed in miles per hour.

But then, "appropriateness" was entirely judged in terms of cultural transmission.

At worst, the mathematics curriculum was abstract, irrelevant, selective and elitist—as indeed it was in Europe—governed by structures like the Cambridge Overseas Certificate, and culturally laden to a very high degree.[17] It was part of a deliberate strategy of acculturation—intentional in its efforts to instruction "the best of the West," and convinced of its superiority to any indigenous mathematical systems and culture. As it was essentially a university-preparatory education, the aspirations of the students were towards attending western universities. They were educated away from their culture and away from their society. For example, Watson quotes Wilkinson, criticising Malayan education at the turn of the century in these terms: "unpractical, to make the people litigious, to inspire a distaste for manual and technical work and to create a class of literary malcontents, useless to their communities and a source of trouble to the Empire."[18] Mathematics and science—subjects which, in fact, could so easily have made connections with the indigenous culture and environment, and which could have been made relevant to the needs of the indigenous society—were just not thought of in those terms, despite many of the teachers' good intentions. They were seen merely as two of the pillars of western culture, significant as part of a cultured person's education in the nineteenth and early twentieth centuries.[19]

So, it is clear that through the three media of trade, administration, and education, the symbolisations and structures of western mathematics would have been imposed on the indigenous cultures just as significantly as were those linguistic symbolisations and structures of English, French, Dutch or whichever was the European language of the particular dominant colonial power in the country.

However, also like a language, the particular symbolisations used were, in a way, the least significant aspect of mathematics. Of far more importance, particularly in cultural terms, were the values which the symbolisations carried with them. Of course, it goes without saying that it was also conventional wisdom that mathematics was value free. How could it have values if it was universal and culture free? We now know better, and an analysis of the historical, anthropological, and cross-cultural literatures suggests that there are four clusters of values which are associated with western European mathematics, and which must have had a tremendous impact on the indigenous cultures.

First, there is the area of rationalism, which is at the very heart of western mathematics. If one had to choose a single value and attribute which has guaranteed the power and authority of mathematics within western culture, it is rationalism. As Kline says: "In its broadest aspect mathematics is a spirit, the spirit of rationality. It is this spirit that challenges, stimulates, invigorates, and drives human minds to exercise themselves to the fullest."[20] With its focus on deductive reasoning and logic, it poured scorn on mere trial and error practices, traditional wisdom and witchcraft. So, consider this quotation, from Gay and Cole in Liberia:

> A Kpelle college student accepted *all* the following statements: (1) the Bible is literally true, thus all living things were created in the six days described in Genesis; (2) the Bible is a book like other books, written by relatively primitive peoples over a long period of time and contains contradiction and error; (3) all living things have gradually evolved over millions of years from primitive matter; (4) a "spirit" tree in a nearby village had been cut down, had put itself back together, and had grown to full size again in one day. He had learned these statements from this Fundamentalist pastor, his college bible course, his zoology course, and the still-pervasive animist culture. He accepted all, because all were sanctioned by authorities to which he feels he must pay respect.[21]

One can understand Gay and Cole's discomfort at this revelation, but one can also understand how much more confusing it must have been to the student to learn that anything which was not "rational" in the western sense was not to be trusted.

Second, a complementary set of values associated with western mathematics can be termed objectism, a way of perceiving the world as if it were composed of discrete objects, able to be removed and abstracted, so to speak, from their context. To decontextualise, in order to be able to generalise, is at the heart of western mathematics and science; but if your culture encourages you to believe, instead, that everything belongs and exists in its relationship with everything else, then removing it from its context makes it literally meaningless. In early Greek civilisation, there was also a deep controversy over "object" or "process" as the fundamental core of being. Heraclitos, in 600–500 BC, argued that the essential feature of phenomena is that they are always in flux, always moving and always changing. Democritus, and the Pythagoreans, preferred the world-view of "atoms," which eventually was to prevail and develop within western mathematics and science.[22]

Horton sees objectism in another light. He compares this view with what he sees as the preferred African use of personal idiom as explanation. He argues that this has developed for the traditional African the sense that the personal and social "world" is knowable, whereas the impersonal and the "world of things" is essentially unknowable. The opposite tendency holds for the westerner. Horton's argument proceeds as follows:

> In complex, rapidly changing industrial societies the human scene is in flux. Order, regularity, predictability, simplicity, all these seem lamentably absent. It is in the world of inanimate things that such qualities are most readily seen. This is why many people can find themselves less at home with their fellow men than with things. And this too, I suggest, is why the mind in quest of explanatory analogies turns most readily to the inanimate. In the traditional societies of Africa, we find the situation reversed. The human scene is the locus *par excellence* of order, predictability, regularity. In the world of the inanimate [by which he means "natural" rather than man-made], these qualities are far less evident. Here being less at home with people than with things is unimaginable. And here, the mind in quest of explanatory analogies turns naturally to people and their relation.[23]

We can see, therefore, that with both rationalism and objectism as core values, western mathematics presents a dehumanised, objectified, ideological world-view which will emerge necessarily through mathematics teaching of the traditional colonial kind.

A third set of values concerns the power and control aspect of western mathematics. Mathematical ideas are used either as directly applicable concepts and techniques, or indirectly through science and technology, as ways to control the physical and social environment. As Schaaf says in relation to the history of mathematics: "The spirit of the nineteenth and twentieth centuries, is typified by man's increasing mastery over his physical environment."[24] So, using numbers and measurements in trade, industry, commerce and administration would all have emphasised the power and control values of mathematics. It was (and still is) so clearly useful knowledge, powerful knowledge, and it seduced the majority of peoples who came into contact with it.

However, a complementary set of values, which is concerned with progress and change, has also grown and developed in order to gain yet more control over one's environment. An awareness of the values of control allied to the rational analysis of problems feeds a complementary value of rational progress, and so there is a concern to question, to doubt and to enquire into alternatives. Horton again points to this value when he contrasts western scientific ideas with traditional African values: "In traditional cultures there is no developed awareness of alternatives to the established body of theoretical tenets; whereas in scientifically oriented cultures such an awareness is highly developed."[25] Whether that conclusion has validity or not, there can be no doubting the unsettling effect of an elitist education which was preaching "control" and "progress" in traditional societies, nor could one imagine that these values were what was needed by the indigenous population in the countries concerned.

Certainly, even if progress were sought by the indigenous population, which itself is not necessarily obvious, what was offered was a westernised, industrialised, and product-oriented version of progress, which seemed only to reinforce the disparity between progressive, dynamic and aggressive western European imperialists and traditional, stable and non proselytising colonised peoples. Mathematically inspired progress through technology and science was clearly one of the reasons why the colonial powers had progressed as far as they had, and that is why mathematics was such a significant tool in the cultural kitbag of the imperialists.

In total, then, these values amount to a mathematico-technological cultural force, which is what indeed the imperialist powers generally represented. Mathematics with its clear rationalism, and cold logic, its precision, its so-called "objective" facts (seemingly culture and value free), its lack of human frailty, its power to predict and to control, its encouragement to challenge and to question, and its thrust towards yet more secure knowledge, was a most powerful weapon indeed. When allied to the use of technology, to the development of industry and commerce through scientific applications and to the increasing utility of tangible, commercial products, its status was felt to be indisputable.

From those colonial times through to today, the power of this mathematico-technological culture has grown apace—so much so that western mathematics is taught nowadays in every country in the world. Once again, it is mainly taught with the assumptions of universality and cultural neutrality. From colonialism through to neo-colonialism, the cultural imperialism of western mathematics has yet to be fully realised and understood. Gradually, greater understanding of its impact is being acquired, but one must wonder whether its all-pervading influence is now out of control.

As awareness of the cultural nature and influence of western mathematics is spreading and developing, so various levels of responses can also be seen. At the first level, there is an increasing interest in the study of ethno-mathematics, through both analyses of the anthropological literature and investigations in real-life situations. Whilst recognising that many now-important ideas may well not have seemed to be so by early generations of anthropologists, there is, nevertheless, still a great deal of information to be gleaned from the existing literature.

This kind of literature analysis is, of course, aided by theoretical structures which help us conceptualise just what mathematics, as the pan-cultural phenomenon, might be. It is reiterated that mathematics is a cultural product—a symbolic technology, developed through engaging in various environmental activities.[26] Six universal activities may be identified, by which I mean that no cultural group has been documented which does not appear to carry out these activities in some form.[27] They are

- Counting: the use of a systematic way to compare and order discrete objects. It may involve body or finger counting, tallying, or using objects or string to record, or special number names. Calculation can also be done with the numbers, with magical and predictive properties associated with some of them.
- Locating: exploring one's spatial environment, and conceptualising and symbolising that environment, with models, maps, drawings and other devices. This is the aspect of geometry where orientation, navigation, astronomy, and geography play a strong role.
- Measuring: quantifying qualities like length and weight, for the purposes of comparing and ordering objects. Measuring is usually used where phenomena cannot be counted (e.g., water, rice), but money is also a unit of measure of economic worth.
- Designing: creating a shape or a design for an object or for any part of one's spatial environment. It may involve making the object as a copyable "template," or drawing it in some conventionalised way. The object can be designed for technological or spiritual uses and "shape" is a fundamental geometrical concept.
- Playing: devising, and engaging in, games and pastimes with more or less formalised rules that all players must abide by. Games frequently model a significant aspect of social reality, and often involve hypothetical reasoning.
- Explaining: finding ways to represent the relationships between phenomena. In particular, exploring the "patterns" of number, location, measure, and design, which create an "inner world" of mathematical relationships which model, and thereby explain, the outer world of reality.[28]

We now have extensive documentary evidence from many different cultures confirming the existence of all of these activities, and this structure is one which is enabling more detailed searches to be undertaken in the research literature. Ethno-mathematics is, however, still not a well-defined term,[29] and, indeed, in view of the ideas and data we now have, perhaps it would be better not to use that term but rather to be more precise about which, and whose, mathematics one is referring to in any context. Moreover, the search should also focus on the values aspect as well. In considering the problems and issues of culture-conflict in education, it is all too easy to remain at the level of symbolisations and language, whereas of much more significance educationally are the differences in cultural values which may exist. They need serious attention in future research.

At the second level, there is a response in many developing countries and former colonies which is aimed at creating a greater awareness of one's own culture. Cultural rebirth or reawakening is a recognised goal of the educational process in several countries. Gerdes, in Mozambique, is a mathematics educator who has done a great deal of work in this area. He seeks not only to demonstrate important mathematical aspects of Mozambican society, but also to develop the process of "defreezing" the "frozen" mathematics which he uncovers. For example, with the plaiting methods used by fishermen to make their fish traps, he demonstrates significant geometric ideas which could easily be assimilated into the mathematics curriculum in order to create what he considers to be a genuine Mozambican mathematics education for the young people there.[30]

Clearly, the ideas of the first level will inform and stimulate work at this second level—another reason why ethno-mathematical research needs to be updated. This activity is not restricted to developing countries either. In Australia with the Aborigines, in North America with the Navajos and other Amerindian groups and in other countries where there exist cultural and ethnic minorities, there is a great deal of interest in discovering and developing local, folk, or indigenous mathematics which may have been lying dormant for many centuries.[31] These ideas may then help to shape a more relevant, and culturally meaningful, curriculum in the local schools.

One of the greatest ironies in this whole field is that several different cultures and societies have contributed to the development of what is called western mathematics: the Egyptians, the Chinese, the Indians, the Arabs, the Greeks, as well as the western Europeans. Yet when western cultural imperialism imposed its version of mathematics on the colonised societies, it was scarcely recognisable as anything to which these societies might have contributed. In Iran, in the early 1970s, for example, there appeared to be little awareness amongst the local mathematics educators of the massive contribution which the Muslim empire had made to the development of the mathematics which they were struggling to teach to their young people. Nowadays, with the rise of fundamentalism, there is growing and increasing awareness of both this contribution and also of an essential Islamic philosophy of education, which will shape the mathematical and scientific curricula in the fundamentalist schools.[32] We are, therefore, beginning to see the assimilation, in place of the imposition, of western mathematics into other cultures. This is a worldwide development and can only help to stimulate cultural regrowth.

The third level of response to the cultural imperialism of western mathematics, is, paradoxically, to reexamine the whole history of western mathematics itself. It is no accident that this history has been written predominantly by White, male, western European or American researchers, and there is a concern that, for example, the contribution of Black Africa has been undervalued.

Van Sertima's book *Blacks in Science* is a deliberate attack on this prejudiced view of mathematical development.[33] Various contributors to this book point to the scientific, technological, and mathematical ideas and inventions developed in Africa centuries ago, yet rarely referred to. Other contributors argue that the contribution of the Greeks to mathematics has been overemphasized; that they only consolidated and structured what had been thoroughly developed by the Babylonians and the Egyptians earlier; that Euclid worked in Alexandria and is more likely to have been African rather than Greek; that the archaeological evidence has either been ignored or misrepresented.[34]

Joseph[35] emphasises the strong role played by the Muslim empire in bringing mathematical ideas from the East to the notice of a wider people, not just in Europe. Needham's work[36] demonstrates very well the contributions which began in China and grew through India where the Muslims made contact with them. There is certainly no reason to claim that what we know as western mathematics was entirely the product of western European culture.

In my view, however, the significance of cultural values has been underestimated in much of this historical analysis so far, and that when that dimension is fully recognised, there will be a great deal more re-analysing to do. The separation of symbolisations from cultural values is difficult to achieve, but we know how even the language of English carries different messages on both sides of the Atlantic because of the different cultural values existing there. The same symbolisations of mathematics may well have carried with them different kinds of values in different cultures in the past. Perhaps the best example of this is with India. Indian mathematics, along with that of other eastern cultural groups, had strong religious and spiritual values associated with it. Western mathematics on the other hand, was identified strongly with western science, with dehumanised, so-called "objective" knowledge, and with empirical and rational interpretations of natural phenomena. Yet, in most Indian schools today, it is western mathematics which is taught and it is the western values that are thereby fostered. Of course, many of the symbolisations (numbers, etc.) are the bases for our own symbolisations, and many of the ideas of arithmetic were developed by the Hindus. The values, though, are markedly different. Some Indian mathematics educators[37] are now arguing for developments to redress the balance, although a further irony is that there may well be more interest in this kind of educational development among the Indian community in, for example, England than in India, where the educational conflicts are apparently felt less deeply. Nevertheless, the relationship between values and symbolisations is likely to be a promising area for further research.

I began by describing the myth of western mathematics' cultural neutrality. Increasingly, modern evidence serves to destroy this naive belief. Nevertheless the belief in that myth has had, and continues to have, powerful implications. Those implications relate to education, to national developments and to a continuation of cultural imperialism. Indeed, it is not too sweeping to state that most of the modern world has accepted western mathematics, values included, as a fundamental part of this education. In Hungary in 1988 the Sixth International

Congress on Mathematics Education (which is held every four years) was attended by around 3,000 mathematics educators. They came from every country in the world that was able to support participation, and those that were not there will now be purchasing copies of the proceedings and the reports. Such is the magnet of western mathematics and its principal acolyte, western mathematics education. Clearly, many societies have recognised the benefits to their peoples of adopting western mathematics, science, and technology.

However, taking a broader view, one must ask: Should there not be more resistance to this cultural hegemony? Indeed, there is some awareness to build on. In addition to the three major responses mentioned earlier, in recent years, as the kinds of evidence and issues referred to in this article have become more widely disseminated and more seriously discussed, so there has grown a recognition of the need to reflect these concerns at such congresses. At the Hungary conference, one whole day was given over to the theme of "Mathematics, education, and society" on which many papers were presented, discussion stimulated and awareness kindled. Included in that day's programme were topics central to the issues discussed here.[38]

Resistance is growing, critical debate is informing theoretical development, and research is increasing, particularly in educational situations where culture-conflict is recognised. The secret weapon is secret no longer.

Notes

1. G.A. Lean, *Counting Systems of Papua New Guinea* (Papua New Guinea, 1986); C. Zaslavsky, *Africa Counts* (Boston, 1973); M.P. Closs, *Native American Mathematics* (Austin, Texas, 1986).

2. K. Menninger, *Number Words and Number Symbols: A Cultural History of Numbers* (Cambridge, Mass, 1969).

3. R. Pinxten, I. van Dooren and F. Harvey, *The Anthropology of Space* (University of Pennsylvania Press, 1983).

4. D.F. Lancy, *Cross-cultural Studies in Cognition and Mathematics* (New York, 1983); H. Philp, "Mathematical education in developing countries" in A.G. Howson (ed.), *Development in Mathematical Education* (Cambridge, 1973).

5. See, for example, U. d'Ambrosio "Ethnomathematics and its place in the history and pedagogy of mathematics," *For the Learning of Mathematics* (1985), and P. Gerdes, "How to recognise hidden geometrical thinking: a contribution to the development of anthropological mathematics," *For the Learning of Mathematics* (1986).

6. "Pan-cultural" is used to convey the sense that all cultures engage in mathematical activities.

7. In the late nineteenth century and early twentieth century, one can also recognise the increasing contribution of American and Australian influences, which nevertheless stem from the western European cultural tradition.

8. A fourth candidate would be "technology." Its influence is clear: see, for example, D.R. Headrick's *The Tools of Empire* (Oxford, 1981); but what is rather less clear is the mathematical relationship with technology. As science and mathematics developed in their power and control, they undoubtedly influenced technology, particularly later in the imperialist era.

9. See Zaslavsky, op. cit. and Menninger, op. cit.

10 J. Jones, *Cognitive Studies with Students in Papua New Guinea* (Papua New Guinea, 1974).

11 See Ascher, op. cit.

12 Even today, the abacus has survived the calculator invasion and is still in prolific use in the countries of Asia.

13 See P.W. Bridgman, "Quo Vadis," *Daedalus* (No. 87, 1958), and L.C.S. Dawe, "The influence of a bilingual child's first language competence on reasoning in mathematics" (unpublished PhD thesis, University of Cambridge, 1982). As Awoniyi points out: "A foreign language is more than a different set of words for the same ideas; it is a new and strange way of looking at things, an unfamiliar grouping of ideas," T.A. Awoniyi, "Yoruba language and the schools system; a study in colonial language policy in Nigeria 1882–1952," *The International Journal of African Historical Studies* (Vol. VIII, 1975).

14 In the main, of course, there was felt to be little need for anything beyond reading, in order to understand either the bible translated into a local language, or simple work instructions. In India, after the orientalist phase, English was the language used predominantly in the schools and the acquisition of English became *the* goal of education to the exclusion of anything else.

15 For example, Budo College, Uganda, the Alliance High School, Kenya, Elphinstone College, India. See M. Carnoy, *Education as Cultural Imperialism* (Longman, 1974) and R.J. Njoroge and G.A. Bennaars, *Philosophy and Education in Africa* (Nairobi, 1986).

16 G.R.V. Mmari, "The United Republic of Tanzania: mathematics for social transformation" in F.J. Swetz (ed.) *Socialist Mathematics Education* (Southampton, PA 1978). He also says: "Textbooks of the period in question indicate the use of foreign units of measure of length, weight, capacity, volume, and currency which support this theory of direct interaction between business practices and the cultural background of the then dominant existing business community."

17 P. Damerow says "The transfer of the European mathematics curriculum to developing countries was closely associated with the establishment of schools for the elite by colonial administrations. Under these circumstances it seemed natural to simply copy European patterns," "Individual development and cultural evolution of arithmetical thinking" in S. Strauss (ed.), *Ontogeny and Historical Development* (Pennsylvania, 1986).

18 J.K.P. Watson *Education in the Third World* (London, 1982).

19 Indeed, there was no great attempt in the "home" countries themselves to make science and mathematics relevant either.

20 M. Kline, *Mathematics in Western Culture* (London, 1972).

21 J. Gay and M. Cole, *The New Mathematics in an Old Culture* (New York, 1967).

22 See C.A. Ronan, *The Cambridge Illustrated History of the World's Science* (Cambridge Press, 1983), and C.H. Waddington, *Tools for Thought* (St Albans, 1977), for a recent analysis.

23 R. Horton, "African traditional thought and Western science" *Africa*, (Vol XXXVII, 1967), also in M.F.F. Young (ed.), *Knowledge and Control* (London, 1971).

24 W.L. Schaaf, *Our Mathematical Heritage* (New York, 1963).

25 Horton, op. cit.

26 For a fuller examination of these ideas, see A.J. Bishop, *Mathematical Enculturation: a cultural perspective on mathematics education* (Dordrecht, Holland, 1988).

27 The caveat may perhaps seem unnecessary, but to a mathematician the word "universal" does cause certain problems. For further discussion of this general issue,

see G.P. Murdoch, "The common denominator of cultures" in R. Linton (ed.), *The Science of Man in the World Crisis* (New York, 1945).

28 In order for mathematical knowledge to develop, it is necessary for these activities to integrate and to interact. Without this integration, the set of activities could be argued to be pre-mathematical.

29 See d'Ambrosio op. cit. and M. Ascher and R. Ascher, "Ethnomathematics," *History of Science* (Vol. XXIV, 1986) for different perspectives. The Aschers argue specifically for ethnomathematics to be the province of "non-literate peoples," while d'Ambrosio's view encompasses all mathematical ideas not exposed by "mainstream" mathematics.

30 See Gerdes (1986) op. cit. and P. Gerdes, "On possible uses of traditional Angolan sand drawings in the mathematics classroom," *Educational Studies in Mathematics* (No. 19, 1988).

31 See P. Harris *Measurement in Tribal Aboriginal Communities* (Northern Territory Department of Education, Australia, 1980), and Closs, op. cit.

32 See S.H. Nasr, *Islamic Science: an illustrated study* (Essex, UK, 1976) and I.R. Al-Faruqi and A.D. Naseef, *Social and Natural Science: the Islamic perspective* (London, 1981).

33 I. van Sertima, *Blacks in Science* (New Brunswick, 1986).

34 For example, B. Lumpkin, "Africa in the mainstream of mathematics history," in van Sertima, op. cit.

35 G.G. Joseph, "Functions of Eurocentrism in Mathematics," *Race and Class* (Vol. XXVIII, 1987).

36 See C.A. Roman, *The Shorter Science and Civilization in China,* Vol. 2 (Cambridge, 1981).

37 See, for example, D.S. Kothari's keynote address in the *Proceedings of the Asian Regional Seminar of the Commonwealth Association of Science and Mathematics Educators* (London, 1978).

38 See A.J. Bishop, P. Damerow, P. Gerdes, and C. Keitel, "Mathematics, Education and Society" in A. Hirst and K. Hirst, *Proceedings of the Sixth International Congress on Mathematical Education* (University of Southampton, 1988); also, there is a special UNESCO publication of the whole day's papers and proceedings (C. Keitel, A.J. Bishop, P. Damerow and P. Gerdes *Mathematics, Education and Society* [Document Series 35, Paris, 1989]).

DISCUSSION QUESTIONS AND ACTIVITIES

1. Take a previously written lesson plan and make it culturally relevant. Be sure to consider both content and instructional strategies (Chapter Four).

2. Brainstorm sources for transformative knowledge in your subject area. Research sources and develop relevant unit or lesson plans. Share your work with other class members.

3. How does Schiele define Afrocentricity? Why does he say that Afrocentricity is good "for all?" Explain your answers. Do you agree?

4. Chapter Five begins with "School Teachers' Blues" and ends with "Steps to becoming a Culturally Relevant Teacher." What might your "blues" be in getting started? Explain your answers.

5. Write a reaction response to the article "Western Mathematics: The Secret Weapon of Cultural Imperialism." How might George Will or Gloria Ladson-Billings respond?

REFERENCES

Banks, J. A. 1996a. The Canon Debate, Knowledge Construction, and Multicultural Education. In J. A. Banks (ed.), *Multicultural Education: Transformative Knowledge and Action.* New York: Teachers College, Columbia University.

Banks, J. A. 1996b. Teaching Social Studies for Decision-Making and Action. In C. A. Grant & M. L. Gomez (eds.), *Making Schooling Multicultural.* Englewood Cliffs, NJ: Merrill.

Banks, J. A. 1997. Approaches to Multicultural Curriculum Reform. In J. A. Banks and C. A. McGee Banks (eds.), *Multicultural Education: Issues and Perspectives,* 3rd ed. Boston: Allyn & Bacon, pp. 229–250.

Barba, R. H. 1995. *Science in the Multicultural Classroom: A Guide to Teaching and Learning.* Boston: Allyn & Bacon.

Boyle-Baise, M. 1995. Teaching Social Studies Methods from a Multicultural Perspective. In J. M. Larkin and C. E. Sleeter (eds.), *Developing Multicultural Teacher Education Curricula.* Albany: State University of New York Press.

Cheung, K. 1994. Reflections on Teaching Literature by American Women of Color. In L. Fio-Matta & M. K. Chamberlain (eds.), *Women of Color and the Multicultural Curriculum.* New York: Feminist.

Diaz, C. 1992. *Multicultural Education for the 21st Century.* Washington, D.C.: National Education Association.

Good, R. 1995. Comments on Multicultural Science Education. *Science Education, 79*(3): 335–336.

Griffin, G. 1995. *Seasons of the Witch: Border Lines, Marginal Notes.* Pasadena, CA: Trilogy.

Ladson-Billings, G. 1995. Challenging Customs, Canons, and Content. In C. A. Grant (ed.), *Educating for Diversity.* Boston: Allyn & Bacon.

Multiculturalism in Mathematics, Science, and Technology: Readings and Activities. 1993. Menlo Park, CA: Addison-Wesley.

National Research Council 1996. *National Science Education Standards.* Washington, D.C. National Academy Press.

Tate, W. F. 1996. Mathematizing and the Democracy: The Need for an Education that is Multicultural and Social Reconstructionist. In C. A. Grant & M. L. Gomez (eds.), *Making Schooling Multicultural.* Englewood Cliffs, NJ: Merrill.

Will, G. 1990. Welcome to the World of Adversarial Pedagogy. *Daily Hampshire Gazette.* December 19, p. 10.

Wood, M. E. 1994. Survey of American Literature to 1865. In L. Fio-Matta & M. K. Chamberlain (eds.), *Women of Color and the Multicultural Curriculum.* New York: Feminist Press.

Chapter Six

Supporting Students' Reading, Writing, and Language

```
        W
        R
READING
        T
SPEAKING
        N
LANGUAGE
```

1 Down: word describing act of constructing meaning
2 Across: word describing act of constructing meanning
3 Across: word describing act of constructing meaning
4 Across: vehicle for conveying meaning

Literacy scholars today underscore the similarities between reading, writing, and speaking by emphasizing the commonalities in cognitive processes required to be a successful reader, writer, or speaker. The purpose of using language, in whatever form, entails the construction of meaning. In addition, because language is intimately tied to culture, instruction in any of these areas must consider the cultural context of the writer, the reader, and the speaker's words.

In standard methods textbooks, a chapter on literacy skills typically begins by extolling the benefits of reading and writing well in our society. Future middle and secondary content area teachers are told that all teachers are teachers of reading and writing and that the work of English teachers must be reinforced

177

by what is done in history, math, and physical education classrooms. Future teachers are reminded that reading, writing, and thinking across the curriculum are important instructional goals. The literacy skills chapter then explains how to integrate this instruction into your curriculum and how to support students' efforts to learn from texts and communicate in a variety of ways. Recent textbooks also include a section on the needs of nonnative speakers of English, "diverse students," and strategies teachers can use to help these students be academically successful.

In the first part of this chapter, we will cover some of the same territory, but our emphasis will be on explaining how culture relates to reading, writing, and language proficiency. Our focus is on the interactions between individual students and texts, and we highlight the processes that influence how readers comprehend, how writers try to communicate, and how culture influences language.

The second part of this chapter approaches the development of literacy skills within a broader social and political context. This perspective is often referred to as the New Literacy movement, critical literacy, or cultural literacy (Willinsky, 1990). We will want to consider the instructional implications of our findings in both sections. Readings at the end of this chapter examine the needs of nonstandard English speakers (that is, nonnative English speakers, speakers of Black Vernacular, and other dialects). This is useful information for future teachers as they develop curricula and work to strengthen their students' communication skills.

As you read, keep in mind the five approaches to multicultural education presented in Chapter One: Teaching the Exceptional and the Culturally Different, Human Relations, Single-Group Studies, Multicultural Approach, and Multicultural and Reconstructionist approach. Pay particular attention to the Multicultural Approach and the fifth approach, multicultural education that is Multicultural and Reconstructionist. Which aspects of literacy instruction respond to the Multicultural Approach and which aspects respond to multicultural education that is Multicultural and Reconstructionist?

Cultural Influences on the Construction of Meaning

Middle and Secondary Teachers as Teachers of Reading

Content-area teachers want their students to comprehend and learn from their reading assignments, a goal that fits well with current definitions of reading comprehension:

> Comprehension can be seen as the process of using one's own prior experiences and the writer's cues to construct a set of meanings that are useful to the individual reader reading in a specific context. This process can involve understanding and selectively recalling ideas in individual sentences (microprocesses), inferring relationships between clauses and sentences (integrative processes), organizing ideas around summarizing ideas (macroprocesses), and making inferences not necessarily intended by the author (elaborative processes). These processes work together (interactive hypothesis) and can be controlled and adjusted by the reader

as required by the reader's goals (metacognitive processes) and the total situation in which comprehension is occurring (situational context). (Irwin, 1991, p. 9)

This definition emphasizes reading comprehension as a mental activity in which the reader processes information at a number of different levels. Through an awareness of these processes, called metacognition, readers can control and adjust their comprehension. This definition also complements a constructivist approach to learning where students are viewed as meaning makers.

How might culture influence the reading process? Certainly, "one's own prior experiences" are influenced by culture and, in fact, research studies support this expectation. Schema theory is often used to describe how prior experiences are organized in the brain. Schemata are nonlinguistic structures representing concepts or generalizations of past experience and data and can be very abstract or very specific. For example, schemata can refer to story structures that provide a framework for understanding "how stories are told," often a cultural variable (Kaplan, 1980), or they may refer to "what makes the letter 'a', 'A', or '*a*' an 'a'."

Readers call on various schemata as they read. Incoming data is matched to slots within a schema. Slots remaining open can, by a process of inference, be filled by default. The term instantiation is used to describe this slot-filling process. Thus, an instantiated schema is one that has been only partially filled by text information and whose remaining slots have been filled by inference or default. Inferences can be based on a variety of factors including culture.

Several studies have shown that the reader's world knowledge influences the reader's comprehension. For example, college students with varying background knowledge read ambiguous passages for which there were two distinctly different interpretations. Results indicated that the schemata—of either two men wrestling or someone escaping from prison—the reader used determined the reader's understanding of the passage. Similar results were found for students reading passages that could be interpreted as four people getting together to play cards or to play music; music majors generally interpreted the passage to be about music (Anderson, Spiro, & Anderson, 1976).

The schema readers use while comprehending can also be the result of cultural knowledge:

Steffenson, Joag-Dev, and Anderson (1979) had American and Indian university students read two letters—one on an American wedding, the other about a wedding in India. The American rituals involve clothing, flowers, and receptions, with the bride the dominant figure. In Indian weddings, the groom's family, financial interests, and the social status of the two families are prominent.

The students read faster the passage that matched their own cultural framework. Asked to recall the culturally unfamiliar text, readers distorted facts and inserted ideas from their own culture. For example, Americans refer to the ceremony as the 'wedding' and the resultant state as the 'marriage.' No such differentiation is made by the Indian culture. Reading about an heirloom dress, an American commented on its sentimental value and the tradition of wearing something old and borrowed, but an Indian reader commented on its being out of fashion. (cited by Andersson & Barnitz, 1984, p. 104)

Another study (Reynolds, Taylor, Steffensen, Shirey, & Anderson, 1982) looked at the interpretations of eighth graders who had read a passage about a school cafeteria incident. Readers from the dominant culture most often interpreted the passage to be about a fight or near fight between the speakers, whereas African American readers interpreted the passage as referring to "sounding, a form of ritual insult and verbal play practiced mainly by teenage boys in many African American communities" (Au, 1993, p. 23).

Teachers must be aware of the influence schemata can have on a student's understanding of a text. Teachers who ask students to explain their thinking, rather than emphasizing a particular answer to a question, might uncover differences in background knowledge that students bring to a reading. Differences in interpretations can lead to more thoughtful class discussions and to greater understanding and awareness of individual comprehension.

Middle and Secondary Teachers as Teachers of Writing

For every reader, there is a writer who is engaged in another meaning-making task. In this case, the writer is working to put on paper (or the computer screen) observations, thoughts, ideas, feelings, and so on in the hope that they will make sense to at least the writer, if not to a wider audience. Writing is also indebted to "one's prior experiences" and thus is subject to an individual's cultural and experiential background. Story structure (how stories are constructed) can vary among cultures. For example, many Japanese folktales do not have major characters who are pursuing some goal (Matsuyama, 1983). Many western stories present a problem that is solved by the end of the story.

How directly writers choose to convey their ideas can also be influenced by culture. Arabic writers are expected to "get off track" (from a western perspective); western writers are admonished to "stick to the point." Korean writers are encouraged to present their ideas in such a way that the "point" is understood at the end of the reading; western expository writing demands a linear structure. You might remember being taught in expository writing to, first, introduce your topic and include a thesis statement; second, support your thesis with detailed evidence, and, third, sum up your ideas, restating your thesis, in your conclusion. Thus, you can see how an individual's writing style is often a function of how she has been taught meaning should be conveyed.

Middle and Secondary Teachers as Teachers of the English Language

Contrary to media hype, most parents in the United States or Canada whose children are non-English speaking say they *want* their children to learn English. Its value in the marketplace and politics is well understood. What parents sometimes ask is "What will be the cost of my child learning English? Will it mean giving up her first language? Will it be the first step to her losing her culture? Does the school see my child's first language as an asset or a deficit?"

Answers to these questions depend on how schools respond to nonnative English speakers or to speakers of non-standard English.[1]

> In all of the research described, the primary barriers to school literacy learning did not lie in the details of sounds, grammar, and vocabulary. Instead, the barriers were those created by schools' failure to acknowledge and appreciate students' home cultures and to build upon the interactional styles and everyday uses of language with which students were already familiar. (Au, 1993, p. 124)

Monolingual teachers can easily forget how closely language usage is linked to culture. Knowing a language also means knowing how to use it appropriately in a context that reflects the values, social relationships, and history of a group.

Heath's research (1983) on differences in language socialization clearly demonstrates how some cultural linguistic environments are more compatible with school linguistic environments. Her research into the literacy patterns of two North Carolina working-class communities (one Black, one White) "discovered that the way children related to the printed word was embedded in their daily life experiences. Meaning was not derived through the learning of isolated pieces of information or individual letters, but through real messages that were usually surrounded by oral communication" (McCaleb, 1994, p. 187). For example, recall Baby Lamees and Baby Nicholas in Chapter Three. Lamees is surrounded by talking relatives. In this environment, she observes language being used and learns to understand it in its social context. She learns to read nonverbal cues as equally important markers of communication. In contrast, Nicholas's first language lessons include him as a participant. Verbal interactions by his mother assume that he can "join in." Remember how his mother taught him to name the objects around him. Later she is likely to help him name their attributes (*brown* bear, *round* cup, *silver* spoon).

As reported in Farr and Daniels (1986), Heath's research in the (Black) Trackton and (White) Roadville communities reflect similar patterns:

> Thus in Roadville, in direct contrast with Trackton, babies begin almost immediately to "participate" in dialogues with others, rather than being left to "figure things out" on their own. The children of both communities, of course, learn to talk at a normal rate of development, but the context in which they learn to do so differs markedly from one community to another.... Since much of the curriculum in early school years is similar to the kinds of language practices pre-schoolers experience in Roadville homes, their initial transition to formal schooling is not a difficult one. This, of course, is not the case for the Trackton children, who experience a sharp discontinuity between language practices at home and those at school. (pp. 29–30)

Although Trackton children have other ways of using language which should serve them well in school (e.g., creativity in the use of rhymes and

---

[1] We recognize that there are potentially several standard forms of English that meet linguists' criteria for rule-based language patterns; however, we use the term *standard English* to refer to the *preferred* standard English taught in schools and used in commerce. Learning standard English is not a requirement to becoming literate.

metaphors), their early experiences in school, where written language is often taught as a series of subskills, confuse and discourage them, so that they never progress to the point in school where these more innovative uses of language are more evident in the school curriculum. Moreover, some students seem to get stuck in the remedial track . . . . (pp. 28–29)

Two other relevant areas of research are sharing time (Michaels, 1981; 1986) and questioning techniques (Heath, 1982). Michaels researched sharing time in a first-grade classroom where the teacher asked students to pick an event or object about which to talk. An important goal of this exercise is to give students an opportunity to construct narrative structures that reflect literate discourse (that is, language found in print). Through teacher comments and questioning, students are moved toward more "book like" talk. Michaels described two styles of sharing: topic-centered sharing and topic-associating sharing. She found that in general European-American students were easily able to meet the teacher's expectations. Students kept to the topic, and the teacher's questions did not intrude on the child's presentation. Many of the African American students, however, used a form of sharing she designated as topic-associating, a rhetorical structure that might have its roots in Africa. In this style a student appears to present several different topics without directly making the connections between the statements. In these situations teachers' comments and questions appeared to be intrusions into the "story" being told. Teachers who are unaware of this oral discourse pattern are not likely to assume that the topics are linked and will not be able to move the child toward a more conventional literate discourse style.

Shirley Brice Heath's research on Trackton and Roadside also led her to examine differences in questioning styles of the two communities. In Trackton, children were more likely to be asked to compare two objects, whereas in Roadside, children might be asked to describe the two objects. Questioning in Trackton required responses that elicited analogies rather than responses that identified attributes, which is often a characteristic of school questions. An awareness of this allows teachers to expand the types of questions used in their discussions and build on the literacy strengths of all students.

LITERACY DEVELOPMENT WITHIN A SOCIOPOLITICAL CONTEXT

Because learning *how* to read is expected to occur at the elementary level, middle and secondary teachers often feel removed from debates about how children should be *taught* to read. If a middle or high school student is reading far below grade level, she is usually assigned to a reading class or required to work with a reading specialist. In the classroom, content-area teachers work hard to employ comprehension strategies based on some of the information we have previously discussed. Nevertheless, they regularly have to contend with students who *can* read, but *do not* or *will not*.

Recent scholarship on literacy, including a discussion of its social and political uses and functions, can shed light on this phenomenon and other factors that influence students' involvement in literacy tasks. What follows is a brief overview of current perspectives on literacy. As you read, think about how this information relates to classroom instruction, in general, and instruction for reluctant readers and writers, in particular.

Definitions of Literacy

The long-held view that reading and writing involve a set of finite, functional skills that can be taught sequentially has been previously challenged by psycholinguists (Goodman, 1986; Smith, 1975) and is "now being challenged across a broad range of fields including psychology, anthropology, linguistics, educational sociology and literary criticism" (Bloome, 1986, p. 71). An essential change has been a reconceptualization of literacy as including both cognitive and social cultural contexts.

Au (1993) proposes this definition of literacy: "The ability and the willingness to use reading and writing to construct meaning from printed text in ways which meet the requirements of a particular social context" (p. 20). She emphasizes several important aspects: willingness *to use,* especially as connected to authentic tasks, both *reading and writing* (with equal emphasis on each); *constructed meaning* in interpreting written text and in creating written text; *printed text* as differentiated from "prescriptivist" (McLaren, 1991) conceptions of literacy [for example, Bloom, 1987, and Hirsch, 1987] and from technological literacy; and *social context* that recognizes the impact of home and community on literacy development. We will come back to these concepts.

According to Gee (1990), defining literacy can only be done as it connects to discourse, "a socially accepted association among ways of using language, of thinking, feeling, believing, valuing and acting that can be used to identify oneself as a member of a socially meaningful group or 'social network,' or to signal (that one is playing) a socially meaningful 'role'" (p. 143). Gee notes that there are many discourses, primary ones and secondary ones; dominant ones (with status) and nondominant ones (without status) respectively. Gee believes that literacy is controlling the language in secondary discourses and the word can be applied to multiple secondary discourses. Applying this in varying situations can be thought of as "code switching," as being able to speak the "Queen's English" in the workplace and being able to communicate "Ebonically" in the appropriate context, or to use and understand "geek speak" while interacting on the Internet.

Clearly, these definitions of literacy place the reader, writer, and speaker within a framework larger than words, print, or individual experience! Middle and secondary school teachers will need to consider several other variables that can affect how, when, or why a student is willing to read or write: What function does literacy perform in a student's family or community? Are literacy practices community events where groups work together to construct meaning as they did in Trackton? Is student reluctance to engage in literacy instruction an act of conscious or unconscious opposition to mainstream institutions? (see Ogbu, 1992).

Cultural Literacy

The media has paid considerable attention to those advocates of **cultural literacy** who McLaren (1991) identifies as "prescriptive," that is, those who propose to itemize what one needs to know to be culturally literate. Such perspectives establish "canons" that are put forth as stately exemplars of what is worth knowing without addressing "the ways in which dominant text constitute an articulation of the societies that produced them" (p. 295). (Recall our discussion on the construction of knowledge in Chapter Five.) These canons advance standards of excellence without examining what factors (political and social) influence their being deemed so and how these factors systematically exclude other "voices." For example, E. D. Hirsch (1987) has written several books outlining what Americans need to know to be culturally literate.

We use the term *cultural literacy* to reflect more pluralistic perspectives that promote "the legitimacy of a broader range of discursive practices which reflect more closely the language practices, values, and interests of racially and economically diverse groups' students" (Bizzell as cited by McLaren, 1991, p. 288). Instructional approaches that incorporate students' language and literacy practices of the home and community would support our definition of cultural literacy.

Literacy is a cultural practice with political, social, and economic roots (Lipson & Wixon, 1997, p. 8). What students produce as readers and writers is intimately intertwined with all their prior experiences. Political, economic, and societal factors are part of the culture students bring to literacy learning. Cole points out that "(b)ooks have been read, ideas have been exchanged, and social interactions have occurred" (cited by Lipson & Wixon, 1997, p. 8). All these experiences effect the literacy orientations brought into the classroom, orientations brought by the student as well as by the teacher. Thus, the concept of cultural literacy is understood in a much broader realm than an "everything one needs to know to be culturally literate" list.

These scholars exemplify the new theoretical conceptualizations of literacy. In addition to an emphasis on active involvement of students' roles in the reading and writing processes (including recognition of their cultural identity), evidence supports psycholinguistic as well as sociolinguistic influences on literacy development (Graff, 1987).[2] Advocates of critical literacy shift the paradigm away from the skills and mechanical processes involved in reading. Instead, they (Friere; Giroux; McLaren; Shor) focus on the recognition of political and social contexts and the practices that reflect those concerns (Willinsky, 1990).

Critical Literacy

Freire's classic, *Pedagogy of the Oppressed* (1970), posited a theory of **critical literacy** that is inextricably connected to political liberation. Freire's insistence that readers adopt critical reading practices moves far beyond the traditional

---

[2] Some whole language scholars prefer to use the term sociopsycholinguistics to incorporate the social/cultural context of literacy.

critical reading skills of analysis, synthesis, and evaluation done for the purposes of intellectually massaging ideas. The context for critical reading practices is viewed in relationship to counteracting notions of colonialization, cultural hegemony, and "cultural reproduction and indoctrination." Any proposal of a canon must acknowledge that "texts are products of the interest that inform dominant social and cultural groups," and furthermore, educators must "probe the canon for what it does not say—for its 'structured silences,' its 'present absences,' its exclusionary politics—as well as for what it actually does say" (McLaren, 1991, p. 300). Teachers who embrace critical literacy will acknowledge such influences and ask their students to investigate the larger context of the material they read. Whose voice is being heard? Whose voice is silent? Who benefits from the story being told in this way?

For Freireans, the aims of literacy need to include "making linkages between bodies of knowledge and the social and political realities that generate them" (Macedo 1995, p. 85). Literacy, therefore, can be radical social thought that encourages "emancipatory" ideals and justifiable social change through collective social action. For Freire (and a legion of his followers) not only is the political pedagogical but the pedagogical is political. *What* we teach has political implications as well as *how* we teach. Although some instructional practices encourage student empowerment, others reinforce or reproduce existing power relationships.

Friere (1987) and Shor (1992; see Chapter One Readings) are literacy scholars who explicitly connect the teaching of reading to a political process.

> Freire has fashioned a theory of cultural power and production that begins with the notion of popular education. . . . he rightly argues for pedagogical principles that arise from the concrete practices that constitute terrain on which people live out their problems, hopes, and everyday experiences. All of this suggests taking seriously the cultural capital of the oppressed, developing critical and analytical tools to interrogate it, and staying in touch with dominant definitions of knowledge so we can analyze them for their usefulness and for the ways in which they bear the logic of domination. (Giroux, 1985, pp. xxi–xxii)

New Literacy

Advocates of **New Literacy** embrace the notion of empowerment suggested by Freire and propose that tension is needed to "shake up the power structure" as a way to more equitable social realities (Willinsky, 1990). New Literacy stands as a challenge to the models of reading and writing programs as the acquisition of skills or "scribal literacy" as Illich (1987) has called it: "The New Literacy introduces a radical program of studies along two dimensions, the one unsettling the school and the other disturbing the acquired habits of the student. This (is) to be a literacy which plays *against* institutional authority and a literacy which works *within* the student" (p. 22, original emphasis).

Such a program calls for new roles for teachers, a more visible and active voice for students and dismantling a system that rewards middle- and upper-class privilege. Crediting the work of Pierre Boudrieu, Willinsky (1990) acknowledges that schools reward those students whose backgrounds provide them with the linguistic "cultural capital" necessary to succeed at literacy tasks defined by the institution (p. 32). New Literacy places reading and writing in a more communal context—meaning making, whether expressed through the creation of a written product or through the interpretation of reading a text, is socially constructed. This requires recognizing the diversity in social reality and not limiting the view represented in most classrooms today.

New Literacy regards meaning making as a cultural process, contested, negotiated, renegotiated, and recreated by the members of the culture. The approach is constructivist in orientation, allowing students to have more of an active role in the information that is learned. They are not empty vessels to be filled or bank accounts waiting for deposits. They are active participants in a dialogue.

These descriptions of the new literacy don't make for light reading! What is common to these perspectives is a recognition that literacy is a powerful tool—not just for individuals, but for society as a whole. Literacy is linked to power and although teachers might choose to focus on the act of comprehending or composing written texts, other equally powerful influences are at work in their classrooms. These influences can affect how comfortable students will be in the learning environment as well as how willing they may be to participate.

EDUCATIONAL IMPLICATIONS FOR COGNITIVE AND CULTURAL PERSPECTIVES ON LITERACY

Experts in the field of reading have had various responses to new directions in literacy research. Advocates of psycholinguistics, sociopsycholinguistics, and whole language approaches that emphasize the links between society, language learning, and learning how to read, might more readily accept research that connects culture and politics to literacy. We want to look at the instructional implications of these perspectives on reading instruction. We believe that many instructional implications coming from this expanded definition of literacy would be acceptable to most reading experts. What follows is a synthesis of those instructional strategies that middle and secondary content-area teachers could use in their classrooms. Finally, we discuss a set of strategies aligned more specifically with proponents of the critical literacy movement.

Given the research demonstrating how an individual's background knowledge, culture and experience can affect comprehension, it is important for teachers to get to know their students in a variety of ways. What experiences do students bring into the classroom? What kinds of knowledge do they have? What are their cultural frames of references? With what communications styles are they most comfortable? How is being literate defined in their communities? As our previous discussion of schema theory pointed out, knowing our students is a basis for knowing what kinds of schemata they might bring to a reading assignment. Teachers who know their students can provide that next bit of assistance, often called **scaffolding,** that allows students to be increasingly more successful understanding written discourse. Scaffolding can be in the form of questioning, elaborating on student responses, supplying relevant information to build on what the student knows, or collaborating with the student to make sense of the task.

Another important function of instruction is to support students' language and develop their awareness (metacognition) of how others communicate and how language is structured—including different discourse styles. This is accomplished best in an environment where a student's own language is accepted and affirmed. Gee (see earlier) talks about primary, secondary, and dominant discourses; teachers who help students understand these distinctions enhance their literacy skills. Middle and secondary methods textbooks as well as textbooks dealing with reading in the content area provide future teachers with several valuable techniques for developing comprehension skills.

STRATEGIES TO ENHANCE LITERACY

Many of the suggested strategies that follow develop students' ability to question, communicate and organize information and should be incorporated into pre-reading/writing, reading/writing, and post–reading/writing activities.

K-W-L

The K-W-L technique has been used for years at the elementary level. Teachers solicit answers from students to the following questions: What do I *know* about topic "x?" What do I *want* to know? What have I *learned*? This strategy is useful as a pre-reading or writing exercise. In responding to the first two questions, students activate their prior knowledge, help set a purpose for the assignment, and model brainstorming and thinking aloud. While students are working, they might jot down answers to their questions, making note of whether their questions are answered explicitly or by inference in the text. After the project is completed, students answer the third question and initiate a process of reflection and self-evaluation. At the end, teachers sometimes add a fourth question: What questions do I still have? This can form the basis for the next unit of study.

Questioning Techniques

As future teachers, we must monitor the kinds of questions we ask in our classes. To put it simply, some questions make us think, and some questions don't. Teachers should ask the former kinds of questions, but there is real skill in being able to do so! Many novice teachers think that good questions come naturally or that they should ask students provocative questions only after quizzing the students for literal comprehension.

Pre-planning is essential. Beginning teachers should prepare questions in advance of their classes. They need to systematically monitor and evaluate the kinds of questions they ask and the depth of student responses. Including a "Question/Discussion Format" in lesson planning helps structure and strengthen a teacher's questioning skills. A question/discussion format includes first, a purpose for questions or discussion. Is the purpose for students to demonstrate an understanding of what has been read, to understand their own opinions on a topic, apply what they have read, or generate issues, ideas, and additional questions that need more research? Second, the format includes a description of the process—will students respond to questions in pairs, small groups, or large groups? Will they write brief responses before exchanging ideas? The third component of the format includes the specific questions or discussion prompts. It is important to link these questions to the overall goals for the discussion. We recall the student teacher who planned a discussion on the pros and cons of cloning and wondered why the small groups were off task fifteen out of the allotted twenty minutes. A quick look at the posed questions showed five questions that could be answered with either a "yes" or "no." The fourth component of the format calls for criteria with which to evaluate students' participation and the process as a whole.

Dialogue

The more students discuss, write about, and struggle with ideas and concepts that they read, the greater will be the improvement in their literacy skills. Dialoguing is the counterpoint to questioning. As students take in new information, they need to build new schemata, create new links in old ones, and gain productive use over the material.

Students need to be engaged in real conversations. This resonates well with proponents of multicultural education and the critical literacy movement, but what is a "real" conversation? We define a real conversation as one in which students actively participate in a discussion, where the topic has some relevance and significance to them, where there is room for both cognitive and affective responses, and where individuals want to hear what their classmates have to say.

Good questions are important to real conversations. In the previous section, we outline a question/discussion format that teachers can use in preparing their lessons. In addition, students can help generate questions. A technique one of us has used has been to ask students to read a section and develop four questions: two school-type questions for which they know the answers and two "real" questions for which they don't know the answers, but would genuinely like to know. Both kinds of questions are brought forward, and students and teacher have the opportunity to discuss differences in the kinds of questions students generated. Finally, teachers who have developed genuine and open connections with their students (see Chapter Four) and have helped students to respect each other will have laid a stronger foundation for student dialogue.

Journal Writing

Journal writing is prevalent in English classes and is used for a variety of purposes. Although we see merit in having students write down their feelings about a topic or reading, we think it is equally as important to use journals to encourage student reflection and analysis. We sometimes describe these as "academic journals" where the entries are more focussed. Students use journals to respond to problems presented in a text before the class discussion. In science logs, students speculate about results of experiments they are going to perform, including any evidence to support their hypotheses.

Students complete double-entry journals as they read. They note specific ideas, paragraphs, and examples from the text. These references to the text are place on the left-hand page of a spiral notebook. Students note the page and the text briefly. On the right-hand page, students respond or react to the text notation. They might have a question about what is being said; they might disagree with what is being presented. Over the year, students' notations should become more detailed and thoughtful. An added benefit of the double-entry journal is that it helps prepare students for class discussions. Teachers can call on students and ask them to read some of their notations.

Finally, dialogue journals are particularly good for nonnative speakers. Students dialogue with the teacher or another student. Controversial issues make good topics; one person writes and the other responds to what has been written and then offers ideas and reactions of his or her own.

Informational Organizers

A fourth type of comprehension strategy deals with helping readers and writers organize information. As we discussed previously, one culture's preferred organizational structure can be another's disarray; however, most types of expository reading and writing found in content-area classrooms present information in a hierarchical and linear format. Writers are encouraged to develop outlines, and readers are given study guides to follow while reading. Teachers often work with students to develop graphic representations of text information, and then after reading, ask students to retell the information using the graphic organizer. Finally, teachers can point out the different rhetorical structures often used in textbook writing. Important rhetorical structures include cause and effect, comparison and contrast, listing, chronological order, generalizations with evidence, description, and question and answer.

At the start of this chapter, we asked you to consider which literacy strategies might be compatible with a Multicultural Approach to multicultural education. The strategies just described seem to fit this category well: They acknowledge the students' active contribution to the learning process—both as creators of knowledge and makers of meaning; they affirm multiple discourse styles and perspectives, and recognize a continuous dialogue among students, text, and teacher. Some would argue, however, that these strategies stop short of asking students to seriously analyze their sociopolitical context or consider avenues for social change.

Strategies that respond to critical and new literacy theories are most likely found within an approach that is both Multicultural and Reconstructionist. For example, teachers advocating this approach make explicit the power dynamics between students and teacher. Power resides with those *who* select what is read or *what* writing tasks are assigned. Students are taught to understand the power of those whose books are published and whose discourse style is given more prestige.

Technological Literacy

With the advent of technological developments come inevitable realizations about the impact that computers and electronic media have on the literacy process. Reading and writing become different tasks. The requisite skills and knowledge to negotiate the hardware and software of technology compound the challenges to the more traditional understanding of literacy. The intimacy of holding a written text in one's own hand and the feel of turning pages is immediately lost. Composing on screen seems simultaneously "screen-flickering" fleeting and "perfectly-presented-printable-in-a-second" permanent. The shape and the look of text take on more importance than the context (Constanzo, 1994, p. 15). One's consciousness about the process of being or becoming literate is transmuted by the interface with technology.

Heralded as the key to negotiating the information age, understanding and using technology is touted as the Rosetta stone to future success. In addition to shaping literacy, technology is shaping the economic base for the future. Friere and Machedo (1987) believe that "literacy becomes a meaningful construct to the degree that it is viewed as a set of practices that functions to either empower or disempower" (p. 141). This is no less true of technological literacy, and empowerment takes multiple forms. Zeni (1994) reports that numerous studies indicate differences in the delivery of instruction in low-income and minority classrooms. "While the haves are doing word processing and programming (learning to gain power over a computer), the have-nots are doing grammar drills (learning to be programmed) . . . If we believe in affirming the stories, minds, and voices of all our students, then we must resist impoverished applications" (p. 83). With so much at stake, there are natural concerns about equal access to these emerging technologies; but even when access is not the issue, patterns of how the technology is used is very telling. "Technology can be as educationally repressive as it can be liberatory. When computers are used as a tool for literacy education, choices regarding technology can privilege one model of literacy while excluding others" (LeBlanc, 1994, p. 22). Issues of access as well as empowerment are critical. In 1996, Bill Clinton issued a literacy challenge advocating inclusion, ensuring that no students would be left behind ("President Clinton's Call . . .," 1997). In his speech, President Clinton also encouraged the development of partnerships to create new ways of using technology for learning.

Does technology have the potential to be culture neutral, a tool that embraces all cultures equally, or are these myths Madison Avenue has created? According to Chandler (1997), those who argue that technology, itself, is value free believe that "what counts is not the technology but the way in which we use it." Does it only take any tool in the "right" hands, used in the "right" way, or do some tools have embedded the influences of those who designed them?

Teachers who are multicultural and social reconstructionist carefully consider the range of benefits and challenges of technology in the classroom. How do issues of race, gender, and socioeconomic status affect the tools? How do the tools enhance or change the literacy process? How do the tools advance pedagogy that is democratic and liberatory? How does one choose hardware/software and instructional practices that are consonant with equitable ideals?

Critical pedagogists extend this discussion to include ways in which students and teachers might share more of the power. What is important is that students become aware of this hidden curriculum. Teachers can share power by learning more about students' language styles and discuss how those language styles differ from status discourses. If students are required to be bi-dialectical, then teachers can also learn another dialect. Students also can learn the analytical skills necessary to look beyond explicit text. Comprehending a text includes understanding the social, cultural, and political background of the material.

Literacy becomes a vehicle for social change. Connections to the community are important here. McCaleb in *Building a Community of Learners* (1994) describes several ways that education can take place within the context of the community. For example, students observe and write about how their community functions, what its strengths and weaknesses are, and offer suggestions for change (p. 42). Using the community as a resource, students construct knowledge that the school sanctions.

Finally, do not overlook the importance of home literacy. "The concept of emergent literacy suggests that all children come to school with certain experiences and interests in literacy . . . The concept of emergent literacy reminds us that literacy begins in the home, not the school, and that school literacy instruction should seek to make connections to the lives children have beyond the walls of the classroom" (Au, 1993, pp. 36–37). For relevant research, see Solsken, Keenan, and Willett (1993) and Keenan, Willett, and Solsken (1993). The significance of family literacy practices and school connections to the community are the focus of Chapter Nine.

READINGS

The readings in this chapter are practical, informative, and thought-provoking. "Instructional Strategies for Second-Language Learners in the Content Areas" offers middle and secondary school teachers practical suggestions for working with nonnative speakers. We have already discussed many of the techniques. Readers will discover that what is helpful to nonnative speakers can also be useful to a much broader group of students. Brian Lewis's synthesis of research surrounding the history of Black English is very informative. The significance of this material presented in "Black English: Its History and Its Role in the Education of Our Children" is twofold: One, it helps to dispel some of the misinformation being circulated in mainstream media, and two, it can help teachers do their jobs better.

The third reading, "Technological Literacy: More Questions Than Answers," is written by Anne Pelak, who has worked with computers in the business and nonprofit sectors for the last ten years. She has been involved in community-based advocacy on issues of equity and computer literacy and has a special interest in the history of computing as it reflects the popular culture. Technological literacy raises thought-provoking questions on the potential for neutrality in technological development and use. In her essay, Pelak examines the theory of neutrality versus technological determinism.

READING 1

Instructional Strategies for Second-Language Learners in the Content Areas

María de la Luz Reyes
Linda A. Molner

The prominent role of content area instruction in secondary schools and the accompanying implications for reading and writing instruction pose both a challenge and an opportunity for teachers with increasingly large numbers of language minority students in their classrooms. In recent years, demographic shifts in many countries have changed the student population from primarily native speaking to linguistically heterogeneous. The increase in the number of learners with mixed levels of proficiency in the language of the classroom calls for a close examination of important factors that contribute to their success in content area classrooms.

The purpose of this article is twofold. First, we will discuss important considerations for teachers as they plan and implement content area instruction with linguistically diverse students. Second, we will review promising strategies for content area instruction that are appropriate and appealing for mixed groups of native and non-native speakers.

Since we are active in the U.S., we focus particularly on practices and strategies that may be effective with Hispanics and Asians (particularly Hmong, Laotian, Cambodian, and Vietnamese)—two of the fastest-growing segments among U.S. student populations. We see important reasons for targeting these two groups. First, despite reports that indicate recent academic improvement among Hispanic students in the U.S., as a group they continue to perform significantly below national norms on reading and writing tasks (Applebee, Langer, & Mullis, 1989). Second, although there is a general perception that Asian students are successful academically, more recent evidence suggests that not all Asians are "model minority" students (Hu, 1989; Nash, 1990). The myth of Asian students' invariable success is especially untrue for the second and third waves of Asian immigrants to the U.S. from war-torn countries who may have considerable gaps in their education.

However, the strategies and principles of instruction that we will discuss here are not limited to use with English. They are basic enough to be usable in many countries with diverse groups of learners.

Important Considerations for Teaching Diverse Learners

To work effectively with language-diverse students, teachers need to know that minority learners are often automatically placed in low ability groups

---

Reprinted by permission of the International Reading Association and the authors.

(Oakes, 1985) where instruction is based on a watered-down version of the curriculum. This puts minorities at a disadvantage. Once they are labeled poor readers, these students receive qualitatively different literacy experiences (Allington, in press; Díaz, Moll, & Mehan, 1986). The problems intensify if their lack of English fluency is erroneously perceived as an indicator of low intellectual ability, resulting in minimal exposure to higher order thinking skills (DeAvila, Duncan, & Navarrete, 1987).

Confounding the situation is the fact that by the time students reach high school they have already been conditioned to view themselves as successful or unsuccessful. Many students "caught in the failure cycle . . . develop their own behaviors to cope with their lack of reading success; these behaviors amount to learned helplessness in the face of repeated failure" (Coley & Hoffman, 1990). A lack of background knowledge coupled with the heavy concept load of many content area texts may also contribute to students' perceptions of themselves as poor readers and to their learned helplessness.

These experiences, common to language minority students, are important to understand because they provide compelling reasons for content area teachers to explore alternative ways of working with these students that are both effective and sensitive to their special needs.

Promising Strategies for Content Learning

Little is known about how language minority students deal with the demands of literacy tasks, especially in the subject areas. A review of the rather limited literature, however, reveals several strategies that have been found to be effective in helping these students make sense of and learn from content materials.

We present here only those that (a) can be introduced to mixed groups of students enrolled in regular subject-area classrooms, (b) have been researched or tried successfully with language minority students, and (c) include features that address the needs and learning styles of linguistically diverse learners.

The strategies presented are context specific—that is, they ground understandings of content in cultural and social contexts (Díaz, Moll, & Mehan, 1986). They also recognize the importance of teacher and peer mediation in learning new information.

Specifically, each strategy includes at least one of three characteristics believed to be important in teaching language minority students: first, that language learning is integrated with content instruction (Snow & Brinton, 1988); second, that students are given access to problem-solving activities in non-threatening, cooperative contexts designed to foster higher order thinking and complex processing of content information (Moll & Díaz, 1987); third, that learning activities are mediated or scaffolded so as to build background and promote learning across the subject areas.

We have organized the strategies under the following categories: background-building strategies, writing-to-learn activities, and cooperative learning approaches. Each is summarized in the Figure, which outlines the research findings and describes how language and content are integrated, how higher order skills are fostered and how mediated/scaffolding techniques are included. This is followed by a description of how each strategy is used.

1. Background-building strategies. Linking new concepts to students' existing background knowledge and experience is an important component of prereading activities that prepare students for learning new content material. For second-language learners, this integration of background and text appears to facilitate the construction of meaning (Block, 1986; Langer, Bartolome, Vasquez, & Lucas, 1990). Semantic mapping the PreReading Plan (PReP) and the Experience-Text-Relationship (ETR) method fall under this category.

- Semantic mapping: Carrell, Pharis, and Liberto (1989) recommended semantic mapping to introduce key vocabulary from a reading passage and to provide teachers with a means for informal assessment of students' prior knowledge. In their research, ESL college students trained in semantic mapping showed increased comprehension of content area texts.

The procedure begins with class brainstorming in which students generate associations on a topic. Because this type of associating triggers attention and builds on students' prior knowledge, brainstorming serves as an advanced organizer for understanding the potentially related information that follows in the reading assignment. The teacher then conducts a discussion in which students organize in a map the information generated by brainstorming. Once reading is completed, students revise their maps, applying knowledge of text structure and important concepts in an organized, visual format.

For second-language learners, the chance to contribute ideas toward the common goal of collecting information, to exchange ideas with others to rehearse the facts, and to revise visual learning aids (in the form of a semantic map) supports limited skills in the target language and provides opportunities for the social construction of learning. Throughout the process students are actively predicting, hypothesizing, and verifying content, all of which contribute to a greater likelihood of recalling information from text.

- PreReading Plan (PReP): Langer's (1984) PReP discussion activity introduces students to reading assignments by moving them through three phases of knowledge development. First, all students in the class are required to generate associations with a key concept presented by a teacher (e.g., "Tell me what comes to mind when you hear the expression 'the arms race'"). All responses, regardless of their quality or "correctness," are written on the board with student initials denoting who provided each response. Next, each student refines and elaborates on these initial associations (e.g., "What made you think of 'missiles'?"). Finally, students reorganize and synthesize their knowledge statements (e.g., "Based on our discussion, what new ideas do you have about the arms race?").

The activity encourages second-language learners to integrate prior experiences with new concepts using informal rather than "school" language, to interact with and learn from other students, and to participate as equals in a nonthreatening environment. Learning in a stress-free environment reduces the risks limited English speakers often perceive in many academic settings (Krashen, 1981).

The opportunity to use informal English appears to lessen the uncertainties experienced by limited English speakers who in other circumstances might be required to produce a more standard type of response. As Cummins and Swain (1986) note, students may learn language skills more effectively in informal, nonacademic settings.

Molner (1989) found that the PReP strategy in conjunction with a reading assignment significantly improved 9th- and 10th-grade Hispanic students' long-term understandings of social studies concepts.

- Experience-Text-Relationship method (ETR): Created as a strategy for tapping into students' prior knowledge and facilitating comprehension, ETR has been used successfully with linguistically diverse students at both the elementary (Au, 1979) and college levels (Carrell, Pharis, & Liberto, 1989). The activity links known information to new concepts presented in texts.

Following a question and discussion period centering on what students already know about key concepts from a text, students read short segments of the material. The teacher then asks questions about the content, clarifies misconceptions, and assists students in perceiving relationships between the text content and prior experiences.

This ETR procedure requires that teachers lead the discussion but allows students to discover answers for themselves so that the thinking processes involved will later transfer to independent reading. The scaffolding aspect of this strategy is particularly helpful for students who may need clarification because of limited English skills and unfamiliarity with technical vocabulary or who may need assistance in finding relationships and relevancy in the text content.

(For more description of literacy scaffolds in second-language reading instruction, see Boyle & Peregoy, 1990).

2. **Writing-to-learn activities.** Many ESL and remedial writing programs approach writing instruction as a series of grammar exercises adhering to strict forms (Raimes, 1980). They provide few opportunities for extended expository writing (Moll & Díaz, 1987). As a result, language minority students may be unprepared for the academic reading and writing demands of high school or college (Snow & Brinton, 1988).

Culturally relevant and authentic forms of expression, such as writing-to-learn activities that promote thinking and learning of content (Tchudi & Huerta, 1983; Trueba, Díaz, & Díaz, 1984), can help linguistically diverse students actively construct meaning and synthesize thinking as they integrate reading and writing tasks.

- Guided Writing Procedure (GWP): The GWP structure includes both idea generation and guided writing in conjunction with content area reading assignments. Using oral language as a tool for integrating reading and writing instruction in the content areas, the GWP (Searfoss, Smith, & Bean, 1981) has been used successfully with middle school Hispanic students in ESL and regular content area classes.

Recommended content literacy strategies of language minority students

Important characteristics

Strategy	Research findings	Integrates language and content learning	Fosters higher order thinking	Includes mediated/scaffolded instruction	Other features
1. Background-building					
Semantic mapping	Significant effects on open-ended comprehension questions and posttest maps for Asian, Arabic, and African ESL college students	Yes—students brainstorm orally and transfer associations to written maps	Yes—students map relationships, use text structure	Yes—mediated by peers and teacher	Incorporates visual aids; students predict and verify content; allows teachers to assess background for topic
PreReading Plan (PReP)	Significant long-term understandings of social studies concepts for 9th and 10th grade Hispanic students	Yes—students use natural language to connect prior knowledge of concepts to assigned reading	Yes—students reorganize, synthesize ideas	Yes—primarily peer mediation; some teacher direction provided if misconceptions exist	Requires equal participation; high level of peer interaction in nonthreatening setting; can be used to assess prior knowledge
Experience-Text-Relationship (ETR)	(See semantic mapping, above)	Yes—students discuss what they know and link it to reading concepts	Yes—requires students to perceive relationships between text and prior knowledge	Yes—teacher scaffolds learning according to need	Requires teacher adeptness in leading discussion
2. Writing to learn					
Guided Writing Procedure (GWP)	Growth in writing ability and positive student reactions with 8th grade Hispanic ESL students	Yes—oral language serves as bridge to other language skills	Yes—students summarize information and synthesize text content with prior knowledge	Yes—teacher creates criteria checklist that students and teacher apply several times during the writing process	Teachers need to create content-centered (vs. editing) checklists; could be adapted for peer learning and interactions

Chapter Six • Supporting Students' Reading, Writing, and Language   **197**

Important characteristics

Strategy	Research findings	Integrates language and content learning	Fosters higher order thinking	Includes mediated/ scaffolded instruction	Other features
Connecting school writing with the community	Improvement in writing fluency and motivation for middle-level Hispanic ESL students	Yes—interview formats develop oral skills; written products emphasize writing as a way to learn	Yes—students synthesize and organize data in written reports	Yes—teacher models structures and provides initial guidance until students are able to self-regulate	Authentic, culturally relevant writing tasks are based on community issues
3. *Cooperative learning*	Gains in achievement for LEP students; dramatic catch-up effects for minority children; increased cooperativeness and cross-ethnic friendships; increase in peer achievement norms; improved status for minority students; increased time on task	Yes—students need to communicate at higher levels; negotiating meaning assists language acquisition	Determined by goals and structure of tasks	Yes—mediated by peers in most cooperative formats; tasks usually assigned in manageable segments	Culturally congruent for most minority students; effects are strongest when group and peer reward structures are included
Student Teams–Achievement Divisions (STAD)	(See above)	Yes—peer tutoring format encourages oral interactions	(See above)	Yes—students monitor progress of peers in group	Rewards based on individual and team improvement
Jigsaw	(See above)	Yes—students must communicate as they teach assigned segments of material to be learned	(See above)	Yes—students evaluate/monitor individual and group learning	Tests or quizzes given individually; lack of group reward structure may affect achievement gains
Descubrimiento (Finding Out)	(See above)	Yes—acquisition of English skills and technical vocabulary emerges naturally in science problem-solving	Yes—thematic assignments are designed to promote thinking skills	Yes—students mediate instruction as they adopt various roles	Hands-on activities provide students access to higher order learning; may be modified for older students

The procedure includes opportunities for students to brainstorm and discuss what they know about a topic, create a brief outline of categories presented, and write a short piece while following the outline. Using a teacher-designed checklist that addresses content, organization, style, and mechanics, the teacher then quickly reads and analyzes first drafts. Students prepare another draft using the same checklist.

The students then read on the topic using other guide materials as appropriate. After reading and discussing the assignment, they write a third draft to include important concepts from the reading. The teacher holds individual conferences with students as necessary.

There are several reasons why the GWP approach seems to facilitate writing in the content areas. First, integrating reading and writing tasks fosters synthesis of ideas and comprehension of content. Second, applying common criteria during the writing process has been found to improve the quality of finished products (Hillocks, 1982; Sager, 1973). A teacher-designed checklist with too much emphasis on form and mechanics, however, could be detrimental to some ESL students with fragile English skills who may not be able to focus on both form and content at once.

Modifications of the GWP could include cooperative formats in addition to the described teacher-directed approach. The opportunity to develop writing skills through content instruction in a cooperative environment assists second-language learners to achieve greater success than they might if they were struggling individually.

- Connecting school writing with community resources: Treuba, Moll, and Díaz (1982) collaborated with teachers in an ambitious writing project designed to meet Hispanic language minority students' writing needs. After observing forms and functions of writing in the home and community, these researchers created a series of modules that linked expository, school-sanctioned writing tasks to community issues and concerns.

For example, middle-level ESL students conducted home and community interviews and surveys on relevant topics (e.g., the value of bilingualism). Then, with careful teacher guidance and modeling in the form of "formula" paragraphs, they created papers that reflected the results of their work in the community. Because the project emphasized relevant, authentic communication and writing as a learning tool and provided initial structured guidance with eventual self-regulation, students' writing, and their attitudes toward writing, improved dramatically.

The importance of cultural relevance was also noted in a 1990 study by Pritchard, who examined the role of cultural schemata in reading comprehension. Making a strong connection between the community and the subjects studied in school can help teachers address the interests and needs of students in heterogeneous classrooms.

3. Cooperative learning activities. Linguistically diverse learners also benefit from content instruction that incorporates cooperative learning activities.

Several of the strategies highlighted here, such as the GWP and ETR, lend themselves to cooperative adaptations.

In an extensive review of the benefits of cooperative learning for language minority students, Kagan (1986) notes that in cooperative classrooms minority students often make strong gains, are more involved in activities, receive more practice with learning concepts, spend more time on task, and become motivated to learn. Kagan offers several explanations for these findings.

First, cooperative learning is more "culturally congruent" with students from Mexican American and Asian backgrounds, for example, because these cultures value cooperation and group interaction. Second, in a cooperative classroom, all students receive equal amounts of teacher attention and have equal opportunities to learn. Finally, peer and group rewards serve as strong motivators. Fortunately, many staff-development programs offer teachers training in cooperative learning.

The types of cooperative learning activities that Kagan recommends for minority students in regular classrooms include the following:

- Student Teams-Achievement Divisions (STAD): STAD (Slavin, 1978) activities involve five components: (a) teacher introduction or presentation of material to be learned; (b) formation of teams comprising four or five students representing a range of ability levels, ethnic backgrounds, English proficiency, and sexes, who use peer tutoring to master the assigned material; (c) individual quizzes on the material; (d) a team scoring system based on improvement; and (e) recognition and rewards for team performance.

Although it is true that STAD is not entirely free of competition, the team aspect of this strategy contributes to the ESL learner's increased opportunities to master content without the added stress of individual English language mastery.

- Jigsaw: In a Jigsaw approach, students develop interdependence. Each student selects one section of a unit to teach to other group members. Each group member is also assigned to an "expert group" of students from other groups responsible for the same assigned material.

Students meet in expert groups to discuss and master the material. Following that, they teach the material to members of their home groups; everyone is ultimately responsible for all the material.

Jigsaw formats usually include extensive initial team-building activities to prepare students to communicate effectively. Jigsaws also use heterogeneous groups of five or six students and a student-selected group leader who facilitates group processes. Students take tests or quizzes individually.

- Finding Out/Descubrimiento: Originally designed for elementary students, Finding out/Descubrimiento (Cohen, DeAvila, & Intiti, 1981; DeAvila, Duncan, & Navarrete, 1987) is a Spanish/English cooperative inquiry-based science program that has potential for older students as well. Weekly activities connected to content area topics are organized by themes (e.g., electricity, measurement) and assignments are designed to promote thinking skills (inquiring, comparing, examining, and drawing conclusions).

Students form linguistically heterogeneous groups and interact cooperatively as they move from one learning center to another through a series of activities related to the theme. Activity cards with instructions are provided in English and Spanish, allowing the students to use the language with which they feel most comfortable to carry out the task. These hands-on activities allow students opportunities to manipulate and work with concepts under study.

In particular, the program was designed to provide limited English speakers with access to higher order learning not often available to them when mastery of English is made the prerequisite. The program assigns different "roles" to students (e.g., facilitator, checker, reporter, clean-up person) so each can be responsible for completing the task. Students are assessed individually.

An interesting byproduct of this program is that students with limited English proficiency quickly learn the English technical terms and appropriate language for conducting the activities. It becomes unnecessary to teach vocabulary in isolation from the task. Acquisition of English emerges naturally and rapidly through its integration in the content areas because it is learned in the context of solving problems.

Although to our knowledge this program has not yet been tested with secondary students, it has great potential as a model for content area curricula in classrooms that include students with limited English proficiency. We present it here simply as a good example of a program that includes the three components that we consider crucial for success.

Benefits for students and teachers

We have presented here only those instructional strategies that have been well researched or appear to match the needs of language minority students, for two reasons: first, the mismatch between students' first language and the language of instruction causes insecurity in teachers unaccustomed to mixed language groups in the same classroom; second, the common practice of limiting second-language students' access to meaningful, higher order content on the assumption that limited English proficiency indicates low intellectual potential is unfounded.

Too often, teachers relegate instruction of limited English speakers to bilingual or ESL specialists in the belief that only specialists have the expertise to teach these students. However, while the ESL teachers may have training in language development, they are not necessarily experts in content area instruction. Furthermore, there are not enough specialists to meet the needs of ESL students in middle and secondary schools where content area learning is central to the curriculum and students spend most of their time in these classes.

Content area teachers must share in the responsibility for making a difference in the academic success of linguistically diverse students. Although willing, they may lack knowledge of strategies to accommodate these students in the context of regular, meaningful instruction. The strategies we have presented here are offered as a way to make their jobs as subject area teachers easier as they work with the growing number of diverse learners and strive to make them an integral part of the learning environment.

References

Allington, R.L. (in press). Children who find learning to read difficult: School responses to diversity. In E.H. Hiebert (Ed.), *Literacy for a diverse society: Perspectives, programs and policies.* New York: Teachers College Press.

Applebee, A.N., Langer, J.A., & Mullis, I.V.S. (1989). *Crossroads in American education.* Princeton, NJ: Educational Testing Service.

Au, K. (1979). Using the experience-test-relationship method with minority children. *The Reading Teacher, 32,* 677–679.

Bock, E. (1986). The comprehension strategies of second language learners. *TESOL Quarterly, 2,* 463–491.

Boyle, O.F., & Peregoy, S.F. (1990). Literacy scaffolds: Strategies for first- and second-language readers and writers. *The Reading Teacher, 44,* 194–200.

Carrell, P.L., Pharis, B.G., & Liberto, J.C., (1989). Metacognitive strategy training for ESL reading. *TESOL Quarterly, 23,* 647–678.

Cohen, E.G., DeAvila, E., & Intiti, J.A. (1981). *Multi-cultural improvement of cognitive ability.* Unpublished manuscript.

Coley, J.D., & Hoffman, D.M. (1990). Overcoming learned helplessness in at-risk readers. *Journal of Reading, 33*(7), 497–502.

Cummins, J., & Swain, M. (1986). *Bilingualism and special education: Issues in assessment and pedagogy.* San Diego, CA: College Hill.

DeAvila, E., Duncan, S., & Navarrete, C. (1987). *Finding out/descubrimiento.* Northvale, NJ: Santillana.

Díaz, S., Moll, L.C., & Mehan, H. (1986). Sociocultural resources in instruction: A context-specific approach. In *Beyond language: Social and cultural factors in school in language minority students.* Los Angeles, CA: Evaluation, Dissemination & Assessment Center, California State University.

Hillocks, G. (1982). The interaction of instruction, teacher comment, and revision in teaching the composing process. *Research in the Teaching of English, 16,* 261–278.

Hu, A. (1989). Asian Americans: Model minority or double minority? *Amerasian Journal, 15,* 243–257.

Kagan, S. (1986). Cooperative learning and sociocultural factors in schooling. In California Department of Education, *Beyond language: Social and cultural factors in schooling language minority students* (pp. 231–298). Los Angeles, CA: California State University.

Krashen, S.D., (1981). *Second language acquisition and second language learning.* New York: Pergamon.

Langer, J.A.(1984). Examining background knowledge and text comprehension. *Reading Research Quarterly, 19,* 461–481.

Langer, J.A., Bartolome, L., Vasquez, O., & Lucas, T. (1990). Meaning construction in school literacy tasks: A study of bilingual students. *American Educational Research Journal, 27,* 427–471.

Moll, L.C., & Díaz, S. (1987). Change as the goal of educational research. *Anthropology and Education Quarterly, 18,* 300–311.

Molner, L.A. (1989). *Developing background for expository prose: The effects of a prereading treatment on comprehension and topic-specific knowledge.* Unpublished doctoral dissertation, University of Colorado, Boulder, CO.

Nash, P.T. (1990). ESL and the myth of the model minority. In S. Benesch (Ed.), *ESL in America: Myths and possibilities.* Portsmouth, NH: Heinemann.

Oakes, J. (1985). *Keeping track: How schools structure inequality.* New Haven, CT: Yale University Press.

Pritchard, R. (1990). The effects of cultural schemata on reading processing strategies. *Reading Research Quarterly, 25*(4), 273–295.

Raimes, A. (1980). Composition: Controlled by the teacher, free for the student. In K. Craft (Ed.), *Readings on English as a second language: For teachers and teacher trainees* (pp. 386–398). Cambridge, MA: Winthrop.

Sager, C. (1973). *Improving the quality of written composition through pupil use of rating scale.* Paper presented at the Annual Meeting of the National Council of Teachers of English. (ERIC Document Reproduction Service No. ED 089 304)

Searfoss, L.W., Smith, C.C., & Bean, T.W. (1981). An integrated language strategy for second language learners. *TESOL Quarterly, 15,* 383–389.

Slavin, R.E. (1978). *Using student team learning.* Baltimore, MD: Johns Hopkins University, Center for Social Organization of Schools.

Snow, M.A., & Brinton, D.M. (1988). Content-based language instruction: Investigating the effectiveness of the adjunct model. *TESOL Quarterly, 22,* 553–574.

Tchudi, S.N., & Huerta, M.C. (1983). *Teaching writing in the content areas: Middle school/junior high.* Washington, DC: National Education Association.

Trueba, H.T., Díaz, S., & Díaz, R. (1984). *Improving the functional writing of bilingual secondary school students* (Final Report; NIE 400-81-0023). Washington, DC: National Institute of Education.

Trueba, H., Moll, L.C., & Díaz, S. (1982). *Improving the functional writing of bilingual secondary school students* (Context No. 400-81-0023). Washington, DC: National Institute of Education.

READING 2: Black English: Its History and Its Role in the Education of Our Children

Brian C. Lewis

The fact that many Black Americans, especially inner-city children, speak in a language of slang is an easily observable fact. The name given to this speech has ranged from "the language of soul" to "the shuffling speech of slavery." Concern has been raised in recent times over the role and implications of this language in trying to educate inner-city African American children who speak in the language of slang. The performance of these children continues to lag behind that of Whites. To examine the role that this lingo plays in the continuing disparity

Copyright ©1995, 1996 and Intellectual Property of Brian C. Lewis. Reprinted by permission between the performance of Black and White children, it is necessary and helpful to examine the history of this language of slang, or Black English, as linguists have come to call it.

Academic and Social Interest in Black English

Interest in the existence of Black English began in the early twentieth century. In 1924, linguist George Philip Krapp published the article "The English of the Negro." A year later he followed up his article with the book *English Language in America*. Krapp attributed the existence of Black English to the "baby-talk" that he felt slave masters must have employed when speaking to their slaves. He hypothesized that slave masters addressed their servants in a simplified English, "the kind of English some people employ when they talk to babies," (Smitherman, 172). The view that Blacks who spoke in Black English were deprived of a real, dynamic, and multi-faceted language continued through the 1960s. In 1968, British sociologist Basil Bernstein wrote that "much of lower-class language consists of a kind of incidental emotional accompaniment to action here and now," (Stoller, 93). In 1966, Karl Bereiter, in his work with four-year-old Black children, concluded that ". . . the children had no language." He continued saying that "The language of culturally deprived children . . . is not merely an underdeveloped version of standard English, but it is a basically non-logical mode of expressive behavior," (Stoller, 93).

It was also in the 1960s that an audible defense of the logic and legitimacy of Black English was launched. The Black Arts Movement of the 1960s featured a long needed appreciation and celebration of Blackness. The language of Black Americans was included in that celebration. Black poet Haki Madhubuti said simply, "Black poets [will] deal in . . . Black language or Afro-American language in contrast to standard English . . . will talk of kingdoms of Africa, will speak in Swahili and Zulu, will talk in muthafuckas and can you dig it," (Smitherman, 180). Around the same time, William Labov, a linguist at the University of Pennsylvania, followed by J.L. Dillard, Geneva Smitherman, and other linguists, mounted an impressive defense of the legitimacy of Black English. Labov published a number of essays and three books in the late 1960s that refuted the language deprivation theories of previous times. Labov described Carl Bereiter as ". . . handicapped by his ignorance of the most basic facts about human language and those who speak it," (Stoller, 127). In his essay "The Logic of Non-Standard English," Labov concludes that "All linguists agree that nonstandard dialects are highly structured systems; they do not see these dialects as accumulations of errors caused by the failure of their speakers to master standard English," (Stoller, 125). With the assistance of linguists and the Black Arts Movement, Black English gained a large amount of legitimacy. The demise of legal segregation brought Blacks and Whites together in the classroom. At first, White children performed better than Black children. This was easily explained by the recently outlawed separate and unequal facilities. Black children, it was thought, would soon fully integrate and perform at parity with White children. Continuing disparity in the performance and test scores had resulted in a dilemma for Black children and the school systems that are charged with the duty of their education.

History and Development of Black English

Many linguists trace the development of Black English back to the time of slavery and the slave trade. Thus, the history of Black English must date back to about 1619 when a Dutch vessel landed in Jamestown with a cargo of twenty Africans (Smitherman, 5). During the slave trade, ships collected slaves from several different nations rather than just trading with one nation. The rationale that justified this action was simple. Africans from different nations spoke different languages and could not communicate with each other, and thus were incapable of uniting to overthrow the ship's crew. In 1744 slave ship Captain William Smith wrote: ". . . the safest way to trade is to trade with the different Nations, on either Side the River, and having some of every sort on board, there will be no more Likelihood of their succeeding in a Plot, than of finishing the Tower of Babel," (Stoller, 19). Upon arriving in America, all the slaves had to be able to communicate with their masters in some way. Thus, all the slaves had to learn at least some degree of English vocabulary. This established English as a common language among slaves. The one language that all the slaves had in common was English. Linguists propose that Africans developed a pidgin language with English language providing the vocabulary.

When the African slaves bore children, they must have taught them this African-English pidgin. It was necessary that they be able to communicate with the slave master, as well as other slaves. This by no means suggests that Africans immediately relinquished their mother tongues. It is probable that the children of slaves were taught original African languages, but they were probably of little use amongst their diverse peer group. The African-English pidgin now had native speakers and would be forced to fill the needs of a normal speech community. Any vocabulary needs would be filled by borrowing from other languages. The pidgin graduated from its role as a language of transaction, and became a creolized language (Stoller, 21). Geneva Smitherman proposed that "this lingo [early Black English] involved the substitution of English for West African words, but within the same basic structure and idiom as that characterized West African language patterns," (Smitherman, 5). In a very real sense, this new language was a mixture of West African languages (such as Ibo, Yoruba, and Hausa) and English. Listed below are some of the West African language rules that were embedded in early Black English that Smitherman notes in her book *Talkin and Testifyin.*

Very little evidence of the speech of slaves exists from the 17th century, the earliest time in the language's history. However, in 1692 Justice Hawthorne recorded Tituba, an African slave from the island of Barbados in the British West Indies, speaking in the pidgin of the slaves. Tituba was quoted as saying "He tell me he God," (Smitherman, 5). The words of the phrase are English, but the structure and grammar of the phrase are congruous with that of the West African Languages that Smitherman identifies. In the eighteenth century, more

Grammar and Structure Rule in West African Language	Black English
Construction of sentences without the form of the verb to be	He sick today. They talkin about school now.
Repetition of noun subject with pronoun	My father, he work there.
Question patterns without do	What it come to?
Same form of noun for singular and plural	one boy; five boy
No tense indicated in verb	I know it good when he ask me.
Same verb form for all subjects	I know; you know; he know; we know; they know

Sound Rule in West African Languages	Black English
No consonant pairs	jus (for just); men (for mend)
Few long vowels or two-part vowel (diphthongs)	rat (for right); tahm (for time)
No /r/ sound	mow (for more)
No /th/ sound	substitution of /d/ or /f/ for /th/; souf (for south) and dis (for this)

records of the speech of slaves and the representation of their speech were produced. In fact, J.L. Dillard claims that "By 1715 there clearly was an African Pidgin English known on a worldwide scale," (Stoller, 23). Dillard justifies this claim by citing the pidgin's utilization in Defoe's *The Family Instructor* (1715) and in *The Life of Colonel Jaque* (1722), as well as in *Robinson Crusoe* (1719). "Yes, yes . . . me know, me know but me want speak, me tell something. O! me no let him makee de great master angry," a Virginia slave was depicted as saying in *The Life of Colonel Jaque* (Stoller, 23). Black characters made their way into show business in 1777 with the comical Trial of Atticus Before Justice Beau, for Rape. In this farcical production, "one of our neighbor's Negroes" says "Yesa, Maser, he tell me that Atticus he went to bus 'em one day, and a shilde cry, and so he let 'em alone," (Smitherman, 8). Much like Tituba's statement, the statements above use English vocabulary, yet the structure and grammar of the statements are well in keeping with that of the West African Languages.

Other informative evidence in tracing the development of Black English lies in newspaper ads reporting runaway slaves. In locating and identifying runaway slaves, the slaves' speech played an instrumental role. It is important to remember that the slave trade was not outlawed until 1808, and even then it was not strictly adhered to. Smitherman reports that "As late as 1858, . . ., over 400 slaves were brought direct from Africa to Georgia" (Smitherman, 12). Consequently, there was a constant influx of Africans who spoke no English at all. This produced a community of people with a broad array of mastery of Black English and even standard English. This is made clear when we look at the newspaper ads that reported runaway slaves. In 1744, an ad in *The New*

York Evening Post read: "Ran away . . . a new Negro Fellow named Prince, he can't scarce speak a Word of English." In 1760, an ad in the *North Carolina Gazette* read: "Ran away from the Subscriber, . . ., African Born . . ., speaks bad English." In 1734, the *Philadelphia American Weekly Mercury* read: "Run away . . .; he's Pennsylvanian born and speaks good English," (Smitherman, 13). This stratification of language is vital in the development and the development of the perception of Black English, if it is remembered that not all Blacks were slaves in Early America. Successful runaways were likely to be those who attained a relative mastery of standard English. The mastery of standard English would prove invaluable to a slave who had to travel a long distance across American soil to win his freedom. Furthermore, early Black writers, such as Frederick Douglass, wrote in the standard English of his time. A mastery of standard English was also beneficial in passing as a free Black. In a very real and disturbing way, Black English became the language of slavery and servitude.

During the civil war period, abolitionists made the speech of slaves known to all serious readers of that era. Writers such as Harriet Beecher Stowe and Thomas Haliburton produced many works that indicated their knowledge of the existence of Black English (Stoller, 31). While the Civil War and the emancipation of slaves were significant historical events, their impact was mitigated severely by the Jim Crow era. Although everyone labeled "Negro" by the Jim Crow laws did not speak Black English, it is safe to assume that those Blacks who did speak Black English far outnumbered those who spoke standard English. It is certain that under these conditions, Black English continued to flourish. *The Shadow of the Plantation* (1934) and B.A. Botkin's *Lay My Burden Down* reveal that Black English was still alive and well (Stoller, 36).

Perhaps the most significant event in the history in the development of Black English, aside from the inception of the European enslavement of Africans, is *Brown v. Board of Education of Topeka, Kansas* and the desegregation at "all deliberate speed" that ensued. Black children speaking Black English in the classroom has placed the language before the feet of educators. That brings us to the present pressing issue concerning the role of Black English in the inability of Black children to perform at parity with White children in our nation's school system. The following tables list the performance of Black and White children on Reading and Writing proficiency and the Scholastic Aptitude Test.

Scores in reading and writing proficiency and the Scholastic Aptitude Test all show the continuing disparity between the performance of Black children and White Children. The statistics do show that the disparity is decreasing at a very small rate. However, the Spring 1994 issue of *The Journal of Blacks in Higher Education* reported that "The racial gap in standardized test Scores is so wide and the rate at which the gap is closing is so small that absent some extraordinary and unforeseen event, Blacks will not catch up to Whites until well into the middle or latter part of the next century," (Cross, 49). The role that Black English plays in this disparity is a dynamic one. A language barrier can create hurdles in the communication between student and teacher, as well as creating barriers for students in comprehending the subject matter to be learned.

Black English & Education—Student Achievement

Reading and Writing Performance on Standardized Tests

Reading	Black	White
students at age 9 (1984)	185.7	218.3
students at age 13 (1984)	236.0	262.6
students at age 17 (1984)	264.2	295.6
students at age 9 (1988)	188.5	217.7
students at age 13 (1988)	242.9	261.3
students at age 17 (1988)	274.4	294.7

Writing	Black	White
students grade 4 (1984)	148.2	177.2
students grade 8 (1984)	188.3	217.9
students grade 11 (1984)	204.2	229.1
students grade 4 (1988)	150.7	180.0
students grade 8 (1988)	190.1	213.1
students grade 11 (1988)	206.1	225.3

UNITS: Reading level shown as score on scale: 150=rudimentary, 200=basic, 250=intermediate, 300=adept, 350=advanced. Writing level shown as score on scale: 100=unsatisfactory, 200=minimal, 300=adequate, 400=elaborate.

Scholastic Aptitude Test (SAT) Scores

Scholastic Aptitude Test (SAT)	Black	White
verbal (1975–1976)	332	451
math	354	493
verbal (1980–1981)	332	442
math	362	483
verbal (1984–1985)	346	449
math	376	491
verbal (1986–1987)	351	447
math	377	489
verbal (1987–1988)	353	445
math	384	490
verbal (1988–1989)	351	446
math	386	491

Source of Data: *Black Americans: A Statistical Sourcebook.* Edited by Alfred Garwood. Boulder, CO: Numbers & Concepts, 1992.

Educators differ over the way to overcome the existing problem that Black English creates in the schools. The traditional method used in dealing with Black English is simply to correct it as incorrect grammar. The *New York Times* reported a Bronx elementary teacher as saying that the problem may lie more with insufficient instruction than Black English. She was quoted as saying, "We need to stop making excuses for not teaching. When my students use bad English, I tell them it is bad English and that it has nothing to do with the color of their skin," (Lee, D22). It was in the same spirit that Ramon Cortines, New York City's Schools Chancellor, said "The problem with American education is we get caught up in fads and don't teach the basics," (Lee, D22). These views are consistent with the New York City Board of Education's decision to set no policy on teaching students who speak Black English (Lee, D22). However, individual teachers and school districts are beginning to lose faith in the traditional method, and are now trying their own innovative techniques to teach students who speak Black English. The *New York Times* reported that Mark Halperin, a Manhattan teacher, has his students create a dictionary of Black English, which he has them translate into standard English (Lee, D22). Some school districts in cities with large Black populations are now developing and using programs to teach students who speak in Black English. The programs are very much like the technique that Mark Halperin uses. The programs attempt to show the children the differences between Black English and standard English.

Regardless of what the schools decide to do in the future concerning teaching students who speak Black English, the fact remains that at present a crisis exists. Those students who do speak Black English are falling by the wayside in America's educational system. Of course, Black English is not the sole reason for this crisis. Blacks who speak the vernacular tend to be those who live in impoverished, inner-city neighborhoods filled with violence. Because all of these issues cannot be tackled is not reason to tackle none of them. The charts that were listed on the previous page suggest that the traditional method is failing speakers of Black English. The reasons for this could be numerous; however, its adherence to the language deprivation theory of Bereiter and others is particularly alarming. If indeed Black English is a legitimate, structured system of communication, which linguists contend that it is, then it is not logical to call that language "incorrect" or "bad." Massey and Denton claim that because of such teaching methods "their [students'] confidence and self-esteem are threatened, thereby undermining the entire learning process" (Massey, 164). However, the new and innovative methods that some teachers and school districts are beginning to use adhere to the theory of the linguists, that Black English is a legitimate and intelligent form of communication. By treating Black English as a separate language, it allows teachers to demand standard English in the classroom without damaging the self-esteem of their students.

With the research of the linguists, it appears obvious that Black English is indeed a language with an enriched and developmental history like Spanish or any other language. It is no doubt that Black English has not been adequately addressed in our nation's school system. This plays a significant role in the disparity between the performances of Black and White Children. Recognition and appreciation of the language, especially in education circles, would only serve to enrich the education of all Americans.

Bibliography

Bernstein, Basil. "Social Class and Linguistic Development: A Theory of Social Learning," *Education, Economy, and Society,* A. H. Halsey, ed., Glencoe: The Free Press, 1961, 288–314.

Black Americans: A Statistical Sourcebook. Edited by Alfred Garwood. Boulder, CO: Numbers & Concepts, 1992.

Cross, Theodore, "Suppose There Was No Affirmative Action at the Most Prestigious Colleges and Graduate Schools," *The Journal of Blacks in Higher Education, 3* (Spring 1994):44–51.

Dillard, J.L. *Black English.* New York: Random House, 1972.

Duneier, Mitchell. "Earning Another Chance," *Chicago Tribune,* 29 December 1994, p1.

Hale, Janice E. *Black Children: Their Roots, Culture, and Learning Styles.* Provo, Utah: Brigham Young University Press, 1982.

Lee, Felicia R. "Lingering Conflict in the Schools: Black Dialect vs. Standard Speech," *New York Times,* 5 January 1994, pA1.

Massey, D.S. and N.A. Denton. *American Apartheid.* Cambridge, Massachusetts: Harvard, 1993.

Smitherman, Geneva. *Talkin and Testifyin: The Language of Black America.* Detroit: Wayne State University Press, 1986.

Stoller, Paul, ed. *Black American English.* New York: Dell Publishing Co., 1975.

READING 3: *Technological Literacy: More Questions Than Answers*

Anne Pelak

Technology, bells and whistles fully charged, inspires the popular notion that we are in the throes of an information revolution that only the computer literate will survive. Getting on the "information superhighway" and hurtling toward the "bridge to the twenty-first century" has become (in addition to an overnight cliché) no less than a presidential directive to our nation's schools.

It should not be terribly surprising that talk of an information revolution generates lots of discussion about wiring, hardware/software needs, and technical training, but very little discussion about "information." It is a given in our digital age that access to massive amounts of information is valuable and desirable. Moving forward from that given, it is tempting (perhaps especially for students) to blur the distinctions between quantity and quality and to

---

Reprinted by permission of the author.

impart a certain objectivity to information simply because it came from "the Web" or some other digitized source. With information available and readily accessible from traditionally published sources, from software and CD-ROM, and from the Internet, the challenge is certainly not in finding information, but in taking the time to critically think about it.

Interestingly, as digital information becomes easier to access and retrieve, much of it also seems to become more generic. Educational and "edutainment" materials rarely include information on authorship. Cyberspace connections on bulletin boards and in chatgroups, newsgroups, discussion lists, and Web pages are often anonymous or selectively constructed (intentionally or not) to filter out real-time social, gender, racial, or class connections. Some might argue that software authorship is of little significance (content is all) or that insight into the context of where and from whom digital information originates is irrelevant in the democratizing environment of digital technology. But that's only true if you believe that content can somehow be separated from a cultural or social context. Or that digital technology has, in fact, a democratizing effect. (Let's not forget that democratization on the Internet means that you can speak your mind because nobody really knows if you're a Black, a woman, a lesbian, a gay, or anything else that makes you "different." Once distinctions of difference emerge, so too does the racism, sexism, and homophobia of real-time.)

It's often suggested that high-speed digital technologies are simply tools that energize and facilitate (and, by implication, improve) both teaching and learning. This belief has its roots in the "bigger, better, faster" school of technocratic thought: Something may have been well taught using a textbook and limited visual aids, but it was better taught using filmstrips, and it will be best taught using digital enhancement. This is an unreflective posture and a potentially harmful one, especially as technology becomes more sophisticated and potentially intrusive. I recently attended a presentation in which an instructor demonstrated the use of VR (virtual reality) technology in the social studies classroom. Computers equipped with powerful processors and fast Ethernet connections took participants to a small Mayan home for a virtual visit. VR software allowed us, as cyberspace visitors, to manipulate the computer screen for a full 360 degree view of the interior of the dwelling. The instructor suggested that the images of poverty depicted in the scene were so powerful that students would get the point immediately—that they should appreciate their own good fortune in living in this country so rich with material benefits. As they say in cyberspace, I was >:-c (bummed out) by this teaching demonstration.

I honestly don't know what disturbed me more—realizing that multiculturally sensitive teachers are not the only ones visiting the little Mayan home on the Web, or the feeling that I had participated in a bit of voyeurism that served little purpose but to show off the technological wonder of VR. On reflection, many more questions than answers come to mind. Regardless of the intent, do we have a right (other than the one granted by technological capability) to shrink a bit of someone's private world in order to examine it in detail on our computer screens? Are we advancing education, or simply serving technology, when we embrace every new digital tool that comes down the information superhighway? Is (or should) computer literacy be about more than knowing how to keyboard and use computer applications? Whose job is it to teach students how to recognize and navigate the social spaces of technology? How long will it take classroom teachers to realize that technology belongs to them, and not the technocrats?

DISCUSSION QUESTIONS AND ACTIVITIES

1. Choose a passage or an article you might have your students read and develop a set of discussion questions to go along with the reading. Develop questions that help students comprehend, as well as critique, what has been written. Practice leading discussions with other members of the class.

2. Select a passage from a textbook or an article and apply some of the reading strategies suggested in this chapter. For example, you might develop a graphic organizer for the selection, or complete a K-W-L chart.

3. What could you do to motivate students who cannot read to read?

4. In what ways is the New Literacy movement compatible with multiculturalism?

5. Develop lesson plans that incorporate reading, writing, and speaking. Be aware of how these lessons support the development of literacy in your students. Review your lessons for their applicability with nonnative English speakers. (See the Reyes and Molner reading.)

6. Pelak ends her essay on technological literacy with a series of questions. Find someone with whom to discuss her questions. How do issues of race, gender, and socioeconomic status affect the tools of technology? How does the technology enhance or change the literacy process? How does it advance pedagogy that is democratic and liberatory?

7. Review the article "Black English: Its History . . . ." What information was new to you? Compare this information with stories about Black English or Ebonics reported in mainstream press. How might a teacher use this information? Make a list of ways in which you could affirm students' language in your class.

REFERENCES

Anderson, R. C., Spiro, R. J., and Anderson, M. C. 1977. Schemata as Scaffolding for the Representation of Information in Connected Discourse. *Technical Report 24.* Champaign: Center for the Study of Reading, University of Illinois.

Andersson, B. V., and Barnitz, J. G. 1984. Cross-cultural Schemata and Reading Comprehension Instruction. *Journal of Reading* 28(2): 102–108.

Au, K. H. 1993. *Literacy Instruction in Multicultural Settings.* Fort Worth, TX: Harcourt, Brace, Jovanovich.

Bloom, A. 1987. *The Closing of the American Mind: How Higher Education Has Failed Democracy and Impoverished the Souls of Today's Students.* New York: Simon & Schuster.

Bloome, D. 1986. Building Literacy and the Classroom Community. *Theory into Practice,* 2(2): 71–76.

Chandler, D. 1997. Technological or Media Determinism: Technology as Neutral or Non-Neutral. http://www.aber ac uk/-dgc/tdet08.html

Constanzo, W. 1994. Reading, Writing and Thinking in an Age of Electronic Literacy. In Cynthia L. Selfe, C. L. and Hillgoss, S. (eds.) *Literacy and Computers: The Complications of Teaching and Learning with Technology.* New York: Modern Language Association, pp. 11–22.

Farr, M., and Daniels, H. 1986. *Language Diversity and Writing Instruction.* Urbana, Illinois: ERIC.

Freire, P. 1970. *Pedagogy of the Oppressed.* New York: Seabury.

Freire, P. 1987. *The Politics of Education: Culture Power and Liberation* (translated by Donaldo Macedo). South Hadley, MA: Bergin and Garvey.

Friere, P. and Macedo, D. 1987. *Literacy: Reading the Word and the World.* New York: Bergin and Garvin.

Gee, J. P. 1987. What is Literacy? *Teaching and Learning,* 2(1): 3–11.

Giroux, H. 1985. Introduction. *The Politics of Education: Culture, Power and Liberation.* Paulo Freire (translated by Donaldo Macedo). South Hadley, MA: Bergin and Garvey, pp. xi–xxv.

Goodman, K. 1986. *What's Whole in Whole Language?* Portsmouth, NH: Heinemann.

Graff, H. J. 1987. *The Legacies of Literacy: Continuities and Contradictions in Western Culture and Society.* Bloomington: University of Indiana Press.

Heath, S. B. 1982. Questioning at Home and at School: A Comparative Study. In G. Spindler (ed.) *Doing the Ethnography of Schooling: Educational Anthropology in Action.* New York: Holt, Rinehart and Winston, pp. 102–131.

Heath, S. B. 1983. *Ways with Words: Language, Life, and Work in Communities and Classrooms.* Cambridge: Cambridge University Press.

Hirsch, E. D. 1987. *Cultural Literacy: What Every American Needs to Know.* New York: Houghton Mifflin.

Illich, I. 1987. A Plea for Research on Lay Literacy. *Interchange, 18:* 9–22.

Irwin, J. W. 1991. *Teaching Reading Comprehension Processes.* 2nd ed. Englewood Cliffs, NJ: Prentice-Hall.

Kaplan, R. B. 1980. Cultural Thought Patterns in Inter-cultural Education. In K. Croft (ed.), *Readings on English as a Second Language.* Cambridge, MA: Winthrop, pp. 401–418.

Keenan, J. W., Willett, J., and Solsken, J. 1993. Focus on Research: Constructing an Urban Village: School/Home Collaboration in a Multicultural Classroom. *Language Arts, 70*(March): 204–214.

LeBlanc, P. J. 1994. The Politics of Literacy and Technology in Secondary School Classrooms. In Cynthia L. Selfe, C. L., and Hillgoss, S. (eds.) *Literacy and Computers: The Complications of Teaching and Learning with Technology.* New York: Modern Language Association, pp. 22–36.

Lipson, M. Y., and Wixson, K. K. 1997. *Assessment and Instruction of Reading and Writing Disability: An Interactive Approach.* New York: Longman.

Macedo, D. 1995. Literacy for Stupidification: The Pedagogy of Big Lies. In Sleeter, C. E., and McLaren, P. L., (eds.) *Multicultural Education, Critical Pedagogy and the Politics of Difference.* Albany: State University of New York Press.

Matsuyama, U. K. 1983. Can Story Grammar Speak Japanese? *The Reading Teacher, 36*: 666–669.

McCaleb, S. P. 1994. *Building Communities of Learners.* New York: St. Martin's.

McLaren, P. 1991. Culture or Cannon? Critical Pedagogy and the Politics of Literature. In Masahiko Minami and Bruce P. Kennedy (eds.), *Language Issues in Literacy and Bilingual/Multicultural Education.* Cambridge, MA: Harvard Educational Review, pp. 286–309.

Michaels. S. 1981. "Sharing Time" Children's Narrative Styles and Differential Access to Literacy." *Language in Society, 10*(3): 423–442.

Michaels. S. 1986. Narrative Presentations: An Oral Preparation for Literacy. In J. Cook-Gumperz (ed.) *The Social Construction of Literacy.* Cambridge, MA: Cambridge University Press, pp. 94–116.

Ogbu, J. U. November 1992. Understanding Cultural Diversity and Learning. *Educational Researcher, 21*(8): 5–14.

President Clinton's Call to Action for American Education in the 21st Century. http://www.ed.gov/updates/Pres/EdPlan/part11.html

Reynolds, R. E., Taylor, M. A., Steffensen, M. S., Shirey, L. L., and Anderson, R. C. 1982. Cultural Schemata and Reading Comprehension. *Reading Research Quarterly, 17*: 353–66.

Shor, I. 1992. *Empowering Education: Critical Teaching for Social Change.* Chicago: University of Chicago Press.

Smith, F. 1975. *Comprehension and Learning.* New York: Holt, Rinehart and Winston.

Solsken, J., Keenan, J. W., and Willet, J. Fall, 1993. Interweaving Stories: Creating a Multicultural Classroom through School/Home/University Collaboration. *Democracy & Education*: 16–21.

Willinsky, J. 1990. *The New Literacy: Redefining Reading and Writing in the Schools.* New York: Routledge.

Zeni, J. 1994. Literacy, Technology and Teacher Education. In Cynthia L. Selfe, C. L. and Hillgoss, S. (eds.) *Literacy and Computers: The Complications of Teaching and Learning with Technology.* New York: Modern Language Association, pp. 76–86.

Chapter Seven

Culturally Responsive Assessment

Immigrants from Asia—almost all from China and Japan—were among the most ghetto-bound of the newcomers, rigidly segregated in their "China town" communities.... Few American officials paid any attention to whether Asian-American children attended public schools.... Almost every American of European ancestry believed Asians were racially inferior. (Wilson, Gilbert, Nissenbaum, Kupperman, & Scott, 1990. *The Pursuit of Liberty,* pp. 633–635)

When one scientist found at the turn of the century that Blacks generally performed better than Whites on tests of memory, he explained that their superior mnemonic ability was "naturally expected" since "in both races... the memory is in decadence from primitive conditions, but... the Blacks are much nearer those conditions." A decade later a famous English researcher found that on tests of memory the sons of the rich displayed "complete superiority" over the sons of the working class, a result that led him to the obvious conclusion that a disciplined memory was characteristic of greater intelligence. Yet when a well-known contemporary psychologist found that poor and Black children with low IQ scores had excellent memories, he concluded that memory should not properly be considered a component of "intelligence." (Tucker, 1994, *The Science and Politics of Racial Research,* p. 3)

[C. Steele and J. Aronson] gave two groups of Black and White Stanford undergraduates a test composed of the most difficult verbal-skills questions from the Graduate Record Exam. Before the test, one group was told that the purpose of the exercise was only to research "psychological factors involved in solving verbal problems," while the other group was told that the exam was "a genuine test of your verbal abilities and limitations.". . . The Blacks who thought they were simply solving problems performed as well as the Whites (who performed equally in both situations). However, the group of Black students who labored under the belief that the test could measure their intellectual potential performed significantly worse than all the other students. . . . [C. Steele and S. Spencer have] run eight additional experiments showing that stereotype vulnerability can negatively affect women who believe a math test shows "gender differences." The negative impact of stereotype vulnerability has even appeared in White men told that Asians tended to outperform Whites on that particular exam. (Watters, 1995)

If we take an honest look at the history of testing in this country, the insidious and cyclical debates of intellectual superiority based on race, and past and present practices of assessment in our schools, we have no choice but to consider race when we talk about assessment. Race has always been an integral part of assessment and to omit it from a chapter on assessment would be a disservice to future middle and secondary school teachers. Teachers find assessment one of their most difficult tasks. Teachers want to be fair, but *(un)fair* has its historical antecedents. Teachers who are aware of past practices are in a much better position to provide their students with fairer assessments.

Our opening quotes offer evidence of how descendants of western European Americans have allowed racist notions to influence their views on the intellectual inferiority or superiority of different groups. The first quote dealing with the "intellectual inferiority" of the Chinese contrasts starkly with today's perception of Asian intellectual superiority! Obviously, views on intellectual capacity develop within a social-political context and, as suggested in our second quote, researchers interpret scientific evidence to support *their* preferred versions of reality. Students don't take tests in a vacuum, and Claude Steele's research demonstrates how even subtle messages or cues about race or gender and ability can affect student performance.

This chapter is organized around a series of questions: What is the historical context of testing in the United States? What are the current trends in assessment? What are the responsibilities of culturally responsive teachers when assessing students? Following a brief overview of testing in the United States and common assumptions underlying our assessment practices, we present several examples of current assessment methods at the national and classroom levels and their implications for fair assessment. Finally, we consider the role teachers must play in developing culturally responsive assessment practices.

WHAT IS THE HISTORICAL CONTEXT OF TESTING IN THE UNITED STATES?[1]

By today's standards, students attending colonial schools were tested rather informally. Testing was often done individually with students reciting their lessons as they were ready. Emphasis was placed on behavior and performance—being able

---

[1] Assessment involves both measurement and evaluation. Measurement provides us with quantifiable data that can then be evaluated. "A test is a means of measuring the knowledge, skills, feelings, intelligence, or aptitude of an individual or group." (Gay, 1985, p. 9)

to read material out loud, respond to teachers' questions during class, or perform mathematical problems at the chalkboard. Assessment was ongoing and informal. Results were shared with parents "incidentally" when teacher and parents saw each other at church or the local store. There was no state or national testing—no figures to let districts know how their students compared with others, or how well teachers were doing their jobs. In southern colonies, only the elite had access to education, and schooling usually took place in the home under the supervision of hired tutors.

As our nation became more industrialized, secondary schooling became more formalized. The private academy was an alternative to Latin grammar schools and offered middle-class children a broader, more practical curriculum. First proposed by Benjamin Franklin in 1751, the academy was most popular during the first half of the nineteenth century. Eventually, the public high school replaced the academy. Legislation allowing states to use tax monies to fund secondary schools brought large numbers of students into classrooms.

"The American population kept pace with industrial growth. For every 100 people living in the United States in 1870, there were 126 in 1880, 158 in 1890, 190 in 1900, and 230 in 1910" (Wilson et al., 1990, p. 633). Most of these immigrants came from southern and eastern Europe. The economic needs of industry for a skilled labor force, and the sociopolitical reality of this increased immigration set the stage for large-scale testing.

Political leaders and captains of industry needed a mechanism (some would say justification) by which people could assume their "rightful places" in society. In the 1900s, Social Darwinism was a popular theory. If natural selection was operating in nature, why not apply it to the human condition? The fittest "naturally" would rise to the top of the economic and social ladder, and competition would ensure that only the best rose to the top. According to Stephen Jay Gould (1996) in *The Mismeasure of Man,* "the initial meaning referred to a specific theory of class stratification within industrial societies, particularly to the idea that a permanently poor underclass consisting of genetically inferior people had precipitated down into their inevitable fate" (p. 368).

This belief coupled nicely with the myth of the American meritocracy that viewed prosperity as the result of individual effort, ambition, and ability. Depending on an individual's perspective, formalized testing grew out of a need to evaluate human potential, to provide appropriate educational instruction, to justify people's "natural" place in society, or to reinforce the present power structure.

Formalized testing developed along two, not mutually exclusive, fronts: one, IQ testing—the measuring of an individual's general intelligence,[2]—and

---

[2] The concept of general intelligence (a "g" figure that represents some general ability level separate from specific cognitive processes) is debatable. Many psychologists (Gardner, 1985; Sternberg, 1985) dispute the legitimacy of such a number regardless of the statistical procedures that make quantifying such a number possible. In addition, the belief in intelligence as an inherited and unchangeable quantity is challenged. Although recognizing that individuals are born with differences in ability, psychologists emphasize the impact of environment on influencing achievement.

two, school-based achievement and aptitude testing. Many students are familiar with the Stanford-Binet Intelligence Test (adapted from the Binet scale) that has been a mainstay in public education for several decades. Developed by Alfred Binet in France to help identify children with special needs, the Binet test consisted of a number of subtests for which he claimed no theoretical underpinnings. He cautioned against its use as a test for "normal" children; the "scale is a rough, empirical guide for identifying mildly retarded and learning-disabled children who need special help" (p. 185). Finally, children's scores were not to be used as limitations on their learning capacity.

H. H. Goddard has the dubious distinction of popularizing Binet's scale in the United States, although he easily disregarded Binet's concerns. Goddard believed that intelligence *was* hereditary and that intelligence tests would yield a number representing a "single, innate entity" (p. 189). Working as the director of research at the Vineland Training School for Feeble-Minded Girls and Boys in New Jersey, he had coined the term *moron* to denote "high-grade" defectives (p. 188).

Almost immediately, Goddard began administering the test to immigrants arriving at Ellis Island. Results could determine an immigrant's status as a moron, imbecile, or feebleminded person, but even Goddard had trouble accepting the high numbers of feebleminded immigrants his research revealed! Eventually he concluded, "It should be noted that the immigration of recent years is of a decidedly different character from the early immigration . . . We are now getting the poorest of each race . . . The intelligence of the average 'third class' immigrant is low, perhaps of moron grade" (as cited in Gould, 1996, p. 197).

In *The Mismeasure of Man,* Gould writes comprehensively of the ways "in which this test was used to reinforce racist beliefs." As evident in the opening chapter quote, test results were often twisted to justify political and social policies. Immigrants, soldiers, Blacks in the North and South, and school children were given the test. Colonel Robert M. Yerkes, once a faculty member at Harvard, was responsible for overseeing the mental testing of 1.75 million recruits during World War I. Although results repeatedly suggested a strong link between scores and environment, findings were interpreted to support a theory of innate intelligence. When results indicated a relationship between schooling and intelligence, Yerkes opined that native intelligence is what made students stay in school longer. Blacks did not attend school because they had low intelligence. Yerkes noted the differences in scores for Blacks from southern and northern states.

> Many years later, Ashley Montagu (1945) studied the tabulations by state that Yerkes had provided. He confirmed Yerkes's pattern: the average score on Alpha was 21.31 for Blacks in thirteen Southern states, and 39.90 in nine Northern states. Montagu then noted that average Black scores for the four highest Northern state (45.31) exceeded the White mean for nine Southern states (43.94). . . . Hereditarians had their pat answer, as usual: only the best Negroes had been smart enough to move North. (Gould, 1996, pp. 249–250)

In 1924, the Immigration Restriction Act was passed, which limited immigration from foreign countries to 2 percent of that group's population noted in the 1890 census. Data obtained from these army tests helped convince Congress that it was in the national interest to limit the numbers of less intelligent people entering the United States.

Today, standardized testing is big business. Most testing companies are for profit; an exception is the Educational Testing Service (ETS), established in 1947 as a nonprofit organization. Nevertheless, the ETS 1996 annual report shows a yearly income of $460,018 and assets of more than $286 million. Concerns about equity and bias in testing are still present in the literature, and arguments for an innate model of intelligence surface on a regular basis.

As thoughtful educators and testing organizations work to eliminate inequities and develop alternative kinds of assessments, others discuss the assumptions of rank-ordering inherent in standardized testing. (See the chapter reading, "Alternative Assessment: Issues in Language, Culture, and Equity.") Given current calls for teacher and student accountability, however, large-scale testing likely will be with us for some time. We should not be naïve regarding the influence national and standardized testing has on *how* and *what* teachers teach. According to Kohn, "'Accountability' usually turns out to be a code for tighter control over what happens in classrooms by people who are not in classrooms . . ." (1999).

We also need to be aware of how political schooling and education have become. Every elected official is expected to have a policy on education—and no one wants to be soft on education! Much of the public discussion revolves around "getting tough," "having high standards," and "holding teachers and schools accountable." As Kohn points out, "In practice, 'excellence,' 'higher standards,' and 'raising the bar' all refer to scores on standardized tests, many of them multiple-choice, norm-referenced, and otherwise flawed. Indeed, much of the discussion about education today is arrested at the level of 'Test scores are low; make them go up.' All the limits of, and problems with, such testing amount to a serious indictment of the version of school reform that relies on these tests" (1999).

You will not be immune from these forces in your classrooms. Scores on standardized tests can result in greater pressure on you to teach a standard curriculum and to turn over more control of what is taught and how it is taught in your classroom. On the other hand, scores on standardized tests can result in greater opportunity for you to bring focus and coherence to your curriculum. Which outcome do you think is more realistic and why? What concerns might a multiculturalist have with a standard curriculum? How might a change agent respond to external pressures for higher test scores?

What Are the Current Trends in Classroom Assessment?

Assessment in the classroom has changed over time. In comparison with colonial methods of oral recitation, assessment instruments have become quite sophisticated. Tracking, the policy of grouping students based on ability, has come under professional and public scrutiny. (See the readings, "Successful

Detracking in Middle and Senior High Schools" and "Detracking Helps At-Risk Students" at the end of this chapter.) As educators have become more aware of the myriad factors affecting student achievement, they have attempted to respond. Assessment has moved beyond paper-and-pencil tests to include projects, portfolios, and media displays; in pre-service training programs, the integration of objectives, instruction, and assessment are emphasized.

New Approaches to Classroom Assessment

Most recent trends in classroom assessment advocate moving away from standardized, norm-referenced testing. Such tests have fallen into disfavor because of vocal criticisms ranging from cultural bias to increased demands on teachers to "teach to the tests" and additional pressures to "make a good showing" (Grant & Gomez, 1996, p. 89) for their school and school district. Recent school scandals involving alleged teacher or administrator altering of student test answers attest to the latter. In addition, reflective teachers need assessment tools that will guide instructional decisions. How students perform on formative (ongoing) assessment measures provides valuable information to teachers, allowing them to evaluate their instructional strategies and make improvements. The alignment of curriculum and assessment is a powerful trend in assessing what has been learned in the classroom.

As a consequence, educators have sought to develop tests that give a more genuine reading of, not only what content students have learned, but also what "approaches and processes" students can demonstrate (Garcia, 1994, p. 64). The terms *authentic assessment, portfolio assessment,* and *rubrics* are used to describe these new evaluation measures.

This new language of assessment can be confusing. Several researchers use some of the terms interchangeably, whereas others try to delineate the terminology with great specificity. Though it is easy to get bogged down in the labeling, the current trends reflect common goals and philosophical basis: a recognition of the shortcomings of commercialized, objective testing; a desire for tests that tap students' ability to demonstrate higher order thinking rather than recognition or recall of information; and assessments that reflect real-life tasks. What follows is a brief overview of the terms and their descriptions.

Alternative Assessment Alternative assessment is, perhaps, the most overarching and inclusive of the terms currently used. It refers to any assessment that differs from traditional paper-and-pencil tests, most particularly objective (rather than subjective) tests (Callahan, Clark, & Kellough, 1995; McMillan, 1997). Therefore, many of the other types of assessments (performance, authentic) fall into this category. Despite the variety of terms used, generally the terms have two major commonalities: "All are viewed as *alternatives* to traditional multiple-choice standardized achievement tests (and) . . . all refer to *direct* examination of student *performance* on significant tasks that are relevant to life outside of school" (Worthen, 1993, p. 445). Diaries, portfolios, writing samples over time, and projects allow teachers to focus on processes and encourage students to become more self-directed and reflective. As criticism of standardized testing grows, more and more educators turn to assessments that provide more relevant evaluation of students.

Authentic Assessment Authentic assessment refers to performance tasks that have some connection to the real world outside the classroom. These tasks can include writing an opinion piece for an editorial page, testing well-water for contaminates, or any activity that reflects skills and knowledge needed to act in ways usually associated with working in an adult setting. Such tasks emphasize skills in thinking, particularly synthesis, analysis and evaluation, and depth rather than breadth of knowledge. Authentic assessments provide "more expansive descriptions of learning" (Zessoules & Gardner, 1991, p. 49), something increasingly more attractive to educators.

Another defining characteristic of authentic assessment is that the procedures of testing must correlate to instruction. The ways in which students have actively engaged in the classroom necessarily becomes a part of assessment. For example, if students spend considerable time in classroom instruction generating solutions to a specific problem, carefully weighing options, and designing rationales for chosen action plan(s), an authentic assessment task would ask them to demonstrate those abilities rather than focus on isolated memorization related to the task. Specific application of higher-order thinking skills provide students with a stronger framework for synthesizing information in contrast to skills-based, decontextualized learning.

Portfolio Assessment Although a familiar term to some disciplines (for example, art, photography, journalism), portfolio assessments have a more recent history in today's middle school and secondary classrooms. Portfolios document students' learning with artifacts (samples of student work) produced as a "result of their regular learning activities" (Grant & Gomez, 1996, p. 100). Portfolios have been described as "purposeful" collections of students' work that "tell a story" of progress and development. Included in the artifacts are materials selected by the students themselves, in addition to self-assessments of one's own growth and productivity. Students must reflect (a metacognitive task encouraging students to think about their own thinking and learning) and evaluate their learning.

Performance-Based Assessment In performance-based assessments, students demonstrate learning through some product, construction, or creation. Proponents highlight the connection between teaching and assessment. What is taught is tested in appropriate ways (generally reflecting constructivist and engaged learning rather than the rote memorization often associated with objective-type tests); what is tested informs instruction. Although not all performance assessments are authentic (Callahan, Clark, & Kellough, 1995; McMillan, 1997), many frequently are, emphasizing "hands on" activities and critical thinking skills. In addition, performance measures use a variety of standards and criteria that students encounter during the teaching/learning process, rather than solely at the end of instruction.

Rubrics Rubrics are a descriptive standard of student performance that evaluate levels of proficiency. Rubrics provide guidelines of what learners should know and should be able to do. "A rubric has three essential features: evaluative criteria, quality definitions, and a scoring strategy" (Popham, 1997, p. 72). Rubrics are primarily used with performance tests or the evaluation of products. Levels or degrees of proficiency (excellent, good, average, and so on) are assigned values based on an analytical or holistic determination of students' mastery of skills being assessed.

> An analytic-scoring rubric generally scores a given response on several different dimensions. For instance, a response might be scored on the basis of the student's mathematical knowledge, strategic knowledge, and level of communication (Cai, Jakabcsin, & Lane, 1996; Cai, Lane, & Jakabcsin, 1996) or on using representations, demonstrating accuracy, and making connections (Petit & Zawojewski, 1997). The response might be scored on the level at which a student understands the problem, the level at which a solution is planned, and the level at which a final solution is obtained (Charles, Lester, & O'Daffer, 1987). A holistic-scoring rubric differs from an analytic-scoring rubric in that a student's response is examined in its entirety and a score is assigned based on the entire response. Holistic-scoring rubrics often use a 0-to-4 or a 0-to-6 scale (Charles, Lester, & O'Daffer, 1987; Kenney & Silver, 1993; Marzano, Pickering, & McTighe, 1993; Stenmark, 1989). (cited by Thompson & Senk, 1998, p. 786)

Rubrics are generally given to students *before* the assessment performance so that students are aware of what is considered quality work for an *A* or *B*. For example, in writing a clear thesis, tight organization and supporting details are often cited as requirements for quality work. As you can see, rubrics can provide students with instructional goals as well as goals for assessment.

WHAT ARE THE TRENDS IN NATIONAL ASSESSMENT?

Another trend gaining some momentum in the 1990s has been national assessment with the federal government leading the way. President Clinton put his support behind national standards for assessment. "Under his plan, fourth-graders would take a rigorous new national test in reading, and eighth-graders would take one in math. Administration officials view the tests as a potentially powerful tool to help states and schools better judge how they are educating children" (Sanchez, 1997, p. A18). With the advent of curriculum reform suggested by Goals 2000 and national standards created by the designated "learned societies" (such as the National Council for the Social Studies, National Council for Teachers of English, National Council for Teachers of Math, National Science Teachers Association), the push for discipline-specific as well as comprehensive national assessments seems a logical result. We will look briefly at three federal initiatives: Goals 2000, national standards, and Title II Higher Education Amendments of 1998 Teacher Quality and Enhancement Grants.

Goals 2000

Under the initial direction of former President Bush and later support from President Clinton, who signed them into law, national educational goals, popularly known as Goals 2000, have tried to implement curriculum reform at the state and local levels. The goals, formalized in the *Goals 2000: Education Act of 1994,* focus on eight areas for all American schools to achieve by the year 2000:

1. *Readiness for school.* All children will start school ready to learn.
2. *High school completion.* The high school graduation rate will increase to at least 90 percent.
3. *Student achievement and citizenship.* All students will leave grades four, six, eight, and twelve with demonstrated competency in math, science, English, history, and geography; all students will learn to be responsible citizens and productive workers.
4. *Teacher education and professional development.* Teachers will have access to programs for the continued improvement of their professional skills and the opportunity to acquire the skills necessary to instruct and prepare all students for the next century.
5. *Science and mathematics.* U.S. students will be the first in the world in science and mathematics achievement.
6. *Adult literacy.* Every adult will be literate and possess the knowledge and skills to compete in a global economy.
7. *Safe, disciplined and drug-free schools.* Every school will be free of drugs and violence and will offer a disciplined environment conducive to learning.
8. *Parental participation.* Every school will promote partnerships that will increase parental involvement and participation in promoting social, emotional, and academic growth of children.

These goals have been criticized in a number of areas. Accomplishing these goals by the year 2000 is highly unrealistic. The nature of school and curricular reform is a slow and uneven process. The 1995 National Education Goals Report was encouraged by some progress, but the report is decidedly mixed:

> Mathematics achievement at Grades 4 and 8 has increased. The general health status of the nation's infants has improved. The proportion of pre-schoolers who are regularly read to and told stories has increased. Incidents of threats and injuries to students at school have declined. At the same time, we have lost ground . . . Reading achievement at Grade 12 has declined. Student drug use and the sale of drugs at school have increased. Fewer secondary school teachers reported holding a degree in their main teaching assignment in 1994 than 1991. The high school completion rate has not increased. Reading achievement in Grades 4 and 8, and mathematics achievement at Grade 12 have remained at

constant levels. There is still a large gap between White and minority students in college enrollment and completion rates. (pp. 4–5)

Title II Teacher Quality Enhancement Grants

In 1999, the U.S. Department of Education allocated $75 million in grant monies to states and K–12/higher education partnerships to address the challenge of ensuring "that every child has the chance to learn from caring, well-prepared teachers" (Department of Education, 1999). The Department of Education funded three types of grants: state grants to promote "comprehensive statewide reforms to improve teacher quality"; partnership grants to promote systemic change in how pre-service teachers have traditionally been prepared; and teacher recruitment grants aimed at "reducing shortages of qualified teachers in high-need districts" (p. 47). The expressed goals of the Title II grant initiatives are impressive: "The programs are designed to make a lasting impact on significant numbers of school districts, institutions of higher education, and new teachers—and ultimately to increase student achievement—through comprehensive approaches to improving teacher quality" (p. 47). We do not yet know how successful these programs will be. Your first teaching job might be in a school that is participating in a Title II grant program. In evaluating program success, it will be important to know how success, defined by increased student achievement, is determined. Fundamental change takes time and progress is, at best, difficult to plot. As a multiculturalist, you will want to investigate what instruments or benchmarks are used to gauge success and which programs result in success and for whom.

Other National Trends

Despite the caveats, state and local reform efforts are making some progress and see even small gains as harbingers of hope (Rothman, 1994). Futrell (1989) notes that new partnerships are now being investigated and formed among and between government, corporate, and educational groups (for example, "school to work" programs, coalitions between public and private schools, and higher education professional development schools). Educators have hailed these developments as exactly the kind of cooperation needed among these entities as more widespread support for change—rather than isolated piecemeal approaches—is developed.

The suggested national reforms have spurred states to evaluate and revise curriculum, establish competencies for teachers and students and determine more comprehensive school standards. Even though these reforms have increased the potential for more uniform accountability, the loss of flexibility in curriculum design is a noticeable drawback. This issue highlights a long-standing tension in American public education: the right of local, regional, and state communities to determine curriculum goals and content versus the federal government's interest in achieving some oversight of public education. Several questions emerge: Whose curriculum should be taught? Are the needs of students in California the same as those of students in Connecticut?

National Standards

The thrust for national standards has been developing along two lines. One is the creation of an organization, the National Board for Professional Teaching Standards (NBPTS), to certify teachers who meet content knowledge and standards of effective teaching pedagogy as set by the board. This board is unique in the teaching profession because it offers an opportunity for teachers to monitor and regulate the certification processes in much the same way as the medical and legal professions do. Diverse assessment tools include such alternative measurements as interviews, portfolios, and computer and video simulations (Smith & Smith, 1994).

The other thrust is toward national standards by discipline created by subject-specific professional organizations that determine what the standards should be. National standards have been proposed for the arts, civics and social studies, English/language arts/reading, foreign languages, geography, history, mathematics, science, and physical education (Callahan, Clark, & Kellough, 1995). These guidelines provide directives for state and local curriculum revisions.

National Curriculum/National Testing

Discussions of national curriculum and national testing are a tag-team event: The concept of national testing goes hand in hand with the development of a national curriculum that the national tests would reflect. Such tests would provide a framework for teachers of what attitudes, skills, and knowledge should be emphasized in the classroom. Comparisons of the educational development of students in the United States with students in other industrialized countries (particularly countries that have more centralized educational systems) have spurred the national curriculum debate. The debate, obviously, has its proponent and opponent viewpoints. Table 7-1, adapted from Ornstein and Levine (1993, p. 591), encapsulates major issues in the discussion surrounding a national curriculum.

It is sometimes difficult for teachers to relate to national issues, especially if the changes promoted "at the higher levels" appear to bear little relationship to what goes on in their classrooms. This would not be true if the United States adopted a national curriculum or national testing precisely for some of the reasons listed in Table 7-1. Future educators and multiculturalists should take the time to become aware of the arguments and consider how they might affect a diverse student population.

WHAT RESPONSIBILITIES DO CULTURALLY RESPONSIVE TEACHERS HAVE WHEN ASSESSING STUDENTS?

Culturally responsive teachers are aware of the history of testing and its racist and sexist underpinnings. Therefore, they are careful to review all assessment instruments and monitor them for bias and equity. These teachers evaluate

Table 7-1 Major Issues Surrounding National Curriculum Proposals

National Curriculum: PRO

- High levels of achievement, especially in areas such as math and science are partially attributed to the use of national curriculum in Japan and Korea.
- A carefully designed national curriculum makes it easier to achieve in-depth teaching of well-sequenced objectives and materials.
- Uniformity of objectives decreases inefficiencies and learning problems when students move from one classroom, school, or district to another.
- A national curriculum would facilitate improvement in teacher education programs.
- A national curriculum could draw on the best current thinking in each subject area.

National Curriculum: CON

- A national curriculum would run counter to some promising trends and would disempower teachers.
- A national curriculum would require using objectives and materials that are too difficult for some students and too easy for others.
- Lack of diversity in national curriculum materials will be unmotivating and uninteresting for some students.
- Teachers would likely feel compelled to use objectives and materials specified nationally, and funding would probably not be available for alternate materials.
- A national curriculum would reinforce tendencies to emphasize low-level skills and uncreative materials.

standardized tests and their uses in their school and school district. They ask, "What is the economic or political impact of students not doing well on these tests?" Moreover, teachers are vigilant and guard against sacrificing their curricula for teaching to the test.

In Chapter Three, we looked at how culture influences learning. If culture influences how students learn, then we can also expect it to affect how students demonstrate that learning. Assessment measures that let students show what they have learned in ways that are compatible to their learning styles should improve their performance. What then are the implications of cultural learning styles on assessment? A sound pedagogical response to different learning styles is to incorporate multiple assessment measures into overall evaluation. Teachers are already familiar with assessments, such as projects, presentations, and portfolios, in which students show what they have learned in a variety of ways. (We discussed several of these measures as current trends in classroom assessment.)

Even though educators often support these multiple measures in theory, they find it difficult to implement them in the classroom. First, there doesn't seem to be enough time to "meet everyone's assessment needs"; second, grading portfolios, group projects, and so on, is work intensive; and, three, teachers aren't convinced that these assessments are really as rigorous or as valid as paper-and-pencil tests. Teachers' assumptions about what it means to be smart and do well affect and are affected by their views of good assessment. In addition, teachers bring their own preferred learning styles to the process of developing assessment measures and can be unaware of how this affects student evaluation. One solution teachers have found useful as they expand their types of assessment is to develop careful criteria for performance. In addition to using rubrics, teachers have used rating/ranking scales and criteria sheets. This helps to validate the worthiness of the assessment measure and allay teacher concerns. A culturally responsive approach to assessment does not mean that students are only assessed using instruments that match their learning styles; rather the goal is to allow all students to expand their skills and validate differences among them.

We have looked at the current trends in assessment and recognized some salient commonalities: a commitment to improving the tools used in assessment, a desire to improve and assess students' critical thinking abilities, and the creation of tools that are more authentic. We have reported how current trends at the classroom level are more culturally responsive, and we see the link between classroom curriculum and instruction and assessment. We believe that classroom assessment requires more cultural responsiveness. Assessments that look at the personal experiences that students bring into the classroom, that use multiple measures, that support students' language and literacy development, and that involve the student in self-assessment all meet the criteria for culturally responsive assessment.

National assessment, national curriculum, and national testing have also fueled the assessment debate. We have concerns about these trends, particularly about their potential for being less culturally responsive beyond surface superficialities. Such measures, by their inherent standardization, allow less creativity and flexibility in curriculum design. The ability to design contextually meaningful measurement tools is seriously compromised by the adoption of national directives.

What else might you as middle and secondary teachers do to create an assessment environment where all students have an opportunity to excel, an environment that eliminates the racial vulnerability described by Claude Steele (April, 1992)? Here we offer several additional suggestions for classroom implementation:

- Be sure to assess your inclusive, multicultural curriculum. Students know what knowledge is important by what is assessed.
- Use authentic assessment to inform your instructional strategies. Using a cultural lens to analyze assessment measures, you can then modify their instructional practices.
- Provide explicit instructions for your tests. This can include the purpose of the test, its relevance to students, and comments on the test format. When appropriate, teachers can explain the structure of test questions and help students develop their metacognitive awareness for test taking.
- Make sure that tests are not tests of language. This is particularly important for nonnative speakers of English. Explaining test questions, providing synonyms, and providing a framework for responding can minimize the interference of language skills.

- Engage in self-reflection and encourage self-reflection and performance assessment by students. Reflection is also an opportunity for dialogue between teacher and student.
- Make final evaluation decisions based on your knowledge of content, students, and the assessment tool. Providing students with timely, specific, positive, and constructive feedback is important.

A chapter on assessment would not be complete without our reminding you of how critical expectations are in the evaluation process. Teachers who implement the latest in authentic assessment, develop rigorous rubrics for evaluation, and champion a "get smart" approach to intelligence must still be vigilant when it comes to assessing individual students. What expectations will you have for individual students? Middle and, especially, secondary school teachers, have many more students and spend less time with their students than elementary teachers do, thus making it more difficult to develop personal relationships and to invest in individual student achievement. High expectations translate into more student-intensive time—time to encourage students, to ask for revised work, and to monitor progress. Sometimes knowing a student and her life's circumstances can, in the name of compassion, result in lowered expectations or higher marks! Good behavior is often rewarded with higher grades even given poor work. Evaluating student work challenges our definitions of fairness and equity. Our hope is that as a culturally responsive teacher, you will have a greater awareness and understanding of yourself and your students as you participate in this process.

READINGS

The readings in this chapter expand our understanding of alternative assessment, current detracting efforts, and the importance of expectations on student achievement. In "Alternative Assessment: Issues in Language, Culture and Equity," Estrin discusses the hopes and concerns educators have in using alternative assessment measures to evaluate the work of students belonging to "nondominant language and cultural groups." Her article provides several examples of how different cultural groups might respond to mainstream assessment practices. She points out that a major goal in the assessment reform movement is to create a more equitable process that does not focus on some students being "winners" and others being "losers."

"Successful Detracking in Middle and Senior High Schools" by Ascher summarizes Wheelock's research findings on successfully detracking schools. Ascher describes standardized testing as "the handmaiden of tracking, assuring teachers, students, and administrators alike that there is a rationale behind the hierarchical sorting of students." Finally, Olsen describes in "Detracking At-Risk Students" how her "stupidity" working with inmate pupils led to their academic success, again underscoring the importance of teacher expectations.

READING 1

Alternative Assessment: Issues in Language, Culture, and Equity

Elise Trumbull Estrin

Within the span of a few years, alternative assessments such as student portfolios, performance tasks, and student exhibitions have captured center stage among proposed education reforms. Also called "authentic" or "performance" assessments, these alternatives have at heart the common notion of a meaningful performance or product. The use of such alternatives with students belonging to non-dominant language and cultural groups is of enormous interest and concern for two principal reasons:

- the hope that alternative assessments will reveal what these students truly know and can do, and
- the fear that the same inequities that are associated with traditional norm-referenced tests will recur.

Although alternative assessments are being developed for widescale uses (such as statewide accountability), many educators believe their most attractive potential is at the classroom and school level. Unlike norm-referenced tests, these new assessments have the potential to inform instructional planning through assessment activities linked directly to students' learning experiences and to the contexts of those experiences—including the cultural contexts of a pluralistic student population. Other desired outcomes are:

- Students will be more intensely engaged as participants in their own learning.
- Student growth and achievement will be communicated more effectively to parents and community.
- Teachers will be stimulated to improve their teaching.

The current assessment reforms can be accomplished meaningfully only in tandem with access to high-level learning experiences for all students. If, indeed, *all* students are to benefit from reforms in assessment, specific attention needs to be paid to issues of equity and access for students from non-dominant languages and cultures—and not as an afterthought once reforms are in place for the "majority."

Finally, as Edmund Gordon, Emeritus Professor at Yale University, has observed, the core of equity in assessment lies in deep attitudes and values regarding the social purposes of assessment. In the past, the central purpose of

---

Reprinted by permission of the author.

assessment has been to sort and rank students according to presumed inherent abilities—in effect to create winners and losers. The current assessment reform movement represents a major shift in values toward using assessment to ensure that all students have equitable opportunities to learn and achieve at the highest possible levels.

Historical Context of the Reform

The negative consequences of norm-referenced test use for students from non-dominant cultures and language groups are well-documented. Despite psychometricians' efforts to address test bias, most such efforts have focused only on statistical or technical adjustment rather than on understanding the *root causes* of differences in performance or how to avoid *invalid uses* of tests—understandings that could guide systemic reforms.

Past attempts to reduce the cultural or linguistic load of tests by eliminating content that might be specific to any culture or by avoiding the use of language have not been very satisfactory. Pictorial or figural tests, for example, are limited in revealing what a student knows and can do. In addition, they, too, rely on skills or experiences that are culturally-based. It is in the context of these past failures to grapple with aspects of test bias that advocates for students from non-dominant linguistic and cultural groups look to alternative assessments with both hope and trepidation.

Equity Issues in the Public Debate on Assessment

Consequential Validity. In the current public debate about the new forms of assessment, concerns about their validity center at least as much on their use for making decisions about students and the consequences of those decisions (i.e., consequential validity) as on content and construct validity. A test can be said to be valid only if the way in which it is *used* is appropriate.

Gatekeeping. Some of the most serious negative consequences of assessment ensue from so-called "high-stakes" testing that determines program placement, certification, or graduation, for example. It is no secret that scores on ability and achievement tests are highly correlated with socioeconomic status and with the quality of schooling to which children have access. Tests thus compound the inequities endured by poor children by foreclosing to them additional learning opportunities.

Tracking. Disproportionate numbers of poor and minority students have long been tracked into low-ability classrooms and special education programs or disproportionately categorized as learning handicapped or language delayed on the basis of norm-referenced tests. Students in such classes do not get the opportunities to practice the kind of thinking associated with solving complex problems or exploring ideas—the kind of thinking called for in particular by many alternative assessments. And research shows that students placed in low-ability groups rarely, if ever, move into higher-ability groups. The damage to students can be argued to be lifelong, both cognitive and emotional, and even economic—in terms of missed opportunities.

Opportunities to Learn. The advent of alternative assessments offers an opportunity to re-examine the whole context of schooling, including what have been called "opportunities to learn." As long ago as the 1930s, critics of the use of norm-referenced tests with Spanish-speaking students argued that they were inappropriate on the grounds that those students were not receiving a *comparable education* (Sanchez, 1934)—that they did not have an equal "opportunity to learn." There are numerous recent studies documenting the effects of what has been taught (one index of opportunity to learn) on achievement (see Winfield, 1987).

It is clear that adequate opportunities to learn need to be ensured for assessment reform to be effective. But there is another consideration. It is apparent that even *equal* opportunity is not the perfect remedy to inequities; what works for some students does not work for others. The real challenge for schools is to be responsive to students' needs in ways that go beyond satisfying legal requirements or demands of public accountability to incorporating culturally responsive practices. Equal treatment may not ensure equal outcome. In fact, some educators caution that the wholesale rejection of instruction in basic skills penalizes students whose home experiences do not prepare them for the demands of school. For such students, a pure "process" approach to writing, for example, may be inadequate; and disciplined instruction in essential skills of writing may be complementary (Delpit, 1986).

The Social Context of Assessment

A Culture-Tinted Lens. Student performance on any assessment cannot be fully understood without reference to the language and culture of that student. "Culture" is used here to mean a group's systems of knowledge, values and ways of living that are acquired and transmitted through symbol systems. Assessment in any form is a communicative event (verbal and non-verbal), representing some set of cultural values and expectations. Test questions and student responses are understood only in terms of the test-taker's background, the testing context, and the cultural lens of the test developer and scorer. (What counts as "intelligence," for example, is so culturally variable that a single test of it cannot be valid for all people.)

Different Social Realities. Not all non-dominant cultural and linguistic groups function similarly in the larger society. Because of differences in their histories, they may have different views of social reality (Gibson & Ogbu, 1991). These differences are reflected in the ways students interact in the classroom. "Involuntary minorities," such as African Americans and American Indians, may find themselves opposed to identifying with the dominant group, a stance which would interfere with their full participation in the classroom. In such groups, cultural and linguistic differences may be regarded as "symbols of identity to be maintained" (Gibson & Ogbu, 1991) rather than barriers to surmount, as many voluntary immigrants view their own cultural and linguistic differences. If, indeed, students' investment in learning and performing is compromised by social identity conflicts, test scores will most surely not be indicative of their ability.

Cultural Conceptions of Assessment. Cultures vary in their methods of teaching and assessing children, both in informal (home/community) and formal settings (school). In the past, research has shown that students from the dominant culture have more "test-wiseness" than their peers from non-dominant groups. But knowledge of and attention to how to pace oneself on a timed test or eliminate unlikely answers are only superficial indices of a more fundamental awareness of the meaning of assessment.

In American schools, it is accepted practice to examine students at steps along the way to mastery of a skill or performance. There is an assumption that "trial and error" is a good strategy that can work for everyone, that successive approximations with feedback from a more competent model represent a good way to learn. This approach is in stark contrast to the way competence is demonstrated in many cultures. For example, in the Navajo culture, a child observes until fairly sure he can do a task without error (Deyhle, 1987). Children receive non-verbal instruction in the form of adult modeling. At home, they learn privately through self-initiated self-testing, and they decide when they are ready to be examined. Navaho children may then be ill at ease if pushed into a premature performance. Among some other American Indian communities as well, failure to learn is considered a private act to be ignored in public (Philips, 1983).

It should not be surprising that research with Navajo elementary students has shown them to develop a school-congruent concept of *test* years later than non-Navajo peers (Deyhle, 1987). By the second grade, while non-Navajo students understood tests to be important learning events that would have consequences for their academic futures, Navajo students still did not.

Even with improved testing, we cannot escape the fact that the very concept of displaying one's competence via formal, often public, assessment according to a prescribed timetable will continue to be incompatible with community practices for some students.

Attitudes and Beliefs about Language, Culture and Learning. "Cultural mismatch" is often invoked by educators as the cause of some students' poor school performance vis-à-vis the dominant culture's norms—which are seen as objective standards to be met. Although overt claims of genetic inferiority and cultural deprivation have largely given way to these more neutral assertions about cultural discontinuity or difference from the dominant culture, the language used to talk about the needs of culturally non-dominant students often belies a belief that they are handicapped by their own culture and background—that they are ultimately responsible for their own lack of success in school. Teachers may regard the "culturally different" child as having inappropriate attitudes toward learning, lacking the necessary experience for school success, and possessing inadequate language skills (DeAvila & Duncan, 1985). In addition, they may blame parents for not valuing education for their children, though parents' educational backgrounds do not provide them with the knowledge of how to help their children in ways valued by the school.

Another assumption underlying much of past testing has been that ability is immutable, some mix of heredity and environment that is virtually fixed by the time the child comes to school. To the contrary, considerable research has shown the reality of "cognitive modifiability," i.e., that children's learning—indeed, what we have called "intelligence"—is responsive to experience.

Invidious assumptions like those above have paradoxically rationalized the provision of lower-level instruction; proponents argue that such students need instruction in basic skills before they can engage in higher-order thinking. Actually, research has shown that higher-order thinking is linked to successful learning of even elementary levels of reading, math, and other content (Shepard, 1991). However, as long as a language other than English and "different" cultural practices are viewed as obstacles to learning rather than assets, the learning potential of many children will continue to be underestimated.

Most educators and many parents share the belief that all students need to learn the ways of the dominant culture to survive in society. However, when other ways of knowing and learning are not capitalized on in the classroom, student strengths are ignored, and bridges that might have been built across cultures remain unbuilt, boundaries reinforced—to use common metaphors (Olsen, 1989; Gallagher, 1993). Moreover, culturally-dominant students and teachers are thus deprived of new ways of understanding themselves and others.

Cultural difference is not situated in particular students, of course. Where one sees difference is relative to where one stands; and all social groups are ethnocentric or communicentric, viewing their own ways of behaving and talking as "normal" and appropriate benchmarks by which to judge others' different behaviors. Though the expectation is that students from non-dominant groups need to accommodate to the dominant norms, if cultural accommodation is necessary, it should be reciprocal and result in a synthesis of cultures (Banks, 1988). Figure 1 illustrates this two-way relationship.

Social Constructivism: Learning, Instruction and Assessment

The alternative assessment approach is compatible with a "constructivist" view of learners, more student-centered than teacher-centered, with its emphasis more on learning than on instruction. Students are seen as active constructors of knowledge, engaged in thinking—not just building skills hierarchically from simple to complex. One "constructivist" orientation often cited is *social* constructivist. Learning is portrayed as a social act in classrooms (and in the community), rather than as a set of strictly intrapersonal psychological processes.

From this standpoint, knowledge itself is conceived of as socially constructed, not a set of objective givens; and access to knowledge is affected by social factors. The meaning of "social" is not merely "interpersonal"; rather it implies that learning takes place within a larger context (the society) that entails differential status for different class, ethnic or cultural groups, as well as purposes for schooling that reflect the values of dominant groups. These factors influence what goes on in the classroom—consciously or unconsciously—

Figure 1 Reciprocity of Cultural Learning

Adapted from Banks, 1988

including the nature of the curriculum, how it is taught, how students are invited to participate in their own learning, and which students are expected to perform well.

Alternative Assessments, Language and Culture

This section presents a more in-depth look at the role of language and culture in instruction and assessment and offers suggestions for "culturally-responsive pedagogy" (Villegas, 1991).

Language Demands of School—Instruction and Assessment. Language is the primary medium of instruction in schools, and even with "multi-intelligence" instruction and assessment, it will continue to be necessary for all students to develop a high level of language proficiency—the ability to use oral and written language to communicate, think critically and create new ideas. Complex problem-solving—even in mathematics—is highly dependent on language. Although visual tools and manipulatives can aid students in solving problems, it is usually through language that students represent problems to themselves. And good solutions depend in part on these representations. Moreover, instruction and assessment as conceived of in current reforms make greater demands on language proficiency than do traditional approaches—something that can make assessment even more daunting for English learners.

Students need to be proficient not only in pronunciation, vocabulary and grammar but proficient with particular academic uses of language. Before coming to school, children learn the language uses their communities value through thousands of interactions over a period of years, but the uses chosen are culturally variable. School uses of language are mirrored in dominant culture homes and communities to a much greater degree than in culturally non-dominant homes and communities, giving dominant culture students an advantage in the classroom.

Unlike social uses of language, school uses tend to be abstracted from context—*decontextualized*. One example of decontextualization of language is formal written text: here the reader must supply some context from his/her own background knowledge and knowledge of how texts "work." However, even classroom routines like "show and tell" in which students are expected to talk about past or future events in a prescribed format require use of decontextualized language. The speaker must gauge what listeners need to know to understand his/her presentation, in the absence of immediate context.

Table 1 Assessment Activities and Their Language Demands

Sample Assessment Activity	Potential Language Demands
Write a report for a friend who was sick today explaining to her the science experiment you did and how you did it. (Third-grade writing task following a classroom science experiment.)	Recount a multi-step past event, sequencing and reinterpreting information; assume role of teacher to a non-present audience. Requires considering what recipient already knows, level of detail she needs to comprehend.
Tell us anything else about your understanding of this story—what it means to you, what it makes you think about in your own life, or anything that relates to your reading of it. (Segment of an elementary reading assessment.)	Give account of own experience(s), linking to text, elaborating story comprehension.
You are a statistician in a political campaign. Design a poll, construct a graph, and analyze data in various forms regarding voter preferences and characteristics. Advise your candidate on a campaign strategy. (Synthesis of an eighth grade mathematics assessment.)	Obtain/select necessary information, recount information through multiple representations, interpret and explain; summarize conclusions.
Imagine that you are a staff writer for a small magazine. One day you are given your "big chance." . . . You are asked to write the final scene of an incomplete story. (Taken from a 12th-grade writing task.)	Complete an account (a story) following prescribed format; comprehend/analyze story so that new segment makes sense. Take on voice of another author, maintaining style.

Tasks are adapted from examples provided by the California Department of Education and the Arizona Student Assessment Plan (The Riverside Publishing Co., 1992). All entail additional context in original but are synthesized to highlight language demands.

Students are often asked to create a story, recount past events, summarize material they have read, explain why they solved a problem as they did, or display their knowledge in a structure considered logical. There is an accepted "formula" for responding to all of these demands—a map for the structure of discourse to be produced (called "discourse genre"). When asked to summarize a passage, the student is expected to do so in a way that follows a specific pattern. For many children entering school, there is minimal fit between language uses and genres they have learned in their home communities and those that school requires. Table 1 gives some examples of the kinds of assessment tasks students may be faced with and their associated language demands.

Cultural Variability. Even when school and community language uses overlap, the formula for the corresponding genre may vary markedly. For example, though storytelling is apparently universal, what counts as a story varies from culture to culture. Some prefer topic-centered stories which are characterized by structured discourse on a single topic that assumes little knowledge about

Table 2   The Recitation Script

Basic pattern:

Teacher *initiates* communication → Student *responds* → Teacher *evaluates* student response

Features:
- Teacher regulates virtually all talk (including topic; who talks, when, and for how long). Teacher can interrupt or re-direct talk to another student.
- All talk is mediated through the teacher, i.e., students do not talk to each other or to the whole group (except when called upon to give accounts).
- Students do not evaluate or elaborate on each other's responses.
- Teacher is transmitter of knowledge; students are receivers.

---

the topic or characters on the part of listeners. Others prefer topic-associating stories, which are characterized by structured discourse on several linked topics with considerable presumption of shared knowledge on the part of listeners.

Expository styles are also culturally variable. The dominant (European-American) written expository style is a linear one. In the linear expository style, an idea is introduced, supporting evidence is given, and conclusions are drawn or events are related in time sequence. When a contrasting holistic/circular style—in which many parallel topics are developed at once—is used by students from non-European cultures, such as Asian, Pacific Island or American Indian, teachers may simply judge their discourse to be disorganized (Clark, 1993).

Methods of argumentation in support of certain beliefs also differ across cultures. Some Chinese speakers prefer to use a format of presenting supporting evidence first, leading up to a major point or claim (in contrast to topic sentence and supporting details). Non-Chinese speakers have judged them to be "beating around the bush" (Tsang, 1989). Unlike European-Americans who use "rational" style in argumentation, some groups freely incorporate emotion and personal belief to seal an argument—and find the former disingenuous (Kochman, 1989, speaking of White vs. Black style). Performance assessments often ask students to state their own views, supported by evidence. It is easy to imagine how students grounded in various communicative/discourse styles might approach such a task differently. In the same way, teachers from different cultural backgrounds could be expected to respond differently (and perhaps unfairly) to students' culturally varied styles.

Classroom Communication Structures. Classrooms have distinctive interpersonal communication patterns. The traditional communication structure is the "recitation script" (Mehan, 1979) (See Table 2). Certain features of the "recitation script" conflict with the communicative style of some students.

For example, domination of talk by a single person (the teacher) is alien to some American Indian students (Philips, 1983). In many Indian communities, a person is expected to address the group rather than a single individual. One-to-one exchanges in the presence of others, as when the teacher asks a single student a question and he answers only to her, are culturally discordant. It is also usual for a speaker to choose when to speak and to speak as long as he/she needs to, thus having more control over his/her own conversational turn. Indian children are often characterized as "quiet" by their non-Indian teachers; yet it is apparent that to participate in the recitation script they may have to violate numerous rules of communication as they know them.

When the communication conventions of the classroom are so different from those that students know, students may fail to participate in "appropriate" ways. Informal assessment via questioning may reveal very little about what students know.

Alternative Strategies. The recitation script is not compatible with the goals of current reforms in instruction and assessment, nor is it compatible with principles of good instruction for English learners or for many students from culturally non-dominant communities. To move away from the recitation script, teachers can:

- Give students more opportunities to take an active role in classroom discourse.

- Allow for variety of ways of participating in classroom discourse. (Students need latitude to select how they will participate. Variation makes learning opportunities more equitable.)

- Increase collaborative learning activities. (Student-to-student communication will increase. Small-group projects in which students work independently allow students to speak at their own determination.)

- Encourage students to use their language of choice in small-group work, if a group is linguistically homogeneous.

- Allow opportunities for group response from students, versus focusing on individual students.

- Encourage students to learn from each other in group discussions, and give evaluative feedback to the group, rather than to individual students.

(These last two strategies will be particularly effective for some students, such as American Indian and Hawaii Native.)

Teachers' direct knowledge of the communication style and patterns of their students' particular communities is critical to their making decisions about appropriate instructional and assessment strategies. There is no catalog of cultural characteristics that can safely be applied to any group (all American Indians, all African-Americans, etc.) for three reasons: 1) there is great variability among people within any cultural group; 2) cultures are not frozen in time but continue to change; and 3) contacts with other cultures cause change within a group.

Moving Toward Equitable Alternatives in Assessment

Table 3 lists some of the most compelling and widely-mentioned criteria for valid classroom assessments, many of them recommended by the National Center for Research on Evaluation, Standards, and Student Testing (CRESST)

Table 3 Criteria for Valid Alternative Classroom Assessments

- are curriculum-linked
- are flexible (form, administration, interpretation)
- reflect opportunities to learn (fairness issue*)
- are cognitively complex*
- call on multiple intelligences
- are authentic (make real-world connections)
- are meaningful in themselves* (are learning opportunities)
- entail opportunities for self-assessment
- are culturally responsive/allow for variation in language, in cognitive and communicative style, and in beliefs and values
- integrate skills
- are used appropriately and are useful for the purpose for which they are designed (informing instruction)

Proposed by CRESST/UCLA

at UCLA. We have focused on classroom assessments here; additional criteria (such as transfer and generalizability and cost-effectiveness) would be more applicable to widescale alternative assessments, although they are of some concern in the classroom.

Assessments used for widescale accountability (e.g., state assessments) will also, necessarily, be less curriculum-linked, less flexible in form, and may offer less opportunity for self-reflection—particularly if students are not allowed to see them after they are scored. For these reasons, as mentioned earlier, many educators believe that the greatest potential for best use of the alternatives discussed here is in the classroom.

One alternative that many educators believe extremely promising for all students is portfolio assessment. If used well, portfolios can meet the criteria for valid, culturally-sensitive assessment. (See Table 4 on page 240.)

Some Recommended Steps to Equity

Although the concerns about ensuring equity for students from non-dominant languages and cultures run deep, there are many positive steps that can be taken to begin to address them. Perhaps the first is to cultivate an attitude toward diversity that moves beyond characterizing students from non-dominant cultures and language groups as inferior (an assimilationist approach) and toward a true commitment to equality of outcomes for all students—a more pluralistic approach. The following are some elements of an agenda for equity in assessment.

Attention to Evidence and Consequences. It is imperative that we have a clear rationale for assessing students via certain products and performances and for the ways we interpret students' performances. We must be vigilant at every step of the way for potential bias, looking at a student's behavior and background as well as test performance to justify interpretations of scores and how they are used. Messick (1992) calls this the "interplay between evidence and consequences."

In addition, we must be extremely cautious in interpreting inadequate performances of students who are still developing proficiency in English or whose cultures do not match that of the school. A low performance cannot be assumed to mean that the student has not learned or is incapable of learning what is being assessed.

Flexibility. A principal key to meeting the assessment needs of a diverse student population is a flexible approach. It should be possible to design assessments that allow for a wide variety of tasks to elicit a single response and single tasks that allow for a wide variety of response types, while maintaining standards. For example, there are many possible ways to assess a student's ability to apply linear measurement skills. A task that reflects a context meaningful to the student should be used; and if appropriate, the student can record her problem solution in writing *or* on audiotape.

Improved Teacher Knowledge Base. If culturally-responsive pedagogy is truly a goal, teachers must be provided with pre-service and in-service education opportunities to learn about issues of language and culture and how they play out in the classroom. The cultures of students should be considered when programs, instructional practices, and materials are designed or selected, so that students' ability to participate in schooling is maximized, rather than attenuated. This means going beyond infusion of multicultural content into existing curricula to the use of culturally-responsive instructional strategies. Teacher preparation and development should address:

- differences in communication and cognitive styles and strategies for promoting inclusion of all students in classroom discourse
- ways of evaluating the language demands of classroom tasks
- frameworks for understanding students' language proficiencies
- a repertoire of ways to group students and work with them
- ways of working with communities
- frameworks for understanding and strategies for intervening with status differences that perpetuate inequities of the larger society in the classroom
- the role of teachers' own languages and cultures in shaping their world views and cognitive and communicative styles as well as their understandings of student performances
- opportunities to develop deep knowledge about particular cultural communities.

Collaboration with Communities. To understand students' classroom performance, teachers need to learn from their local communities what is valued and how it is taught (Nelson-Barber & Mitchell, 1992). Therefore, community members should be included in decision-making about educational goals and assessments and their uses. Linking with the community will be crucial—to see communication patterns firsthand, to understand from parents what they value and why, to learn about how children perform at home, and to share with them a "school perspective." As change occurs, ongoing dialog with parents is vital to gaining their support—something that ultimately affects students' investment in the classroom.

Use of Multiple Sources. As Anastasi (1990) has cautioned, we must beware of using a single assessment score to make decisions about a student. What is needed is a range of assessments administered at different times throughout the school year. Students' performances on different tasks—even within a subject area—can vary considerably, and they change over time. Portfolios have been suggested as a desirable method of unifying in one place multiple indices of student performance that have been gathered over time.

Attention to Student Motivation and Interest. Often overlooked are *conative* variables having to do with motivation and interest—variables that affect learning outcomes. For example, personal interests lead people to seek certain experiences, which in turn contribute to the development of certain aptitudes. Conative information may be particularly important in understanding the performance of students whose cultural backgrounds differ from the dominant culture of the school. Their interests may diverge from what is available to them in school, and they may have developed skills in areas unknown to teachers. Such skills, however, could be linked to school experience by a sensitive teacher.

Other reasons that students may not be motivated to perform at peak capacity include conflicts in social identity and local conditions such as peer dynamics within a single classroom. In addition, some (as in the Navajo example cited) may not understand the meaning of "assessment" or "test" as construed by the school and thus may not be motivated to invest necessary effort.

Mediation of Assessments. Administration of assessments may be mediated in a number of ways: by increasing the amount of time given to complete them, by repeating or rephrasing instructions, by explaining the meaning of terms, by allowing the use of adjunct materials or classroom tools (dictionaries, calculators, etc.), or by translating portions of an assessment into a student's first language.

Translation. Translation is itself a form of mediation of text, between one language and another. Translating an assessment into a student's first language is a positive step. The more that students' first languages can be drawn upon (and maintained and developed) the greater the benefit to their learning. However, assessment translation is a source of many psychometric problems. There are no perfect equivalents across languages; and one is really translating across cultures as well. Some languages, like Spanish, have many dialects. Determining where the overlap of dialects lies so as to produce a translation comprehensible to most speakers of the language presents a considerable challenge. As the American Educational Research Association's Standards for Educational and Psychological Testing notes,

Table 4 Portfolios in the Pluralistic Classroom

Student portfolios are structured collections of student work gathered over time, intended to show a student's development and achievement in one or more subject areas. They are process tools through which teachers and students evaluate student work together. Portfolios offer

- Linkages to classroom experiences and students' personal experiences
- Flexibility to include products in any language or in any form (e.g. tapes, written pieces, drawings, photographs), experience-sensitive tasks, modified to suit student needs; student-chosen activities
- Developmental portrayals of student progress, using multiple measures at frequent intervals
- Self-evaluation opportunities for students
- Parent participation opportunities
- Opportunities to contextualize student performances (annotation)
- Program coordination support (when students have more than one teacher)

A Caveat and Some Recommendations

For portfolios to function well for English learners, in particular, teacher annotation is crucial to understanding the full context in which a performance was obtained. Annotation may include

- explanation of why an activity was selected by teacher and/or student
- information on how much and what kind of teacher support was given; which teacher strategies were helpful
- notes on how the student completed a task, including successful student strategies, amount of time required
- information on difficulties the student had in completing a performance
- observations on the student's expressed feelings while engaged in an activity
- observations about the student's use of language and choice of language (English, other than English)
- the student's own written or dictated commentary about the meaning of the activity of his/her performance
- parents' commentary

"Psychometric properties cannot be assumed to be comparable across languages or dialects. Many words have different frequency rates or difficulty levels in different languages or dialects. Therefore words in two languages that appear to be close in meaning may differ radically in other ways important for the test use intended. Additionally, test content may be inappropriate in a translated version" (AERA. . . ., p. 73).

Other aspects of text such as length may be affected by translation. Perhaps most fundamentally, construct validity is jeopardized with translation, i.e., it is not clear with a translated test that one is still testing the same presumed underlying abilities of knowledge. For all of these reasons, translation has to be regarded as a partial solution only.

Moderation. Moderation is the process of teachers' collectively evaluating student performances so as to ensure that the same standards are being applied. Teacher exchange of scored or graded student work offers the opportunity for teachers to check their interpretations of assessments against those of peers—something that could be particularly valuable in fostering discussion among teachers from different cultural backgrounds.

References

American Educational Research Association (with the American Psychological Association and the National Council on Measurement in Education). 1985. *Standards for Educational and Psychological Testing.* Washington, DC: American Psychological Association.

Anastasi, Anne. 1990. What is Test Misuse? Perspectives of a Measurement Expert. In Anastasi, Anne, et al. (Eds). *The Uses of Standardized Tests in American Education: Proceedings of the 1989 ETS Invitational Conference.* Princeton, NJ: Educational Testing Service.

Banks, James A. 1988. *Multiethnic Education: Theory and Practice.* Boston, MA: Allyn & Bacon.

Clark, Lynne W. (Ed). 1993. *Faculty and Student Challenges in Facing Cultural and Linguistic Diversity.* Springfield, IL: Charles C. Thomas Publisher.

De Avila, Edward A. and Duncan, Sharon. 1985. *Thinking and Learning Skills.* Hillsdale, NJ: Erlbaum.

Delpit, Lisa D. 1986. Skills and Other Dilemmas of a Progressive Black Educator. *Harvard Educational Review,* Vol. 56, No. 4.

Deyhle, Donna. 1987. Learning Failure: Tests as Gatekeepers and the Culturally Different Child. In Trueba, Henry (Ed). *Success or Failure.* Rowley, MA: Newbury House.

Gallagher, Pat. 1993. *Teachers' Cultural Assumptions: A Hidden Dimension of Schoolteaching.* Paper presented at the annual American Educational Research Association conference in Atlanta, Georgia.

Gibson, Margaret A. and Ogbu, John U. 1991. *Minority Status and Schooling: A Comparative Study of Immigrant and Involuntary Minorities.* New York: Garland Publishing, Inc.

Gordon, Edmund. 1993. *Human Diversity, Equity, and Educational Assessment.* Paper presented at 1993 CRESST Assessment Conference.

Kochman, Thomas. 1989. Black and White Cultural Styles in Pluralistic Perspective. In Gifford, B. (Ed). *Test Policy and Test Performance: Education, Language, and Culture.* Boston, MA: Kluwer Academic Publishers.

Linn, Robert L., Baker, Eva L., and Dunbar, Stephen B. 1991. Complex, Performance-Based Assessment: Expectation and Validation Criteria. *Education Researcher,* Vol. 20, No. 8.

Mehan, H. 1979. *Learning Lessons.* Cambridge, MA: Harvard University Press.

Messick, Samuel. 1992. *The Interplay of Evidence and Consequences in the Validation of Performance Assessments.* Princeton, NJ: Educational Testing Service.

Nelson-Barber, Sharon S. and Mitchell, Jean. 1992. Restructuring for Diversity: Five Regional Portraits. In Dilworth, Mary E. (Ed). *Diversity in Teacher Education.* San Francisco, CA: Jossey-Bass.

Olsen, Laurie. 1989. *Bridges.* San Francisco, CA: California Tomorrow.

Philips, Susan Urmston. 1983. *The Invisible Culture: Communication in Classroom and Community on the Warm Springs Indian Reservation.* New York: Longman.

Sanchez, G.I. 1934. Bilingualism and Mental Measures: A Word of Caution. *Journal of Applied Psychology.* No. 18.

Shepard, Lorrie. 1991. Negative Policies of Dealing with Diversity: When Does Assessment Turn into Sorting and Segregation? In Hiebert, Elfrieda H. (Ed). *Literacy for a Diverse Society.* New York: Teachers College Press.

Tsang, Chui Lim. 1989. Bilingual Minorities and Language Issues in Writing: Toward Professionwide Responses to a New Challenge. *Written Communication.* Vol. 9, No. 1.

Villegas, Ana Maria. 1991. *Culturally Responsive Pedagogy for the 1990s and Beyond.* Princeton, NJ: Educational Testing Service, September.

Winfield, Linda F. 1987. Teachers' Estimates of Test Content Covered in Class and First-Grade Students' Reading Achievement. *The Elementary School Journal,* Vol. 87, No. 4.

READING 2

Successful Detracking in Middle and Senior High Schools

Carol Ascher, ERIC Clearinghouse on Urban Education

In tracked schools, students are categorized according to measures of intelligence, achievement, or aptitude, and are then assigned to hierarchical ability or interest-grouped classes. Although most elementary schools have within-class ability grouping, tracking is most common at the middle and high school levels.

Recently, a wide range of national educational and child advocacy organizations have recommended the abolition of tracking. Their reason is that too often tracking creates class and race-linked differences in access to learning. In fact, because of the inequities in opportunity it creates, tracking is a major contributor to the continuing gaps in achievement between disadvantaged and affluent students and between minorities and whites (Oakes, 1992; 1985).

Although tracking has declined nationwide in recent years, it remains widespread. For example, in grade seven about two-thirds of all schools have ability grouping in some or all subjects, and about a fifth group homogeneously in every subject. Moreover, the prevalence of ability grouping increases when there are sizable enrollments of black and Hispanic students (Braddock, 1990).

Not surprisingly, the changeover to heterogeneous groupings—generally called either detracking or untracking—remains controversial. The greatest concern among both parents and educators is that heterogeneous grouping may slow down the learning of high-achieving students, for there is evidence that high achievers do better in accelerated classes for the gifted and talented (Kulick, 1991). Oakes (1992), however, has pointed out that the benefits these students experience are not from the homogeneity of the group, but from their enriched curriculum—which lower-track students would also thrive on, given sufficient support.

It is also clear that tracking can work against high achievers, particularly where a large number of the students are above average. Districts vary enormously in their cut-offs for slow and gifted learners. In fact, suburban, middle-class districts, where students perform above the national average, generally have high cut-offs for their gifted and talented programs, and are therefore most likely to send many capable students to regular or unaccelerated classes (Useem, 1990).

Current Detracking Efforts

There is still much to understand about the ramifications of both tracking and heterogeneous groupings. Yet because the country is quickly shifting toward a belief in heterogeneous groupings, and many schools have already begun

Reprinted by permission of the publisher.

detracking some or all academic subjects, it is useful to summarize those changes necessary for detracking to succeed.

Based on the ethnographic study of schools around the country, Wheelock (1992) outlines six factors which exist in schools that are successfully detracking.

1. **A Culture of Detracking.** Creating a new culture of detracking is probably more important than any specific strategy. Perhaps the key to a detracked culture is the commitment to be inclusive. Teachers, parents, and students alike believe in the right and ability of students from every background to learn from the best kind of curriculum. They are also convinced that all students can gain academically and socially from learning together and from each other.

2. **Parent Involvement.** Since middle-class parents of gifted students can be detracking's most powerful opponents, they must be assured that their children will not be subjected to a watered-down curriculum, but that all students will be offered "gifted" material. They must also be helped to rethink the competitive, individualistic way in which they have come to view schooling, and to see how learning improves when students listen to others from different backgrounds, share knowledge, and teach their peers.

3. **Professional Development and Support.** Because the core of any detracking reform centers on how teaching will occur in the classroom, it is critical that teachers be actively involved in the change. This means not only that discussions about when, where, and how to detrack must include teachers, but that teachers must receive professional development prior to, during, and after the detracking process. Wheelock suggests that teachers must receive three major areas of training for detracking:
   - the risk-taking, communication, and planning skills to work for whole-school change;
   - strategies for working effectively with diverse students in a single classroom; and
   - specific curricula they may not have used or watched others use.

4. **Phase-In Change Process.** Detracking involves large changes at many levels. Even once the commitment to detracking has been made, most schools proceed slowly to allow teachers, students, and parents to adjust. Often detracking begins with a single grade level, student cluster, or subject—say, science, social studies, or language arts. Mathematics, with its aura of appropriateness for only the best and the brightest, often remains the last to be breached by detracking plans. The point is not that there is a certain way to proceed with detracking, or even a definite time schedule. Rather, plans must be flexible enough to respond to hesitations and concrete problems as well as unanticipated openings.

5. **Rethinking All Routines.** Ultimately, detracking should be reflected in all areas of school life. Thus, school routines that separate students from each other, that exclude some students from the opportunity to learn, that

communicate reduced expectations for some, or that undermine a sense of belonging must all be rethought. Instead of pull-out approaches, every attempt should be made to keep all students within the regular classrooms, providing the fast learners with needed stimulation and the slow ones with the necessary support.

6. **District and State Support.** Although detracking takes place at the school level, a supportive policy coupled with technical assistance at the district and state levels can nurture administrators and teachers, enabling more than the most adventurous schools to proceed.

Instruction for Heterogeneous Classes

In a fully detracked school, most instruction is provided in heterogeneous groups. Teachers no longer pace their instruction to the "average" student, but individualize learning through personalized assignments and learning centers. Rather than dominate the classroom, teachers act as directors of learning which takes place through such multiple routines as cooperative learning, complex instruction, and peer and cross-age tutoring.

Developed by Robert Slavin and his associates at Johns Hopkins University, cooperative learning has been heavily researched; it is the most common strategy used in detracked schools and exists in a number of models. In all, students work in heterogeneous groups and share responsibility for one another's learning. While some models insert a competitive element, others stress the building of team scores by mutual cooperation (Slavin, 1990).

The Need for Alternative Assessment

Standardized testing has been the handmaiden of tracking, assuring teachers, students, and administrators alike that there is a rationale behind the hierarchical sorting of students. Although standardized tests will likely continue to be used for some purposes, they tend to work against a detracked culture. First, they see ability as static, not as dynamic, and they suggest what students already know, not where they need help. Second, they create an emphasis on teacher talk, seat work, and rote learning—all of which are antithetical to the interactive, problem-solving and egalitarian workings of a detracked school.

While a variety of performance-based tests are being developed, so far they are expensive, labor intensive, and imprecise (Maeroff, 1991). Thus their growth will be dependent on a commitment not only to new ways of teaching and a problem-solving curriculum, but to egalitarian school organizational structures.

Accelerated Schools

One school restructuring model that results in detracking is Accelerated Schools, developed by Henry Levin and his colleagues at Stanford. Briefly, in an accelerated school, all students receive the enriched curriculum and problem-solving techniques generally reserved for gifted and talented students. As in any successfully detracked school, an accelerated school curriculum is not only fast-paced and engaging, but it includes concepts, analyses, problem-solving and interesting applications. Dewey's notion of "collaborative inquiry" both informs how learning occurs in accelerated schools, and guides the school governance process. Again, as with detracked schools that depend for their success on bringing parents, teachers, and students into the process, accelerated schools involve parents, teachers, and students in formulating both the goals and the interventions (Levin, 1987).

Conclusion

Although tracking remains controversial among both educators and parents, there has been a recent policy consensus that the negative effects of tracking on lower-track students are so severe that schools should move towards detracking.

Successful detracking rests on an "inclusive" school culture. It also depends on a curriculum that is interactive and problem-solving, as well as on assessment processes that support such a curriculum. Schools embarked on detracking must draw in parents, students, and teachers, not only to ensure that these groups buy into the change, but to teach them new egalitarian ways of thinking, and to use them to help reconsider existing school routines.

References

Braddock, J. H. (1990). Tracking: Implications for student race-ethnic groups. Report no. 1. Baltimore, MD: Johns Hopkins University, Center for Research on Effective Schooling for Disadvantaged Students. (*ERIC Abstract*)

Kulick, J. A. (1911, November). Ability grouping. Report to the Office of Educational Research and Improvement, U.S. Department of Education, Grant No. R206R00001.

Levin, H. M. (1987, Fall). New schools for the disadvantaged. Teacher Education Quarterly, 13(4), 60-83.

Maeroff, G. I. (1991, December). Assessing alternative assessment. Phi Delta Kappan, 272–281. (*ERIC Abstract*)

Oakes, J. (1992, May). Can tracking research inform practice? Technical, normative, and political considerations. Educational Researcher, 12-21. (*ERIC Abstract*)

Oakes, J. (1985). Keeping track: How schools structure inequality. New Haven: Yale University Press. (*ERIC Abstract*)

Slavin, R. E. (1990). Cooperative learning: Theory, research and practice. Englewood Cliffs, NJ: Prentice Hall.

Useem, E. (1990). Getting on the fast track in mathematics: School organizational influences on math track assignment. Paper presented at the Annual Meeting of the AERA, Boston, MA, April 16-20, 1990. (*ERIC Abstract*)

Wheelock, A. (192). Crossing the tracks: How 'untracking' can save America's schools. New York: The New Press. (*ERIC Abstract*)

Digest Number 82, October 1992. EDO-UD-92-5. ISSN 0889 8049. This Digest was developed by the ERIC Clearinghouse on Urban Education with funding from the Office of Educational Research and Improvement, U.S. Department of Education, under contract no. RI88062013. The opinions expressed in this Digest do not necessarily reflect the position or policies of OERI or the Department of Education.

READING 3

Detracking Helps At-Risk Students

Susan A. Olsen

People often ask me what my secret is behind the high scores of my students. I have one answer—stupidity. When my colleagues and I began our school in a Maryland state prison, all of us were "green" to corrections. None of us had worked in a prison before; therefore, none of us knew that "prison inmates cannot learn," or that "prison students won't work," or that "inmate pupils don't care about education." All we knew was that we were supposed to begin a school. Naturally, we expected our students to learn, to succeed, and to graduate with General Educational Development diplomas.

We began our school with few supplies. We were still waiting for most of our books to come in, and we had only limited access to a copy machine. I was to teach language arts classes, but I didn't have much of a curriculum. I had just been given a general idea of what would be covered on the GED test. So I did what every good teacher does: I improvised. I was teaching freshman composition in the evening at a local college, so I included many of the same lessons in my GED classes.

The response from my prison students was remarkable. The light bulbs went on; the sparks flew. It was one of those precious moments for teachers when you've really gotten the students' attention.

Four months after we began our program, we had our first GED test. Much to our delight, our students scored at a pass rate of 80 percent—the highest in the state.

Shortly thereafter in my correctional teaching career, I began networking with other prison teachers at meetings and conferences. There I learned that inmates "couldn't learn"; however, it was too late. I had already observed them demonstrate the contrary. Clearly, teacher expectation, my "stupidity," had made the difference.

If teacher expectation can work with the ultimate at-risk students, prison inmates, how much more successful can it be in "detracking" our nation's public schools?

Tracking, placing students in classes according to their perceived ability, undermines achievement because the majority of students are denied access to a challenging curriculum and are not well prepared for higher education. It causes students to develop negative attitudes toward school and lowers self-esteem. I have discovered that my biggest job is convincing my prison students that they can learn. Once we've crossed that hurdle, the rest is easy.

Reprinted by permission of the publisher.

According to the January/February 1997 issue of the *Harvard Education Letter,* teaching all students as though they are the brightest (detracking) extends opportunities to those who never had them before. Detracking involves developing a meaningful curriculum for all students with less emphasis on "basic skills." Lower-ability students are given support so they can stay in class with more successful students. This is accomplished by extra coaching, Saturday school, double classes in weak areas, or training volunteers to help out in the classroom. In my classroom, this is accomplished by hiring inmates with stronger academic backgrounds (often some college credits) to work as classroom aides. (They work for about a dollar a day and good-time credit.) This ensures that all my students get the personal attention and immediate feedback they require to keep them on task and interested in my assignments.

When schools detrack, teachers begin to use exciting methods, such as interdisciplinary curricula, cooperative learning, hands-on activities, and critical thinking. All students—both high- and low-achieving—benefit when teachers and parents have high expectations for them. Surprisingly, all students achieve in a heterogeneous classroom.

The core of detracking is high teacher expectation. This strategy works in prison, where students have a host of learning and emotional problems not encountered in such concentration in the public school system. The students at Eastern Correctional Institution have had the top GED pass rates for nine straight years, frequently in the high 90 percent to 100 percent range.

If correctional educators can take students who "fell through the cracks" and enable them to become successful through high expectations, so can public school teachers. Detracking public schools would push more students toward success and away from our barbed-wire fences.

DISCUSSION QUESTIONS AND ACTIVITIES

1. Anyone who has been a student has had lots of experience with assessment. Moreover, most of us have strong affective and cognitive responses to the topics of teachers' expectations, intelligence, IQ and standardized tests, and tracking. Consider your past experiences with assessment. How have your experiences affected your perspective on assessment? How might this influence how you assess students in your classes?

2. Research has found that parents from different cultural groups explain their children's academic success differently. For example, Asian Americans usually say that their children do well because they work hard, whereas Anglo Americans say that it is because their children are bright. How do these answers reflect different definitions of intelligence? What are the implications of these definitions for teachers? What is your definition of intelligence?

3. Should students be allowed to participate in their own evaluations? If so, in what ways? Is this consistent with the goals of multicultural education?

4. Review a standardized test for cultural, gender, and class bias. You might want to compare the same test using versions published in different years.

5. Review the reading, "Alternative Assessment: Issues in Language, Culture, and Equity." What have you learned about how different cultural/ethnic groups might approach assessment and how would you use this information as a teacher?

6. Imagine that your school has decided to institute schoolwide detracking. Several middle- and upper-class parents have approached you with concerns about their children's education. How would you respond?

REFERENCES

Callahan, J., Clark, L. H., and Kellough, R. D. 1995. *Teaching in the Middle and Secondary Schools,* 5th ed. Englewood Cliffs, NJ: Merrill.

Futrell, M. H. 1989. Mission Not Accomplished: Education Reform in Retrospect. *Phi Delta Kappan,* 7: 8–14.

Garcia, G. E. 1994. Equity Challenges in Authentically Assessing Students from Diverse Backgrounds. *Educational Forum,* 59(1): 64–73.

Gardner, H. 1985. *Frames of Mind.* New York: Basic.

Gay, L. R. 1985. *Educational Evaluation and Measurement: Competencies for Analysis and Application,* 2nd ed. Columbus, OH: Merrill.

Gould, S. J. 1996. *The Mismeasure of Man.* New York: Norton.

Grant, C. A., and Gomez, M. L. 1996. *Making Schooling Multicultural: Campus and Classroom.* Englewood Cliffs, NJ: Merrill.

Kohn, A. 1999. "Tougher Standards" vs. Better Education.www.alfiekohn.org/teaching/standards.htm

McMillan, J. H. 1997. *Classroom Assessment: Principles and Practice for Effective Instruction.* Boston: Allyn & Bacon.

The National Education Goals Report: Building a Nation of Learners [Executive Summary]. 1995. National Education Goals Panel. Evan Bayh, Chair.

Ornstein, A. C., and Levine, D. U. 1993. *Foundations of Education,* 5th ed. Boston: Houghton and Mifflin.

Popham, W. J. 1997. What's Wrong—And What's Right—with Rubrics. *Educational Leadership,* 55(2): 72–77.

Rothman, R. 1994. Assessment Questions: Equity Answers. *Proceedings of the 1993 CRESST Conference.* ED#367 684.

Sanchez, R. 1997. Education Initiatives Off to a Slow Start. *Washington Post.* (July 11): A18.

Smith, J. K., and Smith L. G. 1994. *Education Today: The Foundation of a Profession.* New York: St. Martin's.

Steele, C. M. 1992. Race and the Schooling of Black Americans. *Atlantic Monthly, 269:* 68–78.

Sternberg, R. J. 1985. *Beyond IQ.* New York: Cambridge University Press.

Thompson, D. R., and Senk, S. L. 1998. Using Rubrics in High School Mathematics Courses. *Mathematics Teacher, 91*(9): 786–794.

Tucker, W. H. 1994. *The Science and Politics of Racial Research.* Urbana: University of Illinois Press.

U.S. Department of Education. 1999. CFDA No. 84. 336. OMB No. 1840–0007.

Watters, E. 1995 (Sept. 17). Claude Steele Has Scores to Settle, *New York Times Magazine,* pp. 68, 70.

Wilson, R. J., Gilbert, J., Nissenbaum, S., Kupperman, K. O., and Scott, D. 1990. *The Pursuit of Liberty* (vol. 2). Belmont, CA: Wadsworth.

Worthen, B. R. 1993. Critical Issues That Will Determine the Future of Alternative Assessment. *Phi Delta Kappan, 74*(6): 444–456.

Zessoules, R., and Gardner H. 1991. Authentic Assessment: Beyond the Buzzword and Into the Classroom. In V. Perrone (ed.) *Expanding Student Assessment.* Alexandria, VA: ASCD.

Chapter Eight

School/Family/Community Partnerships

Re-Visioning Teaching Practices Beyond the Classroom

John Gabriel, Ed.D.

We begin this chapter with a scene that might take place in many middle and secondary schools across the country. The scene relates to an administrative proposal to increase the school and its teachers' involvement with parents and the community.

Out of the Classroom Doors and into the Community

Scene: Teacher's Cafeteria
Conversation about latest administrative initiative for the school—its teachers—to find ways to encourage and enlist parent/family/community support to ensure the success of all students.

Players: Mr. Fletcher, a mathematics teacher for twenty years.

Ms. Hernandez, a social studies teacher for five years.

Narrator (cites research related to the topic(s) of discussion)

Mr. Fletcher: It'll never work. Just another fad in education to please the politicians and secure the principal's job until retirement. Besides, I have too much to do already.

Ms. Hernandez: The administration has not asked us to do more; they have asked us to consider doing things differently. Don't you remember what Ms. Johnson said? "I invite you to re-vision the way you do things as teachers. Teaching should be a joint venture with students, their families, and our community." It's an invitation, Mr. Fletcher, not an edict.

Mr. Fletcher: Oh, hogwash. What does that mean? Chanting before trying to solve math problems? She'd turn my classroom into a bazaar.

Ms. Hernandez: No, I don't think she means that. I think what she means is for you to try to find ways to link what you already do with the students' parents, family, or the community. For example, I know a teacher who asked his students to interview local business people. One student interviewed a cabinet-maker and wrote problems about production costs. Another student interviewed a veterinarian and wrote a word problem about how much medicine to administer to a cat. If the pills were each 2 mg. and the cat weighed 8 pounds . . . (Schine, 1996).

Mr. Fletcher: Well, OK, they got lucky with a few old people in town. That wouldn't work with many people. And what about the parents? That's a laugher and you know it. Why, just look at the last parents' night we had. You know how that goes. All the parents of the good students show up, while the ones you really want to see are nowhere to be found. I wanted to see Desiderio's mother or father in the worst way. Think they'd ever show up?

Ms. Hernandez: I happen to know Desiderio's family. His father still lives in the Dominican Republic. His mother works at night and speaks no English. She has three other children, ages 6, 9, and 11.

Mr. Fletcher: You're just making excuses. Most parents just don't want to be involved. They toss their kids out the door and say to the schools, "There you go, do the best you can." That's part of the problem, too. These immigrants have got to learn more English and have fewer children!

Ms. Hernandez: I can't believe you sometimes. No, I can't believe you most of the time. You're an educated man, aren't you? You're a teacher. Where do you get your ideas or beliefs about who your students and their parents are, what they know, what their concerns are? I am not making excuses. Most parents do want to be involved. Have we done all we can to make Desiderio's mother feel welcome here? Was there someone here to translate for her, attend to her children while she spoke with you? How well would you manage if you had to attend an event for your child where you had to get off from your job teaching here, bring two or three of your children with you, find a ride, knowing all the while that when you got there nobody would speak English? How would you hold up, Mr. Fletcher? We in the schools do not do enough to involve parents, families, and the greater community in our students' education. That's the bottom line. Again, they're not asking us to do more; they're asking us to do differently. A re-vision.

Narrator: All involved parties should seek to understand and value the diversity that exists within and between them. Varying economic, cultural, and social backgrounds should be used to shed light on circumstances affecting behaviors, beliefs and attitudes of students at home, community, and school partners (Rutherford, Anderson, & Billig, 1995, p. 33).

Mr. Fletcher: OK, OK, what can I do not more but differently?

Ms. Hernandez: You've taken the first step. You've agreed to listen further and explore the possibilities. That's a terrific first step. Creating teacher, school, parent, family, community partnerships is complex but worth our efforts. With the right approach, it becomes a win-win situation, especially for the students. We are here for the students, remember? The partnership involves the school, the parents, the family, the community, and, most important, you and me, Mr. Fletcher.

Narrator: School/family/community partnerships will amount to little more than empty rhetoric unless teachers help design the partnerships, are devoted to making them work, and eventually find themselves benefiting from them (Davies, 1991, p. 380).

This scenario depicts some of the issues related to school/family/community partnerships. The main goal of the partnerships is to strengthen ties between the schools, parents and families, social agencies, and businesses to ensure success for all students regardless of their background or circumstances. An old African saying, "The whole village educates the child," has been quoted often in the research literature related to such partnerships. The saying succinctly describes the joint nature of partnerships and places the responsibility for the child's academic and social success in the embrace of the entire community.

Forming partnerships is complicated and complex. Everybody has opinions, based on deeply and dearly held beliefs. Not always easy to recognize, let alone change, those beliefs become "the gnarled fidelity of an old habit/that [are] comfortable with us and never want to leave" (Rilke, 1968, p. 3). Partnerships are not a panacea for all students or all schools. Nevertheless, given the right emphasis, support, and mutual participation, they hold promise and potential for greater student achievement and success. Studies over the last twenty-five to thirty years have shown that children benefit when their parents are involved in their education (Hidalgo, Siu, Bright, Swap, & Epstein, 1995).

In this chapter, we will explore some of the main issues related to school/family/community partnerships at the middle and secondary levels. We look briefly at what schools can do, and, within that context, what teachers can do to make connections with families and the greater community. We address issues of equity and empowerment in the complex relationships among schools/families/community and raise questions, if not provide answers, to "what's in it for me, the teacher?" We ask you to consider the same question: "What's in it for me?" We believe, as the authors of *A Nation at Risk* have stated, that all students can succeed. Therefore, in looking at partnerships, we are ultimately asking, "What's in it for our students?"

Historically, a considerable amount of research focused on both schools and families, though it was not necessarily focused on issues of partnership. Patri (1928), for example, has written about his school's efforts to reach out into the community. Nurses and social workers visited families' homes to talk about health, educational, or civic issues. Patri, himself, and other teachers from his school, visited their students' homes and encouraged parents to come to the schools to participate in school activities. Cremin (1988), too, has shown how broadly education and educational institutions at the turn of the century extended beyond the classroom. He has cited the public libraries and museums, social agencies, such as the YMCA, and Jane Addams's Hull House in Chicago as just a few examples of community agencies involved in public education.

Julia Richman, a New York City district superintendent, writing in the early part of the twentieth century, also recognized how important it was to connect the schools to the families, immigrant families in particular.

> If we have given to the child other, and let us hope better, standards, then let us build a bridge between the Americanized child and its [sic] foreign parent, so that the parent can cross the bridge to join the child on the American side. It is for us [educators] who are Americanizing these immigrant children to bring their parents forward with them. But how can this be done? First and most prominent in school activities should be the parents' meetings . . . If the parent will not come to the school, the school or its representative must go to the parent. (Richman, 1905, pp. 119–120)

Though a long tradition of research—and practice—exists about families and schools, only within the last twenty years have researchers turned their attention more to the idea of "partnerships" among schools, parents, the extended family (aunts, uncles, grandparents), and the community (Hidalgo et al, 1995). The partnerships are one of a broader series of educational reforms that have followed the publication of *A Nation at Risk* in 1983. With "top-down" reforms, too many people were left out of the loop: teachers, students, parents and families, and the larger community—the main players. What sounded neat theoretically or seemed politically expedient rarely worked out in the classroom. Johnny still could not read. Current reform efforts focus more on how to involve the principal players more integrally in students' education.

WHO VALUES SCHOOL/FAMILY/COMMUNITY PARTNERSHIPS?

Now we near the end of the twentieth century, a time and a world vastly changed from the end of the nineteenth century. As a nation, we are as committed as we were in the past to educating as much of our citizenry as possible. The average citizen would agree that we all stand to gain from a better-educated populace. Today's adolescents are tomorrow's leaders. Everyone has a personal stake in providing students with the best possible education.

Parents and families want to be involved in their children's education, despite what the Mr. Fletchers of the school world believe. As Hidalgo and colleagues (1995, p. 519) state, "All families—whatever their background, culture, or language—want and need assistance from schools in helping their children succeed each year." Parents involved in the *Tellin' Stories Project* (Ziegler, 1998), one of the readings for this chapter, became integrally involved in their children's education and the life of the classroom. Of all those who participated in the project, including the District of Columbia Public Schools for Systemic Change, the Network of Educators on the Americas, the D. C. Area Writing Project, Howard University, and of course, the parents and students themselves, "no individual described the project in any way but very positive" (Ziegler, 1998, p. 12).

To speak to the complexities of parental involvement in their children's education, we think it is important to talk briefly about some of the difficulties schools might face in getting parents to come to the schools. In some areas of the country, such as California, Texas, and Arizona, or more generally where large immigrant populations exist, an unspecified number of students and their parents live in this country illegally. Despite a school's or an individual teacher's best efforts, parents will not come to the schools because they fear that their immigration status will become known, possibly made public, and they and their families will face deportation. We mention this not to discourage efforts enlisting parental support, but to underscore some of the realities that work against our most thoughtful initiatives. Parents get blamed too often for "not caring" about their son or daughter's education. Closer to the truth, though, is that they live on society's borders, many of them illegally, and would much rather endure the plaintive (and unheard) cries of committed teachers and administrators than face deportation.

How do the school administrators show their interest in school/community relations? How do they welcome parents and families to the school? How do they communicate that welcome message to parents and families? How do administrators support parents and families so they can get to the schools and find assistance when they get there, should they need it? Some family members did not have good school experiences themselves, and coming to school is a painful reminder. Some families whose cultural norms differ from the mainstream might need permission and encouragement to come to the schools. For example, in the Pakistani culture, parents are not encouraged to attend their children's schools (Huss-Keeler, 1997). The school's message to the parents is "You do the parenting and we'll do the schooling." Of course, not all your students will have a Pakistani heritage, but knowing and respecting cultural and class differences becomes part of the dialogue between schools, teachers, and families as they seek ways to conjoin in students' education.

Teachers want parents and families to participate. Even Mr. Fletcher expressed his desire to see Desiderio's parents, and—we'd like to believe—not just to give them a piece of his mind and be done with it. The opportunity just to talk to one another will open possibilities to engage teachers and parents more in their children's education. In one study (Hollifield, 1995), the researcher found that four of five teachers felt that parent/family involvement was important and one of three strongly supported it. Even though one study does not a truth make, our hunch is that these figures represent the larger picture. Teachers want to enlist parent/family support.

Even students want greater school and family involvement, though understandably less perhaps than their teachers or their families do. As they enter the middle school grades and on into high school, young adolescents seek more independence, more autonomy, from authority figures. Teens want to become their own authorities, a natural part of their growth and development. Yet, they still look for support in their efforts to understand their bursting social, biological, and cognitive changes. In an interview (Gabriel, 1997), Elena, an immigrant student from Puerto Rico, spoke about the importance of a close relationship with the teacher, and her former teacher's initiative in building that kind of a relationship:

> She was very friendly. She was real open. That's the main thing I liked about her. She was real open. Teachers in the United States don't have a close relationship with the students. My teachers in Puerto Rico, they actually would go to your house. They would talk to your parents, have a close relationship with the students. Here [in the United States] they don't do that. They keep apart from you.

TIES THAT STRENGTHEN

In a recent statement[1] (IRA, April/May, 1997, p. 16), the national Parent Teacher Association set forth six standards for promoting parent and family involvement in schools. Included are the following:

- Regular, two-way, meaningful communication between home and school
- Parents as welcome volunteer partners in schools
- Parents as full partners in school decisions that affect children and families
- Active parent participation in student learning
- Outreach to the community for resources to strengthen schools

If the majority of teachers, parents, and students want closer ties to bolster students' achievements, what can schools and teachers do to make those important links? Your efforts, the individual teacher's efforts, are situated ideally within a broader context that integrally involves other teachers, the administration, and any other policy or governance coalitions that influence your actions. In short, you are not a lone ranger but, rather, a member of a larger, unified team with clear, comprehensive goals. Within that framework, how can your school and especially you, the teacher, engage parents and families in their young adult's education? First, we return to a question we asked earlier: "What's in it for me?"

---

[1] This information can also be found at Web site: http://www.pta.org

From our own teaching experiences, we recall an initiative several years ago in a Los Angeles high school. Students had nearly taken over the campus, and two beleaguered assistant principals could not handle all the problems that arose in the population of 2,500 students. The school principal wanted to involve parents, many of whom were recent immigrants to the United States, in their children's education and the daily workings of the school. Several fathers volunteered their time and services as part of a school and parent effort to monitor the halls and the school grounds. Their presence ensured that students passed between classes in an orderly way. The fathers wore orange jackets that identified them immediately as parents. Just their *presence* brought smiles and lifted spirits. These fathers helped ensure a safer environment for students, and their efforts supported their sons and daughters, the school, and the teachers. Teachers could stay in their rooms and teach, rather than concern themselves with policing errant bands of students. In sharing the responsibilities that schools have in educating students, which includes making the campus a safe and supportive place to study, parents shared both the responsibility and the burden that educators face. When teachers know that families and communities will support them and share the responsibilities of educating students, "What's in it for me?" becomes clearer. With the support and encouragement that the fathers provided, teachers were able to focus primarily on their teaching. Part of re-visioning your teaching practice means allowing others to shoulder some of the responsibilities that you were either expected or accustomed to doing on your own. We will suggest ways for you to do that as we proceed.

> Sharing responsibility for children's learning and development can reduce the burden, the isolation, and the stress felt by so many hard-working and dedicated school professionals today. (Davies, 1991, p. 382)

The next two sections suggest several ways that schools and teachers can build relationships with parents and families beyond the confines of the classroom. We proceed from simpler activities to more complex ones, recognizing that something is better than nothing when involving families in students' education. We suggest that you think of your involvement as a new or different way to think about teaching itself. We trust that you will not have to do more, just differently.

Though we write this chapter primarily with the teacher in mind, we begin with suggestions for the school. Without a school policy and school support, teachers will face an uphill struggle in trying to enlist parent/family/community support themselves. We still believe, however, that teachers are primary players in these relationships.

What Schools Can Do

Create a parent center in the school. Davies (1991) has suggested placing adult size chairs and tables in the room, a telephone, coffeepot, and occasionally some snacks. Generally, make the room a comfortable place where parents feel welcome. Ask community businesses to donate plants, posters, musical tapes, furniture, and appliances for the room.

Staff the room with teachers, if possible. If participation is voluntary, many teachers will not take part, insisting "I'm too busy. I need my prep time...." This is true. Teachers are always busy and need that preparation time, if only to catch a breath between periods of the hectic school day. But let's say that a school has fifty teachers, 180 days make a school year, and the parent room is open for half the school day, three class periods. If every teacher volunteered, each would be in the parent room roughly ten times during a school year. If teachers voluntarily staffing the room does not seem plausible, then consider as Davies (1991) has suggested, Chapter 1 monies (federal dollars given to schools in financial need for academic improvement) that might be used to pay someone else—or teachers themselves—to staff the room.

Invite parents to come to the room to talk with teachers, administrators, and other parents. Parents might want to talk about their son or daughter's progress in a chemistry class. They might want to talk about the proposed site-based management team the school is considering, block-scheduling, or a proposed year-round school calendar. Generally, they might just want to know "what's happening" and offer assistance—like the fathers who patrolled that Los Angeles high school campus—in ways that best suit the needs of the school and its students. Parents could talk to other parents. "What and how is your son doing in his chemistry class?" "How do you handle child-care when you come here to the parent's room?" "Will you please join me when I talk to Mrs. Sullivan? I don't always understand everything she says." A parent's room is a room where all members of the partnership gather to talk, share information and ideas, and support each other's efforts to educate students. It is a place that facilitates open, two-way communication necessary for successful partnership building. Setting up a parent's room is the school's way of saying to parents, "Welcome. There's a place for you here."

To broaden parent and community involvement even further, plan professional development days that focus on school/family/community partnership. Invite students, teachers, administrators, parents, families, and community members. Hash things out. What does each group want from the partnership? What are the best ways to achieve those goals? At these meetings, use language free from educational jargon that all in attendance can understand. Translators might have to attend these meetings, especially in many larger city school districts with larger immigrant populations. In many ways, not much has changed between Julia Richman's time and our own. We are an immigrant nation, and schools, especially the major city schools, reflect that reality. We still seek ways to invite and engage immigrant students' parents, those (like Desiderio's mother and father in the opening scene), who might need a good deal of encouragement to become involved in their adolescent's schooling.

To widen the net in partnerships, schools can contact local business employers to talk about ways of linking study programs in the schools with potential employment opportunities once students have graduated. With dwindling federal and state dollars, schools will have to solicit more local political and economic resources to support school programs. No one best "model" exists for developing and sustaining school-to-work programs. Although some critics fault school-to-work initiatives for placing too much emphasis on the vocational aspect of these initiatives, several promising programs have been implemented in many states across the country. One vocational high school student we have interviewed spoke highly of his school's links with the work community. He already had a part-time job as an auto mechanic, and the employer agreed to hire him full-time after his graduation. (See Andrus, 1996, and Schine, 1996, for specific examples of connecting school curriculum to business and community.)

As with other initiatives in school/family/community partnerships, school-to-work initiatives should at least be explored. Venturing out into the community and talking with business people opens possibilities; however, it is important that schools do not use school-to-work programs to counsel students away from pursuing post-secondary degrees. Administrators need to monitor these programs to ensure that they offer viable options for students' growth and development, rather than roadblocks to future—lifetime—success.

What Teachers Can Do

Teacher involvement in parent/family/community partnerships ranges from the simple—leaving a recorded message on your voice mail—to the complex—conducting an action research project either on your own, with a parent, or with a member of the business community. Several books and articles have explored ways for teachers, schools, parents, families, and communities to join together to work for students' success (for example, Botrie & Wenger, 1992; Clemens-Brower, 1997; Epstein, 1995; Huss-Keeler, 1997; Rutherford & Billig, 1995; Timpane & Reich, 1997). Having cited some of the available resources from a wealth of published materials, we would like to suggest a few ways for teachers to get started:

1. *Create a daily or weekly voice-mail message* (Clemens-Brower, 1997), *stating what you did in class on a particular day or during the week.* Use your office phone machine, if one is available. This will enable parents to call in at their convenience to get an update of what's going on in their son or daughter's classroom. It also opens the lines of communication, an important aspect of teacher/family relationships.

2. *Ask parents to come in to your class to teach a lesson in their expertise or share an experience they had as a civil rights marcher or Vietnam veteran.* We once asked students to invite their parents who had served in Vietnam to come in and talk to our American Literature class. We were reading Tim O'Brien's book about the Vietnam War, *The Things They Carried* (1990). One student's father, an army captain, and another student's mother, a nurse, came in and talked to the class. Sharing their experiences about the war brought to life the tragic and the human side to the war and deepened our understanding and feeling for those who were part of it.

3. *Write a list of all that you do as a teacher that you would like someone to help you with:* getting library books from the public libraries, scanning the newspapers for articles relevant to what you teach, picking up (free) supplies

from supporting businesses. Send your wish list home to parents. See what they can help you with.

4. *Invite members of the community to come to your class as guest speakers.* You will be surprised how many experts are willing to share that expertise with your students. Inviting guests in also provides students with some direct links from the classroom to the "real world."

5. *Participate in the life of the community.* During an in-service workshop we attended several years ago, a veteran teacher spoke to us about how important it was for teachers to be in the community. "Find out where your students live, where their parents work. Go into the supermarkets, fast-food stores, and garden nurseries. Walk in the neighborhoods." "Checking out" the neighborhoods and communities our students come from provides some context for our teaching, a sense of students' everyday lives. In addition to informally exploring the communities where students and their families live and work, teachers can venture out into their students' communities in other ways. For example, ethnic fairs are often held in communities where our students live. One of the most notable and festive fairs in Los Angeles is "El Cinco de Mayo," May 5th—to celebrate a Mexican victory in a war with the French. A huge affair, the event draws crowds of more than a million people. We have also attended a Lithuanian fair and there, too, learned some of the customs, foods, dress, and music of the Lithuanian people. Latina students we have taught have invited us to attend the celebration of their fifteenth birthdays, "La Quinceanera," an elaborate event proclaiming the young woman's rite of passage from a girl to a young woman. Such sojourns inform our teaching, as we get to understand our students' social and cultural lives, and generally enhance our lives by our participation in community affairs.

6. If you are more adventurous or ambitious, start a joint action-research project that involves parents and members of the community (Burch, 1993). Burch describes the joint project as one where "The team documents the program's development and collects information on its impact on children, families, and school practice. This information is used to make immediate programmatic decisions and as evidence in final program evaluation" (p. 11).[2] For example, if parents are enlisted to work as

---

[2] In her description of the joint effort, Burch provides a useful, working definition of "action research," a term sometimes used synonymously with "teacher research." In one 1996 edition of *Teacher Research,* 4(1), a journal devoted to classroom inquiry, the editors wrote in their "Contributor's Guidelines": "Nietzsche has written that 'Only through chaos can you give birth to the dancing star.' How does teacher research upset the normal order of life in your classroom? How do you cope with the twists and turns of research integrated with teaching? What are the insights that come from not following the expected plan, and looking for the birth of that dancing star?" Part of the implications of this statement, its questions, suggests the complexities of this kind of research. This form of self-study, or study of one's own practice, with a persistent effort, yields deeper insight into one's teaching, because it allows you to view the "dancing star." For further exploration of this topic, see Altrichter, H., Posch, P., & Somekh, B., (Eds.), (1993); Goswami, D., & Stillman, P., (Eds.), (1987); and, Hubbard, R., & Power, B., (Eds.), (1993).

classroom aides, the teacher and the parents could devise an action-research project that documented what was going on in the classroom, share ideas, and make changes in practice based on mutual agreements and decisions. It can be as simple as documenting how many students are tardy and why they are. Or, noting what the homework assignments are, how they connect to classroom instruction, or how many students complete the homework assignments. This information could be distributed among other parents, and in thinking of the "action" part of action research, homework assignments might be modified to better reflect students' and teachers' needs and goals. At the least, an action-research project affirms the importance of teachers and parents collaborating to improve practice.

As you can see, some of the suggestions require little or no extra time, for example, leaving voice mail. Although you will then have to listen to responses to your message, you also realize that you have found a way to enlist the support of those who really want to make a difference in young adult lives. Likewise, even though several of the other suggested activities require additional work, in the long run, you might spend less time on devising ways to recruit parents and community members than finding out what to do with all the help once they arrive. Teaching is—can be—an alienating job. Once inside the classroom, teachers often find little support from other adults. Some teachers like it that way. They do not want to share their power and authority with others. Building relationships with parents and the larger community means that teachers will have to share some of their power and authority, as they find those willing to cooperate in students' education. We teach students to work cooperatively. By inviting other adults into the classroom, we demonstrate what's positive about cooperative learning.

ISSUES OF EQUITY: IS THE PARTNERSHIP FAIR TO ALL PARTICIPANTS?

Issues of equity and empowerment will doubtless arise when schools and teachers invite parents to share in decision making. As Bauch and Goldring (1996, p. 425) have noted,

> The improvement of parent involvement could be threatening to teachers who may not wish to include parents' opinions and ideas in their decisions and how increased teacher decision making could mitigate the influence of parents in school matters.

Forming partnerships is an inclusionary process and demands that participants check their egos—and their beliefs—and talk in good faith, using a common language and common sense.

Yet teachers—trained professionals—might not be willing to compromise their views on what really matters in a student's education: Why should I consult someone who has never taught before, or knows little or nothing about quadratic equations, the double helix, or iambic trimeter?

Fair enough. We are not talking here, though, primarily about methodology or methods of teaching, though even there, teachers could lend an open ear. We are talking more about teachers, families, and communities listening closely to each other, an important skill in the classroom and in life, talking openly, and negotiating in good faith, with students' achievement being the mutual goal. Good teaching, we believe, means continually reflecting on what we do and finding ways to do it better. Changes do not come easily, nor overnight. As the world becomes more global, schools and schoolteachers need to reach out into the (smaller) world to enlist a willing cadre of supporters, parents, grandparents, and business people, waiting for the call to aid in our children's education. Relationships with parents, families, and communities, though complex and potentially difficult (Thompson, 1993), are critical to students' success. Finding ways to engage the broader community in our students' education seems like a win-win situation for all involved.

We do not think that engaging the broader community is a simple task. We would do well to pause here for a moment and recall de Tocqueville (1966):

> Each person, withdrawn unto himself, behaves as though he is a stranger to the destiny of all the others. His children and his good friends constitute for him the whole of the human species. As for his transactions with his fellow citizens, he may mix among them, but he sees them not; he touches them, but does not feel them; he exists only in himself and for himself alone. And if on these terms there remains in his mind a sense of family, there no longer remains a sense of society.

We do not raise the specter of de Tocqueville here, or his proclamations about American society, to douse the spirit of building school/family/community partnerships. Rather, we trust that by looking more deeply into the nature of "the American character," either as perceived by de Tocqueville, or existing in fact, we look squarely at the challenges that face us as individuals, schools, communities, states, and nations, as we seek ways to forge those unions. For de Tocqueville has also stated (p. 541), "[Americans] may often look cold and serious, but never haughty or constrained, and if they do not say a word to each other, it is because they do not want to talk, not that they think it to their interest to keep quiet." Forging school/family/community partnerships might not be an easy task, but, it is possible.

In school/family/community partnerships, students are the ultimate winners or losers. By re-visioning teaching practices beyond the classroom, we show students how their learning is linked to a world they are about to enter. It is a complex world, demanding the best from students if they are to succeed. They will need to know how to read, write, and reason. But they will also need to know how to listen, talk clearly, negotiate, and compromise. When schools, teachers, families, and communities act together responsibly to do what's best for all students, we model what's most important in human interactions. Students will see the benefits of these links and themselves become part of a broader school, teacher, parent, family, community—and now student—partnership in our society's best attempt to educate its citizenry.

READINGS

We have selected four readings for this chapter. The first, "School/Family/Community Partnerships," provides a broad overview of the "theory, framework, and guidelines that can assist schools in building partnerships." It also has a comprehensive bibliography at the end for further reading. The second article, "Tellin' Stories Project," describes a joint effort to "bring together parents, teachers, school administrators, and children to build a community of learners through the art of storytelling and story writing" (Ziegler, 1998, p. 9). Even though this article focuses on elementary schools, we trust that those who teach in secondary schools will be able to adopt the basic principles and insights from the article. Further, knowing what goes on in elementary classrooms provides middle and high school teachers with an understanding of students' development as they move from elementary to secondary schools. The third article, "Eight Lessons of Parent, Family, and Community Involvement in the Middle Grades," targets the middle school specifically. The authors feel we need to devote considerable attention to students at this level, who are both dependent and striving to be independent and require additional support that families and communities can provide. Finally, the fourth reading, "High Schools Gear Up to Create Effective School and Family Partnerships," offers further practical suggestions about what "any high school can do." It also provides an important perspective on school/family/community initiatives in secondary schools, since we have also included readings appropriate for the elementary and middle school in our selections.

READING 1

School/Family/Community Partnerships
Caring for the Children We Share

Joyce L. Epstein

The way schools care about children is reflected in the way schools care about the children's families. If educators view children simply as *students,* they are likely to see the family as separate from the school. That is, the family is expected to do its job and leave the education of children to the schools. If educators view students as *children,* they are likely to see both the family and the community as partners with the school in children's education and development. Partners recognize their shared interests in and responsibilities for children, and they work together to create better programs and opportunities for students.

From *Phi Delta Kappan* (76, May): 701-712. Reprinted by permission of the Center on School, Family, and Community Partnership.

There are many reasons for developing school, family, and community partnerships. They can improve school programs and school climate, provide family services and support, increase parents' skills and leadership, connect families with others in the school and in the community, and help teachers with their work. However, the main reason to create such partnerships is to help all youngsters succeed in school and in later life. When parents, teachers, students, and others view one another as partners in education, a caring community forms around students and begins its work.

What do successful partnership programs look like? How can practices be effectively designed and implemented? What are the results of better communications, interactions, and exchanges across these three important contexts? These questions have challenged research and practice, creating an interdisciplinary field of inquiry into school, family, and community partnerships with "caring" as a core concept.

The field has been strengthened by supporting federal, state, and local policies. For example, the Goals 2000 legislation sets partnerships as a voluntary national goal for all schools; Title I specifies and mandates programs and practices of partnership in order for schools to qualify for or maintain funding. Many states and districts have developed or are preparing policies to guide schools in creating more systematic connections with families and communities. These policies reflect research results and the prior successes of leading educators who have shown that these goals are attainable.

Underlying these policies and programs are a theory of how social organizations connect; a framework of the basic components of school, family, and community partnerships for children's learning; a growing literature on the positive and negative results of these connections for students, families, and schools; and an understanding of how to organize good programs. In this article I summarize the theory, framework, and guidelines that have assisted the schools in our research projects in building partnerships and that should help any elementary, middle, or high school to take similar steps.

Overlapping Spheres of Influence: Understanding The Theory

Schools make choices. They might conduct only a few communications and interactions with families and communities, keeping the three spheres of influence that directly affect student learning and development relatively separate. Or they might conduct many high-quality communications and interactions designed to bring all three spheres of influence closer together. With frequent interactions between schools, families, and communities more students are more likely to receive common messages from various people about the importance of school, of working hard, of thinking creatively, of helping one another, and of staying in school.

The *external model* of overlapping spheres of influence recognizes that the three major contexts in which students learn and grow—the family, the school, and the community—may be drawn together or pushed apart. In this model, there are some practices that schools, families, and communities conduct separately and some that they conduct jointly in order to influence children's learning and development. The *internal* model of the interaction of the three spheres of influence shows where and how complex and essential interpersonal relations and patterns of influence occur between individuals at home, at school, and in the community. These social relationships may be enacted and studied at an *institutional* level (e.g., when a school invites all families to an event or sends the same communications to all families) and at an *individual* level (e.g., when a parent and a teacher meet in conference or talk by phone). Connections between schools or parents and community groups, agencies, and services can also be represented and studied within the model.[1]

The model of school, family, and community partnerships locates the student at the center. The inarguable fact is that students are the main actors in their education, development, and success in school. School, family, and community partnerships cannot simply produce successful students. Rather, partnership activities may be designed to engage, guide, energize, and motivate students to produce their own successes. The assumption is that, if children feel cared for and encouraged to work hard in the role of student, they are more likely to do their best to learn to read, write, calculate, and learn other skills and talents and to remain in school.

Interestingly and somewhat ironically, studies indicate that students are also crucial for the success of school, family, and community partnerships. Students are often their parents' main source of information about school. In strong partnership programs, teachers help students understand and conduct traditional communications with families (e.g., delivering memos or report cards) and new communications (e.g., interacting with family members about homework or participating in parent/teacher/student conferences). As we gain more information about the role of students in partnerships, we are developing a more complete understanding of how schools, families, and communities must work with students to increase their chances for success.

How Theory Sounds in Practice

In some schools there are still educators who say, "If the family would just do its job, we could do our job." And there are still families who say, "I raised this child; now it is your job to educate her." These words embody the theory of "separate spheres of influence." Other educators say, "I cannot do my job without the help of my students' families and the support of this community." And some parents say, "I really need to know what is happening in school in order to help my child." These phrases embody the theory of "overlapping spheres of influence."

In a partnership, teachers and administrators create more *family-like* schools. A family-like school recognizes each child's individuality and makes each child feel special and included. Family-like schools welcome all families, not just those that are easy to reach. In a partnership, parents create more *school-like* families. A school-like family recognizes that each child is also a student. Families reinforce the importance of school, homework, and activities that build student skills and feelings of success. Communities, including groups of parents working together, create *school-like* opportunities, events, and programs that reinforce, recognize, and reward students for good progress, creativity, contributions, and excellence. Communities also create *family-like* settings, services, and events to enable families to better support their children. *Community-minded* families and students help their neighborhoods and other families. The concept of a community school is reemerging. It refers to a place where programs and services for students, parents, and others are offered before, during, and after the regular school day.

Schools and communities talk about programs and services that are "family-friendly"—meaning that they take into account the needs and realities of family life in the 1990s, are feasible to conduct, and are equitable toward all families. When all these concepts combine, children experience *learning communities* or *caring communities*.[2]

All these terms are consistent with the theory of overlapping spheres of influence, but they are not abstract concepts. You will find them daily in conversations, news stories, and deliberations of many kinds. In a family-like school, a teacher might say, "I know when a student is having a bad day and how to help him along." A student might slip and call a teacher "mom" or "dad" and then laugh with a mixture of embarrassment and glee. In a school-like family, a parent might say, "I make sure my daughter knows that homework comes first." A child might raise his hand to speak at the dinner table and then joke about acting as if he were still in school. When communities reach out to students and their families, youngsters might say, "This program really made my schoolwork make sense!" Parents or educators might comment, "This community really supports its schools."

Once people hear about such concepts as family-like schools or school-like families, they remember positive examples of schools, teachers, and places in the community that were "like a family" to them. They may remember how a teacher paid individual attention to them, recognized their uniqueness, or praised them for real progress, just as a parent might. Or they might recall things at home that were "just like school" and supported their work as a student, or they might remember community activities that made them feel smart or good about themselves and their families. They will recall that parents, siblings, and other family members engaged in and enjoyed educational activities and took pride in the good schoolwork or homework that they did, just as a teacher might.

How Partnerships Work in Practice

These terms and examples are evidence of the *potential* for schools, families and communities to create caring educational environments. It is possible to have a school that is excellent academically but ignores families. However, that school will build barriers between teachers, parents, and children—barriers that affect school life and learning. It is possible to have a school that is ineffective academically but involves families in many good ways. With its weak academic program, that school will shortchange students' learning. Neither of these schools exemplifies a caring educational environment that requires academic excellence, good communications, and productive interactions involving school, family, and community.

Some children succeed in school without much family involvement or despite family neglect or distress, particularly if the school has excellent academic and support programs. Teachers, relatives outside of the immediate family, other families, and members of the community can provide important guidance and encouragement to these students. As support from school, family, and community accumulates, significantly more students feel secure and cared for, understand the goals of education, work to achieve to their full potential, build positive attitudes and school behaviors, and stay in school. The shared interests and investments of schools, families, and communities create the conditions of caring that work to "overdetermine" the likelihood of student success.[3]

Any practice can be designed and implemented well or poorly. And even well-implemented partnership practices may not be useful to all families. In a caring school community, participants work continually to improve the nature and effects of partnerships. Although the interactions of educators, parents, students, and community members will not always be smooth or successful, partnership programs establish a base of respect and trust on which to build. Good partnerships withstand questions, conflicts, debates, and disagreements; provide structures and processes to solve problems; and are maintained—even strengthened—after differences have been resolved. Without this firm base, disagreements and problems that are sure to arise about schools and students will be harder to solve.

What Research Says

In surveys and field studies involving teachers, parents, and students at the elementary, middle, and high school levels, some important patterns relating to partnerships have emerged.[4]

- Partnerships tend to decline across the grades, *unless* schools and teachers work to develop and implement appropriate practices of partnership at each grade level.
- Affluent communities currently have more positive family involvement, on average, *unless* schools and teachers in economically distressed communities work to build positive partnerships with their students' families.
- Schools in more economically depressed communities make more contacts with families about the problems and difficulties their children are having, *unless* they work at developing balanced partnership programs that include contacts about positive accomplishments of students.
- Single parents, parents who are employed outside the home, parents who live far from the school, and fathers are less involved, on average, at the school building, *unless* the school organizes opportunities for families to volunteer at various times and in various places to support the school and their children.

Researchers have also drawn the following conclusions.

- Just about all families care about their children, want them to succeed, and are eager to obtain better information from schools and communities so as to remain good partners in their children's education.
- Just about all teachers and administrators would like to involve families, but many do not know how to go about building positive and productive programs and are consequently fearful about trying. This creates a "rhetoric rut," in which educators are stuck, expressing support for partnerships without taking any action.
- Just about all students at all levels—elementary, middle, and high school—want their families to be more knowledgeable partners about schooling and are willing to take active roles in assisting communications between home and school. However, students need much better information and guidance than most now receive about how their schools view partnerships and about how they can conduct important exchanges with their families about school activities, homework, and school decisions.

The research results are important because they indicate that caring communities can be built, on purpose; that they include families that might not become involved on their own; and that, by their own reports, just about all families, students, and teachers believe that partnerships are important for helping students succeed across the grades.

Good programs will look different in each site, as individual schools tailor their practices to meet the needs and interests, time and talents, ages and grade levels of students and their families. However, there are some commonalities across successful programs at all grade levels. These include a recognition of the overlapping spheres of influence on student development; attention to various types of involvement that promote a variety of opportunities for schools, families, and communities to work together; and an Action Team for School, Family, and Community Partnerships to coordinate each school's work and progress.

Six Types of Involvement; Six Types of Caring

A framework of six major types of involvement has evolved from many studies and from many years of work by educators and families in elementary, middle, and high schools. The framework (summarized in the accompanying tables) helps educators develop more comprehensive programs of school and family partnerships and also helps researchers locate their questions and results in ways that inform and improve practice.[5]

Each type of involvement includes many different *practices* of partnership (see Table 1). Each type presents particular *challenges* that must be met in order to involve all families and needed *redefinitions* of some basic principles of involvement (see Table 2). Finally, each type is likely to lead to different *results* for students, for parents, for teaching practice, and for school climate (see Table 3). Thus schools have choices about which practice will help achieve important goals. The tables provide examples of practices, challenges

Table 1   Epstein's Framework of Six Types of Involvement and Sample Practices

Type 1—Parenting	Type 2—Communicating	Type 3—Volunteering
Helps all families establish home environments to support children as students.	Design effective forms of school-to-home and home-to-school communications about school programs and children's progress.	Recruit and organize parent help and support.
Sample Practices	**Sample Practices**	**Sample Practices**
Suggestions for home conditions that support learning at each grade level.	Conferences with every parent at least once a year, with follow-ups as needed.	School and classroom volunteer program to help teachers, administrators, students, and other parents.
Workshops, videotapes, computerized phone messages on parenting and child rearing at each age and grade level.	Language translators to assist families as needed.	Parent room or family center for volunteer work, meetings, resources for families.
Parent education and other courses or training for parents (e.g., GED, college credit, family literacy).	Weekly or monthly folders of student work sent home for review and comments.	Annual postcard survey to identify all available talents, times, and locations of volunteers.
Family support programs to assist families with health, nutrition, and other services.	Parent/student pickup of report card, with conferences on improving grades.	Class parent, telephone tree, or other structures to provide all families with needed information.
Home visits at transition points to preschool, elementary, middle, and high school. Neighborhood meetings to help families understand schools and to help schools understand families.	Regular schedule of useful notices, memos, phone calls, newsletters, and other communications.	Parent patrols or other activities to aid safety and operation of school programs.
	Clear information on choosing schools or courses, programs, and activities within schools.	
	Clear information on all school policies, programs, reforms, and transitions.	

for successful implementation, redefinitions for up-to-date understanding, and results that have been documented and observed.

Charting the Course

The entries in the tables are illustrative. The sample practices displayed in Table 1 are only a few of hundreds that may be selected or designed for each type of involvement. Although all schools may use the framework of six types as a guide, each school must chart its own course in choosing practices to meet the needs of its families and students.

Table 1 • *Continued*

Type 4—Learning at Home	Type 5—Decision Making	Type 6—Collaborating with Community
Provide information and ideas to families about how to help students at home with homework and other curriculum-related activities, decisions, and planning.	Include parents in school decisions, developing parent leaders and representatives.	Identify and integrate resources and services from the community to strengthen school programs, family practices, and student learning and development.

Sample Practices

Type 4:
- Information for families on skills required for students in all subjects at each grade.
- Information on homework policies and how to monitor and discuss schoolwork at home.
- Information on how to assist students to improve skills on various class and school assessments.
- Regular schedule of homework that requires students to discuss and interact with families on what they are learning in class.
- Calendars with activities for parents and students at home.
- Family math, science, and reading activities at school.
- Summer learning packets or activities.
- Family participation in setting student goals each year and in planning for college or work.

Type 5:
- Active PTA/PTO or other parent organizations, advisory councils, or committees (e.g., curriculum, safety, personnel) for parent leadership and participation.
- Independent advocacy groups to lobby and work for school reform and improvements.
- District-level councils and committees for family and community involvement.
- Information on school or local elections for school representatives.
- Networks to link all families with parent representatives.

Type 6:
- Information for students and families on community health, cultural, recreational, social support, and other programs or services.
- Information on community activities that link to learning skills and talents, including summer programs for students.
- Service integration through partnerships involving school; civic, counseling, cultural, health, recreation, and other agencies and organizations; and businesses.
- Service to the community by students, families, and schools (e.g., recycling, art, music, drama, and other activities for seniors or others).
- Participation of alumni in school programs for students.

The challenges shown (Table 2) are just a few of many that relate to the examples. There are challenges—that is, problems—for every practice of partnership, and they must be resolved in order to reach and engage all families in the best ways. Often, when one challenge is met, a new one will emerge.

The redefinitions (also in Table 2) redirect old notions so that involvement is not viewed solely as or measured only by "bodies in the building." As examples the table calls for redefinitions of workshops, communication, volunteers, homework, decision making, and community. By redefining these familiar terms, it is possible for partnership programs to reach out in new ways to many more families.

Table 2 Challenges and Redefinitions for the Six Types of Involvement

Type 1—Parenting

Challenges

Provide information to *all* families who want it or who need it, not just to the few who can attend workshops or meetings at the school building.

Enable families to share information with schools about culture, background, children's talents and needs.

Make sure that all information for and from families is clear, usable, and linked to children's success in school.

Redefinitions

"Workshop" to mean more than a *meeting* about a topic held at the school building at a particular time. "Workshop" may also mean making information about a topic available in a variety of forms that can be viewed, heard, or read anywhere, any time, in varied forms.

Type 2—Communicating

Challenges

Review the readability, clarity, form, and frequency of all memos, notices, and other print and nonprint communications.

Consider parents who do not speak English well, do not read well, or need large type.

Review the quality of major communications (newsletters, report cards, conference schedules, and so on).

Establish clear two-way channels for communications from home to school and from school to home.

Redefinitions

"Communications about school programs and student progress" to mean two-way, three-way, and many-way channels of communication that connect schools, families, students, and the community.

Type 3—Volunteering

Challenges

Recruit volunteers widely so that *all* families know that their time and talents are welcome.

Make flexible schedules for volunteers, assemblies, and events to enable parents who work to participate.

Organize volunteer work; provide training; match time and talent with school, teacher, and student needs; and recognize efforts so that participants are productive.

Redefinitions

"Volunteer" to mean anyone who supports school goals and children's learning or development in any way, at any place, and at any time—not just during the school day and at the school building.

The selected results (Table 3) should help correct the widespread misperception that any practice that involves families will raise children's achievement test scores. Instead, in the short term, certain practices are more likely than others to influence students' skills and scores, while other practices are more likely to affect attitudes and behaviors. Although students are the main focus of partnerships, the various types of involvement also promote various kinds of results for parents and for teachers. For example, the expected results for parents include not only leadership in decision making, but also confidence

Table 2 • *Continued*

Type 4—Learning at Home	Type 5—Decision Making	Type 6—Collaborating with Community
Challenges	**Challenges**	**Challenges**
Design and organize a regular schedule of interactive homework (e.g., weekly or bimonthly) that gives *students* responsibility for discussing important things they are learning and helps families stay aware of the content of their children's classwork. Coordinate family-linked homework activities, if students have several teachers. Involve families and their children in all important curriculum-related decisions.	Include parent leaders from all racial, ethnic, socioeconomic, and other groups in the school. Offer training to enable leaders to serve as representatives of other families, with input from and return of information to all parents. Include students (along with parents) in decision-making groups.	Solve turf problems of responsibilities, funds, staff, and locations for collaborative activities. Inform families of community programs for students, such as mentoring, tutoring, business partnerships. Assure equity of opportunities for students and families to participate in community programs or to obtain services. Match community contributions with school goals; integrate child and family services with education.
Redefinitions	**Redefinitions**	**Redefinitions**
"Homework" to mean not only work done alone, but also interactive activities shared with others at home or in the community, linking schoolwork to real life. "Help" at home to mean encouraging, listening, reacting, praising, guiding, monitoring, and discussing—not "teaching" school subjects.	"Decision making" to mean a process of partnership, of shared views and actions toward shared goals, not just a power struggle between conflicting ideas. Parent "leader" to mean a real representative, with opportunities and support to hear from and communicate with other families.	"Community" to mean not only the neighborhoods where students' homes and schools are located but also any neighborhoods that influence their learning and development. "Community" rated not only by low or high social or economic qualities, but by strengths and talents to support students, families, and schools. "Community" means all who are interested in and affected by the quality of education, not just those with children in the schools.

about parenting, productive curriculum-related interactions with children, and many interactions with other parents and the school. The expected results for teachers include not only improved parent/teacher conferences or school/home communications, but also better understanding of families, new approaches to homework, and other connections with families and the community.

Most of the results noted in Table 3 have been measured in at least one research study and observed as schools conduct their work. The entries are listed in positive terms to indicate the results of well-designed and well-implemented

Table 3 Expected Results of the Six Types of Involvement for Students, Parents, and Teachers

Type 1—Parenting	Type 2—Communicating	Type 3—Volunteering
Results for Students	**Results for Students**	**Results for Students**
Awareness of family supervision; respect for parents.	Awareness of own progress and of actions needed to maintain or improve grades.	Skill in communicating with adults.
Positive personal qualities, habits, beliefs, and values, as taught by family.	Understanding of school policies on behavior, attendance, and other areas of student conduct.	Increased learning of skills that receive tutoring or targeted attention from volunteers.
Balance between time spent on chores, on other activities, and on homework.	Informed decisions about courses and programs.	Awareness of many skills, talents, occupations, and contributions of parents and other volunteers.
Good or improved attendance.	Awareness of own role in partnerships, serving as courier and communicator.	
Awareness of importance of school.		
For Parents	**For Parents**	**For Parents**
Understanding of and confidence about parenting, child and adolescent development, and changes in home conditions for learning as children proceed through school.	Understanding school programs and policies.	Understanding teacher's job, increased comfort in school, and carry-over of school activities at home.
Awareness of own and others' challenges in parenting.	Monitoring and awareness of child's progress.	Self-confidence about ability to work in school and with children or to take steps to improve own education.
Feeling of support from school and other parents.	Responding effectively to students' problems.	Awareness that families are welcome and valued at school.
	Interactions with teachers and ease of communication with school and teachers.	Gains in specific skills of volunteer work.
For Teachers	**For Teachers**	**For Teachers**
Understanding families' backgrounds, cultures, concerns, goals, needs, and views of their children.	Increased diversity and use of communications with families and awareness of own ability to communicate clearly.	Readiness to involve families in new ways, including those who do not volunteer at school.
Respect for families' strengths and efforts.	Appreciation for and use of parent network for communications.	Awareness of parents' talents and interests in school and children.
Understanding of student diversity.	Increased ability to elicit and understand family views on children's programs and progress.	Greater individual attention to students, with help from volunteers.
Awareness of own skills to share information on child development.		

Table 3 • Continued

Type 4—Learning at Home	Type 5—Decision Making	Type 6—Collaborating with Community
Results for Students Gains in skills, abilities, and test scores linked to homework and classwork. Homework completion. Positive attitude toward schoolwork. View of parent as more similar to teacher and of home as more similar to school. Self-concept of ability as learner.	**Results for Students** Awareness of representation of families in school decisions. Understanding that student rights are protected. Specific benefits linked to policies enacted by parent organizations and experienced by students.	**Results for Students** Increased skills and talents through enriched curricular and extracurricular experiences. Awareness of careers and of options for future education and work. Specific benefits linked to programs, services, resources, and opportunities that connect students with community.
For Parents Know how to support, encourage, and help student at home each year. Discussions of school, classwork, and homework. Understanding of instructional program each year and of what child is learning in each subject. Appreciation of teaching skills. Awareness of child as a learner.	**For Parents** Input into policies that affect child's education. Feeling of ownership of school. Awareness of parents' voices in school decisions. Shared experiences and connections with other families. Awareness of school, district, and state policies.	**For Parents** Knowledge and use of local resources by family and child to increase skills and talents or to obtain needed services. Interactions with other families in community activities. Awareness of school's role in the community and of community's contributions to the school.
For Teachers Better design of homework assignments. Respect of family time. Recognition of equal helpfulness of single-parent, dual-income, and less formally educated families in motivating and reinforcing student learning. Satisfaction with family involvement and support.	**For Teachers** Awareness of parent perspectives as a factor in policy development and decisions. View of equal status of family representatives on committees and in leadership roles.	**For Teachers** Awareness of community resources to enrich curriculum and instruction. Openness to and skill in using mentors, business partners, community volunteers, and others to assist students and augment teaching practice. Knowledgeable, helpful referrals of children and families to needed services.

practices. It should be fully understood, however, that results may be negative if poorly designed practices exclude families or create greater barriers to communication and exchange. Research is still needed on the results of specific practices of partnership in various schools, at various grade levels, and for diverse populations of students, families, and teachers. It will be important to confirm, extend, or correct the information on results listed in Table 3 if schools are to make purposeful choices among practices that foster various types of involvement.

The tables cannot show the connections that occur when one practice activates several types of involvement simultaneously. For example, volunteers may organize and conduct a food bank (Type 3) that allows parents to pay $15 for $30 worth of food for their families (Type 1). The food may be subsidized by community agencies (Type 6). The recipients might then serve as volunteers for the program or in the community (perpetuating Type 3 and Type 6 activities). Or consider another example. An after-school homework club run by volunteers and the community recreation department combines Type 3 and Type 6 practices. Yet it also serves as a Type 1 activity, because the after-school program assists families with the supervision of their children. This practice may also alter the way homework interactions are conducted between students and parents at home (Type 4). These and other connections are interesting, and research is needed to understand the combined effects of such activities.

The tables also simplify the complex longitudinal influences that produce various results over time. For example, a series of events might play out as follows. The involvement of families in reading at home leads students to give more attention to reading and to be more strongly motivated to read. This in turn may help students maintain or improve their daily reading skills and then their reading grades. With the accumulation over time of good classroom reading programs, continued home support and increased skills and confidence in reading, students may significantly improve their reading achievement test scores. The time between reading aloud at home and increased reading test scores may vary greatly, depending on the quality and quantity of other reading activities in school and out.

Or consider another example. A study by Seyong Lee, using longitudinal data and rigorous statistical controls on background and prior influences, found important benefits for high school students' attitudes and grades as a result of continuing several types of family involvement from the middle school into the high school. However, achievement test scores were not greatly affected by partnerships at the high school level. Longitudinal studies and practical experiences that are monitored over time are needed to increase our understanding of the complex patterns of results that can develop from various partnership activities.[6]

The six types of involvement can guide the development of a balanced, comprehensive program of partnerships, including opportunities for family involvement at school and at home, with potentially important results for students, parents, and teachers. The results for students, parents, and teachers will depend on the particular types of involvement that are implemented, as well as on the quality of the implementation.

Action Teams for School, Family, and Community Partnerships

Who will work to create caring school communities that are based on the concepts of partnership? How will the necessary work on all six types of involvement get done? Although a principal or a teacher may be a leader in working with some families or with groups in the community, one person cannot create a lasting, comprehensive program that involves all families as their children progress through the grades.

From the hard work of many educators and families in many schools, we have learned that, along with clear policies and strong support from state and district leaders and from school principals, an Action Team for School, Family, and Community Partnerships in each school is a useful structure. The action team guides the development of a comprehensive program of partnership, including all six types of involvement, and the integration of all family and community connections within a single, unified plan and program. The trials and errors, efforts and insights of many schools in our projects have helped to identify five important steps that any school can take to develop more positive school/family/community connections.[7]

Step 1: Create an Action Team

A team approach is an appropriate way to build partnerships. The Action Team for School, Family, and Community Partnerships can be the "action arm" of a school council, if one exists. The action team takes responsibility for assessing present practices, organizing options for new partnerships, implementing selected activities, evaluating next steps, and continuing to improve and coordinate practices for all six types of involvement. Although the members of the action team lead these activities, they are assisted by other teachers, parents, students, administrators, and community members.

The action team should include at least three teachers from different grade levels, three parents with children in different grade levels, and at least one administrator. Teams may also include at least one member from the community at large and, at the middle and high school levels, at least two students from different grade levels. Others who are central to the school's work with families may also be included as members, such as a cafeteria worker, a school social worker, a counselor, or a school psychologist. Such diverse membership ensures that partnership activities will take into account the various needs, interests, and talents of teachers, parents, the school, and students.

The leader of the action team may be any member who has the respect of the other members, as well as good communication skills and an understanding of the partnership approach. The leader or at least one member of the action team should also serve on the school council, school improvement team, or other such body, if one exists.

In addition to group planning, members of the action team elect (or are assigned to act as) the chair or co-chair of one of six subcommittees for each type of involvement. A team with at least six members (and perhaps as many as 12) ensures that responsibilities for leadership can be delegated so that one person is not overburdened and so that the work of the action team will continue even if members move or change schools or positions. Members may serve renewable terms of two to three years, with replacement of any who leave in the interim. Other thoughtful variations in assignments and activities may be created by small or large schools using this process.

In the first phase of our work in 1987, projects were led by "project directors" (usually teachers) and were focused on one type of involvement at a time. Some schools succeeded in developing good partnerships over several years, but others were thwarted if the project director moved, if the principal changed, or if the project grew larger than one person could handle. Other schools took a team approach in order to work on many types of involvement simultaneously. Their efforts demonstrated how to structure the program for the next set of schools in our work. Starting in 1990, this second set of schools tested and improved on the structure and work of action teams. Now, all elementary, middle, and high schools in our research and development projects and in other states and districts that are applying this work are given assistance in taking the action team approach.

Step 2: Obtain Funds and Other Support

A modest budget is needed to guide and support the work and expenses of each school's action team. Funds for state coordinators to assist districts and schools and funds for district coordinators or facilitators to help each school may come from a number of sources. These include federal, state, and local programs that mandate, request, or support family involvement, such as Title I, Title II, Title VII, Goals 2000, and other federal and similar state funding programs. In addition to paying the state and district coordinators, funds from these sources may be applied in creative ways to support staff development in the area of school, family, and community partnerships; to pay for lead teachers at each school; to set up demonstration programs; and for other partnership expenses. In addition, local school/business partnerships, school discretionary funds, and separate fund-raising efforts targeted to the schools' partnership programs have been used to support the work of their action teams. At the very least, a school's action team requires a small stipend (at least $1,000 per year for three to five years, with summer supplements) for time and materials needed by each subcommittee to plan, implement, and revise practices of partnership that include all six types of involvement.

The action team must also be given sufficient time and social support to do its work. This requires explicit support from the principal and district leaders to allow time for team members to meet, plan, and conduct the activities that are selected for each type of involvement. Time during the summer is also valuable—and may be essential—for planning new approaches that will start in the new school year.

Step 3: Identify Starting Points

Most schools have some teachers who conduct some practices of partnership with some families some of the time. How can good practices be organized and extended so that they may be used by all teachers, at all grade levels, with all families? The action team works to improve and systematize the typically haphazard patterns of involvement. It starts by collecting information about the school's present practices of partnership, along with the views, experiences, and wishes of teachers, parents, administrators, and students.

Assessments of starting points may be made in a variety of ways, depending on available resources, time, and talents. For example, the action team might use formal questionnaires[8] or telephone interviews to survey teachers, administrators, parents, and students (if resources exist to process, analyze, and report survey data). Or the action team might organize a panel of teachers, parents, and students to speak at a meeting of the parent/teacher organization or at some other school meeting as a way of initiating discussion about the goals and desired activities for partnership. Structured discussions may be conducted through a series of principal's breakfasts for representative groups of teachers, parents, students, and others; random sample phone calls may also be used to collect reactions and ideas, or formal focus groups may be convened to gather ideas about school, family, and community partnerships at the school.

What questions should be addressed? Regardless of how the information is gathered, some areas must be covered in any information gathering.

- *Present strengths.* Which practices of school/family/community partnerships are now working well for the school as a whole? For individual grade levels? For which types of involvement?

- *Needed changes.* Ideally, how do we want school, family, and community partnerships to work at this school three years from now? Which present practices should continue, and which should change? To reach school goals, what new practices are needed for each of the major types of involvement?

- *Expectations.* What do teachers expect of families? What do families expect of teachers and other school personnel? What do students expect their families to do to help them negotiate school life? What do students expect their teachers to do to keep their families informed and involved?

- *Sense of community.* Which families are we now reaching, and which are we not yet reaching? Who are the "hard-to-reach" families? What might be done to communicate with and engage these families in their children's education? Are current partnership practices coordinated to include all families as a school community? Or are families whose children receive special services (e.g., Title I, special education, bilingual education) separated from other families?

- *Links to goals.* How are students faring on such measures of academic achievement as report card grades, on measures of attitudes and attendance, and on other indicators of success? How might family and community connections assist the school in helping more students reach higher goals and achieve greater success? Which practices of school, family, and community partnerships would directly connect to particular goals?

Step 4: Develop a Three-Year Plan

From the ideas and goals for partnerships collected from teachers, parents, and students, the action team can develop a three-year outline of the specific steps that will help the school progress from this starting point on each type of involvement to where it wants to be in three years. This plan outlines how each subcommittee will work over three years to make important, incremental advances to reach more families each year on each type of involvement. The three-year outline also shows how all school/family/community connections will be integrated into one coherent program of partnership that includes activities for the whole school community, activities to meet the special needs of children and families, activities to link to the district committees and councils, and activities conducted in each grade level.

In addition to the three-year outline of goals for each type of involvement, a detailed one-year plan should be developed for the first year's work. It should include the specific activities that will be implemented, improved, or maintained for each type of involvement; a time line of monthly actions needed for each activity; identification of the subcommittee chair who will be responsible for each type of involvement; identification of the teachers, parents, students, or others (not necessarily action team members) who will assist with the implementation of each activity; indicators of how the implementation and results of each major activity will be assessed; and other details of importance to the action team.

The three-year outline and one-year detailed plan are shared with the school council and/or parent organization, with all teachers, and with the parents and students. Even if the action team makes only one good step forward each year on each of the six types of involvement, it will take 18 steps forward over three years to develop a more comprehensive and coordinated program of school/family/community partnerships.

In short, based on the input from the parents, teachers, students, and others on the school's starting points and desired partnerships, the action team will address these issues.

- *Details.* What will be done each year, for three years, to implement a program on all six types of involvement? What, specifically, will be accomplished in the first year on each type of involvement?

- *Responsibilities.* Who will be responsible for developing and implementing practices of partnership for each type of involvement? Will staff development be needed? How will teachers, administrators, parents, and students be supported and recognized for their work?

- *Costs.* What costs are associated with the improvement and maintenance of the planned activities? What sources will provide the needed funds? Will small grants or other special budgets be needed?

- *Evaluation.* How will we know how well the practices have been implemented and what their effects are on students, teachers, and families? What indicators will we use that are closely linked to other practices implemented to determine their effects?

Step 5: Continue Planning And Working

The action team should schedule an annual presentation and celebration of progress at the school so that all teachers, families, and students will know about the work that has been done each year to build partnerships. Or the district coordinator for school, family, and community partnerships might arrange an annual conference for all schools in the district. At the annual school or district meeting, the action team presents and displays the highlights of accomplishments on each type of involvement. Problems are discussed and ideas are shared about improvements, additions, and continuations for the next year.

Each year, the action team updates the school's three-year outline and develops a detailed one-year plan of the coming year's work. It is important for educators, families, students, and the community at large to be aware of annual progress, of new plans, and of how they can help.

In short, the action team addresses the following questions. How can it ensure that the program of school/family/community partnership will continue to improve its structure, processes, and practices in order to increase the number of families who are partners with the school in their children's education? What opportunities will teachers, parents, and students have to share information on successful practices and to strengthen and maintain their efforts?

Characteristics of Successful Programs

As schools have implemented partnership programs, their experience has helped to identify some important properties of successful partnerships.

- *Incremental progress.* Progress in partnerships is incremental, including more families each year in ways that benefit more students. Like reading or math programs, assessment programs, sports programs, or other school investments, partnership programs take time to develop, must be periodically reviewed, and should be continuously improved. The schools in our projects have shown that three years is the minimum time needed for an action team to complete a number of activities on each type of involvement and to establish its work as a productive and permanent structure in a school.

  The development of a partnership is a process, not a single event. All teachers, families, students, and community groups do not engage in all activities on all types of involvement all at once. Not all activities implemented will succeed with all families. But with good planning, thoughtful implementation, well-designed activities, and pointed improvements, more and more families and teachers can learn to work with one another on behalf of the children whose interests they share. Similarly, not all students instantly improve their attitudes or achievements when their families become involved in their education. After all, student learning depends mainly on good curricula and instruction and on the work completed by students. However, with a well-implemented program of partnership, more students will receive support from their families, and more will be motivated to work harder.

- *Connection to curricular and instructional reform.* A program of school/family/community partnerships that focuses on children's learning and development is an important component of curricular and instructional reform. Aspects of partnerships that aim to help more students succeed in school can be supported by federal, state, and local funds that are targeted for curricular and instructional reform. Helping families understand, monitor, and interact with students on homework, for example, can be a clear and important extension of classroom instruction, as can volunteer programs that bolster and broaden student skills, talents, and interests. Improving the content and conduct of parent/teacher/student conferences and goal-setting activities can be an important step in curricular reform; family support and family understanding of child and adolescent development and school curricula are necessary elements to assist students as learners.

The connection of partnerships to curriculum and instruction in schools and the location of leadership for these partnership programs in district departments of curriculum and instruction are important changes that move partnerships from being peripheral public relations activities about parents to being central programs about student learning and development.

- *Redefining staff development.* The action team approach to partnerships guides the work of educators by restructuring "staff development" to mean colleagues working together and with parents to develop, implement, evaluate, and continue to improve practices of partnership. This is less a "dose of inservice education" than it is an active form of developing staff talents and capacities. The teachers, administrators, and others on the action team become the "experts" on this topic for their school. Their work in this area can be supported by various federal, state, and local funding programs as a clear investment in staff development for overall school reform. Indeed, the action team approach as outlined can be applied to any or all important topics on a school improvement agenda. It need not be restricted to the pursuit of successful partnerships.

It is important to note that the development of partnership programs would be easier if educators came to their schools prepared to work productively with families and communities. Courses or classes are needed in preservice teacher education and in advanced degree programs for teachers and administrators to help them define their professional work in terms of partnerships. Today, most educators enter schools without an understanding of family backgrounds, concepts of caring, the framework of partnerships, or the other "basics" I have discussed here. Thus most principals and district leaders are not prepared to guide and lead their staffs in developing strong school and classroom practices that inform and involve families. And most teachers and administrators are not prepared to understand, design, implement, or evaluate good practices of partnership with the families of their students. Colleges and universities that prepare educators and others who work with children and families should identify where in their curricula the theory, research policy, and practical ideas about partnerships are presented or where in their programs these can be added.[9]

Even with improved preservice and advanced coursework, however, each school's action team will have to tailor its menu of practices to the needs and wishes of the teachers, families, and students in the school. The framework and guidelines offered in this article can be used by thoughtful educators to organize this work, school by school.

The Core of Caring

One school in our Baltimore project named its partnerships the "I Care Program." It developed an I Care Parent Club that fostered fellowship and leadership of families, an *I Care Newsletter,* and many other events and activities. Other schools also gave catchy, positive names to their programs to indicate to families, students, teachers, and everyone else in the school community that there are important relationships and exchanges that must be developed in order to assist students.

Interestingly, synonyms for "caring" match the six types of involvement: Type 1, parenting: supporting, nurturing, and rearing; Type 2, communicating: relating, reviewing, and overseeing; Type 3, volunteering: supervising and fostering; Type 4, learning at home: managing, recognizing, and rewarding; Type 5, decision making: contributing, considering, and judging; and Type 6, collaborating with the community: sharing and giving.

Underlying all six types of involvement are two defining synonyms of caring: trusting and respecting. Of course, the varied meanings are interconnected, but it is striking that language permits us to call forth various elements of caring associated with activities for the six types of involvement. If all six types of involvement are operating well in a school's program of partnership, then all of these caring behaviors could be activated to assist children's learning and development.

Despite real progress in many states, districts, and schools over the past few years, there are still too many schools in which educators do not understand the families of their students; in which families do not understand their children's schools; and in which communities do not understand or assist the schools, families, or students. There are still too many states and districts without the policies, departments, leadership, staff, and fiscal support needed to enable all their schools to develop good programs of partnership. Yet relatively small financial investments that support and assist the work of action teams could yield significant returns for all schools, teachers, families, and students. Educators who have led the way with trials, errors, and successes provide evidence that any state, district, or school can create similar programs.[10]

Schools have choices. There are two common approaches to involving families in schools and in their children's education. One approach emphasizes conflict and views the school as a battleground. The conditions and relationships in this kind of environment guarantee power struggles and disharmony. The other approach emphasizes partnership and views the school as a homeland. The conditions and relationships in this kind of environment invite power sharing and mutual respect and allow energies to be directed toward activities that foster student learning and development. Even when conflicts rage, however, peace must be restored sooner or later, and the partners in children's education must work together.

Next Steps: Strengthening Partnerships

Collaborative work and thoughtful give-and-take among researchers, policy leaders, educators, and parents are responsible for the progress that has been made over the past decade in understanding and developing school, family, and community partnerships. Similar collaborations will be important for future progress in this and other areas of school reform. To promote these approaches, I am establishing a national network of Partnership-2000 Schools to help link state, district, and other leaders who are responsible for helping their elementary, middle, and high schools implement programs of school, family and community partnerships by the year 2000. The state and district coordinators must be supported for at least three years by sufficient staff and budgets to enable them to help increasing numbers of elementary, middle and high schools in their districts to plan, implement, and maintain comprehensive programs of partnership.

Partnership-2000 Schools will be aided in putting the recommendations of this article into practice in ways that are appropriate to their locations. Implementation will include applying the theory of overlapping spheres of influence, the framework of six types of involvement, and the action team approach. Researchers and staff members at Johns Hopkins will disseminate information and guidelines, send out newsletters, and hold optional annual workshops to help state and district coordinators learn new strategies and share successful ideas. Activities for leaders at the state and district levels will be shared, as will school-level programs and successful partnership practices.

The national network of Partnership-2000 Schools will begin its activities in the fall of 1995 and will continue until at least the year 2000. The goal is to enable leaders in all states and districts to assist all their schools in establishing and strengthening programs of school/family/community partnership.[11]

Notes

1. Joyce L. Epstein, "Toward a Theory of Family-School Connections: Teacher Practices and Parent Involvement," in Klaus Hurrelmann, Frederick Kaufmann, and Frederick Losel, eds., *Social Intervention: Potential and Constraints* (New York: DeGruyter, 1987), pp. 121–36; idem, "School and Family Partnerships," in Marvin Alkin, ed., *Encyclopedia of Educational Research,* 6th ed. (New York: Macmillan, 1992), pp. 1139–51; idem, "Theory to Practice: School and Family Partnerships Lead to School Improvement and Student Success," in Cheryl L. Fagnano and Beverly Z. Werber, eds., *School, Family and Community Interaction: A View from the Firing Lines* (Boulder, Colo.: Westview Press, 1994), pp. 39–52; and idem, *School and Family Partnerships: Preparing Educators and Improving Schools* (Boulder, Colo.: Westview Press, forthcoming).

2. Ron Brandt, "On Parents and Schools: A Conversation with Joyce Epstein," *Educational Leadership,* October 1989, pp. 24–27; Epstein, "Toward a Theory"; Catherine C. Lewis, Eric Schaps, and Marilyn Watson, "Beyond the Pendulum: Creating Challenging and Caring Schools," *Phi Delta Kappan,* March 1995, pp. 547–54; and Debra Viadero, "Learning to Care," *Education Week,* 26 October 1994, pp. 31–33.

3. A. Wade Boykin, "Harvesting Culture and Talent: African American Children and Educational Reform," in Robert Rossi, ed., *Schools and Students at Risk* (New York: Teachers College Press, 1994), pp. 116–39.

4. For references to studies by many researchers, see the following literature reviews: Epstein, "School and Family Partnerships"; idem, *School and Family Partnerships;* and

idem, "Perspectives and Previews on Research and Policy for School, Family, and Community Partnerships," in Alan Booth and Judith Dunn, eds., *Family-School Links: How Do They Affect Educational Outcomes?* (Hillsdale, N.J.: Erlbaum, forthcoming). Research that reports patterns of involvement across the grades, for families with low and high socioeconomic status, for one- and two-parent homes, and on schools' programs of partnership includes: Carol Ames, with Madhab Khoju and Thomas Watkins, "Parents and Schools: The Impact of School-to-Home Communications on Parents' Beliefs and Perceptions," Center on Families, Communities, Schools, and Children's Learning, Center Report 15, Johns Hopkins University, Baltimore, 1993; David P. Baker and David L. Stevenson, "Mothers' Strategies for Children's School Achievement: Managing the Transition to High School," *Sociology of Education,* vol. 59, 1986, pp. 156–66; Patricia A. Bauch, "Is Parent Involvement Different in Private Schools?," *Educational Horizons,* vol. 66, 1988, pp. 78–82; Henry J. Becker and Joyce L. Epstein, "Parent Involvement: A Study of Teacher Practices," *Elementary School Journal,* vol. 83, 1982, pp. 85–102; Reginald M. Clark, *Family Life and School Achievement: Why Poor Black Children Succeed or Fail* (Chicago: University of Chicago Press, 1983); Susan L. Dauber and Joyce L. Epstein, "Parents' Attitudes and Practices of Involvement in Inner-City Elementary and Middle Schools," in Nancy Chavkin, ed., *Families and Schools in a Pluralistic Society* (Albany: State University of New York Press, 1993), pp. 53–71; Sanford M. Dornbusch and Philip L. Ritter, "Parents of High School Students: A Neglected Resource," *Educational Horizons,* vol. 66, 1988, pp. 75–77; Jacquelynn S. Eccles, "Family Involvement in Children's and Adolescents' Schooling," in Booth and Dunn, op. cit; Joyce L. Epstein, "Parents' Reactions to Teacher Practices of Parent Involvement," *Elementary School Journal,* vol. 86, 1986, pp. 277–294 idem, "Single Parents and the Schools: Effects of Marital Status on Parent and Teacher Interactions," in Maureen Hallinan, ed., *Change in Societal Institutions* (New York: Plenum, 1990), pp. 91–121; Joyce L. Epstein and Seyong Lee, "National Patterns of School and Family Connections in the Middle Grades," in Bruce A. Ryan and Gerald R. Adams, eds., *The Family-School Connection: Theory, Research, and Practice* (Newbury Park, Calif.: Sage, forthcoming); Annette Lareau, *Home Advantage: Social Class and Parental Intervention in Elementary Education* (Philadelphia: Falmer Press, 1989); and Diane Scott-Jones, "Activities in the Home That Support School Learning in the Middle Grades," in Barry Rutherford, ed., *Creating Family/School Partnerships* (Columbus, Ohio: National Middle School Association, 1995), pp. 161–81.

5. The three tables update earlier versions that were based on only five types of involvement. For other discussions of the types, practices, challenges, redefinitions, and results, see Epstein, "School and Family Partnerships"; Lori Connors Tadros and Joyce L. Epstein, "Parents and Schools," in Marc H. Bornstein, ed., *Handbook of Parenting* (Hillsdale N.J.: Erlbaum, forthcoming); Joyce L. Epstein and Lori Connors Tadros, "School and Family Partnerships in the Middle Grades," in Rutherford, op. cit.; and idem, "Trust Fund: School, Family, and Community Partnerships in High Schools," Center on Families, Communities, Schools, and Children's Learning, Center Report 24, Johns Hopkins University, Baltimore, 1994. Schools' activities with various types of involvement are outlined in Don Davies, Patricia Burch, and Vivian Johnson, "A Portrait of Schools Reaching Out: Report of a Survey on Practices and Policies for Family-Community-School Collaboration," Center on Families, Communities, Schools, and Children's Learning, Center Report 1, Johns Hopkins University, Baltimore, 1992.

6. Seyong Lee, "Family-School Connections and Students' Education: Continuity and Change of Family Involvement from the Middle Grades to High School" (Doctoral dissertation, Johns Hopkins University, 1994). For a discussion of issues concerning the results of partnerships, see Epstein, "Perspectives and Previews." For various research reports on results of partnerships for students and for parents, see Joyce L. Epstein, "Effects on Student Achievement of Teacher Practices of Parent Involvement," in Steven

Silvern, ed., *Literacy Through Family, Community, and School Interaction* (Greenwich, Conn.: JAI Press, 1991), pp. 261–76; Joyce L. Epstein and Susan L. Dauber, "Effects on Students of an Interdisciplinary Program Linking Social Studies, Art, and Family Volunteers in the Middle Grades," *Journal of Early Adolescence,* vol. 15, 1995, pp. 237–66; Joyce L. Epstein and Jill Jacobsen, "Effects of School Practices to Involve Families in the Middle Grades: Parents' Perspectives," paper presented at the annual meeting of the American Sociological Association, Los Angeles, 1994; Joyce L. Epstein and Seyong Lee, "Effects of School Practices to Involve Families on Parents and Students in the Middle Grades: A View from the Schools," paper presented at the annual meeting of the American Sociological Association, Miami, 1993; and Anne T. Henderson and Nancy Berla, *A New Generation of Evidence: The Family Is Critical to Student Achievement* (Washington, D.C.: National Committee for Citizens in Education, 1994).

7. Lori Connors Tadros and Joyce L. Epstein, "Taking Stock: The Views of Teachers, Parents, and Students on School, Family, and Community Partnerships in High Schools," Center on Families, Communities, Schools, and Children's Learning, Center Report 25, Johns Hopkins University, Baltimore, 1994; Epstein and Tadros, "Trust Fund"; Joyce L. Epstein and Susan L. Dauber, "School Programs and Teacher Practices of Parent Involvement in Inner-City Elementary and Middle Schools," *Elementary School Journal,* vol. 91, 1991, pp. 289–303; and Joyce L. Epstein, Susan C. Herrick, and Lucretia Coates, "Effects of Summer Home Learning Packets on Student Achievement in Language Arts in the Middle Grades," *School Effectiveness and School Improvement,* in press. For other approaches to the use of action teams for partnerships, see Patricia Burch and Ameetha Palanki, "Action Research on Family-School-Community Partnerships," *Journal of Emotional and Behavioral Problems,* vol. 1, 1994, pp. 16–19; Patricia Burch, Ameetha Palanki, and Don Davies, "In Our Hands: A Multi-Site Parent-Teacher Action Research Project," Center on Families, Communities, Schools, and Children's Learning, Center Report 29, Johns Hopkins University, Baltimore, 1995; Don Davies, "Schools Reaching Out: Family, School, and Community Partnerships for Student Success," *Phi Delta Kappan,* January 1991, pp. 376–82; idem, "A More Distant Mirror: Progress Report on a Cross-National Project to Study Family-School-Community Partnerships," *Equity and Choice,* vol. 19, 1993, pp. 41–46; and Don Davies, Ameetha Palanki, and Patricia D. Palanki, "Getting Started: Action Research in Family-School-Community Partnerships," Center on Families, Communities, Schools, and Children's Learning, Center Report 17, Johns Hopkins University, Baltimore, 1993. For an example of an organizing mechanism for action teams, see Vivian R. Johnson, "Parent Centers in Urban Schools: Four Case Studies," Center on Families, Communities, Schools, and Children's Learning, Center Report 23, Johns Hopkins University, Baltimore, 1994.

8. Surveys for teachers and parents in the elementary and middle grades and for teachers, parents, and students in high school, developed and revised in 1993 by Joyce L. Epstein, Karen Clark Salinas, and Lori Connors Tadros, are available from the Center on Families, Communities, Schools, and Children's Learning at Johns Hopkins University.

9. Mary Sue Ammon, "University of California Project on Teacher Preparation for Parent Involvement, Report I: April 1989 Conference and Initial Follow-up," mimeo, University of California, Berkeley, 1990; Nancy F. Chavkin and David L. Williams, "Critical Issues in Teacher Training for Parent Involvement," *Educational Horizons,* vol. 66, 1988, pp. 87–89; and Lisa Hinz, Jessica Clarke, and Joe Nathan, "A Survey of Parent Involvement Course Offerings in Minnesota's Undergraduate Preparation Programs," Center for School Change, Humphrey Institute of Public Affairs, University of Minnesota, Minneapolis, 1992. To correct deficiencies in the education of educators, I have written a course text or supplementary reader based on the theory, framework, and approaches described in this article. See Epstein, *School and Family Partnerships.* Other useful readings for a university course include Sandra L. Christenson and Jane Close Conoley, eds., *Home-School Collaboration: Enhancing*

Children's Academic Competence (Silver Spring, Md.: National Association of School Psychologists, 1992); Fagnano and Werber, op. cit.; Norman Fruchter, Anne Galletta, and J. Lynne White, *New Directions in Parent Involvement* (Washington, D.C.: Academy for Educational Development, 1992); William Rioux and Nancy Berla, eds., *Innovations in Parent and Family Involvement* (Princeton Junction, N.J.: Eye on Education, 1993); and Susan McAllister Swap, *Developing Home-School Partnerships: From Concepts to Practice* (New York: Teachers College Press, 1993).

10. See, for example, Gary Lloyd, "Research and Practical Application for School, Family, and Community Partnerships," in Booth and Dunn, op cit.; Wisconsin Department of Public Instruction, *Sharesheet: The DPI Family-Community-School Partnership Newsletter,* August/September 1994; and the special section on parent involvement in the January 1991 *Phi Delta Kappan.*

11. For more information about the national network of Partnership-2000 Schools, send the name, position, address, and phone and fax numbers of the contact person/coordinator for partnerships for your state or district to Joyce Epstein, Partnership-2000 Schools, CRESPAR/Center on Families, Communities, Schools, and Children's Learning, Johns Hopkins University, 3505 N. Charles St., Baltimore, MD 21218.

READING 2

Tellin' Stories Project

Dr. Mary F. Ziegler

The project turns a light on inside of people that was there all along and then the light spills over into everything.

Tellin' Stories is a project of the District of Columbia Public Schools Center for Systemic Change in collaboration with the Network of Educators on the Americas and the D.C. Area Writing Project. The project is based at Howard University and is funded by a three-year grant from the U.S. Department of Education Fund for the Improvement and Reform of Schools and Teaching. This document is the final evaluation report compiled for the Tellin' Stories Project, formerly called the Family Writing Project.

Project Purpose

The purpose of the Tellin' Stories Project is to increase the involvement of economically disadvantaged parents in the educational process of their children. The project connects parents, educators, schools, and communities. A brochure describing the project says, "The Tellin' Stories Project is based on the belief that all parents regardless of their nationality, cultural background, native language, and level of formal education have the knowledge and experience to create their own literature and to serve as sources of literacy at home, in the school, and in the community."

Reprinted by permission of the author.

Project Goals

Six major goals have focused the project's activities for the last three years. The goals of the project are to

- Develop family oriented activities to enable parents with little formal education to involve themselves in literacy activities with their children.
- Build parental collaboration across linguistic, ethnic, and racial barriers.
- Create a school environment which is respectful of the children's culture and family traditions.
- Increase input of low income and immigrant parents in the school policy and practice.
- Increase the comfort level of parents in their child's school and classroom.
- Develop an innovative, affordable, feasible, and easily reproducible model of parental involvement that can be replicated in low-income urban school districts across the country.

The purpose of the evaluation and the methods were defined at the beginning of the project by the Evaluation Team (comprising project staff, co-coordinators, Barbara D'Emilio and Toni Blackman [and later Imani Tolliver] and parent coordinators, Margarita Chamorro and Lashawn Blango, and the evaluator, Dr. Mary Ziegler) at the beginning of the project evaluation process. Evaluation methods are participatory in that the project staff and parent participants (when possible) are involved in the design and implementation of the evaluation.

The third-year evaluation process consisted of four primary data collection methods: (1) a focus group with parents, staff, and a teacher involved in the project, (2) review of project documents, (3) interviews with parents and teachers, and (4) observation of project activities.

Accomplishing the Goals of the Project

The project has made excellent progress in achieving its goals. Goals for the project were established when the project first began more than three years ago. The goals have remained remarkably constant over time and so has the steady progress made in achieving them. Because the project staff is quite small, parent and teachers have taken a leadership role in moving the Tellin' Stories project forward. Project participants report that the project has a different flavor depending on the school or organization that is involved. Following is a description of the way parents, staff, teachers and administrators describe how the project has accomplished its goals.

1. Developing Family Oriented Activities   The first goal of the project is to develop family oriented activities to enable parents with little formal education to involve themselves in literacy activities with their children. Project activities have evolved over the life of the project. Activities have been continuously improved as a result of the suggestions made by parents and teachers. Activities for parents fall into three main categories: workshops, storytelling in classrooms, and the summer institute. Project documents show that more than 450 parents have participated in the project activities over the last three years.

Workshops are conducted weekly over a period of weeks or months depending on the school. In these workshops, parents write stories about their lives and concerns. In some workshops, quilt making is used as a stimulus to begin the writing process. Parents depict their stories graphically on pieces of felt. Squares of felt, each with the story of a parent or a family, are sewn together to make a story quilt. The square also includes a brief statement. The quilt is accompanied by a narrative of the stories that are represented on the quilts. In other writing workshops, parents write their stories and these written stories are printed by the project staff. Selected stories are bound as anthologies and are used as readers in the classroom.

Story telling training workshops are conducted for those parents that want to become equipped to tell stories in classrooms. Parents help select stories (either stories parents have written or stories selected from children's literature) and they create felt characters to depict the stories to children. Parents learn the art of story telling. Since the beginning of the project, ten parents from a variety of cultures and backgrounds, speaking three different languages, have told stories in more than 30 schools citywide. Parent storytellers have reached over 2,200 students. One school, after a storytelling workshop, developed a school-based team of parent storytellers.

Summer Story Telling Institute is an annual event for parents, teachers, and other interested community members. This institute brings expert story tellers together with parents and teachers to explore the various ways to tell stories. The institute also focuses on the way story telling can be used to challenge inequities, understand community, and look at change. More than 40 people attended the last summer institute.

When parents describe the project activities, they describe activities that stimulate writing, storytelling in classrooms, parents teaching children through stories and incentives for parents.

Activities That Stimulate Writing—Project staff selected activities to stimulate ideas that helped make writing interesting for parents who volunteered to attend workshops. Readings were selected and read by project staff and teachers. These included dramatic reading of poetry, stories from literature, oral stories, and stories written by other parents. As one parent said, "The poems and stories related to my life. They helped me tell my own story." Themes for stories came from experiences in peoples' lives, like immigration or discrimination. Parents who immigrated to the United States wrote stories about their native lands. These stories were compiled into personal books. These books were used in story telling activities in classrooms and at home. Parents expressed a great deal of pride in showing their books to others and reading their stories. Parents' written stories were collected into anthologies for teachers to use to stimulate writing activities with children.

Making story quilts was an important activity for many parents. In this activity, parents gathered to tell their story by making pieces for a quilt made up of many felt squares. Parents depicted their story through a picture, words, or other symbols. Along with the graphic depiction, they wrote a summary of what the felt square meant. Project staff wove the felt pieces together to make a quilt. The quilt squares told the story of the individual or the family. Parents said that making a quilt was very stimulating and helped them overcome their fear of writing and speaking publically. As one parent explained it, "It helped relieve our anxiety about writing." As a result of this activity, parents from a particular school were able to tell their collective story and receive recognition for their work from administrators, other parents, teachers, and children. Some of the quilts are displayed in the schools where the parents' children attend.

Storytelling in Classrooms—Parents teach and entertain children in their classrooms by telling stories and by conducting follow-up writing exercises based on the stories. One parent said, "When we tell stories to the children, the stories come alive in a new way." In order to find interesting stories, parents read a broad range of children's books. Once parents became storytellers, they begin searching for and finding stories to tell to the children. Parents choose different ways to tell stories. Some act out the story. Others make flannel pieces to tell the story with felt characters. One parent commented that she loved the stories that had a "moral" or a teaching point. Parents have developed, documented, and stored almost forty stories using felt or other materials. New storytellers have the advantage of a library of stories already prepared for them. In addition to stories from children's literature, parents read from the books they themselves have written in the writing workshops. Parents described how they used their childhood experiences to write stories that were later told to children in classrooms. As one parent said proudly, "Everyone is a story teller."

Parents Teaching Children Through Stories—Through writing and story telling, parents became better teachers. They devised follow-up activities to do with school children that would reinforce both the points of the story and the curriculum focus of the teacher. Words from stories were used to teach vocabulary. Because most of the stories were told by bilingual storytelling teams, children learned to listen to another language and appreciate life in other cultures. Parents and teachers worked together to identify curriculum topics that could be reinforced by the storytelling teams, for example, number concepts, color, and seasons. The stories helped to stimulate the children's ideas for other stories. All participants in the project reported that the children responded enthusiastically to the stories and to the parents (especially the bilingual teams) who came to their classrooms to tell stories. Themes about things that are important to parents and children helped build community.

Parents also reported a significant increase in the literary activities they did with their children in the home. "I told stories to kids to make them understand. We drew pictures at home, the same as the story. My kids drew pictures. My kids made felt stories themselves." Several parents reported that they did not know that it was important to read to their children. Some said that they did not know how to select a book or they did not know that their children would like to listen to stories read by their parents. Parents learned how to write and read their own stories and how to value good stories written by others. This formed the foundation of the parents' increased ability to use literacy activities to teach their children.

2. Building Parental Collaboration Across Linguistic, Ethnic, and Racial Barriers The second goal of the project is to build parental collaboration across linguistic, ethnic, and racial barriers. Parents reported that the storytelling themes cross all boundaries. Storytelling teams are multilingual. Telling stories to children in another language helps children value differences. People of different races and languages met together to tell their stories. People found that they had a lot in common. "Writing exercises helped us understand one another—a poem about colors helped us understand each other's cultures." One parent who was learning English commented that she learned that words in different languages are often similar. "We are very similar in our heritage and how we have so much in common." For parents who were English speaking, they commented that they learned how it felt to not speak the dominant language that was used in the school. All parents commented on the "value of . . . children and parents learning together and being interested because of the multilingual stories." One person commented that he learned, "Color does not determine a language."

A teacher described the activities of the project that were meaningful to parents. "In the workshops, parents discuss themes for the stories. After the discussion they write and read their writings." Multicultural groups of parents, in Tellin' Stories Workshops, practiced writing and reading their stories to one another. Through these stories, they learned a great deal about one another's lives, cultures, traditions, and languages.

In some cases, a teacher reported, "Children and parents write together and then they read the stories." One parent commented that she read her stories to her children and they asked her questions about it. Another person said, "I have been more motivated to learn together with my children." "The community benefits too," said one parent. "When parents work together to learn, all the parents of the community benefit." Parents report that story telling has become part of their lives. At one school where there is a team of parent story tellers, the administration is considering establishing a position for a parent to be the story telling coordinator. Over the course of three years, four of the parent storytellers obtained paid positions as educational aides or parent partners even though this was not a planned outcome of the project.

3. Respect for Children's Culture and Family Traditions The third goal of the project has been to create a school environment which is respectful of the children's culture and family traditions. While creating a respectful environment cannot be done by one project alone, the project has made a significant contribution in the schools where it is active. From its inception, the project has had a multicultural, multilingual focus. This focus enabled parents from different ethnicities, speaking different languages, to come together for a common purpose—to enhance their ability to be their children's teacher and to get involved in their children's education.

A major accomplishment at one of the schools was the translation of PTA meetings into Spanish and Vietnamese for the parents who speak those languages. Parents report that in some cases, teachers are not as insistent that parents speak only English at home. The multicultural aspect of the project led to more teachers including multicultural activities in their classrooms, for example, including information about famous Native Americans, famous African Americans, and famous Asian Pacific Islanders.

Parents acknowledged that the children learned to speak English better or learned to respect other languages and traditions through the story telling. One parent story teller commented, "I went to tell a story in the 6th grade. Some of the children did not know how to write in English. I asked the teacher if the children may write in Spanish. She gave permission. The children wrote beautiful stories in Spanish." Multilingual parent teams were able to validate the children's writing ability in their own language.

A parent commented, "We teach our children about the tradition of our people, the musical tradition, the history, the language. One of my children said, 'I don't want to speak Spanish, only English.' I told him, 'No, this way when you go to Guatemala, you will not be able to communicate with your grandmother or other people. And you will not be able to know the country.' I think he understood." The language is one way to keep the traditional cultures alive.

Almost all parents who have been involved in the project report that their involvement in their child's school has increased as a result of participation in the project activities. They report that they feel welcome in the school building and recognized by teachers and administrators. The enthusiasm with which the multilingual parent storytelling teams were received is an additional indicator of the respect for the children's culture and family traditions in those classrooms.

4. Increasing Input of Parents into School Policy and Practice The fourth goal of the project is to increase input of low income and immigrant parents in the school and classroom. Parents are valuable contributors to the educational process. A noticeable exchange has occurred in the support that the school administrators are giving to the project. According to a principal, "The Tellin' Stories Project has provided a positive environment which has encouraged parents to view themselves as writers and partners in the educative process . . . [Our school] strongly supports the efforts of the Tellin' Stories Project which has increased parental involvement 50% over the previous academic year."

Parents explained that the Tellin' Stories Project is like a first step in school involvement. Getting involved in story telling increases a parent's confidence to get involved in other activities. A teacher commented, "Parents start with telling stories and then get involved in other organized projects. It's a motivator, a catalyst, to start other initiatives." The project equips parents for involvement in their child's school.

Telling stories in classrooms has been a very positive experience for the children, the parents, and the school. The teachers hear the parents and it raises their interest in story telling as an activity. It also raises their awareness of and respect for parents. The literacy level of children is also improved through story telling. Parents commented that their roles as storytellers have raised the awareness of the contribution parents can make. This is influencing policy about activities like story telling. "We have parents who have increased their influence in the school," said a teacher. Parents get other roles, even paid positions because of their involvement in the Tellin' Stories project. One parent commented, "The children of politicians hear the stories and ask their parents to tell stories, so this project influences politicians."

5. Increasing Parents' Comfort Level in the School and Classroom Most of the comments on the accomplishments of the other goals speak to this goal. It is difficult to be comfortable in a school or classroom without receiving respect. Parents often do not know how to become involved, nor how to have their contribution valued. The Tellin' Stories Project acts as a gateway for parents who otherwise do not see themselves as active in their child's education. Gathering to write and read stories is a first step for many parents believing that they are welcome in their child's school.

Most parents are usually called to the school when the child is experiencing difficulty or when the child has broken the rules. Parents with low literacy skills may see their role and the school's role as adversarial rather than collaborative. Even if parents volunteer in their child's school, the efforts are often relegated to supervising in the cafeteria or on the playground. Telling stories in the classroom gives the parents a different status, one that, according to them, generates respect. The project has documented that parents who hesitated even entering the school building became confident contributors to both the school and their child's educational process.

6. Develop a Reproducible Model The final goal of the project is to develop an innovative, affordable, feasible, and easily reproducible model of parental involvement that can be replicated in low-income urban school districts across the country. The project "model" has emerged over the three-year life of the project.

Model Developed by the Tellin' Stories Project

The Tellin' Stories project grew from a desire to involve parents of children from economically disadvantaged neighborhoods in the Washington D.C. Public School System as partners in the educational process. Increased involvement strengthens parents' role as their children's first teacher. Immigrant parents and parents with low literacy skills are reluctant to participate in the educational process of their children for a variety of reasons. Immigrant parents report that they are reluctant because they do not speak the dominant language of the school. Other parents report that they do not believe they are competent to be involved. Teachers often misinterpret parents' lack of involvement as apathy or lack of concern. The goal of the Tellin' Stories project is to bring together parents, teachers, school administrators, and children to build a community of learners through the art of story telling and story writing. In the three years the project has been under way, a model has emerged that is described by project staff, parents, and teachers. Following is a description of the model and the way it works in the District of Columbia Public School System.

When the project began it was called the Family Writing Project. In the first year, two part-time co-coordinators and two parent coordinators held writing workshops for parents of children in the public school system. Project staff made flyers or presentations about the project to encourage parents to participate and encourage teachers to be supportive. Workshops were conducted, and parents began writing their stories which were turned into personal books and anthologies. At the conclusion of the first year, project staff decided that parents without English language skills and with low literacy skills were more attracted to the idea of writing stories rather than simply writing. Stories became the focal point of the project even though writing remained an important component. The project was renamed Tellin' Stories to indicate this emphasis.

The Tellin' Stories project, as it was called in the second year, took on a more definite shape. Successful activities were identified and tested. These activities meaningfully involved parents in their child's school and educational process. Through contributions of parents, teachers, school administrators, project staff and an outside evaluator, a replicable model of the project emerged. This model was validated by a group of parents, teachers, and staff at the end of the third year of the project. Inherent in the model is the fact that it will continue to evolve as it is carried out in a wide variety of school and organizational settings. Each school or group stamps its imprint on the project activities allowing for a wide range of applications. Following are the steps to carry out the project. These steps have been clarified, tested, and modified over three years.

Promoting the project is the first step. The Tellin' Stories Project can be promoted in a wide variety of ways. In the past, project staff made presentations to principals or they spoke at parent/teacher meetings. Teachers who became familiar with the project promoted it to the principals in their schools. Parents who participated in the project in their school spoke to parents and teachers in other schools. Parent storytellers told of their experiences at meetings with administrators of schools and the school system. Project staff located teachers who might be interested in the project.

Initiation is the second step. Usually an inquiry is made about the project to someone already involved or to the project staff. For example, an inquiry has been made by a teacher, a school librarian, a school counselor, a principal and a member of a community-based organization. The initiator is usually interested in bringing the project to a particular school or organization. This individual generally makes the inquiry because he or she sees the value in parent involvement. Project staff give this individual an informal description of the project and provides names of other schools where the project has been active. The initiator often becomes the project "champion," that is, the person who will find support for the project in their school or organization. These individuals tell their principals about the project and get support.

This support is usually in the form of a meeting room for activities. (This is very important as space is at a premium in many schools.)

Coordination is the third step. An event is planned. The event may be a writing workshop, a quilt-making workshop or a story telling training workshop. The event is primarily for a particular school and will involve parents in that school. Project staff will prepare flyers for the initiator to give to parents and other teachers. Initiators understand the value of the project for getting parents involved in the school and their child's education and are enthusiastic to begin. If the initiator is a teacher, the teacher will work with the project staff to decide on the event and make plans for it. At this stage, incentives are planned. Parents reported that incentives to participate were important.

Invitation is the fourth step. Parents are invited to attend an event. The invitation is given by the initiator, project staff, or a parent who has participated in the project in the past. The invitation may be personal or it may be in the form of a flyer or other publicity announcement. For example, one teacher recruited parents of children in her grade. In another school, the librarian recruited parents who wanted to be teacher's aides. Parents are recruited by teachers who know them or they are recruited by other parents through word of mouth. A teacher might take an informal poll among parents to find out what day and time would be most convenient. Parents go to teachers they know to find out more about the Tellin' Stories project. One parent said she looked at a flyer and said, "Hmmm, something might be happening here." She spoke to a teacher to get more information. Incentives are planned to encourage people to participate. Incentives used in the project included food and refreshments, books, or stipends.

Facilitation and/or training event is the fifth step. The Story Tellin' Project staff usually facilitate workshops and training events for a period of time. Parents attend the events and begin thinking about what the project can do for them. Parents say things like, "I can pass this on to my children" or "What I know I can teach." During the event, the project staff encourage parents to express themselves in writing, by making story quilts, and through telling stories. In this process, parents get to know one another better and they get to know teachers in a setting outside their child's classroom. They come to look forward to the event. Project staff prepare an evaluation for the parents to complete. This way the staff can keep in touch with ideas parents have for improving the project. In some cases, the facilitation is taken over by the initiator or another individual on site who is a champion of the project. Storytelling training is provided by the project staff; however, when possible, an on-site coordinator takes over the coordination of the parent story tellers in the classroom. On-site coordinators can be the initiators of the project, parents who have participated, or other interested teachers. In those schools where the initiator planned a story quilt workshop, principals invited the parents to display their quilts in the school as a tribute to their contribution. The quilt display validates the parents' stories and gives them value. The quilts are a tangible symbol of the contribution that parents make to the school community.

Transferring learning is the sixth step. Once parents have participated in project activities, they begin doing similar activities with their children.

Many parents report increased literacy activities in their families. Other parents tell in detail how they have begun to write and read stories with their children at home. Many immigrant parents report that they had not told their children many stories of their homeland and the project gave them an opportunity to do this. For those parents who have taken the storytelling training, they begin to tell stories in classrooms. They also work with the teachers to understand the curriculum topics and the lessons that the teachers would like to have reinforced through the stories. In the process of transferring the learning to their children, parents also learn to navigate their way through the school system. They find their "voice" even if they do not speak English. Several parents report that the outcome of this was their investment in their child's school, a positive relationship with their child's teacher, and for some a commitment to study English or go on to get a GED.

Documenting outcomes is the seventh step. Outcomes of the project are documented through anecdotes by parents to project staff and to school administrators. Outcomes are documented in evaluations and also through presentations to parents who speak about the project to recruit other parents. Because of the small project staff, there is no formal follow-up after a parent has completed the workshop or training event. However, many parents continue to be involved in the project after the particular part they were involved in has finished. When parents were asked about the changes the project has brought about in their lives, they include the following items:

- Parents and children have increased literacy skills and knowledge.
- Parents are better equipped to teach their children.
- Parents write stories and poems and tell these to their children.
- Parents have positive relationships with their child's teacher.
- Parents are trained to assist in classroom activities.
- Parents are trained to tell stories in children's classrooms.
- Parents get to know one another and appreciate their diversity.
- Parents' talents are valued by the school.
- Children have increased literacy activities in the home.
- Children see their parents as their teachers.
- Children are exposed to multicultural teams of parents who enjoy working together.

When teachers and administrators were asked what impact the project has had on their practice or on the school in general, they include the following items:

- Teachers and parents collaborate on a meaningful project.
- Teachers see parents in a supportive teaching role.
- Parents and teachers have respect for people from different cultures.
- Anthologies of parents' stories are published and used in classroom teaching.

- Schools learn a new and valuable way to achieve parent involvement.
- Schools in economically disadvantaged neighborhoods have increased parental involvement.
- The broader community is involved in the life of the school.

Dissemination is the final step and is linked to promotion, the first step. Information about the project is available from dissemination activities including publicity materials, presentations at school meetings and conferences, and annual project celebrations. Dissemination activities also include using the project information to build relationships with school administrators, teachers and other community-based organizations. A parent who had successfully participated in the project said her job was to bring in other parents, "Once they start, everyone has a story to tell."

Project Staff

Throughout the three years of the project, staff consisted of two part-time co-coordinators and one or two parent coordinators. The accomplishments of the project are outstanding when weighed against the small staff and budget.

Project Activities

Storytelling Workshops were conducted in the following schools.

Adams Elementary School	McGogney Elementary School
Bancroft Elementary School	Meyer Elementary School
Brightwood Elementary School	Parkview Elementary School
Bruce Monroe Elementary School	Powell Elementary School
Garrison Elementary School	Richardson Elementary School
K. C. Lewis Elementary School	Shepherd Elementary School

- A school-based storytelling team of fifteen parents worked at McGogney Elementary School and told stories from January to June 1997.
- Over 2,200 students participated in storytelling activities in 30 schools.
- More than 450 parents in D.C. Public Schools have participated in the project.
- Stories were told in three languages: English, Spanish, and Vietnamese.
- Other organizations involved included the Significant Male Taskforce, the Dinner Program for Homeless Women and the Sarah House, and D.C. LEARN.

In the Tellin' Stories project evaluation process, no individual, either in a focus group, interview, or in the project documents described the project in any way but very positive. It is rare that so broad a group of people, parents, teachers, administrators, community members, and project staff react positively to a project. The Tellin' Stories project seems to have filled a niche, a vacuum that encourages community between a diverse group of people who have a stake in the D.C. Public School System.

READING 3

Eight Lessons of Parent, Family, and Community Involvement in the Middle Grades

Barry Rutherford and Shelley H. Billig

In our study of parent and community involvement in education, we examined school/family partnerships in the middle grades (grades 6 to 8). Research on the potential effects of family involvement in early childhood education and in the elementary grades presents a favorable picture,[1] but less is known about the effect of parent and family involvement in the middle grades.

Our research focused on three areas: comprehensive districtwide programs, school restructuring, and adult/child learning programs. Three sites for each focus area were selected and visited twice during the 1993-94 school year. Comprehensive districtwide program sites included the Jefferson County (Kentucky) Public Schools; the Fort Worth Independent School District; and the Minneapolis Public Schools. For our study of family and community involvement in restructuring schools, we visited sites in Lamoni, Iowa; Georgetown, South Carolina; and Shelburne, Vermont. For our study of adult/child learning programs, we visited Community District 3, New York City; the Rochester (New York) Public Schools; and the Chapter 1 Parent Center in Natchez, Mississippi.

Each of these nine sites presented its own unique challenge for family and community involvement.[2] However, two central questions defined the responses at all sites. First, how do schools and districts involve families and the community as partners in education reform? We found many examples at our sites of various ways in which schools or districts met this challenge by providing opportunities and supports for families, school practitioners, community members, and businesses as they assume new roles in education reform. Second, how do schools and districts create partnerships that acknowledge the roles of the family, school, and community in the growth of the child, and how do these systems interact? One teacher to whom we spoke typified the responses to this question. She said, "No one person has the 'big picture' of a child at this age. We try to work with families to construct the picture, to strengthen the partnership, in order to help the children succeed."

Just as each site that we studied faced unique challenges in its efforts to create school/family partnerships, so each site also yielded a unique set of responses.[3] We synthesized our findings across all nine sites and developed a set of eight "lessons." These lessons broaden the scope of our findings beyond the specific context of an individual site. They also move beyond conventional thinking about family and community involvement to enrich our

---

Reprinted by permission of the authors.

understanding of the critical and complex nature of school/family partnerships in the middle grades.

Each of the lessons is described briefly below, along with implications in the form of action statements that highlight what schools, communities, and families can do to implement the lessons. Finally, we offer examples of how specific sites put these lessons into practice.

Lesson 1: The stakes are high and immediate for everyone in the middle grades. During the middle grades, students make personal and educational decisions that have serious consequences. They wrestle with issues of authority, independence, and changing relationships with their families. Their visibility, both as individuals and as members of groups in community settings, requires that students learn and practice productive social skills for community participation. These challenges, coupled with the perception that the years spent in the middle grades are a watershed—and not merely a transition period between elementary school and high school—create a compelling case for the critical importance of the middle grades.[4]

Implications. Schools can create programs that respond to the unique needs of middle-grade families and students. Communities can publicize the success of middle-grade schools and students to emphasize their economic, social, and political importance to the community and they can provide positive interventions for middle-grade students. Families can engage middle-grade children in active decision making. In the Fort Worth Independent School District, Vital Link places sixth-graders in more than 40 businesses for approximately four hours each morning during a one-week internship. In 1993 more than 2,300 students participated in spring or summer pilot internships. The goal of the program is to understand career opportunities in a variety of fields through hands-on experience.

Lesson 2: Challenges can become opportunities for parent/family involvement. In addition to coping with the physical and emotional changes of adolescence, middle-grade students and their families must also deal with changes in the way schools operate. Communication patterns between the school and children and families change; the student's day is fragmented, with many more teachers and subjects, added extracurricular choices, and an increasingly complex curriculum. At the same time, these barriers present a variety of opportunities for families to participate in schools and to interact with their children.

Implications. Schools can create structures that decrease the fragmentation caused by the way schools are organized; they can provide parents with strategies to support the academic success of their middle-grade students; they can make available specific educational opportunities geared to the special interests of middle-grade families. Families can serve as advocates and resources for middle-grade children. Restructuring in Shelburne, Vermont, has focused on organizing elementary and middle grades into a nine-year system divided into three-year "communities." This strategy makes it more likely that students will learn necessary skills and makes the middle school "more inviting and less threatening." In Rochester, New York, many parents take adult basic education courses as part of the Parent/Child Basic Learning Program in that district.

Lesson 3: Relationships are the essence of middle-grade family and community involvement. Schools and communities are ideal contexts for developing and fostering strong relationships with the families of middle-grade students. One-on-one communication between families and teachers, the addition of school personnel to deal with family issues, and community contact with middle-grade students in their roles as consumers and workers all help to build support for middle-grade schools.

Implications. Schools can encourage direct contact between middle-grade families and teachers and can create staffing patterns that support these relationships. Communities can take advantage of middle-school students' relationships with local businesses (as workers and consumers) to make community connections that build support. Families can build personal relationships with members of the school staff.

"I want to be involved," a Minneapolis parent told us. "But I just didn't know how to get involved. If it hadn't been for one of the teachers calling and personally inviting me to come to the school and help, I wouldn't be here today." The efforts of Minneapolis teachers and family support personnel have resulted in increased parent attendance at meetings, a large parent volunteer program, and parents who are being trained as advocates for middle-grade students through the Parent Institute Program.

Lesson 4: Responsibility and decision making are shared by a broad array of players, including the child. Just as adolescents' roles change during the middle grades, so do their responsibilities and their processes of making decisions. School, home, and community are all places where middle-graders learn and are actively involved in either positive or negative ways. Teachers, counselors and service agency personnel, community members, businesspeople, families, and students themselves can and should share responsibility and decision making with regard to the curriculum and the delivery of instruction. The challenge for middle-grade schools comes in coordinating information and efforts across a broad range of stakeholders to create a coherent picture of the student.[5]

Implications. Schools should include middle-grade families, teachers, and students in decisions about curriculum and instruction; involve middle-grade families and students in conferences about coursework and individual progress; and coordinate information from the school to ensure smooth communication with middle-grade families. Families should identify school policies and expectations in preparation for their roles as advocates and supporters of middle-grade students.

Lamoni (Iowa) Middle School has fostered an environment in which, as one administrator put it, "Teachers are comfortable experimenting with structures to see what works." Teacher advisory groups, cooperative learning strategies, interdisciplinary units, and team teaching give students opportunities to make decisions about learning. Frequent contacts with families—both in the school and in the small rural community—allow open communication about curriculum, instruction, and student progress.

Lesson 5: Sustained parent/family involvement and community involvement depend on active advocacy by leaders. Leadership, both within the school and in the community, plays a key role in fostering parent/family involvement and community involvement. Leaders set the tone for involvement, make involvement a priority, and provide the context that enables school personnel, families, community members, and businesspeople to maintain an active role in middle-grade education.

Implications. Schools should look for a whole array of community connections; use creative approaches to "defining" leadership, designing programs, and solving problems; and provide a climate for success that includes making fiscal and human resources available. Communities should take an active role in making connections with schools. Families can represent the interests of middle-grade children, and they can use community connections to advocate for the school.

The principal at Barre Traditional Middle School in Louisville, Kentucky, describes himself as "part instructional leader, part administrator, and part public relations expert." He views his leadership as going beyond the boundaries of the school and into the community. Under his leadership, Barret Traditional Middle School sets expectations for family involvement, implements numerous strategies and activities fostering family involvement and maintains partnerships with community members and businesses.

Lesson 6: A system of supports for frontline workers is critical to parent/family involvement. Frontline workers—teachers and other school personnel—are key players in family involvement. It is through these frontline workers that families are connected to the services provided by the school or the community. In order to be effective, these frontline workers need professional development, the ability and authority to make decisions about services to address family needs, structures that provide the workers themselves with social and emotional support, and a variety of other resources.

Implications. Schools can provide professional development for school personnel that deal with promising practices and programs for family involvement, they can empower frontline workers to make key decisions that connect middle-grade families with needed services, they can create structures that provide social and emotional support for frontline workers, and they can design support systems that outline expectations and give frontline workers resources for family involvement.

The Kentucky Education Reform Act mandates "Youth Service Centers" in middle schools serving economically disadvantaged students. Teachers in Louisville are empowered to refer students and their families to these centers, where a wide range of services are available through local agencies in a "one-stop shopping" atmosphere. In addition, the school district and the parent/teacher organization provide teachers with training. Through teaming efforts, teachers report that they have more time available for connecting with families and that these connections produce powerful results.

Lesson 7: Families need connections to the curriculum. During the elementary grades, the connection of families to curriculum is easier to maintain. In the middle grades, however, multiple teachers, the increase in complexity of course content, and students' growing need for autonomy weaken this connection. It is important for families to remain involved in their children's learning, recognizing that the ways in which they are involved will undergo fundamental changes during the middle-grade years.

Implications. Schools should engage families in meaningful home learning tasks; demonstrate ways for families to work with middle-grade students; and use the content and characteristics of middle-school learning experiences—what and how middle-schoolers learn—as starting points for family connections. Families can create an environment that values and promotes achievement and can communicate with the school and teacher about what is being taught and the progress their middle-schooler is making.

Community District 3 in New York City provides families with home learning "kits" that reinforce classroom instruction. In the Chapter 1 Parent Center in Natchez, Mississippi, staff members demonstrate materials and activities that families can use to work with their children at home.

Lesson 8: Schools need connections to the community. The geographic area served by a school broadens in the middle grades. The school is often located at a greater distance from a student's "home" community; middle-grade school attendance areas often draw students from several different communities. In defining "community," schools must recognize the unique strengths of diverse, multiethnic, and multiracial school populations in both rural and urban settings. They must implement strategies to provide multiple opportunities for the "community" to be involved in the middle grades.

Implications. Schools must recognize and acknowledge the unique characteristics of the community; design programs to build on strengths and needs of the community; seek opportunities to engage and invite the community to participate in school activities; and use a variety of strategies to communicate directly with the community. Communities must take an active role in school decision making. And families must find a variety of ways to participate and adopt new roles for participation.

Project REACH (Rural Education Alliance for Collaborative Humanities) at Beck Middle School in Georgetown, South Carolina, uses community members as instructional resources. Through Project REACH students learn about their own families and about the unique culture and context of their larger community. Community District No. 3 in New York City facilitates family outings to cultural events and art museums.

Educating middle-grade students poses unique challenges to families, schools, and districts as they strive to create strong partnerships to promote education reform. These eight lessons and the examples that accompany them illustrate some of the ways in which districts and middle-grade schools engage families and the community. These partnerships go beyond information exchange to foster school change and the creation of relationships that contribute to student success. Each partnership takes planning and visionary leadership, and each of the sites we studied is still engaged in this process.

However, all of our sites show that, even in schools and districts in which students are considered "at risk," families and communities can and do support the changes in teaching and learning that are at the heart of education reform.

Notes

1. For a review of research on school/family partnerships, see Anne T. Henderson and Nancy Berla, *A New Generation of Evidence: The Family Is Critical to Student Achievement* (Washington, D.C.: National Committee for Citizens in Education, 1994).
2. Barry Rutherford et al., *Final Technical Research Report, Vol. II: Case Studies* (Denver: RMC Research Corporation, 1995).
3. Barry Rutherford et al., *Final Technical Research Report, Vol. I: Findings and Conclusions* (Denver: RMC Research Corporation, 1995).
4. On the critical nature of adolescence, see Carnegie Task Force on the Education of Young Adolescents, *Turning Points: Preparing American Youth for the 21st Century* (New York: Carnegie Council on Adolescent Development of the Carnegie Corporation, 1989). For reviews of middle-grade education and its effects on adolescents, see William M. Alexander and C. Kenneth McEwen, *Schools in the Middle: Status and Progress* (Columbus, Ohio: National Middle Schools Association, 1989); and Joyce L. Epstein and Douglas J. Mac Iver, *Education in the Middle Grades: Overview of National Practices and Trends* (Baltimore: Center for Research on Elementary and Middle Schools, Johns Hopkins University, 1990).
5. An excellent review of the role of responsibilities in school/family partnerships can be found in *Strong Families, Strong Schools: Building Community Partnerships for Learning* (Washington, D.C.: U.S. Department of Education, 1994).

READING 4

High Schools Gear Up to Create Effective School and Family Partnerships

John H. Hollifield

Parent involvement in children's schooling declines dramatically during the high school years, but this doesn't have to be the case. High schools can reach out to increase and improve parent involvement in multiple ways, and students continue to want and need the support of their parents and other adults to help them reach their educational goals.

Joyce L. Epstein and Lori J. Connors, researchers with the Center on Families, Communities, Schools and Children's Learning (Center on Families), are working with six high schools—two urban, two suburban, and two rural—in a collaborative effort to identify what parent-school partnership practices are appropriate at the high school level, how the schools can develop and implement such practices, and how the practices actually affect the students, parents, and teachers involved.

In a series of meetings, Epstein and Connors and teams from each school discussed the schools' current practices—what they were already doing to involve families and their ideas for doing more. Each school also administered surveys to ninth-grade teachers, parents, and students to provide information from each group about attitudes and beliefs about family involvement and the school, current practices considered weak or strong, levels of current parent involvement (including school practices for reaching out to contact parents), and demographic and school-specific information. The researchers have analyzed the data provided by these surveys and summarized the preliminary results, which are being used by the schools to develop multiyear action plans for a comprehensive and responsive set of family partnership practices at the high school level.

Current Practices and Ideas: Some Blue-Chip Stocks in the Trust Fund, but Some Junk Bonds Too

The six high schools are all part of Maryland's Tomorrow—a state dropout prevention initiative that puts family involvement on the school agenda. Thus these high schools already had some practices under way. Epstein and Connors (1994) describe where these schools are starting from—the existing practices in each school—as a "trust fund," recognizing that each school's past practices can be built upon to create further partnerships, and also recognizing that trust is a primary element in the effort to develop comprehensive practices of partnership over time.

An action team from each school and Center on Families researchers Epstein and Connors collaborated to identify their trust funds—a combination of existing practices and ideas for further practices. All the schools were conducting some activities under each area of a six-part typology developed by Joyce Epstein to help schools build strong family, school, and community partnerships.

Type I—School help of families. This refers to schools helping to improve parents' understanding of adolescent development, parenting skills, and the conditions at home for learning. The school also seeks to improve its own understanding of the families of its students. Activities and ideas in the trust funds of the six schools included home visits, family support groups, referrals for special services, social services, providing information to parents about teens, and providing parenting skills for teen parents.

Type II—School-home communication. This refers to the basic obligations of schools to improve the communications from school to home and from home to school about school programs and students' progress, including the use of letters, memos, report cards, newsletters, conferences, and other mechanisms. Activities and ideas included easing the transition to high school (orientation letters, tours for middle-grade students, summer and fall orientations for students and parents), holding back-to-school nights, signing pledges/contracts with parents, using phone and mail communications (including newsletters), holding conferences, and providing information on school policies and programs.

Type III—Family help for schools. This refers to the involvement in school of parent and community volunteers, and the involvement of parents and others who come to the school to support and watch student performances, sports, and other events. School practices and ideas included volunteer activities (parents help other parents, call about attendance, talk about their careers, mentor students), and increasing family attendance at school events.

Type IV—Involvement in learning activities at home. This refers to improving family involvement in learning activities at home, including involvement in homework, classwork, and curricular-related interactions and decisions. Activities and ideas included helping parents to help students set goals and select courses, providing college information, and conducting career transition programs.

Type V—Involvement in governance, decision making, and advocacy. Refers to parent and other community residents in advisory, decision-making, or advocacy roles in parent associations, advisory committees, and school improvement or school site councils. It also refers to parent and community activists in independent advocacy groups that work for school improvement. The six schools' activities and ideas included creating more active parent organizations, and increasing the numbers of parents, students, and community members on advisory and decision-making groups.

Type VI—Collaboration and exchanges with the community. This refers to involvement of any of the community organizations or institutions that share some responsibility for children's development and success. School activities and ideas included community involvement in school-linked health care programs, delineating a clear role for families in business-school partnerships, offering workshops at school about community resources, and informing families about students' community service activities and requirements.

Thus the schools, with their current practices and their ideas for more, had some well-endowed trust funds, but some were better endowed than others, and some of the endowments were more idea based than practice based. Epstein and Connors (1994) note that "in these high schools, as in most others, past efforts have been limited. Few parents are informed about or involved in their teens' education. Even the most basic communications are not systematized to reach all families, and many . . . are limited to negative messages or discussions about students' problems. Families are rarely guided to conduct discussions with their teens about important school decisions or plans for their future" (p. 1).

The next task was to examine the schools' current practices and ideas, make improvements, and add other practices based on the specific needs of their school's teachers, students, and families. These needs were identified through surveys conducted by each school, with the data for each analyzed by the researchers on the project.

Survey Results: Teachers, Students, and Parents Provide Information for Building Partnerships

Teachers, students, and parents, through the surveys, discussed their attitudes toward their school and the importance of family involvement, and contributed their thoughts about the current condition of parent involvement practices at the school, what practices they would like to see put into place, and suggestions for next steps that should be taken.

Four themes emerged from Connor and Epstein's (1994) analyses of the data on attitudes: school and community relationships; importance of parent involvement and willingness to be involved; time and training for school-family partnership activities; and the frequency, amount, and type of homework assigned.

There's much agreement by all three groups in these areas, with some differences. Together, they worry about their communities being unsafe and not having good after-school and evening activities for teens—in general, recognizing that all the schools need to strengthen connections with their communities. At the same time, they tend to rate their school itself as a good place (78 percent of parents, 62 percent of students, and 49 percent of teachers), and more than 90 percent of parents reported being welcome at their teen's high school.

More than 90 percent of the parents and teachers and 82 percent of the students agreed that parent involvement was needed at the high school level. And many parents (more than 80 percent) said they wanted to be more involved, a view supported by more than 50 percent of students, who want their parents to be more involved. Only 32 percent of the teachers, however, felt that it was their responsibility to involve parents.

Further agreement among teachers, students, and parents occurs on the issue of time—nobody has a lot to spare. About 50 percent of the teachers say they don't have enough time to involve families; about 50 percent of students say they don't have enough time to talk to their parent about school or homework, and about 25 percent of parents say they do not have enough time to talk with their teen on a daily basis about school.

School practices. Teachers, parents, and students rate how well their school was conducting activities within the six types of school-family-community partnership practices. They identified practices that were currently strong, needed improvement, or needed to be added, forming a profile of opportunities for growth for each school. Again, there were many areas of agreement among the groups, but some differences.

In all high schools, parents (72 percent), students (61 percent), and teachers (95 percent) believed that the school should start or improve practices to help parents understand more about adolescent development. Teachers, parents, and students also felt that communication practices should be improved in three ways: reach more families with information about school programs and student progress, contact families more often with positive news about students, and provide more information to help students plan their futures.

Teachers clearly supported the idea that more parents and other community members should volunteer to help at school—but 70 percent of the parents noted that they had never been asked to volunteer. Students weren't entirely sold on the idea of their parents being active in the school—40 percent thought it was not important to "invite my parents to become volunteers," 22 percent said it was not important to "invite parents to school programs or events," and 55 percent said "no, don't ask my parent to go on a class trip."

Teachers, parents, and students in all six schools "felt that practices to assist parents in monitoring and improving student homework should be developed or strengthened," note Connors and Epstein (1994, 11). At the same time, most parents say they are doing the four practices that teachers think are most important: checking homework (85 percent of parents say they talk to their teen about homework), talking to the teen about school at home (94 percent of parents say they talk to their teen about school), telling teen that school is important (88 percent of parents say yes, they do this), and helping the teen balance activities (88 percent of parents say they help their teen plan time for homework, chores, and other responsibilities).

All groups agreed that parents should be included on committees to review school policy and the curriculum and in other decision-making groups. Many students (70 percent) said that they too want to be included on committees that make decisions about the school. As for community involvement—parents and students say that the best thing communities can do is provide employment or job training to teens. More than 80 percent of the parents wanted information on summer and part-time jobs for teens, more than 70 percent wanted information on job training, and the students themselves wanted information about job training (56 percent) and after-school jobs (65 percent).

"The activities that parents, students, and teachers would like their school to begin or improve were similar for schools in city, suburban, and rural locations," Connor and Epstein note. "High school teachers, students, and families . . . have a common vision of high schools that inform and involve families in their teens' education" (Connors and Epstein 1994, 26).

Some Topics Are Especially Important for High Schools

There are good reasons why parent involvement drops off drastically in high school. And each of these good reasons becomes a special topic that programs of school-family-community partnerships at the high school level have to deal with. Primarily, these include the needs that adolescents have for more autonomy and responsibility; more working parents who live further from the high schools; the more complex organization of the high school; and high school teachers who have greater numbers of students to teach, more specialized training, and more families to involve.

The school survey results have implications for building partnerships that deal with these topics. For example, more than 70 percent of the students say that they would like to be included in parent-teacher conferences, reflecting their needs to assume responsibility and maintain their autonomy. More than

Table 1 Any High School Can . . .

Type 1—Parenting	Develop a lasting set of workshops on key issues in adolescent development. This could be a videotaped series, developed with the help of a local cable company, community or technical college, or the high school's media department. The guidance office could take leadership for these activities, working with the Action Team, perhaps using the tapes as a forum for a parent workshop series. The tapes can be made available to families through the school, the library, or for free at local video stores on a checkout basis.
Type 2—Communicating	Include students in parent-teacher conferences. Develop one-page guidelines for parents and teens to prepare for the conference. The guidelines would help parents and teens identify common concerns, interests, and talents to discuss with teachers during the conference. The conference could also focus on students' goals and how the teacher and parent could better assist the student.
Type 3—Volunteering	One member of the Action Team or a parent and teacher as cochairs could coordinate parent and community volunteers with school and teacher needs for help. Encourage many to participate by allowing work to be done at home or at school, on the weekends, or before/after regular school hours. Encourage teachers to be creative in their requests for assistance so that the many skills and interests of parents and community members can be tapped.
Type 4—Learning at Home	Design interactive homework that requires students to talk to someone at home about something interesting that they are learning in class or about important school decisions. The homework activity is the students' responsibility, but a parent or other family or community member is used as a *reference source* or *audience* for the student. This enables students to share ideas at the same time that families are informed about the students' curricula and learning activities.
Type 5—Decision Making	Invite parents and students to become members of school committees or councils to review curriculum or specific school policies. In order to encourage diverse representation, ask a more experienced parent or student leader to be a "buddy" to a less experienced parent or student.
Type 6—Collaborating with Community	Develop a community resource directory, perhaps in cooperation with the school nurse, or with a member of the chamber of commerce or other group, which gives parents and students information on community agencies that can help with health issues, job training, and summer or part-time employment for teens, and other areas of need for families and students.

half of the students reported that they make decisions *alone* about their high school courses, perhaps reflecting autonomy, but also implying the need for more parent input in making such truly crucial decisions.

Eighty-one percent of the high school teachers say that family involvement is important, and 33 percent say they personally strongly support it—but only 3 percent of them think that parents strongly support it. A major task of high school partnerships will be to convince these teachers that parents really do want to be involved and that the teachers can effectively involve most families.

Next Steps

The six high schools in this project are already engaged in implementing new and improved practices for ninth-grade students and families, and they'll follow up this work by extending the practices throughout the grades. Examples of the practices they'll be building on include

- a five-session workshop series in which parents discuss teen behavior and appropriate parenting practices;
- "survival packets" given to each ninth-grade parent, which include telephone numbers, school meeting dates, school policies;
- students working on a ten-year plan for their future and discussing their goals with a family member.

Connors and Epstein also suggest some "get started" steps for other urban, suburban, or rural high schools. The creation of a school-family-community partnership action team is the first step. Then some basic funding needs to be secured (the project schools each had a small stipend per semester to work with). Then the team needs to get reactions from and specific information on the needs of the school's teachers, students, and families. While gathering this information, the researchers suggest, the team can begin selecting appropriate practices. The researchers provide a chart of basic practices (see Table 1), covering the six types of school, family, and community partnerships that might be considered by "any high school."

References

Connors, L. J., and J. L. Epstein. 1994. *Taking stock: Views of teachers, parents, and students on school, family, and community partnerships in high schools.* Report no. 25. Baltimore, MD: Johns Hopkins University, Center on Families, Communities, Schools and Children's Learning.

Epstein, J. L., and L. J. Connors. 1994. *Trust fund: School, family, and community partnerships in high schools.* Report no. 24. Baltimore, MD: Johns Hopkins University, Center on Families, Communities, Schools and Children's Learning.

DISCUSSION QUESTIONS AND ACTIVITIES

1. *Brainstorm your possible role(s) in a school/family/community partnership. What actions would you be willing to take to include families and the community in your classroom? Would you be willing to participate in events in the local community? Offer some examples.*

2. *Interview a student, a family member of one of your students, a member of the business community, or a combination of these to find out their ideas about partnerships. Share your "research" with other members of the class. These interviews might spawn ideas for future action-research projects.*

3. When all is said and done, little can be done to bridge cultural, ethnic, linguistic, and socioeconomic gaps that divide teachers in multicultural settings from their students and parents. Teachers who participate in partnerships will not be willing to share power or authority when it comes to their perceived classroom roles. School/community/family partnerships will only replicate the existing social and economic status quo.

   State whether you agree or disagree with these statements and explain your response.

4. Write a dialogue or enact a role-play between Mr. Fletcher and Desiderio's parents. Discuss some of the issues that Mr. Fletcher raised in the play, such as Desiderio's tardiness, his sleeping in class, his not handing in any work.... You might also want to include Ms. Hernandez and Desiderio himself in the scenario. Decide what issues are important to each of the participants. Find ways to resolve those issues if possible, though not too simplistically.

5. In this chapter and in the article, we have used the oft-quoted African proverb, "It takes a village to raise a child." Individualism, however, is strongly rooted in mainstream society and runs counter to the concept of the village or the community. In our recent past, community might even have drawn whispers about the specter of communism. In the context of school/family/community partnerships, discuss whether and how you think it is possible to reconcile these two contrary ways of thinking.

6. Many parents work during school hours and would find it difficult to take time off to come to visit or volunteer. What can schools and teachers do to reach out to them? Some middle and secondary schools have located social services programs (that is, health clinics, public libraries, and swimming facilities) at school sites. Is this a good solution? Explain your answers.

REFERENCES

Altrichter, H., Posch, P., and Somekh, B. (Eds.). 1993. *Teachers Investigate Their Work: An Introduction to the Methods of Action Research.* New York: Routledge.

Andrus, E. November, 1996. Service Learning: Taking Students Beyond Community Service. *Middle School Journal, 28*(2): 10–18.

Bauch, P., and Goldring, E. 1996. Parent involvement and teacher decision making in urban high schools of choice. *Urban Education, 31*(4): 403–431.

Botrie, M., and Wenger, P. 1992. *Teachers and Parents Together.* Ontario, Canada: Pembroke.

Burch, P. 1993. Circles of Change: Action Research on Family-School-Community Partnerships. *Equity and Choice, 10*(1):11–16.

Clemens-Brower, T. J. 1997. Recruiting parents and the community. *Educational Leadership, 54*(5): 58–60.

Cremin, L. 1988. *American Education: The Metropolitan Experience, 1876–1980.* New York: Harper & Row.

Davies, D. Jan., 1991. Schools Reaching Out: Family, School, and Community Partnerships for Student Success. *Phi Delta Kappan,* 72(5): 376–382.

de Tocqueville, A. (trans. G. Lawrence). 1966. *Democracy in America.* New York: Harper & Row.

Epstein, J. 1995. School/Family/Community Partnerships: Caring for the Children We Share. *Phi Delta Kappan,* 76(9):701–711.

Gabriel, J. 1997. *The Experiences of Language Minority Students in Mainstream English Classes in United States Public High Schools: A Study Through In-Depth Interviewing.* Unpublished dissertation.

Goswami, D., and Stillman, P. (Eds.). 1987. *Reclaiming the Classroom: Teacher Research as an Agency for Change.* Portsmouth, NH: Heinemann.

Hidalgo, N., Siu, S-F., Bright, J., Swap, S., and Epstein, J. 1995. Research on Families, Schools, and Communities: A Multicultural Perspective. In J. Banks and C. Banks (eds.), *Handbook of Research on Multicultural Education.* New York: Macmillan, pp. 498–524.

Hollifield, J. 1995. High Schools Gear Up to Create Effective School and Family Partnerships. *New Schools, New Communities,* 11(2): 26–31.

Hubbard, R., and Power, B. (Eds.). 1993. *The Art of Classroom Inquiry.* Portsmouth, NH: Heinemann.

Huss-Keeler, R. 1997. Teacher Perception of Ethnic and Linguistic Minority Parental Involvement and its Relationships to Children's Language and Literacy Learning: A Case Study. *Teaching and Teacher Education,* 13(2): 171–182.

O'Brien, T. 1990. *The Things They Carried.* Boston: Houghton Mifflin.

Patri, A. 1928. *A Schoolmaster of the Great City.* New York: Macmillan.

Richman, J. 1905. The Immigrant Child. *NEA Addresses and Proceedings, 44th Annual Meeting,* 113–121.

Rilke, M. (trans. C. F. MacIntyre). 1968. *Duino elegies.* Los Angeles: University of California Press.

Rutherford, B., Anderson, B., and Billig, S. 1995. *Parent and Community Involvement in Education. Vol. I: Findings and Conclusions. Studies of Education Reform.* ED 397544.

Rutherford, B., and Billig, S. 1995. Eight Lessons of Parent, Family, and Community Involvement in the Middle Grades. *Phi Delta Kappan,* 77(1): 64–66, 68.

Schine, J. 1996. Service Learning: A Promising Strategy for Connecting Students to Communities. *Middle School Journal,* 28(2): 3–9.

Thompson, S. 1993. Two Streams, One River: Parent Involvement and Teacher Empowerment. *Equity and Choice,* 10(1): 17–20.

Timpane, M., & Reich, B. 1997. Revitalizing the Ecosystem for Youth: A New Perspective for School Reform. *Phi Delta Kappan,* (Feb.): 464–470.

Ziegler, M. 1998. *Tellin' Stories Project: Final Evaluation Report.* ED 419967.

Further Reading

Delgado-Gaitan, C. 1994. *Consejos:* The Power of Cultural Narratives. *Anthropology and Education Quarterly,* 25(3): 298–316.

Hidalgo, N. 1994. Profile of a Puerto Rican Family's Support for School Achievement. *Equity and Choice,* 10(2): 14–22.

Chapter Nine

DIVERSITY, SPECIAL EDUCATION, AND MULTICULTURALISM

James Martin-Rehrmann, Ph.D.

Imagine that you have just been hired as a middle school specialist in science. During the interview process, you learned that the school district is committed to inclusive education.[1] You don't have direct experience with inclusion, but you have a basic understanding of its principles and goals. You also have heard that inclusion is controversial, although you know about some communities that are experiencing success with this approach. The middle school where you will be teaching has a very culturally diverse student body, which attracted you in the first place. You were attracted to this position because you believe in the ideal that all children deserve an equitable and effective public education, and you wanted to be a teacher in a school where students of color and of different first languages (other than English) were represented.

Your own cultural background and race very likely influenced your comprehension of the previous paragraph (for example, what specifics you filled in as you read or images you formed). The paragraph is intended to be neutral, thus allowing the reader broad interpretation. Relative to the beliefs and ideals mentioned, some or a lot of the description may be true of you personally for

---

[1] In Inclusion, the general education program retains responsibility for educating all students, including those with disabilities. The educational focus is on the individual goals and abilities of disabled students and how to obtain these goals within the regular educational setting to the fullest extent possible (Kohler & Rusch, 1995; Malloy, 1994).

various reasons including, but not limited to, your own racial identity and cultural background. In addition, other factors that would likely have influenced your interpretation of this hypothetical situation could be your everyday and professional experiences with members of different racial and cultural backgrounds, teaching experience, and biases and prejudices relative to special education programs or adolescents with disabilities.

Why do we begin this chapter about diversity and special education with this type of hypothetical situation? Increasingly, regular education program teachers will work with children with disabilities. Even if the number of school-age children receiving special services were to remain at today's levels of nearly five million, recently enacted legislation will require regular education program teachers to be more directly involved in delivering special education services (Individuals with Disabilities Education Act of 1997). Also, given predictions of the changing demographics of the United States, the school-age population will become increasingly diverse (Day, 1992, cited in Lipson & Wixson, 1997, p. 19). All educators need to consider the issues of diversity and inclusion very carefully. Public Law (PL) 105-17[2] was signed into law on June 4, 1997, as the Individuals with Disabilities Education Act of 1997 (IDEA '97). The Congressional Findings of PL 105-17 indicate that

- By the year 2000, [the United States] will have 275,000,000 people, nearly one of every three of whom will be either African American, Hispanic, Asian American, or American Indian.
- Between 1980 and 1990, the rate of increase in the population for White Americans was 6 percent, while the rate of increase for racial and ethnic minorities was much higher: 53 percent for Hispanics, 13.2 percent for African Americans, and 107.8 percent for [Asian Americans].
- Taken together as a group, minority children comprise an ever-larger percentage of public school students.
- The limited English-proficient population is the fastest growing in [the United States], and the growth is occurring in many parts of [the United States]. (Individuals with Disabilities Education Act of 1997)
- By the year 2050, the present percentage of Latinos in the U.S. population will almost triple; the [Asian American] population will more than triple; African Americans will increase about 3 percent; [and] the non-Hispanic White population will drop from 76 percent to 53 percent (Carger, 1997, p. 39).

In the twenty-two years since the passage of the first United States federal special education legislation, the 1975 Education for All Handicapped Act (PL 94–142), the trend has been to move children and adolescents into general

---

[2] PL stands for Public Law. The first number following PL is the congress that passed the law (105th in this case). The second number identifies the number in the sequence of bills passed during that congressional session (17th in this case).

education programs whenever possible, rather than the reverse (Smith, Polloway, Patton, & Dowdy, 1995; Villa & Thousand, 1995, cited in Lipson & Wixson, 1997, p. 19).

Undoubtedly, individuals entering the field of education today need to be aware of these important issues and be willing to carefully examine their own attitudes and beliefs about special education and diversity.

A Brief History of Special Education Federal Legislation in the United States

Before the passage of the 1975 Education for All Handicapped Act (PL 94–142), several court rulings dealt with the inequities in the public educational system in the United States. The summary effect of these court cases was to provide the legislative platform for a number of laws, beginning in the early 1960s, that established federal programs to aid disabled individuals. This legislative effort led to the passage of the 1975 Education for All Handicapped Act.[3] This now-famous law was the first federal law to mandate that all "handicapped children" should receive a "free appropriate public education" in the "least restrictive environment." Before the passage of this law, children with disabilities were often denied access to public educational services and were sent to special schools, separate from their peers in regular education programs (Allington & McGill-Frazen, 1995, p. 14). The U.S. Department of Education estimates that, in 1975, about one million children with disabilities were denied access to public schools, and hundreds of thousands more in the public schools were being denied appropriate services (Individuals with Disabilities Education Act of 1997). In addition to these provisions, the law also mandated that a child with disabilities has the right to an Individualized Education Plan (IEP); the right to nondiscriminatory evaluation; and the right of parental participation in the process of both identification and evaluation and in the development and review of the IEP itself.

The Individuals with Disabilities Act of 1990 and Secondary Education

The inaugural Education for All Handicapped Act in 1975 (PL 94–142) was reauthorized as the Individuals with Disabilities Education Act of 1990 (IDEA) (PL 101–476).[4] Kohler and Rusch (1995) point out that one of the most important provisions of this reauthorization was "definitions to help guide the delivery of special education services, including a range of outcomes expected as a result of obtaining an effective education" (p. 111). The focus on outcomes is an important emphasis here because, for the first time, IDEA included requirements for transition services (planning and training for post-

---

[3] For a summary of these court cases, see Lipson and Wixson (1997), pp. 13, 14.

[4] In addition to IDEA (1990), other federal legislative initiatives have been designed to improve the educational and postsecondary outcomes of secondary students with disabilities. For more information, see Kohler and Rusch, 1995.

secondary experiences). Before this, school districts did not necessarily include transitional services in a student's IEP; therefore, many secondary special education students did not receive services that would help them plan for postsecondary education and training (Kohler & Rusch, 1995).

The idea of providing transition services for secondary students is not new. Secondary schools have both informal and formal means of helping college-bound students make the transition from high school to college. Even if the transition services are informal, generally teachers, guidance counselors, and administrators move these students through the college-bound curricula and through the various mandatory requirements (for example, SAT exams and letters of recommendation) so that the students accomplish a postsecondary goal: college and later full-time employment. Therefore, it is only fair that non-college-bound students—whether disabled or not—should receive this same type of coordinated transitional planning during their secondary school years. Kohler and Rusch (1995) define transition planning services in the same manner as the 1990 IDEA, "but [we] interpret the 'coordinated set of activities' [34 C.F.R. Section 300.18] to mean *all* [authors' emphasis] the educational activities and programs in which the student participates. This transition perspective does not view 'transition planning' as an add-on activity for students with disabilities once they reach age 16, but rather a fundamental basis of education which guides the development of all educational programs" (pp. 116–117).

The need to emphasize transitional services has occurred primarily as a result of dismal postsecondary employment history, dropout rates, and criminal justice system statistics for individuals with disabilities. For example, the unemployment rate for young adults with disabilities two years after leaving high school exceeds 50 percent (Wagner, 1989, cited in Kohler & Rusch, 1995, p. 107). "Further, as many as 40 percent of all students with disabilities have been reported to drop out of high school" (Bruininks, Thurlow, Lewis, & Larson, 1988; Gajar, Goodman, & McAfee, 1993, cited in Kohler & Rusch, 1995, pp. 107–108). The comparable figures for all students in 1995 was estimated by the National Center for Educational Statistics to be 10.5 percent (Fossey, 1996).[5]

In general, in the United States, although the overall dropout rates for African Americans have improved dramatically in recent years, dropout rates for all students of color is exceedingly high. For example, in some cities, the dropout rate for some groups of color ranges from 50 percent to 80 percent (Grossman, 1995, p. 2). Historically, dropout rates for Hispanics have remained relatively constant at about 30 to 33 percent nationwide. Criminal justice statistics are equally abysmal:

> The arrest rate among youths with disabilities increases as this population of youths gets older. For example, Wagner (1993) reported that almost 30 percent of all youths with disabilities are arrested three to five years out of school, with youths with emotional disturbances accounting for more than half (57.6 percent) of those arrested. (Kohler & Rusch, 1995, p. 109)

---

[5] For a comprehensive review of postsecondary student outcomes, see Kohler and Rusch, 1995.

It is not difficult to see the connection between these bleak statistics and the thrust of the Individuals with Disabilities Act of 1990. This reauthorization, more so than the original law (PL 94–142), focused on secondary education and a need to improve the postsecondary outcomes of students with disabilities.

Disabled secondary students deserve the same level and quality transitional services that most high schools provide for college-bound students. Denying quality transitional services is not only illegal, under IDEA '90, it is immoral. When disabled students leave school without receiving the appropriate training for life after high school, they are at a severe disadvantage when compared to nondisabled peers. Without transitional services, many disabled youth are left to fend for themselves after high school. Our society must meet the challenge of educating all children. Despite federal legislation that dates back to 1975, which has been designed to improve the educational and postsecondary opportunities of all students with disabilities, more needs to be done. For example, programs that plan comprehensively for all middle and secondary students (not just the college-bound) need to be broadly established.[6]

The Individuals with Disabilities Education Act of 1997

The most recent reauthorization of PL 94–142, the Education for All Handicapped Act of 1975, was signed into law by President Bill Clinton on June 4, 1997. This law, the Individuals with Disabilities Education Act of 1997 (IDEA '97), has many provisions designed to improve educational services for students with disabilities. Most of these provisions are intended to be implemented across the full range of educational levels, from pre-school through secondary. Similar to the IDEA of 1990, there is continued emphasis on transition services at the secondary level. Some highlights of the new law are as follows:

- Involve regular education teachers in IEP development and implementation
- Provide improved special education and related services in the regular classroom
- Support professional development of all personnel (including regular education personnel) involved in the education of students with disabilities
- Increase involvement of students with disabilities in extracurricular activities
- Raise academic expectations and performance of students with disabilities
- Strengthen the role of parents
- Provide improved procedural safeguards for parents of disabled students and for the students themselves

---

[6] PL 94–142 was again reauthorized in 1991 (PL 102–119) as the Individuals with Disabilities Education Act of 1991. Generally, the provisions in this law sought to improve the educational opportunities of pre-school children. For a review of this and other legislative acts that attempted to provide improved educational opportunities for pre-school children with disabilities or at-risk, see Fewell (1995).

- Require states and school districts to provide services for pre-school children with disabilities
- Mandate that students with disabilities learn the same curricula and partake in the same assessments as nondisabled students (with appropriate accommodations when necessary)
- Provide a statement of 'transition service needs' in the IEP beginning at age 14 (lowered from age 16 in the IDEA of 1990)

IDEA '97 is the most comprehensive reauthorization of the original law (PL 94–142). Although IDEA '97 is intended to improve special education services from pre-school through secondary education, the "transition service needs" requirement in the IEP by age 14 (Individuals with Disabilities Education Act of 1997, PL 105–17, 20 U.S.C., Section 1414) will likely most directly affect middle and secondary education programs. In fact, the shift in age requirement from 16 to 14 for the onset of transition services would indicate that school districts in many cases will need to provide transition services beginning in middle school.

IDEA '97 defines transition services as the following:

> The term "transition services" means a coordinated set of activities for a student with a disability that:
>
> (A) is designed with an outcome-oriented process, which promotes movement from school to post-school activities, including post-secondary education, vocational training, integrated employment (including supported employment), continuing and adult education, adult services, independent living, or community participation;
>
> (B) is based upon the individual student's needs, taking into account the student's preferences and interests; and
>
> (C) includes instruction, related services, community experiences, the development of employment and other post-school adult living objectives, and, when appropriate, acquisition of daily living skills and functional vocational evaluation. (Individuals with Disabilities Education Act of 1997, PL 105–17, 20 U.S.C., Section 1401)

IEPs for students with disabilities, beginning at age 14, must include planning for postsecondary experiences and may include independent living skills, job training, preparation for higher education and other related post-secondary preparation and training. Changing the onset of postsecondary planning from age 16 to age 14 appears to be one attempt to attenuate the dropout rates for students with disabilities, which is twice as high as that for nondisabled students.[7] Perhaps, if state and local educational agencies are successful in implementing this law, the dropout rates for students with disabilities will decline. This would undoubtedly lead to decreases in unemployment and crime statistics for this group of individuals, which would benefit society as a whole.

---

[7] Source: U.S. Department of Education Web site:
http://www.ed.gov/offices/OSERS/IDEA/overview.html

As a result of the passage of IDEA '97, regular education programs will likely have an increased presence of special educators, related personnel where appropriate (for example, an independent living instructor), and, of course, students with disabilities. IDEA '97 requires that at least one regular education teacher be a member of the IEP team charged with IEP development and periodic review, if the child is involved in any regular education programs. The IEP must address specific involvement in regular education programs, and explain to what extent, if any, a student with disabilities will not participate in the regular classroom and extracurricular and other nonacademic activities. Surely, the emphasis on transition services and involvement of students with disabilities in regular education programs are just two important features of IDEA '97 that will significantly impact middle and secondary education in the United States for years to come.

The local and state educational agencies charged with carrying out the provisions of the law will largely determine the impact of IDEA '97. Since 1975, there has been a change in focus in special education legislation from a deficit perspective and what an individual could not do to an emphasis of what an individual with disabilities is capable of doing. This shift is evident in the IDEA of 1990, when compared with the initial law, PL 94–142 (Kohler & Rusch, 1995). IDEA '97 has moved even further in this direction with its emphasis on early intervention, regular education program involvement in both academic and nonacademic areas, and planning and training for postsecondary experiences.

Laws by themselves, however, do not guarantee results in the sociopolitical environment of our communities and public schools. PL 94–142, the law passed in 1975 that first required free and appropriate education for all children, has benefited millions of children. Nevertheless, many educators and scholars would argue that the implementation of PL 94–142 has not benefited the vast majority of poor students of all backgrounds and students of color in the United States. In fact, these educators contend that the implementation of special education legislation has been detrimental to the educational success and personal well-being of a very large number of these students. Further, some of these educators and scholars believe that special education today is, at best, a mixed blessing for students of color and poor students, regardless of race, gender, or cultural background.

INEQUITIES IN SPECIAL EDUCATION TODAY

In his book, *Special Education in a Diverse Society,* Herbert Grossman (1995), contends that students of color and poor students from diverse backgrounds experience three major areas of difficulty relative to special education:

1. They are misrepresented—overenrolled as well as underenrolled—in special education programs. Those who are misplaced in special education are denied the kind of education they would profit from in regular education programs, whereas those who are inappropriately kept in the regular education system are deprived of the special education services their disabilities require.

2. Those who are correctly placed in special education often receive services that are culturally inappropriate and ill suited to the socioeconomic and geographic factors, as well as other factors that shape the context of their lives.

3. Students who are limited English proficient or who speak a nonstandard English dialect often experience a third problem—linguistically inappropriate services. (pp. 2–3)

Grossman (1995) is not alone in his concerns about the inequities he sees in special education today. He and other scholars (for example, Correa, 1992; Ford, 1992; Ford, Obiakor, & Patton, 1995; Markowitz, 1996; Mayhew & Herbert, 1995) contend that a significant number of poor students, students of color, and students who have limited English proficiency, experience widespread inequities in two main areas: identification and placement and culturally inappropriate instruction. Many students of color who are referred for evaluation are misidentified and, therefore, receive inappropriate placements. For example, a student might have a learning disability or speech impairment and be placed in a class for the educable mentally retarded (EMR). In some cases, such as the following, the individual might not have a disability at all but might be classified as disabled because the professional making a referral failed to consider the cultural background of the child. The following is a personal account by Hiram Zayas:

> At the age of nine, I was referred to a speech therapist for a speech impediment. What really occurred was that my Spanish speaking mother assisted me with my spelling homework, and I would learn to pronounce words according to her instructions. For example, she taught me to say letters *ch* as they are pronounced in the word *cheat*. So when it came to a word like *machine*, I would mispronounce it, and, even after being encouraged to say it correctly, I would only do as I was instructed by my mother. The constant therapy received for this 'speech impediment' eventually created in me a low self-worth for not overcoming this matter. It wasn't until many years later that an English speaking, culturally sensitive teacher informed me that I did not have a speech problem. (Zayas, 1981, cited in Grossman, 1995, p. 5)

This erroneous referral might not have occurred if the professional involved had simply done some rudimentary investigative work beforehand. There is no additional information from this account to confirm it, but it appears that both language and cultural barriers between the professional involved and Hiram Zayas led to this misidentification that had a significant negative impact on this individual during much of his school experience.

Disproportional Representation

Disproportional representation, in the context of this chapter, means that the percentage of a given group enrolled in special education programs is very inconsistent with the overall percentage of this group in a specific population or in the general population. The group of interest can either be overrepresented or underrepresented. For example, "[Disproportionately] large numbers of

Native American children and youth (as high as 33 percent in some Utah schools) have been placed in special education programs, while representation in gifted and talented programs is [disproportionately] low. Native Americans represent approximately 1.5 percent of the K–12 school population of Utah" (Mayhew & Herbert, 1995, p. 2). The disparity between 1.5 percent (the percentage of Native Americans enrolled in the K–12 school population of Utah) and 33 percent (enrollment of Native American children and youth in special education programs in some Utah schools) is obvious. This is a clear example of overrepresentation. In this example, Mayhew and Herbert (1995) also point out that Native Americans are underrepresented in gifted and talented classes.

Other examples of disproportional representation are the following:

- African American children are three times more likely than European American children are to be placed in classes for the educable mentally retarded and one half as likely to be placed in classes for the gifted. (Nieto, 1992, cited in Ewing, 1995, p. 193)

- American students of color, who have limited English proficiency, are even more likely to be misrepresented in special education programs, when compared with students of color who are proficient in English. Before the 1980s, generally, limited English proficiency students were overrepresented in classes for the learning disabled, behavior disordered, and mildly developmentally disabled. Since that time, the results vary across school districts, but misrepresentation is still evident in these same programs. (Martinez, 1981; Pyecha, 1981; U.S. Comptroller General, 1981; Willig, 1986, cited in Grossman, 1995, pp. 4–5; see also Ortiz, 1992)

- The U.S. Department of Education's Office for Civil Rights (OCR) found one school district that had a cut-off IQ composite score of 70 as the highest score allowed for a student to be classified as educable mentally retarded. OCR determined that this district even violated its own rules in addition, of course, to the federal laws against discrimination. They discovered that "28 percent of the Black students had a score *higher* [author's emphasis] than 70 while only *one* [author's emphasis] White student had an IQ higher than 70." (Markowitz, 1996, p. 4)

In IDEA '97, the most recent reauthorization of PL 94–142 discussed earlier, it is reported in the Congressional Findings of the law that

- More minority children continue to be served in special education [programs] than would be expected from the percentage of minority students in the general population.

- Although African Americans represent 16 percent of elementary and secondary enrollments, they constitute 21 percent of total enrollments in special education.

- Poor African-American children are 2.3 times more likely to be identified by their teachers as having mental retardation than their White counterparts are. (Individuals with Disabilities Act of 1997, PL 105–17, 20 U.S.C., Section 1400)

This data reveals widespread and longstanding disproportional representation of students of color, limited English proficiency students, and Native Americans in special education programs. Some research indicates that these gifted and talented programs "enroll no more than 50 percent of [students of color] and poor students than they would if these students were represented proportionally" (Cohen, 1990; Van Tassel-Baska, Patton, & Prillaman, 1989; Yancey, 1990, cited in Grossman, 1995, p. 255). Other scholars have reported similar statistics over a long period (for example, Ewing, 1995; Ford, 1992; Grossman, 1995; Markowitz, 1996; Mayhew & Herbert, 1995; and Obiakor, 1992, who cites Hilliard, 1989, and Samuda, 1975). These studies tell the same story: Disproportional representation of students of color, poor students, and students with limited English proficiency, is an indisputable fact in special education programs across the United States.

Many and varied explanations have been offered for this disproportional representation of the poor, students of color, and students with limited English proficiency. Generally, these explanations can be broken down into deficit and nondeficit explanations. Before providing some discussion of these explanations, however, we will first address gender misrepresentation in special education programs.

Gender Misrepresentation in Special Education   Grossman (1995) reviewed a number of studies in this area. For example, he reports that "males are more likely to be enrolled in special education programs for students with developmental disabilities, behavior disorders, emotional disturbances, and learning disabilities" (DBS Corp., 1986, 1987; Messick, 1984, cited in Grossman, 1995, p. 8). Other research, to date, has focused on possible differences between the genders relative to self-confidence, positive risk-taking behaviors (for example, answering questions in class), emotional problems, reaction to academic challenges, behaviors relative to math and science education, persistence after failure or threat of failure, and seeking adult approval. We do not believe that it is possible to determine generalizations about the traits under study from the collective results of these studies, as reported by Grossman (1995, p. 8–9). Some evidence suggests, however, that females are underrepresented in classes for the emotionally disturbed (for example, Baron & Perron, 1986; Grossman & Grossman, 1994; Marsh, 1987; Reynolds, 1984; Wynstra & Cummings, 1990, cited in Grossman, 1995, pp. 8–9). Ongoing and future research might provide additional information that will further clarify this issue.

Deficit Explanations for Disproportional Representation of Poor Students and Students of Color

Historically, many reasons have been offered that assert the problem of disproportional representation is indicative of the characteristics of the groups who are misrepresented—in other words, these suppositions blame the victims. For example, one explanation that has a long history is that African Americans are intellectually inferior to European Americans based on an old theory of biological determinism (for example, see Gould, 1981, or Minton & Schneider, 1980, cited in Obiakor, 1992, p. 160).

Another theory, cultural deprivation, arose in the 1960s when many educators rejected genetic explanations, like biological determinism. At the time, the cultural deprivation theory was promoted by noted educators such as Benjamin S. Bloom. Poor students and students of color, who did not succeed in regular education, were thought to be lacking the experiences in their homes that were necessary for academic success in school. In other words, the student's culture did not "transmit the cultural patterns necessary for the type of learning characteristics of the schools and the larger society" (Bloom, Davis, & Hess, 1965, cited in Grossman, p. 34).

The term culturally *deprived* was later changed to culturally *disadvantaged* because it was realized that these students were not lacking culture; it was just the *wrong* one. Grossman (1995) points out that few educators today would subscribe, at least publicly, to a theory that states that poor children and children of color are brought up in an *inferior* cultural environment, but many educators still believe "that some students are ill prepared to succeed in school because their culture places them at an educational disadvantage" (p. 34).[8]

The term "educationally disadvantaged" is still used by the U.S. Department of Education. Legally, the term is used as a broad classification of children and adolescents who are eligible for services provided through one or more of the department's compensatory education programs (such as Title I or Head Start). Many educators might not view this term as offensive or think of it as a concept that is similar to culturally disadvantaged. After all, groups of children and adolescents identified as educationally disadvantaged become eligible[9] for the department's compensatory education programs. These same educators might not realize that the idea of labeling groups of students "educationally disadvantaged" still places blame for poor academic performance on the students themselves.[10]

Biological determinism and cultural deprivation, culturally disadvantaged and educationally disadvantaged are several examples of deficit theories for academic failure of poor students and students of color in regular education programs. These and other deficit theories or perspectives have been used to explain the disproportional representation of poor students and students of color in special education programs.[11]

---

[8] Grossman (1995, pp. 62–103) provides a thorough review of research that refutes the theory of educational disadvantage.

[9] *Eligible* does not mean *entitled*. Individuals from groups of students identified as "educationally disadvantaged" are *not entitled* to receive the services the compensatory programs offer. Therefore, many children and adolescents, who are eligible for the U.S. Department of Education's compensatory education programs, do not receive the services they need if the program is underfunded at the federal level.

[10] Some scholars view compensatory education programs as second tier and just another version of separate and unequal education (for example, Ewing, 1995; Grossman, 1995).

[11] For a more comprehensive treatment of deficit explanations of disproportional representation, see Grossman (1995, pp. 1–61).

We believe that collectively these theories do not provide an adequate explanation for disproportional representation of poor students and students of color in special education programs. Although socioeconomic conditions and family circumstances of some poor families (including European American working poor and rural poor) and of some families from diverse cultural backgrounds might contribute to educational failure, it would be incorrect to assume that children and adolescents from these groups are predisposed to educational failure *simply because of membership in a specific cultural or socioeconomic group.* This is called prejudice. It is prejudging an individual's capacity to learn in a school setting, based solely on the condition of being poor or on the condition of membership in a culturally diverse group. You might ask yourself if *all* middle- and upper-class European American children and adolescents possess the prerequisite knowledge, experience, attitudes and motivation, and linguistic ability to succeed in school. Could it be that one reason that many of these students often succeed is that "schools that serve primarily middle-and upper-class European American students have many more resources than schools [that] serve primarily [students of color] and poor students" (Grossman, 1995, p. 31). Or could it be that, for many European American students, educational success is also a result of the coordinated efforts of teachers, administrators, and guidance counselors to provide transition services to postsecondary educational opportunities discussed earlier in this chapter? Obviously, many factors contribute to the educational success and failure of any given individual at any given time. Teachers need to be aware of these factors, but they must not make assumptions about the ability of any individual to learn based primarily on membership in a culturally diverse or socioeconomic group.

Nondeficit Explanations for Disproportional Representation

In the previous section, we presented some deficit explanations for the disproportional representation of the poor and students of color in special education programs. If society as a whole and the education community were to accept deficit explanations for the disproportional representation of the poor and students of color, then we could all look the other way because the society and the educational system could not be blamed. In other words, the inequities observed in special education programs would be the result of the characteristics of individuals in the populations that are disproportionately represented. Deficit perspectives give society an out and allow the status quo to continue.

In this section, we will present nondeficit explanations. These explanations turn the spotlight on the society and the educational system. A basic assumption of these explanations is that, all things being equal (for example, equitable funding of all school districts, full funding of effective compensatory programs such as Head Start,[12] full funding of programs for students with limited English proficiency), we would not observe the present levels of disproportional representation of students

---

[12] We mention Head Start because studies indicate that children who have participated in Head Start programs have lower dropout rates and are more successful academically throughout their schooling when compared with non-Head Start peers.

of color, poor students, and students with limited English proficiency in special education programs.

Numerous societal and educational factors, to a greater or lesser degree, contribute to the disproportional representation of poor students and students of color in special education programs. Undoubtedly, poverty is a critical factor. Other factors, related more specifically to special education programs themselves, are assessment bias, initial referral, classification, retention, and dropout rates.

The Role of Poverty   In 1991, Jonathan Kozol wrote *Savage Inequalities,* which chronicles the devastating effects of poverty on the poor. Norma Ewing (1995) characterizes Kozol's appeal for an equitable system of education as follows:

> His strong appeal is for equity in education of children from poor families—children who are *being starved intellectually* [italics added] in schools. He postulated that schools of today are more segregated and less equal than in 1954, the year of the *Brown v. Board of Education* decision, which mandated an end to separate and unequal educational institutions. Kozol concluded that the rich still get a richer quality of education while the children of the poor get less. (p. 191)

In contrast, according to the theory of a meritocracy, all people have an equal chance at success in the United States (see Chapter Two). Those who fail do so of their own accord because they lack either the ability or motivation to succeed. Meritocracy, in our view, is a deficit explanation for disproportional representation of students of color, poor students, and students with limited English proficiency.

Is the United States a meritocracy? Can an individual "rise up" despite an upbringing in abject poverty after attending, and possibly graduating from, inferior schools that have very limited resources? Yes. One classic example is Claude Brown's (1965) autobiography, *Manchild in the Promised Land,* which chronicles his childhood and adolescence spent in poverty, gangs, drug use, and crime in Harlem, to his days as a law student. Claude Brown overcame tremendous odds to get to law school. It was a tremendous achievement, and there was a happy ending (except that most of his childhood friends were either dead or in jail by the time Claude Brown made it to law school). Like Claude Brown, others have overcome the hurdles of growing up poor. In fact, proponents of the theory of meritocracy would argue that the accomplishments of individuals like Claude Brown are proof that anyone can overcome the odds if he or she has the will and determination. Is this really the case?

Being poor does starve children intellectually. It robs them of opportunities that are available to the vast majority of middle- and upper-class students. Parents of poor children, like all parents, want their children to succeed academically and otherwise, but they lack the financial resources available to parents in the middle- and upper-classes. For example, poor parents aren't able (financially) to provide their children with the same levels of nutrition and health care that children of middle- and upper-class parents receive. Another hurdle to academic success is inequitable funding of the local schools that results in decaying school buildings and facilities. For these, and other reasons discussed earlier, the theory of meritocracy cannot explain away the deleterious effects on academic achievement of growing up poor.

Another deficit theory presented earlier, cultural disadvantage, attributes the lack of academic success of students who are poor to characteristics of the individuals in the group, but these supposed characteristics (such as low aspirations and lack of parental supervision) are the result of a lack of family and community resources.

> Many of the characteristics that are attributed to cultural disadvantage are actually the result of poor peoples' inability to afford and obtain the resources available to the middle and upper classes, and the disadvantages many poor immigrants experience because of their limited English proficiency. Since many more [students of color] . . . come from lower socioeconomic-class backgrounds [than European American students], many of the apparent cultural differences between them are actually the result of financial factors. Although poor parents want their children to do well in school, many of them are unemployed, underemployed, underpaid, and undereducated. Thus, they are unable to provide their children with the childhood experiences needed to prepare them for school or the educational and financial support they require to assist their youngsters during their educational careers. (Grossman, 1995, p. 39)

Students who grow up in poverty do not have the same advantages as students who don't. Poverty adversely affects dreams, hopes, and aspirations of children and adults alike. It limits educational opportunity and contributes to the disproportional representation of poor students and students of color in special education programs. As a teacher, you will need to learn about the consequences of poverty and understand the strong adversarial role it plays in the educational experiences of children and adolescents.

Assessment Bias[13] Reliability and validity are two traditional measures of assessment instruments or procedures. A third, which is a fairly new category, is called absence-of-bias (Popham, 1995). Simply stated, reliability is the consistency of a test or procedure. Validity is more subjective, but in essence, the question being asked is this: Does this test or procedure measure what it purports to measure? In other words, for example, does an Intelligence Quotient (IQ) score accurately measure the overall or *general* intelligence of an individual?

Absence-of-bias is a new category that has arisen from significant criticism of standardized tests in the fields of education and psychology (Allen & Yen, 1979; Kaplan & Saccuzzo, 1982; Popham, 1995). Popham (1995) provides the following explanation:

> During the past couple of decades, educators have increasingly recognized that the tests they use are often biased against particular groups of students. Consequently, students in those groups do not perform as well on the test, *not because the students*

---

[13] One important objective of practitioners who practice culturally responsive assessment is to assess students from diverse backgrounds fairly and equitably. See Chapter Seven for more information about culturally responsive assessment.

are less able [italics added], but because there are features in the test that distort the nature of the students' performance. (p. 63)

Popham's comments suggest that the testing community recognizes that specific groups of students might not perform well on standardized tests because of inadequate features of the test. Indeed, establishing absence-of-bias in standardized tests would be a laudable goal, but it is not yet a reality.

The following examples illustrate that standardized tests are not culturally neutral or free from bias. There are many types of assessment bias, including content bias (such as a mismatch between the curriculum offered in the school or other experiences of the examinees and the curriculum and other experiences that are tested); bias that is introduced through assessment procedures when these procedures are piloted mostly with European American students and the subjects are students of color; rigid scoring procedures that do not allow the individuals being tested to explain reasonable alternatives to the "correct" responses; and dialect bias, where the students being tested are not familiar with the predominate dialect of the test itself or of the administrator of the test or both.

The following is an example of content bias: "Within each socioeconomic class, African-American students who grow up in racially mixed neighborhoods score higher on intelligence tests because they are exposed to the contents of tests that reflect the experiences of European Americans" (Moore, 1987, cited in Grossman, 1995, p. 32). The "feature," in intelligence tests in this case, is "experiences of European Americans." A lack of exposure to European American culture could result in a lower score, and, in this case, the score could be an indicator of a lack of experience with European American culture, *not lack of ability.*

Assessment bias can also be introduced through rigid scoring procedures (Kaplan & Saccuzzo, 1982). Researchers from Johns Hopkins University studied an African American neighborhood in Baltimore with 200 children and found that when the strict guidelines were administered for acceptable responses, many children gave "incorrect" responses. Here is an example with one item from the Wechsler Intelligence Scale for Children (WISC):

> The WISC question "What would you do if you were sent to buy a loaf of bread, and the grocer said he didn't have any more?" was given. The WISC scoring instructions state that the correct answer is "Go to another store." Among the 200 children in the study, 61 percent gave an incorrect response. However, when the examiners probed the children about their responses, they discovered that many children had given replies *that were reasonable considering their circumstances* [italics added]. For instance, the rigid WISC scoring procedures do not allow credit for the response "Go home." Yet many of the inner-city children explained that there were no other stores near their homes and that they were not allowed to go away from home without permission. (Hardy, Welcher, Mellitis, & Kagan, 1976, cited in Kaplan & Saccuzzo, 1982, pp. 447–448)

Many of the children who scored incorrectly by saying "Go home," were indeed providing a reasonable response given the hypothetical circumstances stated in the question. This illustration strongly suggests that rigid scoring procedures can result in assessment bias. Further, this type of assessment bias can be unpredictable. If the test developer is not able to anticipate "incorrect" responses because of differences in the cultural backgrounds of the test developer and the examinees, then assessment bias can distort the results.

Many European American professionals in education are not aware of these types of studies and accept results of IQ tests without question. In some circumstances IQ results, in particular, should be viewed with skepticism when administered to students of color, especially African Americans. The issue of ethnic or assessment bias is longstanding (Allen & Yen, 1979), and some educators, psychologists, and sociologists consider assessment bias to significantly affect the disproportional representation of American Americans in EMR classes (Mercer, 1972, 1979, and Williams, 1974, cited in Kaplan & Saccuzzo, 1982). Also, we must recognize that, even though PL 94–142 (and all the reauthorizations) specifically prohibits the use of any *single* testing procedure for determining classification of disability (Individuals with Disabilities Education Act of 1997, PL 105–17, 20 U.S.C., Section 1414), the U.S. Department of Education's Office for Civil Rights has found evidence where IQ tests alone were used for classification (Markowitz, 1996).

Popham (1995) provides this definition of assessment bias: "*Assessment bias* [author's emphasis] refers to qualities of an assessment instrument that offend or unfairly penalize a group of examinees because of examinees' gender, ethnicity, socioeconomic status, religion, or other such group-defining characteristics" (p. 63). Popham (1995) emphasizes, however, that with individual scores, there isn't necessarily an automatic penalty for individuals from diverse cultural backgrounds. Any individual score is the result of several factors, including something as simple as fatigue. However, standardized test results of students of color should not be accepted without scrutiny.

Initial Referral   In addition to poverty and assessment bias, other factors most likely contribute to the disproportional representation of students of color in special education programs. Initial referral is the action that initiates the process of evaluation for placement in special education programs.

When students are initially referred for evaluation, a process governed by the procedures outlined in IDEA '97 is set in motion. Grossman (1995) writes that this is where bias first enters the process. Even though parents are entitled to make referrals to have their children evaluated, many times a teacher makes the initial referral.

> Bias in the assessment process begins even before students are assessed for special education placement. Depending upon the teachers involved, in comparison to females and European American middle-class students, teachers overrefer or underrefer poor, African American, Hispanic American, and Native American males to programs for students with learning disabilities, emotional/behavioral problems, speech and language disorders, and mild cognitive disabilities. Similarly, teachers underrefer poor, African American, Hispanic American, and Native American students to gifted and talented programs. (Grossman, 1995, p. 255)

Congressional findings, referred to earlier, lend support: "Poor African-American children are 2.3 times more likely to be identified by their teacher as having mental retardation than their White counterpart[s are]" (Individuals with Disabilities Act of 1997, PL 105–17, 20 U.S.C., Section 1400).

Classification After referral, a determination is made about the eligibility of the student for special education services. Classification refers to the outcome of the initial referral and evaluation in the cases where placement is deemed appropriate. Some scholars think many misclassifications and non-identifications occur at this step, which in turn contributes to disproportional representation of many students of color and students with limited English proficiency. One estimate placed the figure for misdiagnosis of all students with disabilities at 75 percent (Reynolds, Wang, & Walberg, 1987, cited in Malloy, 1994).

Misclassifications might very well be the result of the procedures that are implemented inconsistently. Earlier, we indicated that reliability and validity can refer to procedures as well as tests. If procedures are inconsistent (not reliable), then the results will not be valid. Margaret C. Wang (1992) provides this explanation and illustration:

> One of the most significant problems in the state of practice in special education today is the way students with special needs are classified and placed in special education programs. There are serious scientific and practical flaws in classifying students for special programs. For example, there is a substantial amount of evidence that most procedures for the classification of children in special programs are *unreliable and invalid* [italics added]. The same child may be classified as handicapped by one test or diagnostician and not by another. Even a single diagnostician, working from an identical case record on two separate occasions, can offer two different diagnoses and classifications. (Ysseldyke, 1987, cited in Wang, 1992, p. 4)

Inconsistencies in classification procedures, alone, might or might not lead to disproportional representation of the poor, students of color, and students with limited English proficiency. But unreliable and invalid procedures do allow bias to be introduced in the process. This bias can take many forms, including adverse stereotypical viewpoints or outright prejudicial perspectives as part of the classification process. Misclassifications lead to situations where eligible students receive inappropriate services, or they are denied needed special education services.

Probably the single most adverse consequence of misclassification is the high retention rate in special education programs. Historically, once classified, most special education students don't return to regular education programs (Grossman, 1995; Wang, 1992). Those students who are classified, but are not really disabled, are denied an entire school career in regular education programs. Those students who are disabled, but misclassified, receive an entire school career of inappropriate special education—unless they drop out first. Wang (1992) makes a very clear connection between retention rates, dropout rates, and other important statistics.

> [The] statistics for retention rates in special education are especially alarming in view of the significantly higher dropout rate of students in special education programs. A recently completed study commissioned by the U.S. Congress,

entitled *The Education of Students with Disabilities: Where Do We Stand?*, indicates a 36 percent dropout rate for students with disabilities, a 15 percent participation rate in postsecondary education programs, and a 55 percent unemployment rate for Americans with disabilities between the ages of 16 and 64. (National Council on Disability, 1989, cited in Wang, 1992, p. 5)

The dropout rate for students with disabilities apparently has not improved significantly recently. Earlier in this chapter, one study cited from 1993 indicated that the dropout rate was about 40 percent (Gajar, Goodman & McAfee, 1993, cited in Kohler & Rusch, 1995).

Poverty, assessment bias, and misclassification of disabled and nondisabled students all contribute to inequity in special education programs. Students of color, students with limited English proficiency, and poor students often are placed in special education programs that are not appropriate for their needs because of circumstances and other factors related to the non-deficit explanations. Individuals from these same groups of students are also denied access to regular educational programs when placement in special education programs is not warranted.

CULTURALLY RESPONSIVE PRACTICES FOR DISABLED STUDENTS FROM DIVERSE BACKGROUNDS

PL 94–142 and its reauthorizations (Individuals with Disabilities Education Act of 1990, 1991 and 1997) have required *culturally appropriate* instructional special education practices for disabled students from diverse backgrounds. Each time, however, Congress has not defined the term *culturally appropriate*. This has resulted in varying approaches to providing students from diverse backgrounds with culturally appropriate practices. Some issues that should be addressed in culturally appropriate practices would be, for example, efforts to reduce prejudice, increase respect for diversity, and "resolve cultural incompatibilities between students' learning and behavior styles and the special educators' instructional styles" (Grossman, 1995, p.105).

The term *culturally responsive practices*, for the purposes of this chapter, can be divided into three components: instructional practice, special education responsibilities of the regular education teacher, and teaching students with limited English proficiency. Consequently, three themes will be presented in this section: (1) teaching methods designed to reduce the instructional style/learning style gap, referred to earlier, that often exists between the teacher and students of color with disabilities; (2) the role of the regular education teacher as part of the IEP Team; and (3) a brief treatment of issues related to teaching students with limited English proficiency.

Instructional Practices

Readings 1 and 2, at the end of this chapter, discuss culturally responsive instructional practices. In Reading 1, "Multicultural Education: A Challenge for Special Educators," Dean, Salend, and Taylor provide a basic overview of multicultural methods that, although addressed to special educators in the article, generally apply to middle and secondary classrooms. In Reading 2, "Culturally Sensitive Instructional Practices for African-American Learners with Disabilities," Franklin thoroughly examines issues related to the education of AfricanAmerican students with disabilities. Before continuing to read this chapter, we recommend that you read both Readings 1 and 2.

Middle-school teachers can be generalists or content-area specialists. Secondary teachers are most often content-area specialists. No matter what level, or subject, these two readings provide suggestions and principles to remember when you are working with students of color with disabilities. Teacher sensitivity to learning styles, for example, is important for all students. Knowledge of your students' experiences with, and prior knowledge of, the content under study is also important, no matter what their cultural backgrounds.

One method of learning about the background knowledge of students is using pre-reading strategies before students undertake independent reading of a subject area chapter or other reading selection.[14] This serves many purposes. As a result of pre-reading strategies, generally, students are motivated to read and have a specific focus and purpose for their reading. Also, providing students with pre-reading strategies often helps students build confidence because they are able to learn or review something about the concepts before independent reading of the chapter. The teacher also gains information about the students' background knowledge and can plan future lessons accordingly. During the discussions that occur, either in small or whole groups, you can gain insight into preconceived notions or attitudes about the content in the chapter. The students' background knowledge, attitudes, and motivation might be partly the result of their cultural backgrounds. Not only is the use of pre-reading strategies good practice that leads to increased comprehension of content-area textbooks, it is also an opportunity for teachers to learn about their students' prior knowledge, including culturally influenced perspectives, that are critical to the learning of new content (Anderson, 1984; Steffensen, Joag-Dev, & Anderson, 1979).

Using biographies also provides middle and secondary teachers with the opportunity to help students learn content, and biographies can be used simultaneously as a way to introduce students of color to scientists, inventors, or other influential professionals from culturally diverse groups (Daisey, 1997).

Family and community involvement is an important tenet of multicultural education as indicated in Reading 1. Research results suggest that students do better in school when their families are involved in their education. In secondary education, parent involvement is associated positively with higher parental expectations, and higher enrollment in postsecondary vocational and academic programs. Parents can perform several roles in education and are a valuable resource that often remains untapped (Kohler & Rusch, 1995).

---

[14] See Vacca and Vacca (1999) and Alvermann and Phelps (1998) for more information about the effectiveness of pre-reading strategies in subject- (or content-) area reading.

Special Education Responsibilities of the Regular Education Teacher

IDEA of 1997 requires that at least one regular education member be a part of the IEP team of students who participate in the regular education program. The regular education member is required to participate in the development, review, and revision of the IEP (Individuals with Disabilities Education Act of 1997, PL 105-17, 20 U.S.C., Section 1414). This does not mean that every regular education teacher has to be on the IEP team of every special education student in his or her class(es). The law specifies a minimum of one regular education teacher per team. At the middle and secondary levels, special education students most likely will have more than one regular education teacher. Therefore, this requirement will generally be a shared responsibility among a group of regular education teachers.

This requirement has merit. The regular education teacher would most likely bring unique insights and experiences to the IEP team that would benefit the student. In addition, increased collaboration between regular and special education teachers is vital for the success of students enrolled in special education programs.

Collaboration between regular and special educators is a fact of life in many schools today. It has been our experience, however, that regular and special education teachers sometimes have very different perspectives about the goals of special education programs. The regular education teacher might believe that the main responsibility for the education of students placed in special education programs is with that program. On the other hand, the special education teacher's goal generally is to maximize participation in the regular education program and increase this participation when appropriate. When regular education teachers play a more direct role in the special education program, as mandated by IDEA '97, this participation probably will lead to a more shared responsibility for students enrolled in these programs.

Teaching Students with Limited English Proficiency

Dialect differences might be the most critical feature in today's, and increasingly in tomorrow's, classrooms. Earlier in this chapter, we cited demographic predictions about the expected increasingly diverse U.S. population. We have used terms to describe groups from diverse backgrounds, for instance, Asian American, and Hispanic American. But, what do these terms mean relative to country of origin? Asian Americans can be native-born Americans, as can immigrants from a variety of countries, including Cambodia, China, Korea, Japan, Laos, Thailand, and Vietnam. Hispanic Americans too can be native-born, but they are also immigrants from countries such as Honduras, Mexico, Panama, Puerto Rico, and Venezuela. Imagine all the languages that are spoken in these countries, then all the dialects that are spoken as well.

Dialects are variations within a single language. They can occur in three areas: pronunciation, grammar, and vocabulary. Depending on the listener's perspective, the perceived variance from the listener's dialect is either considered just what it is—a difference—or this difference is considered a deficit.

This concept—difference versus deficit perspective—is our focus here. Before continuing, we recommend that you now read Reading 3, "Language Differences: A New Approach for Special Educators," located at the end of the chapter. The article, although addressed to special educators, is appropriate for more general audiences in education. Adger, Wolfram, and Detwyler offer a brief, yet informative introduction to the topic, a rationale for adopting sociolinguistic instructional practices, and some practical instructional suggestions.

Students with disabilities from both culturally and linguistically diverse backgrounds face the challenges of their disability as well as a limited proficiency in English. This places this group of students with disabilities in "double jeopardy" (Dev, 1992, p.11). As educators we must help these students overcome these significant challenges. We believe that adopting a *difference* perspective is the first step, if you have not already done so. Second, learn about the cultures represented in your class(es). These recommendations are necessarily linked by the interwoven nature of language and culture. Individual teachers have the capacity to accomplish both of these recommendations. The first one needs to be accomplished at a personal level. The second recommendation can be accomplished, first, through learning from your students (Gantner, 1997; Williams & Woods, 1997), and, second, in more formal venues like professional development in-service or by taking courses in multicultural education, second-language acquisition, and linguistics.

Cultural responsive practices are essential to the success of students from culturally and linguistically diverse backgrounds. Without them, we will, as a society, continue to leave millions of students out of the mainstream of educational and employment opportunities, as current dropout and unemployment rates for disabled students and students of color indicate.

READINGS

In Reading 1, "Multicultural Education: A Challenge for Special Educators," Dean, Salend, and Taylor review the critical elements of multicultural education and make recommendations for incorporating these features into the classroom. The article is appropriate for general educational audiences, even though special educators are the intended audience.

In Reading 2, "Culturally Sensitive Instructional Practices for African-American Learners with Disabilities," Franklin reviews theoretical assumptions about culturally and linguistically diverse students. Franklin also provides several recommendations for instructional practices that promote high achievement among African American learners.

Reading 3, "Language Differences: A New Approach for Special Educators," provides a rationale for using the students' dialectal differences as a source of strength in the classroom. Adger, Wolfram, and Detwyler provide practical suggestions for learning about dialects in addition to a discussion about the teaching of standard English. Although intended for the special educator, the discussion also applies to middle and secondary regular education settings.

READING 1

Multicultural Education
A Challenge for Special Educators

Ann V. Dean, Spencer J. Salend, and Lorraine Taylor

Multicultural education is an ambiguous concept encompassing the many ways in which educators attempt to acknowledge and understand the increasing diversity in society and in the classroom. The term means widely different things to different interest groups. For example, some humanistic education discourses define multicultural education primarily as the promotion of harmonious relations among students in the classroom (Sleeter & Grant, 1987). At the other end of the spectrum are critical education discourses that define multicultural education as "emancipatory teaching" requiring a critical examination of the relationship between diversity and equality in the classroom (Freire, 1985; Shor, 1992). Critical education theories offer teachers and students a means to disrupt the power relations that exist in the classroom by, for example, asking questions about who is given the authority to talk in the classroom. Teachers can evaluate their own "teacher talk" and begin to create a classroom atmosphere of shared authority in which *all* students are encouraged to find and express their voices.

Because the definition of multicultural education is so controversial, especially when viewed as a social, political, and cultural construct, it is important to be clear about its goals. Multicultural education seeks to make schools examine and address their role in either empowering or disabling students. It serves as a solid platform from which advocacy groups and educators can promote goals of equal opportunity; racial, ethnic, and religious tolerance; and gender and sexual orientation awareness, and it allows them to openly challenge the content and values of the traditional school curriculum.

Whereas students from culturally and linguistically diverse backgrounds are often viewed as the sole focus of the multicultural education movement, we believe that it should target *all* students. For the purposes of this article, culturally and linguistically diverse students are defined as "those whose native or primary language is not English, and/or who are not native members of the Euro-Caucasian cultural base currently dominant in the United States" (Salend, 1994, p. 22).

Critical Elements of Multicultural Education

To achieve the goals of multicultural education, educators, students, parents, and community members need to work collaboratively to restructure schools so that they incorporate the following critical elements of multicultural education.

© 1993 by The Council for Exceptional Children. Reprinted by permission.

Employing Student-Centered Assessment Strategies While the traditional norm-referenced testing model focuses on labeling students and documenting their failure, in a multicultural education approach assessment data serve as the basis for advocating for students and their families (Cummins, 1986). This approach to assessment examines how the educational system and the curriculum contribute to the problems students are experiencing in school (Hamayan & Perlman, 1992).

Proponents of multicultural education view assessment as an ongoing process dealing with real learning experiences that provide a clear and direct relationship between assessment and instruction. Effective assessment also involves collaboration among students, parents, professionals, and administrators and seeks to empower students in the learning process by making them the center of all assessment activities. Student-centered assessment strategies include self-evaluation questionnaires and interviews, student entries in journals or learning logs, think-alouds, and portfolio assessment. For example, Davison and Pearce (1992) assessed and improved the math performance of a group of Native American students by having them maintain journals describing their reactions to lessons and the problems they were experiencing in learning the material.

Using Culturally Responsive Instruction An important component of multicultural education is the use of culturally responsive instruction, in which educators employ instructional strategies and curriculum adaptations that are consistent with students' experiences, cultural perspectives, and developmental ages (Collier & Kalk, 1989; Irvine, 1990). For many students, culturally relevant instruction also means a movement away from traditional teaching models that promote the transmission of information through task analysis, structured drills, teacher-directed activities, and independent seatwork. Figueroa, Fradd, and Correa (1989) and Ortiz and Yates (1989) have suggested that educators consider using reciprocal interaction teaching models such as cooperative learning and whole language, which promote empowerment and learning via verbal and written dialogues between students, as well as between students and teachers.

Culturally responsive instruction also involves use of multicultural instructional materials that reflect and validate students' experiences and aspirations. Educators should carefully evaluate instructional materials in terms of the following questions:

- To what extent do the materials include the various social groups that make up society?
- How are various groups depicted in the material?
- Are the viewpoints, attitudes, reactions, experiences, and feelings of various groups presented accurately?
- Does the material incorporate the history, heritage, language, and traditions of various groups?

- Are the experiences of and issues important to various groups presented in a realistic manner that allows students to recognize and understand their complexities?
- Are the materials factually correct?
- Are the graphics accurate as well as inclusive of and sensitive to various groups?
- Do the materials avoid stereotypes and generalizations about groups?
- Is the language of the materials inclusive and reflective of various groups? (Banks, 1991; Franklin, 1992; Gollnick & Chinn, 1990).

Transforming the Curriculum One means of making learning relevant for all students is to create a multicultural curriculum that acknowledges the voices, histories, experiences, and contributions of all groups, rather than focusing solely on the needs of students from racial minority groups and students who speak languages other than English (Banks, 1991). A transformative approach to revising the multicultural education curriculum changes the basic structure of the curriculum by encouraging the examination and exploration of concepts, issues, problems, and concerns from a variety of cultural perspectives (Banks, 1991). Students learn to think critically and reflect upon the viewpoints of a variety of cultural, gender, religious, and social class groups. For example, Banks and Sebata (1982) developed a lesson that allows students to examine and compare the traditional textbook representation of Christopher Columbus and the Arawak Indians from two different perspectives, thereby allowing students to envision the arrival of European explorers in the New World from the viewpoint of both the explorer and the indigenous peoples.

Teaching Students to Accept and Appreciate Individual Differences

An integral part of a multicultural education curriculum is teaching students to accept and appreciate diversity. An appreciation of and respect for individual differences helps students understand and empathize with the experiences and feelings of their classmates, which can enhance the learning and socialization of all students (Schniedewind, 1992).

Teachers should offer student learning activities that help them understand, accept, and appreciate individual differences related to culture, language, disability, gender, religion, sexual orientation, and socioeconomic status (Salend, 1994). For example, Derman-Sparks (1989) has developed an antibias curriculum that deals with the issues of color, language, gender, and disability. The curriculum includes a variety of activities to teach students to be sensitive to the needs of others, think critically, interact with others, and develop a positive self-identity based on their own strengths rather than on the weaknesses of others. Teachers also should help students understand that "difference exists in the context of inequality when some groups of people have more power and resources than those labeled 'different,' and when the dominant group's culture, values, and practices, being the norm, tend to maintain that inequality" (Schniedewind, 1992, p. 4).

The following guidelines can assist teachers in helping students overcome misunderstandings and negative attitudes toward other cultures by teaching them about different cultures and the value of cultural diversity:

- Examine cultural diversity from the standpoint that all individuals have a culture that is to be valued and affirmed.
- Help students view the similarities among groups through their differences.
- Make cultural diversity activities an ongoing and integral part of the curriculum rather than a 1-day "visit" to a culture during holidays or other special occasions.
- Relate cultural diversity experiences to real-life and hands-on experiences that address the students' interests.
- Teach students about the variance of individual behavior within all cultures and emphasize the notion that families and individuals experience their cultures in personal ways (Derman-Sparks, 1989; Martin, 1987).

Teaching Social Responsibility A common goal of educators committed to multicultural education is to open up possibilities of social change, which can be accomplished by "affirming plurality and difference and . . . working to create community" (Greene, 1993, p. 17). To accomplish this, educators must recognize the need to raise all students' cultural consciousness and teach them to analyze critically the ways in which the culture perpetuates inequality and maintains the status quo (Adams, Pardo, & Schniedewind, 1992). For example, Reissman (1992) used group discussions and projects to help students learn about the biased ways newspapers cover various cultural and linguistic groups and to investigate ways of challenging various forms of discrimination. This approach to teaching involves challenging the assumptions educators, parents, and students hold about traditional school practices and the cultural norms of schools and encouraging an enhanced awareness of social responsibility.

Promoting Family/Community Involvement and Empowerment Multicultural education also targets the school's interactions with family and community as an important area in need of change and seeks to promote active involvement and empowerment of families and communities in the educational process. This requires schools to examine the historical, economic, social, and political variables that have shaped their interactions with parents and communities and establish coalitions of mutuality and support with the communities they serve (Roberts, Bell, & Salend, 1991).

Rather than viewing parents and communities as disinterested, ineffective, and deficient, a multicultural education approach promotes a collaborative, equal-status dialogue among professionals, parents, and community members (Harry, 1992). Parents are empowered to perform a variety of roles that provide them with a voice in the decision-making process (Cheng, 1992). Salend and Taylor (in press) have identified a variety of strategies and programs that educators can employ to empower parents and establish a reciprocal connection among the family, school, and community.

Understanding Behavior in a Social/Cultural Context Schools, and therefore the behavioral expectations of teachers, are rooted in the mainstream, middle-class culture. It is important that educators be aware of this potential cultural bias and assess the impact of cultural and class perspectives and language background on student behavior. For example, Boykin (1986) noted that African-American students may engage in a variety of passive and active behaviors to cope with social institutions primarily based on mainstream perspectives. Therefore, educators need to increase their understanding of the ways in which behavior and communication work within a specific social/cultural context, expand their acceptance of individual differences, and promote competence in all students, regardless of cultural, class, or language backgrounds.

Countering Resistance to Change

Educators who hope to create classrooms that affirm diversity and promote a sense of community must be prepared to face many challenges (Greene, 1993). The first challenge is the resistance to change they may encounter from peers, administrators, school board members, parents, students, and other groups who have a vested interest in what goes on in schools. These groups will work to protect their own interests through control of the existing curricula and everyday school practices. As educators begin to recognize and respond to the needs of an increasingly diverse group of students, these changes may be perceived by some individuals and groups as an attempt to usurp their power and upset the status quo.

The second, less obvious challenge is the resistance to change educators might experience within themselves. They must be willing to examine subtle forms of personal resistance. For example, it is not easy for teachers to take a frank look at the power they wield and examine how they use that authority to disable or empower students. It is easier to resist acknowledging the social and political aspects of teaching. Through a thoughtful examination of their assumptions and pedagogical practices, it is possible for teachers to confront their resistance to change and create possibilities for inclusive, multicultural classrooms by asking questions such as the following:

- Am I willing to reflect on the way I use power in the classroom?
- Am I defensive when the assumptions of multicultural education are discussed?
- Is it possible for me to accept that the knowledge made legitimate in schools may not be meeting the needs of my students?
- Am I willing to try to understand the racial, ethnic, linguistic, gender, and class dimensions of teaching?
- Will my authority as a teacher be threatened if I look at how my teaching supports or does not support concepts such as acceptance of individual differences, equality, and justice?

Conclusion

Many of the challenges encountered in advocating for multicultural education are also faced by those who support inclusion. As proponents of educational reform, the multicultural and inclusion movements share mutual goals and seek to provide equality, equity, and excellence for all students. The movements also share common affective goals for students, including developing positive attitudes toward their cultures and the cultures of others, understanding and accepting individual differences, and appreciating the interdependence among diverse groups and individuals.

Many of the critical elements of multicultural education also coincide with those identified for inclusion. Best practices in terms of assessment, culturally responsive instruction, curriculum reform, and an appreciation of individual differences are common to both movements. The empowerment and support of families and communities is another important component that is shared by advocates of both philosophies. By recognizing their commonalities, proponents of these philosophies can create a unified school system in which *all* students are welcomed and affirmed in classrooms that are based on acceptance, belonging, and community.

References

Adams, B. S., Pardo, W. E., & Schniedewind, N. (1992). Changing the ways things are done around here. *Educational Leadership, 49*(4), 37–42.

Banks, J. A. (1991). *Teaching strategies for ethnic studies* (5th ed.). Boston: Allyn & Bacon.

Banks, J. A., & Sebesta, S. L. (1982). *We Americans: Our history and people* (Vols. 1 & 2). Boston: Allyn & Bacon.

Boykin, A. W. (1986). The triple quandary and the schooling of Afro-American children. In U. Neisser (Ed.), *The school achievement of minority children* (pp. 57–92). Hillsdale, NJ: Lawrence Erlbaum.

Cheng, L. L. (1992, November). *Difficult discourse: Making home-school-student connections.* Paper presented at The Council for Exceptional Children's Topical Conference on Culturally and Linguistically Diverse Exceptional Children, Minneapolis.

Collier, C., & Kalk, M. (1989). Bilingual special education curriculum development. In L. M. Baca & H. T. Cervantes (Eds.), *The bilingual special education interface* (2nd ed.) (pp. 205–229). Columbus, OH: Merrill.

Cummins, J. (1986). Empowering minority students: A framework for intervention. *Harvard Education Review, 56,* 18–36.

Davison, D. M., & Pearce, D. L. (1992). The influence of writing activities on mathematics learning of American Indian students. *The Journal of Educational Issues of Language Minority Students, 10,* 147–157.

Derman-Sparks, L. (1989). *Anti-bias curriculum.* Washington, DC: National Association for the Education of Young Children.

Figueroa, R. A., Fradd, S. H., & Correa, V. I. (1989). Bilingual special education and this special issue. *Exceptional Children, 56,* 174–178.

Franklin, M. E. (1992). Culturally sensitive instructional practices for African-American learners with disabilities. *Exceptional Children, 59,* 115–122.

Freire, P. (1985). *The politics of education: Culture, power and liberation.* South Hadley, MA: Bergin & Garvey.

Gollnick, D. M., & Chinn, P. C. (1990). *Multicultural education in a pluralistic society.* Columbus, OH: Merrill.

Greene, M. (1993). The passions of pluralism: Multiculturalism and the expanding community. *Educational Researcher, 22*(1), 13–18.

Hamayan, E., & Perlman, R. (1992). Assessment of language competencies. In Illinois State Board of Education (Eds.), *Recommended practices in the identification, assessment, and provision of special education for culturally and linguistically diverse students* (pp. 46–60). Springfield: Illinois State Board of Education.

Harry, B. (1992). *Culturally diverse families and the special education system.* New York: Teachers College Press.

Irvine, J. J. (1990). *Black students and school failure: Policies, practices and prescriptions.* New York: Praeger.

Martin, D. S. (1987). Reducing ethnocentrism. *TEACHING Exceptional Children, 20*(1), 5–8.

Ortiz, A. A., & Yates, J. R. (1989). Staffing and the development of individualized educational programs for the bilingual exceptional student. In L. M. Baca & H. T. Cervantes (Eds.), *The bilingual special education interface* (2nd ed.) (pp. 183–203). Columbus, OH: Merrill.

Reissman, R. (1992). Multicultural awareness collages. *Educational Leadership, 49*(4), 51–52.

Roberts, G. W., Bell, L. A., & Salend, S. J. (1991). Negotiating change for multicultural education: A consultation model. *Journal of Educational and Psychological Consultation, 2*(4), 323–342.

Salend, S. J. (1994). *Effective mainstreaming: Creating inclusive classrooms.* New York: Macmillan.

Salend, S. J., & Taylor, L. (In press). Working with families: A cross-cultural perspective. *Remedial and Special Education.*

Schniedewind, N., (1992). Appreciating diversity: Promoting equality. *Cooperative Learning, 12*(3), 4–7.

Shor, I. (1992). *Empowering education: Critical teaching for social change.* Chicago: University of Chicago Press.

Sleeter, C. E., & Grant, C. A. (1987). An analysis of multicultural education in the U.S. *Harvard Education Review, 57,* 421–444.

READING 2

Culturally Sensitive Instructional Practices for African-American Learners with Disabilities

Mary E. Franklin, University of Cincinnati

American public schools have traditionally used a monolithic model of instruction, in which the organization of teaching, learning, and performance is compatible with the social structure of the dominant culture (Tharp, 1989). This traditional model, which is also adopted in the field of special education, emphasizes three patterns of cognitive functioning: (1) analysis of academic tasks, (2) the establishment of sequential learning objectives based on each task analysis, and (3) direct instruction of individual task components (Cummins, 1984). According to Tharp, teachers tend to expect that *all* students will learn based on these traditional patterns of cognitive functioning and instructional practices. The truth is, however, only learners whose cognitive functioning corresponds to these patterns are likely to succeed. Tharp and others (Cummins; Poplin, 1988) have asserted that many African-American, Hispanic, Native American, and Asian-American learners have difficulty with traditional patterns of cognitive functioning because the patterns ignore the impact culture has on language, learning, and thinking.

Despite the pervasive literature asserting that culture and language affect learning (Banks, 1981; Boykin, 1982; Hale-Benson, 1986; Hilliard, 1989; Piestrup, 1973; Tharp, 1989; Villegas, 1991), most special education teachers continue to plan instruction and activities based on their students' disabilities, with little consideration given to the diverse cultural and linguistic backgrounds of the students (Almanza & Mosley, 1980; Clark-Johnson, 1988; Cummins, 1984). In view of the disproportionate overrepresentation of culturally and linguistically diverse learners in special education classes, we cannot ignore the impact that culture and language have on learners' cognitive styles.

The goal of public education must be the same for *all*, that is, *to help students achieve their fullest potential*. The crucial question is, however, How can this task be best accomplished for African-American learners with disabilities? This article identifies effective teaching, learning, and performance strategies that are compatible with the social/cultural background of African-American learners (with or without disabilities). First, I examine six theoretical assumptions about culturally sensitive instructional practices. Second, I review the literature showing the relationship between affective, culturally sensitive instructional practices and high academic achievement among African-American learners. Last, I recommend ways to organize teaching, learning, and performance to be compatible with the social structure of African-American students with disabilities.

© 1992 by The Council for Exceptional Children. Reprinted by permission.

Theoretical Assumptions

Educators must consider culture and language when they plan instruction and develop activities for students from diverse backgrounds. The following assumptions undergird recommendations for culturally sensitive instructional practices.

Assumption 1: Quality instruction should incorporate resources from the learner's environments outside the school parameters. The learner's immediate cultural environment is the home and the local community (Bronfenbrenner, 1979). In this environment, the learner interacts and develops language and interrelationship skills that may challenge the school culture.

Cultural-difference theory attributes the academic problems of culturally and linguistically diverse students to the discontinuity between home and school. Discontinuity exists in relation to differences in dialects (Piestrup, 1973) and in cognitive styles (Almanza & Mosley, 1980; Cummins, 1984) when the method of instruction is incompatible with the cognitive and interactive styles of culturally and linguistically diverse learners. The solution to cultural discontinuity between home and school is not necessarily having the school replicate every cultural condition of the home and community (Villegas, 1991), but rather requiring teachers to adapt and infuse cultural variables in their interactions with African-American learners and in their instructional practices.

Assumption 2: Special education should **not** ***be the primary solution for African-American learners whose cognitive and behavioral patterns are incompatible with schools' monocultural instructional methods.*** Chinn and Hughes (1988) reported that of all ethnic groups, African Americans were the most represented in special education programs, and African-American males were the most overrepresented in classes for students with behavior disorders and mental retardation. Traditional instructional methods tend to be unrelated to or incompatible with the experiences of culturally and linguistically diverse learners. Consequently, Tharp (1989) and others (Cummins, 1984; Poplin, 1988) found that many African-American, Hispanic, Native American, and Asian-American learners are much less successful in regular education programs than are white-American learners.

Assumption 3: African-American learners' differences should not be perceived as genetic deficiencies but, rather, as sources of strength. The notion that minority learners' low achievement is due to genetic intelligence deficiencies has been disputed throughout the literature (e.g., Feuerstein, 1979; Mercer, 1973; Villegas, 1991). According to Sternbeg (1983), there is great diversity in a culture's conception of intelligence. He explains: "People's personal experiences in various cultures almost invariably suggest that what is adaptive and 'intelligent' in one culture can be maladaptive and even 'unintelligent' in another culture" (p. 8). Thus, people's experiences within a culture formulate their definition of intelligence. Without an understanding of various cultures, well-meaning teachers may ignore cultural definitions that are peculiar to the learners' cultural backgrounds.

Assumption 4: Culturally sensitive teachers will identify and build on the learner's strengths and interests. Poplin's (1988) theory of constructivism/holism lends support to this assumption. This theory suggests that a learner's context for learning begins with what is currently known. Hence, special education teachers must develop a knowledge of learners' cultures and must design meaningful experiences around *what learners know* rather than *what learners do not know.*

Assumption 5: Language and dialectical differences are important cultural influences that affect communication and interaction between the teacher and learner (Piestrup, 1973; Poplin, 1988; Tharp, 1989). The required language in the school may differ from that used in the home—or may be the same (language) but differ in the way it is used (Villegas, 1991). Hence, language activities presented in the classroom may generate many different interpretations based on how the learner views the world. Teachers who lack cross-cultural sensitivity may view the responses of culturally and linguistically diverse learners as "wrong" and academically incompetent. The question then becomes, What use is prior experience to learners whose established ways of using language and making sense of the world are deemed unacceptable or prohibited by the classroom?

Assumption 6: Culturally sensitive instruction should be integrated with activities that provide learners opportunities to learn and practice new skills. The constructivist theory posits that learning is a process in which new meanings are created by the learner within the context of his or her current knowledge (Poplin, 1988). If a new experience is unrelated to a learner's developmental levels, interests, and problems, the learner will naturally reject and ignore the information. Teachers must understand the importance of knowing their learners' interests, hobbies, music, and so forth.

When learners are provided many opportunities to negotiate their cultural background, interests, and cognitive styles in the learning environment, they are more inclined to experience academic success. The following review of literature explores the cultural values and practices of African Americans, the effect these values and practices have on the cognitive and interactive styles of African-American learners, and the characteristics of effective teachers of African-American learners.

Impact of African-American Cultural Values on Learning and Instruction

A review of 23 years of research shows *some* common cultural values of African Americans and the effect these values have on the learning and interactive styles of African-American learners. Further, an examination of teaching practices used with African-American students delineates certain teacher attitudes, perceptions, and interactive styles that have successfully facilitated continuity between the school and home and community environments.

African-American Child-Rearing Practices   In a study examining child-rearing practices of white families and African-American families, Young (1970) found that white children were more object-oriented, having available to them as infants numerous manipulative objects and discovery properties.

Conversely, African-American children were person-oriented. As infants, they were held by their mothers or another family member most of the time, and few objects were given to them. When African-American infants reached for an object or felt a surface, their attention was immediately redirected to the person holding them, thereby reducing the value of material objects. Similarly, Lewis (1975) and Dougherty (1978) observed extensive interaction among African-American family members and infants involving touching, kissing, and holding the baby's hands.

Young (1970) observed other interactive techniques between African-American mothers and their children. For example, a "contest" style of speech was used between the mothers and children in which they "volleyed" rhythmically, and the children were taught to be assertive and to develop their individual styles. African-American mothers gave directions for household chores in a "call-and-response" pattern, an interactive style found in some African-American churches (Lein, 1975) and in some African-American music (Hale-Benson, 1986).

Other African-American values regarding child rearing included the value of strictness and the expectation that children assume responsibility early (Bartz & Levine, 1978). African-American parents also valued creative functioning in their children; that is, they were not immediately frustrated by their children's "typical" childhood behavior and encouraged its development (Greathouse, Gomez, & Wurster, 1988).

Engram (1982) found that African-American children were also socialized early regarding the realities of racism and poverty in society and told they must be twice as good if they were to succeed. In summary, researchers have found that child-rearing practices help form and shape the child's view of self and how he or she fits in the world. These practices also serve to establish the cognitive and interactive characteristics of learners.

Some Characteristics of African-American Learners The emotional and social characteristics of African-American learners and their families have important implications for teacher-student relationships. Silverstein and Krate (1975) classified over half of the African-American students they studied as being "ambivalent." They explained that these students needed—and sought rather aggressively—teacher attention, nurturance, and acceptance. Students needed constant encouragement, recognition, warmth, and reassurance to continue participating in the class activities. However, when positive attention and affirmation were not given, students often became frustrated, angry, and disruptive.

Regarding African-American students' motivation and interests, Silberman (1970) reported that observers were struck by the liveliness and eagerness demonstrated by African-American learners in the early grades and by their passivity and apathy in the later grades. Lefevre (1966) reported that by the fifth grade, African-American students had become cynical and preoccupied with blatant attempts to confound the constrictions of the traditional instructional environment. Boykin (1982) explained that African-American learners were not inherently apathetic and cynical, but inherently eager and had become "turned off" by the nature of their school experiences. Many African-American children are exposed to high-energy, fast-paced home environments, where there is simultaneous variable stimulation (e.g, televisions and music playing simultaneously and people talking and moving in and about the home freely). Hence, low-energy, monolithic environments (as seen in many traditional school environments) are less stimulating.

In 1982, Boykin studied the effects of task variability on African-American and white students. Each learner's home stimulation level was assessed, based on the total number of adults and children in the home, total number of rooms in the home, and the total number of televisions, radios, and stereos. Findings indicated that African-American students experienced home environments higher in stimulation than did white students. Further, the difference in home environment was reflected in differential responsiveness to variability in task presentation format. African-American learners' performance was markedly better in the more varied condition than when there was less variability. White learners' performance was not affected by task variability.

Rohwer and Harris (1975) also studied task variability of African-American and white students—specifically, the effect of teaching prose by using multimedia variations. Again, the results indicated that the performance of African-American learners when using multimedia, especially oral plus visual media, was greater than when using single media. The performance of white learners generally was not affected when combined or single media were used.

Some Characteristics of Effective Teachers of African-American Learners Teacher attitudes and perceptions both affect and moderate learners' academic achievement. According to Villegas (1991), an effective teacher has the ability to create meaningful and successful learning activities that take into consideration the learner's culture and background experiences.

Researchers examining teacher-student interactions found that affective-oriented teachers were more successful than task-oriented teachers in improving African-American students' academic achievement (Collins & Tamarkin, 1982; Cureton, 1978; Dillon, 1989; St. John, 1971). Affective-oriented teachers were described as being kind, optimistic, understanding, adaptable, and warm. They also were group conscious, cooperative, and sociocentric.

In a microethnographic study, Dillon (1989) found that effective teachers were "affective" and were successful in bridging home and school cultures. These teachers were able to create learning environments that were open and risk free; they planned and structured activities that met the interests and needs of the students.

Instructional planning should also incorporate small groups. According to Hale-Benson (1986), this practice provides African-American learners the human interaction they are familiar with in their families. Hale-Benson has encouraged teachers to incorporate peer- and cross-age grouping and cooperative learning groups in instructional planning.

Research on cooperative learning in the classroom showed that small, heterogeneous-ability groups working together on learning tasks and activities were particularly effective for African-American learners (Slavin & Madden, 1979; Slavin & Oickle, 1981). For example, Slavin and Oickle found that cooperative learning groups made significantly greater gains in academic achievement than did nonteam classes, largely because of the outstanding gains made by African-American learners.

Effective teachers also bridge African-American students' home and school cultures by using stimulus variety, greater verve, and verbal interaction. Piestrup (1973) identified varied techniques that were effective when teaching reading to African-American first graders who spoke a Black English dialect. Results revealed that when teachers used a culturally sensitive approach, African-American children demonstrated a high proficiency level. That is, the teacher spoke rhythmically, varied intonation, and engaged in verbal interplay with the learners. Similarly, Delpit (1988) observed a teacher successfully integrating today's learners' music (e.g., rap) into a lesson that included very complex science factors.

In summary, many African-American learners are reared in people-focused families and communities where human interaction and simultaneous stimulus variability are highly valued. Therefore, effective teachers of African-American students, with or without disabilities, will develop a repertoire of instructional practices that involve cultural aspects that are valued by these students and that will enhance their development. Teaching and learning should be compatible with the cultural characteristics of African-American learners with disabilities.

Teaching and Learning That Is Compatible With the Cultural Characteristics of African-American Learners With Disabilities

The literature reviewed previously suggests that the following instructional strategies are effective with African-American learners: task variability; culturally sensitive teacher-student interaction; and social learning in peer groups, cross-age groups, and cooperative learning groups. Researchers' findings, however, should be viewed not as rigid prescriptions, but as suggestions for guiding instructional decisions for African-American learners with disabilities. To be effective, educators must exercise their freedom to adapt instruction to meet the needs of local circumstances and individual students.

Stimulus Variability Stimulus variability includes varying the format of instruction presentation and increasing the classroom energy. Many African-American students prefer a faster pace, with techniques that incorporate body movement.

Greater Verve and Rhythm. Variety in instruction provides the spirit and enthusiasm for learning. When instructional strategies facilitate stimulus variety, using combinations of oral, print, and visual media, African-American students perform better (Boykin, 1982; Rohwer & Harris, 1975). Instructional activities should include music, singing, and movement. For example, teachers can vary instructional activities to incorporate different media (e.g., film, filmstrip, transparencies, and pictures), instructional materials, and study locations. Teachers can also use multimedia test materials.

Verbal Interaction. Through verbal activities, teachers can encourage learners to treat the text material orally. Motivation increases when teachers encourage the use of many expressive, creative activities (Collins & Tamarkin, 1982). Such activities could include rap (Delpit, 1988), choral reading (Collins & Tamarkin; Young, 1970), chants, and responsive reading (Piestrup, 1973).

Divergent Thinking. A method of problem solving, divergent thinking requires students to think in ways that differ from conventional thinking and problem solving (Boykin, 1982; Poplin, 1988). Teachers should provide experiences for students to explore various ways of arriving at a particular solution. These experiences include activities that require brainstorming, open-ended responses, and critical thinking. Learners need to practice making conjectures, gathering evidence, and building arguments to defend or refute their conjectures. The teacher's responsibility is to help students realize they have the power to make sense of a new question or problem situation. This can be accomplished by allowing students the opportunity to gather information about what they will study and to draw from information they already have in their cultural backgrounds. Teachers may also find it helpful to connect problems and activities to other subject areas of interest to the African-American learner (Boykin, 1982; Poplin, 1988; Tharp, 1989).

Teachers' Interactions With African-American Learners Research reveals that interacting with African-American learners may require teachers to model affective behavior (e.g., affirming, giving positive reinforcements, etc.) (Collins & Tamarkin, 1982; Dillon, 1989; St. John, 1971).

Use of Dialect. Teachers may *at times* integrate aspects of the Black English dialect into their conversations with African-American learners, for example, "jive talkin'," which is based on African-American improvisation of the English language. This form of interaction should be used only by those educators who have established a rapport with learners; otherwise this form of interaction could be perceived as condescending. Teachers should inform African-American learners that although the Black English dialect is useful in their home and community environment, it is not accepted in all environments. Nevertheless, when the teacher uses the learner's dialect from time to time, the learner may be more inclined to engage in tasks he or she might otherwise reject (Collins & Tamarkin, 1982; Villegas, 1991).

Presenting Real-World Tasks. Teachers should include activities that are realistic to the African-American learners' cultural environment (i.e., school, home, and community). Teachers should become familiar with African-American culture and integrate learners' real-life experiences in instructional materials, resources, and techniques (Boykin, 1982; Gay, 1978; Hale-Benson, 1986; Poplin, 1988; Tharp, 1989).

Including a People Focus. Person-to-person interaction is a learning-style preference of many African-American learners (Collins & Tamarkin, 1982; Cureton, 1978; Diloon, 1989; Doughtery, 1978; Young, 1970). This characteristic has implications for how teachers interact with African-American students with disabilities and how instruction is planned and implemented. As mentioned previously, for example, African-American students may benefit from small-group work (Cureton, 1978; Hale-Benson, 1986; Slavin & Oickle, 1981) and peer tutoring (Hale-Benson, 1986). Other examples include selecting reading textbooks and materials that include credible young people with whom African-American learners, of either gender, can relate (Franklin & Mickel, in press). Materials may emphasize the student's lifestyle, values, motives, speech, and mannerisms (see also Boykin, 1982; Piestrup, 1973; Poplin, 1988; Tharp, 1989; Villegas, 1991). Teachers should also examine instructional materials carefully to ensure that the materials selected include African Americans, as well as other ethnic groups (Franklin & Mickel).

Grouping Patterns Instructional activities for small groups can be organized to allow students to work together. This means that the room will not always be quiet, and some students may even be off task at times. Nevertheless, students need to have opportunities to work on problem situations together and to talk about ways of doing an activity or finding a solution to the problem. Further, this method gives students a chance to stimulate others' thinking and to realize that there may be many methods of accomplishing a task. Group activities also encourage social growth and cross-racial friendships.

Cooperative Learning. In this instructional strategy, students work together in teams. Specific methods include Student Team Learning, Jigsaw, Group Investigation, and Learning Together (Slavin & Madden, 1979; Slavin & Oickle, 1981). Teachers divide the class into small, heterogeneous-ability groups in which each member is expected to contribute to an assigned task, and each group should work cooperatively on assigned, content-related tasks.

Peer/Cross-Age Grouping. In these groups, students of the same or different age work together informally. Learners in such groups may be working on different assignments (Hale-Benson, 1986).

Peer Tutoring. This person-to-person interaction fosters helping relationships between learners (Hale-Benson, 1986). In this technique, the teacher encourages learners to tutor each other and problem solve together as part of a small group (e.g., a cooperative group or peer or cross-age grouping).

To connect culturally with African-American learners' home and community, effective special education teachers may use stimulus variability, affective methods of interaction, and variable grouping patterns. Teachers must be especially mindful of these practices when they systematically plan successful learning experiences for African-American learners with disabilities. Although some of these instructional practices appear in the effective teaching literature, recognition and understanding of a learner's culture will expand the teacher's range of practices.

Conclusion

The Council for Exceptional Children (CEC, 1978) has strongly urged special educators to develop sensitivity, awareness, and insight into the needs of learners from diverse ethnic and cultural groups. As part of this initiative, this article has provided a review of the literature relating to African-American culture and its influence on the learner. This research has suggested culturally sensitive instructional practices, with specific suggestions for the instruction of African-American students with disabilities. The inclusion of these or similar practices in curriculum and instruction may enhance the learning experiences of African-American students with disabilities.

References

Almanza, H. P., & Mosley, W. J. (1980). Curriculum adaptation and modifications for culturally diverse handicapped children. *Exceptional Children, 46,* 608–614.

Banks, J. A. (1981). *Multiethnic education: Theory and practice.* Boston: Allyn & Bacon.

Bartz, K., & Levine, E. (1978). Childrearing by Black parents: A description and comparison to Anglo and Chicano parents. *Journal of Marriage and the Family, 40,* 709–719.

Boykin, A. W. (1982). Task variability and the performance of Black and White children: Vervistic explorations. *Journal of Black Studies, 12*(4), 469–485.

Bronfenbrenner, U. (1979). *The ecology of human development.* Cambridge: Harvard University Press.

Chinn, P. C., & Hughes, S. (1988, October). Representation of ethnic minorities in special education for the mentally retarded and learning disabled. In L. Olion (Chair), *Reaching new horizons.* Symposium conducted at The Council for Exceptional Children Symposia on the Education of Culturally Diverse Exceptional Children, Denver.

Clark-Johnson, G. (1988). Special focus: Black children. *TEACHING Exceptional Children, 20*(4), 46–47.

Collins, M. & Tamarkin, C. (1982). *Marva Collins' way.* Los Angeles: Jeremy P. Tarcher.

Council for Exceptional Children. (1978). Minorities position policy statements. *Exceptional Children, 45,* 57–64.

Cummins, J. (1984). *Bilingual and special education: Issues in assessment and pedagogy.* San Diego: College-Hill Press.

Cureton, G. O. (1978). Using a Black learning style. *The Reading Teacher, 31,* 751–756.

Delpit, L. D. (1988). The silenced dialogue: Power and pedagogy in educating other people's children. *Harvard Educational Review, 58*(3), 280–297.

Dillon, D. R. (1989). Showing them that I want them to learn and that I care about who they are: A microethnography of the social organization of a secondary low-track English-reading classroom. *American Educational Research Journal, 26*(2), 227–259.

Dougherty, M. C. (1978). *Becoming a woman in rural Black culture.* Nashville, TN: Vanderbilt University Press.

Engram, E. (1982). *Science, myth, reality: The Black family in one-half century of research.* Westport, CT: Greenwood Press.

Feuerstein, R. (1979). *The dynamic assessment of retarded performers: The learning potential assessment device, theory, instruments and techniques.* Baltimore: University Park Press.

Franklin, M. E., & Mickel, V. (in press). Are publishers of reading textbooks for intermediate-students sensitive to the learning characteristics of African-American students. *SENGA: Sensitive to the Educational Needs of Growing Americans.*

Gay, G. (1978). Multicultural preparation and teacher effectiveness in desegregated schools. *Theory Into Practice, 11,* 149–156.

Greathouse, B., Gomez, R., & Wurster, S. (1988). An investigation of Black and Hispanic parents' locus of control, childbearing attitudes and practices and degree of involvement in Head Start. *Negro Educational Review, 39*(1-2), 4–17.

Hale-Benson, J. E. (1986). *Black children: Their roots, culture and learning styles.* Baltimore: Johns Hopkins University Press.

Hilliard, A. (1989). Teachers and cultural styles in a pluralistic society. *NEA Today, 7*(6), 65–69.

Lefevre, C. (1966). Inner city schools: As the children see it. *Elementary School Journal, 7,* 8–15.

Lein, K. (1975). Black American migrant children: Their speech at home and school. *Council on Anthropology and Education Quarterly, 6,* 1–11.

Lewis, D. K. (1975). The Black family: Socialization and sex roles. *Phylon, 36,* 221–237.

Mercer, J. (1973). *Labeling the mentally retarded.* Berkeley, CA: The University of California Press.

Piestrup, A. (1973). *Black dialect interference and accommodation of reading instruction in first grade* (Monograph No. 4). Berkeley, CA: University of California, Language Behavior Research Laboratory.

Poplin, M. S. (1988). Holistic/constructivist principles of the teaching/learning process: Implications for the field of learning disabilities. *Journal of Learning Disabilities, 21*(7), 401–416.

Rohwer, W. D., & Harris, W. (1975). Media effects on prose learning in two populations of children. *Journal of Educational Psychology, 67,* 651–657.

Silberman, C. (1970). *Crisis in the classroom.* New York: Vintage Books.

Silverstein, B., & Krate, R. (1975). *Children of the dark ghetto: A developmental psychology.* New York: Praeger.

Slavin, R. E., & Madden, N. A. (1979). School practices that improve race relations. *American Educational Research Journal, 16,* 169–180.

Slavin, R. E., & Oickle, E. (1981). Effects of cooperative learning teams on student achievement and race relations: Treatment by race interactions. *Sociology of Education, 54,* 174–180.

Sternberg, R. J. (1983). Criteria for intellectual skills training. *Educational Researcher, 12*(2), 6–12.

St. John, N. (1971). Thirty-six teachers: Their characteristics and outcomes for Black and White pupils. *American Educational Research Journal, 8,* 635–648.

Tharp, R. G. (1989). Psychocultural variables and constants: Effects on teaching and learning in schools. *American Psychologist, 44*(2), 349–359.

Villegas, A. M. (1991). *Culturally responsive pedagogy for the 1990s and beyond* (Trends and Issues Paper No. 6). Washington, DC: ERIC Clearinghouse on Teacher Education.

Young, V. H. (1970). Family and childhood in a southern Georgia community. *American Anthropologist, 72,* 269–288.

READING 3

Language Differences
A New Approach for Special Educators

Carolyn Temple Adger, Walt Wolfram, and Jennifer Detwyler

One of the hallmarks of multicultural societies, schools, and classrooms is the coexistence of multiple language and language varieties, or dialects. Communication problems arise not only when people do not share a language, but also when a variation exists within a single language. The problems associated with language variation, however, appear to result more from social attitudes about dialects than from authentic comprehension difficulties. The preferred, or "standard," variety of English is considered superior in some way and somehow better suited for communication than the disfavored nonstandard English, or vernacular varieties. In fact, Standard English is standard because it is used by the more powerful segment of the society, those whose opinions can be imposed on the less powerful. Crucial as it is that students become proficient in the standard dialect so that they can have access to the culture of power, there is no linguistic reason to discard or devalue vernacular dialects, which are natural human systems. Discrimination against individuals based on their dialect is as destructive as other kinds of discrimination against human variation, yet it seems to be much more tolerated than other forms of prejudice (Milroy & Milroy, 1985).

Traditional education typically rejects any role for language variation in English, since differences are viewed simply as obstacles to be overcome in the acquisition of a standard variety. However, language and dialect difference need not merely be endured as an unfortunate fact of life in multicultural schools. Students' implicit knowledge of their own and other dialects offers a valuable educational resource. Teachers can use the natural occurrence of multiple dialects in the school and community as a laboratory for teaching children about the nature of language in society.

A Rationale for Sociolinguistic Education

Many students have grown up in multicultural settings. To them, culturally based language variation may seem usual, if they are even conscious of it. But because they live in a society that holds unwarranted attitudes toward language variation, it is important to give students the tools to identify and examine language contrasts and to counter negative attitudes. If they are to avoid perceiving others' dialects simplistically as grammatical mistakes or "funny accents," students need to become aware of the fact that language varieties spoken by members of the society are regular linguistic systems that differ systematically from each other.

© 1993 by The Council for Exceptional Children. Reprinted by permission.

We need to give students an information base to counter dialect prejudice. Those who speak socially favored language varieties may view their dialectically different peers as linguistically deficient, and those who speak stigmatized dialects are at risk for adopting the negative social attitudes about their language expressed in both subtle and conspicuous ways at school. Because ways of speaking are such strong markers of social group identity, attitudes toward language reinforce other social attitudes. Harmonious relationships among students and teachers in culturally diverse schools depend not just on good will, but also on opportunities to examine the nature of social differences and the stereotypical interpretations that sometimes accompany them.

Another reason for the study of language differences is to infuse current knowledge about language into the language arts curriculum. Language differences offer a window through which the fascinating, dynamic nature of language can be viewed scientifically. In examining language data, students can discover generalizations about language regularity within dialects and develop hypotheses about certain forms of language that they can then test in actual language use.

This process of scientific inquiry is generally untapped in language instruction. Language is still viewed in terms of fossilized grammatical definitions and prescriptive rules for language use that presume a single "correct" English. Language arts lessons may focus on memorizing and applying the abstractions of traditional grammar in written activities: identifying parts of speech or writing synonyms and antonyms. The skills students learn from this traditional approach are relevant to other school activities such as passing standardized tests and discussing written work, but they have little value for understanding the language that occurs naturally in everyday life. The traditional approach to language study is at odds with current methods of teaching literature, writing, math, and science, which discourage rote learning and simple taxonomic classification in favor of careful observation and the development of critical thinking skills.

The Special Educator and Language Awareness

In a sense, special educators have always been involved with language differences. The lack of appropriate assessment for distinguishing dialect differences from language disorders has meant that special education and related services, especially speech/language pathology, have served disproportionate numbers of students from various ethnic and racial groups who speak vernacular dialects. By taking a proactive role in revising language education, special education teachers can directly address the language difference issue that may figure in their own students' classification, in addition to addressing the educational needs of all students.

In discussions of cultural diversity, educators sometimes hesitate to identify differences among cultural groups for fear that differences will be equated with deficits. Because they have focused on the difference/deficit issue, however, special educators are well situated to insist that cultural differences be acknowledged honestly and that they not be confused with deficits. Assuming a proactive role in educating children about language differences is a logical extension of the special educator's position. Involving other teachers in the endeavor is one way to open up the diversity dialogue. In pilot testing the dialect lessons described in this article, we found that teachers who participated in co-teaching the lessons not only found it a productive line of inquiry for their students, but also developed new ways of thinking about dialects and dialect discrimination themselves.

The proactive role we advocate presents some difficulties. Special education teachers' training in language areas traditionally has focused on problems related to learning disabilities, rather than on normal language. Furthermore, not every teacher has critically examined the stereotype that Standard English is inherently better than other dialects, rather than merely socially favored. Certainly, sociolinguistic training should be emphasized in teacher education for multicultural schools, but the need to modify language study is immediate. One resource of teaching about language variation is the school speech language pathologist, who is likely to have had sociolinguistic training. Another resource is the instructional unit on dialect described in this article, which supplies some background knowledge and lists references. Since it uses the scientific method to examine data, the process, if not the content, is familiar.

Learning About Dialects

We have been experimenting with a five-lesson unit on language variation for middle-grade students that addresses humanistic, scientific, and cultural objectives (Wolfram, Detwyler, & Adger, 1992).

Humanistic Objectives

On a humanistic level, the objective is to introduce students to elementary notions of language variation that contrast with some of the typical prejudices and stereotypes associated with dialect differences in popular culture. Through selected excerpts from a popular video, *American Tongues* (Alvarez & Kolker, 1987), students are inductively introduced to the naturalness of culturally based and regionally based linguistic diversity. The video juxtaposes natural samples of linguistic diversity with a set of excerpts from real-life interviews about language attitudes in which people resort to unjustified stereotypes in describing other people's speech.

Scientific Objectives

Another goal of the dialect curriculum is scientific: The students examine patterns of language variation in a systematic way and make generalizations from carefully describe sets of data. The boxed example is a student exercise that concerns the disappearance of the contrast between two vowel sounds when they precede nasal sounds in Southern varieties of English, classically illustrated in the identical pronunciation of *pin* and *pen* in these varieties. First the students look at a data set in which the vowel merger takes place, and then they compare it with another set of data showing where the merger does *not* take place. They are then asked to formulate a hypothesis that specifies the surrounding sounds that trigger the merger. Finally, they are asked to predict where the merger does and does not occur for a new set of data.

In addition to pronunciation differences, students learn to identify two other elements of dialect—vocabulary and grammar—by listening to recorded stories told in a dialect different from their own. The lessons include exercises on examining dialect grammar, such as the prefix *a-* in some rural dialects (e.g., "They went a-hunting and a-fishing"), and vocabulary contrasts (e.g., "rubber band" vs. "gumband").

Cultural Objectives

A third major goal of the curriculum is cultural-historical. Students are introduced to the historical development of language varieties to show the continuity of current dialects with their historical roots. For example, African-American vernacular English (AAVE) is traced from its presumed pidgin and creole language roots in West Africa through concrete, participatory activities as well as historical exposition. In one group activity, students make up a skit simulating language contact between groups that speak mutually unintelligible languages. In this way, they inductively learn to appreciate the circumstances that give rise to language pidginization. Following the skit, they view a video segment profiling the development, distribution, and migration of pidgins and creoles in the African diaspora to see the historical continuity between AAVE (assumed to be a "creolized" variety), Caribbean, and West African-based creoles. Through this process, all students gain an appreciation for the roots of different sociolinguistic groups, replacing myths about language change and development with authentic sociohistorical information, while African-American students connect with their own sociolinguistic heritage in a positive, empowering way (Cummins, 1986).

As an important by-product of this type of inquiry, we have found that students and teachers begin to develop an authentic respect for the intricacy of language patterning in dialects (including their own and those of other people) regardless of the social status of those dialects. This is a necessary starting point in promoting the truth about dialects.

Teaching Standard English

Introducing students to facts about language variation also sets the stage for teaching Standard English as a second dialect to those who do not already speak it proficiently. Current language instruction typically suggests that there is only one acceptable variety of English and that vernacular dialects should be replaced by Standard English in all social settings. A more realistic appraisal is that Standard English is used in some settings and events that are important to students and that they can benefit from Standard English proficiency in addition to proficiency in the dialect that is appropriate for other settings.

Our ethnographic research in five elementary schools within an urban school system where many students speak AAVE or a European-American vernacular dialect has shown that teachers usually use Standard English for instructional discourse, while students often use the vernacular dialect (Adger, Wolfram, Detwyler, & Harry, in press). However, students' language shifts naturally toward Standard English on certain predictable occasions: when they are producing text and when they are taking on the teacher's or another adult's role. For example, students dictate Standard English sentences for the teacher to write on a story grammar chart, and they shift toward the standard dialect in improvising radio advertisements during a "store" activity in math. Interestingly, teachers do not direct students to speak Standard English in these cases, students make the shift naturally when the communicative situation demands it. The fact that this shifting between dialects rarely draws comments from teachers suggests that teachers and students implicitly agree on domains for the standard and vernacular dialects during instructional discourse.

This patterned dialect shifting in our research site has some implications for teaching Standard English. If teachers in other locations observe that their students demonstrate such sophisticated sociolinguistic knowledge about when Standard English is expected and that they are able to produce Standard English to some extent, teachers can focus on any Standard English forms with which students have difficulty when they have shifted. The goal is to build on students' demonstrated sociolinguistic awareness and their capacity for producing situationally appropriate speech, and not to replace the vernacular dialect in the domains in which it is implicitly considered appropriate in school.

Once students have studied language variation and acquired skills for comparing varieties of a language in a nonjudgmental way, they can use this knowledge in comparing structures of their own vernacular dialects and Standard English. For example, if students sometimes omit the plural marker when they have shifted into Standard English, then a minilesson becomes timely. While vernacular dialects may omit the plural suffice sometimes (e.g., "All the girl want pizza"), Standard English requires it ("All the girls want pizza").

Conclusion

As cultural diversity increases, so does the need to teach students about what diversity entails. To ensure that their knowledge of the world is accurate and to help them avoid adopting the baseless beliefs about differences that prevail in society, teachers must take a proactive role in leading the investigation into culturally and socially based human variation. Because dialects are a form of culturally patterned behavior in which everyone participates, they offer a rich, easily accessed research site for investigating one kind of cultural diversity.

References

Adger, C., Wolfram, W., Detwyler, J., & Harry, B. (In press). Confronting dialect minority issues in special education: Reactive and proactive perspectives. *Proceedings of OBEMLA Research Conference.* Washington, DC: U.S. Government Printing Office.

Alvarez, L., & Kolker, A. (Producers). (1987). *American tongues.* New York: Center for New American Media.

Cummins, J. (1986). Empowering minority students: A framework for intervention. *Harvard Educational Review, 56,* 18–36.

Milroy, J., & Milroy, L. (1985). *Authority in language: Investigating language prescriptivism and standardization.* London: Routledge & Kegan.

Wolfram, W., Detwyler, J., & Adger, C. (1992). *All about dialects: Instructors' manual.* Washington, DC: Center for Applied Linguistics.

A Southern Vowel Pronunciation

In some Southern dialects of English, words such as *pin* and *pen* are pronounced the same. Usually, both words are pronounced as *pin*. This pattern of pronunciation is also found in other words. List A gives words in which the *i* and *e* are pronounced the *same* in these dialects.

List A: I and E Pronounced the Same
1. *tin* and *ten*
2. *kin* and *Ken*
3. *Lin* and *Len*
4. *Windy* and *Wendy*
5. *sinned* and *send*

Although *i* and *e* words in List A are pronounced the *same*, there are other words in which *i* and *e* are pronounced differently. List B gives word pairs in which the vowels are pronounced *differently*.

List B: I and E Pronounced Differently
1. *lit* and *let*
2. *pick* and *peck*
3. *pig* and *peg*
4. *rip* and *rep*
5. *litter* and *letter*

Compare the word pairs in List A with those in List B. Is there a pattern that can explain why the words in List A are pronounced the *same* and why the words in List B are pronounced *differently*? To answer this question, you have to look at the sounds that are next to the vowels. Look at the sounds that come after the vowel. What sound is found next to the vowel in all of the examples given in List A?

Use your knowledge of the pronunciation pattern to pick the word pairs in List C that are pronounced the *same* (S) and those that are pronounced *differently* (D) in this Southern dialect.

List C: Same or Different?
___1. *bit* and *bet*
___2. *pit* and *pet*
___3. *bin* and *Ben*
___4. *Nick* and *neck*
___5. *din* and *den*

How can you tell where *i* and *e* will be pronounced the same and where they will be pronounced differently?

DISCUSSION QUESTIONS AND ACTIVITIES

1. Interview two special educators of adolescent special-needs students. Also, interview two parents of adolescent special-needs students. Compare their perspectives on a number of issues related to special education (for example, placement, inclusive education, IEPs, and parent advocacy).

2. What is inclusion? Discuss the pros and cons of teaching in an inclusion classroom. Discuss how you, as a regular education middle or secondary education teacher, can prepare yourself for teaching in today's diverse schools.

3. An African American sociologist, Adrian Dove, developed the Dove Counterbalance General Intelligence Test (the Chitling Test) in 1968 to demonstrate that

there is a body of information unfamiliar to European Americans. Dove also demonstrated that there is an area of content where African Americans outperform European Americans. Review the Johns Hopkins' study summarized earlier where the issue of rigid scoring procedures is discussed. The issue of content bias and acceptability of "incorrect" but logical answers is relevant to Dove's notion that traditional intelligence tests do not accurately measure the general knowledge of African Americans. Discuss the implications of Dove's results in light of the discussion of assessment bias presented earlier.

For additional information, see the following:

Kaplan, R. M., & Saccuzzo, D. P. (1982). Psychological testing: Principles, applications, and issues. *Monterey, CA: Brooks/Cole, pp. 448–450.*

Dove, A. (1968). Taking the chitling test. Newsweek, 72, 51–52.

4. *IDEA '97 mandates more collaboration between regular and special educators. Discuss the implications of this law for middle and/or secondary schools. Will "mandating" more involvement of regular educators be effective? Why or why not?*

ADDITIONAL READINGS

Anderson, J. P., Floisand, B., Martinez, D., and Robinson, D. P. 1997. Horizonte: Where students come first. *Educational Leadership, 54*(7): 50–52.

Cusher, K., McClelland, A., & Safford, P. 1996. *Human diversity in education: An integrative approach,* 2nd ed. New York: McGraw Hill.

Garcia, S. B., and Malkin, D. H. 1993. Toward defining programs and services for culturally and linguistically diverse learners in special education. *Teaching Exceptional Children, 26*(1): 52–58.

Harry, B. 1992. Restructuring the participation of African-American parents in special education. *Exceptional Children, 59*(2): 123–131.

Harry, B. 1992. Making sense of disability: Low-income, Puerto Rican parents' theory of the problem. *Exceptional Children, 59*(1): 27–40.

Holman, L. J. 1997. Meeting the needs of Hispanic immigrants. *Educational Leadership, 54*(7): 37–38.

Mahony, M. 1997. Small victories in an inclusive classroom. *Educational Leadership, 54*(7): 59–62.

Martin, D., and Cherian, M. 1999. Children, schools, and social class. In V. R. Fu & A. J. Stremmel (eds.), *Affirming diversity through democratic conversations* (pp. 105–123). Upper Saddle River, NJ: Prentice-Hall.

The National Information Center for Children and Youth with Disabilities. URL: http://www.nichcy.org

NICHCY News Digest. 1996, October. *The education of children and youth with special needs: What do the laws say?* Washington, D.C.: Author, pp. 1–15.

Pool, C. R., & Hawk, M. 1997. Hope in Chicago. *Educational Leadership, 54*(7): 33–36.

Sileo, T. W., Sileo, A. P., and Prater, M. A. 1996. Parent and professional partnerships in special education: Multicultural considerations. *Intervention in School and Clinic, 31*(3): 145–153.

Sleeter, C. E., and Grant, C. A. 1999. *Making choices for multicultural education,* 3rd ed. Upper Saddle River, NJ: Prentice-Hall.

REFERENCES

Allen, M. J., and Yen, W. M. 1979. *Introduction to measurement theory.* Belmont, CA: Wadsworth.

Allington, R. L., and McGill-Franzen, A. 1995. Individualized Planning. In M. C. Wang, M. C. Reynolds, & H. J. Walberg (Eds.), *Handbook of special and remedial education,* 2nd ed. New York: Pergamon, pp. 5–36.

Alvermann, D. E., and Phelps, S. F. 1998. *Content reading and literacy: Succeeding in today's diverse classrooms,* 2nd ed. Needham Heights, MA: Allyn & Bacon.

Anderson, R. C. 1984. Role of the reader's schema in comprehension, learning, and memory. In R. C. Anderson, J. Osborn, & R. Tierney (eds.), *Learning to read in American schools: Basal readers and content texts.* Hillsdale, NJ: Erlbaum, pp. 243–258.

Baron, P., and Perron, L.M. 1986. Sex differences in Beck Depression Inventory scores of adolescents. *Journal of Youth and Adolescents, 15*(2): 165–171.

Bloom, B. S., Davis, A., and Hess, R. 1965. *Compensatory education for cultural deprivation.* New York: Holt, Rinehart & Winston.

Brown, C. 1965. *Manchild in the promised land.* New York: New American Library.

Bruininks, R. H., Thurlow, M. L., Lewis, D. R., and Larson, N. W. 1988. Post-school outcomes for students one to eight years after high school. In R. H. Bruininks, D.R. Lewis, & M. L. Thurlow (eds.), *Assessing outcomes, costs and benefits of special education programs.* Minneapolis: University of Minnesota, University Affiliated Programs, pp. 9–111.

Carger, C.L. 1997. Attending to new voices. *Educational Leadership, 54*: 39–43.

Cohen, L. (1990). *Meeting the needs of gifted and talented minority language students.* Reston, VA: ERIC Clearinghouse on Handicapped and Gifted.

Correa, V. I. 1992. Cultural accessibility of services for culturally diverse clients with disabilities and their families. *Rural Special Education Quarterly, 11*: 6–12.

Daisey, P. 1997. Promoting literacy in secondary content area classroom with biography projects. *Journal of Adolescent & Adult Literacy, 40*(4): 270–278.

Day, J. D. 1992. *Population projections of the United States by age, sex, race, and Hispanic origin: 1992–2050.* Washington, D.C.: Bureau of Census.

DBS Corporation. 1986. *Elementary and secondary school civil rights survey, 1984. National Summaries.* ERIC ED 271 543.

DBS Corporation. 1987. *Elementary and secondary school civil rights survey, 1986. National Summaries.* ERIC ED 304 485.

Dev, P. C. 1992. *Multicultural education: What do we need to know to better meet our students' needs?* ERIC ED 387 956.

Ewing, N. 1995. Restructured teacher education for inclusiveness: A dream deferred for African American children. In B. A. Ford, F. E. Obiakor, & J. M. Patton (Eds.), *Effective education of African American exceptional learners.* Austin, TX: Pro-Ed, pp. 189–207).

Fewell, R. C. 1995. Early education for disabled and at-risk children. In M. C. Wang, M. C. Reynolds, & H. J. Walberg (eds.), *Handbook of special and remedial education,* 2nd ed. New York: Pergamon, pp. 37–60.

Ford, B. A. 1992. Multicultural education training for special educators working with African-American youth. *Exceptional Children, 59*: 107–114.

Ford, B. A., Obiakor, F. E., and Patton, J. M. (eds.) 1995. *Effective Education of African American exceptional learners.* Austin, TX: Pro-Ed.

Fossey, R. (1996). School dropout rates: Are we sure they are going down? *Phi Delta Kappan, 78*: 140–144.

Gajar, A., Goodman, L., and McAfee, J. 1993. *Secondary schools and beyond: Transition of individuals with mild disabilities.* New York: Merrill.

Gantner, M. W. 1997. Lessons learned from my students in the Barrio. *Educational Leadership, 54*(7): 44–45.

Gould, S. J. 1981. *The mismeasure of man.* New York: Norton.

Grossman, H. G. 1995. *Special education in a diverse society.* Boston: Allyn & Bacon.

Grossman, H., and Grossman, S. 1994. *Gender Issues in Education.* Boston: Allyn & Bacon.

Hardy, J. B, Welcher, D. W., Mellitis, E. D., and Kagan, J. (1976). Pitfalls in the measurement of intelligence: Are standardized intelligence tests valid for measuring the intellectual potential of urban children? *Journal of Psychology, 94*: 43–51.

Hilliard, A.G. 1989, December. Cultural style in teaching and learning. *The Education Digest, 55*: 21–23.

Individuals with Disabilities Education Act of 1990. Pub. L. No. 101–476, Sections 1400 *et seq.,* 1824 Stat. 1990)

Individuals with Disabilities Education Act of 1991. Pub. L. No. 102–119, Sections 1400 *et seq.,* 1106 Stat. 1991.

Individuals with Disabilities Education Act of 1997. Pub. L. No. 105–17, Sections 1400 *et seq.,* 111 Stat. 1997.

Kaplan, R. M., and Saccuzzo, D. P. 1982. *Psychological testing: Principles, applications, and issues.* Monterey, CA: Brooks/Cole.

Kohler, P. D., and Rusch, F. R. 1995. Secondary educational programs and transition perspectives. In M. C. Wang, M. C. Reynolds, and H. J. Walberg (eds.), *Handbook of special and remedial education,* 2nd ed. New York: Pergamon, pp. 107–130).

Kozol, J. 1991. *Savage inequalities: Children in America's schools.* New York: Crown.

Lipson, M. Y. and Wixson, K. K. (1997). *Assessment and instruction of reading and writing disability,* 2nd ed. New York: Longman.

Malloy, W. W. 1994. *Inclusion: An educational reform strategy for all children.* ERIC ED 379 856.

Markowitz, J. 1996. *Disproportional representation: A critique of state and local strategies.* ERIC ED 392 195.

Marsh, H. W. 1987. *The content specificity of math and English anxieties: The high school and beyond study.* ERIC ED 300 402.

Martinez, H. (Ed.) 1981. *Special education and the Hispanic child, proceedings from the second annual colloquium on Hispanic issues.* ERIC ED 210 404.

Mayhew, J., and Herbert, M. 1995. *Preparing special educators to work with culturally diverse exceptional learners: A rural case study.* ERIC ED 394 772.

Mercer, J. R. 1972, September. *Anticipated achievement: Computerizing the self-fulfilling prophecy.* Paper presented at the meeting of the American Psychological Association: Honolulu, Hawaii.

Mercer, J. R. 1979. In defense of racially and culturally non-discriminatory assessment. *School Psychology Digest, 8*(1): 89–115.

Messick, S. 1984. Assessment in context: Appraising student performance in relation to instructional quality. *Educational Researcher, 13*(3): 3–8.

Minton, H. L., and Schneider, F. W. 1980. *Differential psychology.* Prospect Heights, IL. Waveland.

Moore, E. G. J. 1987. Ethnic social milieu and Black children's intelligence achievement. *Journal of Negro Education, 56*(1): 44–52.

National Council on Disability. 1989. *The education of students with disabilities: Where do we stand?* Washington, D.C.: Author.

Nieto, S. 1992. *Affirming diversity: The sociopolitical context of multicultural education.* New York: Longman.

Obiakor, F. E. 1992. Self-concept of African-American students: An operational model for special education. *Exceptional Children, 59*(2): 160–167.

Ortiz, A. A. 1992. *Assessing appropriate and inappropriate referral systems for LEP special education students.* ERIC ED 349 819.

Popham, W. J. 1995. *Classroom assessment: What teachers need to know.* Boston: Allyn & Bacon.

Pyecha, J. A. 1981. A study of the implementation of Public Law 94–142 for handicapped migrant children. In *Disparities still exist in who gets special education* (GAO Report). Gaithersburg, MD: General Accounting Office, U.S. Government.

Reynolds, M. C., Wang, M. C., and Walberg, H. J. 1987. Restructuring "special" school programs: A position paper. *Policy Studies Review, 2*: 189–212.

Reynolds, W. 1984. Depression in children and adolescents. *School Psychology Review, 13*: 171–182.

Samuda, R. J. 1975. *Psychological testing of American minorities: Issues and consequences.* New York: Harper & Row.

Smith, T. E., Polloway, E. A., Patton, J. R., and Dowdy, C. A. 1995. *Teaching children with special needs in inclusive settings.* Boston: Allyn & Bacon.

Steffensen, M., Joag-Dev, C., and Anderson, R. 1979. A cross-cultural perspective on reading comprehension. *Reading Research Quarterly, 15*: 10–29.

U.S. Comptroller General. 1981. *Disparities still exist in who gets special education* (GAO Report). Gaithersburg, MD: General Accounting Office, U.S. Government.

Vacca, R. T., and Vacca, J. A. L. 1999. *Content area reading,* 6th ed. New York: Addison-Wesley.

Van Tassel-Baska, J., Patton, J., and Prillaman, D. 1989. Disadvantaged gifted learners at-risk for educational neglect. *Focus on Exceptional Children, 22*(3): 1–16.

Villa, R. A., and Thousand, J. S. (eds.) 1995. *Creating an inclusive school.* Alexandria, VA: ASCD.

Wagner, M. 1989, May. *Youth with disabilities during transition: An overview of descriptive findings from the National Longitudinal Transition Study.* Menlo Park, CA: SRI International.

Wagner, M. 1993. *The secondary school programs of students with disabilities.* Menlo Park, CA: SRI International.

Wang, M. C. 1992. *Effective school responses to student diversity: Challenges and prospects.* ERIC ED 360 446.

Williams, B., and Woods, M. 1997. Building on urban learners' experiences. *Educational Leadership,* 54(7): 29–32.

Williams, R. L. 1974. Scientific racism and I.Q.: The silent mugging of the Black community. *Psychology Today,* 7: 32–41.

Willig, A. C. 1986. Special education and the culturally and linguistically different child: An overview of issues and challenges. *Reading, Writing, and Learning Disabilities, 2*: 161–173.

Wynstra, S., and Cummings, C. 1990. *Science anxiety: Relation with gender, year in chemistry class, achievement, and test anxiety.* ERIC ED 331 837.

Yancey, E. 1990. *Increasing minority participation in gifted programs.* Washington, D.C.: Mid-Atlantic Equity Center.

Ysseldyke, J. E. 1987. Classification of handicapped students. In M. C. Wang, M. C. Reynolds, & H. J. Walberg (Eds.), *Handbook of special education: Research and practice: Vol. 1. Learner characteristics and adaptive education.* Oxford, England: Pergamon, pp. 253–271).

Zayas, H. 1981. *Bilingual special education personnel preparation national task oriented seminar.* Washington D.C.: Association for Cross-Cultural Education and Social Studies, Inc.

Chapter Ten

CHALLENGES FOR CHANGE AND DIVERSITY

Verse 29: Tao Te Ching
Do you want to improve the world?
I don't think it can be done.
The world is sacred.
It can't be improved.
If you tamper with it, you'll ruin it.
If you treat it like an object, you'll lose it.

There is a time for being ahead,
a time for being behind;
a time for being in motion,
a time for being at rest;
a time for being vigorous,
a time for being exhausted;
a time for being safe,
a time for being in danger.

The Master sees things as they are,
without trying to control them.
She lets them go their own way,
and resides at the center of the circle.

Tao Te Ching. 1998. Translation by S. Mitchell
Translation © 1988 by Stephen Mitchell. Reprinted by
permission of HarperCollins Publishers, Inc.

A recurring theme throughout our text has been asking future teachers to see themselves as change agents, teachers who know their convictions and accept a role of leadership within their schools and communities. In Nieto's (1996) vision of multicultural education, social change is an integral part of the definition. "Because it uses critical pedagogy as its underlying philosophy and focuses on knowledge, reflection, and action (praxis) as the basis for social change, multicultural education promotes the democratic principles of social justice" (p. 307).

We have encouraged you, as future teachers, (1) to look within to better understand yourselves; (2) to examine and evaluate the influences of race, class, and gender in the classroom; (3) to broaden your understanding of cultural differences and of how you connect with students from different backgrounds; (4) to embrace instructional practices and curricula that set the highest standards for student performance; and (5) to take this instruction into students' homes and communities.

Critics might accuse us of promoting ivory tower solutions that serve lofty ideals but are unworkable in reality; however, we believe educators need a vision for change while they work in the trenches. We have tried to open your minds to new ideas, hoping that you would weigh our suggestions and take the best for your classrooms. Our suggestions are consistent with culturally relevant pedagogy and multicultural education. These questions logically follow: Will implementing these practices constitute an act of social change? If so, how do we structure that change to be most effective? How do we serve as catalysts who are transformed, rather than destroyed, in the process? How do we maintain lofty ideals, live in the real world, *and* achieve change?

A quick interpretation of verse 29 from the *Tao Te Ching* might imply that we can do nothing; orchestrating change is not within our power. On the other hand, we believe its paradoxical message of action and nonaction relates to our roles as change agents. We are called to be leaders as well as team players, to work within the school culture and to change the school culture, to take risks but get good teaching evaluations, to be silent but speak up, to be committed but take "time to smell the roses." The *Tao Te Ching* cautions us that although we can participate fully in life, we cannot control it. As change agents, our task is not to control the world, but to do right by it. For aspiring change agents, balance becomes the challenge.

In this chapter, we look at the issue of educational reform and change. Several national reports on education have been released during the last fifteen years. In 1983, the Reagan-appointed National Commission on Excellence in Education published *A Nation at Risk,* a document stressing the "rising tide of mediocrity" in our schools (Tozer, Violas, & Senese, p. 368). This report was followed by President Bush's *America 2000: An Education Strategy,* in which national educational goals, unified curriculum, and rigorous standards were recommended along with local control over implementation. *What Matters Most: Teaching for America's Future* was released in 1996, with its emphasis on teacher excellence making a difference. Together, these reports provide a broad context in which teachers are working and within which they will advocate for change. In the next section, we briefly outline some of the major educational reform themes of the past two decades. Then, we consider the day-to-day reality of beginning teachers, some of the challenges/obstacles to change they face, and their potential role as change agents. We conclude with a review of "first steps" for becoming change agents that were presented in the Introduction, "Teaching in the 21st Century—Becoming a Change Agent" and consider possible "next steps." You might want to return to the Introduction and reread that before going on.

REFORM THEMES

Two major educational reform themes are strengthening standards for teacher certification and mandating continued teacher professional development. In response to national reports, teacher preparation programs have raised standards for admittance into their programs—most programs now require students to have a liberal arts or science major in addition to their education major. In addition, grade-point requirements for student teaching have been raised, and most states have mandated teacher tests in basic skills and subject-matter content. Individuals obtain an initial certification and then, with continued course work, typically a masters degree, they are granted advanced or standard certification. Lifetime certification is increasingly rare; teachers must continue their professional development to be re-certified. (In some states, politicians are even interested in having veteran teachers pass reading, writing, and subject matter tests to keep their jobs.)

Another area of reform focuses on making schools and teachers more accountable for students' academic achievement. Many states have developed curriculum frameworks that inform teachers' goals for student learning and guide the content of what and when material is taught. Given that the inclusion or omission of specific content makes powerful statements about what a society values, several educational stakeholders, including multiculturalists, have voiced concern over a statewide or national curriculum.

To hold schools accountable, states have introduced new measures of assessing student learning with follow-up "report cards" and potential sanctions for underperforming schools and districts. The trend is to develop assessment measures that include more open-ended response items and test students' critical thinking and problem-solving skills. Critics are concerned that these standardized tests too heavily influence what and how teachers teach; advocates say that as long as there is agreement about what should be taught, teaching to the test is a good thing.

The theme of school choice includes charter schools, school vouchers, magnet schools, and home schooling. In general, school vouchers offer parents a sum of money to apply to a school of their choice—most often another public school. The marketplace assumption behind this approach is that vouchers will create competition among schools and consequently improve educational quality. Opponents believe that vouchers draw monies away from schools already in financial distress and "choice systems are political processes that preserve the social reproduction function of schools" (Parish & Aquila, 1996,

p. 301). Magnet schools are organized around different themes such as visual and performing arts, technology, or business and are open to students from several school districts. These schools are typically middle and secondary schools. Some magnet schools are developed to help de-segregate schools, and the trend has been to make magnet schools less elite and more accessible to students of all abilities and different socioeconomic status.

Charter schools receive grants from state boards of education or local school boards. State monies are given to groups of parents, teachers, or community organizations to set up schools, frequently with specialized curriculum such as an Afrocentric curriculum or a sports academy. Although these schools do not have to adhere to many of the rules and regulations mandated by school boards, they are accountable for specific academic results. Students apply to a charter school and are selected by lottery. Charter schools have been criticized by teachers' unions because teachers are not required to have certification and, in effect, schools receive state funds to operate as private schools.

Home schooling is on the rise with an estimated 200,000 to 300,000 students receiving instruction at home (McNergney & Herbert, 1995, p. 111). Parents are required to demonstrate compliance with a state-approved curriculum and must meet standards for instructional time and achievement on standardized tests. Some states require the home school instructor to be certified; however, the trend is toward greater flexibility. Some school districts allow students to come to the school to participate in sports and extra curricular activities. The reasons for home schooling tend to be ideological or religious with most home schooled students coming from White, middle-class, European-American families.

The School-to-Work Opportunities Act of 1994 targets those often referred to as "the 'forgotten half' of American youth—the more than 50 percent of high school students who do not go on to college and whose life chances have been diminished by changes in the American economy" (Kantor, 1995, p. 215). These programs range from job shadowing opportunities, to ongoing mentoring relationships, to paid apprenticeships (that is, on-the-job training for the last two years of high school). Proponents of school-to-work programs are persuaded by the links students can make between what they are learning and future occupations, whereas opponents are concerned about creating a two-tiered educational system where large numbers of working class students and students of color are tracked into dead-end jobs.

Middle and high school teachers need to think seriously about school-to-work initiatives. For example, what does the research show about follow-up employment of students and particularly students of color? Teachers can find themselves caught up in wanting to support the future employment opportunities of their students while feeling uneasy about the overall equity of these programs. This is a reform effort in which teachers are directly involved; therefore, they need to be mindful of its ramifications. (See Table 10–1, The Pros and Cons of School to Work.)

A final reform effort encompasses empowerment of a variety of stakeholders: teachers, principals, parents, and students. With site-based management,

Table 10-1 The Pros and Cons of School to Work

Pros:
- Improves skills of future workers.
- Links instruction with authentic experiences of future occupations.
- Increases students' motivation and maturation.
- Improves job opportunities for students of color, providing a much needed system of networking that appears to be lacking in communities of color.

Cons:
- Creates a two-tier system within the school leading to *de facto* tracking of students of color and students of lower socioeconomic status.
- Ignores underlying reality of barriers such as racism or sexism that ultimately keep students at poorly paid entry-level positions. This is more problematic for students of color than for Whites.
- Limits students' opportunities to develop broader problem solving and higher order critical thinking skills.

principals have greater control over their schools (that is, the hiring and firing of teachers, implementing curriculum initiatives). They also have greater accountability and can be fired if their schools do not perform satisfactorily on state mandated exams. Teacher empowerment gives teachers a greater voice in school decisions, the induction of new teachers, and decisions about content and methods of instruction; however, state requirements for a standard curriculum and achievement levels of students on state tests mitigate this empowerment.

School districts have created professional development opportunities for their teachers to meet the new regulations for re-certification. In addition, schools have responded to national reports stressing the need for greater collaboration between public schools and institutions of higher education. These collaborations are structured around collegiality where both teachers and college faculty are recognized as experts working together democratically to improve teacher preparation, professional development, and student instruction. Professional development schools are often the result of such collaboration. Pre-service students are welcomed into a school to observe and teach; school faculty members develop mentoring expertise and join with education faculty to offer on-site professional development courses.

The establishment of school improvement committees encourages parents, business leaders, and students to become involved in the school governing process. The success of these committees varies according to the school's commitment and the value school administrators and teachers place on this form of input.

Obviously, educational reforms are not all created equally, and they bring a variety of issues and concerns for multicultural educators who seek meaningful, democratic change. One observation from the literature is that "systemic reform and effective leadership efforts are rooted in middle-class, Eurocentric cultural frames of reference and organizational structures. A Eurocentric perspective omits alternative frames of reference, experiences, and *funds of knowledge* that many students bring to the educational process" (McCullough, Lavadenz, & Martin 1996, p. 47). As the authors of this text, we admit a bias toward reforms that clearly come from a social justice paradigm. Reforms must be critiqued for who gets included, and who does not. Who has access to resources and opportunities? Whose voices are allowed to contribute? When data is collected, whose worldview frames the research questions? Who is in charge of creating information, and who controls its flow? And does the reform perpetuate existing inequities by merely disguising them in a new practice?

CHALLENGES AND OBSTACLES TO CHANGE

Beginning high school or middle school teachers do more than walk into their classrooms and meet their students on the first day of school. They step into a flowing river where no two days are the same—developing adolescents guarantee that. However, the river has an undertow—strong political, social, economic, and bureaucratic forces define much of a teacher's daily life: Some educational reforms drain teachers' time and energy; a scarcity of funds leads to larger class sizes and a reduction in resources; a variety of social problems affects student academic achievement; and demands for great accountability for both students and teachers take their toll in data collection and record keeping. Many teacher tasks detract from instructional time and create mounds of paper. High stakes accountability—including assignments, attendance, and assessment—adds its own stress.

Your first year of teaching can feel more like a cold shower than a wade in that river. Your worst fears are reinforced in the frequent venting sessions in the teachers' lounge. In the face of reality, being a multiculturalist or a change agent seems like a noble, but fading, goal of your last education methods course.

"Consider the dilemma of a high school teacher who wants to teach creatively. Her class sizes range from twenty-six to thirty-three students and her total student load is between 130 and 170. She may be able to memorize all her students' names, but she won't have the time to get an in-depth understanding of their individual strengths and weaknesses. Nor will she have the time to implement the kind of labor-intensive activities and assessment essential to good teaching. Against her idealistic aspirations, she will be drawn by the practical constraints of her situation into the mass-production techniques of overreliance on the textbook and standardized tests" (Levine, 1995, p. 59).

The tension between what you learn in your education courses and day-to-day teaching reality is an integral part of professional teacher training even when your professors make every effort to bring the real world into your classroom. Education is not the only profession where practitioners speak of the gap between the learning and its application. For example, learning the proper procedures for stitching up open wounds of a crash victim is not a substitute for doing it while the patient struggles in pain. Mock court scenes do not compare with a lawyer's first case. Veteran teachers, battling the external forces we've discussed, justifiably seek to warn new teachers of what is in store. As educators working in teacher education programs at the college level, we also want to prepare future teachers for reality; *and,* we want to give them the tools to address that reality. Becoming a change agent means understanding the dynamics that surround your circumstances (see Datnow in the Introduction), recognizing the challenges inherent in this complex social-political-economic institution and becoming active. It is a process whose products will take time to bear fruit. Our hope is that you move forward, despite the challenges. Being aware of and understanding the challenges is a first step to maintaining activism.

We have already described some of the external and institutional challenges teachers face. You might also recall the words from *School Teacher Blues* in Chapter Five. In addition, resistance can come from you, your colleagues, and your students. We all know how to talk the language of change; willingly venturing out of our comfort zone—whether it is really comfortable or not—is harder.

Part of your job as a new teacher is to fit into the existing school culture. It is human to want to belong. Where faculty and administrators have created a climate open to change and where collaboration is encouraged, a first-year teacher may be expected to speak up. In fact, this ability might have been part of the reason she was hired. On the other hand, first-year teachers, entering schools where teachers feel isolated, don't share common goals for students, and have experienced considerable frustration in effecting change in the past, will find more pressure to conform to the status quo. Colleagues have a personal stake in convincing you that conditions aren't as bad as you think or as bad as they are elsewhere. Your suggestions for trying something new will be countered with "We've already tried that and it didn't work."

Resistance to change can come from a variety of sources—teachers, students, principals, school boards, and parents. Alfie Kohn (1998) has written extensively about how parents—predominantly White, middle-class parents—of academically successful students block educational reforms intended to raise the academic performance of poor students, students of color, and academically average students. Most affluent parents send a message that creating a fairer system is unacceptable; they want their children to be "'winners." This message "reverberates through the offices of administrators and effectively discourages meaningful change" (p. 571). Fried (1998) extends Kohn's argument to incorporate the systemic aspects of the problem and feels that high schools and colleges must also be held accountable. "What enables certain parents to intervene in the public schools on behalf of their children? . . . What does it take for school leaders to create and protect initiatives that 'raise the floor' for low-achieving students without 'lowering the ceiling' for high achievers?" (p. 266).

Students offer their own unique brand of resistance. They may not like the way things are, but they have developed skills to negotiate the system. They want learning to be exciting, but they don't want it to interfere with their social lives. They want to be included in making plans, but don't want to be accountable for the follow-through. They want good grades, but would rather not have to work for them. One of us recalls a high school student saying "If you keep on giving me these bad grades, you're going to ruin my self-esteem." Students won't necessarily stop by after class and thank you for raising your expectations, much like the way you didn't thank your parents for imposing any restrictions on you when you were a teenager.

Some scholars express greater concern about students' intrinsic motivation: "Whether it's high standards or the basics, whether it's in suburban schools or urban schools, whether parents choose the schools or not, today's young people are less motivated to learn. An increasingly serious side effect of our consumer-driven, high-tech age is the addiction of many students to passive consumption and instant gratification. Like an atrophied muscle, students' capacity for concentration has been diminished by this addiction to the no-effort, multimedia drug. Many students are truly lost in cyberspace, caught half-way between television fantasies of fame and fortune and the netherworld of Nintendo" (Wagner, 1996, p. 145).

STEPPING FORWARD: BEING A CHANGE AGENT

Given this picture of reality, how can teachers mount the institutional, collegial, and personal obstacles to initiate change? We know that there are no simple, quick, or immediate action plans that ensure success, but it is helpful to know something about how institutions are changed and how individuals contribute to that process. John P. Kotter, a well-known professor at the Harvard Business School, has written comprehensively in *Leading Change* (1996) about how to facilitate organizational change. It might be ironic that as advocates of educational restructuring, we look for guidance from the corporate sector; however, the process of producing lasting change in policies, procedures, and culture is remarkably similar. In addition, we draw on ideas from *The Courage to Teach* by Parker Palmer (1998) who outlines an individual path to effecting change. The following are a synthesis of the two perspectives:

- *Make change a priority.* Palmer would describe this as making a decision "to live divided no more." For example, a teacher decides that in addition to teaching standard English, a student's home language should be validated. She believes that this change is important for the integrity and viability of the institution and its students. Remember the goal is not to destroy the institution; after all, it is our enduring belief in the value of educational institutions that motivates us to want to change them. But change will not happen without effort.

- *Build coalitions.* Both Kotter and Palmer recognize the need to find support within the organizations. Go-it-alone leaders will soon burn out and their actions can be easily marginalized. Their practices might even be supported on a limited basis (for example, "Isn't it nice that Mr. Freeman lets students speak Spanish during group work."). Colleagues or administrators offer partial support for an innovative practice, although institutional practices remain intact.

You can form coalitions within or across departments, with parents, students, community leaders, and administrators—wherever mutual understandings and common ground can be forged and where individual ideas can be shared and understood. The purpose of coalition-forming is not to reinforce frustration or negativity, but to reaffirm purpose and keep focussed on the benefits of the change. If you hope for systemic change, then you need a solidified effort. Kotter points out the need for credible and powerful advocates within the group. Although teachers are often credible, they don't see themselves as powerful advocates; however, the hierarchical relationships in corporations and lines of authority aren't quite the same in public schools. In the schools, a small group of respected teachers can more easily serve as powerful advocates for change.

- *Go public (Palmer) and communicate the vision (Kotter).* Let's take an example: A group comprising two teachers, a parent, and a local Mexican businessman have been meeting and discussing the need for second-language affirmation within the school. They've worked to develop a set of specific events that they believe will help to educate the school at-large of the benefits of being bilingual. They approach the school's parent-teacher organization with a request to support a Spanish poetry writing contest—the winner to be given a gift certificate to a local restaurant. The group proclaims the event a success only to find out that a number of disgruntled parents feel as though their youngsters have been excluded.

  Having gone public the group now receives valuable feedback that helps them "check and correct its values" (Palmer, 1998, p. 175). "As a movement goes public, the identity and integrity of its participants are tested against the great diversity of values and visions at work in the public arena. We must stay close to our own integrity in this complex field of forces, where we can easily lose our way. But we must also risk opening ourselves to conflicting influences, for in that way both the movement and our integrity can grow" (p. 179).

- *Set short-term and long-term goals.* Small wins are important. We need to realize that change takes time and small victories should be recognized and celebrated. In our scenario, our coalition members naïvely thought that a series of events highlighting the Spanish language would result in everyone recognizing its value. They weren't prepared for the opposition and felt defeated. In reality, three small victories came out of this event. One, the students who participated in the event saw a marginalized culture and language affirmed; two, in getting support from the parent-teacher organization, the group expanded its number of allies; and, three, the disgruntled parents offered the coalition an opportunity to hold a follow-up meeting with parents and administrators on issues surrounding bilingualism.

- *Don't be overwhelmed.* Change takes time, and resistance to change is an expected reaction. If institutions changed by themselves, there would be no need to go further. Some claim that change takes place *only* in the presence of opposition. At first, our second-language coalition members were disheartened; they felt misunderstood, unappreciated, and not a little bit self-righteous. Committed to their vision, however, they were able to step back, reflect and, understanding the nature of change, begin again.

- ***Make new changes a way of life.*** Kotter refers to this as "anchoring changes in the culture." New changes must become an integral and sustained part of the way things are done. Actions taken cannot be one-time deals. Palmer suggests that one way you anchor change is by making sure there are alternative rewards for those participating in change.

Our second-language coalition must consider its steps as an expansion of "how things operate around here. This is the way things are. We are going to be a school that respects and affirms second languages. We and the changes are here to stay." For rewards, change agents might have to look at intrinsic factors—the knowledge that they are learning about themselves and are part of a supportive community.

It is easy to be overwhelmed by the magnitude of changes we hope to make, especially if our plans are not consistent with current educational practices, even if school rhetoric is. (See Sleeter's discussion of multicultural education as a social movement in the readings section at the end of this chapter.) Recognizing the complexity of educational problems facing us and their inextricable links to sociopolitical and economic forces, we understandably wonder what one individual or a group of individuals can accomplish. As teachers in our classrooms with connections to our academic departments, to the school at-large, to the local district, the state, the nation and the world, we see complex problems situated in complex organizational systems. Orchestrating change seems difficult, and outcomes seem unpredictable. *System dynamics*[1]— the analysis of the behavior of systems—can offer change agents another tool in planning and understanding the nature of change. "System dynamics is a method for studying the world around us. Unlike other scientists, who study the world by breaking it up into smaller and smaller pieces, system dynamicists look at things as a whole. The central concept to system dynamics is understanding how all the objects in a system interact with one another. A system can be anything from a steam engine, to a bank account, to a basketball team. . . . What system dynamics attempts to do is understand the basic structure of a system, and thus understand the behavior it can produce. Many of these systems and problems which are analyzed can be built as models on a computer" (Systems Dynamics, 1999).

Forrester makes a distinction between systems thinking and system dynamics: Systems thinking means thinking about systems whereas system dynamics involves working through some of the computer models. Most applications of systems thinking have been in models of economic behavior,

---

[1] J. Forrester has been a pioneer in this field and founded the System Dynamics Group at the Sloan School at the Massachusetts Institute of Technology in 1956.

corporate management education, and K–12 curricula development (for example, the System Dynamics in Education Project—SDEP). We aren't aware of any computer models that attempt to explain the consequences of changes within educational institutions (system dynamics); however, we feel that change agents can benefit from understanding the conceptual framework of systems thinking. (See the chapter reading, "System Dynamics and Learner-Centered Learning in Kindergarten through 12th Grade Education" by Jay W. Forrester for an example of how system dynamics is being used in the content areas.) Understanding the theory helps to place proposals for change within a larger dynamic context. The theory also explains some of the discouraging outcomes of planned change (that is, years of work resulting in little improvement, or good solutions making matters worse).

Concluding Thoughts

We are reminded of our interpretation of the *Tao Te Ching* verse quoted at the beginning of this chapter: The *Tao Te Ching* cautions us that although we can participate fully in life, we cannot control it. As change agents, our task is to do right by it. Perhaps the notion that we *could* control our world is indicative of being human—or of being trained in human Western thought! Nevertheless, we see problems and want to solve them; we see potential in our students and want them to achieve; we see schools that need to change and want to lead the way. Tatum (1997) speaks compellingly of a sphere of influence. "While many people experience themselves as powerless, everyone has some sphere of influence in which they can work for change, even if it is just in their own personal network of family and friends" (p. 204) and co-workers (our addition). It is also important to value collective incremental changes that foster greater and greater change and consider the complex organizational systems in which we live and work.

Moving in the right direction is a worthy goal. As "Moms" Mabley, a famous Black comedienne always says, "If you always do what you always did, you will always get what you always got." What specific actions you take in your role might change over time; much will depend on your ability to maintain a commitment and strength for the long haul. There is wisdom in moving fast slowly.

> What is rooted is easy to nourish.
> What is recent is easy to correct.
> What is brittle is easy to break.
> What is small is easy to scatter.
>
> Prevent trouble before it arises.
> Put things in order before they exist.
> The giant pine tree
> Grows from a tiny sprout.
> The journey of a thousand miles
> Starts from beneath your feet.
>
> *Tao Te Ching (verse 64)*
> Translation © 1988 by Stephen Mitchell. Reprinted by permission of HarperCollins Publishers, Inc.

READINGS

In the first reading, "Why Teachers Must Become Change Agents," Michael G. Fullan argues that moral purpose and change agentry must be linked, if we hope to bring about true teacher professionalism: "Moral purpose keeps teachers close to the needs of children and youth; change agentry causes them to develop better strategies for accomplishing their moral goals." He examines present teacher education programs and calls on teachers to be sure they practice what they preach. Although Fullan's writing links change with educational reform in general, Sleeter's "Multicultural Education as Social Movement" links change with the goals of multicultural education. Remember that we discussed Sleeter and Grant's (1998) five approaches to multicultural education in Chapter One. In this reading, Sleeter "examines four different metaphors for conceptualizing the form multicultural education often takes" and discusses the merits of multicultural education as a social movement. Multicultural education as a social movement is predicated on the teacher as change agent who recognizes "vested interests in unequal relations of power." The final reading, by Jay W. Forrester, describes "System Dynamics and Learner-Centered Learning in Kindergarten Through 12th Grade Education"—an innovative approach to learning that develops the abilities of students to synthesize information, to develop "a framework for giving cohesion, meaning, and motivation to education at all levels from kindergarten upward." The approach uses computer modeling and a learner-centered teaching pedagogy that Forrester views as a "new kind of education." The reading is valuable in two ways: One, we read about a relatively new innovation in teaching, and, two, we learn more about how models for change are explained in system dynamics. Would computer models adapted to address educational issues (that is, areas of change) be useful to change agents?

READING 1

Why Teachers Must Become Change Agents

Michael G. Fullan

Teaching at its core is a moral profession. Scratch a good teacher and you will find a moral purpose. At the Faculty of Education, University of Toronto, we recently examined why people enter the teaching profession (Stiegelbauer 1992). In a random sample of 20 percent of 1,100 student teachers, the most frequently mentioned theme was "to make a difference in the lives of students." Of course, such statements cannot be taken at face value because people

---

Reprinted by permission of the publisher from *Eduational Leadership,* March 1993, vol. 50, no. 6, pp. 12–17.

have a variety of motives for becoming teachers. Nonetheless, there is a strong kernel of truth to this conclusion.

What happens in teacher preparation, the early years of teaching, and throughout the career, however, is another story. Those with a clear sense of moral purpose often become disheartened, and those with a limited sense of purpose are never called upon to demonstrate their commitment. In an extensive study of teacher burnout, Farber (1991) identifies the devastating effects of the growing "sense of inconsequentiality" that often accompanies the teacher's career. Many teachers, says Farber, begin their careers "with a sense that their work is socially meaningful and will yield great personal satisfactions." This sense dissipates, however, as "the inevitable difficulties of teaching . . . interact with personal issues and vulnerabilities, as well as social pressure and values, to engender a sense of frustration and force a reassessment of the possibilities of the job and the investment one wants to make in it" (1991, p. 36).

A Natural Alliance

Certainly calls for reestablishing the moral foundation of teaching are warranted, but increased commitment at the one-to-one and classroom levels alone is a recipe for moral martyrdom. To have any chance of making teaching a noble and effective profession—and this is my theme here—teachers must combine the mantle of moral purpose with the skills of change agentry.

Moral purpose and change agentry, at first glance, appear to be strange bedfellows. On closer examination they are natural allies (Fullan 1993). Stated more directly, moral purpose—or making a difference—concerns bringing about improvements. It is, in other words, a *change theme*. In addition to the need to make moral purpose more explicit, educators need the tools to engage in change productively. Moral purpose keeps teachers close to the needs of children and youth; change agentry causes them to develop better strategies for accomplishing their moral goals.

Those skilled in change appreciate its volatile character, and they explicitly seek ideas for coping with and influencing change toward some desired ends. I see four core capacities for building greater change capacity: personal vision-building, inquiry, mastery, and collaboration (see Senge 1990 and Fullan 1993). Each of these has its institutional counterpart: shared vision-building; organizational structures, norms, and practices of inquiry; the development of increased repertoires of skills and know-how among organizational members; and collaborative work cultures.

But we are facing a huge dilemma. On the one hand, schools are expected to engage in continuous renewal, and change expectations are constantly swirling around them. On the other hand, the way teachers are trained, the way schools are organized, the way the educational hierarchy operates, and the way political decision makers treat educators results in a system that is more likely to retain the status quo. One way out of this quandary is to make explicit the goals and skills of change agentry. To break the impasse, we need a new conception of teacher professionalism that integrates moral purpose and change agentry, one that works simultaneously on individual and institutional development. One cannot wait for the other.

Personal Vision-Building

Working on personal visions means examining and re-examining why we came into teaching. Asking "What difference am I trying to make personally?" is a good place to start.

For most of us, the reasons are there, but possibly buried. For the beginning teacher, they may be underdeveloped. It is time to make them front and center. Block emphasizes that "creating a vision forces us to take a stand for a preferred future" (1987, p. 102). To articulate our vision of the future "is to come out of the closet with our doubts about the organization and the way it operates" (p. 105).

Personal vision comes from within. It gives meaning to work, and it exists independently of the organization or group we happen to be in. Once it gets going, it is not as private as it sounds. Especially in moral occupations like teaching, the more one takes the risk to express personal purpose; the more kindred spirits one will find. Paradoxically, personal purpose is the route to organizational change. When it is diminished, we see in its place group-think and a continual stream of fragmented, surface changes acquired uncritically and easily discarded.

Inquiry

All four capacities of change are intimately interrelated and mutually reinforcing. The second one—inquiry—indicates that formation and enactment of personal purpose are not static matters but, rather, a perennial quest. Pascale (1990) captures this precisely: "The essential activity for keeping our paradigm current is persistent questioning. I will use the term *inquiry*. Inquiry is the engine of vitality and self-renewal" (p. 14, emphasis in original).

Inquiry is necessary for forming and reforming personal purpose. While the latter comes from within, it must be fueled by information and ideas in the environment. Inquiry means internalizing norms, habits, and techniques for continuous learning. For the beginner, learning is critical because of its formative timing. Lifelong learning is essential because in complex, ever-changing societies mental maps "cease to fit the territory" (Pascale 1990, p. 13). Teachers as change agents are career-long learners, without which they would not be able to stimulate students to be continuous learners.

Mastery

Mastery is a third crucial ingredient. People *behave* their way into new visions and ideas, not just think their way into them. Mastery is obviously necessary for effectiveness, but it is also a means for achieving deeper understanding. New mind-sets arise from mastery as much as the reverse.

It has long been known that expertise is central to successful change, so it is surprising how little attention we pay to it beyond one-shot workshops and disconnected training. Mastery involves strong initial teacher education and career-long staff development, but when we place it in the perspective of comprehensive change, it is much more than this. Beyond exposure to new ideas, we have to know where they fit, and we have to become skilled in them, not just like them.

To be effective at change, mastery is essential both in relation to specific innovations and as a personal habit.

Collaboration

There is a ceiling effect to how much we can learn if we keep to ourselves (Fullan and Hargreaves 1991). The ability to collaborate on both a small- and large-scale is becoming one of the core requisites of postmodern society. Personal strength, as long as it is open-minded (that is, inquiry-oriented), goes hand-in-hand with effective collaboration—in fact, without personal strength collaboration will be more form than content. Personal and group mastery thrive on each other in learning organizations.

In sum, the moral purpose of teaching must be reconceptualized as a change theme. Moral purpose without change agentry is martyrdom; change agentry without moral purpose is change for the sake of change. In combination, not only are they effective in getting things done, but they are good at getting the *right* things done. The implications for teacher education and for redesigning schools are profound.

Society's Missed Opportunity

Despite the rhetoric about teacher education today, there does not seem to be a real belief that investing in teacher education will yield results. With all the problems demanding immediate solution, it is easy to overlook a preventive strategy that would take several years to have an impact.

Currently, teacher education—from initial preparation throughout the career—is not geared toward continuous learning. Teacher education has the honor of being the worst problem and the best solution in education. The absence of a strong publicly stated knowledge base allows the misconception to continue that any smart person can teach. After visiting 14 colleges of education across the U.S., Kramer (1992) concludes:

> Everything [a person] needs to know about how to teach could be learned by intelligent people in a single summer of well-planned instruction (p. 24).

In a twisted way, there is some truth to this observation. It is true in the sense that many people did and still do, take such minimal instruction and manage to have a career in teaching. It is true also that some people with a strong summer program would end up knowing as much or more as others who take a weak yearlong program. In her journey, Kramer found plenty of examples of moral purpose—caring people, committed to social equality. What she found wanting was an emphasis on knowledge and understanding. Caring and competence are of course not mutually exclusive (indeed this is the point), but they can seem that way when the knowledge base is so poorly formulated.

Teacher education institutions themselves must take responsibility for their current reputation as laggards rather than leaders of educational reform.

I will not take up the critical area of recruitment and selection in the profession (for the best discussion, see Schlechty 1990, chapter 1). In many ways an "if you build it, they will come" strategy is called for. It is self-defeating to seek candidates who turn out to be better than the programs they enter. What is needed is a combination of selection criteria that focus on academics as well as experience (related, for example, to moral purpose), sponsorship for under-represented groups, and a damn good program.

Teacher educators like other would-be change agents must take some initiative themselves. Examples are now happening on several fronts. At the University of Toronto, we embarked on a major reform effort in 1988. With a faculty of some 90 staff and 1,100 full-time students in a one-year post-baccalaureate teacher certification program, we piloted a number of field-based options in partnerships with school systems (see University of Toronto, *Making a Difference* Video, 1992a). In 1991 I prepared a paper for our strategic planning committee, taking as a starting point the following premise: *Faculties of Education should not advocate things for teachers or schools that they are not capable of practicing themselves.* Using a hypothetical "best faculty of education in the country" metaphor, I suggested that such a faculty would:

1. commit itself to producing teachers who are agents of educational and social improvement,
2. commit itself to continuous improvement through program innovation and evaluation,
3. value and practice exemplary teaching,
4. engage in constant inquiry,
5. model and develop lifelong learning among staff and students,
6. model and develop collaboration among staff and students,
7. be respected and engaged as a vital part of the university as a whole,
8. form partnerships with schools and other agencies,
9. be visible and valued internationally in a way that contributes locally and globally,
10. work collaboratively to build regional, national, and international networks (Fullan 1991).

To illustrate, consider items 3 and 6. It would seem self-evident that faculties of education would stand for exemplary teaching among their own staff. Faculties of education have some excellent (and poor) teachers, but I would venture to say that hardly any have effective *institutional* mechanisms for improving their own teaching. Regarding item 6, many faculties of education advocate collaborative work cultures for schools, and some participate in professional development schools. This leads to two embarrassing questions. First, to what extent are teacher preparation programs designed so that student teachers deliberately develop and practice the habits and skills of collaboration? Even more embarrassing, to what extent do university professors (arts and science, as well as education) value and practice collaboration in their own teaching and scholarship?

Key Images for Teacher Preparation

With such guiding principles, and some experience with them through our pilot projects, we at the University of Toronto have recently begun redesigning the entire teacher preparation program. Our Restructuring Committee has proposed that:

> Every teacher should be knowledgeable about, committed to, and skilled in:
> 1. working with *all* students in an equitable, effective, and caring manner by respecting diversity in relation to ethnicity, race, gender, and special needs of each learner;
> 2. being active learners who continuously seek, assess, apply, and communicate knowledge as reflective practitioners throughout their careers;
> 3. developing and applying knowledge of curriculum, instruction, principles of learning, and evaluation needed to implement and monitor effective and evolving programs for all learners;
> 4. initiating, valuing, and practicing collaboration and partnerships with students, colleagues, parents, community, government, and social and business agencies;
> 5. appreciating and practicing the principles, ethics, and legal responsibilities of teaching as a profession;
> 6. developing a personal philosophy of teaching which is informed by and contributes to the organizational, community, societal, and global contexts of education (University of Toronto, B.Ed. Restructuring Committee, 1992b).

We are now developing the actual program, curriculum, and teaching designs. Everything we know about the complexities of change applies in spades to the reform of higher education institutions. Nonetheless, after four years, we have made good progress and look forward to the next four years as the ones when more comprehensive and systematic reform will be put into place (see also Goodlad 1991, Howey 1992, and the third report of the Holmes Group, forthcoming).

To summarize: Faculties of education must redesign their programs to focus directly on developing the beginner's knowledge base for effective teaching *and* the knowledge base for changing the conditions that affect teaching. Sarason puts it this way: "Is it asking too much of preparatory programs to prepare their students for a 'real world' which they must understand *and seek to change* if as persons and professionals they are to grow, not only to survive" (in press, p. 252, my emphasis). Goodlad (1991) asks a similar question: "Are a large percentage of these educators thoroughly grounded in the knowledge and skills required to bring about meaningful change?" (p. 4). The new standard for the future is that every teacher must strive to become effective at managing change.

Redesigning Schools

One of the main reasons that restructuring has failed so far is that there is no underlying conception that grounds what would happen within new structures. Restructuring has caused changes in participation, in governance, and in other formal aspects of the organization, but in the majority of cases, it has not affected the teaching-learning core and professional culture (Berends 1992, Fullan 1993). *To restructure is not to reculture.*

The professional teacher, to be effective, must become a career-long learner of more sophisticated pedagogies and technologies and be able to form and perform productive collaborations with colleagues, parents, community agencies, businesses, and others. The teacher of the future, in other words, must be equally at home in the classroom and in working with others to bring about continuous improvements.

I do not have the space to elaborate—indeed many of the details have not been worked out. The general directions, however, are clear. In terms of pedagogy, the works of Gardner (1991) and Sizer (1992)—in developing approaches to teaching for understanding—exemplify the kinds of knowledge and skills that teachers must develop and enlarge upon throughout their careers.

Beyond better pedagogy, the teacher of the future must actively improve the conditions for learning in his or her immediate environments. Put one way, teachers will never improve learning in the classroom (or whatever the direct learning environment) unless they also help improve conditions that surround the classroom. Andy Hargreaves and I developed 12 guidelines for action consistent with this new conception of "interactive professionalism":

1. locate, listen to, and articulate your inner voice;
2. practice reflection in action, on action, and about action;
3. develop a risk-taking mentality;
4. trust processes as well as people;
5. appreciate the total person in working with others;
6. commit to working with colleagues;
7. seek variety and avoid balkanization;
8. redefine your role to extend beyond the classroom;
9. balance work and life;
10. push and support principals and other administrators to develop interactive professionalism;
11. commit to continuous improvement and perpetual learning;
12. monitor and strengthen the connection between your development and students' development (Fullan and Hargreaves 1991).

We also developed eight guidelines for principals that focus their energies on reculturing the school toward greater interactive professionalism to make a difference in the educational lives of students. However, as important as principals can be, they are a diversion (and perhaps a liability) as far as new conceptions of the professional teacher are concerned. In a real sense, what gives the contemporary principalship inflated importance is the absence of leadership opportunities on the part of teachers (Fullan 1993).

A New Professionalism

Teacher professionalism is at a threshold. Moral purpose and change agentry are implicit in what good teaching and effective change are about, but as yet they are society's (and teaching's) great untapped resources for radical and continuous improvement. We need to go public with a new rationale for why teaching and teacher development are fundamental to the future of society.

Above all, we need action that links initial teacher preparation and continuous teacher development based on moral purpose and change agentry with the corresponding restructuring of universities and schools and their relationships. Systems don't change by themselves. Rather, the actions of individuals and small groups working on new conceptions intersect to produce breakthroughs (Fullan 1993). New conceptions, once mobilized, become new paradigms. The new paradigm for teacher professionalism synthesizes the forces of moral purpose and change agentry.

References

Berends, M. (1992). "A Description of Restructuring in Nationally Nominated Schools." Paper presented at the Annual Meeting of the American Educational Research Association, San Francisco.

Block, P. (1987). *The Empowered Manager.* San Francisco: Jossey-Bass.

Farber, B. (1991). *Crisis in Education.* San Francisco: Jossey-Bass.

Fullan, M. (1991). "The Best Faculty of Education in the Country: A Fable." Submitted to the Strategic Planning Committee. Faculty of Education, University of Toronto.

Fullan, M. (1993). *Change Forces: Probing the Depths of Educational Reform.* London: Falmer Press.

Fullan, M., and A. Hargreaves. (1991). *What's Worth Fighting for in Your School?* Toronto: Ontario Public School Teachers' Federation; Andover, Mass.: The Network; Buckingham, U.K.: Open University Press; Melbourne: Australian Council of Educational Administration.

Gardner, H. (1991). *The Unschooled Mind.* New York: Basic Books.

Goodlad, J. (1991). "Why We Need a Complete Redesign of Teacher Education." *Educational Leadership* 49, 3: 4–10.

Holmes Group. (In press). *Tomorrow's Colleges of Education.* East Lansing, Mich.: Holmes Group.

Howey, K. R. (1992). *The Network of Fifteen.* Columbus: Ohio State University.

Kramer, R. (1992). *Ed School Follies.* New York: Foss Press.

Pascale, P. (1990). *Managing on the Edge.* New York: Touchstone.

Sarason, S. (In press). *The Case for a Change: The Preparation of Educators.* San Francisco: Jossey-Bass.

Schlechty, P. (1990). *Reform in Teacher Education.* Washington, D.C.: American Association of Colleges of Education.

Senge, P. (1990). *The Fifth Discipline.* New York: Doubleday.

Sizer, T. (1992). *Horace's School: Redesigning the American High School.* Boston: Houghton Mifflin.

Stiegelbauer, S. (1992). "Why We Want to Be Teachers." Paper presented at the Annual Meeting of the American Educational Research Association, San Francisco.

University of Toronto, Faculty of Education. (1992a). *Making a Difference* Video, Toronto, Ontario.

University of Toronto, Faculty of Education. (1992b). "B.Ed. Restructuring Committee Report," Toronto, Ontario.

READING 2

Multicultural Education as Social Movement

Christine E. Sleeter

As argued in Chapter 1, multicultural education originated in the context of social movement during the 1960s, the civil rights movement. In the 1990s, however, one commonly finds multicultural education as it is practiced severed from any sort of social movement. This phenomenon struck me forcefully several years ago when I was working with some schools to help them restructure for multicultural education. By restructure, I mean they were not to "add a program" in multicultural education, but to change the schools' processes so that they would better support the concerns, abilities, and perspectives of culturally diverse students.

The change process that my colleagues and I were using involved having a team of teachers investigate and assess structures and processes within their own school, such as placement of students (by race and sex) in remedial and special education, connections between students' interests and the curriculum, relationships between commonly used teaching strategies and students' preferred ways of learning, and the representation of diverse groups in the curriculum. We designed a series of instruments to guide data collection for this self-study. To help teachers interpret their data and plan for change, we gave them a library of literature on multicultural education and had several staff development sessions that focused on issues with which they were grappling. In retrospect, we had packaged multicultural education largely as depoliticized teaching techniques, although at the time did not realize this.

A part of the self-study was to find out more about communities the school served, including community leaders and organizations, issues facing the communities, and community members' feelings about education. The teams in each school seemed to be putting this part of the study off, so my colleagues and I organized an all-day meeting that connected the teachers with various leaders of local communities of color that their schools served. In that meeting, it was apparent that there was little communication between the teachers and communities of color. And in other contexts, as teachers talked about the implications of their findings (such as reasons for racial discrepancies in achievement in their own schools), I saw some large gaps between their interpretations and those of people of color I knew locally.

So, we helped the teachers add community members to their study teams, particularly to help them interpret the data they had collected about their schools and to develop change plans. These efforts helped only minimally, however. The teachers were used to making decisions about the school in-house,

---

Reprinted by permission of the State University of New York Press, from *Multicultural Education as Social Activism* by Christine Sleeter. © 1996, State University of New York. All rights reserved.

and while they did not resist occasional visits by community people, neither did they regard their input as essential to the project. As their reform plans developed, although the plans reflected interests of the teachers, they did not embody a spirit of community renewal and uplift through an education that is multicultural. It was clear to me that multicultural education as conceptualized in these schools had little (if any) connection with community-based movements that aim toward equality and social justice.

This chapter will examine four different metaphors for conceptualizing the form multicultural education often takes: multicultural education as therapy, as teaching techniques, as academic discourse, and as a social movement. I argue that although multicultural education grew out of a social movement, today it usually takes the first three forms. I then suggest the sorts of activities with which we should be engaged if we were to take the social movement metaphor more seriously.

Multicultural Education as Therapy

Multicultural education is viewed as therapy when racism, sexism, heterosexism, or classism are conceptualized as psychological diseases requiring a healing process. Prejudice, stereotypes, hatred, or low self-esteem are its symptoms. Many teachers talk about multicultural issues in ways such as the following, which are interview responses from the same study as reported in chapter 4, in which I asked teachers how multicultural education fit with their teaching goals:

> When we were studying Martin Luther King, one of the kids didn't want to study Martin Luther King. They were sick of that holiday and they didn't want Black History Month either. You know, getting rid of that kind of an attitude.

> [Kids] need to realize that everybody else needs to belong and to have some self-esteem and that you don't build yourself up by ripping other kids down, and that there's a way that you can all work together and everybody can win instead of winning at so-and-so's expense.

These two comments stressed using multicultural education to eliminate negative attitudes and hurtful behavior such attitudes provoke.

When multicultural education is viewed as a form of therapy for prejudice and stereotyping—which is a very common way it is viewed—teachers or counselors take on the role of therapist, helping students to examine their prejudices and attitudes, to identify negative feelings about themselves and/or others, to identify misconceptions they use to judge people, and to replace negative with positive images. The healing process involves expunging "sick" attitudes from the individual. This is done by helping one to admit one has a problem and confess the sins of one's prejudices, then helping one engage in a long, painful process of healing by examining one's own feelings and working to replace negative feelings with positive ones (Peck, 1994).

In this view, young children are more easily "cured" than adults, and teachers can prevent prejudice by providing appropriate information and experiences. For example, the authors of *Cultural Awareness for Young Children* explained in the preface that they were concerned about "the lack of acceptance of the diversity of the traditional customs and lifestyles of a culture by many of the citizens of this country" (McNeill, Schmidt, & Allen, 1981, p. 5). They went on to explain that,

> To accomplish an acceptance of diversity, adults working with young children need to be aware of their stereotypic views of cultures and share authentic information about each culture with children. Racist attitudes need to be changed to positive feelings toward others. (p. 5)

To attempt to replace racist attitudes with positive feelings, lessons introduce children to artifacts and customs of traditional non-European people. To develop appreciation of black cultures, for example, children build traditional Zulu houses, make dashikis and masks, and learn some words in Swahili.

Most advocates of multicultural education criticize such "tourist curricula" that exoticize difference (Banks, 1984; Derman-Sparks, 1989). The problem is not that tackling prejudice and stereotypes is a useless endeavor, but rather that this endeavor so often is completely disconnected from political engagement. Such depoliticized approaches to prejudice reduction

> translate the political into the psychological: prejudice and stereotyping are simply operations of human cognition that can be corrected by educating people to new patterns of thinking (with better information, we will reject stereotypes and discard prejudices). (Peck, 1994, p. 101)

Reducing racism, sexism, or institutionalized poverty to psychological feelings and misconceptions that individuals can overcome may help individuals interact with others in a more positive manner and may provide a context for teaching worthwhile concepts. However, this reduction camouflages the main issues and does not necessarily lead to action directed toward real change (Gurnah, 1984).

> In terms of the material conditions of the workless, homeless, school-less, welfare-less blacks of slum city, all this paroxysm of activity [in racial awareness training] has not made the blindest bit of difference. (Sivanandon, 1985, p. 22)

The material conditions with which oppressed groups struggle, in a context of unequal power relations, are a major focus on social justice movements, and a major impetus behind school reform in such communities. The next metaphor focuses more directly than the first on school improvement.

Multicultural Education as Teaching Techniques

Multicultural education is viewed as a set of teaching techniques when it is regarded as a set of curricular and instructional strategies to add to one's classroom repertoire, particularly to use with culturally diverse students. This view can overlap with the therapeutic view above, but it emphasizes the acquisition of particular techniques for teaching "them." And it is also a very common conception among many teachers. Several of the teachers I interviewed about multicultural education responded in terms of teaching techniques to use with children culturally different from themselves. One, for example, articulated an "individual differences" perspective about children, in which teachers make adaptations to individual children's problems or characteristics, culture being one such "problem":

> It doesn't have to be just race, everybody comes in with some sort of, maybe they're left-handed or maybe they have something else, a problem at home or that sort of thing, so I think each child, if you look at each child individually and don't say, Well this is a minority group or this is a Hispanic group or that sort of thing, I think every child has something that's a problem.

Other teachers talk about specific techniques they learned. One emphasized the value of a staff development program teaching

> more about the Hispanic families, the Black families, the Puerto Rican families, but also what incites getting those students happy, how they interact with their parents, what their parents are like when they interact with schools. . . . We have to learn to gear down our languages so that we can communicate effectively when we're dealing with their children.

Another discussed the usefulness of adding teaching strategies to her repertoire:

> More of the cooperative learning activities, I think. By doing more types of hands-on things. . . . Just more types of incorporating, I should say, more of the cooperative learning styles, you know, where they are working together.

As these interviews suggest, multicultural teaching techniques in this view help teachers manage diversity.

Lin Goodwin (1994) surveyed 120 preservice teachers to find out how they conceive of multicultural education. Seventy-one percent discussed it as therapy for racial disharmony; another 16% defined it as a way of addressing individual differences among children. As a whole, the majority described multicultural education as a set of techniques teachers should use to respond to diverse students. "They define it as primarily procedural or technical, requiring knowing and doing something" to adapt the regular curriculum to one's own students (p. 128). Further, the preservice teachers' "emphasis on each child implicitly identifies the individual as the fulcrum of change; multicultural pedagogy becomes idiosyncratic and dependent on the needs of single students" (p. 128).

One certainly cannot argue that teachers should not develop technical skills to respond to students' diversity and teach them effectively. However, Goodwin observed that the vast majority in her study did not connect such skills with broader political issues. Indeed, only one of the 120 preservice teachers argued that multicultural education should include "the ability to look critically at existing political, economic and social structures" (p. 122). Such critical analysis might include critiquing how schools reproduce hierarchies of privilege and advantage (such as through tracking) and working to change such structures and processes. It might also include recognizing that most oppressed people do not wish to remain oppressed and that one should engage in dialog with members of oppressed communities regarding their own wishes for their children's education. This is a very different orientation from one in which a teacher adopts techniques from a book or workshop to apply to children with whom the techniques are supposed to "work" in order to gain greater compliance from them.

Multicultural Education as Academic Discourse

Multicultural education takes the form of academic discourse when intellectuals engage in a great deal of talk about multicultural issues without also actually engaging in social change processes (Platt, 1993). Until recently, multicultural education was rarely a topic of academic debate; over the past few years it has become a hot topic, and in some circles, in vogue. As Gates (1992) put it,

> Academic critics write essays, "readings" of literature, where the bad guys (for example, racism or patriarchy) lose, where the forces of oppression are subverted by the boundless powers of irony and allegory that no prison can contain, and we glow with hard-won triumph. We pay homage to the marginalized and demonized, and it feels almost as if we've righted a real-world injustice. (p. 19)

But engaging in battles of words, by itself, does not necessarily bring social change. Gates commented that, "it sometimes seems that blacks are doing better in the college curriculum than they are in the streets" (p. 19).

Discussions that clarify thinking, share ideas, and persuade are of value. But the frequent substitution of texts and words for genuine dialog and struggle concerns scholar-activists. Carby, for example, asked, "Have we as a society successfully eliminated the desire for achieving integration through political agitation for civil rights and opted instead for knowing each other through cultural texts?" (in Platt, 1993, p. 75).

These observations do not mean that academicians should not work toward the reform of the entire university. Indeed, there is a great deal of work to be done not only to make universities truly multicultural institutions, but also to strengthen their capacity to help us address injustices in the broader society.

> Multiculturalism has to be more than a special project or piecemeal reform to diversify students, faculty, and ideas. We need to engage the whole university in acknowledging that the existing institutions and discourse of race relations are inadequate to the crisis we face. (Platt, 1993, p. 77)

The problem with academic discourse is that it often consists of little more than words and often contributes nothing to improving the real conditions of life for disenfranchised peoples. "The relation between our critical postures and the social struggles they reflect upon is far from transparent. That doesn't mean there's no relation, of course, only that it's a highly mediated one" (Gates, 1992, p. 20).

This book, for example, consists of academic discourse. Academic discourse, like examination of attitudes and development of multicultural teaching skills, is not inherently worthless. The problem is that so often none of these is directly connected with any organized movement for social justice. It is the fourth metaphor, multicultural education as a social movement, that should refocus our energies and actions, and provide the grounding and direction for future work in multicultural education.

Multicultural Education as a Social Movement

If multicultural education were viewed as a movement or as connected with other related social movements, discussions about it would be quite different from those above. Let us examine the various dimensions of social movements, then draw implications of those dimensions for multicultural education.

Dimensions of Social Movements   A social movement is a "sustained challenge to powerholders in the name of a population living under the jurisdiction of those powerholders by means of repeated public displays of that population's numbers, commitment, unity, and worthiness" (Tilly, 1993, p. 7). Movements aim to redistribute power and resources by confronting power relations in which a dominant collective has attained the power to define the society for the masses, to construct an ideology in which that definition makes sense, and to achieve hegemony—to get most people to accept that ideology and act in accordance with it, viewing it as natural (Eyerman & Jamison, 1991; Gramsci, 1971; Touraine, 1988). In a social movement, the goal is not just to effect a particular policy change, but more importantly to shift the power to control decisions, define situations, and allocate resources (Staples, 1984).

Social movement theorists distinguish among four main kinds of actors in a movement: the constituent base, the powerholders, the activists, and the general public who are not directly involved. The base of a social movement consists of a constituency who share common problems or concerns; movements aim toward empowering this base. Initially, would-be members of the constituent base may not necessarily identify with each other, a common set of problems and concerns, or an action agenda. Movements need continued work at building a sense of shared identity and a common definition of shared concerns and at developing networks for communication within the constituency (Eyerman & Jamison, 1991). The movement's constituency can be connected partly through print or electronic media, but regular face-to-face contact through social and cultural organizations serves this purpose most effectively (Aronowitz, 1992; Minkoff, 1993; Shields, 1994). Sometimes a symbol that has meaning to various segments of the constituency is used to represent the whole collective in order to build a common identity; for example, language serves as such as symbol for bridging various Latino communities (Padilla, 1985). But the formal organizational structure of the movement is less important to its success and longevity than are cultural activities that bring people together to cultivate, nurture and sustain solidarity and identification with the movement (Ingalsbee, 1993; Minkoff, 1993; Staggenborg, Eder & Sudderth, 1993).

This constituency stands in opposition to the powerholders who must be confronted in order for the constituent base to achieve better life conditions and self-determination. A movement must have a clear sense of who the opposition is and what issues differentiate "them" from "us." Without that, movements tend to dissipate, since many different sectors, including the dominant society, can articulate interpretations of problems and recommended agendas for action; then people who are unclear about the issues and the power differential often end up supporting the regime currently in power (Eyerman & Jamison, 1991; Touraine, 1988). A problem with many recent "movements" for improvement of life in the U.S. and Western Europe, such as liberal feminism or populist politics, is that they are actually attached to the existing political parties and capitalist structure, rather than opposing these groups and systems (Aronowitz, 1992; Bobbs, 1986).

Movements must differentiate the constituent base from the opposition, but it is necessary to be aware of problems associated with binary opposition thinking that constructs each as a monolithic group (Popkewitz, 1991). Neither the powerholders nor the constituency is a unified monolith, which renders the process of defining the constituency and the opposition to be quite complex, particularly when we are talking about "multicultural" which articulates problems defined around race, gender, sexual orientation, social class, and disability. As argued shortly, it is at this point that multicultural education loses its social movement character.

Activists stand between the constituent base and the powerholders; activists often but not always come from the constituent base (Tilly, 1993). The role activists play is to organize constituents, articulate their concerns, and negotiate on their behalf with powerholders. Activists who come from the powerholder group may be listened to more readily by powerholders than those from the constituent base of the movement. In this way, they can be helpful allies. It is important to realize that activism is a role more so than a group; one may be an activist in some contexts but not in others. What one actually does, and with whom one works, identifies one as an activist.

The primary basis for power of a social movement is its ability to organize and mobilize the "marching millions" as needed (Staples, 1984). Movement organizers generally mobilize the constituent base most effectively by networking with existing local, political and cultural groups that identify with the broader movement (Staggenborg, Eder & Sudderth, 1993; Tilly, 1993) Increasingly important also is a movement's ability to mobilize the general public, who may identify with neither the movement nor the powerholders. Touraine (1988) argues that movements today depend more on mobilizing public opinion than engaging in direct action and that those that grasp importance of public opinion tend to be more successful. To do this, movements must link political advocacy with moral issues and conditions of everyday life, tap into the discontent of large segments of the public, and help them to see a connection between the movement's action agenda and their own discontent. In this way, the public can be mobilized as an additional pressure group (Staples, 1984).

At this point, readers should stop and mentally locate themselves as either members of the constituent base of multicultural education, powerholders, activists, or the general public. Quite likely many readers will identify themselves as activists—as educators who are attempting to change other educators on behalf of children from disenfranchised groups. It is possible for activists to evolve into a loose group unto itself, in which they "spend a major part of their energy making claims not on powerholders but on themselves" (Tilly, 1993, p. 15). When this happens, activists move away from direct affiliation with the movement's constituent base, affiliating largely with each other. This is a growing problem in multicultural education, which is a point I will return to later. The connection between activists and the movement's constituents is critical; when this connection breaks down, the movement does also.

Social movements articulate counter-ideologies that frame issues and group identity differently from the dominant ideology. A counter-ideology attempts to situate the group historically in a manner that articulates a group consciousness and redefines its relationship with the dominant society in a way that suggests changing that relationship (Aronowitz, 1992). This includes articulating a vision for the future, goals, and some sort of structure through which to achieve the group's goals. In articulating this counter-ideology, the movement's activists attempt to re-orient the thinking of both the constituency and the dominant society (Touraine, 1988), and to "portray [the movement] as numerous, committed, unitary, and worthy" (Tilly, 1993, p. 17). Movements need someone to do the intellectual work of creating such a counter-ideology although there are debates about who should do this. While some argue that intellectuals should develop the movement's theoretical and ideological underpinnings (e.g., Laclau, 1988, p. 26–27), others are more skeptical, stressing the importance of ideas coming from the movement's constituents—its everyday people—rather than an intellectual elite. As Staples (1984) put it, an organizer "must be able to translate people's dreams for a better life into reality" (p. 8) and those dreams need to come from the people themselves. In fact, many argue that the movement's meaning cannot come from anywhere else except the peoples' day-to-day work and interactions (Ingalsbee, 1993).

A movement develops a repertoire of action strategies, with the long-term aim of shifting power and getting powerholders to act in the direction desired by the constituents (Eyerman & Jamison, 1991; Tilly, 1993). Strategies may include routine advocacy, education and persuasion, negotiation, and non-violent or violent direct action. Movements that use advocacy strategies within routine institutional channels tend to have longer lives than those that use direct action strategies (Minkoff, 1993); activists must weigh the relative advantages and trade-offs of protest as opposed to more routine strategies. Whatever approach is chosen, however, action strategies and pressure tactics must get the constituents directly involved, so that they see a direct connection between their own actions and organization, and results—that is empowerment (Staples, 1984).

The 1960s and the 1990s: Different Decades As an outgrowth of the civil rights movement, multicultural education arose as a part of struggles by African Americans, then other racial minority groups, to control decisions about education of their own children. In this regard, education was viewed as a social resource connected with other resources such as jobs, power, and community vitality, and the goal was to gain power to define how education for children of oppressed racial groups should be conducted. In the 1960s, communities and educators of color actively demanded or tried to persuade the white education establishment to make specific changes in the conduct of education. Glenn

Omatsu (1994), for example, described activism as the Asian American community confronted San Francisco State University during the 1960s. During that time, a coalition of working class Third World students who were closely linked with their communities made specific demands on the university that not only attempted to change education, but also "confronted basic questions of power and oppression in America" (p. 26). This example, plus many others from this time period, were clearly movements in which educational change was part of a larger quest by oppressed communities to gain control over their own lives.

As the social movements of the 1960s became dispersed and marginalized, and conservatism gained ideological ground, links between educational change and community-based movements that began in the 1960s have become obscured. Clearly articulated calls for political changes to benefit large groups have waned; "empowerment" commonly now means individual advancement rather than collective empowerment and mobility. This is not, of course, simply the fault of educators or activists; many activists have noted the degree to which activism in oppressed communities has taken on the individualism and conservatism of the larger society. For example, Omatsu (1994) pointed out that while activism in Asian American communities during the 1960s was aimed toward empowerment of the community by challenging structures of oppression, today it is oriented toward upward mobility of young Asian professionals who are more concerned about the glass ceiling than about structural racism and poverty. Similarly, Bronski (1994) contrasted the Gay Liberation Front and Stonewall Riots of 1969 with today's gay rights movement. Twenty-five years ago, gay activists confronted restrictions on sexual behavior; and many also "understood that racism was part of our fight" (p. 22). Today the gay rights movement has shifted away from affirming the right of people to engage in homosexual behavior—one can "be" gay in terms of identity, but not necessarily "act" gay; in behavior and action, confronting racism has been replaced by sporadic talk about "diversity."

Political systems increasingly are closed to social movements; movements need political expression but find it increasingly difficult to connect with any political party (Touraine, 1988). In the U.S., for example, the political system increasingly is controlled by a wealthy elite; ordinary Americans are disaffected from politics, but do not see a clear alternative, and social movements tend to be fractured and marginalized. On a global level, "state-supported global capitalism" increasingly controls political systems (Brecher, Childs & Cutler, 1993, p. xvi). Partly through control of media, the dominant elite directs discontent and anger of various segments of society against each other, rather than against the existing economic and political system and the elite itself. The current anti-immigrant furor is an example. As people's economic situations have eroded, their frustration has been channeled against immigrants, Americans of color, and poor women rather than against a wealthy elite that has been profiting. As a system for producing and distributing wealth, capitalism has achieved such a degree of hegemony that it is very difficult to organize people around opposition to it (Aronowitz, 1992; Boggs, 1986).

In response to the marginalization of movements, many movement activists stress the need to build organic coalitions among grassroots communities who have built a clear sense of their own identity, but also see connections between their own interests and those of other oppressed communities. Childs (1994), for example, calls such coalitions "transcommunal alliances." Further, he and others argue that such grassroots organizations are growing, and many models of effective coalition-building exist (Brecher, Childs, & Cutler, 1993). There is a danger, however, in coalitions becoming "catch-all" parties that attempt to please a wide variety of interests, since these kinds of formations tend to be reabsorbed into existent political structures and ideological formations (Boggs, 1986). Coalitions are necessary, but must retain a clear sense of who and what they are supporting and opposing and what their transformative vision is. For example, coalitions organized around wage improvement, housing improvement and access to jobs and health care can pull very different communities together to address very real, common concerns.

During the early 1970s, multicultural education struggled to be noticed by the education establishment. While its advocates were mainly educators, they were also usually closely connected with community movements and social protest politics. When I began teaching in the early 1970s and first attended multicultural education workshops, I could not distinguish workshop leaders from community activists.

By the mid-1980s, however, as classrooms across the U.S. became more culturally diverse and teachers increasingly began asking for help and as many turned to the growing literature base in multicultural education, more and more Euro-American teachers who had never been involved in social movements took ownership in multicultural education. While some teachers who gravitate toward the field are longtime "boat rockers" (Boyle-Baise & Washburn, 1994), many are simply good people who care about children and who want to improve their effectiveness in teaching the students they now have. By itself, this is not a problem, but it has contributed to a shift in what multicultural education often means. As Euro-American educators who have never been engaged in social activism join the ranks of multicultural education advocates, they filter its meaning through their own ideas about difference and inequality. Further, as multicultural education has adopted an increasingly wide agenda of change, focusing not only on racism but also on gender, social class, disability, and other issues, a still wider array of people have found elements to which they can relate. And by itself this also would not necessarily be a problem. But many have claimed ownership in multicultural education without necessarily taking seriously the needs and claims of other constituents. This leads to the formation of groups of white teachers who are interested in multicultural education (but not in challenging racism), who view it as adding some "divesity" to the day-to-day routines of teaching, and to whom it may not occur to collaborate with community grassroots organizations. Therefore, in the last section of this chapter, I wish to return to the metaphor of multicultural education as a social movement, in order to suggest where our emphases and efforts should be if we were to renew this as the primary metaphor.

Multicultural Education as a Social Movement Viewing multicultural education as a social movement has implications for how one conceptualizes school change, which in turn has far-reaching ramifications. Most educators do not think in terms of collective action aimed toward institutional change. For example, when I asked sixteen teachers how much power they believed a cadre of teachers had to change schools, only two discussed the change process in terms of organizing to press collectively for change. Most of the others discussed school change as involving a process of attempting to persuade other teachers as individuals to change their attitudes (Sleeter, 1992). As a teacher educator, I find my work structured in this manner; every day when I enter the classroom, I am trying to persuade future teachers (who are overwhelmingly white and are in the process of becoming professionals) to teach differently.

The social movement metaphor suggests a very different change process from that educators tend to use—that parents and other concerned community people, as well as educators, organize to pressure schools to serve their interests and those of their children. In a thoughtful discussion of neighborhood organizing for urban school reform, Michael Williams (1989) argued that most communities have the potential to bring about significant changes. "This assumption is warranted by the presence in most of these neighborhoods of leaders and organizations already at work on neighborhood problems" (p. 2). However, most communities do not use that potential as well as they could to reform their schools. Williams instructs community people to go into the schools and observe carefully such variables as teachers' attitudes toward students, the handling of disciplinary issues, the handling of homework, and so forth. As community members identify specific problems and generate ideas for school improvement, they should communicate these directly to the school, collectively using pressure to hold the school accountable. He concluded that,

> The goals of organizing for urban school reform are twofold. Neighborhood organizing should promote change in the school as a result of documentation and the application of collective political pressure, and it should build among parents agreement on what their schools should do for their children. (p. 147)

Educators may become resources and collaborators in this process, but should not own the process. Williams' discussion and the social movement metaphor has important ramifications for multicultural education, which this section will elaborate.

Social movements attempt to shift power from powerholders whom the movement opposes, toward the movement's constituent base. Since the 1970s, a distinction between powerholders and the constituent base of multicultural education has become highly blurred, if not lost. We must recapture this distinction and reorient the field in ways that such a distinction suggests.

The constituent base of multicultural education consists of disenfranchised people in this society, particularly parents and children of color and/or of low-income backgrounds; children who are disabled, gay or lesbian, and their parents or adult supporters; and girls. This is a highly diverse lot including groups who do not identify at all with each other and engage in various forms of exclusion and oppression themselves, a problem that can lead to fragmentation if not addressed directly. I will discuss this issue shortly. However, in many arenas of multicultural activity, predominantly white groups of educators look to ourselves as if we were the constituent base of multicultural education, which misses the entire point of power-redistribution. *Most college-educated white people are not multicultural education's natural constituency.* We can certainly become allies, but we need to recognize the power of our own self-interest and point of view, which often leads us to reshape multicultural education to fit our own needs. In our communities, we need to view children of oppressed groups, their parents, their communities, and their grassroots advocacy organizations as the natural constituency of multicultural education. Multicultural education ought to be about empowering this natural constituency.

Powerholders are mainly the education establishment: administrators, classroom teachers, university professionals, and community constituents who support school policies and practices that multicultural education advocates wish to change. Many readers of this book, as well as its author, could more accurately be thought of as powerholders in education institutions rather than as members of the constituent base of multicultural education. We may be activists and allies to the constituent base, but we do not comprise that base.

The distinction between powerholders and the constituent base of multicultural education is one of relative power and position, rather than strictly one of group membership. Robert Terry (1993) clarified this point very simply and well in his essay "A Parable: The Ups and Downs", writing: "What makes an up an up and a down a down is that an up can do more to a down than a down can do to an up. That's what keeps an up up and a down down" (p. 61). He went on to point out that most people are ups and downs relative to someone else at various times, but some are downs in most relationships while others are ups most of the time. As white women, many of us who are educators are "downs" relative to the patriarchal, bureaucratic education establishment and may see ourselves largely as "downs." We have much more difficulty viewing ourselves *also* as "ups"—as powerholders who someone else would like to change. Yet, relative to our students and their communities, to a large extent, we are powerholders. We may be able to learn to share power and collaborate but must remain vigilant about how our own power and vested interests influences us.

Many readers will regard distinguishing between the constituent base and the powerholders as divisive. Historically in an effort to be inclusive, multicultural activists have offered a wide embrace, arguing that multicultural education is for everyone. While I believe that its ideals are for everyone, everyone does not benefit equally from schooling as it currently operates which is what multicultural education is trying to change. Movements dissipate when they lose a sense of who is their constituency and who is the opposition (Boggs, 1986; Touraine, 1988). The argument that multicultural education includes everyone may accurately articulate a long-range vision and help to draw in otherwise reluctant educators and members of the public, but it also obscures analysis of power and the politics of institutional change. As long as power relations are not addressed, those with the least power to change schools remain relatively powerless. And as long as "everyone" can define multicultural education, it will frequently continue to take forms that white middle class people find least threatening.

Locally, the action agenda for multicultural education should come largely from oppressed communities, not from white educators. White educators can be helpful allies, but if we control decision-making, we are the ones who are exercising power. Terry (1993) writes that leadership in social justice issues should come from "downs" much more so than from "ups." "Ups are too busy trying to maintain the system, rather than generate insight about what's really going on or how to change it. So our source of new insightful information comes from downs, not from ups" (p. 62). The goal is not to get rid of ups, but rather "to get rid of arbitrary up-down power relationships" (p. 63). As educators who are part of a system we are trying to change, we do have a vested interest in protecting our own position and the processes that worked for us. That does not make us bad people, but it does position us differently from the students and parents for whom we advocate. Further, most school systems have the capacity to absorb and contain pressures for change without actually changing in fundamental ways (Skrtic, 1991). Getting rid of arbitrary up-down power relationships means collaborating with oppressed communities. "The neighborhood organization is a political instrument whereby residents can make their educational and other public needs known and have them answered" (Williams, 1989, p. 148). Educators can collaborate with such organizations but cannot tell them what they need.

What about all the many books and articles that have been written over the past twenty-five years, discussing what multicultural education means and how schools should change? Does locating the primary agenda for school change with parents and leaders of oppressed communities mean that we reject the usefulness of this body of knowledge? It does not, although I suggest refocusing its use. Currently such literature—which contains a rich array of conceptual frameworks, research, and specific teaching strategies—often substitutes for dialog between educators and community people, and currently educators have greater access to it than do community people. The reduction of multicultural education to teaching techniques is symptomatic of this gap. In its inception, the action agenda for multicultural education came largely from parents and educators of color, who articulated changes they would like to see in schools. Over time, as academicians have elaborated on that agenda, we have both developed it and to some extent disconnected it from its natural constituent base. Currently, multicultural education is being defined by a wide array of people, including white conservatives (e.g., Bernstein, 1994; Ravitch, 1990a and b; Schlesinger, 1992; Stotsky, 1992). If one depends on professionals to define it, one might be quite bewildered, and even see multicultural education as meaning something contrary to what oppressed groups in one's own community actually want. Further, professional educators use professional knowledge to position ourselves above lay-people. As an activist has pointed out, "school staff can heighten the social distance between themselves and working-class parents by emphasizing that what they teach and how they teach it is beyond the understanding of parents; therefore, parents should stay out of the whole process" (Williams, 1989, p. 130). Professionals may use good ideas with good intentions, but, in an absence of dialog with the communities they serve, still not respond to the concerns of such communities.

The point is that the multicultural education literature should be written for and available to a wider community audience, and oppressed communities should decide for themselves what ideas are most useful. Professionals can help through dialog and information-sharing. Two examples illustrate. A couple of years ago I was talking with an African American parent who was very frustrated about how the school was treating her precocious primary-grade son. As she talked, I suggested that she may be describing cultural differences in learning style between African American and white children and negative reactions that white teachers often have toward African American learning and communication styles. She was completely unaware of this line of argument, so I gave her several articles and books to read. She returned about two weeks later, having devoured that material, and told me that it had given her a vocabulary to describe her concerns, demonstrated that her "gut feelings" were accurate and that she was not "crazy" or imagining things, and suggested ways she might interact more effectively with the teacher. The material I gave her about culture and learning and about multicultural education enriched her own analysis of a problem and strengthened her power to intervene on behalf of her son. (It did not strengthen her power enough to change the teacher or the classroom, however; she eventually transferred her son to another school.)

Concha Delgado-Gaitan (1993) discussed how she worked with a Mexican American parent organization and how this work transformed her understanding of her own position as a scholar. Initially, she viewed her role as an informed, neutral outsider, studying family-school relationships. In the process of meeting with parents to share her research findings, she realized that "not knowing how to connect with the schools had clearly traumatized some of the parents" (p. 397). The parents "tried very hard to do the best for their children, and . . . had the desire and commitment to support their children in their education both at home and at school" (p. 400). What they lacked was the expertise Delgado-Gaitan had about how schools work, what teachers respond to, what program possibilities exist. Over time, she shifted her role with them from researcher to resource. She did not tell the parents what they should want, but rather provided information that would assist them in advocating for themselves. "Although my involvement in their meetings unquestionably influenced their orientation and knowledge base about the schools, the COPLA parents themselves defined their organizational goals and their sociopolitical awareness and identity" (p. 407). In the process, the parents' ability to advocate for themselves grew.

> COPLA moved from conceptualizing change as a list of outcomes, to a list of books they could read to their children, to interacting with each other, to learning the process by which to inquire and access information that would lead them to obtain the resources they desired. (p.408)

These examples illustrate how the body of knowledge called "multicultural education" can be useful to oppressed communities. The teaching techniques and abstract discourse of multicultural education are not irrelevant. On the contrary, there is a great deal of helpful work available that provides ways of conceptualizing issues, research findings that support what oppressed communities want, and specific practices and materials for classroom use.

At the same time, however, communities must themselves define their own goals and develop the capacity to move the goals forward. As long as this body of literature is controlled primarily by professionals, it is subject to being used as a tool for managing and controlling "diversity" in schools. That is quite different from dialoguing with parents and other community members, using the literature mutually to inform thinking and knowledge of possibilities. Redirected toward parents and community activists from oppressed groups, this literature can serve as an empowering resource.

The flow of ideas in multicultural education has been more toward educators, however, than toward constituent communities. In my own community, for example, I and other local educators occasionally disseminate articles or resource materials through community centers and local organizations such as the Urban League. And I place my teacher education students in community centers for field experiences, where I have them practice listening to and dialoguing with "downs" rather than telling "downs" what to do. However, the networks of communication make it much easier for me to talk about multicultural education with other educators at times, in locations and in discourse styles that exclude multicultural education's natural constituent base.

This is true of conferences as well as professional literature. Viewing multicultural education as a social movement suggests broader uses for conferences and other gatherings than is often the case. I have been involved in many conferences and meetings for multicultural education in which the organizers have lamented that we are simply "preaching to the choir"—that those who need to "hear the message" did not come, reducing the conference's effectiveness. This view suggests that educators who are "for" multicultural education are its constituency and do not need to network among ourselves; that is, we hold gatherings to enlighten the unenlightened. Viewing multicultural education as a social movement suggests that we distinguish among three rather different purposes for gatherings: 1) networking the constituent base for multicultural education (who are mostly non-educators), 2) developing the knowledge-base of educator/activists, and 3) communicating desired changes for schools to powerholders. Some organizations and conferences, such as the National Association for Multicultural Education (NAME) attempt comprehensively to address all three purposes. In addition to such large-scale, comprehensive conferences, other gatherings should be clearly organized based on which purpose they are trying to serve.

For the first purpose, some conferences and meetings might provide opportunities for the much-needed face-to-face contact and identity-building among members of a constituent base. If the constituent base for multicultural education is primarily families and other community members from communities of color and low-income white communities, then such people ought to be actively involved in multicultural education's activities—whether they have education credentials or not. Such involvement would help develop flow of communication between local grass-roots organizations and professional educators, as well as building community empowerment across differences. Face-to-face involvement across differences such as gender, ethnicity, sexual orientation, or language is necessary in order to build a powerful constituency that can function together and work toward the development of a pluralistic, democratic polity. Outside education, there are good models of such grass-roots organizations that bridge differences. For example, Childs (1994) described several "Transcommunal" organizations such as the National Urban Peace and Justice "Gang Truce" Summit in Kansas City and the African American/Korean Alliance in Los Angeles. Many labor organizers are recognizing that "fighting all forms of discrimination is the very foundation of building unity between organized labor and women and people of color" (Oppenheim, 1993, p. vi). Such bridge-building requires that people come to grips with their own prejudices as well as deepen their knowledge about issues of concern to others in their communities, which requires face-to-face contact. As an experienced cross-cultural labor organizer explained,

> People just can't be told to not be racist or to love such-and-such—that's mere polemics. We gotta get out there and DO. Overcoming racial and ethnic divisions starts by asking each other questions, housecalling together, going to events together. (Russo, 1993, p. 41)

Similarly, in a discussion of homophobia within communities of color, activists discussed re-education strategies they use, such as the following:

> We can hold town-house meetings for everyone, not just Indian organizations. I compare it to squaw dances on the rez . . . three-day ceremonies. Everyone from the surrounding area comes and shares. They talk about their lives, what's going on, what's bothering them. . . . We look at the community as a whole. (Garcia, 1994, p. 16)

These are examples of face-to-face cross-difference community-building at local levels. To build capacity for community organizing for school reform, educators should be involved, but not necessarily dominate. I cannot overemphasize the importance of such face-to-face gatherings of members of the constituent base of multicultural education. If the constituent base does not identify with the movement and its action agenda and does not help to move that agenda forward, the experience of social movements indicates that the action agenda and the movement itself will dissipate.

The second purpose for conferences and other gatherings is to deepen educator/activists' analysis of the issues and knowledge of how to make social change. This is rather different from the purpose of community-building, in that it specifically involves seasoned educator/activists and focuses on development of our own knowledge-base and repertoire of strategies for institutional change. Often we are so busy trying to "convert" the "unconverted" that we do not use conferences and other gatherings as well as we might to develop our own knowledge. We assume that those who have become involved in multicultural education know all we need to know about its issues and the processes for making institutional change, when that is rarely the case. One important focus for conferences of activists should be developing our analysis of the political process of making school change, and sharpening our ability to use various political change strategies such as networking and organizing, persuasion, and pressure politics. Another focus could be examining forms of institutional inequality outside the classroom such as tracking and school funding, and developing strategies to address these issues. An example of an organization that uses meetings for this second purpose is the National Coalition of Education Activists.

The third purpose for conferences and meetings is to communicate desired changes in schools to educators and other relevant publics—to the powerholders whom we wish to change, and/or to the broader public at large. From the perspective of the social movement metaphor, in such meetings activists and community representatives communicate specific changes to powerholders, backing up their desire for change with the potential for pressure from the constituent base. An example is a conference in which I was involved in 1991, in which the largest school districts in New York State convened to communicate to textbook publishers that their texts fell far short from a multicultural perspective, and that districts would begin to produce their own materials if publishers did not respond. Workshops may also serve the purpose of trying to change the behavior of powerholders but too often there is no one—particularly no one outside the schools—holding teachers accountable for using the training they have received.

Finally, viewing multicultural education as a social movement suggests that effort must be expended to cultivate support among segments of the broader public who currently are unaware of or indifferent to multicultural education. Currently the New Right, having control over far greater financial and media resources than progressives have, is educating the public to regard multicultural education as divisive, intellectually weak, and un-American (Sleeter, 1994). Carl Boggs (1986) argued that increasingly, the development of "a viable counterhegemonic politics will depend, in the final analysis, upon essentially subjective factors" which include

> the capacity of disparate groups to unite in a common outlook, and the success of activists in making concrete—making alive—issues that can attract the vast majority of people to the ideal of a democratic, egalitarian, nonviolent world. (p. 249)

Multicultural education activists do need to develop access to mainstream media and do need to connect the goals and processes of multicultural education with the ideals of democracy and justice that most Americans espouse, as well as the public's concerns about a shrinking job market, an uncertain future, and public safety.

Social Movement Metaphor for Classroom Teachers

What does a classroom teacher do who takes the social movement metaphor seriously? This metaphor has several implications for teachers.

First, it suggests that a teacher recognize the ethical dimensions of teaching other people's children, and work to provide them with the highest quality of education one would wish one's own children to have. This means that such a teacher recognizes the aspirations oppressed groups have for their children and the barriers, both interpersonal and institutional, that persistently thwart their efforts. Low teacher expectations and systems such as tracking that institutionalize those expectations are an example of such barriers. Without necessarily meaning to, through our routine participation in schools as institutions, most of us as teachers contribute to the barriers children from oppressed groups face, partly by not recognizing them as barriers. Teachers who take seriously the social movement metaphor find out in what ways the school hinders the success of children from marginalized groups, then work to change processes and structures that serve as barriers.

Second, a teacher who takes the social movement metaphor seriously learns to work as an ally with the community. In the classroom, this means that the teacher shapes pedagogy on the basis of both professional expertise and ongoing dialog with parents and other community members. Professional expertise alone is not enough since perspectives of "experts" sometimes contradict those of marginalized groups. Lisa Delpit's (1988) discussion is an excellent example illustrating a major disjuncture between how African American educators and progressive Euro-American educators view the teaching of language arts to African American children. Delpit calls for dialog and power-sharing so that teachers will use pedagogy that fits the children they are teaching, with the recognition that adults who are members of the community the children grow up in understand a great deal about the children's learning.

The suggestion that teachers share power with marginalized communities is often met with the objection that many parents from marginalized groups have too many problems of their own to be of much help. While this is true, a teacher also should not equate individual parents' abilities to provide for their children with the community's aspirations and resources. Impoverished parents often face debilitating situations and some do not cope well with those situations. However, within the community are networks of strength and resilience, as well as visions of hope for children's futures. The social movement metaphor suggests that teachers seek out these networks; this is, in fact, what successful teachers do (Ladson-Billings, 1994).

Third, taking the social movement seriously by becoming an ally to marginalized communities means acting as an advocate for children from these communities in the broader civic life. This can involve voting for candidates who support the needs of such children and their communities, supporting agencies and social action groups who work on their behalf, persuading other people to support rather than blame adults in the children's lives, and so forth. Allies find out what issues are of concern to the community and how those issues can be supported. For example, some teacher education students whom I have placed in community centers for field experiences have come to realize the lack of recreation opportunities in low-income neighborhoods, and have begun to support local political action aimed toward enriching available recreation activities. In this way, they are beginning to act as advocates for children.

Fourth, a teacher who takes the social movement metaphor seriously teaches children and youth to act politically, to advocate both individually and collectively for themselves and for other marginalized people. Young people can learn to affect their social world quite powerfully. For example, in Nebraska the students of a high school teacher became so interested in learning about America's cultural diversity that they decided to advocate for a state law requiring curricula in Nebraska to be multicultural. With the teacher's guidance, they were able to persuade the state legislature to pass such a law. This is a rather dramatic example of the impact children and youth can have on institutions around them, under the guidance of a politically astute teacher. Children and youth who learn to use the democratic process effectively to advance ideals of social justice can become adults who are able to actualize the ideals of justice and equality through the political process.

Conclusion

Social movements are based on an analysis of vested interests in unequal relations of power. Movement activists assume that, while to a limited degree people will "do the right thing" on moral grounds, people are more likely to act in accordance with their vested interests. Those who have the most obvious and immediate vested interest in school reforms that challenge racism, classism, patriarchy, ablism, and heterosexism, are those highly diverse publics that occupy the "down" side of unequal relations of power in our own local communities.

I believe that concerned educators generally do want to do the right thing for students. However, all of us conceptualize what that means from our own social locations and in the context of an ideological field that shapes meaning. The social locations, vested interests, and ideology of professional educators usually differs in significant ways from that of oppressed communities. Viewing multicultural education as a social movement directs us to look to such communities as the natural constituents of multicultural education, with whom we professional educators may ally ourselves. That alliance, however takes work—work that recognizes the politics of social change in a racist, capitalist, patriarchal society.

READING 3

System Dynamics and Learner-Centered Learning in Kindergarten through 12th Grade Education

Jay W. Forrester

Secondary education is under increasing attack for not preparing students to cope with modern life. Failures appear in the form of corporate executives who misjudge the complexities of growth and competition, government leaders who

Copyright © 1992 Jay W. Forrester. Reprinted by permission.

are at a loss to understand economic and political change, and publics that support inappropriate responses to immigration pressures, changing international conditions, rising unemployment, the drug culture, governmental reform, and inadequacies in education.

Growing criticism of education may direct attention to incorrect diagnoses and ineffective treatments. Weakness in education arises not so much from poor teachers as from inappropriateness of material that is being taught. Students are stuffed with facts without having a frame of reference for making those facts relevant to the complexities of life. Responses to educational deficiencies are apt to result in public demands for still more of what is causing the present educational failures. Pressures will increase for additional science, humanities, and social studies in an already overcrowded curriculum, a curriculum that fails to instill enthusiasm and a sense of relevance. Instead, an opportunity exists for moving toward a common foundation that pulls all fields of study into a more understandable equity.

1. Sources of Educational Ineffectiveness

Much current dissatisfaction with pre-college education arises from past inability to show how people interact with one another and with their physical environment, and to reveal causes for what students see happening. Because of its fragmentary nature, traditional education becomes less relevant as society becomes more complex, crowded, and tightly interconnected.

Education is compartmentalized into separate subjects that, in the real world, interact with one another. Social studies, physical science, biology and other subjects are taught as if they were inherently different from one another, even though behavior in each rests on the same underlying concepts. For example, the dynamic structure that causes a pendulum to swing is the same as the core structure that causes employment and inventories to fluctuate in a product-distribution system and in economic business cycles. Humanities are taught without relating the dynamic sweep of history to similar behaviors on a shorter time scale that a student can experience in a week or a year.

High schools teach a curriculum from which students are expected to synthesize a perspective and framework for understanding their social and physical environments. But that framework is never explicitly taught. Students are expected to create a unity from the fragments of educational experiences, even though their teachers have seldom achieved that unity.

Missing from most education is direct treatment of the time dimension. What causes change from the past to the present and the present into the future? How do present decisions determine the future toward which we are moving? How are lessons of history to be interpreted to the present? Why are so many corporate, national, and personal decisions ineffective in achieving intended objectives? Conventional educational programs seldom reveal the answers. Answers to such questions about how things change through time lie in the dynamic behavior of social, personal, and physical systems. Dynamic behavior, common to all systems, can be taught as such. It can be understood.

Education has taught static snapshots of the real world. But the world's problems are dynamic. The human mind grasps pictures, maps, and static relationships in a wonderfully effective way. But in systems of interacting components that change through time, the human mind is a poor simulator of behavior. Mathematically speaking, even a simple social system can represent a tenth-order, highly nonlinear, differential equation. Mathematicians can not solve the general case for such an equation. No scientist, citizen, manager, or politician can reliably judge such complexity by intuition. Yet, even a junior high school student with a personal computer and coaching in computer simulation can advance remarkably far in understanding such systems.

Education faces the challenge of undoing and reversing much that people learn by observing simple dynamic situations. Experiences in everyday life deeply ingrain lessons that are deceptively misleading when one encounters more complex social systems (Forrester, 1971). For example, from burning one's fingers on a hot stove, one learns that cause and effect are closely related in both time and space. Fingers are burned here and now when too close to the stove. Almost all understandable experiences reinforce the belief that causes are closely and obviously related to consequences. But in more complex systems, the cause of a difficulty is usually far distant in both time and space. The cause originated much earlier and arose from a different part of the system from where the symptoms appear.

To make matters even more misleading, a complex feedback system usually presents what we have come to expect, an apparent cause that lies close in time and space to the symptom. However, that apparent cause is usually a coincident symptom through which little leverage exists for producing improvement. Education does little to prepare students for succeeding when simple, understandable lessons so often point in exactly the wrong direction in the complex real world.

2. Cornerstones for a More Effective Education

Two mutually reinforcing developments now promise a learning process that can enhance breadth, depth, and insight in education. These two are system dynamics and learner-centered learning.

2.1. Precursors of System Dynamics System dynamics evolved from prior work in feedback-control systems. The history of engineering servomechanisms reaches back several hundred years. Popular writing, religious literature, and the social sciences have grappled with the closed-loop circular nature of cause and effect for thousands of years (Richardson, 1991). In the 1920s and 1930s, understanding the dynamics of control systems accelerated. New theory evolved during development of electronic feedback amplifiers for transcontinental telephone systems at the Bell Telephone Laboratories and work at MIT on feedback controls for analog computers and military equipment.

After 1950, people became more aware that feedback control applies not only to engineering systems but also to all processes of change—biological, natural, environmental, and social.

2.2. System Dynamics in Pre-College Education During the last 30 years, those in the profession of system dynamics have been building a more effective basis than previously existed for understanding change and complexity. The field rests on three foundations:

1. Growing knowledge of how feedback loops, containing information flows, decision making, and action, control change in all systems. Feedback processes determine stability, goal seeking, stagnation, decline, and growth. Feedback systems surround us in everything we do. A feedback process exists when action affects the condition of a system and that changed condition affects future action. Human interactions, home life, politics, management processes, environmental changes, and biological activity all operate on the basis of feedback loops that connect action to result to future action.

2. Digital computers, now primarily personal computers, to simulate the behavior of systems that are too complex to attack with conventional mathematics, verbal descriptions, or graphical methods. High school students, using today's computers, can deal with concepts and dynamic behavior that only a few years ago were restricted to work in advanced research laboratories. Excellent user-friendly software is now available (High Performance Systems, 1990; Pugh, 1986).[1]

3. Realization that most of the world's knowledge about dynamic structures resides in people's heads. The social sciences have relied too much on measured data. As a consequence, academic studies have failed to make adequate use of the data base on which the world runs—the information gained from living experience, apprenticeship, and participation. Students, even as early as kindergarten, already have a vast amount of operating information about individuals, families, communities, and schools from which they can learn about social, business, economic, and environmental behavior.

The system dynamics approach has been successfully applied to behavior in corporations, internal medicine, fisheries, psychiatry, energy supply and pricing, economic behavior, urban growth and decay, environmental stresses, population growth and aging, training of managers, and education of primary and secondary school students.

Nancy Roberts first demonstrated system dynamics as an organizing framework at the fifth and sixth grade levels (Roberts, 1975). Her work (Roberts, 1978) showed the advantage of reversing the traditional educational sequence that normally progresses through five steps:

1. Learning facts
2. Comprehending meaning

---

[1] For most work at the pre-college level, STELLA™ on Macintosh computers is easiest to use. It includes an excellent manual with learning exercises and an introduction to the philosophy of system dynamics. Some other system dynamics software packages are being developed with special attention to use in secondary schools. For more advanced professional use, software exists for system dynamics modeling, such as DYNAMO™ from Pugh-Roberts and Vensim™ from Ventana Systems.

3. Applying facts to generalizations
4. Analyzing to break material into constituent parts
5. Synthesizing to assemble parts into a whole.

Most students never reach that fifth step of synthesis. But, synthesis—putting it all together—should be placed at the beginning of the educational sequence. By the time students are in school they already possess a wealth of observations about family, interpersonal relations, community, and school. They are ready for a framework into which the facts can be fitted. Unless that framework exists, teaching still more facts loses significance.

In his penetrating discussion of the learning process, Bruner states, "the most basic thing that can be said about human memory . . . is that unless detail is placed into a structured pattern, it is rapidly forgotten" (Bruner, 1963, p. 24). For most purposes, such a structure is inadequate if it is only a static framework. The structure should show the dynamic significance of the detail—how the details are connected, how they influence one another, and how past behavior and future outcomes arise from decision-making policies and their interconnections.

System dynamics can provide that dynamic framework to give meaning to detailed facts. Such a dynamic framework provides a common foundation beneath mathematics, physical science, social studies, biology, history, and even literature.

In spite of the potential power of system dynamics, it could well be ineffective if introduced alone into a traditional educational setting in which students passively receive lectures. System dynamics can not be acquired as a spectator sport any more than one can become a good basketball player by merely watching games. Active participation instills the dynamic paradigm. Hands-on involvement is essential to internalizing the ideas and establishing them in one's own mental models. But traditional classrooms lack the intense involvement so essential for deep learning.

2.3. Learner-Centered Learning   Those who have experienced the excitement and intensity of a research laboratory know the involvement accompanying new discoveries. Why should not students in their formative years experience similar exhilaration from exploring new challenges? That sense of challenge exists when a classroom operates in a "learner-centered-learning" mode.

Learner-centered learning is a term I first encountered from Mrs. Kenneth Hayden of Ideals Associated.[2] It substantially alters the role of a teacher. A teacher is no longer a dispenser of knowledge addressed to students as passive receptors. Instead, where small teams of students explore and work together and help one another, a "teacher" becomes a colleague and participating learner. Teachers set directions and introduce opportunities. Teachers act as guides and

---

[2] Ideals Associated, 2570 Avenida de Maria, Tucson, AZ 85718 USA is a small foundation that for two decades has fostered an approach to learning that enlists students themselves in an active participation that contributes to the momentum of the educational process.

resource persons, not as authoritarian figures dictating each step of the educational process. The relationship is more like being a thesis adviser than a lecturer.

3. The Gordon Brown Influence

The thread leading to system dynamics started when I was introduced to feedback systems in the early 1940s by Gordon S. Brown, then director of the MIT Servomechanisms Laboratory. Later, Brown became head of the MIT Electrical Engineering Department and then Dean of Engineering before retiring in 1973. In the late 1980s, he completed the circle he had originally launched by picking up system dynamics and introducing it into the Orange Grove Junior High School in Tucson, Arizona (Brown, 1992).

Friends of Brown have established the "Gordon Stanley Brown Fund," administered through the System Dynamics Society. The fund will support released time and summer time for teachers who have applied system dynamics, so that they can put into transmittable and usable form the materials and methods that can help others. It will also support communication of experiences that did not meet expectations so that others can be forewarned of difficulties and paths to be avoided.

Brown describes his role as the "citizen champion" engaged in drawing all participants in the school system together in their search for a new kind of education.

> "the use of computers in the classroom (not in a computer lab) has, for us in Tucson resulted in a very unique learning environment . . . (students) learn what they need to know as the teacher guides them in conducting a simulation in class. They work in groups, two or three to a computer—certainly not one per computer—and thereby help one another. Dr. Barry Richmond says that this situation, in effect, multiplies the number of teachers by the number of students. Before doing a simulation the students spend several class periods gathering information about the topic; they take notes during lectures, learn about a library and read references, and, working as a group, plan the simulation. By working this way Draper's student do not merely try to remember the material for a test but actually have to use it in a project simulating real life situations. This has led us to identify a new teaching paradigm which we define as SYSTEM THINKING with LEARNER-CENTERED LEARNING." (Brown, 1990)

Gordon Brown started by loaning the STELLA software for a weekend to Frank Draper, an 8th grade biology teacher. Draper returned with the comment, "This is what I have always been looking for, I just did not know what it might be." At first, Draper expected to use system dynamics and computer simulation in one or two classes during a term. Then he found they were becoming a part of every class. With so much time devoted to system dynamics and simulation, he feared he would not have time to cover all the required biology. But, two thirds of the way through the term, Draper found he had completed all the usual biology content. He had a third of the term left for new material. The more rapid pace had resulted from the way biology had become more integrated and from the greater student involvement resulting from the systems viewpoint. Also, much credit goes to the "learner-centered learning" organization of student cooperative study teams within the classroom. To quote Draper, "There is a free lunch." He writes of his classroom experience:

> Since October 1988 our classrooms have undergone an amazing transformation. Not only are we covering more material than just the required curriculum, but we are covering it faster (we will be through with the year's curriculum this week and will have to add more material to our curriculum for the remaining 5 weeks) and the students are learning more useful material than ever before. 'Facts' are now anchored to meaning through the dynamic relationships they have with each other. In our classroom students shift from being passive receptacles to being active learners. They are not taught about science per se, but learn how to acquire and use knowledge (scientific and otherwise). Our jobs have shifted from dispensers of information to producers of environments that allow students to learn as much as possible.
>
> We now see students come early to class (even early to school), stay after the bell rings, work through lunch and work at home voluntarily (with no assignment given). When we work on a systems project—even when the students are working on the book research leading up to system work—there are essentially no motivation/discipline problems in our classrooms. (Draper, 1989)

A dynamic framework can even organize the study of literature (Hopkins, 1992). Classes taught by Pamela Hopkins are from an underprivileged section of the city and many had been labeled as slow learners. Simulation opened the door to a new way of capturing student interest and involvement. In a seminar for teachers taught by Barry Richmond and Steve Peterson of High Performance Systems, she participated in developing a model of psychological dynamics in Shakespeare's *Hamlet:*

> (when we used) a STELLA model which analyzed the motivation of Shakespeare's Hamlet to avenge the death of his father in HAMLET. . . The students were engrossed throughout the process . . . The amazing thing was that the discussion was completely student dominated. For the first time in the semester, I was not the focal point of the class. I did not have to filter the information from one student back to the rest of the class. They were talking directly to each other about the plot events and about the human responses being stimulated. They talked to each other about how they would have reacted and how the normal person would react. They discussed how previous events and specific personality characteristics would affect the response to each piece of news, and they strove for precision in the values they assigned for the power of each event. My function became that of listening to their viewpoints and entering their decisions into the computer. It was wonderful! It was as though the use of precise numbers to talk about psychological motives and human responses had given them power, had given them a system to communicate with. It had given them something they could handle, something that turned thin air into solid ground. They were directed and in control of learning, instead of my having to force them to keep their attention on the task." (Hopkins, 1990)

Several months after the experience related in the Hopkins article, I received a letter from Louise Hayden, director of Ideals Associated:

> Pam and I are so pleased and surprised at the ongoing involvement and depth of interest the high school students in her workshop of last June are showing. They are meeting with her weekly after school, eager to learn more about system

dynamics and to use their advances to help younger students learn. They are arousing considerable teacher interest as they try to use causal loops in all their class rooms. Information is flowing upward—and from students who varied in achievement from high to very low.

We attribute the enthusiasm and commitment to their sense of the potential of systems thinking, and other feelings of self-worth from being regarded as educational consultants. It is their first experience in learner-centered learning. This may well be the first time they have considered themselves a responsible part of the social system." (Hayden, 1990)

Many people assume that only the "best" students can adapt to the style of education here suggested. But who are the best students? Results so far indicate no correlation between students who do well in this program and how they had been previously labeled as fast or slow learners. Some of the so-called slow learners find traditional education lacks relevance. They are not challenged. In a different setting they come into their own and become leaders. Some of the students previously identified as best are strong on repeating facts in quizzes but lack an ability to synthesize and to see the meaning of their facts. Past academic record seems not to predict how students respond to this new program.

4. The Present Status

System dynamics is developing rapidly, but does not yet have widespread public visibility. The international System Dynamics Society was formed in 1985. Membership has grown to some 300. Annual international meetings have been held for fifteen years in locations as widely spread as Norway, Colorado, Spain, China, California, Germany, and Thailand. System dynamics books and papers are regularly translated into many languages including Russian, Japanese, and Chinese.

Six hundred people attended a recent conference on systems thinking organized by Pegasus Communications.[3]

After 30 years of development, several dozen books present the theory, concepts, and applications of system dynamics. Some have exerted surprising public impact (Forrester, 1969; Forrester, 1971). *The Limits to Growth* book (Meadows, et al., 1972), showing interplay among population, industrialization, hunger, and pollution, has been translated into some 30 languages and has sold over three million copies. Such wide-spread readership of books based on computer modeling testifies to a public longing to understand how present actions influence the future. *Limits to Growth* has been recently updated as *Beyond the Limits* (Meadows, et al., 1992).

Early leaders in system dynamics were educated at M.I.T. But competence is now appearing in many places. Talent exists on which to build a new kind of education, even though system dynamics is so broadly applicable throughout physical, social, biological, and political systems that the present small number of experts are thinly dispersed over a wide spectrum of activities.

---

[3] Pegasus Communications, 1696 Massachusetts Ave., Cambridge, MA 02138, publisher of the monthly *The Systems Thinker*.

System dynamics is now becoming well established in some thirty junior and senior high schools. Several hundred schools have started exploratory activity.

Part of the educational emphasis focuses on "generic structures." A rather small number of relatively simple structures appear repeatedly in different businesses, professions, and real-life settings. Students can transfer insights from one setting to another. For example one of Draper's eighth grade students grew bacteria in a culture dish, then looked at the same pattern of environmentally limited growth through computer simulation. From the computer, the student looked up and observed, "This is the world population problem, isn't it?" Such transfer of insights from one setting to another will help to break down barriers between disciplines. It means that learning in one field becomes applicable to other fields.

There is now promise of reversing the trend of the last century toward ever greater fragmentation in education. There is real hope of moving back toward the "Renaissance man" idea of a common teachable core of broadly applicable concepts. We can now visualize an integrated, systemic, educational process that is more efficient, more appropriate to a world of increasing complexity, and more supportive of unity in life.

Several high schools, curriculum-development projects, and colleges are using a system dynamics core to build study units in mathematics, science, social studies, and history. But such programs have not yet reached the point of becoming fully integrated educational structures.

The most advanced United States experiment in bringing system dynamics and learner-centered learning together into a more powerful educational environment appears to be in the Catalina Foothills School District of Tucson, Arizona. In that community the necessary building blocks for successful educational innovation have come together. Progress in that school system rests on:

1. Fundamental new concepts of education,
2. A receptive community,
3. Talented teachers who are willing to try unfamiliar ideas and who are at least in the nonauthoritarian environment of learner-centered learning,
4. A school administration that is applying a systems viewpoint in seeking total quality, mutual understanding, and continuous improvement,
5. A supportive school board,
6. And a "citizen champion" who, without a personal vested interest in the outcome except for a desire to facilitate improvement in education, has helped by inspiring teachers, finding funding, arranging for computers, and above all, facilitating convergence of political differences in the community.

The Catalina Foothills district did not have its own high school. Students went into the Greater Tucson system. After seeing the impact on several hundred students of the new educational philosophy embedded in the Orange Grove junior high school, parents became reluctant to have children revert to a traditional high school. The District in 1990 voted a $30 million bond issue to create a high school in the education pattern that had been pioneered in the junior high school.

In March 1992 a "Systems Thinking in Education Conference" was held in Tucson. Two hundred people attended six plenary sessions and seven sequences of parallel sessions. Enthusiasm was high with reports of systems activity from fourth to twelfth grades.

The Educational Testing Service has established the Systems Thinking and Curriculum Innovation Network Project (STACI) involving about a dozen schools to explore the use of system dynamics in classrooms.[4]

> "The approach consists of three separate but interdependent components: system dynamics, the theoretical perspective; STELLA, a simulation modeling software package; and the Macintosh computer.... The STACI Project is an implementation and research effort that examines the cognitive and curricular impact of using the systems thinking approach in pre-college instruction.... Because it is critical for teachers to be able to seek assistance easily from experts and other teachers, an electronic mail network using AppleLink has been established among the schools ... the project focuses on the examination of cognitive and learning outcomes.... the systems approach is being used in courses that reach a range of students. Contrary to initial beliefs, the perspective can be used to facilitate instruction of low- as well as high-ability students.... from initial results, the use of the systems approach for less able learners seems to be yielding promising outcomes." (Mandinach and Cline, 1989)

Some other countries are moving ahead rapidly in using system dynamics as a foundation for an educational system below the college level. The Scandinavian countries are working together. Davidsen[5] describes their guiding philosophy:

> "System dynamics is a method, used in the study of complex, dynamic systems. Its pedagogical qualities are under investigation in several countries.... Our final goal is to provide our students with an effective way of thinking about complex, dynamic systems. Thus we want to change their cognitive style. Far beyond establishing a basis of values, attitudes, and factual knowledge, our schools significantly influence the way each one of our students will be thinking. ... we encourage our students to become critical users of models and to question assumptions underlying models, used for professional and political purposes. They should gain respect for real life complexity and variety and question simple solutions to complex problems.... In Norwegian and Nordic schools, we have chosen to utilize the conceptual framework offered by system dynamics for our educational purposes ... When we have established an understanding of the basic dynamic processes, we are ready to address ourselves to reality. Then we will have to tackle systems of far greater complexity, typically characterized by feedback, delays, nonlinearities, and noise.... (pursuing) causal chains until they close upon each other, leads us to a multi-disciplinary approach.... Academic boundaries no longer constitute the boundaries of our imagination or our

---

[4] Ellen B. Mandinach and Hugh F. Cline, Educational Testing Service, Princeton, NJ 08541, USA.

[5] Pål I. Davidsen, Department of Information Science, University of Bergen, Thormøhlensgt 55, N-5006 Bergen, NORWAY.

investigation. Historic and economic considerations are merged with physics and chemistry in our study of ecological issues." (Davidsen, 1990)

I have received a German book detailing their experimental use of system dynamics and the STELLA software for teaching high school physics (Bethge and Schecker, 1992).[6]

Several schools are making good progress with system dynamics and learner-centered learning below the level of junior high school students. In the public schools of Ridgewood, New Jersey, Timothy Lucas and Rich Langheim have been focusing on first through fifth grades.

5. The Future

Over the next several decades, an improved kind of education can evolve. The growing frustrations in corporate, economic, social, political, and international organizations demonstrate the need for better understanding. The basis now exists for a far more effective educational process. But a vast amount of work remains to build on the present foundation. Adequate educational materials are yet to be developed. One book was written especially for high schools (Roberts, et al., 1983). Although not written specifically for pre-college use, other introductory system dynamics books are available (Forrester, 1961; Forrester, 1968; Forrester, 1969; Forrester, 1975; Goodman, 1974; Richardson and Pugh, 1981). Nevertheless, the published material does not yet adequately convey the background, simulation models, related teacher-support materials, and guidance on teaching methods. Much material already exists in places ranging from files at MIT to work of teachers who are pioneering in systems thinking and learner-centered learning. But most existing materials are not now widely accessible.

No network has existed before 1992 interchanging information among all interested innovators in pre-college education. But that missing link is now being remedied by a new office, the Creative Learning Exchange,[7] established by John R. Bemis, to receive, print, and distribute system dynamics educational materials. That office will maintain communications among schools, encourage training seminars for teachers, advise teachers in preparing new materials for wider dissemination, and assist in maintaining the integrity and practicality of the system dynamics content of emerging curricula.

A group of students in the MIT Undergraduate Research Opportunities Program are working with me to develop educational materials for use in schools. They are working with teachers in the Cambridge Rindge and Latin High School to test materials and acquire experience in the real world of teachers and classrooms. In a current project they are creating a "Road Maps" agenda for self study in system dynamics as applied to education. The agenda is a guide to using available published material, which will be supplemented by

---

[6] Horst Schecker, Institute of Physics Education, Department of Physics, University of Bremen, Postbox 330440, D-2800 Bremen 33, GERMANY.

[7] Ms. Lees Stuntz, Executive Director, Creative Learning Exchange, 1 Keefe Road, Acton, MA 01720, USA, tel: 508-287-0070, fax: 508-287-0080.

papers written by the students and some selections from more than 4000 memoranda in the files of the MIT System Dynamics Group. The material from this "System Dynamics in Education Project" will be distributed through the Creative Learning Exchange. This project is creating examples of quality systems work to help establish standards for educational programs. It is not the intention to create entire unified courses of study, but rather to generate examples that teachers can use in a wide range of educational settings.

Many private individuals are moving ahead to provide financial assistance to the development of systems education, rather than waiting for public political organizations to innovate. Private support can operate with a freedom and a clarity of purpose that is seldom possible with the bureaucratic processes of government and large foundations.

I believe that the immediate goal is to reach a point where at least twenty schools have been unambiguously successful and have achieved self-sustaining momentum. Thus far, many schools are making good progress but are still relying on outside guidance to assist when barriers are encountered. Some are beginning to emerge from such dependence on external assistance, but there are not yet sufficient examples of on-going, independent successes to over-shadow failures that are almost certain to occur. Preliminary results from system dynamics in primary and secondary schools show such promise that too many schools without the ingredients for success may begin, then fail. As a result, systems education might be discredited unless sufficient successes have been demonstrated to sustain the hope and promise of a more effective education.

The politics and processes of moving from a traditional school to a radically different style of education must be better understood. No one yet knows what percentage of present teachers can make the transition from traditional teacher-dominated classrooms to the free-wheeling, research atmosphere of a learner-centered classroom. To some teachers, the transition is threatening. Little is known about how to evaluate students coming out of this different kind of education. Standardized evaluation probably is not desirable or possible in a program that emphasizes individual development and diversity.

Creating a new kind of education will take substantial time. Planning and funding should provide for long-run continuity based on step-by step progress. Funding will be needed for developing materials, retraining teachers, and launching demonstration schools.

A core of system dynamics experts should monitor progress and continually nudge the activities toward higher quality. There are many ways in which erroneous concepts can creep into such an education. If such fallacies go uncorrected, systems education may be perceived as superficial and unsound and lead to negative backlash. Contributions are essential from experienced teachers, who understand the problems and opportunities in classrooms, and can translate ideas into effective teaching materials. "Citizen champions" can serve an important role to draw together teachers, school administrators, school boards, parents, concerned public, and governmental officials. Such influential groups are beginning to coalesce around the combined concepts of system dynamics and learner-centered learning.

6. References

Bethge, Thomas, and Horst Schecker, 1992. *Materialien zur Modellbildung und Simulation im Physikunterricht,* Bremen, Germany: Institut fur Didaktik der Physik, Universitat Bremen. 238 pp.

Brown, Gordon S., 1990. *The Genisis of the System Thinking Program at the Orange Grove Middle School, Tucson, Arizona.* Personal report. 6301 N. Calle de Adelita, Tucson, AZ 85718: March 1, 8 pp.

Brown, Gordon S., 1992. "Improving Education in Public Schools; Innovative Teachers to the Rescue." *System Dynamics Review,* Vol. 8, no. 1, pp. 83–89.

Bruner, Jerome S., 1963. *The Process of Education,* New York: Vintage Books.

Davidsen, Pål I., 1990. "System Dynamics, a Pedagogical Approach to the Teaching of Complex, Dynamic Systems by Means of Simulation (draft copy)." In *for EURIT 90, The European Conference on Technology and Education,* 12 pp.

Draper, Frank, 1989. *Letter to Jay Forrester.* Personal communication, Orange Grove Junior High School, 1911 E. Orange Grove Rd., Tucson, AZ 85718. May 2.

Forrester, Jay W., 1961. *Industrial Dynamics,* Cambridge, MA: Productivity Press. 464 pp.

Forrester, Jay W., 1968. *Principles of Systems,* (2nd ed.). Cambridge, MA: Productivity Press. 391 pp.

Forrester, Jay W., 1969. *Urban Dynamics,* Cambridge, MA: Productivity Press. 285 pp.

Forrester, Jay W., 1971. "Counterintuitive Behavior of Social Systems." *Technology Review,* Vol. 73, No. 3, pp. 53–68. Also appears as Chapter 14, pages 211–244, in the author's *Collected Papers* 1975; and as Chapter 1, pp. 3–30, in *Toward Global Equilibrium: Collected Papers,* 1973, Dennis L. Meadows, ed., both from Cambridge MA: Productivity Press.

Forrester, Jay W., 1971. *World Dynamics,* (1973 second ed.). Cambridge, MA: Productivity Press. 144 pp. Second edition has an added chapter on physical vs. social limits.

Forrester, Jay W., 1975. *Collected Papers of Jay W. Forrester,* Cambridge, Ma: Productivity Press. 284 pp.

Goodman, Michael R., 1974. *Study Notes in System Dynamics,* Cambridge, MA: Productivity Press. 388 pp.

Hayden, Louise, 1990. *Letter of October 2, 1990 to Jay Forrester.* Personal communication, 1 pp.

High Performance Systems, 1990. *STELLA II Users Guide.* Macintosh. 45 Lyme Road, Hanover, NH: High Performance Systems.

Hopkins, Pamela Lee, 1990. *Classroom Implementation of STELLA to Illustrate Hamlet.* Description of computer model and classroom experience. Desert View High School, 4101 East Valencia Rd., Tucson, AZ 85706. March. 7 pp.

Hopkins, Pamela Lee, 1992. "Simulating *Hamlet* in the Classroom." *System Dynamics Review,* Vol. 8, No. 1, pp. 91–98.

Mandinach, Ellen B., and Hugh F. Cline, 1989. "Applications of Simulation and Modeling in Precollege Instruction." *Machine-Mediated Learning,* Vol. 3, pp. 189–205.

Meadows, Donella H., Dennis L. Meadows, and Jørgen Randers, 1992. *Beyond The Limits,* Post Mills, VT: Chelsea Green Publishing Co. 300 pp.

Meadows, Donella H., Dennis L. Meadows, Jørgen Randers, and William W. Behrens III, 1972. *The Limits to Growth,* New York: Universe Books. 205 pp.

Pugh, Alexander L., III, 1986. *Professional DYNAMO Plus Reference Manual.* IBM PC computers. 5 Lee St, Cambridge, MA: Pugh-Roberts Associates.

Richardson, George P., 1991. *Feedback Thought in Social Science and Systems Theory,* Philadelphia, PA: University of Pennsylvania Press. 374 pp.

Richardson, George P., and Alexander L. Pugh III, 1981. *Introduction to System Dynamics Modeling with DYNAMO,* Cambridge, MA: Productivity Press. 413 pp.

Roberts, Nancy, 1975. *A Dynamic Feedback Approach to Elementary Social Studies: A Prototype Gaming Unit.* Ph.D. thesis, available from University Microfilms, Ann Arbor, Michigan: Boston University.

Roberts, Nancy, 1978. Teaching Dynamic Feedback Systems Thinking: An Elementary View. *Management Science,* Vol. 24. No. 8, pp. 836–843.

Roberts, Nancy, David Andersen, Ralph Deal, Michael Garet, and William Shaffer. 1983. *Introduction to Computer Simulation: A System Dynamics Modeling Approach,* temporarily out of print, successor publisher not yet know. 562 pp.

DISCUSSION QUESTIONS AND ACTIVITIES

1. What educational reforms are being implemented in your community or state? Who has access to resources and opportunities provided by these reform? Whose voices are incorporated? Who is in charge of creating information and who controls its flow? When data is collected, whose worldview frames the research questions? Finally, does the reform perpetuate existing inequities by merely disguising them in a new practice?

2. How do your state regulations for certification incorporate multicultural education? (You might need to consult state licensure regulations.) Are state certification regulations informed by any national reports? (for example, are they in line with findings in What Matters Most: Teaching for America's Future?)

3. How are K–12 teachers held accountable in your state? How are K–12 students held accountable? What assumptions about teaching and learning are reinforced by these measures of accountability?

4. What are the underlying assumptions about teaching, learning, and content in system dynamics? How effective do you think this approach might be for student learning? Do you think the use of system dynamics would support culturally relevant teaching? Explain your answer.

5. Interview a novice teacher or a veteran teacher or both. Do they consider themselves change agents? How does change come about in their schools? What kinds of changes have they seen implemented? Have these changes lasted?

6. Consider a change you would like to implement at the middle or high school level. (You might want to base it on a school you previously attended or one in which you have done field work.) What would you change—the curriculum,

teaching practices, or school structure? Imagine that you work with three other colleagues to devise an action plan. Describe the steps you might take to introduce this change.

7. Write down your current definition of multicultural education. How has this definition changed since reading Chapter One?

REFERENCES

Fried, R. L. 1998. Parent anxiety and school reform. *Phi Delta Kappan, 79* (December): 265–271.

Kantor, H. 1995. The hollow promise of youth apprenticeships. In Levine, D., Lowe, R., Peterson, B., & Tenorio, R. (eds.), *Rethinking schools: An agenda for change.* New York: New Press, pp. 215–229.

Kohn, A. 1998. Only for my kid: How privileged parents undermine school reform. *Phi Delta Kappan, 79* (April): 568–577.

Kotter, J. P. 1996. *Leading change.* Boston: Harvard Business School Press.

Levine, D. 1995. Building a vision of curriculum reform. In Levine, D., Lowe, R., Peterson, B., & Tenorio, R. (eds.), *Rethinking schools: An agenda for change.* New York: New Press, pp. 52–60.

McCullough, M. K., Lavadenz, M., and Martin, S. P. 1996. Sociocultural factors affecting school reform in culturally diverse settings. In Grant, C.A. (ed.), *National Association for Multicultural Education.* San Francisco: Caddo Gap.

McNergney, R. F., and Herbert, J. M. 1995. *Foundations of education.* Needham Heights, MA: Allyn & Bacon.

National Commission on Teaching & America's Future. 1996. *What matters most: Teaching for America's future, summary report.* New York: NCTAF. ERIC ED 395 931.

Nieto, S. 1996. *Affirming diversity: The sociopolitical context of multicultural education,* 2nd ed. London: Longman.

Palmer, P. J. 1998. *The courage to teach.* San Francisco: Jossey-Bass.

Parish, R. and Aquila, F. 1996. Cultural ways of working and believing in schools: preserving the way things are. *Phi Delta Kappan, 78*(4): 298–305.

Sleeter, C. E., and Grant, C.A. 1988. *Making choices for multicultural education: Five approaches to race, class, and gender,* 2nd ed. New York: Macmillan.

System Dynamics. 1999. http://sysdyn.mit.edu/sd-intro/home.html

Tatum, B. D. 1997. *Why are all the Black kids sitting together in the cafeteria?* New York: Basic.

Tozer, S. E., Violas, P.C., and Senese, G. 1993. *School & society: Educational practice as social expression.* New York: McGraw-Hill.

Wagner, T. 1996. Bringing school reform back down to earth. *Phi Delta Kappan, 78*(2): 145–149.

INDEX

achievement, 53
Adger, C. T., Wolfram, W., and Detwyler, J., 348-353
African American,
   learning styles, 62-63
   racial identity, see People of Color
Afrocentric-education, 6,8, 26
Afrocentricity for All, 160-162
Agency, xiii
Alternative Assessment: Issues in Language, Culture and Equity, 228-241
Americanization, 2
Anderson, J., 123-128
Anderson, R.C., Spiro, R. J., and Anderson, M. C., 179
Anglos, 76-81
Any Town High School: A Profile of Pluralism, 52-55
Ascher, C., 242-245
Asian Americans
   learning styles, 64
   racial identity, see People of Color
assessment, 214-227
   current trends, 218
      alternative assessment, 219, 233-236
      authentic assessment, 220
      performance-based assessment, 220
      portfolio assessment, 220
      rubrics, 221
   equitable alternatives to, 236-237
   history of testing, 215
   national trends, 221
      goals 2000, 223
      national curriculum/national testing, 224
      national standards, 224
      teacher quality enhancement grant, 223
   social context of assessment, 230-232
   assessment bias, 323-325
      reliability, 323, 326
      standardized tests, 323-324
      validity, 323, 326
assimilation, 2, 7, 33, 51, 54
Au, K. H., 181. 183

Baker, A., 84-87
Banks, J. A., 5, 24-29, 133, 135, 149
   levels of multicultural curriculum, 137-140
      additive, 137-138
      contributions, 137
      social action, 140
      transformation 138-140
Bethune, M. M., 4
biological determinism, 320
biracial identity, 69-71
Bishop, A., 162-175
Black English: Its History and its Role in the Education of Our Children, 202-209
Bloome, D., 183
Branch, R., Goodwin, Y., & Gualtieri, J., 149-154
Brown, P., 67, 87-89

change
   obstacles, xv, 365-366
change agent, xiii-xvii,17-23, 359-396
charter schools, 362
Christensen, L., 118-123
Civil Rights Movement, 4
class, 39-41
classroom climate
   pointers, 102, 103
   physical appearance, 95
   teacher interactions, 96
classroom management, 106-107

Collins, M., 102
community, see School-Family-Community Relations
communication styles
   and background, 96-99
   and body language, 99-100
constructing meaning
   cultural influences in, 178-180, 232-233
   on teaching English language, 180-181
   on teaching writing, 180
constructivism, 232
cooperative learning, 104
   Some Quick Cooperative Starters, 108-110
critical thinking, 12, 13, 18
Cross, W., 66
cultural capital, 7
cultural deprivation, 320
cultural disadvantage, 323
Cultural Identity Groups, 87-89
culturally disadvantaged, 320
culturally relevant teaching
   steps, 147-148
   see also culturally responsive teaching
culturally responsive teaching, 94-105
   in academic areas: English, 141-142; Math and Science, 144-147, 154-160; Social Studies/History, 142-144
Culturally Sensitive Instructional Practices for African-American Learners with Disabilities, 338-347
   for disabled students from diverse backgrounds, 327-330
   for students with Limited English Proficiency, 329-330

Seven Strategies to Support Culturally Responsive Pedagogy, 110–116
culture, 5

Dangerous Minds: Decoding a Classroom, 118–123
Datnow, A., xiii, xv, xvi
Davidman, L. M. and Davidman, P. T., xiii, 5–6
Dean, A. V., Spencer, J. S., and Taylor, L., 331–337
Delpit, L, 112
democracy, 46
demographics, xii, 144
Detracking Helps At-Risk Students, 246–247
Dewey, J., 3, 10
dialogue, 74–75
Do You Know Why They All Talk at Once?: Thoughts on Cultural Differences between Hispanics and Anglos, 76–81
dropout rates, see special education
Du Bois, W.E.B., 3

education
   and politics, 13–15
   and socialization, 15
educational reform, 360–364
Educational Testing Service (ETS), 218
Eight Lessons of Parent, Family, and Community Involvement in the Middle Grades, 296–301
empowerment, 9, 13–15, 17–23, 88, 362–363
Epstein, J. L., 262–285
equity, 6, 40
Estrin, E. T., 228–241
ethnic group, 66
ethnic identity, 66
ethnic minority group, 66
ethnicity, 5
European Americans
   learning styles, 76–81, 81–84
   racial identity, 68–69, 84–87
   see also Whites
expectations, 36–37, 40, 53

families and schools, see School-Family-Community Relations

feminist pedagogy, 19–20
field-dependent/sensitive, 60–61, 65, 78
field independent, 60–61, 65, 78
fishbowl technique, 103
Forrester, J. W., 396–409
Franklin, M. E., 338–347
Friere, P., 19–20, 184–185
Fullan, M. G., 370–377

Gardner, H., 81–84, 216
Gay, G., xiii
gay and lesbian, 53, 123–128
   see homosexuality
gender, 37–38, 40–41, 52
   learning style, 64–65
   misrepresentation in special education, 319
   research by Sadker, M. and Sadker, D., 38
Gender Balance: Lessons from Girls in Science in Mathematics, 154–160
generalizations, 61–62, 77
Giroux, H., 185
global education, 6
Goals 2000, 222–223
Gould, S.J., *The Mismeasure of Man*, 216–217
Griffin, G., 141
Grossman, H., 61, 98, 104, 105, 319–320
Grossman, H. and Grossman, S., 61

Heath, S. B., 181–182
Helms, J., 66
Hidalgo, N., 253
High Schools Gear Up to Create Effective School and Family Partnerships, 301–307
Hispanic
   See Latino/a
Hollifield, J. H., 301–308
home schooling, 361–362
homosexuality, 53
   see gay and lesbian
How Schools Shortchange Girls, 38

IDEA, see Individuals with Disabilities Education Act of 1990
IDEA '97, see Individuals with Disabilities Education Act of 1997

If Poverty is the Question... 43–46
immigration, 2
inclusion, 310
Incorporating Cultural Pluralism into Instruction, 149–154
Individual Education Plan (IEP), 312, 329
   transition services, 312–316
Individuals with Disabilities Education Act of 1990 (Public Law 101–476), 312–314
   transition services, 312–314
Individuals with Disabilities Education Act of 1991 (Public Law 102–119), 314
Individuals with Disabilities Education Act of 1997 (Public Law 105–17), 311, 316, 318, 329
   transition services, 314–316
   also see, Individual Education Plan (IEP)
instantiation, 179
institutional power, 34
instructional decisions continuum, 94–95
instructional strategies
   culturally responsive teaching and, 101
Instructional Strategies for Second-Language Learners in the Content Areas, 192–202
   revision, 105
   stories, skits and simulations, 105
Irujo, S., 76–81
Irwin, J. W., 178–179

Jackson, F. R., 110–117
Johnson, W. W. and Johnson, R., and Holubec, E. J., 108–109

Kallen, H., 3
knowledge construction, 134–135
Kohn, A., 365
Kotter, J. P., 366–368

Ladson-Billings, G., 4, 143–144
language and culture
   and assessment, 233
   dialect differences, 329–330
Language Differences: A New Approach for Special Educators, 348–353

Latino/a
  learning style, 63, 78–84
  racial identity, see People of Color
learning styles, 59–66
  and African Americans, 64, 81–84
  and Asian Americans, 62–63
  and European Americans, 76–81, 81–84
  and gender, 64
  and Latino/a Americans, 63, 78–84
  and Native Americans, 63
Learning, Chinese-Style, 81–84
lesson plans, 22
Lewis, B. C., 202–209
Limited English Proficiency (LEP), 317–318, 321–322, see culturally responsive teaching
literacy, 183
  cognitive and cultural perspectives, 186
  critical literacy, 184
  cultural literacy, 185
  dialogue, 188
  emergent literacy, 191
  enhancing, 187–189
  k-w-l, 187
  journal writing 188
  questioning techniques, 187
  technological, 191, 209–210
locus of control, 63

magnet schools, 361–362
Manchild in the Promised Land, 322
McIntosh, P., 35–36, 46
meritocracy, 36, 40, 323
model minority, 53, 64
motivation, 105–106
  Motivating Future Educators through Empowerment: A Special Case, 17–23
multicultural education
  approaches, 7–10
  as academic discourse, 382
  as a social movement, 383–396
  as teaching technique, 380–382
  as therapy, 379–380
  critical thinking, 12
  criticism of, 15–17, 24–25
  definitions, 4–12
  developing a definition, 6, 10
  democracy, 4, 7, 24–29
  diversity, 4

  early Black scholars, 3
  history, 2–5
Multicultural Education: A Challenge for Special Educators, 331–337
Multicultural Education as Social Movement, 378–396
Multicultural Education for Freedom's Sake, 24–29
Multicultural Me, 48–51
Multiculturalism as Compulsory Chapel, 15–17
multi-ethnic education, 6

National Commission on Teaching & America's Future, 23
Native Americans
  learning style, 63
  racial identity, see People of Color
Nativist, 2
Nieto, S., 12, 60, 66, 100, 359
1975 Education for All Handicapped Act (Public Law 94–142), 311–312, 327
non-verbal behavior, 33, 76–81

Ogbu, J., 9, 10
Olsen, S. A., 246–247
Olson, R. A., 46–48
oppositional identity, 10

Palmer, P., 366–368
parental involvement, 256, also see School-Family-Community Relations
Peake, M., 4
pedagogy
  critical, 19–21
  feminist, 19–21
Pelak, A., 209–211
people of color
  definition, 66
  racial identity, 67–68, 71
Pickron, C., 103
pluralism, cultural, 2, 3, 4, 6, 33, 52–55
pluralizing curriculum content, 130
  reasons given for not pluralizing (school teacher blues), 130–134
  literary curriculum 141, 146
  social studies curriculum, 142–144

  math/science curriculum 144–147
Pollina, A. 154–160
positionality, 21, 35, 41, 48–57
Poston, C.W.S., 69–71
poverty, 39–40, 42–46, 56, 322–323
Praising My Individuality, 84–87
privilege, 21, 35, 41, 46–48, 49, 57
professional development, 363
professionalism, 376–377
Public Laws
  Public Law 94–142, 311–312, 327
  Public Law 101–476, 312–314
  Public Law 102–119, 314
  Public Law 105–17, 311, 314–316, 318, 329
  Also see 1975 Education for All Handicapped Act and Individuals with Disabilities Education Act (1990, 1991, 1997)

questioning, 101
  and cultural differences, Chapter 6
Questioning the Status Quo: The Politics of Empowerment, 13–15

race, 5, 32–37, 40–41
  definition, 34
racial identity, 48–51
  and teacher interaction, 96
  application in school settings, 71–73
  definition, 66
  groups, 73, 87–89
  theory, 66–75
racism, 32–37, 50
  discussing, 33
reading comprehension, 178
reflection, 41, 49, 51, 73
reliability, 323, 326
Report: U.S. Gap between Rich, Poor is Widening, 32
Reyes, M. L. and Molner, L. A., 192–202
rubrics, 221
Rutherford, B. and Billig, S. H., 296–307

Savage Inequalities, 322
scaffolding, 186–187

schema theory, 179–180
Schiele, J. H., 160–162
School/Family/Community Partnerships: Caring for the Children We Share, 262–285
School-Family-Community Relations
  action plans, 275–279
  complexity of developing, 260–262
  history, 253
  value of, 253–255
  fostering relationships, 256–258
  successful programs, 279–281
  teachers, 258–260
School-to-Work Opportunities Act 1994, 362–363
Seven Strategies to Support a Culturally Responsive Pedagogy, 110–117
sex definition, 37
sexism, 38
Shade, B. J, Kelly, C., and Oberg, M., 100
Shor, I., 13–15, 19–20, 184
Simpson, L., 103
Sleeter, C., 378–396
Sleeter, C. and Grant, C., 5–10, 135,
social justice, 9,
social reconstructionism, 6, 9
Some Quick Cooperative Starters: Cooperation in the Classroom, 108–110
special education
  classification, 326–327
  dialect differences, 329–330

disproportional representation, 317–321
dropout rates, 326–327
theories explaining disproportional representation, 319–327
standardized tests, 361, 323–324
standards, 361
stereotypes, 61–62
Successful Detracking in Middle and Senior High Schools, 242–245
Supporting the Invisible Minority, 123–128
Suzuki, B., 2–3, 9, 11–12, 64
systems dynamics, 368–369, 396–407
System Dynamics and Learner-Centered Learning in Kindergarten through 12th Grade Education, 396–408
systems thinking, 368–369, 396–407

Tatum, B. D., x–xi, 67, 68, 72, 369
teacher expectations, 100, 246, Chapter 8
teachers
  as change agents, xiii–xvii, 17–23, 359–396
  mismatch with students, xiii
  new and veteran, xii
teaching as a moral activity, 370–377
technology, 190, 209–211
Technological Literacy: More Questions Than Answers, 209–210
Tellin' Stories Project, 285–295
tracking, 242–247

Detracking Helps At-Risk Students, 246–247
Successful Detracking in Middle and Senior High Schools, 242–245
transition services, 312–316, 321
  Also see Individual Education Plan (IEP) and Individuals with Disabilities Education Acts of 1990 and 1997
triggers, 74–75
Tyler, R., 22

validity, 323, 326
vouchers, 361

Walsh, C., 99
Washington, B. T., 3
wealth, 42–46, 56
Wellstone, P., 43–46
West, C., 36
Western Mathematics: The Secret Weapon of Cultural Imperialism, 162–176
Will, G., 15–17
White
  racial identity, 68–69
  see also European American
White Privilege in Schools, 46–48
Willinsky, J., 184, 185
Wlodkowski, R. J. and Ginsberg, M. B., 94–95, 106
Why Teachers Must Become Change Agents, 370–396

Ziegler, M. F., 285–295